ARTIFICIAL INTELLIGENCE QUESTION BANK

(For CLASS X)
(Based on CBSE Syllabus Code 417)

S P Verma

www.bpbonline.com

FIRST EDITION 2022

Copyright © BPB Publications, India

ISBN: 978-93-5551-155-3

To View Complete
BPB Publications Catalogue
Scan the QR Code:

Dedicated to

In The Fond Memory
Of
Late Mr Suraj Bali ji
(Father-In-Law),
Late Mrs. Jain Kumari ji
(Mother-In-Law)
and
Late Mr Brijesh Kumar Verma
(Brother-In-Law)

About the Author

 S P Verma, M.Sc; M.Ed; PGCPM has been working in the field of education since last 35 years. As a seasoned educationist, teacher trainer, career counsellor, academic auditor, motivator, mentor, author and editor, he has authored 55 school books, 6 research papers, 10 research articles, more than 70 articles on careers and edited more than 200 educational products. More than 20k educators (teachers and principals) attended his training sessions across the country. More than 200k students were career counselled and inspired to take right career plan by him.

Formerly holding the positions like Principal, Kendriya Vidyalaya Sangathan, New Delhi; Regional Director, Teacher Sity, New Delhi; Regional Director, iDC, New Delhi; and Director (School Trg), Vidya Institute of Training and Development, VKP, Meerut; he is now serving as Director (Trg and Innovation), GEM Foundations, Bengaluru. Besides Associate Life Member of Computer Society of India (CSI), he is associated with a number of professional bodies as Life Member, like Vigyan Parishad, Allahabad; Hindi Vigyan Sahitya Parishad, BARC, Mumbai; InSc, Bengaluru, PTAI, New Delhi, etc.

Acknowledgements

I would like to acknowledge the contributions of all the educationists (teachers and principals), professionals, and reviewers, who provided their feedback and suggestions on the MS of this book. Especially, I am grateful to **Mr. Pavnesh Kumar**, Former Controller of Examinations, CBSE; **Dr DK Sharma**, Dean (School of Engineering and Technolgy), IIMT University, Meerut; **Prof. RC Singh**, Controller of Examinations, Sharda University, Greater Noida; **Mr. Akshay Sharma**, B.Tech., ONGC, Mehsana and **Mrs. Shweta Agrawal**, MCA for their specific suggestions.

It's my proud privilege to put on record my sincere gratitude to my publisher **M/s BPB Publications**, New Delhi, for accepting my vision and plan of writing Coding books for classes VI to VIII and providing me the opportunity for the same. The initial interaction with **Mr. Manish Jain**, CEO, and **Mr. Varun Jain**, Director was fruitful in making a long-term association and bonding. I am grateful to them and the entire team of BPB Publications for bringing out these publications in a short span of time.

I am grateful to my well-wishers namely **Mr. RL Jamuda**, Former Commissioner KVS; **Dr. MM Swami**, Former Deputy Commisioner, KVS; **Mr VK Gupta**, Former Deputy Commissioner, KVS; **Mr. DK Saini**, Former Deputy Commissioner, KVS; **Mr AK Verma**, CEO, Eduwix, New Delhi; **Mr NK Verma**, AGM, BHEL HQ; **Mr AK Pattnaik**, SrGM (Academic), Kalorex Group of Institutions, Ahmedabad; **Mr YP Sharma, Mr Vipin Agrawal**; **Mr. Matin Ahmed, Mr. NK Giri, Mr NK Bansal** and **Mr SC Sharma** for their constant support, help and motivation to do something good to the society.

I am touched by the love, patience and tolerance shown, during the completion of this project, by my family members- **Mrs. Rekha Verma** (Life Partner), **Sqn Ldr Anuj Verma** (Son), Dearest **Atharv** (Grandson) and **Mrs. Shelja Sharma**, B.Tech. (Daughter in Law). I am grateful to them as well as to all my friends and relatives supporting me in all the creative tasks.

While preparing the manuscript of this book, I have gone through a number of books and different websites. I am grateful to all those authors, contributors, editors, freelancers whose articles are read and used in one or another way in this book. And last but not least, I am indebted to God for keeping my brain alive and my health sound even at the time of the Covid Pandemic so that He could get completed this task through me.

— S P Verma

Preface

It is a matter of great pleasure and satisfaction to put the first edition of **"Artificial Intelligence Question Bank (for class X)"** before the enthusiastic learners. Artificial intelligence is getting more attention in the world day by day. It is touching almost all fields related to the development of the human-beings. AI based Technology using coding and its applications is changing at a very fast rate influencing day-to-day life positively. AI and coding are nowadays applied in almost all fields, be it education, transport management, air traffic control, medicine manufacturing, space research, customer care, pandemic control, or entertainment.

After understanding the importance and demand of AI, the Govt of India, through CBSE, has launched Skills Development subjects from class VIII onwards, including Coding, Artificial Intelligence, Data Science, etc. CBSE has introduced *'Artificial Intelligence'* as a skill subject in classes IX-XII from the Session 2019-2020 onwards to simplify the AI learning experience. It is an attempt to nurture design thinking, logical flow of ideas and apply this across the disciplines.

This resource book is written according to the latest guidelines and syllabus of AI issued by CBSE. The main objective of writing this series of books for classes IX to XII is to provide test items on technical knowledge with all examination aspects of AI. Thus, the learners will become fully competent to face the challenges of living in an AI-based applications-equipped futuristic society. Moreover, emphasis on the development of 21st Century Life Skills through a variety of test items is laid down.

The resource book contains twelve chapters and three annexures. The salient features of the book are as follows:

➤ It is based on the syllabus and guidelines issued by CBSE.

➤ Simple, easy, and understandable language is used to clarify the content through a variety of test items.

➤ Each unit is divided into four sections, viz Unit in Brief, CBSE/NCERT Section, Solved Exercises, and Unsolved Exercises.

➤ It explains the concepts of each unit in lucid language in the form of **"Unit In Brief"**.

➤ **'CBSE/NCERT Section'** contains all solved questions appeared in CBSE/NCERT textbook or manual.

➤ **'Solved Exercises'** section provides all sorts of the test items including MCQs, Fill in the Blanks, True/False Type, Statements Based Questions, Assertion Reason Type Questions, VSAQs, SAQs, LAQs, and HOTS related to the content of the unit.

➤ **'Unsolved Questions'** section provides additional unsolved questions for practice.

➤ **"Competency Based Questions"** are incorporated in all units for enhancing and evaluating competencies among learners as per NEP 2020.

➤ It incorporates a pictorial setup in presenting the content by using tables, charts, graphs, pictures, photographs, etc.

➤ **Solved Board Papers, Solved CBSE Sample Papers, Solved Sample Papers** and **Unsolved Sample Papers** for **Term 1** and **Term 2** are provided.

I am sure that the sincere efforts put in by the author and publication team will be well received by the dynamic, dedicated and passionate teachers, and energetic learners. The author will appreciate all sorts of feedback from the readers to improve the quality of the content.

Dated 01 Sept. 2021

SP Verma

E-mail: spv1962@gmail.com

Coloured Images

Please follow the link to download the
Coloured Images of the book:

https://rebrand.ly/c719bc

We have code bundles from our rich catalogue of books and videos available at **https://github.com/bpbpublications**. Check them out!

Errata

We take immense pride in our work at BPB Publications and follow best practices to ensure the accuracy of our content to provide with an indulging reading experience to our subscribers. Our readers are our mirrors, and we use their inputs to reflect and improve upon human errors, if any, that may have occurred during the publishing processes involved. To let us maintain the quality and help us reach out to any readers who might be having difficulties due to any unforeseen errors, please write to us at :

errata@bpbonline.com

Your support, suggestions and feedbacks are highly appreciated by the BPB Publications' Family.

Did you know that BPB offers eBook versions of every book published, with PDF and ePub files available? You can upgrade to the eBook version at www.bpbonline.com and as a print book customer, you are entitled to a discount on the eBook copy. Get in touch with us at :

business@bpbonline.com for more details.

At **www.bpbonline.com**, you can also read a collection of free technical articles, sign up for a range of free newsletters, and receive exclusive discounts and offers on BPB books and eBooks.

Piracy

If you come across any illegal copies of our works in any form on the internet, we would be grateful if you would provide us with the location address or website name. Please contact us at **business@bpbonline.com** with a link to the material.

If you are interested in becoming an author

If there is a topic that you have expertise in, and you are interested in either writing or contributing to a book, please visit **www.bpbonline.com**. We have worked with thousands of developers and tech professionals, just like you, to help them share their insights with the global tech community. You can make a general application, apply for a specific hot topic that we are recruiting an author for, or submit your own idea.

Reviews

Please leave a review. Once you have read and used this book, why not leave a review on the site that you purchased it from? Potential readers can then see and use your unbiased opinion to make purchase decisions. We at BPB can understand what you think about our products, and our authors can see your feedback on their book. Thank you!

For more information about BPB, please visit **www.bpbonline.com**.

Table of Contents

Syllabus

ARTIFICIAL INTELLIGENCE (SUBJECT CODE 417)
Class X (Session 2020-21)
Total Marks: 100 (Theory-50 + Practical-50)

	TERM	UNITS	NO. OF HOURS for Theory and Practical 200	MAX. MARKS for Theory and Practical 100
PART A		**Employability Skills**		
	Term I	Unit 1: Communication Skills-II	10	5
		Unit 2: Self-Management Skills-II	10	
		Unit 3: ICT Skills-II	10	
	Term II	Unit 4: Entrepreneurial Skills-II	15	5
		Unit 5: Green Skills-II	05	
		Total	**50**	**10**
PART B		**Subject Specific Skills**		**Marks**
	Term I	Unit 1: Introduction to Artificial Intelligence		10
		Unit 2: AI Project Cycle		10
		Unit 3: Advance Python* (*To be assessed in Practicals only)		
	Term II	Unit 4: Data Science* (*To be assessed in Practicals only)		
		Unit 5: Computer Vision* (*To be assessed in Practicals only)		
		Unit 6: Natural Language Processing		10
		Unit 7: Evaluation		10
		Total		**40**
PART C		**Practical Work:** • Unit 3: Advance Python • Unit 4: Data Science • Unit 5: Computer Vision		20
		Practical Examination		10
		Viva Voce		5
		Total		**35**
PART D		Project Work/ Field Visit/ Practical File/ Student Portfolio		10
		Viva Voce		5
		Total		**15**
		GRAND TOTAL	**200**	**100**

UNIT 1
Communication Skills II

1.1 UNIT IN BRIEF

✦ Communication is defined as the process of sharing information, ideas, attitude, and feelings.

✦ Communication is defined as a process of sharing information between two or more people through an exchange of thoughts, messages, and information, using the medium of speech, visuals, symbols, writing, attitude, and/ behaviour.

✦ Speech, vocabulary, rhythm, tone, and pitch are some of the factors that enhance oral communication.

✦ There are three basic types of communications-verbal, non-verbal and visual communication.

✦ Verbal communication use linguistics to convey the message/information/feelings.

✦ There are two primary mediums of verbal communication-Oral Communication and Written Communication.

✦ Verbal communication is further classified into two sub-categories: Intrapersonal Communication and Interpersonal Communication.

✦ Written communication means communicating through written words.

✦ Verbal communication helps us to think, maintain relationships, define reality, and organise complex ideas and experiences into meaningful experiences.

✦ Non-verbal communication occurs in the absence of any oral or composing words.

✦ Non-verbal communication uses other forms like tactile, auditory, kinaesthetic channels to transmit information/knowledge.

Figure 1.1

✦ Non-verbal communication uses different non-verbal prompts like body movements, gestures, facial expressions, symbols, images, signals charts, and soon to express sentiments, attitudes, or information.

✦ People use non-verbal communication to emphasize, replace, or complement verbal communication, communicate emotions, and give feedback to the other person.

✦ In visual communication, visuals are used to communicate information/ideas/feelings.

✦ The conveyance of ideas and information in forms that can be seen through the eye is termed visual communication.

✦ The communication cycle comprises seven elements: sender, message, encoding, communication channel, receiver, decoding, and feedback.

✦ The communication cycle describes how an idea, impression, or feeling is made known to others.

✦ Feedback is defined as the response that a receiver gives after the message is received and understood by him.

✦ Feedback may be provided verbally or in written form. Feedback may be specific or non-specific.

✦ Feedback is required to continue the process of active communication. It can be effective only when it is heard, interpreted, and accepted.

✦ Formation or summative feedback may be given to someone about one's progress.

✦ Descriptive feedback gives detailed input, while general feedback is not so important.

✦ Specific feedback helps to improve the thought process.

✦ Feedback should be task-oriented that allows the students to refine their skills, re-engage in their learning, and concentrate on their goal.

✦ Specific feedback provides detailed analysis/ information about something particular relating to a task or the individual's performance.

Figure 1.2

✦ Non-specific feedback provides a vague response to the receiver.

✦ A communication barrier is defined as an obstacle that prevents the receiver from receiving and understanding the message sent by a sender.

✦ When a message is not understood clearly, then it may lead to communication gaps, causing confusion and misunderstanding between the sender and receiver.

✦ Barriers related to the message occur due to problems in the composition or formation of the message itself.

Figure 1.3

✦ The factors that cause barriers related to the message being conveyed include lengthy messages, language problems, intonation issues, or the non-verbal communication used.

✦ Internal barriers occur due to some inherent traits or the frame of mind of any of the communicators.

✦ Factors influencing internal barriers include intense emotions, poor listening skills, prejudice, different viewpoints, or different cultural backgrounds.

✦ External barriers occur due to the factors which are outside our body and mind. We have no control over them.

✦ Factors like noise, cultural differences, different time zones and distance, faulty communication equipment or technologies, etc., are responsible for non-effective communication.

✦ Physical disabilities and physical barriers are some of the causes of external barriers.

✦ Effective communication implies that the transmitted content has been received and understood well by the receiver.

✦ Effective communication also means that what you want to say, what you say, and what the receiver interprets are consistent.

✦ The goals of effective communication are to establish trust and understanding, change behaviour, and acquire information.

✦ The three important points to be considered in communication are content, process, and context.

+ The principles of communication are based on the 7 C's-Clear, Concise, Concrete, Correct, Coherent, Complete, and Courteous.

+ Effective communication reduces misunderstandings. Also, it prevents us from overlooking important information.

+ It allows the communicators to build trust and remove any negative emotions.

+ Effective communication skills increase our self-confidence.

+ The most important benefit of using effective communication techniques is that it improves our relationships with others.

+ For professional growth, writing skills are essential.

+ Essential elements for persuasive writing include reading comprehension, transcription, sentence construction, content knowledge, planning, and self-regulation.

+ Two types of articles-definite and indefinite, are used.

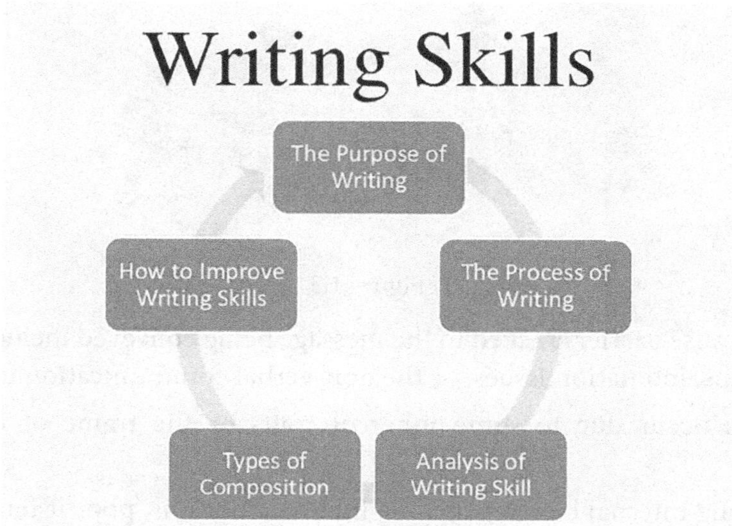

Figure 1.4

+ Elements for paragraph writing are unity, order, coherence, and completeness.

1.2 CBSE/NCERT SECTION (SOLVED CBSE/NCERT EXERCISE QUESTIONS)

(A) Multiple Choice Questions

Read the questions carefully and circle the letter(s) (a), (b), (c) or (d) that best answer(s) the question. (Note: There may be more than one correct choice in some questions).

1. Which of the following is NOT an element of communication within the communication process cycle?

   a) Channel   b) Receiver   c) Sender   d) Time

2. If you need to apply for leave at work, which method of communication will you use?

   a) e-mail   b) Poster   c) Newsletter   d) Blog

3. By which action can senders send their messages?
    a) Gestures   b) Speaking   c) Reading   d) Writing

4. Which of the following is an example of oral communication?
    a) Newspapers   b) Letters   c) Phone call   d) e-mail

5. What are the types of words we should use for verbal communication?
    a) Acronyms   b) Simple   c) Technical   d) Jargons

6. Why do we use e-mails?
    a) To communicate with a large of people at the same time.
    b) To share documents and files.
    c) To talk to each other in real-time.
    d) To keep a record of communication.

7. Which of the following is a positive (good) facial expression?
    a) Frowning while concentrating   b) Maintaining eye contact
    c) Smiling continuously   d) Rolling up your eyes

8. What does an upright (straight) body posture convey or show?
    a) Pride   b) Professionalism   c) Confidence   d) Humility

9. Which of these is NOT an appropriate non-verbal communication at work?
    a) Keeping hands in pockets while talking
    b) Talking at moderate speed
    c) Sitting straight
    d) Tilting head a bit to listen

10. Which of the following statement is true about communication?
    a) 50% of our communication is non-verbal
    b) 20% of total communication is done using body movements, face, arms, etc.
    c) 5% of total communication is done using voice; tone pauses, etc.
    d) 7% of total communication is done using words

11. Which of these are examples of positive feedback?
    a) Excellent, your work has improved.
    b) I noticed your dedication to the project.
    c) You are always doing it the wrong way.
    d) All of the above

12. Which of these are examples of negative feedback?
    a) I hate to tell you this, but your drawing skills are poor.
    b) You can surely improve your drawing.
    c) This is a good drawing, but you can do better.
    d) None of the above

13. Which of the following are effective components of good feedback?
    a) Detailed and time-consuming
    b) Direct and honest
    c) Specific
    d) Opinion-based

14. Which of these is NOT a common communication barrier?
    a) Linguistic barrier
    b) Interpersonal barrier
    c) Financial barrier
    d) Organizational barrier

15. Which of these are ways to overcome communication barriers?
    a) Respecting each other's differences
    b) Using a translator
    c) Not communicating at all
    d) Using your own language for comfort

16. In which of the following, the underlined word is an adjective?
    a) Radha has a red dress.
    b) I can speak French.
    c) The Girl on the Train is a best-seller.
    d) Abdul can swim fast.

17. Which of these sentences is capitalized correctly?
    a) Ravi and I are going to the movies.
    b) Salim is visiting India in July.
    c) The Tiger is a strong animal.
    d) She is arriving on Monday.

18. Which of these sentences are punctuated correctly?
    a) When is the party!
    b) I had a bread omelet and a Banana for breakfast.
    c) I am so excited about my first foreign trip!
    d) This is Abdul's notebook.

19. In which of these sentences can you find an adverb?
    a) Divya drinks milk every day.
    b) Sanjay gifted me a new pen.
    c) I opened the door lock.
    d) Sita is 5-feet tall.

20. Identify the object, verb, and subject in the sentence, 'The car crashed into a tree.'
    a) Object: a tree; Verb: crashed; Subject: the car
    b) Object: The car; Verb: crashed; Subject: a tree
    c) Object: crashed; Verb: the tree; Subject: the car
    d) Object: crashed; Verb: the car; Subject: the tree

21. Identify the indirect object in the sentence, 'The band played music for the audience.'
    a) The band
    b) played
    c) music
    d) audience

22. Which of these is an imperative sentence?
    a) Switch off the fan.
    b) Sheila has gone to the market.
    c) Where are my pen and colours?
    d) Oh no! I missed my flight.

23. Which of these sentences is in active voice?
    a) A movie is being watched by them.
    b) The car was repaired by Raju.

c) He is reading a book.

d) The thief was being chased by a policeman.

ANSWERS
1. d   2. a   3. c   4. c   5. b   6. a, b and d   7. b   8. c   9. a
10. d   11. a and b   12. a and b   13. b and c   14. c   15. a and b
16. a and c   17. a, b and d   18. c and d   19. a   20. a   21. d   22. d
23. c

(B) Subjective Questions

1. Put an X mark against the actions below, which are examples of bad non-verbal communication:

Figure 1.5

a) Laughing during formal communication

b) Scratching head

c) Smiling when speaking to a friend

d) Nodding when you agree with something

e) Standing straight

f) Yawning while listening

g) Sitting straight

h) Maintaining eye contact while speaking

i) Biting nails

j) Firm Handshake

k) Clenching jaws

l) Looking away when someone is speaking to you

m) Intense stare

Ans. a) Laughing during formal communication X

b) Scratching head X

c) Smiling when speaking to a friend

d) Nodding when you agree with something

e) Standing straight

f) Yawning while listening to X

g) Sitting straight

h) Maintaining eye contact while speaking

i) Biting nails X

j) Firm handshake X

k) Clenching jaws X

l) Looking away when someone is speaking to you X

m) Intense stare X

2. List the different types of verbal communication. Include examples for each verbal communication type.

Ans. The following types of Verbal Communication are used:

a) **Interpersonal Communication**: This form of communication takes place between two individuals and is hence a one-on-one conversation. It may be formal or informal.

Examples:

i.   A principal discusses the performance of students with the teachers.

ii. Two school friends are discussing a project.

iii. Two girls are chatting to each other over mobile/phone.

b) **Written Communication**: This form of communication uses writing words. It can be letters, reports, circulars, manuals, social media chats,SMS, etc. It can be between two persons among or more people.

Examples:

i.   A General Manager is writing an appreciation e-mail to core team members.

ii. Hema is writing a letter to grandfather enquiring about his health.

c) **Small-Group Communication**: This communication takes place when there are more than two people involved in a small group. Each participant can interact and converse with the other members.

Examples:

i.   Board meetings   ii. Team meetings   iii. Press conferences

d) **Public Communication**: This communication takes place when one individual addresses a large gathering.

Examples:

i.   Election campaigns initiated by political leaders

ii. Public speeches by dignitaries, like Prime Minister, Cabinet Minister, etc.

3. Draw any five common signs used for Visual Communication. Explain what each conveys and where did you see it?

Ans. i.   Under construction (at construction sites or on roads)

Figure 1.6

ii.   Under CCTV surveillance (at the school gate, at society gate)

Figure 1.7

iii. No pets allowed (in hospitals)

Figure 1.8

iv.   No parking zone (in VIP areas)

Figure 1.9

v.   No mobile phone (in hospitals/silent zones)

Figure 1.10

4.   What do you mean by feedback?

Ans.   Feedback is one of the most important factors in the process of communication since it is defined as the response given by the receiver to the sender.

5.   Write down the common communication barriers you may come across when you move to a new city or country.

Ans.   The following types of communication barriers may be faced while moving to a new city or country:

1.   **Linguistic Barriers:** The inability to communicate using a language is called the language barrier to communication. Language barriers are the most common communication barriers, which cause misunderstandings and misinterpretations between people.

2.   **Cultural Barriers:** Cultural barriers are when people of different cultures are unable to understand each other's customs, resulting in inconveniences and difficulties. People sometimes make stereotypical assumptions about others based on their cultural background and this leads to a difference in opinions and can be a major barrier to effective communication.

3.   **Physical Barriers:** A 'Physical barrier' is the environmental and natural condition that may act as a barrier in communication in sending or receiving a message from sender to receiver or vice versa. Not being able to look at gestures, posture, and general body language can make communication less effective.

4.   **Interpersonal Barriers:** Barriers to interpersonal communication occur when the sender's message is received differently from how it was intended. It is also very difficult to communicate with someone who is not willing to talk or express his/her feelings and views.

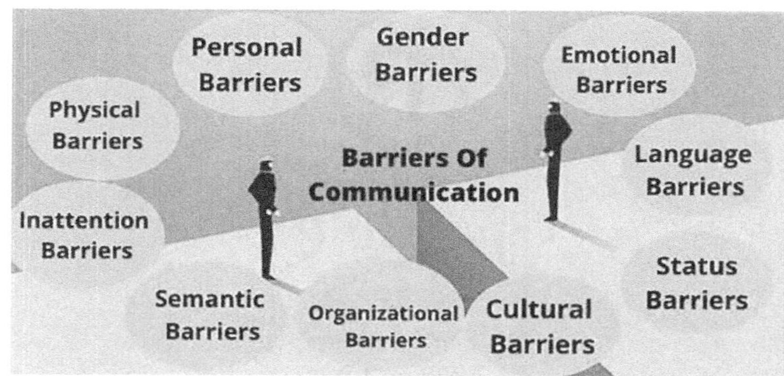

Figure 1.11

6. Fill correct nouns and verbs from the given options to complete the sentence in table given below:

Nouns: Boy, Mr S Sen, Rahim, Children, Cat, Students   **Verbs:** Swimming, Driving, Writing, Teaching, Eating, Playing
a. The _____________ is _____________.   b. The _____________ are _____________.   c. The _____________ are _____________.   d. _____________ is _____________ the car.   e. _____________ is _____________.   f. The _____________ is _____________.

ANSWERS
a. The boy is swimming.   b. The children are playing.   c. The students are writing.   d. Rahim is driving the car.   e. Mr S Sen is teaching.   f. The cat is eating.

7. Identify the conjunctions and prepositions from the list below and write these in the different boxes.

Over, Because, Under, And, Since, In, At, Although, Or, Up, On, Beside

Ans.

Conjunction	Preposition
Because, And, Since, Although, Beside.	Over, Under, In, At, Or, Up, On

1.3 SOLVED EXERCISES

1.3.1 Multiple Choice Questions

Tick (√) is the correct option.

1. Which statement is true about communication?
    a) About 25% of communication is done using voice, tone, and pauses, etc.
    b) About 50% of our communication is non-verbal.
    c) About 75% of communication is done using words.
    d) About 85% of communication is done using body movements, face, arms, etc.

2. What is the most significant benefit of using effective communication techniques?
    a) It improves our relationships.   b) It helps us earn more money.
    c) It makes us famous.   d) None of these

3. An example of positive feedback is:
    a) You are mostly doing it the wrong way.
    b) I noticed your non-dedication towards the project.
    c) Excellent, your work has improved.
    d) All of these

4. A smile and a nod is an example of:
   a) Oral Communication
   b) Written Communication
   c) Verbal Communication
   d) Non-verbal Communication

5. Why should one prefer e-mails over other methods?
   a) To talk to each other in real-time.
   b) To communicate with many people simultaneously.
   c) To share documents and files with one or more persons within seconds.
   d) To keep a record of communication.

6. Which factor(s) should be considered while a medium of communication is selected?
   a) Timing
   b) Distance between the sender and the receiver
   c) Nature of the interaction
   d) None of these

7. What is given in the descriptive feedback in the form of written comments or verbal conversations?
   a) General guidance
   b) Specific information
   c) General rules
   d) None of these

8. Which refers to communication that is believable and credible in order to create trust between the communicators?
   a) Concreteness
   b) Completeness
   c) Conciseness
   d) None of these

9. The goal(s) of effective communication is/are:
   a) Creating understanding
   b) Changing attitude
   c) Sharing information
   d) All of these

10. An example of oral communication is:

Figure 1.12

   a) Blogs
   b) e-mail
   c) Phone call
   d) Letters

11. What refers to explaining things in a brief yet comprehensive manner?
   a) Clarity
   b) Conciseness
   c) Concreteness
   d) Correctness

12. Which of the following is not correct function of verbal communication?
    a) It helps us define reality.
    b) It can be used to reward and punish.
    c) It hinders the maintenance of relationships.
    d) It helps to organise complex ideas and experiences into meaningful categories.

13. The important factors of communication is/are:
    a) Content   b) Process   c) Context   d) All of these

14. What is about avoiding the use of complex words, sentences, and confusing language?
    a) Accuracy   b) Fluency
    c) Punctuation   d) Clarity

15. Which of these is an example(s) of negative feedback?
    a) I do not like to tell you this, but your communication skills are poor.
    b) Rakes! You can't improve your drawing.
    c) This is a good drawing, but you can do better.
    d) None of the above

16. What is a group of words that forms a unit within a sentence but is incomplete independently known as?
    a) Predicate   b) Phrase   c) Noun   d) Subject

17. Which is not a form of non-verbal communication?
    a) Facial expressions   b) Hand gestures
    c) Oral expressions   d) Eye contact

18. Which form of communication is known as extremely private communication?
    a) Interpersonal   b) Intrapersonal
    c) Small group   d) None of the above

19. With which of the following words, the article 'an' cannot be used?
    a) Euro   b) MLA   c) Hour   d) Egg

20. Which barrier does occur due to some inherent traits or the frame of mind of the communicator?
    a) Internal   b) External   c) Emotional   d) Cultural

21. What is used to keep our record of the communication for future reference?
    a) Spoken words   b) Written words
    c) Hand movements   d) Symbols

22. The information that the sender wishes to convey is called:
    a) Feedback   b) Message
    c) Noise   d) Communication barrier

23. What is the final component in the process of communication as it defines the response given by the receiver to the sender?
    a) Notice
    b) Response
    c) Feedback
    d) Request

24. Which of the following words does refer to a word or phrase that expresses a strong emotion?
    a) Interjection
    b) Conjunction
    c) Verb
    d) Preposition

25. Which of the following components is an effective component of good feedback?
    a) Direct and honest
    b) Detailed and time taking
    c) Specific
    d) Non-specific

26. The information provided in the communication should be:
    a) Complete
    b) Incomplete
    c) Short and Neat
    d) None of these

27. Which type of communication brings personal warmth and friendliness between the sender and receiver?
    a) Written Communication
    b) Visual Communication
    c) Oral Communication
    d) None of these

28. Effective communication results in:
    a) Building trust
    b) Reducing misunderstandings
    c) Resolving conflicts
    d) All of these

29. Which mode of communication is used to convey a message consisting of spoken words?
    a) Oral Communication
    b) Visual Communication
    c) Written Communication
    d) Non-verbal Communication

30. Communication is required:
    a) At no time
    b) Sometimes
    c) Frequently
    d) At all time

31. During communication, the sender should be:
    a) Unruly
    b) Rude
    c) Polite
    d) None of these

32. Which element is NOT an element of communication within the communication process cycle?
    a) Receiver
    b) Sender
    c) Time
    d) Channel

33. Which process is related to sharing information between two or more people?
    a) Communication
    b) Description
    c) Transition
    d) Transcription

34. The ____________ the response, the more effective it is the communication cycle.
    a) Clear
    b) Slower
    c) Quicker
    d) Vague

35. The information provided in the communication should be:
    a) Complete
    b) Incomplete
    c) Short and Neat
    d) None of these

36. Why should one prefer e-mails over other methods of communication?
    a) To communicate with many people simultaneously.
    b) To talk to each other in real-time.
    c) To keep a record of communication.
    d) To share documents and files with one or more persons.

37. Which parts of speech do refer to a word that exhibits the relationship of a noun, pronoun, or noun phrase to other word?
    a) Verb
    b) Interjection
    c) Preposition
    d) Conjunction

38. By which action can senders not send their messages?
    a) Gestures
    b) Speaking
    c) Writing
    d) Reading

39. Which refers to the situation or environment in which the message is delivered?
    a) Process
    b) Content
    c) Context
    d) All of these

40. An upright (straight) body posture conveys:
    a) Confidence
    b) Professionalism
    c) Pride
    d) Humility

41. Which is NOT an appropriate non-verbal communication at the workplace?
    a) Tilting head a bit to listen
    b) Keeping hands in pockets while talking
    c) Sitting straight
    d) Talking at moderate speed

ANSWERS									
1. (b)	2. (a)	3. (c)	4. (d)	5. (c)	6. (c)	7. (b)	8. (a)	9. (d)	10. (c)
11. (a)	12. (c)	13. (d)	14. (d)	15. (b)	16. (b)	17. (c)	18. (b)	19. (b)	20. (a)
21. (b)	22. (b)	23. (c)	24. (a)	25. (c)	26. (a)	27. (c)	28. (d)	29. (a)	30. (d)
31. (c)	32. (c)	33. (a)	34. (c)	35. (a)	36. (d)	37. (c)	38. (d)	39. (c)	40. (a)
41. (b)									

1.3.2 Fill in the blanks

1. ___________ communication occurs in the absence of any oral or composing words.

2. A coherent message is ___________ and makes sense to the receiver.

3. In ___________ communication, information is exchanged between two individuals.

4. ___________ is the loudness and softness of a speaker's voice.

5. Poor listening skills are the type of ___________ barriers.

6. The conversion of ideas and information in forms that can be seen through the eyes is referred to as ___________ communication.

7. Technological problems with equipment used for communication are an example of ___________ barrier.

8. ___________ deals with how the receiver interprets the message, depending on his/her circumstances and understanding.

9. The communicator must seek ___________ to check whether the message was clearly understood or not.

10. An ___________ sentence is a sentence that describes a fact.

11. A ___________ is a person for whom the message is intended.

12. ___________ feedback gives a wrong or vague response to the receiver.

13. ___________ Communication enables people to symbolically represent objects, ideas, etc.

14. ___________ feedback does not include grades, marks, or coded symbols.

15. The interferences which occur due to accent, speech disorders, or symbols having multiple meanings for the sender and the receiver are called ___________ Barriers.

ANSWERS				
1. Non-Verbal	2. Logical	3. Interpersonal	4. Pitch	5. internal
6. Visual	7. external	8. Decoding	9. Feedback	10. Assertive
11. Receiver	12. Non-Specific/General		13. Visual	14. Descriptive
15. Linguistic				

1.3.3 True or False

1. Effective communication enhances our confidence.

2. Press conferences, board meetings, and teleconferences are examples of Small-Group Communication.

3. Non-Specific feedback provides a direction for the students to identify the steps taken to fulfill their goals.

4. Non-verbal communication means communicating through written words.

5. The communication process enlists the steps users take to comprehend each other properly.

6. Coding refers to how the receiver interprets the message and translates it into thoughts.

7. Descriptive feedback reduces the gap between the present level of performance and the learning goal.

8. The Effectiveness of a communication cycle depends on how long it takes for feedback to be received by the initial sender.

9. Right feedback given at the right time may lead the communicators towards their desired goal.

10. Encoding deals with how the sender wishes to communicate the message.

11. Negative Feedback can enhance a student's confidence, self-awareness, and enthusiasm for learning.

ANSWERS			
1. (T)	2. (T)	3. (F, specific feedback)	4. (F, written communication)
5. (T) 6. (F, Decoding)	7. (T) 8. (T) 9. (T) 10. (T) 11. (F, Positive feedback)		

1.3.4 Matching type

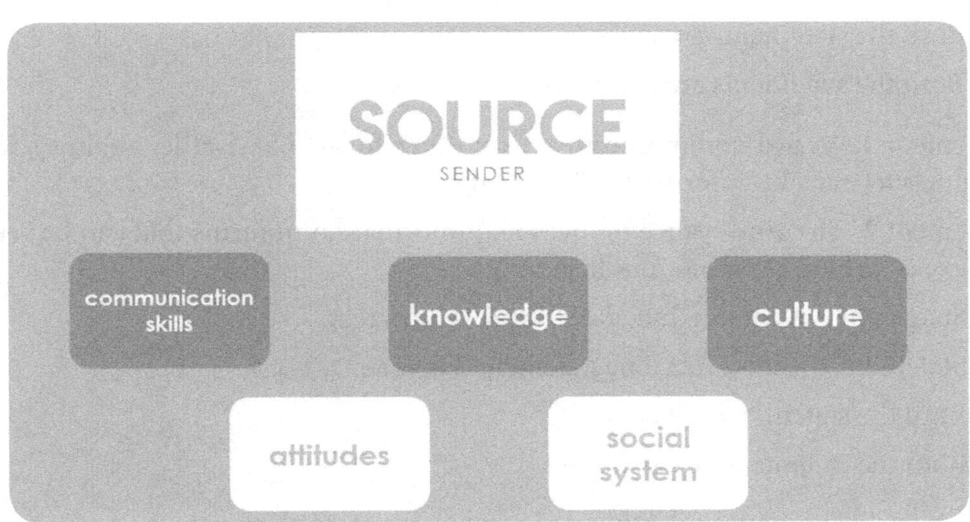

Figure 1.13

I. Match the items of column A with those of column B correctly.

Column A

1. Sender
2. Receiver
3. Message
4. Channel
5. Feedback

Column B

(a) The means by which the information is sent.

(b) The information that the sender wants to convey.

(c) The receiver's acknowledgment and response to the message

(d) The person to whom the message is sent.

(e) The person beginning the communication.

ANSWERS				
1. e	2. d	3. b	4. a	5. c

1.3.5 Statements Based Questions

1. Statement 1: Speech, vocabulary, rhythm, tone, and pitch are some of the factors that enhance oral communication.

   Statement 2: Verbal communication use linguistics to convey the message/information/feelings.

   a) Statement 1 is correct, but statement 2 is incorrect.

   b) Statement 1 is incorrect, but statement 2 is correct.

c) Both the statements are correct.

d) Both the statements are incorrect.

2. Statement 1: Verbal communication helps us to think, maintain relationships, define reality, and organise complex ideas and experiences into meaningful experiences.

   Statement 2: Verbal communication occurs in the absence of any oral or composing words.

   a) Statement 1 is correct, but statement 2 is incorrect.

   b) Statement 1 is incorrect, but statement 2 is correct.

   c) Both the statements are correct.

   d) Both the statements are incorrect.

3. Statement 1: Verbal communication uses other forms like tactile, auditory, kinaesthetic channels to transmit information/knowledge.

   Statement 2: The conveyance of ideas and information in forms that can be seen through the eye is termed verbal communication.

   a) Statement 1 is correct ,but statement 2 is incorrect.

   b) Statement 1 is incorrect ,but statement 2 is correct.

   c) Both the statements are correct.

   d) Both the statements are incorrect.

4. Statement 1: The communication cycle comprises three elements.

   Statement 2: In visual communication, visuals are used to communicate information/ideas/feelings.

   a) Statement 1 is correct, but statement 2 is incorrect.

   b) Statement 1 is incorrect, but statement 2 is correct.

   c) Both the statements are correct.

   d) Both the statements are incorrect.

5. Statement 1: Feedback is the response that a receiver gives after the message is received and understood by him.

   Statement 2: Feedback may be provided verbally or in written form. Feedback may be specific or non-specific.

   a) Statement 1 is correct, but statement 2 is incorrect.

   b) Statement 1 is incorrect, but statement 2 is correct.

   c) Both the statements are correct.

   d) Both the statements are incorrect.

6. Statement 1: Written communication means communicating through visuals and written words.

   Statement 2: Barriers related to the message occur due to problems in the composition or formation of the message itself.

a) Statement 1 is correct, but statement 2 is incorrect.

b) Statement 1 is incorrect, but statement 2 is correct.

c) Both the statements are correct.

d) Both the statements are incorrect.

ANSWERS					
1. (c)	2. (a)	3. (d)	4. (b)	5. (c)	6. (b)

1.3.6 Assertion Reason Type Questions

1. Assertion (A): Feedback is required to continue the process of active communication.

    Reason(R): Feedback can be effective only when it is heard, interpreted, and accepted.

    a) Both A and R are correct, and R is the correct reason for A.

    b) Both A and R are correct, and R is not the correct reason for A.

    c) A is correct, but R is incorrect.

    d) Both A and r are incorrect.

2. Assertion (A): Communication is defined as a process of sharing information between two or more people through an exchange of thoughts, messages, and information, using the medium of speech, visuals, symbols, writing, attitude, and/ behaviour.

    Reason (R): People use verbal communication to emphasize, replace, or complement verbal communication, communicate emotions, and give feedback to the other person.

    a) Both A and R are correct, and R is the correct reason for A.

    b) Both A and R are correct, and R is not the correct reason for A.

    c) A is correct, but R is incorrect.

    d) Both A and R are incorrect.

3. Assertion (A): A specific feedback provides detailed information about something particular relating to a task or the individual's performance.

    Reason (R): Specific feedback is required to improve the thought process.

    a) Both A and R are correct, and R is the correct reason for A.

    b) Both A and R are correct, and R is not the incorrect reason for A.

    c) A is correct, but R is incorrect.

    d) Both A and R are incorrect.

4. Assertion (A): A communication barrier is an obstacle that prevents the receiver from receiving and understanding the message sent by a sender.

    Reason (R): Factors like noise, cultural differences, different time zones and distance, faulty communication equipment or technologies, etc., are responsible for non-effective communication.

    a) Both A and R are correct, and R is the correct reason for A.

b) Both A and R are correct, and R is not the correct reason for A.

c) A is correct, but R is incorrect.

d) Both A and R are incorrect.

5. Assertion (A): Factors influencing external barriers include intense emotions, poor listening skills, prejudice, different viewpoints, or different cultural backgrounds.
   Reason (R): A specific feedback gives a vague response to the receiver.
   a) Both A and R are correct, and R is the correct reason for A.
   b) Both A and R are correct, and R is not the correct reason for A.
   c) A is correct, but R is incorrect.
   d) Both A and R are incorrect.

ANSWERS
1. (b)   2. (c)   3. (a)   4. (b)   5. (d)

1.3.7 Competency Based Questions

1. A Russian group visited **GolumJa AIProducts Ltd**. The Indian team of the company communicated with Russian group using different prompts like body movements, gestures, facial expressions, symbols, images, signals charts, and to express sentiments, attitudes, or information. This type of communication is called:
   a) Verbal Communication
   b) Non-verbal Communication
   c) Visual Communication
   d) None of the above

2. Consider the following limitations/disadvantages:
   i. It is more expensive.
   ii. More time and effort are required to produce them.
   iii. It has limited scope.
   iv. Complete and detailed information is not conveyed.
   v. Sometimes there may be a design issue.

   These limitations are related to:
   a) Verbal Communication
   b) Non-verbal Communication
   c) Visual Communication
   d) All of the above

3. Surjeet Khumman belongs to Manipur and he has a friend AK Unni Krishanan from Kerala. Both have ethnic, religious, and social differences that can often create misunderstandings during communication. These differences can also affect one's perception and create confusion in getting a message correctly. This type of communication barrier is known as:
   a) Linguistic barriers
   b) Cultural barriers
   c) Attitudinal barriers
   d) Perceptual barriers

ANSWERS
1. (b)   2. (c)   3. (b)

1.3.8 VSA

1. Define communication.

Ans. Communication is the process of sharing information, ideas, altitude, and/ feelings between two or more people.

2. What do you mean by communication barriers?

Ans. A communication barrier is defined as an obstacle that prevents the receiver from receiving and understanding the message sent by a sender.

3. Why is feedback necessary in communication?

Ans. To improve the quality of communication, feedback is necessary.

4. Define visual communication.

Ans. The conversion of ideas and information in forms that can be seen through the eye is termed visual communication.

5. Enlist the factors responsible for enhancing oral communication.

Ans. Speech, vocabulary, rhythm, tone, and pitch are some of the factors that enhance oral communication.

6. What are the three basic types of communication?

Ans. Three basic types of communication are verbal, non-verbal, and visual communication.

7. What is used in verbal communication to convey the message?

Ans. Verbal communication use linguistics to convey the message/information/feelings.

8. What are the two primary mediums of verbal communication?

Ans. Oral Communication and Written Communication.

9. When is Non-verbal communication used?

Ans. Non-verbal communication occurs in the absence of any oral or composing words.

10. Define feedback.

Ans. Feedback is the response that a receiver gives after the message is received.

11. How is feedback given?

Ans. Feedback may be provided verbally or in written form. Feedback may be specific or non-specific.

12. What is descriptive feedback?

Ans. Descriptive feedback gives detailed input, while general feedback is not so important.

13. Mention the main purpose of specific feedback.

Ans. Specific feedback helps to improve the thought process.

14. What is achieved through specific feedback?

Ans. Specific feedback provides a detailed analysis /information about something particular relating to a task or the individual's performance.

15. Why is non-specific feedback considered not good?

Ans. Non-specific feedback provides a vague response to the receiver.

16. Define internal barrier?

Ans. Internal barriers occur due to some inherent traits or the frame of mind of any of the communicators.

17. Define external barriers?

Ans. External barriers occur due to the factors which are outside our body and mind. We have no control over them.

18. Define effective communication.

Ans. Effective communication implies that the transmitted content has been received and understood well by the receiver.

19. What is reduced ineffective communication?

Ans. Effective communication reduces misunderstandings.

20. Define verbal communication.

Ans. Sounds and words to express by someone, especially in contrast to using gestures or mannerisms (non-verbal communication), are used in verbal communication.

21. Define a Sentence.

Ans. A group of words giving complete meaning to the ideas is called a sentence. A sentence should be grammatically correct.

22. Define paragraph.

Ans. In a paragraph, a group of sentences dealing with a single topic is used. Thus, a paragraph is a series of sentences that are organised and coherent and are all related to a single topic.

1.3.9 Short Answer Type Questions

1. How do non-verbal communications occur?

Ans. Non-verbal communication uses different non-verbal prompts like body movements, gestures, facial expressions, symbols, images, signals charts, and to express sentiments, attitudes, or information.

2. Enlist seven elements of the communication cycle.

Ans. The communication cycle comprises seven elements: sender, message, encoding, communication channel, receiver, decoding, and feedback.

3. What will happen when a message is not understood clearly by the receiver?

Ans. When a message is not understood clearly, then it may lead to communication gaps, causing confusion and misunderstanding between the sender and receiver.

4. What are the factors responsible for causing barriers?

Ans. The factors that cause barriers related to the message being conveyed include lengthy messages, language problems, intonation issues, or the non-verbal communication used.

5. What are the factors that influence internal barriers?

Ans. Factors influencing internal barriers include intense emotions, poor listening skills, prejudice, different viewpoints, or different cultural backgrounds.

6. What are the factors that cause non-effective communication?

Ans. Factors like noise, cultural differences, different time zones and distance, faulty communication equipment or technologies, etc., are responsible for non-effective communication.

7. What are the main goals of effective communication?

Ans. The main goals of effective communication are to establish trust and understanding, change behaviour, and acquire information.

8. What are the three important points to be considered in communication?

Ans. Content, process, and context.

9. What are the seven principles of communication?

Ans. The principles of communication are based on the 7 C's-Clear, Concise, Concrete, Correct, Coherent, Complete, and Courteous.

10. What are the essential elements for writing?

Ans. Essential elements for persuasive writing include reading comprehension, transcription, sentence construction, content knowledge, planning, and self-regulation.

11. What are the elements for paragraph writing?

Ans. Elements for paragraph writing are unity, order, coherence, and completeness.

12. What is the purpose of feedback?

Ans. Feedback is mainly required to continue the process of active communication. It can be effective only when it is heard, interpreted, and accepted.

13. Differentiate between specific and non-specific feedback.

Ans.

Specific Feedback	Non-specific Feedback
1. Specific feedback provides a detailed analysis or specific information on a particular topic.	1. General feedback is termed non-specific feedback. It may be vague.
2. Specific feedback helps in modifying the behaviour or thinking for the purpose of learning by influencing the thought process.	2. Non-specific feedback is not so helpful in modifying the behaviour or thinking process.

14. Explain descriptive feedback.

Ans. Descriptive feedback is defined as the specific information in the form of written comments or verbal communications that help the sender understand what he/she needs to do in order to improve communication. It can be taken in the form of checklists/evaluations through standard rubrics. Therefore, descriptive feedback is specific information in the form of written comments or verbal conversations. It strengthens communication. For providing descriptive feedback, listening to the message properly by the receiver is must. Age, qualification, religion, region, etc., of the receiver is also important to get the correct feedback.

15. What are the techniques to hone active listening skills?

Ans.   The following five-step approach may be used:

Figure 1.14

a)   Acknowledge the other person's ideas, thoughts, or feedings

b)   Paraphrase, the other person's words to ensure understanding.

c)   Ask questions without judging.

d)   Summarize and classify what you hear.

e)   Offer your opinion if it is required.

16. Define the phrase and give two examples of it.

Ans.   A group of words that are used together is called a 'Phrase.' A phrase does not contain a full verb. A phrase may be short or long, but it does not include the subject.

Examples,

a)   A black rose

b)   A white cat

c)   At the bus station

d)   Very beautiful flower

e)   Clarify effective communication.

Ans.   Effective communication requires an understanding that:

a)   A message is conveyed clearly between communicators so that it is effective and serves the desired purpose.

b)   The communication environment at work or in the community is conducive, and there are no barriers to prevent messages from being sent and received successfully.

c) To communicate successfully, one must know what barriers to communication exist and ensure that they do not obstruct communication.

d) Communication barriers create misunderstandings, and hence, misinterpretations of messages are possible.

17. Give two examples of gestures.

Ans. (a) Raising a hand for greeting or to say goodbye.

(b) Pointing the finger at someone.

1.3.10 Long Answer Type Questions

1. Explain the communication process.

Ans. The following are the five elements of the communication process:

a) Sender: This is the person who is starting communication.

b) Message: The information that the sender intends to communicate is called message.

c) Channel: This is the means or medium by which the information is to be sent.

d) Receiver: The person(s) who receives the message is known as receiver.

e) Feedback: The acknowledgment and response of the receiver to the message.

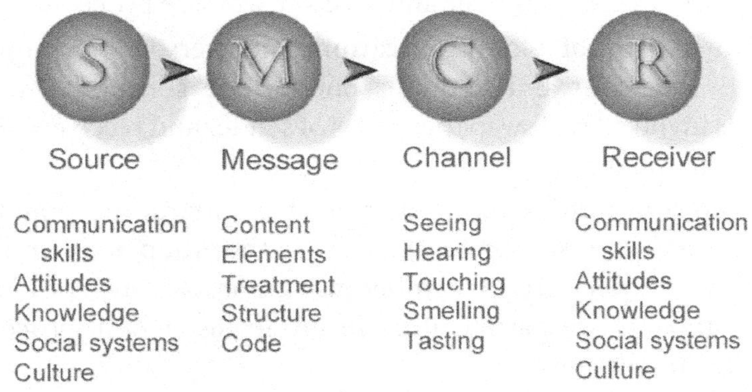

Figure 1.15

2. Explain the SMCR Model of Communication with the help of an example.

Ans. Communication is a two-way process. It means that a minimum of two persons is required during communication. There may be one-to-one communication (between two persons) or one to many communication (one is speaking, and many persons are listening like in a class, the teacher is speaking, and children are listening) or many to one communication (many persons are speaking to one person like crowed is saying something to an individual leader).

A communication message or piece of information is sent or communicated through a channel (or medium) by a sender to the receiver. This is called the SMCR (Sender/Source-Message- Channel -Receiver) model of communication.

ELEMENTS OF COMMUNICATION

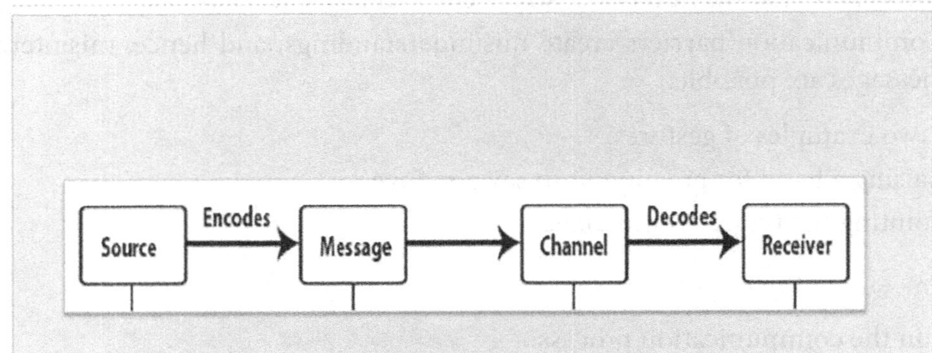

Figure 1.16

For example, if Sangeet Pandey wants to communicate a piece of information to his friend Nikhil, he may choose the channel of speaking or writing. Five senses of human beings are used as channels. Here, Sangeet Pandey will be the sender, and Nikhil will be the receiver.

3. Explain the four types of Verbal Communication.

Ans. Verbal communication is of four types:

a) **Intrapersonal verbal communications:** Intrapersonal communication is extremely private. It includes the silent conversations people have with themselves, wherein they juggle roles between the sender and receiver who are processing their thoughts.

b) **Interpersonal, verbal Communication:** Interpersonal communication takes place between two persons and is thus a one-on-one conversation. In this case, the two individuals involved will swap their roles of sender and receiver in order to communicate in a clearer manner.

c) **Small group communication:** This type of communication can take place where there are more than two persons involved. Here in the group number of persons will be small so that each and every group member may communicate. For example, a teacher in the class, 4-6 students are participating in group discussion, process conferences, board meetings team meetings.

d) **Public Communication:** This form of communication takes place where one individual address a large gather of people. For example, election campaigns, public speeches by the leader, etc.

4. Explain components of effective verbal communication.

Ans. The following are the basic elements for effective verbal communication.

a) **Listening:** It is an important component of the hearing process and to respond properly in communication. Listening is the key to success and removes a lot of misunderstandings.

b) **Language:** It matters a lot of use of appropriate language is must in the world more than 6000 languages are spoken.

c) **Voice Tone:** Voice tone is very basic, and it can come into play every when you are not uttering words. Even when you are making a laugh, your voice tone modifies how it is likely to be interpreted.

d) **Voice Speed:** Speaking too fast can convey an excited or agitated feel. Speaking slightly slower can convey a steady, reliable feel.

e) **Vocabulary:** It reflects how comfortable you are with your wordy language. It helps in the usage of suitable words in different contexts. Using the correct words as per the requirements of the situation is required.

f) **Voice Volume:** Volume of voice may vary from a whisper to a scream and everything in between. A very cool and quiet voice can represent that you are shy, something you don't want to be overheard, that you are depressed, or you are mischievous. A very loud voice may express great joy. A humorous voice demonstrates a lively atmosphere.

g) **Grammar:** Grammar is defined as the set of rules for how words connect into phrases and phrases into sentences, and so on. Using grammatically correct sentences is preferred for effective communication.

h) **Learned Awareness:** It is your awareness about your surroundings include the latest events in the world, because it gives you the confidence to communicate effectively.

i) **Subject knowledge:** Your expertise in the chosen area like arts, science, commerce, etc. will enhance the Effectiveness of the Communication.

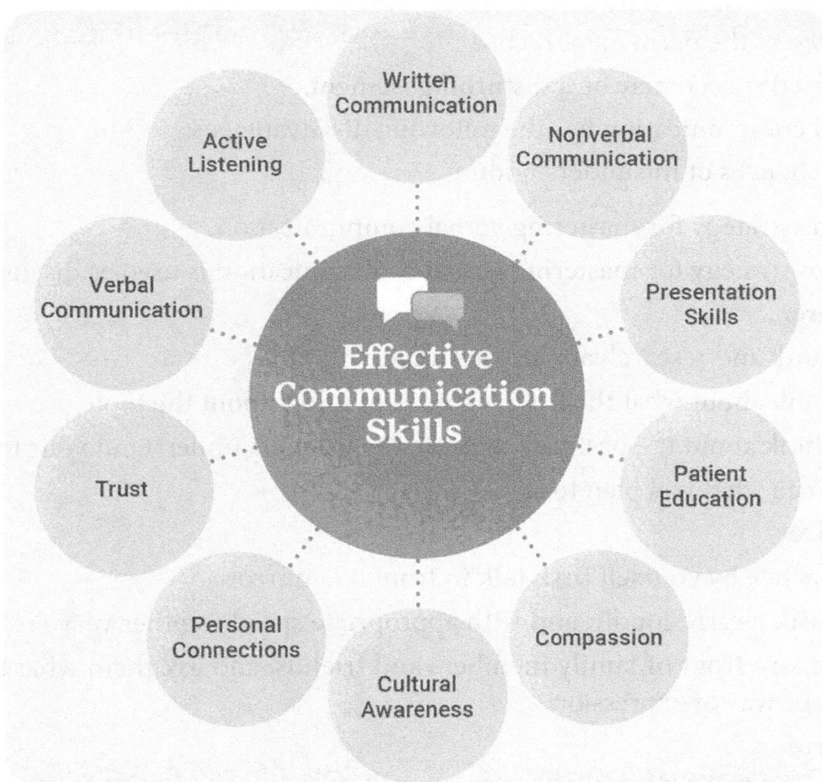

Figure 1.17

5. Enlist the main advantages of verbal communication.

Ans. Verbal communication has the following advantages:

a) Quick and flexible

b) Time-saving

    c) Immediate feedback

    d) Economical

    e) Synergy and mutual creativity

    f) Developing better relationship

    g) An effective tool for motivation

    h) An effective tool for group communication / public address

    i) Understanding, clarity, and transparency

6. Enumerate disadvantages of verbal communication.

Ans. Verbal communication has the following disadvantages:

    a) Verbal communication uses written or spoken words, and hence sometimes, the meanings of the words used can be confusing and difficult to understand.

    b) Distortion of the meaning of words used

    c) Not suitable for the lengthy message

    d) No legal validity

    e) Cultural differences may create problems.

    f) Absence of the permanent record

    g) Confused speech may be a disturbing element.

    h) Verbal communication has the following disadvantages:

    i) More chances of misunderstanding

7. Discuss the strategy for mastering verbal communication.

Ans. Three steps strategy for mastering verbal communication is used as discussed below:

(a) Prepare:

    (i) Think and research about your topic.

    (ii) Think about what the listeners need to know about the topic.

    (iii) Think about the best way to make the listeners understand your topic.

    (iv) Write what you plan to say.

(b) Practice

    (i) Practice by yourself first, talk in front of a mirror

    (ii) Speak clearly, loudly, and with appropriate speed (neither very fast nor very slow)

    (iii) Talk in front of family members and friends, and ask them what they think about your way of expression

(c) Perform

    (i) Take a deep breath in case you are feeling nervous.

    (ii) Have confidence in yourself and start speaking confidently.

    (iii) Speak slowly and clearly but in a loud voice.

    (iv) Have voice modulation and make eye contact with the audience.

8. Explain the various types of non-verbal communication.

Ans. Various types of non-verbal communications relying on various non-verbal means, like physical movements, tasks, colours, signs, symbols, signals, charts, etc., are used to express feelings, attitudes, and information.

a) **Body Language:** It includes biting nails, washing hair, etc.

b) **Eye Contact:** It helps regulate the flow of communication.

c) **Facial expressions:** It conveys what someone is feeling.

d) **Gestures:** These are the movements of the arms, legs, hands, and head.

e) **Touch:** It conveys the feelings (good touch, bad touch).

f) **Symbols:** These are used to represent an idea, a physical entity, or a process.

g) **Humour:** It makes the atmosphere lively.

h) **Silence:** It conveys both positive and negative messages.

i) **Proximity:** Maintain a comfortable distance for interaction, keeping in mind the cultural differences.

j) **Posture and body orientation:** Messages are conveyed by the way you walk, talk, stay, and sit.

k) **Personal appearance:** Your costume/dress conveys about you.

l) **Chromatics:** It uses colours for communication.

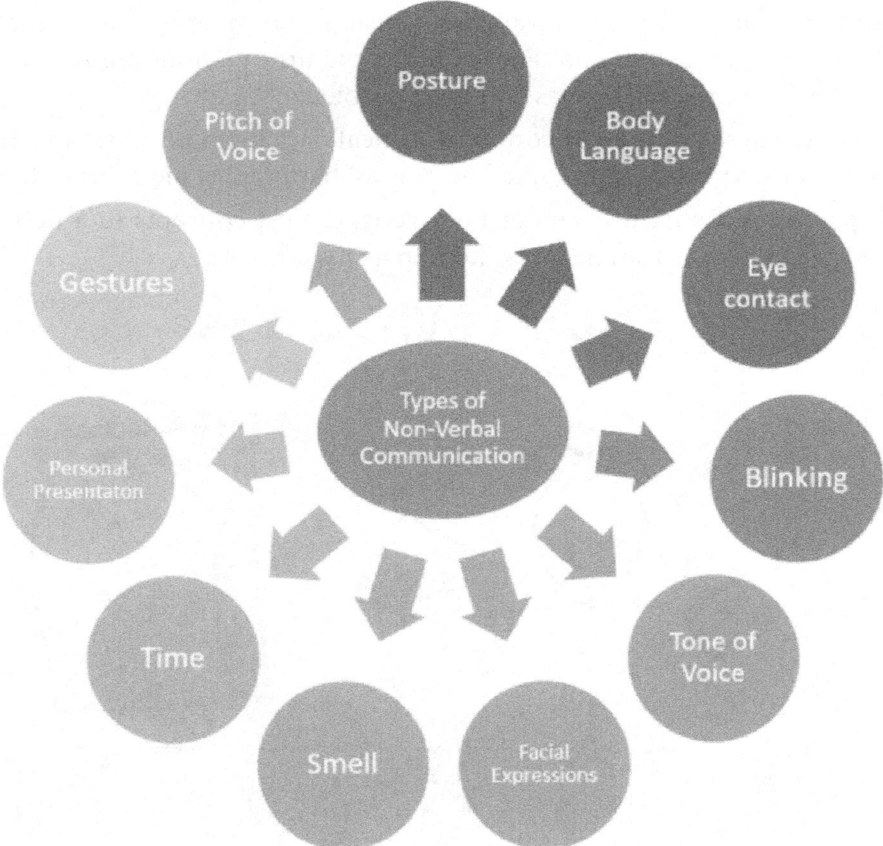

Figure 1.18

9. Discuss various tips for Improving Non-verbal Communication.

Ans. The following methods/tips may be used to improve non-verbal communication:

   a) Use good eye contact.

   b) Pay attention to non-verbal signals.

   c) Look at signals as a whole.

   d) Ask questions about non-verbal signals.

   e) Consider the context.

   f) Look for incongruent behaviours.

   g) Concentrate on the tone of voice while speaking.

   h) Be aware that signals can be misread.

   i) Use signals to make communication more meaningful.

   j) Practice, practice, and practice.

10. Explain five types of visual communication.

Ans. There are five types of visual communication:

   a) **Objects:** Various types of objects are used for visual communication to clear the concept. If we want to convey something about an apple, it is better to show it.

   b) **Models:** Various types of models in place of living things are used in visual communication.

   c) **Photographs:** The main advantage of using photographs is to clear all points or to explain minute details too. For example, pictures of slum areas can give an accurate description of the slum areas and their problems.

   d) **Graphs:** These are used to convey statistical data in an understandable manner. There are various types of graphs, like line graphs, bar graphs, pie charts, etc.

   e) **Maps:** Maps are used to understand geographical concepts in a better way. It can be used to show the locations of an item in a city/country.

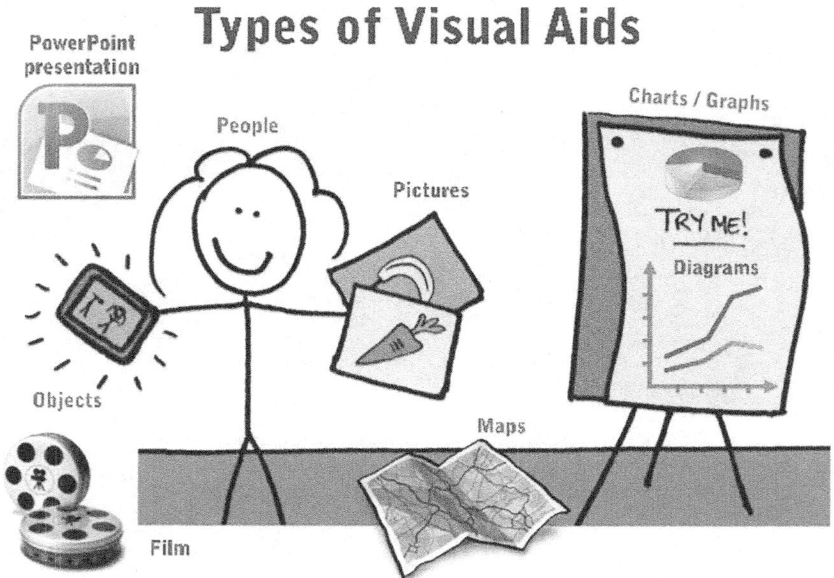

Figure 1.19

11. Discuss the importance of visual communication.

Ans. Visual communication is very important in the following manner:

    a) Visual communication helps in re-enforcing oral communication.

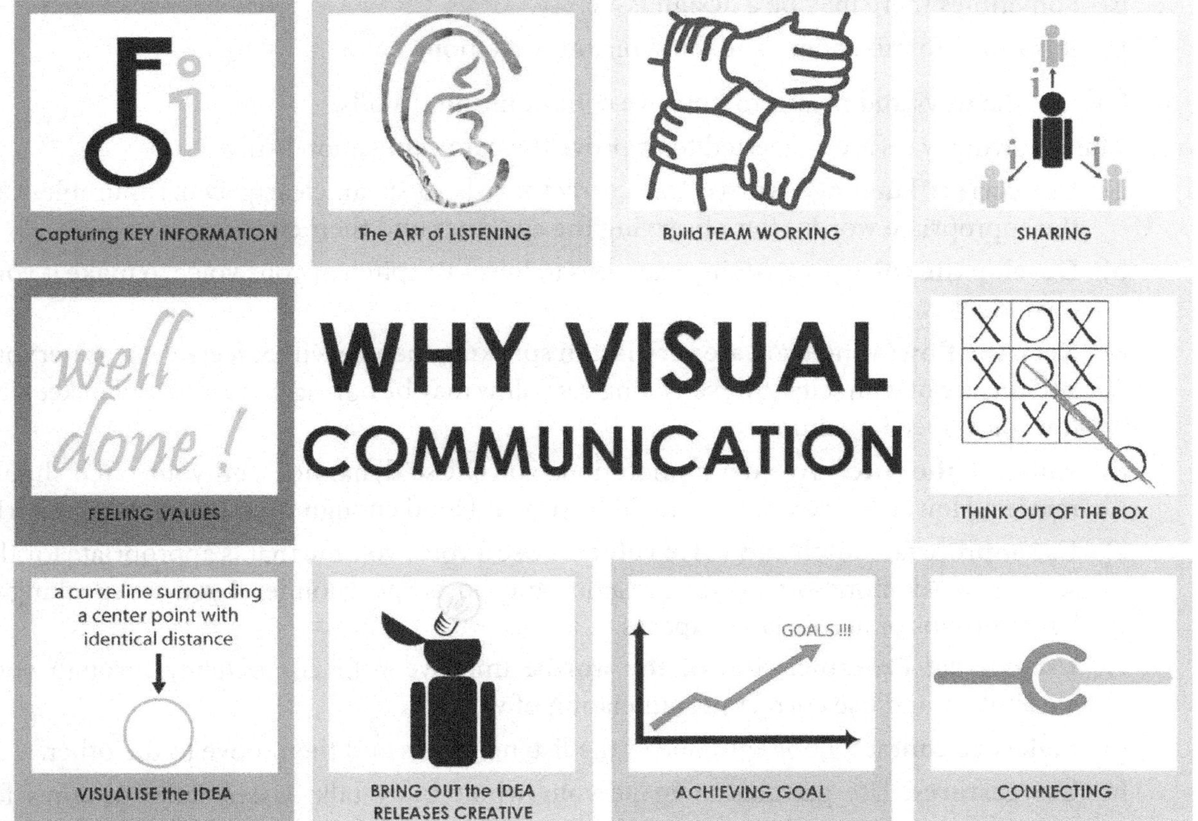

Figure 1.20

    b) It supports the information.

    c) It classifies the meaning of the discussion.

    d) It can be understood by both illiterate and literate people.

    e) It is universal and easy to remember.

    f) It adds variety to our written or oral presentations.

    g) Visual Communication jumps over the hurdles of language difference/regional difference.

    h) It has a stronger impact than words. Pictures tell things that words do not have the strength to tell.

12. What are the limitations/disadvantages of visual communication?

Ans. Visual communication has the following limitations/disadvantages:

    a) It is more expensive.

    b) Storing is quite costly.

    c) More time and effort are required to produce them.

d) Sometimes visuals are not easy to understand.

e) Visual communication has limited scope.

f) Complete and detailed information is not conveyed.

g) Sometimes there may be a design issue.

h) It is prone to misunderstandable /misinterpretation.

13. Discuss the ways and means to improve communication skills.

Ans.   The following ways are suggested to improve the communication skills:

a) **Use correct language/words:** Use correct words to speak clearly. Don't mumble. Use the appropriate words after observing the audience and their cultures.

b) **Develop the voice:** Keep doing exercises to lower the pitch of your voice to make it your own identity.

c) **Keep the flow:** When you are very fast in speaking, people will perceive you as nervous and unsure of yourself; however, being very slow may be boring. So, be careful in keeping the voice-speed medium.

d) **Animate the voice:** Avoid a monotonous voice. Use dynamics, and your pitch should raise and lower. Voice volume should be soft and loud enough to be listened to properly.

e) **Use appropriate pitch and voice volume:** Use a voice volume that is appropriate for the setting. Speak more softly if you are alone and close. Speak louder if you are speaking to larger groups or across larger spaces.

f) **Use correct Pronunciation of the words:** Improve your competency through your vocabulary and use correct pronunciation of words.

g) **Make eye contact:** Look into one of the listener's eyes and then move to the other.

h) **Use gestures:** Use gestures to make your whole body talk. Use smaller gestures for individuals and a small group, and use larger gestures for the larger group.

i) **Don't send mixed messages:** Make your words, gestures, facial expressions, tone, and message match. Avoid a mixed message. If you want to deliver a positive or negative message, make sure that your words, facial expressions, and tone match the message.

14. Explain the seven elements of the communication cycle.

Ans.   The communication cycle has mainly seven elements:

a) **Sender:** This is a person who starts communication.

b) **Message:** This is the information that the sender wants to send or share.

c) **Encoding:** This is how the sender chooses to send the message into a form appropriate for sending.

d) **Channel:** This means by which medium the message is sent.

e) **Receiver:** The person who receives the message

f) **Decoding:** This is how the receiver interprets and understands the message

g) **Feedback:** The receiver's response to the message.

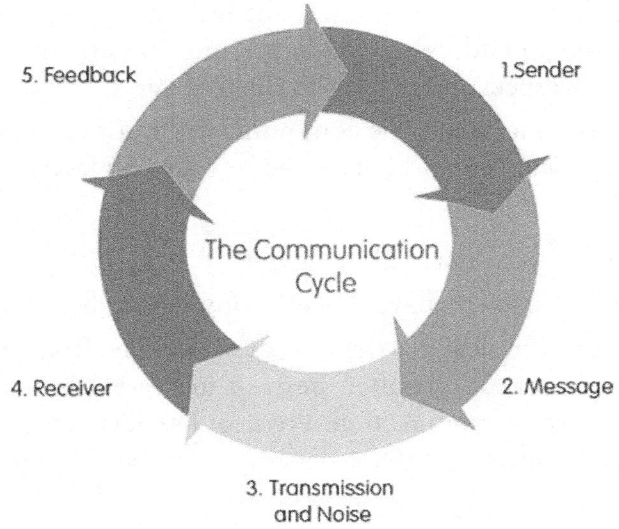

Figure 1.21 Communication Cycle

In the communication cycle, there may be some barriers, which are sometimes known as noise.

15. Give two examples of each: positive feedback and negative feedback.

Ans. The examples are as follows:

(a) Examples of Positive Feedback:

i.   Excellent job!

ii. I noticed you completed the work nicely.

iii. I appreciate you for accepting that challenge.

(b) Examples of Negative Feedback:

i.   You keep forgetting to smile at the hotel guests when you talk to them.

ii. You take a long to reply to e-mails! Are you always so busy?

16. Throw light on 7Cs of communication.

Ans. The 7Cs of communication is also termed the seven principles of communication, which ensure effective communication.

i.   **Clarity:** Clear and simple language is characterised by explicitness, short sentences, and concrete words. Avoid fuzzy language.

ii. **Correctness:** We correct language free from grammatical errors and stylists' lapses. The use of correct language increases trustworthiness.

iii. **Concreteness:** The message should be supported by factual material such as data and figures.

iv. **Conciseness:** Clear and concise message with facts should be preferred in place of a long message to avoid confusion.

v.   **Coherent:** Wary Communicating with the target group, it is important to relate to the target group and be involved. Factors playing a role here are professional knowledge, level of education, age, interest, etc.

vi. **Courtesy:** In addition to understanding the feelings and opinions of the target group, it is also important to address the audience in a friendly manner. Use the terms and phrases that show respect and regards to the receiver(s).

vii. **Completeness:** The message to be communicated must be complete and geared to the receiver's perception of the world. It should be based on facts, and a complex message is to be explained.

17. Explain various types of communication barriers.

Ans. Mainly, communication barriers have the following types.

a) **Physical Barriers:** Physical barriers separate people from each other by marking territories. These barriers can often be seen in the workplace, where offices as well as closed doors stop communication. Physical barriers can stop a person from being comfortable communicating with a person whom he/she does not come face to face with often.

b) **Language Barriers:** When a person is not familiar with the language used by another person in communication, misinterpretation will occur. The accents and dialect (use of words) of people belonging to different cultures/places differ even if their language is the same and may become barriers to communication. For example, the abbreviation "LOL" used in social media is used for Lots of Love and Laugh Out Loud. If a person says LOL, the second person can interpret the meaning in any way he wants.

c) **Gender Barriers:** There are distinct differences between the communication patterns in a man and those in a woman. Variations may exist among masculine and feminine styles of communication. While women often emphasise politeness, empathy, and rapport building, male communication is often more direct and to the point. This means that a man may talk in a linear, logical, and compartmentalised way, which are the features of left-brain thinking, while a woman talks more freely, mixing logic and emotion, features of both sides of the brain. If someone meshes these two styles without awareness, then it could become a barrier.

d) **Attitudinal Barriers:** As those behaviours or perceptions that are divisive in nature lead to nagging doubt, disagreement, or even overt conflict, they all interfere with and undermine communication. These are barriers that distance one from others. These are visible through withdrawal, meaningless rituals that keep one devoid of real contact, superficial activities, etc.

e) **Perceptual Barriers:** People tend to interpret messages from their own points of view or ideologies. Without thinking, one might only view a message from his or her own mindset rather than looking at it from another viewpoint. Different world views can create misunderstanding. The main problem in communicating with others is that all persons see the world differently.

f) **Cultural Barriers:** Ethnic, religious, and social differences can often create misunderstandings during communication. These differences can also affect one's perception and create confusion in getting a message correctly.

g) **Emotional Barriers:** When someone is consumed with emotion, then he/she will have difficulty understanding the message communicated well. Emotions like fear, hostility, anger, love, empathy, etc., make it hard to hear outside one's own self. The roots of the emotional mistrust of others lay in our childhood and infancy when we were taught by our parents to be careful about what we say to others. People must have been often warned- "Mind your P's and Q's." "Don't speak until you're spoken to." That's why many people hold back from communicating their thoughts and feelings to others. While some caution may be wise in some relationships, excessive fear of what others might think of us can stop our development as effective communicators.

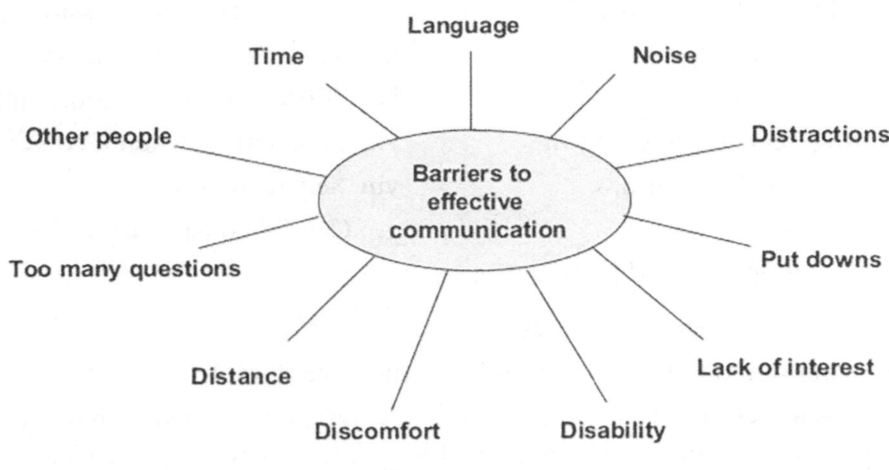

Figure 1.22

18. Discuss the various methods to overcome barriers to communication.

Ans. The following are some methods to overcome barriers to communication:

a) **Use simple language:** Simple and easy language is to be used during communication.

b) **Keep the message short:** Communicate to the point and keep messages short, succinct, and packed with only the information a person needs to do his job.

c) **Communicate as per need:** Noise and distractions can up the communication process at all levels. So, communicate what is necessary or needed.

d) **Be respectful to others' opinions:** Show respect to the opinions expressed by other people.

e) **Remain aware of cultural differences:** Various words in different cultures have different meanings. We must be careful in using these types of words. Using the correct words as per the culture should be encouraged while communicating with a group of people.

f) **Avoid slang:** Slang and casual language can be fun with friends, but with elders and co-workers, it can create a significant barrier to effective communications. Slang differs significantly across generations and cultures. Slang can cause confusion, and it can be a source of frustration.

g) **Stay open-minded for open-house session:** To communicate effectively, one needs to be open-minded and willing to ask and answer questions that may seem frustrating sometimes. Be helpful in the problem-solving process of others.

h) **Stereotyping:** We often form stereotypes about those whom we know the least. Once our mental sets are created, all our transactions are affected by their sets, preventing us from effective listening.

i) **Practice listening:** Listen to the speaker carefully is required to understand him/her and the message.

j) **Not listening as a status or gender issue:** Some persons in positions listen less to those who are lower in a hierarchy. How well do the parents listen to their children or the juniors in age or experience? If a woman employee is speaking, are men employees as attentive as they would be when a male colleague speaks up?

19. Discuss the essential skills needed for written expressions.

Ans. The following are the essential skills that are needed for written expressions:

i. Use simple language
ii. Reading comprehension
iii. Explain in clear terms
iv. Effective sentence construction
v. Planning, revising, and editing
vi. Less is more when it comes to length.
vii. Select the right medium.
viii. Self-regulation
ix. Transcription
x. Candid consistency to have focus.
xi. Use good grammar and punctuation.

20. Discuss the steps for writing a paragraph.

Ans. The following steps are to be followed in writing a paragraph:

i. **Topic Sentence:** The first sentence of the paragraph is termed 'Topic sentence.' It should be a general statement by introducing the overall idea without giving detail. It should be indented. The topic sentence is also termed as the "main idea" of the paragraph.

ii. **Body Sentences:** The body of the paragraph contains sentences that follow the topic sentences. Here, the additional details are provided to give a clear, coherent idea of what the paragraph is about. Insert facts, make arguments, and analyse the issue in the body sentences.

iii. **Conclusion:** The final sentence should sum up all of the information found mainly in the topic and body sentences. By this point, we should have made our case. This is where connections are made. Think of the conclusion sentence as the reverse of the topic sentence; the final statement should be general but sum up the entire paragraph.

iv. **Coherent Details:** All three elements: topic sentence, body sentences, and conclusion, should be presented in a clear and concise manner. The details in your paragraph should be clear enough so that a reader follows what you've written and understands it.

Figure 1.23

21. Explain the elements essential for paragraph writing.

Ans. There are four essential elements for paragraph writing, namely unity, order, coherence, and completeness.

   a) **Unity:** Unity in a sentence starts with the subject phrase. Every sentence has one individual, managing concept that is indicated in its subject phrase. A sentence is specific around this main concept, with the assisting phrases offering details and conversation. For creating a good subject phrase, think about the style and all the details to be made.

   b) **Order:** Order represents the way in which the phrases are arranged. Whether you choose the date order, the order of importance, or another reasonable demonstration of detail, a solid sentence always has a certain organization. In a well-ordered sentence, people follow along easily with the design you've established. Order helps people understand the indicating and avoid misunderstandings.

   c) **Coherence:** Coherence is the quality that makes the writing understandable. Sentences within a paragraph need to be connected to each other, and they should work together as a whole. One method to achieve coherency is to use transition words, which create bridges from one sentence to the next. Moreover, in writing a paragraph, using a consistent verb tense is an important ingredient for coherency.

   d) **Completeness:** Completeness means that an expression is well-developed. When all words clearly and properly assist the significant idea, then the expression is complete. When there are not enough words or enough information to confirm the dissertation, then the expression is partial. The last expression of expression should sum up the significant idea by strengthening the topic.

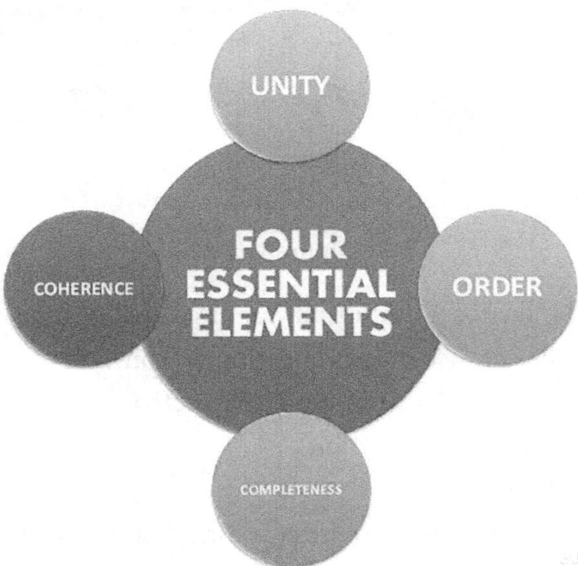

Figure 1.24

1.3.11 HOTS Questions

1. In your opinion, what may be the purpose of Verbal communication?

Ans. Verbal communication helps us to think, maintain relationships, define reality, and organise complex ideas and experiences into meaningful experiences.

2. Which three parts of communication are considered important and why?

Ans. Communication has three important parts, as follows:

    (i) Transmitting: The sender transmits the message through one medium or other.

    (ii) Listening: The receiver listens or understands the message.

    (iii) Feedback: The process in which receiver conveys his/ her understanding of the message to the sender in the form of feedback completes the communication cycle.

    Without these three parts, no communication is considered complete. That's why these are important.

3. How are 'Attitudinal Barriers' creating misunderstanding during communication?

Ans. As the behaviours or perceptions that are divisive in nature lead to nagging doubt, disagreement, or even overt conflict, they all interfere with and undermine communication. These are barriers that distance one from others. These are visible through withdrawal, meaningless rituals that keep one devoid of real contact, superficial activities, etc. These barriers create misunderstandings during communication.

Figure 1.25

4. Why do you consider feedback important for effective communication?

Ans. Feedback is important because of the following reasons:

    a) It makes communication meaningful and effective.

    b) It helps to remove misinterpretation.

    c) It builds a relationship.

    d) It improves performance as it can help to form better decisions to improve and increase performance.

    e) It helps with networking.

    f) It completes the communication cycle.

    g) It generates new ideas.

    h) It boosts learning as it is important to remain focused on goals, plan better, and develop improved products and services.

1.4 PRACTICE QUESTIONS

1. Give an example of a cultural barrier.
2. Enlist the elements of communication.
3. What do you mean by indefinite and definite articles? Give examples.
4. Illustrate the SMCR model of communication with a suitable example.
5. Why are we using different methods of communication?
6. Explain the components of verbal communication.
7. Define and illustrate the different types of non-verbal communication.
8. Discuss the advantages and limitations of visual communication.
9. Throw light on the elements of paragraph writing.
10. Write any three functions of verbal communication.
11. Differentiate between interpersonal and intrapersonal communication.
12. Why is written communication used for official purposes?
13. Explain the 'Communication Cycle.
14. Discuss the barriers to communications.
15. List some factors that enhance our oral communication skills.
16. What are the 7Cs of effective communication? Explain.
17. 'Non-verbal cues complement verbal communication.' Justify the statement.
18. Why is effective communication required at all? Explain.
19. Discuss the importance of feedback in communication.
20. Discuss the importance of the use of correct phrases and sentences in communication.

UNIT 2

Self Management II

2.1 UNIT IN BRIEF

✦ Stress means pressure, tensions, worries, and problems of life, affecting the balance in life.

✦ The most important thing about stress is that it can be managed.

Figure 2.1

✦ Stress may be defined as a reaction to any external stimuli that trigger changes in one's personality.

✦ Stress may be positive or negative. Everyone reacts to stress differently.

✦ Stress may be of two types: acute and chronic.

✦ Common responses to stress may be aches and pains, energy levels and sleep, feelings, and other emotional signs.

✦ Stress management is required to lead a peaceful and meaningful life.

✦ Stress-causing agents are known as stressors, which can be self-induced or external.

✦ Stressors are factors that have an adverse effect on the physical, emotional, behavioural, and mental health of a human being.

SELF-REGULATION RUBRICS

Figure 2.2

+ Stressors can be categorised as positive, dangerous, and irrelevant stressors.

+ Stress management techniques may include physical exercise, yoga, meditation, spending time with friends and family, talking, etc.

+ Setting realistic goals with proper time management may produce less stress.

+ Stress may have a positive impact on people. It can sometimes be useful, helping us to accomplish great things. This is known as 'eustress.'

+ Eustress provides us with the energy and motivation to achieve our goals.

+ Stress management includes a set of techniques that assist individuals in eradicating anxiety and negative thoughts and work on their well-being.

+ Our body is equipped with a natural 'fight or flight' response, in which it reacts spontaneously to protect itself from any unfavourable situation.

+ Doing exercise helps to release endorphins (chemicals in the brain that act as natural painkillers) and eradicate insomnia.

+ Yoga helps in relieving stress and uplifting our mood.

+ Regular practice of meditation reduces stress, anxiety, and depression.

+ Vacation with friends and family can be a refreshing experience that can help in relieving stress.

+ Nature walk also acts as a stress reliever.

+ Being independent teaches you how to be self-regulated and self-motivated.

+ Independent people are likely to be more confident in handling problems affecting their lives, tend to rely less on others, easily make decisions, and are emotionally independent.

+ Self-motivation drives a person to attempt and accomplish tasks.

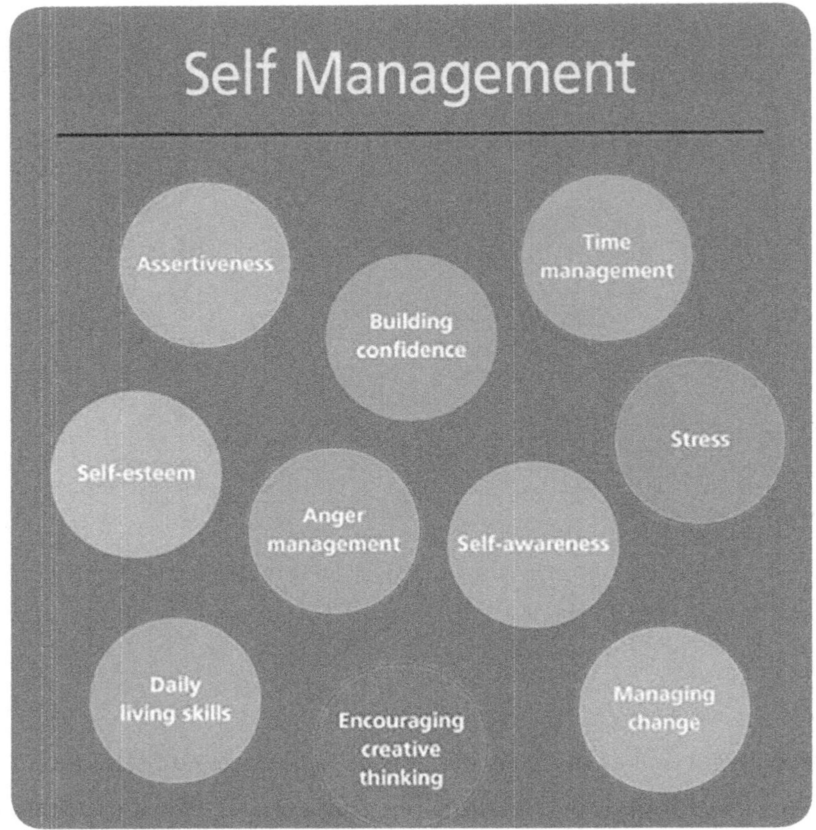

Figure 2.3

✦ There are two main types of motivation-intrinsic and extrinsic.

✦ Intrinsic motivation refers to the behaviour of a person that is driven by his innate desire to do something for his own sake and personal rewards.

✦ Extrinsic motivation refers to the behaviour of a person that is driven by the desire to achieve some sort of external reward, including money, power, and good grades.

✦ In order to work independently, a person must possess certain skills-self-motivation, organisational skills, multitasking ability, discipline, communication skills, and resourcefulness.

✦ The keys to becoming self-reliant are self-awareness, self-motivation, and self-regulation.

✦ Self-awareness means being aware of your personality, including your strengths, weaknesses, thoughts, beliefs, emotions, and motivations.

✦ There are two types of awareness-External self-awareness and Internal self-awareness.

✦ External self-awareness requires understanding how other people perceive us.

✦ Internal self-awareness represents how clearly one sees one's own values, passions, aspirations, thoughts, feelings, behaviours, strengths, weaknesses, and their impact on others.

✦ Self-regulation involves being able to control reactions to emotions like frustration or excitement.

✦ The fundamentals of being independent are the ability to work on your own, with minimal direction, confidence, self-awareness, self-motivation, and self-regulation.

Figure 2.4

2.2 CBSE/NCERT SECTION (SOLVED CBSE/NCERT EXERCISE QUESTIONS)

(A) MCQs

Choose the correct option out of the four options given for each question.

1. What makes you complete work or studies without others cheering you?

   a) Self-confidence   b) Communication   c) Self-motivation   d) Self-esteem

2. Which of the following are types of motivation?

   a) Internal   b) Intermediate   c) External   d) Extensive

3. Ravi works hard to get the best student award at the end of the year. What type of motivation is this?

   a) Internal   b) External

   c) Both internal and external   d) Not any specific type of motivation

ANSWERS
1. (c)   2. (a)   3. (c)

(B) Subjective Questions

1. Define stress and stress management in your own words.

Ans. Stress is defined as the emotional, mental, physical, and social reaction to any perceived demands or threats. These demands or threats are called stressors which are the reason for stress.

Stress Management is all about making a plan to be able to cope effectively with daily pressures. The main goal of stress management is to strike a balance between life, work, relationships, relaxation, and fun.

2. List your favourite stress management technique and elaborate on why you find it the most effective.

Ans. The following Stress Management Techniques (SMT) may be used:

   a) **Time management:** Managing one's time properly is one of the most effective stress-relieving techniques.

b) **Positivity:** Focussing on positive aspects of life will add more joy and pleasure and can reduce stress.

c) **Healthy diet:** Having a healthy diet will help to reduce stress. Eating a balanced diet, like Dal, Roti, vegetables, and fruits, will give you the strength to do your daily work efficiently.

d) **Sleep:** Have a good night's sleep for at least 7 hours so that our brain and body get recharged to function better the next day.

e) **Exercise and fresh air:** A healthy lifestyle is useful for everyone. Stress is normally lower in people who maintain a healthy lifestyle. Doing yoga, meditation, playing, and deep breathing exercises help in proper blood circulation and relax the body.

f) **Organising academic life;** no delaying: By keeping class notes organised, finishing in assignments on time, and keeping track of all deadlines, stress can be reduced to a great extent.

g) **Vacations/Holidays with family and friends:** Going to a picnic or to relative's place, like the grandparents' house, or a new place during the summer vacations, can help you break from the normal routine and come back afresh

These techniques are useful to reduce stress.

Figure 2.5

3. What is Goal Setting?

Ans. Goal setting is about finding and listing the goals and then planning on how to achieve them.

4. In SMART goals, what does 'S' stand for? Explain.

Ans. S in SMART means 'Specific'. A specific and clear goal answers the following six questions:

a) Who is involved in the goal?

b) What do I want to do?

c) Where do I start?

d) When do I start and finish?

e)   Which means do I use?

f)   Why am I doing this

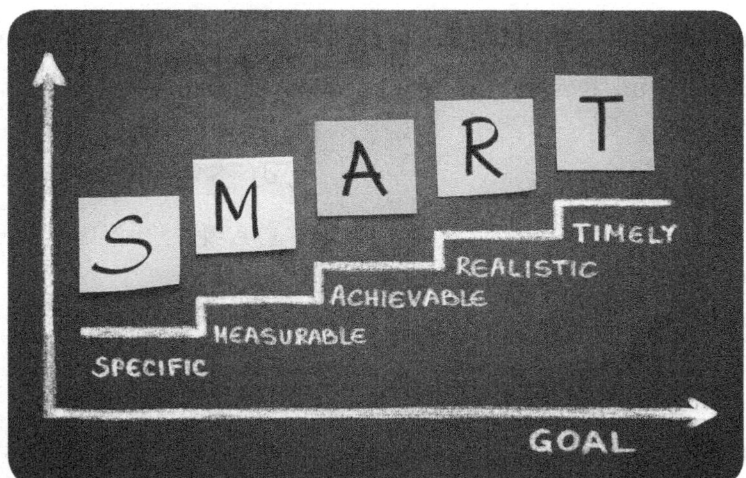

Figure 2.6

5.   What is the best way to work on long-term goals?

Ans.   The best way to work on long-term goals is to set goals as SMART goals, plan and work for the goals, check the progress of the goals, and change the strategy as per the need.

6.   What is time management, and how can you manage your time?

Ans.   Time management is the ability to plan and control how one spends the hours of the day well and do all that one wants to do.

The following steps may be taken for effective time management:

a)   To prepare a 'To-do' list.

b)   To prioritise the activities and actions.

c)   To avoid delay or postponing any planned activity.

d)   To organise the working place, room and school desk properly.

e)   To develop a 'NO DISTURBANCE ZONE,' where one can sit and complete important tasks.

f)   To use waiting time productively.

g)   To replace useless activities with productive activities.

7.   How can tracking your time help you?

Ans.   Tracking the time (Time management) is helpful to:

a)   make a daily timetable.

b)   Complete tasks on time.

c)   Make a time guess for at how long it will take one to do something.

d)   Submit homework and assignments on time.

e)   Waste no time on useless activities.

2.3 SOLVED EXERCISES

2.3.1 Multiple Choice Questions

Choose the correct option out of the four options given for each question.

1. Which of the following is referred to as the "wear and tear" of human body experiences?

   a) Stress

   b) Eustress

   c) Motivation

   d) Self-awareness

2. Consider the following examples and choose the examples of strengths.

   I.   I am good at creative poems.

   II. I have a fear of the crowd.

   III. I play table very well.

   IV. I am good at speaking Hindi and English.

   V.   I find it challenging to solve physics problems.

   VI. I am good at writing in Hindi.

   a) (ii) (iiii) (iv)   b) (iv) (v) (vi)   c) (iii) (iv) (vi)   d) All of them

3. Which of the following statement exhibit an example of weaknesses?

   a) I have a fear of swimming in rivers.

   b) I would like to speak English fluently.

   c) I do not like to lose in any game or sports.

   d) All of the above

4. Which statement related to an independent person is incorrect?

   a) He/she tends to rely more on others.

   b) He/she is resourceful.

   c) He/she is wholly responsible for the outcome of the task which he has undertaken.

   d) He/she is self-aware.

5. What makes Rehan complete his studies without others cheering him?

   a) Self-confidence

   b) Self-motivation

   c) Communication

   d) Self-esteem

6. Meditation brings a sense of:

   a) Depression

   b) Anxiety

   c) Self-awareness

   d) Stress

7. Benson George won first prize at Inter-School Karate Tournament. Now, he is more focused on getting the same prize at State level Tournament. Which type of motivation does Benson George has?

   a) Internal

   b) External

   c) Intermediate

   d) Both internal and external

8. Which of the following is the key skill for becoming an independent person?
   a) Self-awareness
   b) Self-regulation
   c) Self-motivation
   d) All of these

9. Which of the following options provides the people with the energy and motivation to achieve the goals?
   a) Stress
   b) Eustress
   c) Distress
   d) Anxiety

10. Which of the following words is a stressor?
    a) Dangerous
    b) Useless fellow
    c) Irrelevant
    d) All of these

11. Which types of chemicals in the brain are raised due to physical exercise that act as natural painkillers?
    a) Enzymes
    b) Hormones
    c) Endorphins
    d) Ectomorphines

12. Which of the following statements related to self-regulation is correct?
    a) Self-regulation helps people to cope with strong feelings.
    b) Self-regulation makes people more independent.
    c) Self-regulation helps people to behave in socially acceptable ways.
    d) None of these

13. While vacationing with family and friends, one is able to:
    a) Deepen social relations
    b) Break the monotonousness of life
    c) Admire nature's beauty
    d) All of these

14. Navya Sridharan works hard to get the 'Best Anchor' award at the annual day function. What type of motivation is this?
    a) Internal
    b) External
    c) Both internal and external
    d) None of the above

15. Which factor does create a chaotic atmosphere in a person's life leading to 'stress'?
    a) Pressure from family and society
    b) Endless greed
    c) Achieving our goals
    d) All of these

16. Physical exercise helps in:
    a) Proper functioning of organ systems
    b) Building immunity
    c) Both a and b
    d) None of the above

17. Which element is not used to keep a person motivated?
    a) Personal drive to achieve goals
    b) Initiative or readiness to act on opportunities
    c) Being aware of the personality
    d) Commitment to personal or organizational goals

18. The factor(s) that may bring about negative changes in a person suffering from stress is/are:
    a) Peer pressure
    b) Threat
    c) Financial loss
    d) All of these

19. A person who is wholly responsible for the outcome of the task which he has undertaken is called:
    a) Resourceful person
    b) Independent person
    c) Self-motivated person
    d) Confident person

20. Stress management is helpful for:
    a) Focus and complete tasks on time.
    b) Be more energetic
    c) Be able to spend quality time with your friends and family.
    d) All the above

21. Which of the following skills is more important than others in getting success in a professional career?
    a) Intelligence Quotient (IQ)
    b) Emotional and social skills
    c) Communication skills
    d) None of the above

<table>
<tr><td colspan="10" align="center">ANSWERS</td></tr>
<tr><td>1. (a)</td><td>2. (c)</td><td>3. (d)</td><td>4. (a)</td><td>5. (b)</td><td>6. (c)</td><td>7. (b)</td><td>8. (d)</td><td>9. (b)</td><td>10. (d)</td></tr>
<tr><td>11. (c)</td><td>12. (b)</td><td>13. (d)</td><td>14. (a)</td><td>15. (d)</td><td>16. (c)</td><td>17. (c)</td><td>18. (d)</td><td>19. (b)</td><td>20. (d)</td></tr>
<tr><td>21. (b)</td><td></td><td></td><td></td><td></td><td></td><td></td><td></td><td></td><td></td></tr>
</table>

2.3.2 Fill in the blanks

1. Nature walk also acts as a ______________.

2. There are two types of awareness- ______________ self-awareness and internal self-awareness.

3. Yoga helps in relieving ______________ and uplifting our mood.

4. ______________ includes a pool of techniques that assist individuals in eradicating anxiety and negative thoughts and work on their well-being.

5. ______________ referred to an automatic response of the nervous system to any threat, challenge, or problem.

6. Stress can make you feel hot due to a rise in ______________.

7. ______________ motivation refers to the behaviour of a person that is driven by his innate desire to do something for his own sake.

8. ______________ means being aware of your personality, including your strengths, weaknesses, thoughts, beliefs, emotions, and motivations.

9. Systematic efforts to direct thoughts, feelings, actions to attain the required success in the assigned task is termed ______________.

10. ______________ people are likely to be more confident in handling problems affecting their lives.

11. ______________ self-awareness requires understanding how other people perceive us.

12. The keys to becoming ______________ are self-awareness, self-motivation, and self-regulation.

13. Stress-causing agents are known as ______________.

14. ______________ is a natural and inexpensive way that provides immunity to stress.

15. ______________ is the ability to do the things that need to be done without the need for external influence.

<table>
<tr><td colspan="4" align="center">ANSWERS</td></tr>
<tr><td>1. stress reliever/de-stressor</td><td>2. External</td><td>3. stress</td><td></td></tr>
<tr><td>4. Stress management</td><td>5. Stress</td><td>6. blood pressure</td><td>7. Intrinsic</td></tr>
<tr><td>8. Self-awareness   9. self-regulation</td><td>10. Independent</td><td></td><td>11. External</td></tr>
<tr><td>12. self-reliant   13. stressors.</td><td>14. Meditation</td><td>15. Self-motivation</td><td></td></tr>
</table>

2.3.3 True or False

1. Stress Management covers all the tools that all available to deal with chronic stress, which could otherwise prove to be a lethal disease.

2. The most important thing about stress is that it cannot be managed.

Figure 2.7

3. Introspections are clear on who they are but don't challenge their views, often harming their relationships and limiting their success.

4. Our body is equipped with a natural 'fight or flight' response, in which it reacts spontaneously to protect itself from any unfavourable situation.

5. Nature walk induces the basic qualities of living in harmony, peace, and cooperation.

6. The first step for a positive outlook is having a long-term goal and short-term goals.

7. In 'Fight or Flight' response, the body reacts spontaneously to protect itself from any unfavourable situation.

8. Stress is a charged-up internal condition of our body in response to some repulsive external or internal situations.

9. The force within someone that drives him to do things is called self-regulation.

10. Stress can be viewed as a disease that is afflicting people of all age groups.

11. Self-regulation involves being able to control reactions to emotions like frustration or excitement.

12. Stress may be defined as a reaction to any external stimuli that trigger changes in our personality.

13. Stress always has a negative impact on people.

14. Stress management includes a pool of techniques that assist individuals in eradicating anxiety and negative thoughts.

15. Yoga reduces the level of cortisol, which is the stress hormone.

ANSWERS							
1. (T)	2. (F)	3. (T)	4. (T)	5. (T)	6. (T)	7. (T)	8. (T)
9. (F, self-motivation)		10. (T)	11.	12. (T)	13. (F)	14. (T)	15. (F)

2.3.4 Matching type

I. Match the items of column A with those of Column B correctly.

Column A	**Column B**
i. Emotional awareness	(a) Ability to regulate one's own emotions
ii. Harnessing emotions	(b) Ability to identify and name one's own emotions.
iii. Managing emotions	(c) Ability to apply emotions to tasks like thinking and problem-solving.

ANSWERS
I. (i)-b   (ii)-c   (iii)-a

2.3.5 Statements Based Questions

1. Statement 1: Stress may be defined as a reaction to any external stimuli that trigger changes in one's personality.

    Statement 2: Stress will be a negative impact always.

    a) Statement 1 is correct, but statement 2 is incorrect.

    b) Statement 1 is incorrect but statement 2 is correct.

    c) Both the statements are correct.

    d) Both the statements are incorrect.

2. Statement 1: Stress means pressure, tensions, worries, and problems of life, affecting the balance in life.

    Statement 2: Setting realistic goals with proper time management may produce less stress.

    a) Statement 1 is correct but statement 2 is incorrect.

    b) Statement 1 is incorrect but statement 2 is correct.

    c) Both the statements are correct.

    d) Both the statements are incorrect.

3. Statement 1: Extrinsic motivation refers to the behaviour of a person that is driven by his innate desire to do something for his own sake and personal rewards.

    Statement 2: Yoga does not help in relieving stress and uplifting our mood.

Figure 2.8

    a) Statement 1 is correct but statement 2 is incorrect.
    b) Statement 1 is incorrect but statement 2 is correct.
    c) Both the statements are correct.
    d) Both the statements are incorrect.

4. Statement 1: Confidence is not required for completing all tasks.

    Statement 2: Self-regulation involves being able to control reactions to emotions like frustration or excitement.

    a) Statement 1 is correct but statement 2 is incorrect.
    b) Statement 1 is incorrect but statement 2 is correct.
    c) Both the statements are correct.
    d) Both the statements are incorrect.

5. Statement 1: Common responses to stress may be aches and pains, energy levels and sleep, feelings, and other emotional signs.

    Statement 2: Stress management techniques may include physical exercise, yoga, meditation, spending time with friends and family, talking, etc.

    a) Statement 1 is correct but statement 2 is incorrect.
    b) Statement 1 is incorrect but statement 2 is correct.
    c) Both the statements are correct.
    d) Both the statements are incorrect.

6. Statement 1: Intrinsic motivation refers to the behaviour of a person that is driven by the desire to achieve some sort of external reward, including money, power, and good grades.

    Statement 2: Internal self-awareness represents how clearly one sees one's own values, passions, aspirations, thoughts, feelings, behaviours, strengths, weaknesses, and their impact on others.

    a) Statement 1 is correct but statement 2 is incorrect.

b) Statement 1 is incorrect but statement 2 is correct.

c) Both the statements are correct.

d) Both the statements are incorrect.

ANSWERS
1. (a)   2. (c)   3. (d)   4. (b)   5. (c)   6. (d)

2.3.6 Assertion Reason Type Questions

1. Assertion (A): Eustress may have a positive impact on people.

    Reason(R): Eustress provides us with the energy and motivation to achieve our goals.

    a) Both A and R are correct and R is the correct reason for A.

    b) Both A and R are correct and R is not the correct reason for A.

    c) A is correct but R is incorrect.

    d) A is incorrect but R is correct.

2. Assertion (A): Stress can sometimes be useful, helping us to accomplish great things. This is known as 'eustress.'

    Reason(R): The most important thing about stress is that it can be managed.

    a) Both A and R are correct and R is the correct reason for A.

    b) Both A and R are correct and R is not the correct reason for A.

    c) A is correct but R is incorrect.

    d) A is incorrect but R is correct.

3. Assertion (A): Stress management includes a set of techniques that assist individuals in eradicating anxiety and negative thoughts and work on their well-being.

    Reason(R): Regular practice of meditation increases stress, anxiety, and depression.

    a) Both A and R are correct and R is the correct reason for A.

    b) Both A and R are correct and R is not the correct reason for A.

    c) A is correct but R is incorrect.

    d) A is incorrect but R is correct.

4. Assertion (A): Stressors are factors that have an adverse effect on the physical, emotional, behavioural, and mental health of a human being.

    Reason(R): Vacation with friends and family can be a refreshing experience that can help in relieving stress.

    a) Both A and R are correct and R is the correct reason for A.

    b) Both A and R are correct and R is not the correct reason for A.

    c) A is correct but R is incorrect.

    d) A is incorrect but R is correct.

5. Assertion (A): Doing exercise acts as a stress reliever.

    Reason(R): Doing exercise helps to release endorphins (chemicals in the brain that act as natural painkillers) and eradicate insomnia.

    a) Both A and R are correct and R is the correct reason for A.

b) Both A and R are correct and R is not the correct reason for A.

c) A is correct but R is incorrect.

d) A is incorrect but R is correct.

6. Assertion (A): Our body is not equipped with a natural 'fight or flight response, in which it reacts spontaneously to protect itself from any unfavourable situation.

   Reason(R): Stressors can be categorized as positive, dangerous, and irrelevant stressors.

   a) Both A and R are correct and R is the correct reason for A.

   b) Both A and R are correct and R is not the correct reason for A.

   c) A is correct but R is incorrect.

   d) A is incorrect but R is correct.

ANSWERS
1. (a)   2. (b)   3. (c)   4. (b)   5. (a)   6. (d)

2.3.7 Competency-Based Questions

1. Narendra Pratap Bansal is more confident in handling problems affecting their lives, tends to rely less on others, easily makes decisions, and is emotionally independent. He represents:

Figure 2.9

a) Independent people   b) Confident people

c) Stressed people   d) Democratic people

2. Yogita possesses the skills like self-motivation, organisational skills, multitasking ability, discipline, communication skills, and resourcefulness and works independently. Which of the following is the key in order to work independently?

   a) Self-awareness   b) Self-motivation

   c) Self-regulation   d) All of the above

3. Suppose Sudhanshu Pandey studies in class X and he is aware of his personality, including his strengths, weaknesses, thoughts, beliefs, emotions, and motivations. Which of the following skills does he possess?

   a) Communication skills   b) Empathy

   c) Self-awareness   d) Critical Thinking

ANSWERS
1. (a)   2. (d)   3. (c)

2.3.8 VSA

1. Which skill is required to lead a happy and successful life?

Ans. By mastering self-management skills, one will be on track to a happy and successful life both personally and professionally.

2. Define self-awareness.

Ans. Self-awareness is understanding the causes of your own behaviour.

3. What is the right step towards true self-management?

Ans. Taking responsibility for the actions is the right step towards true self-management.

4. What is stress?

Ans. Stress means pressure, tensions, worries, and problems of life, affecting the balance in life.

5. Define self-development?

Ans. Self-development is about expanding your horizons, and that comes with responsibility.

6. What are the two types of stress?

Ans. Stress may be positive or negative. Stress may be of two types: acute and chronic.

7. Why is stress management required?

Ans. Stress management is required to lead a peaceful and meaningful life.

8. What are stress-causing agents called?

Ans. Stress-causing agents are known as stressors, which can be self-induced or external.

9. Define stressors.

Ans. Stressors are factors that have an adverse effect on the physical, emotional, behavioural, and mental health of a human being.

10. What are the types of stressors?

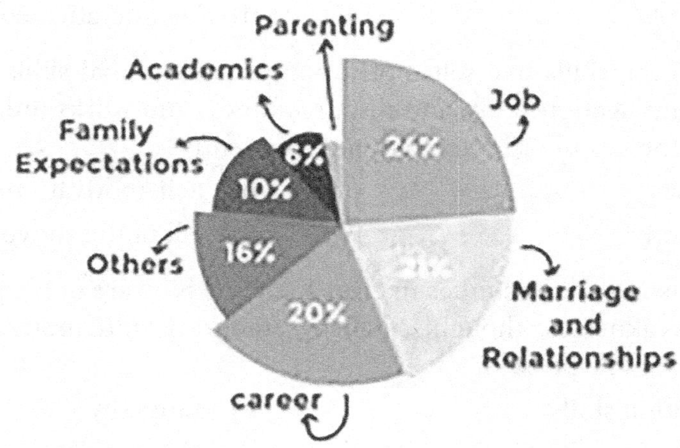

Figure 2.10

Ans.   Stressors can be categorized as positive, dangerous, and irrelevant stressors.

11. What are the common responses to stress?

Ans.   Common responses to stress may be aches and pains, energy levels and sleep, feelings, and other emotional signs.

12. What are the main stress management techniques?

Ans.   Stress management techniques may include physical exercise, yoga, meditation, spending time with friends and family, talking, etc.

13. What is the main advantage of setting realistic goals?

Ans.   Setting realistic goals with proper time management will produce less stress.

14. What is eustress?

Ans.   Stress may have a positive impact on people. It can sometimes be useful, helping us to accomplish great things. This is known as 'eustress.'

15. Why is eustress necessary?

Ans.   Eustress provides us with the energy and motivation to achieve our goals.

16. What is the impact of exercise on the secretion of endorphins?

Ans.   Doing exercise helps to release endorphins (chemicals in the brain that act as natural painkillers) and eradicate insomnia.

17. What is the main benefit of yoga and meditation with respect to stress?

Ans.   Regular practice of yoga and meditation reduces stress, anxiety, and depression.

18. What part is played by enjoying a vacation in reducing stress?

Ans.   Vacation with friends and family can be a refreshing experience that can help in relieving stress.

19. What do you mean by independent people?

Ans.   Independent people are likely to be more confident in handling problems affecting their lives, tend to rely less on others, easily make decisions, and are emotionally independent.

20. What skills are required to work independently?

Ans.   In order to work independently, a person must possess certain skills-self-motivation, organizational skills, multitasking ability, discipline, communication skills, and resourcefulness.

21. What are the keys to becoming self-reliant?

Ans.   The keys to becoming self-reliant are self-awareness, self-motivation, and self-regulation.

22. What do you mean by self-awareness?

Ans.   Self-awareness means being aware of your personality, including your strengths, weaknesses, thoughts, beliefs, emotions, and motivations.

23. Mention the types of self-awareness.

Ans.   There are two types of awareness-External self-awareness and Internal self-awareness.

24. What is external self-awareness?

Ans. External self-awareness requires understanding how other people perceive us.

25. Define internal self-awareness.

Ans. Internal self-awareness represents how clearly one sees one's own values, passions, aspirations, thoughts, feelings, behaviours, strengths, weaknesses, and their impact on others.

26. What is the main purpose of self-motivation?

Ans. Self-motivation drives a person to attempt and accomplish tasks.

27. Mention the types of motivation.

Ans. There are two main types of motivation-intrinsic and extrinsic.

28. Define intrinsic motivation.

Ans. Intrinsic motivation refers to the behaviour of a person that is driven by his innate desire to do something for his own sake and personal rewards.

29. What is extrinsic motivation?

Ans. Extrinsic motivation refers to the behaviour of a person that is driven by the desire to achieve some sort of external reward, including money, power, and good grades.

30. What are the keys to getting the most out of your day?

Ans. Proper planning and time management are the two keys to getting the most out of your day.

31. Define self-regulation.

Ans. Self-regulation involves being able to control reactions to emotions like frustration or excitement.

32. Define Emotional Intelligence (EI).

Ans. Emotional intelligence may be defined as the ability to identify and manage one's own emotions and the emotions of others.

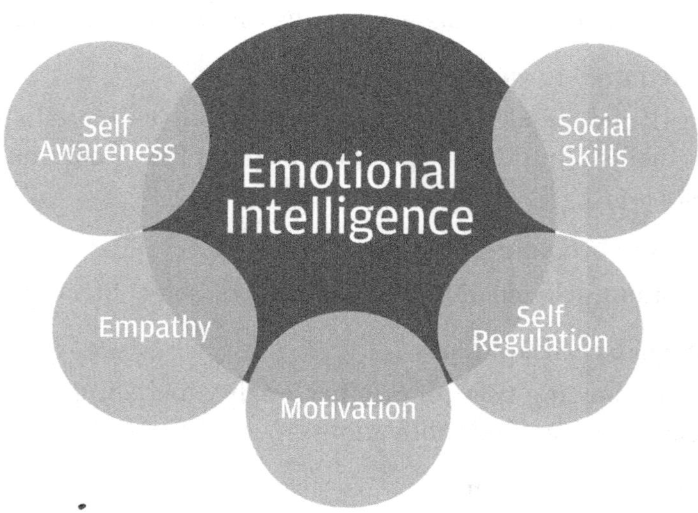

Figure 2.11

2.3.9 Short Answer Type Questions

1. What are the fundamentals of being independent?

Ans. The fundamentals of being independent are the ability to work on your own, with minimal direction, confidence, self-awareness, self-motivation, and self-regulation.

2. Differentiate between eustress and negative stress.

Ans. Positive stress or eustress motivates the person to achieve more. At the same time, negative stress or having stress for a long duration of time is harmful as it may cause health problems and mental troubles as well.

3. What are the various disease-causing factors caused by stress?

Ans. Stress may cause disease-causing factors, like headaches, upset stomach, rashes, insomnia, ulcers, high blood pressure, heart diseases, and stroke, etc.

4. How can stress be beneficial? Illustrate with an example.

Ans. All stress is not bad to disrupt body balance. A mild degree of stress can be beneficial. For example, Anushka is feeling mildly stressed when carrying out a project or assignment. She is compelled to do a good job, focus better, and work energetically.

5. Explain the role of hormones in stress.

Ans. Stress is defined as a hormonal response from the body, and this response starts with a part of our brain called the hypothalamus. When someone is stressed, the hypothalamus sends signals throughout his/her nervous system and to our kidneys.

6. Give some examples/situations from daily life, which may cause stress to people.

Ans. Some of the situations which may cause stress to a person may like price hikes, parental pressure, peer pressure, demanding health conditions, a quarrelsome classmate or neighbour, strict teacher or principal, highly demanding parents, a strict environment at home, no talking by the friends, etc.

7. Differentiate between acute stress and chronic stress.

Ans. Stress is mainly divided into two categories- acute and chronic stress.

Acute stress	Chronic stress
(i) It is associated with the pressures of the future or dealing with the very recent past.	(i) Chronic stress is a wearing effect on people that can become a serious health problem if it continues for a longer period of time.
(ii) Acute stress is often misinterpreted for being a negative impact, but sometimes it is good also.	(ii) It can lead to memory loss, special damage recognition, etc.
(iii) Acute stress is short-term stress.	(iii) It is long-term stress.

8. What are the general causes of stress?

Ans. The cause of stress is highly individual. It depends upon the personality, general outlook on life, problem-solving abilities, and social support system. Many different things cause stress, physical to emotional.

9.   What are the most common health disabilities caused by stress?

Ans.   Anxiety and depression are the most common health disabilities that are increased by long-term stress.

10.   Explain ABC stress management.

Ans.   The ABC of stress management represents:

A: means 'Adversity' or the stressful event

B: means 'Beliefs' or the way you respond to the event

C: means 'Consequences' or actions and outcomes of the event

Figure 2.12

11.   Why is stress management needed?

Ans.   Stress management refers to deal stress using a variety of techniques and psychotherapies for improving everyday functioning. Learning and practicing the techniques for stress management is necessary to lead a happy and meaningful life. Stress management is required to achieve the desired success.

12.   Why is stress called a silent killer?

Ans.   Stress is also referred to as the "silent killer" because it can cause many diseases, like heart disease, chest pain, high blood pressure, an irregular heartbeat, etc.

13.   What are the skills that are included in emotional intelligence? Explain.

Ans.   EI includes three skills:

a)   **Emotional awareness:** This is the ability to identify and name one's own emotions.

b)   **Harnessing emotions:** This is the ability to harness and apply emotions to tasks like thinking and problem-solving.

c)   **Managing emotions:** This is the ability to regulate one's own emotions when necessary and help others to do the same.

14. Why is emotional intelligence required?

Ans. Knowledge of managing one's emotions is required in life. When one can keep one's emotions in a balanced form, then he/she can manage stress, keep the brain active and open-minded, and easily overcome failures. EI is required to have better relations with friends and family. Being emotionally intelligent enhances the chances of success and balanced life.

15. Explain the steps to manage emotional intelligence.

Ans. The steps to manage emotional intelligence are as follows:

a) **Understanding the emotions:** Observe your behaviour to identify the things you need to work on. Work on the emotions you need to improve.

b) **Rationalising thinking in the decision-making:** Do not take decisions abruptly or in haste. Always try to be rational in critical and creative thinking.

c) **Practicing:** Practice meditation and yoga to keep yourself cool and calm.

16. Differentiate between abilities and skills.

Ans. The capacity to perform a task is called ability, while a skill is the ability to perform a task with perfection. Abilities can be converted into skills by practicing them.

17. Which abilities are owned by a person capable of working independently?

Ans. Working independent means that one has the following abilities:

a) Self-awareness (knowing self-knowing strengths, weaknesses, likes, dislikes, etc.).

b) Self-motivating and self-monitoring

c) Knowing your requirements

d) Searching for different options

e) Planning according to the need and requirements

f) Doing the work as per your plan without any fear.

g) Learning through the mistakes and not looking for excuses or blame game

h) Empowering yourself by overcoming the negative thoughts and feelings

18. Differentiate between Interests and Abilities (Strengths).

Ans. The difference between interests and abilities is given below:

Interests	Abilities
(i) Things or activities that you like to do in your free time that makes you happy.	(i) The capacity to perform a task is called ability.
(ii) Things or activities you are curious about or would do even if no one asked you to do it.	(ii) It enables you to perform a particular job or task with considerable proficiency.
(iii) Things or activities you want to learn or would like to do in the future.	(iii) There will be no choice available.

19. Explain the goal with an example.

Ans. A goal is defined as an idea of the future that a person or a group of persons visualize, plan, and commit to achieving. A goal is a set of dreams with a deadline to get them. Example: Saving pocket money to purchase a favourite item on a particular occasion.

20. When is someone called a self-motivated person?

Ans. When any person has the ability to move ahead after identifying effective methods, planning, and making a decision on his own, it is called that he/she is a self-motivated person.

21. Explain the importance of self-regulatory skills.

Ans. When someone is a self-controlled and self-motivated person, then he/she is self-regulatory. It requires critical and creative thinking with effective communication skills. Self-regulation is a must skill to convert the goals of life into reality.

22. Enlist the elements of Self- Motivation.

Ans. The following are the elements playing an important role in self-motivation:

   a) Positive attitude

   b) Commitment to goals

   c) Personal drive to achieve

   d) Initiative (ability to take advantage of opportunities when they occur)

Figure 2.13

   e) Optimism (ability to look on the bright side)

23. Define and illustrate two types of motivation.

Ans. Various people are motivated by different things and at different times in their lives. Following the types of motivation:

   a) **Internal Motivation-Love:** When you do things because they make you happy, healthy, and feel good, then it is internal motivation. For example, when you perform a dance at an annual day function, and you learn some dance steps, then you feel good.

   b) **External Motivation-Reward:** When we do things because they give us respect, recognition, and appreciation, then it is external motivation. For example, you participated in a 200m race and won first prize. This motivated you to go for practice every morning.

24. Define goal-setting and explain its importance.

Ans. Goal setting is about finding and listing the goals and then planning on how to achieve them. Goals allow us to separate out what's important. Goal setting helps us to focus on the end result instead of less important work. This will make us successful in our careers and personal life. Goal setting is an essential factor in our personal life. The process of goal setting in our life helps us decide on how to live our lives, where we want to be, and how we want to be in the future.

25. Define time management.

Ans. Time management is defined as the ability to plan and control how the time is spent well to do all the desired things. In other words, time management is utilizing the available time with a mission to complete the assigned jobs effectively.

26. Explain the importance of Time Management.

Ans. Time management is important as it helps people to:

a) Make a daily timetable.

b) Complete tasks on time.

c) Submit homework and assignments on time.

Figure 2.14

d) Make a time guess for completion of some work/assignment.

e) Do not waste time on unproductive works.

27. What are the tips for Practicing for Effective Time Management? Explain.

Ans. The following tips may be used for effective time management:

a) Avoid delay or postponing any planned activity.

b) Organise your work, room and school desk.

c) Develop a 'NO DISTURBANCE ZONE' to sit and complete important tasks.

d) Use waiting time productively.

e) Prepare a 'To-do' list and prioritise the tasks at hand.

f) Replace useless activities by the productive activities.

2.3.10 Long Answer Type Questions

1. Discuss the four types of sources that cause stress.

Ans. There are four different types of sources that may cause stress.

a) **Survival Stress:** It is created by a do or die situation, which may put the individual in danger of immediate harm-physical or psychic.

b) **Internal Stress:** Worries, frustration, and apprehension in the inner side of someone may cause internal stress. This type of stress keeps on building up inside the body and hinders the open outlook towards life.

c) **Environmental stress:** It is generated by uncomfortable feelings due to environmental factors like noise, extreme hot or cold climate, crowd, quarrelsome neighbour, strict teacher, etc.

d) **Fatigue and Overwork Stress:** It is normally generated by fatigue and overwork when the routines are disturbed due to increased ambitions, setting unrealistic goals, etc.

2. Explain Common Responses to Stress.

Ans. Some common responses to stress are given below:

(i) **Aches and Pains**

- Headache,
- Backache,
- Neckache,
- Stomach-ache,
- Tight muscles,
- Clenched jaws, etc.

(ii) **Energy Level and Sleep**

- Feeling tired without a good reason
- Trouble sleeping

(iii) **Feelings**

- Anger
- Anxiety
- Tense
- Depression
- Helplessness
- Out of Control

(iv) **Other Emotional Signs**

- Easily irritated
- Impatient
- Forgetful

3. Discuss the skills required to succeed in life.

Ans. The following skills are the key skills required to succeed in life:

a) **Self-awareness:** Understanding the reasons/causes of your own behaviour is an important skill that is called self-awareness. Self-awareness is a valuable skill that takes years of effort to truly achieve. Knowing self (strengths and weaknesses of oneself) is called self-awareness. This may be understood well by asking for honest feedback from yourself and as well as from others coming in close contact and gathering insights on the personality and work-specific proficiencies. A self-aware person knows well what he/she can do well.

b) **Positivity:** Positivity must come from the inside in order to be seen on the outside. The first step to developing a positive outlook is having long-term and short-term goals. Motivate yourself to achieve your goals with a constant stream of positivity, and don't allow negativity into your mind.

c) **Responsibility:** Being responsible means taking care of all your actions and their consequences. This can be achieved by prioritizing the tasks at hand, doing proper planning, and taking ownership.

d) **Time Management:** Completing the tasks in the given time frame by prioritizing the tasks is called time management. This can be achieved by removing the waste and redundancy from work and making and adhering to a timetable diligently.

e) **Stress Management:** Implementing effective stress management techniques will allow you to be proactive in managing the things in life, rather than reacting in negative ways.

f) **Adaptability:** Adaptability means having the ability to prepare oneself for new changes so that you can transition seamlessly. This can be achieved by staying updated with best practices and new information always.

4. Discuss the symptoms of Stress.

Ans. All persons react to stress differently, but there are common symptoms of stress, like people may shake uncontrollably, breathe faster, deeper than normal, or even vomit. Some of the symptoms of stress may be as follows:

- Heart palpitations
- High blood pressure
- Sleeplessness
- Overreacting to an unexpected problem
- Eating more or less
- Depression
- Restlessness
- Confusion
- Fatigue
- Memory problem
- Sleep disturbance
- Difficulty in making a decision
- Nervous habits
- Poor judgment
- Lack of concentration
- Digestive problem
- Skin problems
- Asthma or shortness of breath
- Neglecting responsibilities
- Lack of confidence
- Isolation
- Losing temper

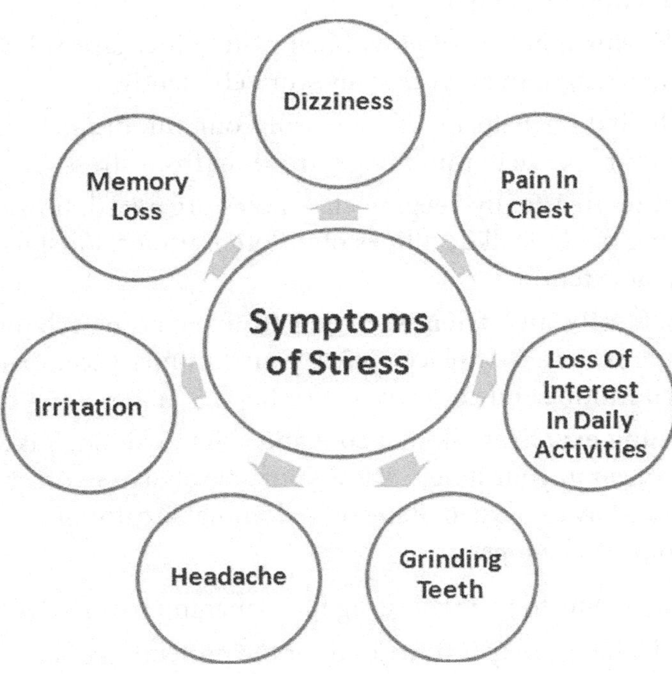

Figure 2.15

5. Discuss the three steps to manage stress.

Ans. The following three steps are used to manage stress:

Step 1: Be aware in case you are stressed:

Look out for various signs of stress, as discussed earlier (like headache, sleeplessness, sadness, excessive worrying, nervousness, etc.). When we are aware of stress, we can manage it well.

Step 2: Identify Stress-causing Elements:

Search out the stress-causing agents/elements. It may be any reason like exams, pressure, family pressures, emotional issues, behaviour and treatment of other people, money issues, food habits, etc.

Step 3: Apply Stress Management Methods and Techniques:

Many techniques are employed for stress management prior to applying any technique. The cause of stress is to be found out to deal with it properly. Some of the techniques are as follows:

a) **Positivity:** Focusing on only negative aspects of life will add more stress. Learn to look at the good things of life and stay positive in all situations. Example: Imran is feeling upset over scoring less in a test. Instead, he should try to maintain a positive attitude and find ways to improve the score next time.

b) **Time Management:** Managing time properly is one of the most effective stress-relieving techniques.

c) **Physical Exercises:** When someone is stressed, he/she may feel exhausted. So, relaxation exercises may be used. Sit in a proper noise-free environment and cool down your body. Doing some light exercises, like walking is a good technique.

d) **Sleep:** One should get a good night's sleep for at least 7 hours, so that brain and body get recharged to function in a better way.

e) **Healthy diet:** Having a healthy diet will help you reduce stress. Eating a balanced diet will give you the strength to do your daily work efficiently.

f) **Meditation:** Meditation help us in increasing our mindfulness. Regular meditation practice brings more peace to mind to get freedom from stress.

g) **Organizing academic life:** By keeping class notes organised, finishing assignments on time, and keeping track of all deadlines of different projects/assignments, stress can be reduced to a great extent.

h) **Holidays with family and friends:** Going to a picnic or relative's place, like your grandparents' house, or a new place during your summer vacations can help you break from the normal routine and come back afresh.

i) **Yoga for breathing exercises:** Sit in a cool and calm position. Take some deep breaths to have more oxygen in your lungs. Allow yourself inhalation of a breath of full oxygen to bring a good supply of oxygen. Belly or abdominal breathing can be very soothing to overcome discomfort feelings.

6. What are the healthy habits to be inculcating for managing stress? Discuss.

Ans. The following healthy habits may be nurtured for the protection of harmful effects of stress:

   i.   Spend time with family and friends.

   ii. Give up bad habits.

Figure 2.16

    iii. Remember to laugh a lot.

    iv. Engage in daily physical activity (walking/swimming/biking/dancing, etc.)

    v. Embrace the things you are able to change

    vi. Slow down try to pace instead of race

    vii. Get enough sleep

    viii. Practice giving back by doing some volunteering work

    ix. Try not to worry

    x. Have a positive approach towards life

    xi. Get organised-have a good timetable.

7. Explain the seven necessary skills required to work independently.

Ans. The following seven skills are required for working independently.

    i. **Decision-making skills** to know what to do and to plan and decide the action plan by keeping in mind the final outcome.

    ii. **Discipline** to keep on the right track for successful completion of a task.

    iii. **Communication skills** to better connect with other people to get their help or support.

    iv. **Flexibility** to adapt your work to suit other people who work with you or for you.

    v. **Negotiation skills** to accommodate other ideas for the benefit in a larger context.

    vi. **Multitasking skills** to perform many tasks at a time to meet the time schedule of the project.

    vii. **Analytic skills** to see the positive and negative aspects of every situation or action and to handle the rejection.

8. Explain four types of self-awareness.

Ans. There are four types of self-awareness:

    i. **Self-Awareness of Your Strengths:** Every person has more than 80 qualities, but one may not be 100% perfect or outstanding in all abilities. Everyone has some outstanding qualities. Sit in a calm position and list out your strengths, i.e., the best qualities you have.

    ii. **Self-awareness about Your Weakness:** You may have some qualities for which you want improvement. These may be called weaknesses. Some of them may be lack of self-confidence, low self-esteem, not speaking fluently in a language, fear of the face of the crowd, etc.

    iii. **Self-awareness about Your Dark side:** Some of your weaknesses and the dark side of your life may be brought out into the light by your family or friends. Talk to them.

    iv. **Self-awareness about Your Emotional Triggers:** Emotional balance is required in life. We have so many emotions. Emotional stability is achieved by having a positive attitude towards life.

9. Explain the techniques for identifying the strengths and weaknesses.

Ans. The techniques given below may be used to search Strengths (or abilities):

    i. Think of all things that you are always successful at.

    ii. Think about what other people like you.

   iii. List what do you do better than others.

   iv. List the things other people admire you.

   v. Think about what you do well.

   vi. How am I different from others?

   vii. List the things that make you stand out.

   viii. The steps given below may be used to search weaknesses:

   ix. List the things where do you worry and struggles.

   x. List the things where, how, and why do others perform better than you.

   xi. Point out the areas where you struggle.

   xii. List the things you find difficult to do.

   xiii. Look at the feedback others usually give about you.

   xiv. Be open to feedback and accept the weaknesses without feeling low about them. Take it as an area of improvement.

   xv. List the advice for improvement do you often receive from others.

10. Enumerate Self-Regulation Strategies.

Ans. The following methods for managing myself may be used:

   i. Awareness of body sensations   ii. Consciously breathing,

   iii. Relaxing   iv. Exercises

   v. Meditation and prayer

   vi. Self-expression through art, music, and dance

   vii. Caring, nurturing self-task.   viii. Movement/walking/biking etc.

11. Enlist the steps to keep yourself Self-Motivated.

Ans. The following steps are needed to keep oneself self-motivated:

   i. Keep learning   ii. Know yourself   iii. Help others

   iv. Start simple and keep motivators around your work area.

Figure 2.17

    v. Keep good company of positive and like-minded people.

    vi. Have a positive attitude

    vii. Stop thinking, just do.

    viii. Track your programs

12. Throw light on the qualities of Self-motivated People.

Ans. The following typical behaviours are seen in self-motivated people:

    i. They are optimistic.

    ii. They are visionary.

    iii. They know what they want from life.

    iv. They are focused and committed.

    v. They possess good self-esteem.

    vi. They know what is important.

    vii. They are highly energetic.

    viii. They are dedicated to fulfilling their dreams.

    ix. They are humble and life-long learners.

    x. They are willing to accept when they are wrong.

13. Enlist the methods/techniques for building Self-motivation

Ans. The following methods and techniques may be used to build self-motivation:

    i. Write down your goals and reasons for their selection.

    ii. Set a large and specific goal. Small goals will follow it.

    iii. Stay loyal to your goals and work towards achieving them, even in a difficult time.

    iv. Be empathetic and focus on the positive.

    v. Remember your successes, not failures.

    vi. Monitor yourself and keep faith in yourself.

    vii. Remember to have fun.

    viii. Make use of your creativity in your projects.

14. Explain in detail the meaning of SMART Goals.

Ans. In SMART Goal, SMART stands for Specific, Measurable, Achievable, Realistic, and Time-bound.

    i. **Specific:** A specific and clear goal answers the following six questions:

        ▲ Who is involved in the goal?   ▲ What do I want to do?

        ▲ Where do I start?   ▲ When do I start and finish?

        ▲ Which means do I use?   ▲ Why am I doing this?

    ii. **Measurable:** A measurable goal answers the question, "How much?" "How many?" and "How do I know that I have achieved results?"

       Not measurable goal: "Matin Ahmed wants to be rich."

       Measurable goal: "Matin Ahmed wants to have ten times more money than what he has today in his hand by the end of 2024."

iii. **Achievable:** By breaking down, big goals into smaller parts will make the big goal achievable.

Bigger goal: "Suhana wants to become a Senior school teacher (Physics) in her life."

Breaking it into smaller goals:

- Completing Senior secondary with maths
- Completing Graduation (PCM)
- Completing Post Graduation (Physics)
- Completing B.Ed.
- Applying for the job in the school
- Getting and starting the job

iv. **Realistic:** A realistic goal is an achievable goal.

Example of unrealistic goal: "Indumati will revise the entire year's syllabus in one day to get 90% marks in the exams."

Realistic goal: "After school time, Indumati will spend 3-4 hours each day of the year to revise the subjects to get 90% marks in the exams."

v. **Time-bound:** A SMART goal should have a timeframe for achieving the goal. The time frame encourages the individual to take action to fulfill the plans completely.

Example: Not a time-bound goal: " Shubhi wants to lose 10 kg weight someday."

Time-bound goal: "Shubhi wants to lose 10kg weight within the next three months."

Figure 2.18

2.3.11 HOTS Questions

1. How is Working Independently useful?

Ans. Some of the benefits of working independently are given below:

a) It ensures creativity.

b) It ensures greater learning.

c) Individuals become assets to the organisation, groups, and nation.

d) It enhances the feeling of empowerment and responsibility among individuals.

e) It provides flexibility to define and choose the working hours and working mechanism.

f) Failure and success of the assignments/tasks/projects are accounted for by individuals.

g) It enhances the satisfaction level amongst individuals.

2. Why is the four Steps strategy for Effective Time Management used?

Ans. The four steps strategy for effective time management is important because it makes the work easier and effective due to the following steps:

i. **Organise**

a) Plan your day-to-day activities.

b) Make a timetable that you follow.

c) Keep your surroundings and study table clean and organised.

d) Put things back where they belong.

e) It helps people save their precious time.

ii. **Prioritise**

a) Make a to-do list that has all the activities and give rank them in the order of importance.

b) It helps people to get the most important task done first and to track what is pending.

iii. **Control**

a) Have control over your activities and time.

b) Avoid time wasters like chatting on the phone for a longer duration, surfing gossip sites, etc., and focus on more important things.

iv. **Track**

a) Identify and note where you have spent your time.

b) Analyse whether the time was used effectively or not.

c) It helps people to identify time-wasting activities and to avoid them.

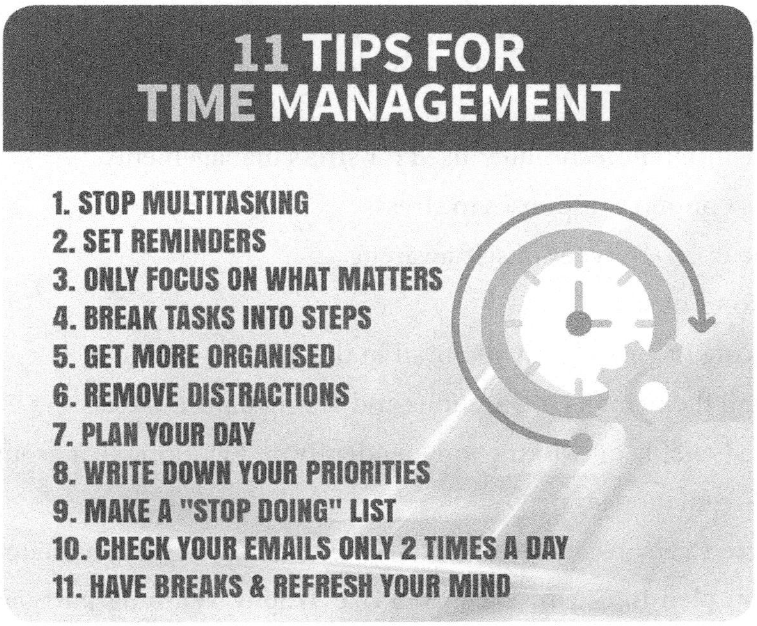

Figure 2.19

2.4 PRACTICE QUESTIONS

1. What is meant by 'Stress Management'?

2. Define stressors and de-stressors.

3. 'Sometimes, stress can be helpful.' Explain it by giving an example.

4. Mention two benefits of physical exercise.

5. Why is self-regulation considered necessary for getting success in life?

Figure 2.20

6. What are the two main types of stress?

7. Differentiate between self-motivation and self-regulation.

8. 'Stress Management is need of the hour.' Justify the statement.

9. What are the different types of stressors? Give examples.

10. 'Stress is like a gateway that provides a free passage to a heap of diseases.' Explain with suitable examples.

11. What are the different techniques used for stress management?

12. What are the common responses to stress?

13. What are the different types of self-awareness?

14. List 8 symptoms of stress.

15. Why is working independently required in the modern world?

16. Write in detail the benefits of vacations and taking nature walks.

17. What are the benefits of working independently and working in a group?

18. Explain self-regulation strategies.

19. ''Self-motivated persons are assets to the organisation.'' Justify the statement.

20. How will you plan to organise a First Prize Trophy Winning party at your home in the evening?

UNIT 3

ICT Skills II

3.1 UNIT IN BRIEF

+ An operating system is the first program that gets loaded into computer memory.

+ The operating system acts as an interface between hardware and software.

+ GUI is more user-friendly as it lets the user interact with the computer by using visual tools.

+ A desktop is the first screen that is displayed after switching on Windows.

Figure 3.1

+ A File System defines the ways in which files are named and placed for storage and retrieval.

+ In a hierarchical file system, the files are organised into folders and sub-folders in a tree-like structure.

+ A computer virus is a program or a set of programs that disrupt the normal operation of a computer.

+ VIRUS stands for Vital Information Resources Under Seize.

+ Antivirus software is a computer program designed to identify, prevent, and remove viruses from a computer.

+ Proper working of the hardware components of a computer can be ensured by physically cleaning them, keeping them in a proper manner, and repairing them whenever required.

+ Cleaning of the software installed on the computer involves the scheduled disk clean-up tasks, protection against viruses, deleting the temporary and unwanted files, etc.

+ Mydoom virus in Jan 2004 infected about a quarter-million computers in a day. It caused 38.5 billion$ in damages.

+ Storm -a worm appeared in January 2007, which infected about 50 million computers by October 2007.

✦ The first Windows virus was named WinVer 1.4, the first .exe file was Groove, and the first boot virus was created by the Farooq Alvi brothers.

✦ The worst ever MS-DOS virus was called Michelangelo that worked in the background and created duplicate copies to spread itself.

✦ 90% of emails contain some type of malware, and most people are unaware of it.

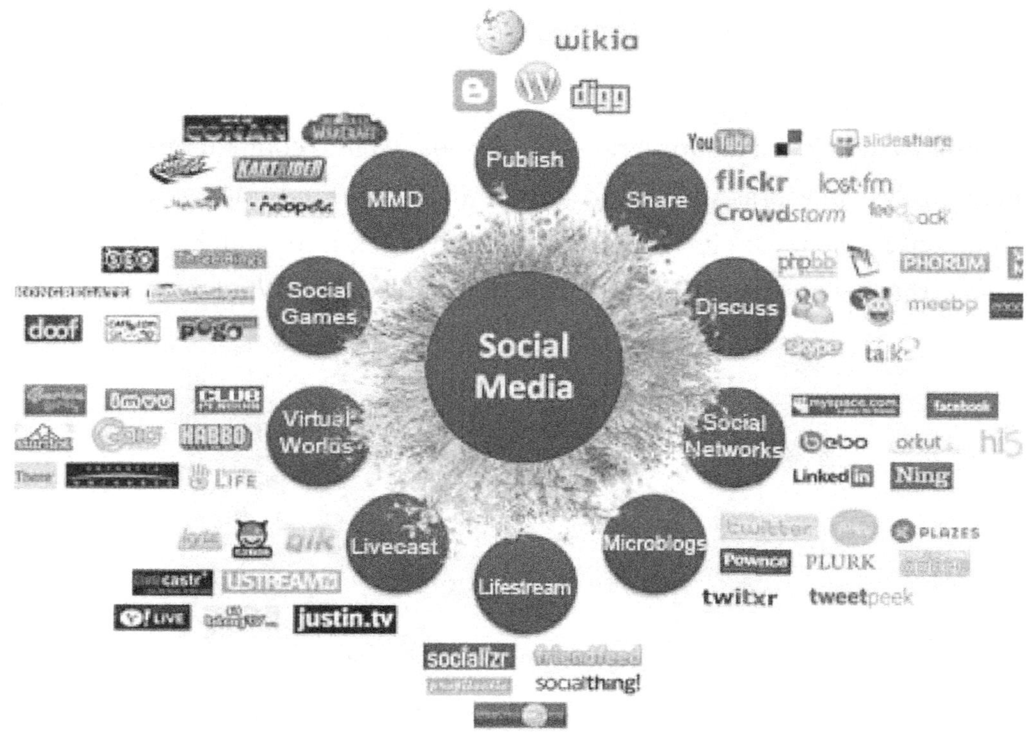

Figure 3.2

3.2 CBSE/NCERT SECTION (SOLVED CBSE/NCERT EXERCISE QUESTIONS)

(A) MCQs

Choose the correct option out of the given four options:

1. Which of the following functions is not performed using a mouse?

   a) Turn on

   b) Hover

   c) Right-click

   d) Drag and Drop

2. What is the term used when you press and hold the left mouse key and move the mouse around?

   a) Highlighting   b) Dragging   c) Selecting   d) Moving

3. Which one of the following shortcut keys is used to paste a file?

   a) Ctrl + c   b) Ctrl + p   c) Ctrl + v   d) Ctrl + x

4. Which of the following is a valid file extension for Notepad file?
   a) .jpg
   b) .doc
   c) .text
   d) .txt

5. What key do you use to copy something?
   a) Ctrl+x
   b) Ctrl+c
   c) Ctrl+z
   d) Ctrl+y

6. What happens if you leave a device plugged in even after it is charged 100%?
   a) It can break.
   b) It can stop functioning.
   c) It can over-heat.
   d) Data can get corrupt.

7. How can an anti-virus protect your device?
   a) It can protect it from over-heating.
   b) It can increase its performance.
   c) It can prevent data from getting corrupt.
   d) It can backup data.

8. Which option is not required to keep a device cool?
   a) Keep the device unplugged when in use.
   b) Don't cover a laptop with a blanket.
   c) See the computer's CPU fan is working.
   d) Avoid leaving the device in the sun.

9. Which of the following condition is essential for maintaining the keyboard?
   a) Turn the keyboard upside down and shake it to remove foreign material.
   b) Remove dust and other particles with the help of a blower.
   c) Use a very dilute combination of soap and water applied with a non-abrasive cloth to remove stains from the keycaps.
   d) All of the above.

10. What should you do to ensure secure online transactions?
    a) Lock your computer
    b) Give credit card or bank details only on safe websites
    c) Use anti-virus
    d) Do not use pirated software

11. Which of the following trap small children into inappropriate relations?
    a) Online predators
    b) Worms
    c) Trojan Horse
    d) Anti-Virus

12. What should a strong password consist of?
    a) Only letters
    b) Numbers and special characters
    c) Name of a person
    d) Letters, numbers, and special characters

ANSWERS									
1. a	2. b	3. c	4. d	5. b	6. c	7. c	8. a	9. d	10. b
11. a	12. d								

(B) Subjective Questions

1. Here are the steps that take place when starting a computer. Rearrange the steps in the correct order.

   (a) Desktop appears after login
   (b) Login screen appears
   (c) Power on Self-Test (POST) starts
   (d) Operating system starts
   (e) Welcome screen appears

Ans. e>>d>>c>>b>>a.

2. What is the function of the ENTER key?

Ans. The ENTER key or the RETURN key is used to move the cursor to the beginning of a new line.

3. How will you prevent others from using your computer?

Ans. We can prevent others from using our computer by locking it and opening it with a password.

4. How is a computer file system similar to our physical file system in a school?

Ans. The information stored in a computer is kept in files. Various files store different types of information. Each file is given a file name. It has a file name extension that identifies the file type. This is almost similar to a physical file system where each file having a specific name contains specific information on papers.

5. What are the steps you will perform to save a text file in Ubuntu?

Ans. The following steps are performed to save a text file in Ubuntu:

   - To open a text editor, type 'editor' in the search dialog box. Then double-click the text editor option. This will open a blank document.
   - Here you can add text, such as 'Prem.'
   - To save the file, click Save. In the Save As dialog box, browse to the Desktop folder, type the name as 'Prem,' and click Save.

6. Explain how to clean a computer on a daily basis.

Ans. A computer can be cleaned on a daily basis as follows:

   - Clean up your email inbox.
   - Download email attachments and save them in proper folders.

7. How can you increase the performance of a computer?

Ans. When we use a computer for a long time, a lot of unnecessary files and data, such as temporary files and images, are added to the computer memory. When these files use too much hard-disk space, the performance of the computer decreases. It is important to keep the computer clean by removing any extra files. We can use some disk cleaner software. This process helps us clean up the unnecessary files to get free space on computer memory.

8. Explain how the Trojan Horse virus works.

Ans. A Trojan Horse looks like a useful software program, but once it enters a computer, it starts behaving like a virus by destroying data.

9. List the various ways you can use to protect your data.

Ans. The following measures can be used to protect data:

a) **Install Anti-virus and Firewall:** Anti-viruses and Firewalls monitor the data coming in and out of a computer and prevent and viruses from entering. Anti-virus software can also detect and clean viruses that may have entered a computer.

b) **Use passwords to login to the computer:** Use passwords that are difficult to guess. Passwords are difficult to hack if they have a mixture of small (For example, 'a, b, c, d') and capital letters (For example, 'H, J, E, R'), numbers (For example '2, 7, 6, 5') and special characters (For example, '%, ^, #, $'). This will prevent unauthorised persons from using your computer.

c) **Secure sites:** Give details of the credit card or bank account only on secure sites. For this, see in the address bar of the browser. When the site address starts with https://and a lock symbol, then it is safe to use or share the details, like credit card details, bank details, etc.

d) **Encrypt Data:** This is usually done by organisations, like banks and security companies, in which important customer information is stored. Organisations may encrypt their entire hard disk data using the encrypting feature in Windows (Bitlocker). This will force users to use a decryption password (or key) before starting the computer and hence, preventing unauthorized usage of data.

Figure 3.3

3.3 SOLVED EXERCISES

3.3.1 Multiple Choice Questions

Choose the correct option out of the four given options for each question.

1. Which of the following software is not used in mobiles?

a) Microsoft Windows,

b) Ubuntu,

c) Mac OS,

d) None of these

2. Consider the following are the functions performed by an OS?
   i.   It keeps track of the status of the device, whether it is busy or not.
   ii. It makes users capable of sharing data among themselves.
   iii. It prevents users from interfering with one another.
   iv. It facilitates making errors.
   v.   It implements the user interface.
   a) (ii) (iii) (iv)   b) (iii) (iv) (v)
   c) (v) (iii) (ii) (i)   d) All of these

3. Which of the following is a punctuation key?
   a) Single quotation marks key.   b) F1 key
   c) Caps Lock key   d) PgUp key

4. Which of the following is not a Navigation key?
   a) HOME   b) END   c) PAGE UP   d) Tab

5. Which of the following is not a function of an OS?
   a) It manages all the devices of the computer.
   b) It shares hardware among users.
   c) It facilitates parallel operations.
   d) It facilitates input/output.

6. Which of the following keys is not a command key?
   a) Insert (INS)   b) Delete (DEL)   c) Home   d) Backspace

7. Which device is a small electronic device that is used to move, select, and open items on the computer screen?
   a) Mouse   b) Monitor   c) Printer   d) PD

8. Which method is required to keep a computer cool?
   a) Keep the device unplugged when not in use.
   b) Do not cover a laptop with a cloth or blanket.
   c) Make sure that the computer's CPU fan is working.
   d) All of these

9. What must you do to ensure secure online transactions?
   a) Lock the computer
   b) Use antivirus
   c) Do not use pirated software
   d) A transaction with the credit/debit card on safe websites only.

10. Which one of the following is not malware?
    a) Virus   b) OS   c) Trojan horse   d) Worm

11. Which part of the computer has a television-like shape?
    a) Keyboard   b) Mouse   c) Monitor   d) System Unit

12. Antivirus is a:
    a) Hardware   b) Software   c) Program   d) None of these

13. What is the full form of CUI?
    a) Clever User Interface   b) Common User Interface
    c) Character User Interface   d) Create User Interface

14. What are McAfee and Quick Heal?
    a) Hardware   b) Software
    c) Antivirus   d) None of the above

15. Which of the functions is not performed by an OS?
    a) It allows the user to create, copy, move, and delete files.
    b) It organises s the structure of the files and directories on a computer.
    c) It ruptures the software resources of the computer.
    d) It manages the computer memory and keeps track of memory space.

16. Which of the following functions is related to OS?
    a) It tracks the amount of disk space used by a specific file.
    b) It schedules resources among users.
    c) It organises data for secure and rapid access.
    d) All the above.

17. Which of the following software is not an Operating System?
    a) DOS   b) Excel   c) Unix   d) Linux

18. Which shortcut key is used to cut/delete a file?
    a) Ctrl + w   b) Ctrl + c   c) Ctrl + x   d) Ctrl + d

19. Which of the mouse buttons is used to drag an item?
    a) Left mouse button   b) Right mouse button
    c) Both a and b   d) Scroll button

20. Which of the following keys enables us to take a screenshot of the computer screen?
    a) Esc key   b) Insert key
    c) Print Screen key (PrtScr)   d) Backspace key

21. What are unwanted bulk emails, or unwanted commercial emails, or junk mail named?
    a) Blog   b) Spam   c) Attachments   d) Malware

22. Where are deleted files and folders moved to?
    a) Desktop   b) Recycle Bin   c) My Computer   d) Favorites

23. Which of the following is not a monitor?
    a) LCD   b) LED   c) LDD   d) CRT

24. CAM stands for
    a) Common-Aided Manufacturing   b) Computer-Aided Manufacturing
    c) Computer-Aided Manufacturer   d) Computer Allowed Manufacturing

25. How can an antivirus protect your device?
    a) It can protect it from over-heating.
    b) It can prevent data from getting corrupt.
    c) It can increase its performance.
    d) It can backup data.

26. What is the term used for the action when you press and hold the left mouse key and move the mouse around?
    a) Selecting   b) Moving   c) Dragging   d) Highlighting

27. Which of the following keys enables us to type a letter in uppercase?
    a) Caps Lock key   b) Ctrl key   c) Page Up key   d) Home key

28. Which of the following is not a source of a computer virus?
    a) CD and PD   b) Email attachments
    c) Downloading files   d) Typing through keyboard

29. Which of the following trap small children in making inappropriate relations?
    a) Online predators   b) Antivirus   c) Trojan Horse   d) Worms

30. Which of the following steps is essential for maintaining a keyboard?
    a) Blow dust and other small particles by using a blower.
    b) Turn the keyboard upside down in the air, and shake it to remove any foreign material.
    c) Use a dilute solution of soap and water and a non-abrasive cloth to remove stains from the keycaps.
    d) All of these.

31. Which software is not malware?
    a) Application Software   b) Virus
    c) Worm   d) Spam

32. What should a strong password consist of?
    a) Only letters
    b) Both numbers and special characters
    c) Name of a person
    d) Letters, numbers, and special characters

33. Which component is not related to the Windows desktop?
    a) Virus   b) Wallpaper   c) Icons   d) Taskbar

34. Which component is not a part of a computer?
    a) Monitor   b) Mouse   c) Keyboard   d) Windows

35. What is the name given to Keys from F1 to F12?
    a) Numeric keys   b) Function keys
    c) Shift key   d) Cursor Control keys

36. Which function is not performed by using a mouse?

    a) Hover   b) Turn on   c) Right-click   d) Drag and Drop

37. By right-clicking on a folder icon, which folder operation cannot be performed?

    a) Renaming folder   b) Deleting folder

    c) Copying folder   d) Entering data in the folder

38. Which of the following extensions is a valid file extension for a picture file?

    a) .jpg   b) .doc   c) .text   d) .txt

39. What shortcut keys are used to copy something in a document?

    a) Ctrl+x   b) Ctrl+p   c) Ctrl+c   d) Ctrl+d

40. Which file extension is used for Linux files?

    a) .sql   b) .tar   c) .xml   d) .exe

41. Which of the following is not an example of a Trojan horse?

    a) Bifrost   b) Magic Lantern

    c) Tiny Banker   d) None of the above

42. Which file extension is used for Python files?

    a) .py   b) .gif   c) .ico   d) .png

ANSWERS

1. (d)	2. (c)	3. (a)	4. (d)	5. (b)	6. (c)	7. (a)	8. (d)	9. (d)	10. (b)
11. (c)	12. (b)	13. (c)	14. (c)	15. (c)	16. (d)	17. (b)	18. (c)	19. (a)	20. (c)
21. (b)	22. (b)	23. (c)	24. (b)	25. (b)	26. (c)	27. (a)	28. (d)	29. (a)	30. (d)
31. (a)	32. (d)	33. (a)	34. (d)	35. (b)	36. (b)	37. (d)	38. (a)	39. (c)	40. (b)
41. (d)	42. (a)								

3.3.2 Fill in the blanks

Figure 3.4

1. The main screen of Windows is called ______________.

2. A ______________ is an application that is used to access or retrieve information or resources from the Internet.

3. A website is regarded as a collection of related ______________ linked to each other by hyperlinks.

4. The Web pages are stored on a computer, which is called a ______________.

5. In Windows 10, Microsoft Edge (codenamed Project Spartan) replaces the Internet ______________.

6. ______________ represents a mode of communication in which a user can send electronic messages to other users through the Internet.

7. Trojan horse is a ______________ that acts as a useful computer program Emails from unknown sources should be deleted.

8. An ______________ acts as an interface between hardware and software.

9. ______________ button has a Cross (x) symbol.

10. The word ______________ is derived from a real-life table-top where you may find files, Notepad, pen stand, clock, calculator, etc.

11. ______________ software is General-purpose software.

12. ______________ feature helps to prevent spam messages from being delivered to your inbox.

13. The virus infects or destroys ______________ of the computer without the permission or knowledge of the owner.

14. A ______________ is defined as a website or part of a website containing the thoughts and ideas of a user.

15. A ______________ is like a container that can store similar types of files.

ANSWERS				
1. wallpaper	2. Web browser	3. web pages	4. Server	5. Explorer
6. Electronic mail (Email)		7. virus	8. operating system	
9. Close]	10. Desktop	11. Presentation	12. Filter	13. data
14. blog	15. Folder			

3.3.3 True or False

1. A computer virus may be defined as a program or a set of programs that disrupt the normal operation of a computer.

2. 50% of emails contain some type of malware, and most people are unaware of it.

3. All virus programs do not cause harm to data or programs.

4. WhatsApp is a free mobile app that is used for exchanging text messages, sharing images or videos, and making free voice/video calling.

5. Facebook is a platform on the Internet that allows users to share different news items. Also, it enables them to vote for these items.

6. Digital India is a campaign launched by the Government of India for providing government services to citizens electronically.

7. Mydoom virus in Jan 2004 infected about a quarter-million computers in a day. It caused 38.5 billion$ in damages.

8. Storm -a worm appeared in January 2007, which infected about 50 million computers by October 2007.

Figure 3.5

9. The virus infects or destroys data in the computer with permission or knowledge.

10. The first Windows virus was named WinVer 1.4, the first .exe file was Groove, and the first boot virus was created by the Farooq Alvi brothers.

11. The worst ever MS-DOS virus was called Michelangelo that worked in the background and created duplicate copies to spread itself.

12. The 32-bit system storage footprint can be reduced by 1.5 GB, and for 64-bit, it can be reduced by 2.6 GB.

13. VIRUS stands for Vital Information Resources Under Seize.

14. Antivirus software is a computer program designed to identify, prevent, and remove viruses from a computer.

15. When we use a computer for a long time, a lot of unnecessary files and data, such as temporary files and images, are added to the computer memory.

ANSWERS							
1. T	2. F (90%)	3. F	4. T	5. F	6. T	7. T	8. T
9. F (without)	10. T	11. T	12. T	13. T	14. T	15. T	

3.3.4 Matching type

(I) Match the extension with correct description of file

Extension	Description of file
(i) .ods	(a) audio file
(ii) .xls	(b) MPEG-2 audio file
(iii) .aif	(c) CD audio track file
(iv) .cda	(d) AIF audio file
(v) .mp3	(e) OpenOffice Calc spreadsheet file
(vi) .mpa	(f) Microsoft Excel file

(II) Match the action with correct meaning.

Action	Meaning
(i) Drag Move	(a) Touch surface for an extended period of time
(ii) Flick	(b) Touch the surface with two fingers and bring them closer together.
(iii) Pinch	(c) Quickly brush the surface with a fingertip.
(iv) Spread	(d) Fingertip over the surface without losing contact
(v) Press	(e) Touch surface on the screen with two fingers and move them apart

ANSWERS					
(I) (i) - ,	(ii) - f,	(iii) - d,	(iv) - c,	(v) - a,	(vi) - b
(II) (i) - d,	(ii) - c,	(iii) - b,	(iv) - e,	(v) - a	

3.3.5 Statements Based Questions

1. Statement 1: A desktop is the first screen that is displayed after switching on Windows.
   Statement 2: A File System defines the ways in which files are named and placed for storage and retrieval.
   a) Statement 1 is correct but statement 2 is incorrect.
   b) Statement 1 is incorrect but statement 2 is correct.
   c) Both the statements are correct.
   d) Both the statements are incorrect.

2. Statement 1: An operating system is the second program that gets loaded into computer memory.
   Statement 2: Antivirus software is a computer program designed to identify, prevent, and remove viruses from a computer.
   a) Statement 1 is correct but statement 2 is incorrect.
   b) Statement 1 is incorrect but statement 2 is correct.
   c) Both the statements are correct.
   d) Both the statements are incorrect.

3. Statement 1: The operating system acts as an interface between hardware and software.

   Statement 2: Cleaning of the software installed on the computer involves the scheduled disk clean-up tasks, protection against viruses, deleting the temporary and unwanted files, etc.

   a) Statement 1 is correct but statement 2 is incorrect.
   b) Statement 1 is incorrect but statement 2 is correct.
   c) Both the statements are correct.
   d) Both the statements are incorrect.

4. Statement 1: The first Windows virus was named WinVer 1.4.

   Statement 2: The first Windows virus was created by the Farooq Alvi brothers.

   a) Statement 1 is correct but statement 2 is incorrect.
   b) Statement 1 is incorrect but statement 2 is correct.
   c) Both the statements are correct.
   d) Both the statements are incorrect.

5. Statement 1: 20% of emails contain some type of malware, and most people are unaware of it.

   Statement 2: GUI is not user-friendly as it lets the user interact with the computer by using visual tools.

   a) Statement 1 is correct but statement 2 is incorrect.
   b) Statement 1 is incorrect but statement 2 is correct.
   c) Both the statements are correct.
   d) Both the statements are incorrect.

6. Statement 1: Linux is an operating system that was designed for personal computers. It is free and open-source software.

Figure 3.6

Statement 2: A device used to transfer information between computer networks is called a router.

   a) Statement 1 is correct but statement 2 is incorrect.
   b) Statement 1 is incorrect but statement 2 is correct.
   c) Both the statements are correct.   d) Both the statements are incorrect.

ANSWERS
1. (c)   2. (b)   3. (c)   4. (a)   5. (d)   6. (c)

3.3.6 Assertion Reason Type Questions

1. Assertion (A): VIRUS (Vital Information Resources Under Seize) is dangerous.

   Reason(R): A computer virus is a program or a set of programs that disrupt the normal operation of a computer.
   a) Both A and R are correct and R is the correct reason for A.
   b) Both A and R are correct and R is not the correct reason for A.
   c) A is correct but R is incorrect.
   d) A is incorrect but R is correct.

2. Assertion (A): In a hierarchical file system, the files are organised into folders and sub-folders in a tree-like structure.

   Reason(R): The first .exe file was Groove.
   a) Both A and R are correct, and R is the correct reason for A.
   b) Both A and R are correct, and R is not the correct reason for A.
   c) A is correct but R is incorrect.
   d) A is incorrect but R is correct.

3. Assertion (A): The worst ever MS-DOS virus was called Michelangelo.

   Reason(R): Michelangelo worked in the background and created duplicate copies to spread itself.
   a) Both A and R are correct, and R is the correct reason for A.
   b) Both A and R are correct, and R is not the correct reason for A.
   c) A is correct but R is incorrect.
   d) A is incorrect but R is correct.

4. Assertion (A): Proper working of the hardware components of a computer can be ensured by physically cleaning them, keeping them in a proper manner, and repairing them whenever required.

   Reason(R): Mydoom virus in Jan 2014 infected about a quarter-million computers in a day and caused 38.5 billion$ in damages.
   a) Both A and R are correct and R is the correct reason for A.
   b) Both A and R are correct and R is not the correct reason for A.
   c) A is correct but R is incorrect.
   d) A is incorrect but R is correct.

5. Assertion (A): An operating system is a set of programs that control a computer.

   Reason(R): Basic computer operations are controlled by operating systems.
   a) Both A and R are correct, and R is the correct reason for A.
   b) Both A and R are correct, and R is not the correct reason for A.
   c) A is correct but R is incorrect.
   d) A is incorrect but R is correct.

6. Assertion (A): Briefly touching the surface with a fingertip is called rovering.

   Reason(R): Tapping activates a control or selects an item.

   a) Both A and R are correct, and R is the correct reason for A.

   b) Both A and R are correct, and R is not the correct reason for A.

   c) A is correct but R is incorrect.

   d) A is incorrect but R is correct.

ANSWERS					
1. (a)	2. (d)	3. (a)	4. (c)	5. (b)	6. (b)

3.3.7 Competency Based Questions

1. Suppose Rakesh Asthana carries the following cleaning strategy for his computers:

   i. Scan the computer to check the entry of any possible virus into the system.

   ii. Remove temporary Internet files.

   iii. Clean up an email inbox

   iv. Remove Windows temporary files.

   v. Download email attachments and save them in proper folders

   This cleaning strategy should be applied:

   a) Daily   b) Weekly   c) Monthly   d) Annual

2. Dinesh Pathak owns *Sai CompuSolutions* and he carries a process that is meant for the following tasks:

   i. For keeping them in proper running condition

   ii. For enhancing their efficiency

   iii. For finding problems and issues at an early stage

   iv. For their safety and enhancing their life span

   v. For prevention against viruses and malware

   vi. For increasing the working speed of the computers

   vii. For maximising the computer software efficiency

   viii. For preventing data loss

   This process is known as:

   a) Up dation of computers   b) Corrective measures for computers

   c) Evaluation of computers   d) Maintenance of computers

3. Which of the following tasks is not included in annual cleaning strategy of computers?

   a) Open the computer case, and clean it from inside.

   b) Clean up contact list on social media accounts.

   c) Execute Disk Defragmenter utility.

   d) Update/Renew antivirus software.

ANSWERS		
1. (a)	2. (d)	3. (c)

3.3.8 VSA

1. Define operating system.

Ans. An operating system is the first program that gets loaded into computer memory.

2. What is the function of an operating system?

Ans. The operating system acts as an interface between hardware and software.

3. Why is GUI called user-friendly?

Ans. GUI is called user-friendly as it lets the user interact with the computer by using visual tools.

4. Define desktop.

Ans. A desktop is the first screen that is displayed after switching on Windows.

5. What is a file system?

Ans. A File System defines the ways in which files are named and placed for storage and retrieval.

6. Which virus in Jan 2004 infected about a quarter-million computers in a day, causing a damage of 38.5 billion$?

Ans. Mydoom virus.

7. What is Storm in computer science?

Ans. Storm is a worm that appeared in January 2007, which infected about 50 million computers by October 2007.

8. Who created the first Windows virus named WinVer 1.4 and the first boot virus?

Ans. Farooq Alvi brothers.

9. Define a computer virus.

Ans. A computer virus may be defined as a program or a set of programs that disrupt the normal operation of a computer.

10. What is the full form of VIRUS?

Ans. VIRUS stands for Vital Information Resources Under Seize.

11. What do you mean by antivirus software?

Ans. Antivirus software is a computer program designed to identify, prevent, and remove viruses from a computer.

12. Windows is an operating system that is developed by Microsoft.

Ans. An operating system is also defined as the set of programs that control a computer.

13. Which device controls the basic computer operations?

Ans. Basic computer operations are controlled by operating systems.

14. What is the meaning of 'Tap' and its action?

Ans. Briefly touching the surface with a fingertip is called tap. It activates a control or selects an item.

15. What is Linux?

Ans. Linux is an operating system that was designed for personal computers. It is free and open-source software.

16. Give two examples of Mobile Operating systems.

Ans. Android, Symbian, Windows Phone, iOS, etc.

17. Define router.

Ans. A device used to transfer information between computer networks is called a router.

18. What is the main function of the Keyboard?

Ans. A keyboard is an input device that is used to type text, numbers, and commands into the computer.

19. Why is the normal 101 keyboard called QWERTY keyboard?

Ans. The first six alphabets of the first row of alphabet keys in a 101 keyboard contain alphabets Q, W, E, R, T, Y., and hence, it is known as the QWERTY keyboard.

Figure 3.7

20. How many function keys are present on a keyboard?

Ans. 12 Keys from F1 to F12 in the keyboard are function keys.

21. Why are function keys called so?

Ans. The function keys are used to perform specific functions. Their functions differ from program to program. For example, the function of the F1 key in most programs is to get help on that program.

22. What are spams?

Ans. All people using email get mails from companies and organisations which are advertising a product or trying to attract users to their website. Such mails are known as SPAM.

23. What do you mean by VIRUS in computer science?

Ans. A computer virus is defined as a piece of software code written to enter the computer system and infect files. It can damage or even destroy precious data.

24. Who launched the first Norton Antivirus in 1990?

Ans. Symantec launched its first Norton Antivirus.

25. Name the first polymorphic computer virus created in 1991.

Ans. Tequila.

26. What is 'drag and drop'?

Ans. To move an item, click it, and then hold the mouse button down, move the item to a new location and release it. This action is known as drag and drop.

27. What do you mean by files on a computer?

Ans. The Files in computers are used for storing the Data of the users for a long time period, and the files can contain any type of information, which means that they can store the text, or images or Pictures, or any data in any format.

28. Define a folder in computer science.

Ans. A folder is like a container in which similar types of files can be stored. It helps in arranging the files into organised groups, which makes it easy for the user to locate any particular file.

29. What is a Mac Operating System?

Ans. It is a UNIX-based operating system which is developed by the Apple company and is mainly used by Mac users.

30. What do you mean by Linux?

Ans. Linux is a freeware and open-source software that can be installed and used on a variety of computers ranging from mobile phones, tablet computers, video game consoles, mainframes, and supercomputers. Linux is a high-level secured operating system.

31. What is Android?

Ans. Android is a Linux-based operating system that is designed basically for mobile phones, which is also used for devices such as notebooks and tablets. The first version of the Android launched in 2007 was Android OS 2.1.

32. Define Symbian.

Ans. Symbian is an OS developed by Symbian Limited, and it uses GEOS (Graphical Environment Operating System). It is used by most advanced smartphones. It allows the user to install applications on the phone, just like Windows allows installing applications onto a computer.

33. What are 'Worms' in computers?

Ans. Worms are viruses that replicate. Worm viruses regenerate themselves and spread to all files once they attack a computer. Since they replicate, and hence this makes it very difficult to remove them.

34. What do you mean by Online Predator?

Ans. Online predators are persons who trap the user to make inappropriate relationships. An online predator may be older people posing to be young, bullying the user into doing illegal activities online or face to face.

35. Who gave the idea of a computer virus?

Ans. The idea of a computer virus was first given in 1949 by John von Neumann.

36. What is Trojan?

Ans. Trojan (Trojan horse) is any malicious PC program that misdirects clients of its actual goal. The term is taken from the Ancient Greek story of the tricky wooden steed that prompted the fall of the city of Troy.

37. What is Zeus?

Ans. Zeus is a crimeware toolkit used to build customised financial services Trojan horses.

38. Give four examples of programming languages.

Ans. The programming languages are C++, Java MIDP, Java Personal profile, OPL, Visual Basic, Python, Simkin, and Flash Lite.

39. Which programming language is mostly used for Symbian OS?

Ans. C++,

40. Which interface is used in Win 3. x?

Ans. Graphical User Interface.

41. Explain the main features of Windows NT.

Ans. Windows NT operating system was built for the server as it was more reliable, stable and offered a large number of system features to the operating system, namely encryption, file/folder level security, auditing, etc.

42. Which OS was also called a Plug and Play (PnP) operating system?

Ans. Windows 95

43. Which Microsoft OS added some updates to the GUI and built-in new features like Internet Connectivity, Firewall Support, etc.?

Ans. Windows XP

44. What is the full form of FAT?

Ans. File Allocation Table.

45. What is Microsoft Edge?

Ans. Microsoft Edge is a new web browser introduced in Windows 10.

46. Name Microsoft's intelligent personal assistant.

Ans. Cortana, which is included in Windows 10 to replace Windows' embedded search feature and support both text and voice input.

47. Can a computer work without software?

Ans. No. No hardware would be able to function without software.

48. What do you mean by backup the data?

Ans. Backing up data is a process to save the information present on your computer on another device, like CD/DVD drives or hard disk.

3.3.9 Short Answer Type Questions

1. How will you ensure the proper working of the hardware components of a computer?

Ans. Proper working of the hardware components of a computer can be ensured by physically cleaning them, keeping them in a proper manner, and repairing them whenever required.

2. What is the purpose of cleaning the software?

Ans. Cleaning of the software installed on the computer involves the scheduled disk clean-up tasks, protection against viruses, deleting the temporary and unwanted files, etc.

3. What is the function of real-time systems?

Ans. Real-time systems are used to navigate in which computers react to a steady flow of new information without interruption. Flight Simulators, Submarine, etc., uses such type of operating system. Examples: Windows CE, Lynx OS, etc.

4. Enlist four software.

Ans. System Software, Operating System, Language Processors, Compiler Assembler Interpreter, Utility Software, Application Software, General Purpose, Customized Software, etc.

5. What are the five basic operations a computer performs?

Ans. A computer performs five basic operations to carry out any task: Input, Process, Output, Storing, and Controlling.

6. What is the meaning of 'Double-tap' and its action?

Ans. Double-tap means rapidly touching the surface twice with a fingertip. Its action includes zooms in and centers content or an image, or zooms out it already zoomed in or select items.

7. Why will a computer be useless in the absence of an OS?

Ans. An Operating System (OS) performs basic tasks, like recognising input from the keyboard, sending output to the screen, keeping track of files and directories, controlling the devices (like disk drives and printers), etc. Without a computer Operating System, a computer would be useless.

8. Explain Interactive or Graphical User Interface (GUI) Operating System.

Ans. In GUI operating system, commands can be entered by clicking/double-clicking/right-clicking a mouse. Examples: MS-DOS, MS-Windows, OS/2, Windows/NT, UNIX, Mac-OS, etc.

9. Explain Character User Interface (CUI).

Ans. CUI Operating System: This type of Operating System requires the user to interact by typing commands. Examples: UNIX, DOS, etc.

10. What should be the daily cleaning strategy for computers?

Ans. The following cleaning of computer on a daily basis should be done:
- Scan the computer daily to check the entry of any possible virus into the system.
- Remove temporary Internet files.
- Clean up an email inbox
- Remove Windows temporary files.
- Download email attachments and save them in proper folders

11. What should be the weekly cleaning strategy for computers?

Ans. The following cleaning of computer on a weekly basis should be done:
- Clean the keyboard
- Update the operating system weekly to check any new offerings.
- Update the software (programming software, Flash, antivirus software, Adobe, etc.)
- Clean the monitor
- Keeping CPU and printer dust-free
- Backup the data to an external drive
- Empty the Recycle Bin folder.
- Delete temporary cookies

12. Why is the maintenance of computers important?

Ans. Maintenance of computers is important for the following reasons:

a) For keeping them in proper running condition

b) For enhancing their efficiency

c) For finding problems and issues at an early stage

d) For their safety and enhancing their life span

e) For prevention against viruses and malware

f) For increasing the working speed of the computers

g) For maximizing the computer software efficiency

h) For preventing data loss

13. Explain Corrective Maintenance.

Ans. When Preventive maintenance is not found working well, then corrective maintenance is used. When the operating system fails to work, and we want it in a working state again in the same condition, then the necessary measures and use the PC further with no mistakes in its running are required. During the corrective support options, we find out the reason and cause of the malfunctioning of an instrument and fix it.

14. What are the cleaning tools used for cleaning computers and peripherals?

Ans. The following things may be needed while cleaning the computer and its peripherals:

a) **Cloth:** A cotton material is the best device utilized when scouring down computer segments.

b) **Water:** When diluting a material, it is ideal to utilize water or scouring liquor.

c) **Portable Vacuum Cleaner:** Sucking the residue, earth, hair, dust particles, and different particles out of a computer can probably be the best technique for cleaning a computer.

d) **Cotton swabs:** Cotton swabs dampened with scouring liquor or water are brilliant instruments for cleaning hard.

15. How will you clean CD-ROM and DVD drive?

Ans. A filthy CD-ROM drive or other circle drives can cause read mistakes when understanding plates. These read blunders could cause software installation issues or issues while running the program. Use CD-ROM cleaner for cleaning the CD-ROM drive to remove dust, residue, earth, hair, etc. Use a fabric hosed with water to clean the plate that discharges from the drive.

16. What should be the monthly cleaning strategy for computers?

Ans. The following cleaning on a monthly basis should be done:

- Execute Disk Defragmenter utility.

- Unused applications should be uninstalled.

- Transfer photographs to the computer and delete them from the drive.

- Organise photos into folders or albums.

- Clean up the 'Download' folder

- Uninstall unused programs and apps.

- Run disk-cleaner software

- Run a full system virus scan

17. What should be the annual cleaning strategy for computers?

Ans. The following cleaning on an annual basis should be done:
- Open the computer case, and clean it from inside.
- Clean up contact list on social media accounts.
- Update/Renew antivirus software.
- Clean up an email contact list
- Update the operating system

18. What is to be done to stop entry and downloading malicious code and viruses in the computer?

Ans. Turn on the Windows Firewall feature in your computer to stop entry and downloading malicious code and viruses to the computer from the Internet.

19. Mention some steps to ensure safety against computer virus infection.

Ans. Some of the steps to avoid virus infection are as follows:
- Get good virus scanning software.
- Scan frequently.
- Update scanning software.
- Stay informed of virus alerts.

20. How is trojan harmful to computers?

Ans. Once a Trojan enters into the system, it can harm the system in the following ways:
- It provides the hacker backdoor control over the system.
- Silently observes keyboard strokes to capture users' account data and passwords.
- To exploit the vulnerability of a computer system, it downloads and installs a virus.
- To extort money from the user for the decrypting key, it installs ransomware to encrypt the user's data.
- Work on the device's camera and recording capabilities.
- Capture computer information illegally relevant to a criminal investigation.

21. Mention the guidelines to avoid the entry of Trojan in the computers.

Ans. The following guidelines assist the administrator in avoiding a Trojan attack on a system:
- Install strong antivirus on your system
- Take regular backups of your sensitive data.
- Deploy hardware-based firewalls on computer systems.
- Must have some idea, how the structure of a malicious program looks like.
- Be very specific while opening a suspicious email.
- Avoid third-party downloads.
- Any stuff should be downloaded from trusted sites.
- Disable the Autorun feature of the computer system. First, scan a device, then open its content.

22. Explain theft in respect of computers.

Ans. Theft means stealing of information or hardware, which may be of three types:

a) **Physical:** Here, a person may steal the desktop computer, laptop, or mobile.

b) **Identity:** Here, a hacker steals your personal information and assumes your identity. By using a false identity, the hacker can gain access to your account information or perform illegal activity.

c) **Software Piracy:** The stealing of software and using or distributing unlicensed and unauthorized copies of a computer program or software is called software piracy.

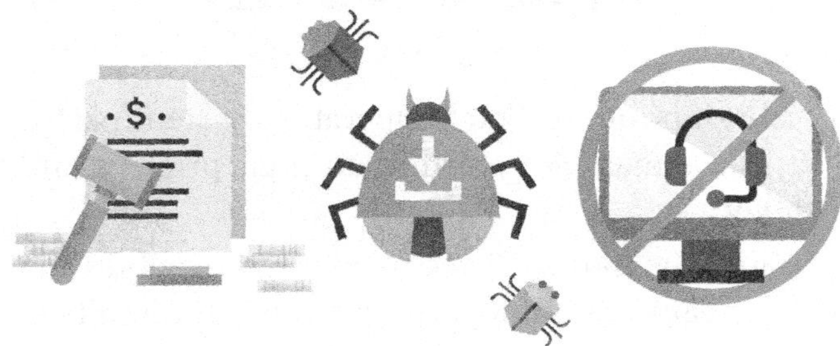

Figure 3.8

23. How can you save the computer from Viruses?

Ans. For the Personal Computer, get a good, dependable, highly rated Anti-Virus Software package. Update your software's virus definition frequently. Another method that can be used is to monitor the byte size of your files and programs, especially your .exe and .com files.

24. What are the different ways of attacking computers by hackers?

Ans. The following are the ways of attacking computers by hackers:

a) Viruses   b) Trojan   c) Malware   d) Phishing

e) Spyware   f) Ransomware   g) Adware

3.3.10 Long Answer Type Questions

1. Discuss the main features of OS.

Ans. Some features of an operating system are as follows:

(i) **Single-user/ Single-task Operating System:** This operating system is used by one user to do a task on the computer.

(ii) **Multi programming:** Multiprogramming system allows more than one program to reside in the memory simultaneously. As one program is executed, the CPU executes the other program.

(iii) **Multi-user Operating System:** A multi-user operating system enables multiple users to work on the same computer at different times or simultaneously. Multi-terminal or nodes are attached to a host computer, and more than one user can work on the nodes.

(iv) **Single-user and Multi-task Operating System:** This type of operating system is used in PC, Desktop computers, and laptops, where a single user can operate on several programs at the same time. Examples: Windows, Apple macOS, etc.

Figure 3.5

(v) **Batch Processing/Spooling:** Batch Operating System places the task in a queue for execution. Tasks are marked according to their priority, and the computer executes them accordingly.

(vi) **Multi-Processing:** A multi-Processing system enables several processes to run concurrently. It means that multi-processing has the ability to execute more than one process at the same time.

(vii) **Multi-threading:** Different parts of a program are called threads. Multithreading executes different parts of a program simultaneously. It means that multithreading allows different parts of a software program to run concurrently.

(viii) **Real-Time OS:** A real-time operating system is a computing environment that reacts to input within a specific period of time. A real-time operating system is used to control machinery, scientific instruments, like robots, in complex animations and computer-controlled automated machines. It manages the resources of the computer to execute an operation in the same amount of time every time it is executed.

(ix) **Distributed Operating System:** This operating system runs on a set of computers that are interconnected by a network. It combines all the different computers in the network, forming a single integrated computer and storage location. Some examples: Windows, UNIX, LINUX, etc.

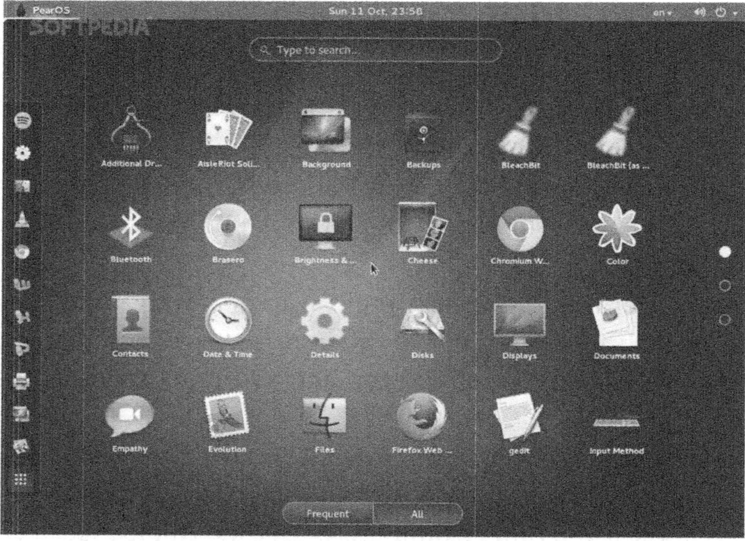

Figure 3.9

2. Differentiate between smartphone and tablet.

Ans. The difference between smartphones and tablets is enlisted below:

Smartphone	Tablet
(i) It is a phone with additional features like a camera, Internet surfing, sending and receiving email.	(i) It is considered a useful device like a computer. Most of the tablets do not offer a phone (calling) feature.
(ii) It is mainly considered as a communication device.	(ii) It is considered an entertainment platform.
(iii) The screen display is smaller than a tablet.	(iii) The screen display is larger than a smartphone and smaller than a notebook.
(iv) It is handy and safe to carry anywhere.	(iv) It is not carried everywhere except for meetings or on long trips.
(v) It requires to be charged (depends on usage).	(v) It has a longer battery life than a smartphone.
(vi) Editing, watching movies, reading e-books is difficult.	(vi) Editing, watching movies, reading e-books is easier.

3. Mention the various steps to create a new folder.

Ans. The steps to create a new folder are as follows:

   i. Double-click the Computer icon.
   ii. Choose/Select the drive in which you want to create a new folder. Say, Local Disk D.
   iii. A window will open up showing files and folders in Local Disc D.
   iv. Click New Folder on the toolbar.

Or

Right-click anywhere in the blank area of the right column, and a shortcut menu appears. Select New Folder from the shortcut menu and click, a new folder is created with the name 'New Folder.'

4. Discuss the steps to copy/cut, and paste a file or folder.

Ans. The following steps are used to copy and paste a file or folder:

Step 1: Click the file/folder that you want to copy/cut.

Step 2: On the Home tab, in the Clipboard group, click the Copy button.

Step 3: Click the folder where you want the file/folder to be placed.

Step 4: On the Home tab, in the Clipboard group, click the Paste button.

The file/folder will be placed at the selected place.

5. Discuss the various types of Computer Maintenance.

Ans. The following types of computer maintenance are required:

   a) **Predictive Maintenance:** In this type of maintenance, a computer user turns on the diagnostic tools to prevent possible problems with the computer. The diagnostic tools are used to monitor computer systems and check whether they are functioning in a normal state or not. For example, the tools controlling and informing about the temperature of the CPU, battery levels, etc.

b) **Preventive Maintenance:** In this type of maintenance, prevention of possible failures, improvement of the functioning of a system, lengthening the life of various components of the computer, etc., is done. The main features of this type of maintenance are that it allows to notice weak points in the system and thus, leads to a lesser number of repairs. In Preventive maintenance of software, the creation of the backups, scanning and cleaning through antivirus, the freeing up of space of hard disk and RAM (random access memory) is done. In the case of hardware preventive maintenance, the actual periodic cleaning of equipment and its components is initiated.

c) **Corrective Maintenance:** In case the Preventive maintenance is not found working well, then corrective maintenance is used. When the operating system fails to work, and we want it in a working state again in the same condition, then the necessary measures and use the PC further with no mistakes in its running are required. During the corrective support options, we find out the reason and cause of the malfunctioning of an instrument and fix it.

d) **Evolutionary Maintenance:** This type of maintenance intends to develop the system of the computer so that the computer may perform more efficiently. Updating of the framework and changes in different pieces of the computer for better execution are initiated. As the laptop is continually developing with time, and we have to catch up with the system so that it works well. Thus, we update the system and sometimes change various parts of the computer, if needed, for better performance.

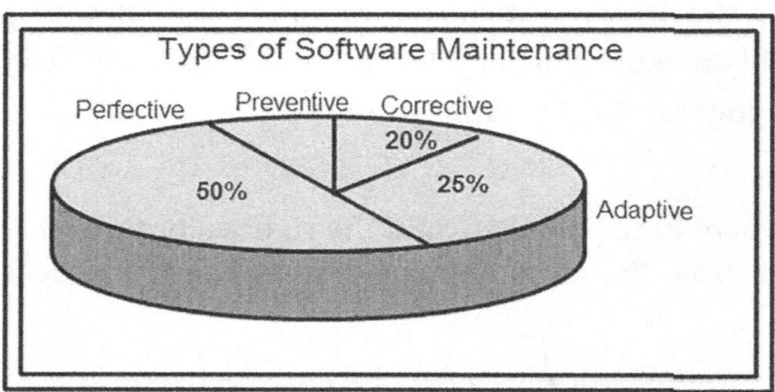

Figure 3.10

6. What are the basic tips for taking care of computer devices?

Ans. Some simple ways to take care of the computers are discussed as below:

a) **Keep the device Clean:** Cleaning a device (a computer or mobile) means keeping the screen, keyboard, and mouse clean.

   ▲ Do not eat anything over a keyboard because crumbs can damage the internal parts of a keyboard. Use a soft brush to clean a keyboard to remove crumbs and dust particles.

   ▲ Clean the mouse with a soft cloth.

   ▲ Wipe off the screen with a soft cloth to remove dust and finger marks.

b) **Handle the device carefully:** Handle and move the computer/laptop carefully and avoid dropping or banging it against a hard surface. Even a shortfall can damage the screen or the hard disk and make the device useless. Use a cover for the mobile and a padded case for moving the laptop to protect the device from any damage.

c) **Avoid overcharging the battery:** Keep a device plugged in for charging till it is fully charged. Don't overheat the battery because it will reduce battery life. Cultivate a habit to unplug the device once it is charged 100%.

d) **Keep the computer cool:** Keep the computer, laptop, or mobile device cool to avoid overheating and to avoid damage to the internal parts. Cooling of a computer is done by an internal fan. Ensure the proper functioning of a fan. Use an external fan if required. Avoid leaving the device in the sun or in a closed car. Be careful while using a laptop while sitting in bed, and ensure that the fan is not covered.

e) **Plug-in devices carefully:** Connect any device, like a USB drive or headphones, to a laptop or computer gently. Do not insert it forcedly into the port. When it is difficult to plug in a device, then change the direction and try instead of trying to force it in.

f) **Don't run many programs simultaneously:** Avoid running too many programs at a time. When many programs are running simultaneously, the computer can become slow and even crash. Close the program when it is not in use so that other programs can work smoothly.

Figure 3.11

g) **Computer case or CPU Tower Cleaning:** While cleaning, on the off chance that you see ventilation openings, these can be cleaned or cleared to help keep a relentless wind stream into the computer for keeping all parts cool. The plastic case that contains the PC parts can be cleaned with a somewhat moist build of the free fabric.

7. Discuss the general guidelines for computer cleaning.

Ans. The following is the list of tips to keep your computer clean:

- Never spray any fluid onto any part of a computer. Spray the fluid onto a cloth in case a splash is required.

- Don't use a vacuum to suck earth, residue, or hair around the computer/laptop because it creates friction-based electricity that can harm the computer.

- Turn off the computer before starting the cleaning of any segment.

- Use water or an exceptionally weak chemical/solvent for cleaning purposes.

▲ During the cleaning of fans, hold the fan or spot something in the middle of the fan with sharp edges to keep it from turning.

▲ Don't eat or drink around the computer.

8. What are the different types of a computer viruses? Discuss.

Ans. Mainly viruses are divided into four categories:

a) **Boot Sector Viruses:** These are usually transmitted from a disk or a CD when it is left in the drive and the computer is booted up. The virus is read from the boot sector, then written to the master boot record of the computer hard disk. Every time when the infected computer is booted up, the virus is loaded into its memory and infects the disk.

b) **Program or File viruses:** These are pieces of viral code that attach themselves to executable programs. When the infected program runs, the virus is transferred to memory, and then it tries to replicate itself further.

c) **Macro viruses:** These are the most common viruses which are found in computer systems today. Files run by applications that use Macro languages, like Word, Excel, PowerPoint, etc., are infected with these types of viruses. The virus looks like a macro in a file, and when the computer is run, the virus may execute commands understood by the application's macro language.

d) **Multipartite viruses:** These have the characteristic of both boot sector viruses and program/file viruses. Viruses can be written into almost any type of file, so it is important to be aware of this when installing software that has been obtained from illegal sources.

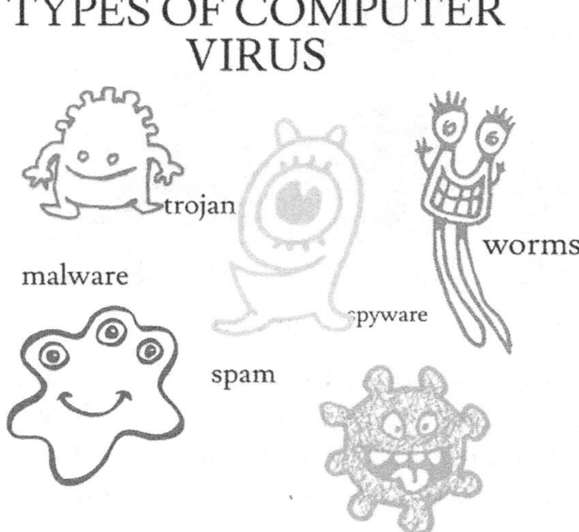

Figure 3.12

3.3.11 HOTS Questions

1. How is the data recovered from the backup data?

Ans. Data can be recovered from the backup data when the computer stops working completely or computers crash due to human mistakes and / natural disasters, like floods. Hence, it is essential for companies, hospitals, banks, etc., to keep their information safe so that their business can function smoothly and the customers do not face any problems.

2. How does FakeAV Trojan work?

Ans. FakeAV inserts into the Windows system tray and continuously encourages users to change the computer's settings for better experiences. When the user follows instructions, it downloads more malware.

3. How will you remove temporary files from the computer?

Ans. Click on the 'Computer' (Windows 7) or 'This PC' (Windows 10) icon on the desktop/File Explorer in order to remove temporary files from the computer system. Then, a window will open. Now, right-click on the Local Disk (C:) icon and a menu will be opened. Select the Properties option from the menu, and a dialog box 'Local Disk (C:) Properties' will appear on the screen.

Click on the Disk Clean-up button. Further dialog box 'Disk Clean-up for (C:)' will appear. Select the checkbox, Temporary Files and Temporary Internet Files, etc. Press the OK button. A confirmation window will appear. Select the 'Delete files' option to delete temporary files from the system.

4. How can you increase computer performance?

Ans. On using a computer for a long time, a lot of unnecessary files and data, such as temporary files and images, is gathered in the computer. When these files use too much hard-disk space, the performance of the computer degrades. It is important to keep cleaning by removing any extra files. Use some disk cleaner software to clean up the unnecessary files.

3.4 PRACTICE QUESTIONS

1. What Is Spam?
2. What is the GUI?
3. What do you mean by CUI?
4. What do you mean by malware?
5. Define an operating system.
6. What is a hierarchical file system?
7. Why is Spam harmful?
8. Why is data back up necessary?
9. What are the temporary files?
10. Why should we delete Spam?
11. Explain the working of the Trojan Horse virus.
12. Enlist the various methods used to protect the data.
13. Which are the common icons present on the Windows taskbar?
14. How is GUI better than CUI?
15. Mention any four-antivirus software available in the market.
16. Enlist different types of malware.

17. What types of information are gathered by spyware?

18. What precautions will you take when there is a spyware attack on your system?

19. What is the online data backup? What are its advantages?

20. Explain the various ways of protecting a computer against viruses.

21. How does ICT impact society? Explain.

Figure 3.13

UNIT 4

Entrepreneurial Skills II

4.1 UNIT IN BRIEF

✦ An entrepreneur is a person who establishes a business or a venture that generates some value for the customers and proves to be profitable for him.

Figure 4.1

✦ Entrepreneurship can be described as starting a business by using the resources available to a person.

✦ Entrepreneurship has a crucial role in the functioning of society.

✦ A business venture needs to have a novel element or process to make it acceptable and thrive in the market.

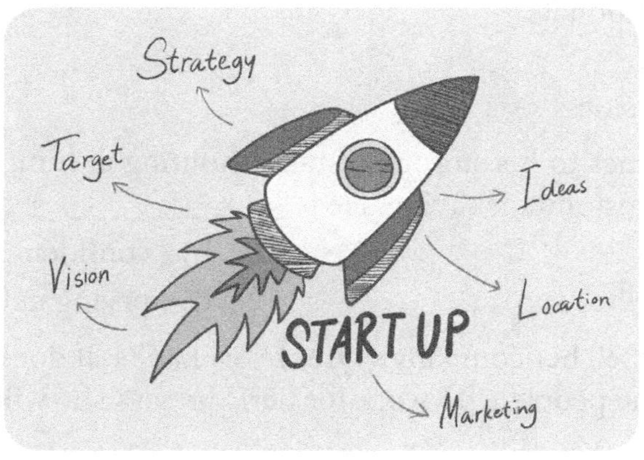

Figure 4.2

+ New and improved products, services, and technology from entrepreneurs enable to development of new markets and create new wealth.

+ The job creation by new and existing businesses is one of the primary goals of economic development.

+ Entrepreneurs play an important role in increasing the quality of living in a community.

+ Entrepreneurs are often seen as visionaries and risk-takers who take well-calculated risks.

+ The two important personality traits that entrepreneurs possess are perception and intuition.

+ Developed countries are moving from 'managerial' to 'entrepreneurial' economies.

+ Being an entrepreneur teaches life skills, increases creativity and problem-solving skills, provides a better understanding of business and market economics, improves communication, teamwork, and networking skills, and hence, enhances employability.

4.2 CBSE/NCERT SECTION (SOLVED CBSE/NCERT EXERCISE QUESTIONS)

(A) MCQs

Choose the correct option out of the four given options for each question.

1. Ali has a diamond factory. He pays his employees on the 1st of every month.
   a) Creates a new product
   b) Manages the business
   c) Takes risk

2. Mary buys bulbs for her business from Noida. She learns that bulbs are cheaper in Faridabad. So, she decides to start buying bulbs from there.
   a) Makes decisions
   b) Divides income
   c) Takes risk

3. Rehnuma has two people who work for her. Every day, she spends one hour with them to learn about what they've done that day.
   a) Creates a new product
   b) Divides income
   c) Manages the business

4. Ravi's customer comes to his store and starts shouting at him. He does not get angry. He listens to what his customer is saying. He is _____________.
   a) hardworking   b) confident
   c) patient   d) prying new ideas

5. Susheela decides to sell her company's tyres in Sri Lanka. It does not sell, and she has a loss. She apologises to the people who work for her. She says she will plan better next time. She _____________.
   a) takes responsibility for your mistakes

b) thinks before making a decision

c) does not give up

d) is creative

ANSWERS
1. (b)   2. (a)   3. (c)   4. (c)   5. (a)

(B) State whether the following statements are True or False.

1. Entrepreneurs can create jobs in the market.

2. When many entrepreneurs sell mobiles in a market, the prices of mobiles increase.

3. Entrepreneurs identify a need in the market and build a product or service for it.

ANSWERS
1. True   2. False   3. True

(C) Matching type Questions

(I) Match the story below with the misconception about entrepreneurship.

Story	Misconception
(i) Ramu owns a large clothes shop. Shamu has a small store selling handmade sarees. Shamu does not call himself an entrepreneur.	(a) Every business idea needs to be unique or special.
(ii) Anna has a great idea for a website. She has `5,000. She is waiting for `20,000 more so that she can start it.	(b) Entrepreneurs are born, not made.
(iii) In a city of thousands of tailoring shops, Gauri is a tailor who stitches good quality clothes and has a very successful business.	(c) A person needs to have a big business to be called an entrepreneur.

(II) Match the columns

1. Surabhi has opened five painting stores across India.   A. Enter

2. There are many coaching classes in Mumbai. Jacob owns one of them. He is starting morning batches to attract more students to his classes.   B. Survive

3. Salma has started her clothing line on the Internet.   C. Grow

ANSWERS		
(I) 1. c	2. b	3. a
(II) 1. C	2. B	3. A

(D) Subjective Questions

1. List the ways in which an entrepreneur affects society.

Ans. An entrepreneur affects society in the following manners:

i. **Fulfill Customers' Needs:** Demand reffers to a product or service that people want. Entrepreneurs realise what people's needs. Then, they use their creativity to bring an novel business idea that will meet the demand of people.

ii. **Use Local Raw Materials:** Entrepreneurs use the raw material and people available around them to make products at a low cost.

iii. **Create Jobs:** With the growth of a business, all entrepreneurs hire more local people to help them. They buy more raw material from more local people. They also hire more people to work for them. In this way, more people have jobs.

iv. **Help Society for a social cause:** Entrepreneurs exhibit a close relationship with society. They make profits through activities and spends for the benefit of society. Some entrepreneurs work towards saving the environment while some give money to build new schools and hospitals. By this way, the people and area around them become better. These are the roles that entrepreneurs play in society.

v. **Sharing of Wealth:** Wealth referrs having enough money to live a comfortable life. As entrepreneurs grow their business, the people working for them and in related businesses also grow. They have more money to live a better quality of life.

vi. **Lower Price of Products:** As more entrepreneurs sell the same product, the price of the product goes down. For example, when more mobile phones were getting sold in India, the cost of the phone became lesser.

2. What is the difference between a misconception and reality? Give an example.

Ans. A myth, or a misconception, is a false belief or opinion about something but the reality is the truth.

Example: People think that tall people run faster than short people, which is a misconception. It is not true. The reality/truth is that short people can also run fast.

3. Which is the most important function of an entrepreneur? Write your answer giving suitable examples.

Ans. The most important functions performed by an entrepreneur are as follows:

Figure 4.3

i.   **Managing new venture/the Business:** An entrepreneur plans the future of his/her business. He/she make arrangements for raw material, hires people for work, and tells everyone in the team what to do. He/she also check if the plan is being followed.

ii. **Making Decisions:** An entrepreneur makes decisions every day. This includes decisions like what to produce or sell, how much, and where to sell.

iii. **Create a new product/idea/method:** An entrepreneur is always trying new things. He/she does this to increase the importance of iy and income.

iv. **Divide Income:** The entrepreneur divides the business profit money into various groups. He/she spends money to buy raw material, pays rent of the building, salaries to people, etc.

v.   **Taking Risk:** Risk is defined as the chance of something going wrong during the process. An entrepreneur takes risks against theft, fires, lost items, etc.

4. Write against the option if the business idea is self-employment or wage employment.
   (a) Cooking in a restaurant
   (b) Owning a clothing business
   (c) Having a dosa selling stall

Ans. (a) wage employment, (b) self-employment (c) self-employment

4.3 SOLVED EXERCISES

4.3.1 Multiple Choice Questions

Choose the correct option out of the four given options for each question.

1. Who defined entrepreneurship as 'the creation of new business' in 1985?
   a) Peter F. Drucker
   b) Richard Cantillon
   c) Amartya Sen
   d) SP Kulkarni

2. Anyone who manages to establish a new business is called:
   a) Visionary
   b) Businessman
   c) Entrepreneur
   d) Entrepreneurship

3. A method for accepting credit card payments is:
   a) SQUARE
   b) TRIANGLE
   c) CIRCLE
   d) None of the above

4. Which of the following is a microblogging and social networking service?
   a) Twitter
   b) Olax
   c) Facebook
   d) Brooks

5. Which of the following options is the correct set of tasks of an entrepreneur?
   i.   Owning the full income/profit
   ii. Creating a New Method, Idea, or Product
   iii. Making Effective Decisions
   iv. Managing the Business
   v.   Taking Risk
   vi. Distributing the dividend

a) (i) (ii) (iii) (iv) (v)   b) (ii) (iii) (iv) (v) (vi)

c) (i) (iii) (iv) (v) (vi)   d) All of the above

6. Suppose Deepika Jain runs a Fresh Vegetable shop. A customer comes to her shop and starts shouting at her. She does not get angry, but she listens to what her customer is saying. She is:

a) Hardworking   b) Patient   c) Confident   d) Creative

7. Which of the following myths about entrepreneurs is correct?

a) Entrepreneurs are born, not made.   b) All entrepreneurs have great ideas.

c) Talent is more important than the industry.   d) All of the above

8. Entrepreneurship has a critical role in the _______________ of society.

a) Evolution   b) Functioning   c) Demolition   d) Planning

9. Which of the following is the role of entrepreneurship?

a) It aids the transfer of technology.

b) It creates employment opportunities by initiating new ventures.

c) It increases productivity through technical and other innovative approaches.

d) All of these.

10. A business set up by the communities facing challenges together in developing the business. For example, shops, call centers, farms, etc. is called:

a) Business   b) Community business

c) Entrepreneur   d) Industrial unit

11. Which of the following abilities allows an entrepreneur to put everything at stake to convert his idea into a reality?

a) Self-confidence   b) Self-motivation

c) Risk-taking ability   d) Time management

12. Which company is headed by Azimji Premji as its chairman?

a) Wipro Limited   b) Infosys

c) Mahindra Group   d) OIL

13. Study the following statements to choose the correct set of myths about entrepreneurs.

i. A person who has a big business is an entrepreneur.

ii. Entrepreneurs are not in the industry for the money.

iii. Entrepreneurs take lots of risks.

iv. An entrepreneur cannot borrow from banks.

v. A new business always flourishes.

vi. One must be young and restless to be an entrepreneur.

vii. The only requirement to become an entrepreneur is a good idea.

a) (ii) (iii) (iv) (v)   b) (iii) (iv) (v) (vi)

c) (iii) (iv) (v) (vii)   d) All of the above

14. _______________ are the entrepreneurs who offer a piece of advice and help to customers.

    a) Builders

    b) Advisors

    c) Administrators

    d) Communicators

15. Which of the following businesses involves more than one type of business?

    a) Manufacturing Business

    b) Hybrid Business

    c) Service Business

    d) None of these

16. Suppose Prem Nath Pandey has a Pharmaceutical company in Chhota Mawana. He decides to sell his company's products in the Maldives. It does not sell, and he has a loss. He apologises to the people who work for him. He says that he will plan better next time and will bring new products. This incident shows that he:

    a) Does not give up

    b) Thinks before making a decision.

    c) Takes responsibility for his actions

    d) Both a and c

17. Entrepreneurs also invest in community projects, and they provide financial support to:

    a) Industry

    b) Communal disharmony

    c) Charities

    d) Collaboration

18. All the industrialists are not called entrepreneurs. This statement is:

    a) True

    b) False

    c) It may be true or false

    d) None of these

19. Which of the following steps involves the support for the establishment of a business enterprise?

    a) Training   b) Pre-training   c) Post-training   d) All of these

20. Entrepreneurship is not only beneficial for the Entrepreneur itself, but it is also essential for the _______________ of the economy.

    a) Decline

    b) Flexibility

    c) Growth

    d) None of these

21. Which pair is incorrect?

    a) Tilak Mehta - Papers N Parcels

    b) Advait Thakur- Piramal Enterprises Ltd

    c) Farhad Acidwala - Rockstar Media.

    d) Sunil Mittal - Bharti Enterprises

22. Aman Ahmed has a Cold Storage to keep the produce of farmers and employs more than 30 persons. He pays his employees on the 7th of every month. He:

    a) Do nothing special.

    b) Takes risk

    c) Manages the business

    d) Creates a new product

23. Who reaps the most benefits of Entrepreneurship?

    a) Society

    b) Entrepreneur

    c) Entrepreneur and his family

    d) Entrepreneur and society

24. Which of the following abilities refers to the ability of an entrepreneur to bring out the new ways to run a business?

    a) Creativity

    b) Hard work

    c) Patience

    d) Self-motivation

25. How many steps are involved in an entrepreneurial process?

    a) Two   b) Three   c) Six   d) Ten

26. Entrepreneurship is a good option as:

    a) Making quick money

    b) Leading an easy life

    c) A career choice

    d) Doing charity

27. The main reason among 90% of start-ups failed is lack of:

    a) novel idea   b) experience in the chosen industry

    c) money   d) human force

28. Who is an entrepreneur?

    a) A person born with a silver spoon in their mouth

    b) A notorious person

    c) A visionary

    d) A deceptive person

29. Jag Jeet Singh Rana lives in Sonipat and buys bulbs for his business from New Delhi. He finds that bulbs are cheaper in Karnal than in New Delhi. Hence, he decides to start buying bulbs from there. He:

    a) is creative.

    b) Makes decisions

    c) Takes risk

    d) Divides income

30. Entrepreneurs play an important role in increasing the ____________ of living in a society.

    a) Confidence   b) Gender gap   c) Efforts   d) Quality

31. For becoming a successful entrepreneur, one must be:

    a) Rich   b) Smart   c) Goal-oriented   d) Illiterate

32. The two important personality traits that entrepreneurs must possess are:

    a) Creative and illiterate

    b) Hardworking and visionary

    c) Optimistic and Uncertain

    d) Hardworking and Distrust

33. Sneha Agrawal has employed ten people in her business of Ahmedabad News Services. Every day, she spends half an hour with them to listen and learn about what they've done that day. She:

    a) Takes risks

    b) Creates a new product

    c) Manages the business

    d) Divides income

34. Study the following statements and choose the correct set of roles of an entrepreneur.

    i.   Coordinating role to coordinate the various factors for production.

    ii. Risk Assumption role in taking a risk in the new venture.

iii. Capital formation role in mobilizing the idle savings for carrying business
iv. Balancing role to provide development in the big cash of nation-building
v. Employment Generation role in providing employment to the youths
vi. Society's interest protector role to safeguards the interest of society
vii. Catalytic role in increasing the rate of economic development of the region

a) (i) (ii) (iii) (iv) (v)
b) (ii) (iii) (iv) (v) (vi)
c) (i) (iii) (iv) (vi) (vii)
d) All of the above

ANSWERS									
1. (a)	2. (c)	3. (a)	4. (a)	5. (b)	6. (b)	7. (d)	8. (b)	9. (d)	10. (b)
11. (c)	12. (a)	13. (d)	14. (b)	15. (b)	16. (d)	17. (c)	18. (a)	19. (d)	20. (c)
21. (b)	22. (c)	23. (d)	24. (a)	25. (c)	26. (c)	27. (b)	28. (c)	29. (b)	30. (d)
31. (c)	32. (b)	33. (c)	34. (d)						

4.3.2 Fill in the blanks

1. _______________ are visionary, hardworking, and creative persons.

2. _______________ is the entrepreneur who imitates the methods and technologies innovated by others to begin his own business.

Figure 4.4

3. _______________ is designed as a unique, integrated approach for providing instructions and counseling from the selection stage to the main operation process.

4. _______________ has a crucial role in the functioning of society.

5. Entrepreneurs are often seen as visionaries and _______________ who take well-calculated risks.

6. _______________ is defined as the ability of an entrepreneur to provide things in a Novel or creative manner.

7. The job creation by new businesses is the primary goal of _______________ development.

8. _______________ is the entrepreneur who is cautious and sceptic about bringing any change in his enterprise.

9. _______________ is a type of business that deals with intangible products, such as accounting, banking, consulting, cleaning, etc.

10. _______________ is the entrepreneur who makes profits through commissions obtained by customer purchases.

11. Entrepreneurs play a key role in increasing the _____________ of living in a community.

12. When many entrepreneurs sell the same product in the same market, the prices of the product _____________.

13. There is a _____________ relationship between the Entrepreneur and entrepreneurship.

14. Successful entrepreneurs _____________ any distraction that might stop them from achieving their goals.

15. _____________ may be described as starting a business by using the local resources available to a person.

ANSWERS			
1. Entrepreneurs	2. Imitative Entrepreneur	3. Entrepreneurship Development Plan (EDP)	
4. Entrepreneurship	5. risk-takers	6. Innovation	7. Economic
8. Fabian Entrepreneur	9. Service business	10. Trader	11. quality
12. decrease	13. direct	14. eliminate	15. Entrepreneurship

4.3.3 True or False

1. An entrepreneur is a person who establishes a business or a venture that generates some value for the customer, and it is profitable for him.

2. Entrepreneurs may create unemployment.

3. Entrepreneurship can be described as starting a business by using the resources available to a person.

4. Entrepreneurs play no role in increasing the quality of living in a community.

5. A business venture needs to have a novel element or process to make it acceptable and thrive in the market.

6. New and improved products, services, and technology from entrepreneurs enable to development of new markets and create new wealth.

7. The job creation by new and existing businesses is the primary goal of economic development.

8. Entrepreneurs are not considered visionaries and risk-takers.

9. EDP focuses more on enhancement in operations than academic training to fulfill certain requirements of the participants.

10. The Indian Government has started offering various incentives and concessions, which comprise capital subsidy, marketing facilities, technical know-how, industrial facilities, etc.

11. Government regulations play a significant role in promoting entrepreneurship.

12. Entrepreneurs do not realize that every event and situation is a business opportunity.

13. Entrepreneurs identify a need in the market to build a product or service for it.

14. The growth of industries and businesses in backward areas leads to Infrastructure improvements.

15. Entrepreneurs do research to find out the need of customers and plan to introduce an innovative product to meet the demand.

ANSWERS

1. T	2. F	3. T	4. F	5. T	6. T	7. T	8. F	9. T	10. T
11. T	12. F	13. T	14. T	15. T					

4.3.4 Matching type Questions

(I) Match the items of column A with those of column B correctly.

Column A Entrepreneurship	Column B Description
(i) Facebook	(a) An e-commerce, cloud computing company
(ii) Apple	(b) World's first, twenty-four-hour, cable news channel.
(iii) Microsoft	(c) A social networking service
(iv) Amazon	(d) A technology company dealing in computer software
(v) Google	(e) A technology company dealing in computers, mobile, etc
(vi) CNN	(f) A technology company dealing in the internet, Search engine

(II) Match the items placed in column A with those of column B correctly.

Column A Entrepreneur	Column B Associated Company
(i) Adar Poonawalla	(a) Wipro
(ii) Ritesh Agrawal	(b) Balaji Telefilms
(iii) Azim Premji	(c) Paytm
(iv) Bhavish Aggarwal	(d) OYO Rooms
(v) Ekta Kapoor	(e) Serum Institute of India
(vi) Vijay Shekhar Sharma	(f) Ola Cabs

(III) Match the items of column A with those of column B correctly.

Column A	Column B
(i) Sudha opens four more restaurants in her state.	a. Survive
(ii) Out of many coaching classes in Dehradun, Chandan started morning batches in his coaching center to attract more students to his classes.	b. Enter
(iii) Deepa Solanki has started her boutique on the Internet.	c. Grow

ANSWERS

(I).	(i)-c	(ii)-e	(iii)-d	(iv)- a	(v)-f	(vi)-b
(II).	(i)- e	(ii)-d	(iii)- a	(iv)-f	(v)-b	(vi)- c
(III).	(i)- c	(ii)-a	(iii)-b			

4.3.5 Statements Based Questions

1. Statement 1: Small scale entrepreneurs are called the backbone of our country and many other developing countries.

   Statement 2: The job creation by new and existing businesses is the secondary goal of economic development.

   a) Statement 1 is correct, but statement 2 is incorrect.

   b) Statement 1 is incorrect, but statement 2 is correct.

   c) Both the statements are correct.

   d) Both the statements are incorrect.

2. Statement 1: Fabian Entrepreneur is an entrepreneur who is cautious and sceptic about bringing any change in his enterprise.

   Statement 2: Mr. Deep Kalra initiated the company" MakeMyTrip".

   a) Statement 1 is correct, but statement 2 is incorrect.

   b) Statement 1 is incorrect, but statement 2 is correct.

   c) Both the statements are correct.

   d) Both the statements are incorrect.

3. Statement 1: 'Make in India' initiative of the Government of India was launched on 25th September 2021.

Figure 4.5

   Statement 2: A service entrepreneur is an entrepreneur who is involved in manufacturing and rendering services rather than goods.

   a) Statement 1 is correct, but statement 2 is incorrect.

   b) Statement 1 is incorrect, but statement 2 is correct.

   c) Both the statements are correct.

   d) Both the statements are incorrect.

4. Statement 1: A Minor Innovator is an Entrepreneur who participates in economic growth by efficiently utilising the existing resources.

   Statement 2: Entrepreneurship has a crucial role in the functioning of society.

   a) Statement 1 is correct, but statement 2 is incorrect.

   b) Statement 1 is incorrect, but statement 2 is correct.

   c) Both the statements are correct.

   d) Both the statements are incorrect.

5. Statement 1: The two important personality traits that entrepreneurs possess are critical thinking and laziness.

   Statement 2: Developed countries are moving from 'entrepreneurial' to 'managerial' economies.
   a) Statement 1 is correct, but statement 2 is incorrect.
   b) Statement 1 is incorrect, but statement 2 is correct.
   c) Both the statements are correct.
   d) Both the statements are incorrect.

6. Statement 1: A 'Private Entrepreneur' is an entrepreneur who establishes and operates private enterprises without any government control. He works for personal interest.

   Statement 2: A business venture does not need to have a novel element or process to make it acceptable and thrive in the market.
   a) Statement 1 is correct, but statement 2 is incorrect.
   b) Statement 1 is incorrect, but statement 2 is correct.
   c) Both the statements are correct.
   d) Both the statements are incorrect.

ANSWERS
1. (a)   2. (c)   3. (b)   4. (c)   5. (d)   6. (a)

4.3.6 Assertion Reason Type Questions

1. Assertion (A): Entrepreneurs are called the community life-change agents.

   Reason(C): Entrepreneurs play an important role in improving the quality of living in a community.
   a) Both A and R are correct, and R is the correct reason for A.
   b) Both A and R are correct, and R is not the correct reason for A.
   c) A is correct but R is incorrect.
   d) A is incorrect but R is correct.

2. Assertion (A): Entrepreneurship development is defined as the process of strengthening the skills and knowledge of upcoming and existing entrepreneurs by hand-holding them during their entrepreneurial journey.

   Reason (C): Entrepreneurs are often seen as visionaries and risk-takers who take well-calculated risks.
   a) Both A and R are correct, and R is the correct reason for A.
   b) Both A and R are correct, and R is not the correct reason for A.
   c) A is correct but R is incorrect.
   d) A is incorrect but R is correct.

3. Assertion (A): An entrepreneur is a person who establishes a business or a venture that generates some value for the customer and proves to be profitable for him.

   Reason (C): Being an entrepreneur teaches life skills, increases creativity and problem-solving skills, provides a better understanding of business and market economics, improves communication, teamwork, and networking skills, and hence, enhances employability.

a) Both A and R are correct, and R is the correct reason for A.

b) Both A and R are correct, and R is not the correct reason for A.

c) A is correct but R is incorrect.

d) A is incorrect but R is correct.

4. Assertion (A): A Fabian Entrepreneur is the Entrepreneur who imitates the methods and technologies innovated by others to begin his own business.

   Reason (C): An innovative Entrepreneur is an entrepreneur who regularly intends to bring in new products in the market, new technologies, etc.

   a) Both A and R are correct, and R is the correct reason for A.

   b) Both A and R are correct, and R is not the correct reason for A.

   c) A is correct but R is incorrect.

   d) A is incorrect but R is correct.

5. Assertion (A): Entrepreneurship can be described as starting a business by using the resources available to a person.

   Reason (C): Manufacturing Entrepreneur looks forward to developing alternative projects by giving responsibility to run the business to someone else and moves on to a new idea or a new venture after selling the running business.

   a) Both A and R are correct, and R is the correct reason for A.

   b) Both A and R are correct, and R is not the correct reason for A.

   c) A is correct but R is incorrect.

   d) A is incorrect but R is correct.

6. Assertion (A): New and improved products, services, and technology from entrepreneurs enable to development of new markets and create new wealth.

   Reason (C): Manufacturing Entrepreneur is an entrepreneur who manufactures goods, mobilizes resources and supplies to sell those products.

   a) Both A and R are correct, and R is the correct reason for A.

   b) Both A and R are correct, and R is not the correct reason for A.

   c) A is correct but R is incorrect.

   d) A is incorrect but R is correct.

ANSWERS
1. (a)   2. (b)   3. (b)   4. (d)   5. (c)   6. (b)

4.3.7 Competency Based Questions

1. Consider the following features of a process:

   i. It fosters creativity.

   ii. It accelerates economic growth.

   iii. It encourages the welfare of society.

   iv. It provides solutions to the problems of society.

   v. It stimulates innovation and efficiency.

   vi. It creates jobs and employment opportunities.

This process is termed:

a) Entrepreneurship

b) Questioning

c) Innovation

d) Data mining

2. Government of India launched a policy whose objective is to meet the challenge of skilling at scale with speed and standard, and it aims to provide an umbrella framework to all skilling activities being carried out within the country, for aligning them to common standards and link the skilling with demand centres. This is called:

a) Start-up India

b) Ujjavala Yojana

c) PMJDY

d) Pradhan Mantri Yuva Udyamita Vikas Abhiyan

3. Which of the following is not a phase of entrepreneurship process?

a) Stimulatory phase

b) Support phase

c) Elimination phase

d) Sustenance phase

Figure 4.6

ANSWERS
1. (a)   2. (d)   3. (c)

4.3.8 VSA

1. Who is an entrepreneur?

Ans. An entrepreneur is a person who establishes a business or a venture that generates some value for the customer, and it is profitable for him.

2. What is entrepreneurship?

Ans. Entrepreneurship can be described as starting a business by using the resources available to a person. Entrepreneurship has a crucial role in the functioning of society.

3. What is the main feature of a business to be successful in the market?

Ans. A business venture needs to have a novel element or process to make it acceptable and thrive in the market.

4. Define entrepreneurship.

Ans. Entrepreneurship may be defined as the creation of a new business, expansion of an existing one, new business organization, or established business.

5. Define 'Small Scale Entrepreneurship.'

Ans. Small Scale Entrepreneurship refers to starting industries in which manufacturing, trading, providing services, productions are done on a small scale or micro scale.

6. Who is called the backbone of our country and many other developing countries?

Ans. Small scale entrepreneurs.

7. What do you mean by 'Serial Entrepreneurship'?

Ans. Serial Entrepreneur looks forward to developing alternative projects by giving responsibility to run the business to someone else and moves on to a new idea or a new venture after selling the running business.

8. Define Entrepreneurship development.

Ans. Entrepreneurship development is defined as the process of strengthening the skills and knowledge of upcoming and existing entrepreneurs by hand-holding them during their entrepreneurial journey.

9. Who is a Fabian entrepreneur?

Ans. Fabian Entrepreneur is an entrepreneur who is cautious and sceptic about bringing any change in his enterprise.

10. Who initiated the company" MakeMyTrip"?

Figure 4.7

Ans. Mr. Deep Kalra

11. Who initiated the idea of 'Nirma' washing powder?

Ans. Mr Karsanbhai Patel

12. Who is an Imitative entrepreneur?

Ans. Imitative Entrepreneur is the entrepreneur who imitates the methods and technologies innovated by others to begin his own business.

13. Who is called an Innovative entrepreneur?

Ans. An innovative entrepreneur is an entrepreneur who regularly intends to bring in new products in the market, new technologies, etc.

14. Who is known as a manufacturing entrepreneur?

Ans. Manufacturing entrepreneur is an entrepreneur who manufactures goods, mobilises resources and supplies to sell those products.

15. Who is a minor innovator?

Ans. Minor innovator is the entrepreneur who participates in economic growth by efficiently utilizing the existing resources.

16. Who is a 'private entrepreneur'?

Ans. A 'Private Entrepreneur' is an entrepreneur who establishes and operates private enterprises without any government control. He works for personal interest.

17. Which entrepreneur is called a service entrepreneur?

Ans. A service Entrepreneur is an entrepreneur who is involved in manufacturing and rendering services rather than goods.

18. When was National Skill Development Mission launched?

Ans. The Mission was launched in 2015.

19. When was the 'Make in India' initiative launched by the Govt of India?

Ans. 'Make in India' initiative of the Government of India was launched on 25th September 2014.

20. What is Instagram?

Ans. Instagram is a photo-sharing app (social media) that uses filters to enhance photos.

21. What is Agricultural Entrepreneurship?

Ans. Agricultural Entrepreneurship is defined as being primarily related to the marketing and production of inputs and products used in agricultural activities.

22. What do you mean by 'BETTER WORKS'?

Ans. It is a workplace recognition and rewards platform that lets businesses engage their staff through innovative rewards through local partners.

23. What is Pinterest?

Ans. It is a pinboard that allows the user to share their image quickly and easily.

24. Who is a trading entrepreneur?

Ans. A trading entrepreneur is an entrepreneur who carries out trading activities only.

25. Who is known as a drone entrepreneur?

Ans. Drone entrepreneur is the entrepreneur who does not change his approach to doing business and maintains conservatism even when he is suffering losses.

26. Who is a trader?

Ans. A trader is an entrepreneur who makes profits through commissions obtained by customer purchases.

27. How do entrepreneurs contribute to creating new wealth?

Ans. New and improved products, services, and technology from entrepreneurs enable to development of new markets and create new wealth.

28. What is the primary goal of economic development?

Ans. The job creation by new and existing businesses is the primary goal of economic development.

29. Why are entrepreneurs considered visionaries and risk-takers?

Ans. Entrepreneurs are considered visionaries and risk-takers because entrepreneurs play an important role in increasing the quality of living in a community by bringing improvised products and services.

30. What are the two important personality traits that entrepreneurs must possess?

Ans. The two important personality traits that entrepreneurs must possess are perception and intuition.

31. Define entrepreneurship development plan?

Ans. Entrepreneurship Development Plan (EDP) is designed as a unique, integrated approach for providing instructions and counseling from the selection stage to the main operation process.

32. What is the main focus of EDP?

Ans. EDP focuses more on enhancement in operations than academic training to fulfill certain requirements of the participants.

33. Define EDP.

Ans. EDP is an ongoing process of training and motivating entrepreneurs to establish profitable enterprises.

34. What types of incentives are provided by the Indian govt for entrepreneurs?

Ans. The Indian Government has started offering various incentives and concessions, which comprise capital subsidy, marketing facilities, technical know-how, industrial facilities, etc.

35. What is entrepreneurship, according to Richard Cantillon-an Irish French economist?

Ans. He defined entrepreneurship as self-employment of any kind and entrepreneurs as non-fixed income wage earners and risk-takers as they invest a known amount without knowing how much amount it will generate.

4.3.9 Short Answer Type Questions

1. What are the main advantages of being an entrepreneur?

Ans. Being an entrepreneur imbibes life skills, increases creativity and problem-solving skills, provides a better understanding of business and market economics, improves communication, teamwork, and networking skills, and hence, enhances employability.

2. Differentiate between an industrialist and an entrepreneur.

Ans. An industrialist is a person who owns and manages a large industrial unit/ company, whereas an entrepreneur is a person who makes profit by starting a new venture or running businesses involving financial risks. Thus, all industrialists who manufacture goods may be called a businessman. The basic difference between industrialists and entrepreneurs is that an industrialist is a person involved in the ownership or management of an industrial unit, while an entrepreneur is a person who organises and operates a business and assumes much of the associated risk.

3. Who are wagers and self-employed people?

Ans. Wage-employed people are people who work for a person or an organization for a fixed salary or emoluments. Self-employed people start their businesses to satisfy the needs of society. A self-employed person always tries to make his/her business better by taking risks and trying new ideas.

4. Explain social entrepreneurship.

Ans. Social entrepreneurship is about recognising the social problems and achieving social change by employing entrepreneurial principles, processes, and operations. This entrepreneurship research is conducted to completely define a particular social issue and then organise, creating and manage a social enterprise/venture to achieve the desired change. Many social problems are taken up by social entrepreneurs, such as the low reach of quality education, child labour, health, and sanitation, unemployment, etc.

5. Write a short note on 'Women Entrepreneurship.'

Ans. Women entrepreneurship is the process where women undertake all the factors of production, undertake risks, and provide employment to others. Women entrepreneurship may be defined as "an enterprise owned and controlled by one or more women who have a minimum financial investment of 51% of the capital, and are giving at least 51 % of the total employment generated in the enterprise to only women employees."

6. Discuss the importance of Entrepreneurs.

Entrepreneurs are associated with the following important tasks in the economic development process of the country:
   a) Free market evolution is encouraged by entrepreneurs.
   b) Efficiency improvements as initiated by entrepreneurs
   c) New values are developed and nurtured in the market for professional growth.
   d) A catalyst for bringing prosperity to society
   e) Promoters of research and development for fostering economic development

7. What are the different phases a person goes through to become an entrepreneur?

Ans. Any person who becomes an entrepreneur goes through a career process having the following phases:
   a) **ENTER:** When an entrepreneur is starting, then he/she is just entering the market to do business. This is the 'Enter' phase.
   b) **SURVIVE:** When there are many entrepreneurs in the market having the same business, and the new entrepreneur has to survive in a competitive market, then it is called the survival phase.
   c) **GROW:** Once the business of the entrepreneur becomes stable, and the Entrepreneur thinks about expanding his or her business, then it is called the 'Grow' phase.

8. What are the phases of the entrepreneurship process?

Ans. Following are the phases of the process of entrepreneurship:
   a) Stimulatory phase
   b) Support phase
   c) Sustenance phase

9. Write a short note on the Ministry of Skill Development and Entrepreneurship.

Ans. It started as a department of skill development and entrepreneurship but was transformed into a Ministry in 2014. The Ministry of Skill Development and Entrepreneurship (MSDE) is responsible for implementation and coordination of all skill development initiatives and efforts across the country, like removal of disconnect between demand and supply of skilled manpower, the building of a vocational and technical framework for training and skilling, implementation of training programs, sensitisation of people on entrepreneurship and large execution of entrepreneurship development programs. National Skill Development Agency (NSDA), National Skill Development Corporation (NSDC), and National Skill Development Fund (NSDF) operate as functional arms of the ministry.

Figure 4.8

10. What is the objective of National Policy on Skill Development and Entrepreneurship 2015 (Pradhan Mantri Yuva Udyamita Vikas Abhiyan)?

Ans. The objective of this policy is to meet the challenge of skilling at scale with speed and standard, and it aims to provide an umbrella framework to all skilling activities being carried out within the country, for aligning them to common standards and link the skilling with demand centers. The objective of the entrepreneurship framework in the policy is to foster the growth of entrepreneurship across the country.

11. What are the aims of 'Start-Up India'?

Ans. The main aim of Start-up India is to encourage entrepreneurship among the youth of India. The 'Start-up India: Stand up India' promotes bank financing for start-ups and offers incentives to enhance entrepreneurship and job creation. This initiative aims to provide a new dimension to entrepreneurship and help in setting up a network of start-ups in the country.

12. Explain Digital India.

Ans. Digital India is an important program of the Government of India with a vision to transform India into a digitally empowered society and sound economy. It is a campaign launched to ensure that the Government's services are made available to all citizens electronically by using improved online infrastructure and by improving the facility of Internet connectivity.

13. Discuss the impact of Entrepreneurship on Society.

Ans. Entrepreneurship has the following impact on society:
   a) It fosters creativity.
   b) It accelerates economic growth.
   c) It encourages the welfare of society.

d) It provides solutions to the problems of society.

e) It stimulates innovation and efficiency.

f) It creates jobs and employment opportunities.

14. How can society contribute towards the development of entrepreneurship?

Ans. Society also plays the following role in boosting entrepreneurship:

a) Creating needs and demands

b) Enabling financial support

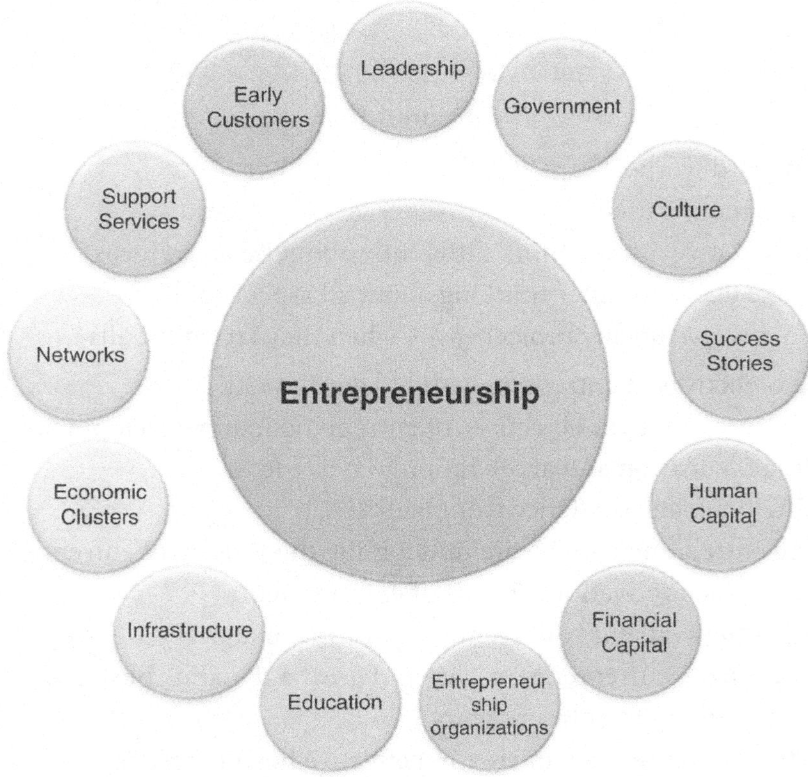

Figure 4.9

c) Providing raw materials

d) Facilitating networking

e) Creating a need for education

f) Supporting infrastructural development

4.3.10 Long Answer Type Questions

1. Discuss the qualities of successful entrepreneurs.

Ans. Successful entrepreneurs have the following qualities:

a) They are self-confident.

b) They take responsibility for their actions.

c) They try new ideas in their business.

Figure 4.10

    d) They are hard workers.

    e) They have more patience.

    f) They are creative as they think differently about business ideas.

    g) They make decisions after thinking about all aspects of them.

    h) They do not give up any project easily when they face difficulty.

2. Explain the objectives of entrepreneurship development.

Ans. The following are the main objectives of entrepreneurship development:

    a) Providing incubation and acceleration to new ideas

    b) Providing financial assistance from banks

    c) Assisting entrepreneurs who are undergoing the process of entrepreneurship.

    d) Developing the motivational needs of entrepreneurs

    e) Helping in the availability of technology or raw material

    f) Helping aspiring entrepreneurs start and grow a dynamic business.

    g) Imparting training to entrepreneurs

    h) Supporting entrepreneurs in creating effective business plans

    i) Encouraging research and development across industries

    j) Providing incentives, subsidies , and tax benefits to new enterprises

3. How are entrepreneurs contributing to the developmental process of society? Explain.

Ans. Basically, an entrepreneur performs the following roles to help society:

    a) **Improving Quality in Life by Sharing of Wealth**

Wealth may be defined as having enough money to live a comfortable life. Because entrepreneurs grow their business, the people working for them and in related businesses also grow. They have more money to live a quality life.

    b) **Fulfilling Customer Needs:**

Demand may be defined as a product or service that people want. Entrepreneurs search and research what people want. Then, they use their creativity to nurture a business idea that will meet that particular demand. Example: During the time of COVID19, many entrepreneurs started the manufacturing of low-cost masks and sanitizers because these items were required for the safety of people.

Figure 4.11

c) **Helping society**

Entrepreneurs make profits through activities that benefit society, and hence, they have a positive relationship with society. Many entrepreneurs work towards saving the environment by making bio-degradable products; some start schools and hospitals for the weaker section of society.

d) **Using Local Resources and Materials:**

Entrepreneurs use the material and people available locally to make their manufacturing cost of the products low and to supply the products at reasonable prices to society.

e) **Create Jobs**

With the growth of a business, entrepreneurs employ more people to help them, and they buy more material from more people. They create jobs and also hire more people to work for their venture. Thus, more people get jobs.

f) **Lowering Price of Products**

As the entrepreneurs are using the materials and resources available locally for manufacturing their products, the price of the product goes down. Moreover, when a large number of entrepreneurs do the same business, the cost of products goes down. For example, when more mobile phones are getting sold in India, the price of the mobile became lesser.

4. Discuss the role of entrepreneurship.

Ans. Entrepreneurship plays the following roles:

   a) It enhances the living standards of people.
   b) It aids the effective utilisation of local resources.
   c) It increases productivity through technical and other innovative approaches.
   d) It helps in transforming the economy.
   e) It involves a strategic role in commercialising new products and inventions.
   f) It creates employment opportunities by developing new enterprises.
   g) It aids the transfer of technology.

    h) It creates new markets for enabling expansion into global markets.

    i) It drives the industries forward by bringing in innovative products.

5. Enlist the qualities of an entrepreneur.

Ans. The following characteristics/qualities are required in an entrepreneur.

    a) **Leadership:** Capacity to lead a team

    b) **Innovativeness/Initiative:** Ability to initiate new plans

    c) **Goal-Oriented:** Self-motivated to set his goals

    d) **Risk Taking:** Ability to take risks

    e) **Highly optimistic:** With a positive attitude to see the brighter part.

    f) **Motivation:** Ability to motivate the team

    g) **Creative:** Full of new ideas and plans

    h) **Self-confident:** having confidence and trust in himself

    i) **Decision maker:** Ability to make correct decisions

    j) **Action-Oriented:** Ability to take actions after proper planning

    k) **Dynamic agent:** Capable of changing the scene by proper actions

    l) **High achiever:** Capable of achieving higher goals

6. Discuss the various types of functions performed by an entrepreneur.

Ans. Four types of main functions of an entrepreneur are as follows:

(a) Entrepreneurial Function

These include the following tasks:

- Developing Organisation and its Management
- Risk-Taking
- Innovation

(b) Promotional Functions

These include the following tasks:

- Idea discovery
- Detailed investigation
- Assembling the requirements
- Financing

(c) Managerial Functions

These include the following tasks:

- Planning
- Organising
- Directing
- Supervision
- Motivation
- Staffing
- Leadership
- Communication
- Controlling
- Coordination
- Negotiation

(d) Commercial Function

These include the following tasks:

- Production and operations
- Finance and Accounting
- Human Resource Management
- Marketing

7. Describe the tasks of an entrepreneur.

Ans. An entrepreneur has to perform the following tasks:

a) **Creating a New Method, Idea, or Product:** An entrepreneur is always trying new ideas to create things. He/she does this to increase his/her importance and income.

b) **Making Effective Decisions:** An entrepreneur makes many decisions each day as per his daily planning/weekly planning/monthly planning/ annual planning. This may include what to produce or sell, how much and where to sell, etc.

c) **Managing the Business:** An entrepreneur make futuristic plans of his/ her business. Through this process, he/she arranges raw material, hires people for work, and tells everyone what to do. He/she also checks if the plan is being followed.

d) **Taking Risk:** Risk is defined as the chance of something going wrong. All entrepreneurs take risks against fires, lost items, theft, etc.

e) **Dividing Income:** The entrepreneur divides business profit money into many groups. He/she spends money to buy raw materials, pays rent of the building,salaries to people, etc.

8. Explain the advantages of entrepreneurship.

Ans. Following are the advantages of entrepreneurship:

a) **Work satisfaction:** One can choose the work he/she like to do, use their strengths and skills, and follow their own style of working and doing things. This can result in more work satisfaction.

b) **Excitement:** Entrepreneurship may be exciting as many entrepreneurs find their work highly enjoyable. Each day is filled with new hopes and opportunities to challenge one's abilities, skills, and determination.

c) **Freedom:** It gives freedom to work whenever they want, wherever they want, and however they want, draws many people. Most entrepreneurs don't consider their work as actual work because they are doing something they love.

d) **Flexibility:** Entrepreneurs may schedule their work hours around other commitments, including spending quality time with their families.

e) **Rational salary:** As an entrepreneur, one's income is directly related to their efforts and the success of the business.

9. Discuss the main disadvantages of entrepreneurship.

Ans. Following are the main disadvantages of entrepreneurship:

a) **No regular salary:** Being an entrepreneur means giving up the security of a regular paycheque. If business slows down, one's personal income can be at risk.

b) **No Set Work schedule:** The work schedule of an entrepreneur may be unpredictable. A major disadvantage for an entrepreneur is that it requires more work and longer hours than being an employee.

c) **Administration:** While making all the decisions that can be taken as a benefit, it may also be taken as a burden. Becoming an entrepreneur involves a lot of paperwork that can take up time and energy.

d) **Loneliness:** He/she will be lonely and scared to be completely responsible for the success or failure of his/her business.

e) **Competition:** Staying competitive in the market is critical as a small business owner. One needs to differentiate their business from others in order to build a solid customer base and be profitable.

4.3.11 HOTS Questions

1. What step are considered important for the entrepreneurial process?

Ans. The entrepreneurial process comprises six steps as mentioned below:

    a) Deciding to become an entrepreneur

    b) Identifying and evaluating the opportunities

    c) Developing a business plan

    d) Determining the required resources

    e) Converting the idea to an enterprise

    f) Managing and growing the enterprise

2. Why was ATAL Innovation Mission (AIM) initiated?

Ans. AIM was initiated through the 2015 budget within National Institution for Transforming India (NITI) to provide an innovation promotion platform involving academicians for drawing upon national and international experiences to foster a culture of innovation, research, and development. Entrepreneurs are still facing certain problems like motivational challenges, lack of formal education, lack of availability of finance, technical knowledge, managerial skills, availability of resources and infrastructure, awareness about entrepreneurship schemes and regulatory framework, market linkage, etc.

Figure 4.12

4.4 PRACTICE QUESTIONS

1. Which person will be called an entrepreneur?

2. What do you mean by entrepreneurship?

3. How many steps are there in an entrepreneurial process?

4. What are the types of entrepreneurs?

5. Mention two myths about entrepreneurship.

6. Differentiate between entrepreneur and entrepreneurship.

7. 'It is only money that motivates employees. 'Is this a myth or a reality? Justify your answer.

8. Differentiate between Entrepreneur and entrepreneurship.

9. What does an entrepreneur do? Write the four main functions of an entrepreneur.

10. How will you justify the impact of entrepreneurship on society?

11. What are the four main qualities required in an entrepreneur?

12. 'Entrepreneurs are job creators, not job seekers.' Justify your answer.

13. State the characteristics of entrepreneurship.

14. Why is entrepreneurship considered a good option for earning a livelihood in the present time?

15. 'Entrepreneurs are high risk-takers.' Express your views on the topic.

16. Discuss the importance of entrepreneurs and entrepreneurship development.

17. What are the career options for entrepreneurship?

18. Describe the advantages and disadvantages of entrepreneurship as a career.

19. Discuss the two initiatives taken by the Government to encourage the creation and growth of new ventures.

20. Enlist the five suggestions that will be helping new entrepreneurs in making their venture successful.

Green Skills II

5.1 UNIT IN BRIEF

- Sustainable development is defined as the development that ensures the needs of the present generation without compromising the needs of future generations too.

- Conventionally, the environment was taken as a separate entity detached from human emotions or actions, while development was a term used for describing political goals and economic progress.

Figure 5.1

- The objectives of sustainable development are economic growth, environmental protection, social inclusion, and cultural diversity.

- The objectives to achieve effective and sustainable development must be applied simultaneously, interacting with one another in a consistent and committed effort.

- The principles of sustainable development are based on the integration of environmental, social, and economic concerns into all aspects of decision-making.

- Sustainable Development Goals (SDGs) are the collection of 17 global goals set by the United Nations General Assembly in 2015, which are to be achieved by the year 2030. These goals were implemented with effect from 1 Jan. 2016.

- The green economy is also defined as the economy that results in improved human wellbeing and social equity by reducing environmental risks and ecological scarcities.

- The skills used to promote a green economy are called green skills.

- The projects which are initiated to manufacture products or to do something to save the environment are called green projects.

- The major challenges of sustainable growth are eradicating extreme poverty, promoting consumption and production, and managing the planet's natural resource base.

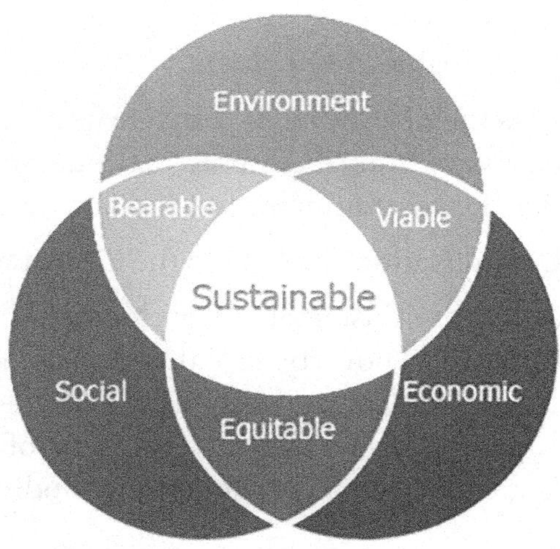

Figure 5.2

5.2 CBSE/NCERT SECTION (SOLVED CBSE/NCERT EXERCISE QUESTIONS)

(A) MCQs

Choose the correct option out of the four options given for each question.

1. How many sustainable development goals are given by the United Nations?

    a) 18   b) 17   c) 15   d) 20

2. Choose the option which defines sustainable development.

    a) Taking care of future generations

    b) Taking care of only ourselves

    c) Taking care of ourselves and the future generations

    d) Wellbeing of all

3. Which organization has made the Sustainable Development Goals.

    a) United Nations   b) League of Nations

    c) UNICEF   d) World Health Organisation

4. Which of the following sources of energy is from a renewable source?

    a) Solar energy   b) Wood   c) Coals   d) Petrol

5. Choose the option which is not a sustainable development goal according to United Nations.

    a) Clean Water and Sanitation   b) Gender Equality

    c) Population   d) Reduced Inequalities

ANSWERS
1. (b)   2. (c)   3. (a)   d. (a)   5. (c)

(B) Subjective Questions

1. What is the meaning of sustainable development?

Ans. Sustainable development is the development that satisfies the needs of the present without compromising the capacity of future generations, guaranteeing the balance between economic growth, care for the environment, and social wellbeing.

2. Why do you think the United Nations had made the 17 Sustainable Development Goals?

Ans. United Nations had made the 17 Sustainable Development Goals (SDGs) that were taken as a universal call of action to end poverty, save the planet, and ensure that all people enjoy peace and prosperity. These 17 SDGs have been made with the aim to take care of important issues facing businesses, governments, and society. Some of these issues include poverty, water use, gender equality, climate change, energy, and biodiversity.

Figure 5.3

3. List some ways in which we can use resources sensibly.

Ans. We can take the following steps to use the resources sensibly:
   a) Use the local resources when needed but do not waste them.
   b) Save energy by switching off lights and fans when not in use.
   c) Use natural light as much as possible.
   d) Use energy-efficient lights (LED bulbs) and appliances.
   e) Avoid wastage of food items.
   f) Use water as much as required, don't wastewater.

4. Explain the importance of education towards sustainable development.

Ans. Education is regarded as one of the most important factors for sustainable development. Children who have gone to a school will be able to do jobs in the future so that they may take care of themselves and their families properly. Education helps people become aware of our role as responsible world citizens. People should use the facilities present in their areas.
   a) Help friends study.
   b) Take our friends to school.
   c) Stop friends from dropping out of school.

5.3 SOLVED EXERCISES

5.3.1 Multiple Choice Questions

1. Which of the following R's is not part of Three R's principle?

   a) Reproduction   b) Reduce   c) Reuse   d) Recycle

2. The term 'ecology' was first coined in 1866 by a German scientist 1866.

   a) Goldsmith   b) Ernst Haeckel   c) JW Guttenberg   d) Huxley

3. What is the combination of sustaining and boosting the economy, environment, and social welfare?

   a) Green Skills   b) Green Economy   c) Environment   d) Resource

4. The technical skills, knowledge, values, and attitudes required in the people to develop and support sustainable economic, social, and environmental results in business, industry, and the community are collectively called:

   a) Social skills   b) Green skills

   c) Emotional intelligence   d) None of the above

5. _____________ satisfies the needs of the present generations and that's too without compromising the capacity of future generations, ensuring the balance between economic growth, care for the environment, and social wellbeing.

   a) Sustainable development   b) Green development

   c) Affordable development   d) None of the above

6. What was the name of the report released by the World Commission on Environment and Development in 1987?

   a) Future of Our Planet   b) Futuristic Approach towards Earth

   c) Our Common Future   d) Brundtland's Final Report

7. How many are sustainable development goals (SDGs) approved by the United Nations?

   a) 15   b) 17   c) 19   d) 21

8. Which one of the following is not an example of an abiotic resource?

   a) Water   b) People   c) Plants   d) Forest

9. Deforestation is the clearance or removal of a forest or trees to convert the land for non-forest use, such as:

   a) Mining
   b) Agriculture
   c) Construction of houses or developing industrial units
   d) All of these

10. Which international organisation has launched the Sustainable Development Goals?

    a) AEC   b) UN   c) UNICEF   d) UNEP

11. Which of the following is an example of an exhaustible resource of energy?

    a) Wind energy   b) Solar energy   c) Hydro energy   d) Coal energy

12. When was the United Nations Commission on Environment and Development (UNCED) created?

    a) 1973　　　　　b) 1983　　　　　c) 1993　　　　　d) 2003

13. Which one of the following is a man-made resource?

    a) Forest　　　　b) Pond　　　　c) Railways　　　　d) Air

14. Which of the following consists of the living organisms that reciprocally take advantages and benefits from each other?

    a) Ecosystem　　　　　　　　　　b) Culture

    c) Green skills　　　　　　　　　　d) Natural resource

15. WCED represents:
    a) World Committee on Environment and Development
    b) World Commission on Environment and Development
    c) Weird Commission on Environmental Detoxification
    d) None of the above

16. Which factor is not responsible for causing soil erosion?

    a) Uncontrolled runoff of surface water

    b) Grazing of land

    c) Deforestation

    d) Improper farming techniques

17. The United Nations formed the World Commission on Environment and Development. What was the other name given to this commission?

    a) Huxley Commission　　　　　　b) Geneva Commission

    c) Brundtland Commission　　　　　d) Tom and Hillary Commission

18. Which is not a benefit from the green economy?

    a) Reduce waste and inefficiency　　b) Environmentally-friendly

    c) Create a blue job　　　　　　　　d) Generate healthful society

19. According to the UNO, which of the following options is not a sustainable development goal?

    a) Clean Water and Sanitation　　　b) Population

    c) Gender Equality　　　　　　　　d) No poverty

20. Which option is one of the objectives of sustainable development in addition to economic growth, environmental protection, and cultural diversity?

    a) Social Security　　　　　　　　b) Social Inclusion

    c) Social Exclusion　　　　　　　　d) Food security

21. What is described by using the term development?

    a) Political goals

b) Economic progress

c) Social justice

d) Political goals and economic progress

22. Which option is related to sustainable development?

a) Taking care of future generations

b) Taking care of only ourselves

c) Taking care of ourselves and future generations

d) None of these

23. What is the process of building sensitivity towards all cultures and celebrating diversity called?

a) Social inclusion   b) Cultural diversity

c) Cultural inclusion   d) Environmental protection

24. Which of the following form the important components of an ecosystem?

a) Energy and air   b) Water and soil

c) Land, air, and water   d) both (a) and (b)

25. Sustainable development is a long-term, ____________ approach to development.

a) Integrated   b) Inclusive   c) Exclusive   d) Submissive

26. Which report was issued in 1987, which highlighted that equity, growth, and environmental maintenance are simultaneously possible?

a) The Brundtland Report   b) Future of Earth

c) Stockholm Report on Environment d) None of the above

27. Which country has completed the Sustainable Developmental Goals first in the world?

a) Norway   b) Sweden   c) USA   d) Switzerland

28. Which of the following statements are related to sustainable development?

i.   Use of digital media instead of paper

ii. Deforestation

iii. Use of energy-saving devices like LED.

iv. Use of drip irrigation

v.   The practice of crop rotation

a) (ii) (iii) (iv)   b) (ii)(iii)(iv)(v)

c) (iii) (iv) (v)   d) All of these

29. Which statement is related to the promotion of sustainable development?

a) Use of hybrid cars instead of conventional cars to reduce air pollution

b) Use of biofuels (biogas in the kitchen)

c) Treatment of Industrial waste and sewage before releasing in the water bodies

d) All of the above

ANSWERS
1. (a) 2. (b) 3. (b) 4. (b) 5. (a) 6. (c) 7. (b) 8. (a) 9. (d) 10. (b)
11. (d) 12. (b) 13. (c) 14. (a) 15. (b) 16. (a) 17. (c) 18. (c) 19. (b) 20. (d)
21. (d) 22. (c) 23. (b) 24. (d) 25. (a) 26. (a) 27. (b) 28. (c) 29. (d)

5.3.2 Fill in the blanks

1. One of the main principles of …………….. is to improve human wellbeing and to sustain these improvements over time without damaging the environment and natural resources.

Figure 5.4

2. The SDGs have been adopted by 193 member countries of the _____________.

3. Vegetable waste, sewage waste, wood, cattle dung, agriculture waste, etc., are examples of _____________ pollutants.

4. Kitchen dry waste should be utilised to make compost that can be used as an _____________ fertilizer.

5. A _____________ aims to improve human wellbeing and social equity and also supports the environment and ecological system.

6. _____________ are the abilities, knowledge, and attitudes that are needed in the manpower to support economic, social, and environmental outcomes in the business and industry.

7. In 1987, the Brundtland Commission released the report entitled _____________.

8. There are _____________ Sustainable Development Goals (SDGs) were adopted by world leaders in 2015 in the Agenda 2030.

9. _____________ resources include living beings and organic material.

10. _____________ refers to foster economic growth and development while ensuring that natural assets continue to provide the resources and environmental services.

11. The term 'ecology' was coined by German scientists _____________ in 1866.

12. The undesirable development has resulted in the depletion of the limited _____________ resources globally.

13. The contamination of the environment with harmful (toxic and poisonous) substances due to some natural phenomena and human activities is called environmental _____________.

14. The protection, restoration, preservation, and rational use of all the natural resources in the total environment is collectively known as natural resource _____________.

15. The concept of sustainable development was first noticed at the international level at the UN Conference on the Human Environment held in _____________.

ANSWERS		
1. sustainable development	2. United Nations	3. biodegradable
4. organic	5. green economy	6. Green skills
7. Our Common Future	8. seventeen	9. Biotic
10. Green development	11. Ernst Haeckel	12. Non-renewable
13. pollution	14. conservation	15. Stockholm

5.3.3 True or False

1. Gro Harlem Brundtland was the chairperson of the Brundtland Commission.

2. There is an urgent need to conserve resources for future generations by using more environmentally friendly materials.

3. Careers in Green construction are related to constructing new green (eco-friendly) buildings.

4. There is no need to conserve resources for future generations by using more environmentally friendly materials.

5. As per the concept of sustainable development, the environment and development are separable issues.

6. Conventionally, the environment was considered as a separate entity, detached from human emotion or action.

7. People's participation creates a feeling of ownership in the development work and environmental conservation activities among the local population.

8. The skills used for promoting a green economy are known as red skills.

9. Sustainable development may be defined as economic development that is conducted without the depletion of natural resources.

10. Green Economy is defined as the economy that results in the growth and development of social wellbeing and that also aims at improving the safety of the environment.

11. Sustainable development demotes prosperity and economic opportunity, greater social wellbeing, and protection of the environment.

12. In sustainable development, the objective of social inclusion is attained by creating high-quality development with accessible local services for the community.

13. The key to using resources in sustainable development is the optimum use of resources for the maximum benefit without wastage.

14. The major challenges of sustainable growth are eradicating extreme poverty, promoting consumption and production, and managing the planet's natural resource base.

15. The most critical areas to achieve a green economy are responsible resource management, access to energy, and good governance.

ANSWERS
1. (T) 2. (T) 3. (T) 4. (F) 5. (F, inseparable) 6. (T) 7. (T)
8. (F, green skills) 9. (T) 10. (T) 11. (F, promotes) 12. (T) 13. (T) 14. (T) 15. (T)

5.3.4 Matching type

Match the SDG with the related field correctly.

SDG	**Related Field**
(i) No Poverty	(a) Actions to reduce inequality within and among countries
(ii) Zero Hunger	(b) Eradicating extreme poverty
(iii) Reduced Inequality	(c) Empowering all women and girls
(iv) Quality Education	(d) Achieving food security, and improved nutrition
(v) Gender Equality	(e) Free, equitable, and quality education

ANSWERS				
1 (i)-b	(ii) -d	(iii) -a	(iv) -e	(v) -c

5.3.5 Assertion Reason Type Questions

1. Assertion (A): Sustainable development is defined as the development that ensures the needs of the present generation without compromising the needs of future generations too.

   Reason (R): Sustainable development is meant for economic growth, environmental protection, social inclusion, and cultural diversity.

   a) Both A and R are correct, and R is the correct reason for A.

   b) Both A and R are correct, and R is not the correct reason for A.

   c) A is correct but R is incorrect.

   d) A is incorrect but R is correct.

2. Assertion (A): The environment was taken as a separate entity detached from human emotions or actions.

   Reason (R):: The green economy is defined as the economy that results in improved human wellbeing and social equity by reducing environmental risks and ecological scarcities.

   a) Both A and R are correct, and R is the correct reason for A.

   b) Both A and R are correct, and R is not the correct reason for A.

   c) A is correct but R is incorrect.

   d) A is incorrect but R is correct.

3. Assertion (A): The principles of sustainable development are based on the integration of environmental, social, and economic concerns into all aspects of decision-making.

   Reason (R):: The projects which are initiated to manufacture products or to do something by harnessing the environment are called green projects.

   a) Both A and R are correct, and R is the correct reason for A.

   b) Both A and R are correct, and R is not the correct reason for A.

   c) A is correct but R is incorrect.

   d) A is incorrect but R is correct.

4. Assertion (A): Development was not used as a term for describing political goals and economic progress.

   Reason (R):: The major challenges of sustainable growth are eradicating extreme poverty, promoting consumption and production, and managing the planet's natural resource base.
   a) Both A and R are correct, and R is the correct reason for A.
   b) Both A and R are correct, and R is not the correct reason for A.
   c) A is correct but R is incorrect.
   d) A is incorrect but R is correct.

5. Assertion (A): Green economy is a boon to mankind.

   Reason (R): The green economy is the economy that results in improved human wellbeing and social equity and simultaneously reduces environmental risks and ecological scarcities significantly.
   a) Both A and R are correct, and R is the correct reason for A.
   b) Both A and R are correct, and R is not the correct reason for A.
   c) A is correct but R is incorrect.
   d) A is incorrect but R is correct.

6. Assertion (A):: The green economy is also defined as the economy that results in improved human wellbeing and social equity and simultaneously reduces environmental risks and ecological scarcities significantly.

   Statement 2: Economic development refers to give people what they need without compromising their quality of life, especially in the developing world.
   a) Both A and R are correct, and R is the correct reason for A.
   b) Both A and R are correct, and R is not the correct reason for A.
   c) A is correct but R is incorrect.
   d) A is incorrect but R is correct.

ANSWERS					
1. (a)	2. (b)	3. (c)	4. (d)	5. (a)	6. (b)

5.3.6 Statements Based Questions

1. Statement 1: The objectives to achieve effective and sustainable development must be applied simultaneously, interacting with one another in a consistent and committed effort.

   Statement 2: Sustainable development may be defined as the development that ensures the needs of the present generation without compromising the needs of future generations too.
   a) Statement 1 is correct, but statement 2 is incorrect.
   b) Statement 1 is incorrect, but statement 2 is correct.
   c) Both the statements are correct.
   d) Both the statements are incorrect.

2. Statement 1: The three objectives of sustainable development are economic growth, environmental protection, social inclusion, and cultural diversity.

   Statement 2: The skills used to demote a green economy are called green skills.

   a) Statement 1 is correct, but statement 2 is incorrect.

   b) Statement 1 is incorrect, but statement 2 is correct.

   c) Both the statements are correct.

   d) Both the statements are incorrect.

3. Statement 1: The objectives to achieve effective and sustainable development must be applied simultaneously, interacting with one another in a consistent and committed effort.

   Statement 2: Green skills are also known as skills for sustainability.

   a) Statement 1 is correct, but statement 2 is incorrect.

   b) Statement 1 is incorrect, but statement 2 is correct.

   c) Both the statements are correct.

   d) Both the statements are incorrect.

4. Statement 1: The principles of sustainable development does not require the integration of environmental, social, and economic concerns into all aspects of decision-making.

   Statement 2: Sustainable Development Goals (SDGs) are the collection of 17 global goals set by the United Nations General Assembly in 2015, which are to be achieved by the year 2030.

   a) Statement 1 is correct, but statement 2 is incorrect.

   b) Statement 1 is incorrect, but statement 2 is correct.

   c) Both the statements are correct.

   d) Both the statements are incorrect.

5. Statement 1; Clean drinking and usable water is called effluent.

   Statement 2: SDGs are not required for the welfare of people and the environment at all.

   a) Statement 1 is correct, but statement 2 is incorrect.

   b) Statement 1 is incorrect, but statement 2 is correct.

   c) Both the statements are correct.

   d) Both the statements are incorrect.

ANSWERS
1. (c)   2. (a)   3. (c)   4. (b)   5. (d)

5.3.7 Competency Based Questions

1. Consider the following benefits of a type of economy:

   i.   It makes the quality of life better.

   ii. The environmental balance becomes harmonized.

   iii. The resource efficiency increases.

   iv. It accelerates the development of new technologies.

   v.   New economic commodities generate in conformity with the environment.

   All these benefits are related to

   a) Command economy

   b) Traditional economy

   c) Green economy

   d) Market economy

2. Which of the following actions is not required to save 'Marine Life'?
   a) Reduce waste because most of the waste that we produce on land ends up in the oceans.
   b) Never buy bottled water; instead, use boiled and filtered water or stored rainwater.
   c) Stop using plastic bags because the wrong disposal of plastic is a major cause of marine pollution.
   d) Use natural light as much as possible.

3. Consider the following actions:
   i. Use energy-efficient lights (LED bulbs) and appliances.
   ii. Save energy by switching off electrical appliances, like tube lights and fans, when these items are not used.
   iii. Use energy-saving and water-saving techniques.
   iv. Use biodegradable items.
   v. Use natural light as much as possible.

   The actions required for developing 'Sustainable Cities' are:

   a) (i) (ii) (iii)   b) (ii) (iii) (iv)
   c) (iii) (iv) (v)   d) All of these

ANSWERS
1. (c)   2. (d)   3. (d)

5.3.8 VSA

1. Define sustainable development.

Ans. Sustainable development may be defined as the development that ensures the needs of the present generation without compromising the needs of future generations too.

2. Define the relationship between environment and development.

Ans. Conventionally, the environment was considered a separate entity detached from human emotion or action, while development was a term used to describe both political goals and economic progress.

3. What are the main objectives of sustainable development?

Ans. The objectives of sustainable development are economic growth, environmental protection, social inclusion, and cultural diversity.

4. How do we achieve sustainable development?

Ans. The objectives to achieve effective and sustainable development must be applied simultaneously, interacting with one another in a consistent and committed effort.

5. On which points, the principles of sustainable development are based?

Ans. The principles of sustainable development are based on the integration of environmental, social, and economic concerns into all aspects of decision-making.

6. What are SDGs?

Ans. Sustainable Development Goals (SDGs) are the collection of 17 global goals set by the United Nations General Assembly in 2015, which are to be achieved by the year 2030.

7. When was SDGs implemented?

Ans. SDGs were implemented with effect from 1 Jan. 2016.

8. Define green economy.

Ans. The green economy is also defined as the economy that results in improved human wellbeing and social equity and simultaneously reduces environmental risks and ecological scarcities significantly.

9. What are green skills?

Ans. The skills used to promote a green economy are called green skills.

10. Define green projects.

Ans. The projects which are initiated to manufacture products or to do something to save the environment are called green projects.

11. What is the term used for 'skills for sustainability'?

Ans. Green skills are also known as skills for sustainability.

12. Define economic development.

Ans. Economic development refers to give people what they need without compromising their quality of life, especially in the developing world.

13. What do you mean by potable water?

Ans. Clean drinking and usable water.

5.3.9 Short Answer Type Questions

1. What are the major challenges of sustainable growth?

Ans. The major challenges of sustainable growth are as follows:
   - eradicating extreme poverty,
   - promoting consumption and production,
   - managing the planet's natural resource base.

2. Illustrate with an example the importance of sustainable development.

Ans. Sustainable development is important. For example, Sustainable agriculture uses environmentally friendly methods of farming that allow the production of agricultural crops or livestock without damage to natural systems or humans. It also involves preventing the excessive use of chemicals to avoid adverse effects and damage to soil, water, and biodiversity.

3. Explain social development.

Ans. Social development is about awareness of and legislation protection of the health of people from pollution and other harmful activities of a business. Social development deals with encouraging people to participate in environmental sustainability and teaching them about the effects of environmental protection.

4. What is the 4Rs concept used in environmental protection?

Ans. The protection of the environment is suggested by applying the concept of 4 Rs (reduce, recover, recycle, and reuse) in businesses. It encourages the use of technologies for keeping their carbon emissions low and defines the ways and means to protect ecosystems, air quality, integrity, and sustainability of our resources.

5. What are the three pillars of sustainable development?

Ans. Three pillars of sustainable development are economic development, social development, and environmental protection.

6. Enlist five ways for enhancing sustainable development.

Ans. Five methods for enhancing sustainable development are as follows:
   a) Tree plantation to prevent soil erosion
   b) Use of solar energy, wind energy, and other alternative sources of energy
   c) Rainwater harvesting
   d) Use of bio-fuels
   e) Recycling of wastes

7. What are the major advantages gained by using 'Kulhads' in place of plastic cups on railway stations?

Ans. The major advantages gained by using 'Kulhads' in place of plastic cups on railway stations are as follows:
   a) To reduce plastic waste.
   b) To reduce the cutting of trees for making paper cups.
   c) To create jobs for potters,
   d) To enhance contributions to the economy.

8. What actions are required from a responsible consumer?

Ans. A responsible consumer will take the following small acts:
   a) Stopping leakage in taps and pipes to avoid wasting water.
   b) Taking cloth bags to market for carrying fruits and vegetables.
   c) Reusing paper, glass, plastic, water, etc.
   d) Buying and eating seasonal fruits and vegetables from local farmers.
   e) Donating things we do not use, such as clothes, books, furniture, food, etc.
   f) Sorting and treating garbage before properly disposing of it.

9. What is the main purpose of Sustainable Development Goals (SDGs)?

Ans. The 17 Sustainable Development Goals (SDGs) are a universal call of action from the United Nations to protect the planet, end poverty, and ensure that all people enjoy peace and prosperity. The Sustainable Development Goals (SDGs) have pre-decided targets that the countries have to should work towards and achieve by 2030.

10. Name a few sustainable practices used by Indians?

Ans. Some sustainable practices, such as organic farming, vermicomposting, and rainwater harvesting, are being used by Indians to help preserve the environment.

11. Explain organic farming.

Ans. Organic farming is farming where farmers do not use chemical pesticides and fertilisers to enhance soil fertility and to increase their crop production. The farmers use organic and natural fertilisers, like cattle dung, to help in growing crops.

12. How is organic farming contributing towards sustainable development?

Ans. The use of organic and natural fertilisers during organic farming helps in better quality chemical-free crops and at the same time maintaining the soil quality for future use. This is an example of sustainable development in which humans are using the Earth's resources, and at the same time, they are also preserving them for our future generations.

13. What are the three primary goals of Sustainable Development?

Ans. There are three primary goals of SD:

a) To minimise the depletion of natural resources while creating new developments.

b) To provide methods to retrofit the existing developments to make them environmentally friendly facilities and projects.

c) To create and promote a development that can be maintained and sustained without causing any further harm to the environment.

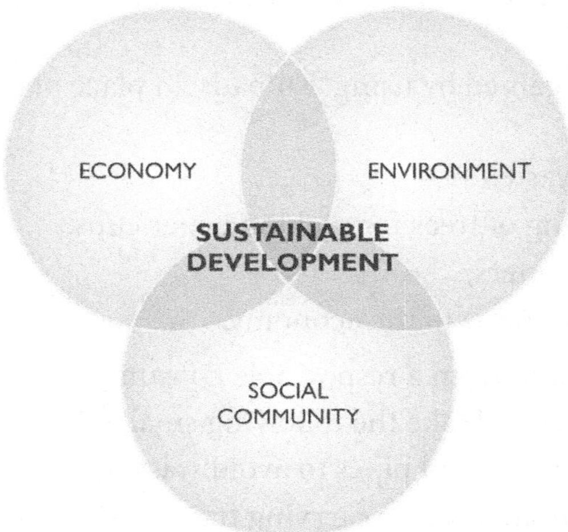

Figure 5.5

14. Explain recycling with suitable examples.

Ans. Recycling is defined as reusing some components of the waste having some economic value. Some materials, such as aluminium, copper, gold, silver, iron, etc., can be recycled many times. Metal, paper, glass, and plastics are recyclable. Plastic items are recycled to make new plastic products. Wet garbage includes most kitchen wastes, which can be used for preparing vermicompost. Most dry garbage is recyclable. Several innovative technological breakthroughs have recently been made to extract material from industrial waste. Non-toxic solid waste should be properly segregated and disposed of in landfills that are properly sealed to avoid leakage and contamination of surrounding land and groundwater.

15. Why are solar power and wind power called clean fuels?

Ans. When we use solar power, wind power, or hydropower, then the power generation process does not cause pollution as it does not require the burning of non-renewable fuels, like coal, and hence, these are called clean fuels/energy sources. The use of biogas and hydro energy is also an eco-friendly alternative to natural gas.

16. What steps can be taken to reduce inequalities?

Ans. The following steps may be undertaken to reduce inequalities:

    a) Behave in a friendly manner with everyone.

    b) Be helpful to one another.

    c) Include everyone while working or playing.

    d) Help others without any bias, whether they are small or big, girl or boy, belong to any class or caste.

5.3.10 Long Answer Type Questions

1. Discuss the main features of Sustainable Development.

Ans. The main features of sustainable development are as follows:

    a) Improving the quality of human life.

    b) Careful utilisation of resources and promoting recycling and reusing waste materials

    c) Caring for all forms of life on Earth

    d) Conserving the Earth's vitality and diversity

    e) Conserving resources for future generations by using more environmentally friendly material or biodegradable material

    f) Enabling communities to care for the environment.

    g) Minimising the emission of greenhouse gases

    h) Minimising the depletion of natural resources.

    i) Promoting eco-friendly and biodegradable products

    j) Changing personal attitudes and practices towards the environment.

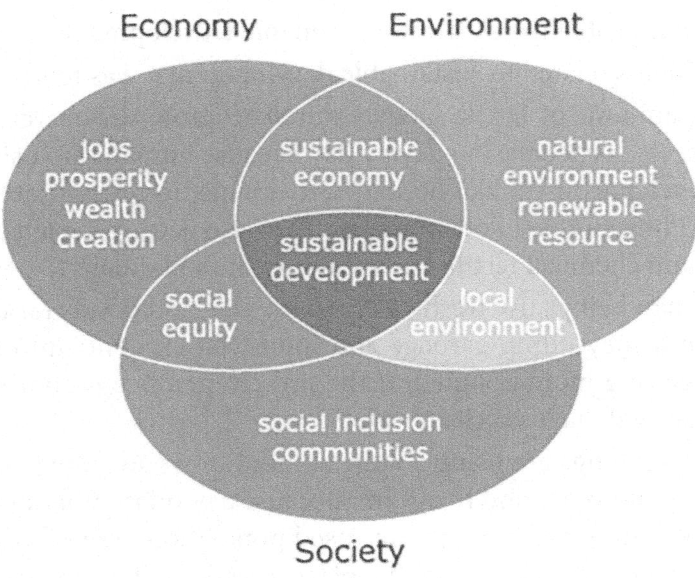

Figure 5.6

2. Why is Sustainable Development important? Explain.

Ans. Economic development is using up the resources of the world at a very fast pace, and it is assumed that future generations will face more environmental problems than the present age is facing. Since most of the natural resources are limited and hence, careful and optimum utilisation of these resources is necessary. Sustainable Development ensures the utilisation of natural resources with care towards nature.

As the population and income of the world are increasing, the consumption of goods is also increasing day by day. This has increased the production and utilisation of natural resources mercilessly, which are required for producing goods. Environmental problems like pollution, the greenhouse effect, etc., are posing a threat to human beings for their existence. Therefore, sustainable development plays an important role.

Sustainable development is important because of the following facts:

a) Sustainable Development ensures the protection of the Earth and Earth's resources.

b) Sustainable Development is not limited to a particular community or country; rather, it is for all without any bias.

c) Sustainability may also be defined as a concept that refers that natural systems are crucial essential to provide both economic needs and quality of life.

d) Sustainable Development (SD) considers the needs of future generations.

e) Sustainable Development is not contradictory to the growth profit and development; rather, it helps in planning out limits.

f) Sustainable Development is a continuous process.

g) Sustainable Development needs cooperation and coordination amongst people from different societies, communities, and countries.

h) Sustainable Development helps in developing an eco-friendly global culture.

i) Sustainable Development ties together the concern for the carrying capacity of natural systems with the social challenges facing the world today.

3. Discuss the major problems related to Sustainable Development.

Ans. The major problems related to sustainable development are as follows:

(i) **Food:** The amount of fertile land required to grow various crops, like wheat, corn, pulses, rice, etc., is decreasing day by day because humans are using up more and more land for other purposes, like human settlements, industrialisation, etc. Soil nutrients (Nitrogen, Phosphorous, Potassium, etc.) are also getting depleted. The excessive use of chemicals and chemical fertilisers is spoiling the soil quality.

(ii) **Water:** Human beings use freshwater from rivers and ponds for drinking and cleaning purposes, but they dump garbage and industrial effluents into them. The rivers and ponds are getting more polluted. If the present practice is continued, then after some time, humans will have no clean water.

(iii) **Fuel:** Human beings are using a large amount of wood from trees as fuels and for the construction of homes and furniture. Because a good number of trees are being cut for meeting the requirements of an increased population, more forest area is diminishing, and it is affecting the climate of the place adversely. Extreme weather conditions, like floods, extreme cold or heat, etc., are seen in many places, and this is affecting the people living in these areas.

An environment-friendly way for the production of power is using wind energy, hydropower, solar energy/energy from the sun, etc., which are unlimited.

4. Give some methods for creating sustainable development?

Ans. The various methods for creating sustainable development may include:

a) Recycling and reuse of waste materials;

b) Reducing excessive use of natural resources and enhancing resource conservation;

c) Scientific management of renewable resources, especially bio-resources;

d) Emphasising afforestation (planting more trees);

e) Developing green grassy patches and planting small trees between concrete buildings;

f) Using more environmentally friendly material or biodegradable material;

g) Use of environmentally friendly technologies that are based on efficient use of resources.

5. How will you justify that sustainable development is must nowadays?

Ans. Consumption of natural resources has increased many folds due to a drastic increase in population and developmental activities. For more population, we need more food, more energy, and more water. We grow more crops to meet the demand of the increased population, then the soil's nutrients are also consumed, and the soil becomes unusable day by day. Moreover, more fossil fuels, like coal, oil, natural gas, etc., are used, and it seems that very soon, we will run out of these natural resources.

During the manufacturing process, industrial units and factories give out smoke and toxic gases that pollute the air. Industrial waste is also dumped in rivers and lakes, which is creating a serious problem of water pollution. Garbage collected from homes and industries is dumped into landfills creating soil pollution. Untreated garbage is leading to the spread of disease and making the environment unhealthy.

This clearly shows that human beings are using natural resources without considering the condition of the environment. They are doing nothing to give back to nature. All this shows that sustainable development is the need of the hour.

Figure 5.7

6. What steps are required for effective water management?

Ans. The following steps are required for effective water management:

a) All citizens must take measurable steps by promoting awareness to keep water sources clean and to minimize water pollution.

b) Conservation and management of water are crucial requirements for the survival of humanity, plants, and animals. This can be done by using the following methods:

c) Industrial wastes (effluents) should be treated in effluent treatment plants to prevent chemical and thermal pollution of freshwater bodies.

d) Sewage should be treated, and only the treated and clear water should be released into the rivers.

e) Growing vegetation in the catchment areas holds water in the soil and allows it to percolate into deeper layers and contribute to the formation of groundwater.

f) Constructing dams and reservoirs is required to regulate the supply of water to the fields, as well as to enable the generation of hydroelectricity.

g) Careful use of water in our day-to-day life is to be promoted.

h) Rainwater harvesting should be encouraged for storing rainwater and recharging groundwater.

i) A Watershed is a single unit of land with a water drainage system and includes soil and water management for developing vegetative cover in the area.

7. What methods are adopted for energy conservation?

Ans. The following methods may be adapted to conserve energy:

a) Switch off electrical appliances like, lights, fans, TV, etc. when not in use.

b) Keep the bulbs and tubes clean.

c) Keep cooking vessels covered with a lid during cooking. It is useful in cooking food faster and saving energy.

d) Use tube lights and energy-efficient bulbs that save energy rather than bulbs.

e) Use a pressure cooker to save the energy required for cooking.

f) Use methods of cooking that use less energy, like using a pressure cooker or solar cooker to cook food.

g) Remove dust from the tubes and bulbs to improve lighting levels by 10 to 20%.

h) Electrical items like air conditioners, geysers, heaters, and dryers use a lot of electrical power. Use them when necessary.

i) Do not keep the door of a refrigerator open for a long time.

j) Cool the hot food before putting it in the refrigerator.

k) Traveling in a public transport vehicle, like roadways bus or traveling in a group using a carpool, etc. is better than using a car.

8. Discuss the concept of 3Rs.

Ans. The 3 Rs is a concept of modern waste management at the workplace and for economic growth.

(i) **Reduce:** Use what you need. If we reduce at source, then there is a lesser chance of waste generation. Thus, the pressure on our already stretched natural resources is reduced.

Every citizen may work at an individual level also like storing fewer items, reducing the purchasing of unnecessary items while shopping, buying items with minimal packaging, avoiding disposable items, avoiding asking for plastic carry bags, etc.

(ii) **Reuse:** Reuse the items/materials for other purposes, such as making pillow covers or rags out of used shirts or ladies' suits.

(iii) **Recycle:** Recycling is defined as the reusing of some components of the waste having some economic value. Recycling has easily visible benefits, like conservation of resources, reduction in energy used during manufacture, reducing pollution levels, etc. Some materials, such as aluminium, copper, gold, silver, iron, etc., can be recycled many times. Metal, paper, glass, and plastics are recyclable.

Figure 5.8

9. What norms may be applied to convert cities into sustainable cities?

Ans. For creating Sustainable Cities, apply the following norms:

a) Use energy-efficient lights (LED bulbs) and appliances.

b) Save energy by switching off electrical appliances, like tube lights and fans, when these items are not used.

c) Use energy-saving and water-saving techniques.

d) Use biodegradable items.

e) Use natural light as much as possible.

10. How can we save marine life?

Ans. We can take /involve in the following actions to save marine life:

a) Reduce waste because most of the waste that we produce on land ends up in the oceans.

b) Run and participate in a campaign on the effects of plastic use on the seas and oceans.

c) Never buy bottled water; instead, use boiled and filtered water or stored rainwater.

d) Stop using plastic bags because the wrong disposal of plastic is a major cause of marine pollution.

e) Keep yourself informed about the latest happenings of Global Goals online or on social media by visiting the site.

f) Organise/participate in a clean-up project for rivers and oceans at the national or international level.

g) Involve the whole community to clean up a local river, lake, seaside, or ocean.

h) Buy local and certified fish. You can support small-scale producers by shopping in local markets and shops.

11. How can we save lives on land?

Ans. Preserving life on land requires well-planned actions to promote terrestrial ecosystems and to promote their sustainable use for the future. A flourishing life on land is required, which is the foundation for our life on our planet.

We can participate in the following actions:

a) Raise your voice to conserve wildlife.

b) Organise/participate in mass awareness campaigns for protecting wildlife.

c) Show/see documentary films on Raising awareness with friends and colleagues.

d) Have a united voice for the continued existence of wildlife.

e) Advocate for stern punishment for poachers

f) Follow the conventions written by the forest department while visiting a forest or protected wildlife area (national park/sanctuary).

g) During the visit to protected areas/ forests, dispose of the garbage in the dustbin or at an appropriate place to keep the environment clean and green.

h) During a forest trip, don't disturb the serenity of the jungle with the sound of the horn.

Figure 5.9

5.3.11 HOTS Questions

1. Why is sustainable development considered one of the most difficult challenges?

Ans. Sustainable development is considered one of the most difficult challenges that humanity has ever faced because attaining sustainability requires solving many fundamental issues at local, regional, national and global levels. Achieving sustainable development goals is a great challenge for all sectors of society.

2. Why is Green Economy important?

Ans. Green Economy is important because of the following reasons:

a) It makes the quality of life better.

b) The environmental balance becomes harmonized.

c) The resource efficiency increases.

    d) It accelerates the development of new technologies.

    e) New economic commodities generate in conformity with the environment.

3. How does sustainable development helpful in enhancing economic, social, and environmental wellbeing?

Ans. The sustainable development of the environment is a way to enhance the long term economic, social, and environmental wellbeing of people and social communities by:

    a) Promoting social justice and equality of opportunity, and

    b) Enhancing the natural and cultural environment.

    c) Enhancing natural resource conservation,

    d) Reducing excessive use of natural resources,

    e) Recycling and reuse of waste products/materials,

    f) Promoting afforestation/planting more trees,

    g) Scientific management of renewable resources, especially bio-resources,

    h) Using more environmentally friendly material promoting products made of biodegradable material,

    i) Using environmental-friendly technologies based on the efficient use of resources.

5.4 PRACTICE QUESTIONS

1. Write the full form of SDG.

2. What is SDG no 15?

3. What are green constructions?

4. What are the principles of sustainable development?

5. Sustainable development is not necessary. Are you agree or disagree with the statement? Explain.

6. List the ways in which human beings can save energy resources.

7. Suggest some methods to save life on land.

8. Why is creating awareness towards sustainable development important?

9. What is sustainable development?

10. Mention the two key concepts of sustainable development.

11. Define the green economy.

12. In which year was the sustainable development agenda adopted by the United Nations?

13. What is SDG no 1?

Figure 5.10

14. What is the main aim of the member countries of the United Nations in implementing sustainable goals?

15. What is the name of the report drafted by the Brundtland Commission?

16. Differentiate between the conventional approach to address environmental issues and sustainable development.

17. Name any three sustainable goals which you think are relevant to your country. What should the country do in order to implement these?

18. Sustainable development is an opportunity for the world communities to come together for a common cause. Justify the statement.

19. How does sustainable development ensure economic growth?

20. What do sustainable resources teach us about the use of resources?

21. What are the significant challenges of sustainable growth?

22. Discuss the objectives of sustainable development.

23. How has unrestricted development in the last two decades destroyed the environment?

24. Discuss some of the social and economic challenges facing the world today.

25. Discuss the problems faced by developing countries with regard to sustainable development?

26. What are some changes that you would like to adopt to contribute towards achieving sustainable development?

Introduction To AI

6.1 UNIT IN BRIEF

✦ Intelligence may be defined as the capacity to learn and solve problems.

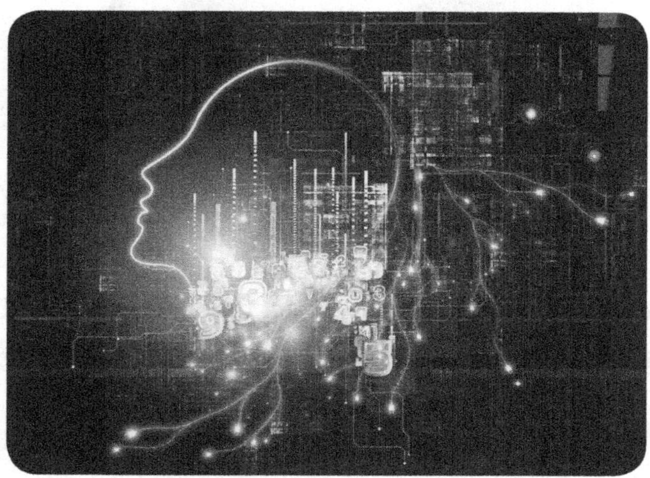

Figure 6.1

✦ Mathematical and logical reasoning is defined as a person's ability to regulate, measure, and understand numerical symbols, abstraction, and logic.

✦ Linguistical Intelligence is language processing skills both in terms of understanding or implementation in writing or verbally.

✦ Spatial Visual Intelligence is defined as the ability to perceive the visual world and the relationship of one object to another.

✦ Kinaesthetic Intelligence is the ability that is related to how a person uses his limbs in a skilled manner.

✦ Musical Intelligence is about a person's ability to recognise and create sounds, rhythms, and sound patterns.

✦ Intrapersonal Intelligence describes how high the level of self-awareness someone has is—starting from realising weakness, strength to his own feelings.

✦ Interpersonal Intelligence: It is the ability of humans to communicate with others after understanding other people's feelings and influence on the person.

✦ Naturalist Intelligence is an additional category of Intelligence relating to the ability to process information on the environment around us.

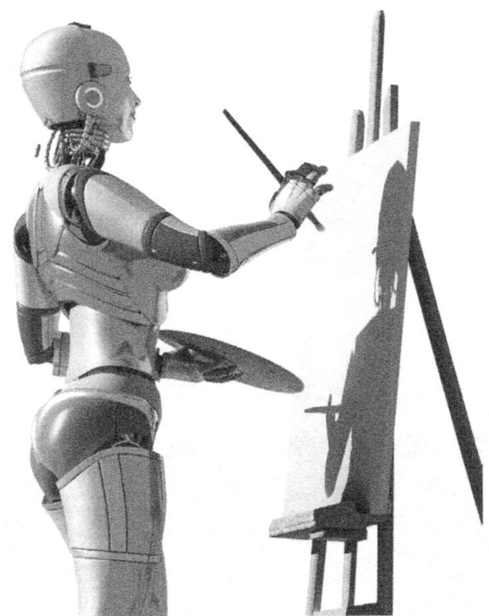

Figure 6.2

+ Artificial Intelligence (AI) may be defined as the simulation of human intelligence by machines. It has the ability to solve problems, the ability to act rationally, and the ability to act like humans.

+ Affective computing is the development of such systems that can recognise, interpret, simulate human effects.

+ Emotion and social skills are essential to an intelligent agent to understand others and to make better decisions.

+ Intelligence is needed for robots to handle tasks like object manipulation and navigation.

+ AI's value is with practical usage, both in the enterprise world and industrial world.

+ Data comes from multiple disparate systems and sources.

+ The business context may not be obvious based on data alone.

+ There are higher demands and expectations for seeing data quality in context.

+ Speech Recognition is the process of converting sound signals captured by a microphone or mobile/telephone to a set of words (70-100 words/minute with an accuracy of 90%).

+ Computer Vision is defined as the ability of a machine to extract information from an image that is necessary to solve a task.

+ Deep Learning is considered the most advanced form of Artificial Intelligence.

+ Machine perception is defined as the ability to use input from sensors to deduce aspects of the world.

+ Expert Systems are Software used for decision-making.

+ Natural Language Processing is responsible for machine's ability to read and understand human language.

+ Semantic indexing is a common method of processing meaning from natural language.

+ AI still leaves many forms of Intelligence to people, such as creativity and innovation, gut feeling, emotion, intuition, strategy, etc.

+ Computer Vision (CV) related projects translate digital visual data into descriptions.

+ The main objective of CV is to teach machines to collect information from pixels.

+ Natural Language Processing inputs machines the ability to read and understand human language.

+ Sophia is a humanoid robot developed in 2015 by "Hanson Robotics," Hong Kong.

+ Sophia was the first humanoid given Citizenship by a country-Saudi Arab in Oct. 2017.

+ Smart assistants like Google Assistant, Apple's Siri, Amazon's Alexa, etc., recognize patterns in speech and then understand their meaning and provide a useful response.

Figure 6.3

6.2 CBSE/NCERT SECTION (SOLVED CBSE/NCERT QUESTIONS)

(A) Fill in the blanks:

1. One of the major sources of data for many major companies in the device which all of us wear in our hands all the time is _____________.

2. The world of Artificial Intelligence revolves around _____________.

Ans. 1. Smartphone/ Mobile Phones   2. Data

(B) True/False

1. All the apps collect some kind of data.

Ans. True

(C) MCQs

1. Snapchat filters use _____________ and _____________ to enhance your selfie with flowers, cat ears, etc.

   a) machine learning and deep learning   b) data and image processing

   c) augmented reality and machine learning   d) NLP and computer vision

2. Based on the image below, choose the correct domain or domains of AI required for it:

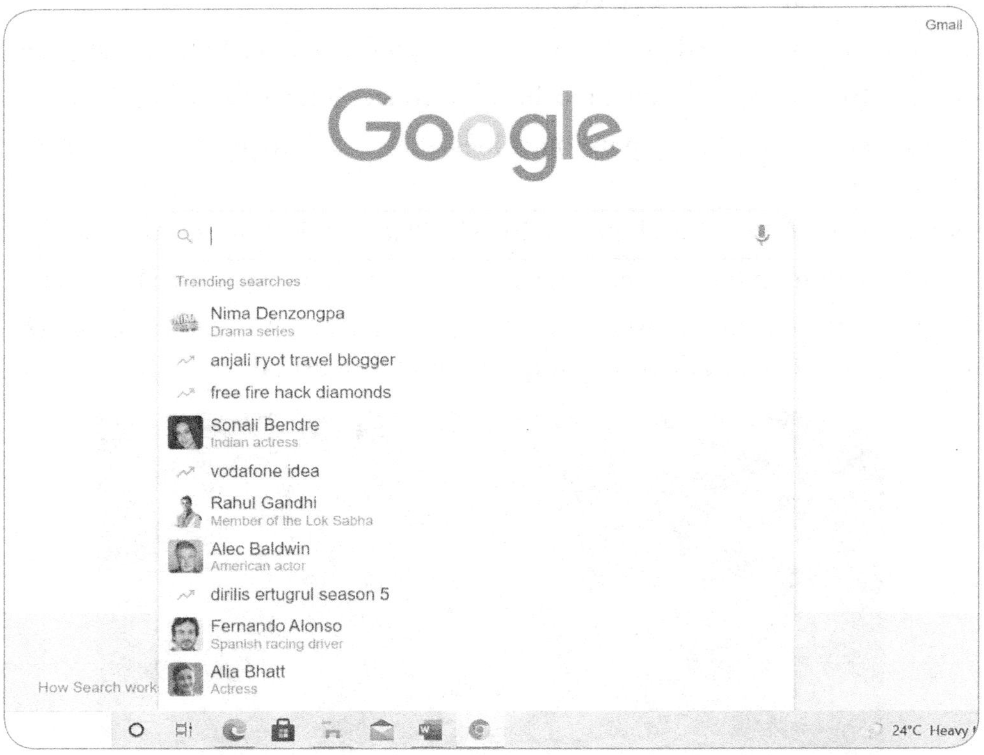

Figure 6.4

a) Data   b) NLP

c) Computer Vision   d) Both (a) and (b)

3. Rock paper and scissors game is based on the following domain:

a) Data for AI   b) Natural Language Processing

c) Computer Vision   d) Image processing

4. Select a game that is based on the Data Science domain of AI:

a) Rock Paper and Scissors   b) Mystery Animal

c) Emoji Scavenger Hunt   d) Pokémon

5. Identify the domain of AI in the following image:

Figure 6.5

a) Data Science b) Natural Language Processing

c) Computer Vision d) Rule-Based

ANSWERS
1. (c)   2. (d)   3. (a)   d. (a)   5. (c)

(D) One Mark Questions

1. What do you understand by Machine Learning?

Ans. Machine Learning is a subset of Artificial Intelligence that enables machines to improve at tasks with experience with large data.

2. What do you understand by Deep Learning?

Ans. In Deep Learning, the computer/machine is trained with large data that help it in training itself around the data.

3. What are the three domains of AI?

Ans. Data Science/ Big Data, Computer Vision (CV), and Natural Language Processing (NLP).

4. Name any two examples of Data Science?

Ans. Fraud and Risk detection, Price Comparison Websites, image tagging, Website Recommendations, Internet search, Personalized healthcare recommendations, Optimizing Traffic routes in real-time. (Any two).

5. Name any two examples of Computer vision?

Ans. Self-Driving cars, Face Lock in Smartphones, Autonomous vehicles, Medical Imaging (CT Scan), Facial recognition, Security Systems, Waste Management, Satellite imaging. (Any two).

6. Name any two examples of Natural Language Processing?

Ans. Email filters, Digital phone calls, Sentiment Analysis, Automatic Summarisation, Smart assistants, Search results, Language translation. (Any two).

7. Name any two examples of Machine Learning?

Ans. Virtual Personal Assistants, Online Fraud Detection, Recommendation systems like Netflix, Face Apps, (Any two)

(E) SAQs (Two/Three Mark Questions)

1. What is Data Science? Give an example of it.

Ans. Data science is a domain of AI dealing with data systems and processes, used for the collection of numerous data, maintains data sets, and derives meaning out of them. The information extracted through data science may be used to make a decision about it.

2. How do we collect data from?

Ans. Data can be collected from the following methods:

- Surveys
- Sensors

- Observations
- Web scrapping (Internet)
- Interviews
- Documents and records.
- Oral histories

3. What is Computer Vision? Give an example of it.

Ans. Computer Vision (CV) is a domain of AI that depicts the capability of a machine to get and analyse visual information to predict a few decisions about it. The entire process of CV involves image acquiring, screening, analysing, identifying, and extracting information.

4. Is Data that is collected by various applications ethical in nature? If no, justify your answer.

Ans. No. The data collected by many applications is not necessarily ethical in nature. Sometimes, the users just share their data to non – trusted third-party applications without reading what happens to their data. Sometimes, companies collect data without the consent of the users leading to unethical use of our data. If the user does not want to share his/her Data with any organisation/individual, he/she can opt for some alternative applications which are of similar usage to keep the data private.

5. What is Natural Language Processing? Give an example of it.

Ans. Natural Language Processing, abbreviated as NLP, is a branch of Artificial Intelligence that deals with the interaction between machines/computers and human beings using the natural language. Natural language is the language that is spoken and written by humans, and natural language processing (NLP) deals with extracting information from the spoken and written word using algorithms.

6. Why do we need to collect data?

Ans. Data to a machine is like food for human beings. Data is required in Artificial Intelligence. Each small or big company collects data from many sources. Data is called the 'New Gold' today. Through data collection, a business or management has the quality information they need to make informed decisions for further analysis, study, product improvement, and research. Data collection and analysis allow them to stay on top of trends, analyze the situations, provide answers to problems, and analyze new trends/insights to great effect.

7. Is Data that is collected by various applications ethical in nature? If yes, justify your answer.

Ans. Yes. Most of the time, the data collected by many applications is ethical in nature because the users agree to it when they click on allow button when the app asks for various permissions. They ask for users' data to provide various facilities - to show users personalized recommendations and advertisements as per their needs and requirements and to make their app more accurate and efficient.

8. What is data mining? Explain with example.

Ans. Data mining is defined as the process of analysing large datasets and extracting useful information from them. Data mining is normally used by companies/organisations to turn raw data into useful information and to find out the trends. It is regarded as an interdisciplinary subfield of computer science and statistics with an overall goal to extract information.

9. What do you understand by Data Privacy?

Ans. The world of Artificial Intelligence requires authentic and reliable Data. Proper and ethical handling of own data of organisation or users' data is called data privacy. Simply, it is all about the rights of individuals with respect to their personal information/data. Data privacy/ information privacy is a branch of data security dealing with the proper handling of data – consent, notice, and legal/regulatory obligations. Practical data privacy concerns often deal with consent: Whether or how Data is shared with third parties.

10. Fill in the blanks for the image given below:

Figure 6.6

Ans. The completed picture is as follows:

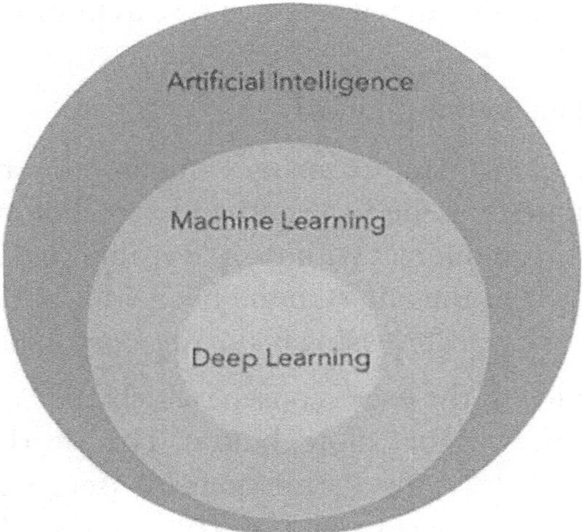

Figure 6.7

(F) LAQs (Four (04) Mark Questions)

1. What are AI, ML, and DL? How are they different from each other?

Ans. a) **Artificial Intelligence (AI):** AI is defined as the incorporation of human Intelligence into machines. Artificial Intelligence (AI) may be defined as the simulation of human intelligence by machines.

b) **Machine Learning (ML):** ML is considered a subset of AI that uses statistical learning algorithms to build smart machines/systems. The ML systems may automatically learn and improve themselves without being programmed.

c) **Deep Learning (DL):** In Deep Learning, the machine is imparted training with large data (training data). These machines/computers become intelligent enough to develop algorithms for improving themselves.

Deep Learning is considered the most advanced form of Artificial Intelligence out of these three. After that comes Machine Learning (ML) which is intermediately intelligent, and at last, Artificial Intelligence covers all the concepts and algorithms which mimic human Intelligence.

Thus, AI is the umbrella term to cover ML and DL.

2. What do you understand by AI bias? Discuss in detail with some examples.

Ans. AI bias is defined as the underlying prejudice in Data used to create AI algorithms, which may ultimately result in discrimination and other social consequences. AI Bias may creep into algorithms in many ways. AI systems learn to make decisions after training with huge data, which may include biased human decisions /reflect historical or social inequities, sensitive variables, like gender, race, or sexual orientation, etc. Another source of bias is defected/flawed data sampling, in which groups are over or under represented in the training data.

Examples: Most of the virtual assistants are given a female voice. Now, some companies have understood this bias, and they have started giving options for male voices too. But female voices are always preferred for them over any other voice since their inception.

On searching on Google for salons, the first few searches are mostly for female salons. This bias is based on the assumption that if a person is searching for a salon, it would be a female. But this is a bias.

3. Why do apps collect data on our phones?

Ans. One of the major sources of data for many companies is the most common device, i.e., Smartphone. Smartphones have become part and parcel of human lives. Most of them use smartphones more than we interact with people around us. For providing the facilities by smartphones, Apps fitted in the Smartphone need a lot of data that is collected from the user, like details about the face, browsing history, geographic location, contact list, etc.

All the data is collected with the user's consent which he/she gives at the time of installing an app by clicking on the "yes" or "allow" button. This clearly shows that users themselves are giving permissions to the Apps. Permissions by users are harmless and even useful to provide users with a good mobile experience. This Data is collected to provide users with a lot of facilities and features that have made their lives easier. Another reason to collect the data is to provide users with customized recommendations and notifications as per their choices. One important reason to collect the Data is to make their app more accurate and efficient.

4. What do you understand by Data Privacy? Discuss in detail with some examples.

Ans. Data privacy/ information privacy is an area of data protection that concerns the proper handling of sensitive data, including personal data, confidential data, such as some financial data and intellectual property data, to meet legal/regulatory requirements as well as protecting the confidentiality and immutability of the data. Data privacy focuses on how to collect, process, share, archive, and delete data in accordance with the law of the State. Privacy is defined as the right of individuals, groups, or organizations to control who can access, observe, or use something they own, like their bodies, property, ideas, data, or information. So, Control is established through physical, social, or informational boundaries to prevent unwanted access, observation, or use of users' data. For example:

A physical boundary, like a locked front door, helps prevent others from entering a building without proper permission in the form of a key to unlock the door or a person inside opening the door.

A social boundary, like a members-only club, only allows members to access and use club resources.

An informational boundary, like a non-disclosure agreement, restricts what information is to be disclosed to others. Privacy of information is important in this digital age, where everything is interconnected and can be accessed and used easily. The possibilities of private information being extremely vulnerable are very real. That's why we require data privacy.

5. Read the following passage and answer the question that follows:

As Artificially Intelligent machines become more and more powerful, their ability to accomplish tedious tasks is becoming better. Hence, it is now that AI machines have started replacing humans in factories. While people see it in a negative way and say AI has the power to bring mass unemployment and, one day, machines would enslave humans, on the other hand, other people say that machines are meant to ease our lives. If machines overtake monotonous and tedious tasks, humans should upgrade their skills to remain their masters always.

Should AI replace laborious jobs? If no, justify your answer.

Ans. No, AI should not replace laborious jobs completely because when it replaces laborious jobs completely, then there will not be any source of income for the daily wage workers due to unemployment. So, industrial units' owners can use some machines but more manpower. Hence, production will not be affected because humans are always smarter than machines.

6. List down various sensors that are present in a smartphone. Also, list down the type of data that gets collected through them.

Ans. a) **Accelerometer:** It helps run AR applications and track steps.

b) **GPS:** Location Data.

c) **Gyroscope:** Orientation Data

d) **Magnetometer:** Direction and Magnetic Field Data

e) **Biometric Sensors:** Fingerprint, Iris, Face data

7. Should AI replace laborious jobs? Is there an alternative for major unemployment?

Ans. Yes, AI should replace laborious jobs.

a) AI can replace laborious jobs like the lifting of heavy items, working in mines, etc.

b) AI can automate most repetitive and physical tasks.

c) In the future, AI would be a good option in the field of architecture and construction.

Alternative for major unemployment: AI taking over laborious jobs will not create unemployment. It is just a baseless fear. The standard view of technical change is that some jobs are displaced by the substitution of machines for labour. The main fear is that total displacement of labour by machines will create total unemployment, while the truth is that new jobs are created due to the technology-fuelled increase in productivity. Human beings have always shifted away from work suitable for machines and to other jobs.

The basic fact remains the same, i.e., the technology eliminates jobs, not work. If this level of AI revolution happens, lots of job opportunities will be created. Example: 20-30 years ago, being an accountant was a lucrative job, but AI took over this job, but this created a lot of opportunities, it raised the demand of a software engineer, data scientist, etc.

It will open doors to skillful jobs rather than doing laborious tasks. Thus, we will be able to cope with the level of major unemployment if AI takes over laborious jobs.

8. **Case Study:** *AI and robotics have raised some questions regarding liability. Take, for example, the scenario of an 'autonomous' or AI-driven robot moving through a factory. Another robot surprisingly crosses its way, and our robot draws aside to prevent the collision. However, by this maneuver, the robot injures a person.*

   a) Who can be held liable for damages caused by autonomous systems?

   b) List two AI Ethics.

Ans. a) It is not an easy task to blame anyone in such a scenario. Here is the situation where AI Ethics comes into the picture. Each person has a different perspective, and hence he/she takes decisions according to his/her moralities. When someone is to be liable, then it should be the programmer/developer who has designed the algorithm of the autonomous vehicle because he/she should have thought all the exceptional conditions that could arise.

   b) AI Bias, Data privacy, AI Access, AI for kids (any two).

9. What, according to you, is a better approach towards this ethical concern? Justify your answer.

Ans. AI taking over laborious jobs won't create unemployment. It is just a groundless fear. Now, some jobs are displaced by the substitution of machines for labour. This will not create total unemployment, but new jobs are created due to the technology-fuelled increase in productivity. Humans have always shifted away from work suitable for machines and to other jobs.

The basic fact is that technology eliminates jobs but not work. If this level of AI revolution happens, lots of new job opportunities will be created. For example: 20-30 years ago, a number of accountants were in demand, AI took over this job, but simultaneously it created a lot of new opportunities like the demand of a software engineer, data scientist, data entry operators, etc.

AI will open doors to skillful jobs in place of laborious tasks. Thus, we will be able to cope with the level of major unemployment when AI takes over laborious jobs.

6.3 SOLVED EXERCISES

6.3.1 Multiple Choice Questions

1. Which of the following languages is one of the most popular languages for AI nowadays?

    a) C+   b) Python   c) Ruby   d) C++

2. Which of the following robots is India's first 3D printed humanoid robot that was developed in 2014 by Diwakar Vaish-an alumni of Sharada University, Noida, UP?

Figure 6.8

    a) Rashmi   b) Satya   c) Shalu   d) Manav

3. Which is not a type of Artificial Intelligence?

    a) ATI   b) ASI   c) AGI   d) ANI

4. Which of the following is associated with the study of computer algorithms that improve their efficiency automatically through experience?

    a) Data science   b) Machine Learning (ML)

    c) Deep Learning (DL)   d) None of the above

5. Which Intelligence has the capacity and capability to understand or learn any intellectual task that a human being can.?

    a) Artificial Narrow Intelligence (ANI)   b) Artificial General Intelligence (AGI)

    c) Artificial Super Intelligence (ASI)   d) None of the above

6. Which of the following fields is associated with enabling computers for identifying and processing images as humans do?

    a) DL   b) Face Recognition

    c) Computer Vision   d) ML

7. What is the full form of NLP in connection with AI?

    a) Neural Learning Presentation   b) Neuro-Linguistic Programming

    c) Natural Language Processing   d) Natural Logic Protection

8. Which program does allow the computer to simulate conversation with a human being?

    a) Speech Application Program Interface
    b) Speech Recognition
    c) Chatbot
    d) Voice Recognition

9. Which of the following is responsible for the machine's ability to read and understand human language?

    a) CV
    b) NLP
    c) AI
    d) DL

10. Which Intelligence is associated with language processing skills both in terms of understanding or implementation in writing or verbally?

    a) Linguistical Intelligence
    b) Kinaesthetic Intelligence
    c) Musical Intelligence
    d) Interpersonal Intelligence

11. ___________ is a set of algorithms and Intelligence that tries to mimic human Intelligence.

    a) Deep Learning
    b) Machine Learning
    c) Artificial Intelligence
    d) None of the above

12. Which type of Artificial Intelligence is used in Chatbots (Alexa, Siri, Cortana, Watson) and image / facial recognition software?

    a) ANI
    b) AGI
    c) ASI
    d) None of the above

13. It is an Indian realistic lip-syncing multilingual humanoid robot that can speak four languages (English, Hindi, Bhojpuri, and Marathi), and it was developed in 2019 by Ranjit Srivastava. What is its name?

Figure 6.9

    a) China
    b) Rashmi
    c) Manavi
    d) Sheela

14. Which Intelligence describes how high the level of self-awareness someone has?

    a) Kinaesthetic Intelligence
    b) Interpersonal Intelligence
    c) Intrapersonal Intelligence
    d) Spatial Intelligence

15. Which system of Programs and Data-Structures is identified to mimic the operation of the human brain?

    a) Intelligent Network
    b) Neural Network
    c) Decision Support Network
    d) Genetic Programming

16. Which of the following is a sub-category of Machine Learning?

    a) Unsupervised Learning

    b) Supervised Learning

    c) Reinforcement Learning

    d) All of the above

17. Which Indian robot developed by a teacher of Kendriya Vidyalaya, IIT Mumbai (Mr. Dinesh Patel) can speak 9 Indian and 37 foreign languages?

Figure 6.10

    a) Rashmi

    b) Manavi

    c) Shalu

    d) Sophia

18. Which one of the following applications is not considered an application of AI?

    a) Robot drones

    b) Remote-controlled Drone

    c) Google search

    d) Self-Driving Car

19. Which website is not a price comparison website?

    a) Junglee

    b) Facebook

    c) Shopzilla

    d) DealTime

20. What are the drawbacks of AI?

    a) Limited Ability and High Cost

    b) Can't Handle Emergency Situation

    c) Difficult code and Machine Ethics

    d) All the above

21. In which analysis ML is not used?

    a) Predictive analysis

    b) Regression analysis

    c) Reaction analysis

    d) Action analysis

22. How many Sustainable Development Goals (SDGs) are identified by UNO?

    a) 15

    b) 16

    c) 17

    d) 19

23. ______________ is not one of the SDGs as proposed by UNO.

    a) No Poverty

    b) Zero illiteracy

    c) Reduced inequalities

    d) Quality education

24. Which Intelligence is about a person's ability to recognise and create sounds, rhythms, and sound patterns?

    a) Spatial Intelligence

    b) Kinaesthetic Intelligence

    c) Musical Intelligence

    d) None of the above

25. What is a common method of processing meaning from a natural language known as?

    a) CV   b) Semantic indexing

    c) Semantic analysis   d) HB

<table>
<tr><td colspan="10" align="center">ANSWERS</td></tr>
<tr><td>1. (b)</td><td>2. (d)</td><td>3. (a)</td><td>4. (b)</td><td>5. (b)</td><td>6. (c)</td><td>7. (c)</td><td>8. (a)</td><td>9. (b)</td><td>10. (a)</td></tr>
<tr><td>11. (c)</td><td>12. (b)</td><td>13. (b)</td><td>14. (c)</td><td>15. (b)</td><td>16. (d)</td><td>17. (c)</td><td>18. (b)</td><td>19. (b)</td><td>20. (d)</td></tr>
<tr><td>21. (c)</td><td>22. (c)</td><td>23. (b)</td><td>24. (c)</td><td>25. (b)</td><td></td><td></td><td></td><td></td><td></td></tr>
</table>

6.3.2 Fill in the blanks

1. Computer vision-related projects translate _____________ visual data into descriptions.

2. _____________ works to implement human Intelligence in machines: creating systems that understand, learn, think, and behave like humans.

3. _____________ is responsible for the machine's ability to read and understand human language.

4. _________ is the ability to understand social situations and the behaviour of other people.

5. _____________ refers to the ability of machines to interact with the world (speech, vision, motion, manipulation), ability to model the world and to reason about it, ability to learn, ability to make decisions, and to adapt.

6. _____________ in the office can recognize shadows or movements, but that doesn't make them an example of artificial Intelligence.

7. An automatic Washing machine is an example of _______________, not AI.

8. Most _____________ items are ordinary things outfitted with sensors and connected to the Internet.

9. __________ is the first humanoid given citizenship by a country-Saudi Arab in Oct. 2017.

10. Machines also become _____________ once they are trained with some information that helps them achieve their tasks.

11. _____________ like Google assistant, Apple's Siri, Amazon's Alexa, etc., recognize patterns in speech and then understand its meaning and provide a useful response.

12. _____________ is a common method of processing meaning from natural language.

13. AI machines also keep updating their knowledge to optimize its _____________.

14. _____________ is language processing skills both in terms of understanding or implementation in writing or verbally.

15. _____________ is defined as the ability to perceive the visual world and to find the relationship of one object to another.

Figure 6.11

ANSWERS

1. digital   2. Artificial Intelligence   3. Natural Language Processing
4. Interpersonal intelligence   5. Intelligence   6. Sensors   7. automation
8. IoT (Internet of Things)   9. Sophia   10. intelligent   11. Smart assistants
12. Semantic indexing   13. output   14. Linguistical Intelligence
15. Spatial/ Visual Intelligence

6.3.3 True or False

1. Artificial Intelligence means a human-made interface with the power to reason and integrate knowledge.
2. The AI devices must be trained with information / large data to produce the best possible accurate results.
3. The main objective of CV is to teach machines to collect information from pixels.
4. Rashmi is a humanoid robot developed in 2015 by "Hanson Robotics," Hong Kong.
5. Semantic analysis is a common method of processing meaning from natural language.
6. It makes sense to have as large a dataset as is required to include variety, subtlety, and nuance to make the model viable for practical use.
7. A fully automatic washing machine may work on its own, and it does not require human intervention to select the parameters of washing.
8. An AI-enabled machine should not only recognize but should also do something with its gathered information.
9. AI is considered a form of Intelligence, a type of technology, and a field of study.
10. Expert Systems are Software used for decision-making.
11. AI theory and development of computer systems (both machines and software) are capable of performing tasks that normally require human Intelligence.
12. Deep Learning is considered the most advanced form of Artificial Intelligence.
13. CV inputs machine the ability to read and understand human language.
14. Artificial Intelligence may be defined as a technique that enables computers to mimic human Intelligence.
15. Speech Recognition is the process of converting sound signals captured by a microphone or mobile/telephone to a set of words (70-100 words/minute with an accuracy of 90%).

Figure 6.12

ANSWERS					
1. T	2. T	3. T	4. F (Sophia)	5. F(Semantic indexing)	6. T
7. F (requires)	8. T	9. T	10. T	11. T	12. T
13. F (Natural Language Processing, not CV)			14. T	15. T	

6.3.4 Matching type

(I) Match the bank with the digital assistant used by it correctly.

Bank	**Digital assistant**
(i) Bank of America	(a) iPal
(ii) HSBC Hong Kong	(b) SIA
(iii) SEB Sweden	(c) Ceba
(iv) Commonwealth Bank, Australia	(d) Amy
(v) SBI India	(e) Aida
(vi) ICICI India	(f) Erica

ANSWERS					
(I) (i) f	(ii) d	(iii) e	(iv) c	(v) b	(vi) a

6.3.5 Assertion Reason Type Questions

1. Assertion (A): Artificial Intelligence (AI) may be defined as the simulation of human intelligence by machines. It has the ability to solve problems, the ability to act rationally, and the ability to act like humans.

    Reason (R): Intelligence may be defined as the capacity to learn and solve problems.

    a)   Both A and R are correct and R is the correct reason for A.

    b)   Both A and R are correct and R is not the correct reason for A.

    c)   A is correct but R is incorrect.

    d)   A is incorrect but R is correct.

2. Assertion (A): Linguistic reasoning is defined as a person's ability to regulate, measure, and understand numerical symbols, abstraction, and logic.

Reason (R): Emotion and social skills are essential to an intelligent agent to understand others and to make better decisions.

a) Both A and R are correct and R is the correct reason for A.

b) Both A and R are correct and R is not the correct reason for A.

c) A is correct but R is incorrect.

d) A is incorrect but R is correct.

3. Assertion (A): Linguistical Intelligence is language processing skills both in terms of understanding or implementation in writing or verbally.

Reason (R): NLP is defined as the ability of a machine to extract information from an image that is necessary to solve a task.

a) Both A and R are correct and R is the correct reason for A.

b) Both A and R are correct and R is not the correct reason for A.

c) A is correct but R is incorrect.

d) A is incorrect but R is correct.

4. Assertion (A): The main objective of CV is to teach machines to collect information from pixels.

Reason (R): Computer Vision (CV) related projects translate digital visual data into descriptions.

a) Both A and R are correct and R is the correct reason for A.

b) Both A and R are correct and R is not the correct reason for A.

c) A is correct but R is incorrect.

d) A is incorrect but R is correct.

5. Assertion (A): Kinaesthetic Intelligence is the ability that is related to how a person uses his limbs in a skilled manner.

Reason (R): Shalu was the first humanoid given Citizenship by a country-Saudi Arab in Oct. 2017.

a) Both A and R are correct and R is the correct reason for A.

b) Both A and R are correct and R is not the correct reason for A.

c) A is correct but R is incorrect.

d) A is incorrect but R is correct.

6. Assertion (A): Data science is a multidisciplinary field that combines mathematics, statistics, and computer science to apply machine learning algorithms to numbers, images, text, video, audio, etc., to produce artificial intelligence (AI) systems that perform tasks as a human does.

Reason (R): Data comes from multiple disparate systems and sources.

a) Both A and R are correct and R is the correct reason for A.

b) Both A and R are correct and R is not the correct reason for A.

c) A is correct but R is incorrect.

d) A is incorrect but R is correct.

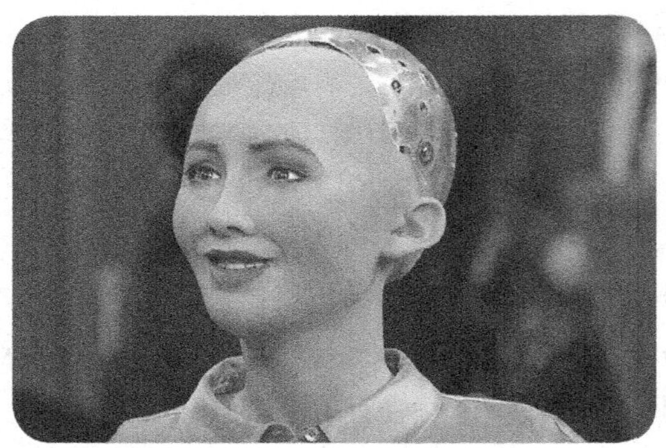

Figure 6.13 Robot Sophia

ANSWERS
1. (a)   2. (d)   3. (c)   4. (b)   5. (c)   6. (b)

6.3.6 Statements Based Questions

1. Statement 1: Deep Learning is considered the most advanced form of Artificial Intelligence.

   Statement 2: Machine Learning is defined as the ability to use input from sensors to deduce aspects of the world.

   a) Statement 1 is correct but statement 2 is incorrect.
   b) Statement 1 is incorrect but statement 2 is correct.
   c) Both the statements are correct.
   d) Both the statements are incorrect.

2. Statement 1: Goggle has produced Chatbot Alexa.

   Statement 2: Machine perception is the ability to use input from sensors to deduce aspects of the world.

Figure 6.14

   a) Statement 1 is correct but statement 2 is incorrect.
   b) Statement 1 is incorrect but statement 2 is correct.
   c) Both the statements are correct.
   d) Both the statements are incorrect.

3. Statement 1: Semantic indexing is a common method of processing meaning from natural language.

   Statement 2: Affective computing is the development of such systems that can recognize, interpret, simulate human effects.

a) Statement 1 is correct but statement 2 is incorrect.

b) Statement 1 is incorrect but statement 2 is correct.

c) Both the statements are correct.

d) Both the statements are incorrect.

4. Statement 1: NLP is defined as the ability of a machine to extract information from an image that is necessary to solve a task.

   Statement 2: Shalu is the first humanoid robot of India that can communicate in 37 languages.

   a) Statement 1 is correct but statement 2 is incorrect.

   b) Statement 1 is incorrect but statement 2 is correct.

   c) Both the statements are correct.

   d) Both the statements are incorrect.

5. Statement 1: Intrapersonal Intelligence is the ability of humans to communicate with others after understanding other people's feelings & influence on the person.

   Statement 2: Intelligence is not needed for robots to handle tasks like object manipulation and navigation.

   a) Statement 1 is correct but statement 2 is incorrect.

   b) Statement 1 is incorrect but statement 2 is correct.

   c) Both the statements are correct.

   d) Both the statements are incorrect.

6. Statement 1: NLP is responsible for a machine's ability to read and understand human language.

   Statement 2: Speech Recognition is the process of converting sound signals captured by a microphone or mobile/telephone to a set of words (70-100 words/minute with an accuracy of 90%).

   a) Statement 1 is correct but statement 2 is incorrect.

   b) Statement 1 is incorrect but statement 2 is correct.

   c) Both the statements are correct.

   d) Both the statements are incorrect.

ANSWERS
1. (a)　　2. (b)　　3. (c)　　4. (b)　　5. (d)　　6. (c)

6.3.7 Competency Based Questions

1. Rahul Pandey owns an AI firm **"Saksham AI Solutions,"** where the firm imparts training to the machines with the help of huge amounts of data (training data) for helping it in training itself around the data. After the training, the machines become intelligent enough to develop algorithms for themselves. This is an example of:

   a) NLP

   b) Deep Learning

   c) Data Sciences

   d) Advance Learning

2. In **'AnuJa AI RoboCreations'**, Prof RK Patel is working on the hypothetical concept where machines become self-aware and surpass the capacity of human intelligence and ability. These machines will supersede the humans in intelligence. With which of the following intelligence is he working?

    a) ANI

    b) ASI

    c) AGI

    d) None of the above

3. Suppose Ramita Nagpal is efficient in the process involving the selection of a course of action from among two or more possible options in order to arrive at a solution for a given problem. Which skills are possessed by her?

    a) Critical Thinking

    b) Creative Thinking

    c) Empathy

    d) Decision-making

<table>
<tr><td colspan="3" align="center">ANSWERS</td></tr>
<tr><td>1. (c)</td><td>2. (b)</td><td>3. (d)</td></tr>
</table>

6.3.8 VSA

1. Name one test used to measure Intelligence.

Ans. The Stanford-Binet Intelligence Test.

2. Who identified three types of Intelligence: practical, creative, and analytical?

Ans. Sternberg

3. What is the other name given to Practical Intelligence?

Ans. Street smartness.

4. What does it mean to be practical?

Ans. Being practical means that you find solutions that work in your everyday life by applying knowledge based on your experiences.

5. Who developed The Stanford-Binet test?

Ans. The American psychologist Lewis Terman (1877-1956)

Figure 6.15 Lewis Terman

6. For which purpose expert systems are used?

Ans. Expert Systems are Software used for decision-making.

7. Define Existential Intelligence.

Ans. Existential Intelligence is an additional category of Intelligence relating to religious and spiritual awareness.

8. Define Intelligence.

Ans. Intelligence may be defined as the ability to interact with the real world to perceive, understand and act.

9. Define decision-making.

Ans. Decision-making is defined as the process of deciding about something that is important, especially in a group of people or in an organization.

10. Who developed the first time machine with a full set of cognitive abilities?

Ans. Russel and Norvig.

11. Define AGI.

Ans. Artificial General Intelligence (AGI) is defined as the Intelligence that has the capacity and capability to understand or learn any intellectual task that a human being can perform.

12. Name India's first 3D printed humanoid robot, which was developed in 2014 by Diwakar Vaish (an alumni of Sharada University, Noida, UP)?

Ans. 'Manav.'

13. Define Narrow Artificial Intelligence.

Ans. Artificial narrow intelligence (ANI) is the type of artificial Intelligence that is goal-oriented and is designed to perform singular tasks, i.e., facial recognition, driving a car, speech recognition/voice assistants, or searching the internet.

14. Define ASI.

Ans. Artificial superintelligence (ASI) is the hypothetical concept that a machine with ASI doesn't just mimic or understand human Intelligence and behaviour, but it becomes self-aware and surpasses the capacity of human intelligence and ability.

15. Define Machine Learning (ML).

Ans. ML is a part of Artificial Intelligence that enables machines to improve at tasks with experience (Data).

16. What is the purpose of ML?

Ans. The purpose of Machine Learning is to enable machines to learn by themselves using the provided Data for making accurate Predictions/ Decisions.

17. What are fuzzy logic systems?

Ans. Fuzzy Logic Systems are devices that are based on human reasoning. Examples: Consumer electronics, automobiles, etc.

18. Define Deep Learning (DL).

Ans. In Deep Learning, the machine is trained with the help of huge amounts of data (training data) for helping it in training itself around the data. The machines become intelligent enough to develop algorithms for themselves.

19. What are the three domains of AI?

Ans. Domains of AI are Data, CV, and NLP.

20. Define Data Sciences.

Ans. Data science is a multidisciplinary field that combines mathematics, statistics, and computer science to apply machine learning algorithms to numbers, images, text, video, audio, etc., to produce artificial intelligence (AI) systems that perform tasks as a human does.

21. Name the technique/way of making a computer, a computer-controlled robot think intelligently, in a similar manner to how intelligent humans think.

Ans. Artificial Intelligence

22. What is Intelligence?

Ans. The ability to think, solve problems, learn from experience, and adapt to new situations is called Intelligence.

23. What is the ability to use input from sensors to deduce aspects of the world known as?

Ans. Machine perception

24. What is speech recognition?

Ans. Speech Recognition is the process of converting sound signals captured by a microphone or mobile/telephone to a set of words (70-100 words/minute with an accuracy of 90%).

25. Which company has produced Chatbot Alexa?

Ans. Amazon

26. Which Intelligence is an additional category of Intelligence relating to religious and spiritual awareness?

Ans. Existential Intelligence

27. What do you mean by Artificial Super Intelligence?

Ans. Artificial superintelligence (ASI) is the hypothetical concept where machines become self-aware and surpass the capacity of human intelligence and ability.

28. What do you mean by decision-making?

Ans. The process of decision-making involves the selection of a course of action from among two or more possible options in order to arrive at a solution for a given problem.

29. Define naturalist intelligence.

Ans. Naturalist Intelligence is an additional category of Intelligence relating to the ability to process information on the environment around us.

30. Which is the first humanoid robot of the world that is given citizenship of a country?

Ans. Sophia

31. Define computer vision (CV).

Ans. Computer Vision is defined as the ability of a machine to extract information from an image that is necessary to solve a task.

32. What is the purpose of Machine Learning?

Ans. To enable machines to learn by themselves using the training Data for making accurate Predictions/ Decisions is the purpose of ML.

33. What is the most common source of data collection by many companies?

Ans. Smartphones

34. What is the full form of IoT?

Ans. Internet of Things

Figure 6.16

35. What do you mean by AI Ethics?

Ans. The ethics of AI lies in the ethical quality of its prediction, the ethical quality of the end outcomes drawn out of that, and the ethical quality of the impact it has on human beings.

36. Which Intelligence is known as the ability related to how a person uses his limbs in a skilled manner?

Ans. Kinaesthetic Intelligence

37. What do you mean by interpersonal Intelligence?

Ans. The ability to communicate with others after understanding other people's feelings & influence on the person.

38. What is Deep Learning?

Ans. Deep Learning deals with a large amount of data which enables software to train itself to perform tasks dealing.

39. Define Fuzzy Logic Systems.

Ans. Fuzzy Logic Systems are devices that are based on human reasoning.

40. Robot Shalu can speak 9 Indian and 37 Foreign languages. It was developed by Mr. Dinesh Patel. Who is he?

Ans. A teacher in Kendriya Vidyalaya, IIT, Mumbai.

41. Why is intelligence needed for robots?

Ans. Intelligence is needed for robots to handle tasks like object manipulation and navigation.

42. What is mathematical and logical reasoning?

Ans. Mathematical and logical reasoning is defined as a person's ability to regulate, measure, and understand numerical symbols, abstraction, and logic.

43. What do you mean by Spatial Visual Intelligence?

Ans. Spatial Visual Intelligence is defined as the ability to perceive the visual world and the relationship of one object to another.

44. In how many ways can AI Bias creep into algorithms?

Ans. Three: Existing bias, technical bias, and emergent bias.

45. What is the full form of NLP?

Ans. Natural Language Processing

46. Name two common machine learning applications.

Ans. Targeted marketing, recommendation engine, Customer churn prevention, Sentiment analysis, Risk Management, Anti-money laundering, Fraud detection (any two).

47. Give two examples of price comparison websites.

Ans. PriceGrabber, Junglee, Shopzilla, PriceRunner, DealTime, etc.

48. What is the main focus of ML?

Ans. Machine learning mainly deals with a focus on the development of computer programs that can access data and use it to improve.

49. What is KDD?

Ans. Data mining is also termed Knowledge Discovery in Data (KDD)

50. What is included in the study of data sciences?

Ans. Data science is defined as the field of study that combines programming skills, domain expertise, and knowledge of mathematics and statistics to explore data to have meaningful decisions.

51. Explain Data Sciences with a suitable example.

Ans. Data Sciences is a concept to unify data analysis, statistics, machine learning, and the related methods to understand and analyses actual phenomena with data. Example: a company has petabytes of user data may use data science to develop effective ways to store, manage, and analyse the data.

52. What is mainly dealt with in Computer Vision?

Ans. Computer Vision is an interdisciplinary field dealing with how computers can be made to gain a high-level understanding of digital images or videos.

53. Mention two examples of smart machines.

Ans. Smartwatches, smart TV, smart (automatic) washing machine, etc.

54. Explain Computer Vision with suitable examples.

Ans. CV is a domain of Artificial Intelligence that enables machines to see-through images or visual data, process and analyze them on the basis of algorithms and methods to analyze actual phenomena with images. Example: Self-Driving cars/ Automatic Cars, Face Lock in Smartphones

55. Define the term "robot ethics."

Ans. The term "robot ethics" (sometimes "roboethics") is related to the morality of how human beings design, construct, use and treat robots.

56. Define linguistic intelligence.

Ans. Linguistic intelligence is defined as the ability of an individual to understand both written and spoken language and to write and speak the language.

57. What is included in linguistic intelligence?

Ans. Linguistic intelligence includes the ability to speak, articulate, and express, and convey one's thoughts and feelings to other people in one or more languages. This can be at an oral or written level. It includes the ability to listen to and understand other people.

58. What is the relation between deep learning (DL) and decision-making?

Ans. Deep learning is an artificial intelligence (AI) function to imitate the workings of the human brain in processing data and creating and analyzing patterns for use in decision making.

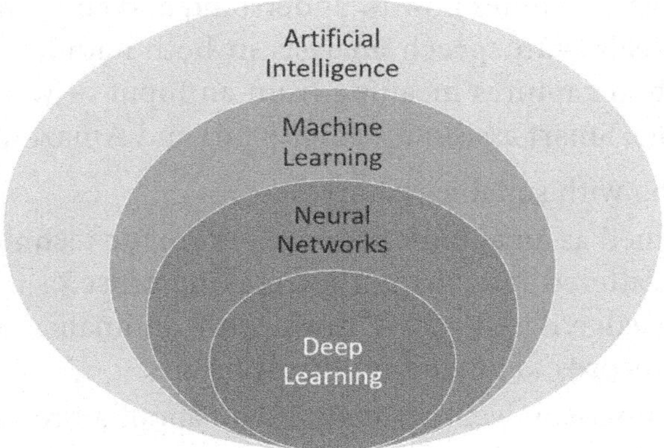

Figure 6.17

6.3.9 Short Answer Type Questions

1. Differentiate between human Intelligence and artificial Intelligence.

Ans. Human Intelligence is the mental quality that consists of the abilities to learn from experience, adapt to new situations, understand and handle abstract concepts, and use knowledge to manipulate one's environment. However, Artificial Intelligence is a set of algorithms and Intelligence that try to mimic human Intelligence.

2. What are the four different types of fundamental Intelligence?

Ans. Mark Oliver identified four fundamental bits of intelligence which are as follows:

   a) IQ (Intelligence Quotient),   b) EQ (Emotional Intelligence),

   c) PQ (Physical Intelligence), and   d) SQ (Spiritual Intelligence).

3. What are the eight types of intelligence as described by Howard Gardner?

Ans. Visual-spatial Intelligence, linguistic-verbal Intelligence, logical-mathematical Intelligence, bodily-kinaesthetic Intelligence, Musical Intelligence, interpersonal Intelligence, intrapersonal Intelligence, and naturalistic Intelligence.

4. Differentiate between 'Fluid Intelligence' and 'Crystallized Intelligence.'

Ans. Fluid Intelligence is the capacity of machines to learn new methods of solving problems and performing activities, whereas Crystallized Intelligence is the accumulated knowledge of the world humans have acquired throughout their lives.

Thus, Crystallized Intelligence increases with age, whereas fluid Intelligence tends to decrease with age.

5. Explain NLP.

Ans. Natural Language Processing, or NLP, is the sub-field of AI that deals with the process of enabling machines/computers to understand and process human languages. Thus, AI is a subfield of Linguistics, Information Engineering, Computer Science, and Artificial Intelligence concerned with the interactions between computers and natural languages. In particular, how to program computers to process and analyze large amounts of natural language data.

6. Explain NLP with suitable examples.

Ans. In NLP, humans train machines how to understand and communicate in human language. Natural language deals with speech analysis in both audible speeches and the text of a language. NLP system captures meaning from an input of words (sentences, paragraphs, pages, etc.). Example: Smart assistants: Apple's Siri and Amazon's Alexa and Email filters.

7. Explain Data mining with suitable examples.

Ans. Data mining is defined as an automatic /semi-automatic technical process used to analyse large amounts of scattered information for making sense of it and turning it into useful information/ knowledge/decisions. It deals with anomalies, patterns, and correlations among millions of records to predict results/decisions.

Example: Price Comparison websites collect data about a product from different sites and then analyze trends/patterns out of it and show up the most appropriate results.

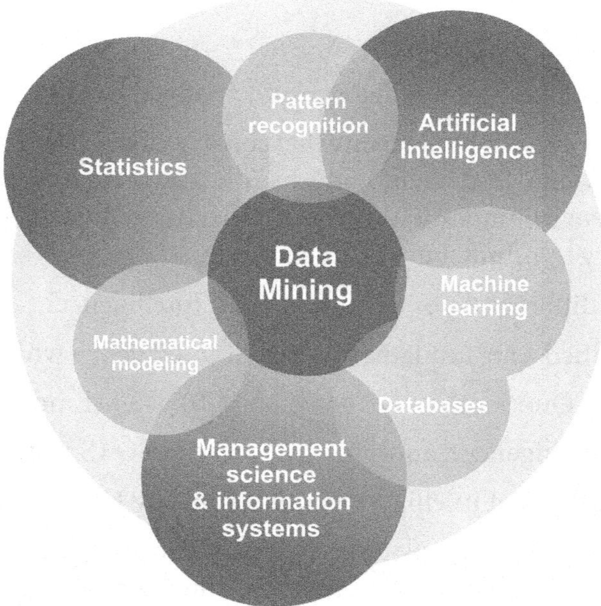

Figure 6.18

8. What are the types of AI?

Ans. There are three types of Artificial Intelligence (AI):

    a) Narrow or weak AI (ANI)

    b) General or strong AI (AGI)

    c) Artificial superintelligence (ASI)

9. Why is ANI called weak AI?

Ans. While the machines using ANI may seem intelligent, they operate under a narrow set of constraints and limitations. That's why this type of Intelligence is commonly known as weak AI. Weak/Narrow AI doesn't mimic or replicate human Intelligence; it only simulates human behaviour based on a narrow range of parameters and contexts.

10. What is the basis for good decision-making?

Ans. The basis of decision-making depends upon the availability of information, one's experience, and understanding. Here, 'information' means our past experience, intuition, knowledge, and self-awareness. We will be able to make effective decisions with correct and valid information because then we have to deal with unknown factors.

11. Why should we not fear ASI?

Ans. Most of the researchers/scientists agree that a super-intelligent AI is not likely to exhibit human emotions like love or hate and hence there is no reason to expect AI to become intentionally benevolent or malevolent.

12. Explain the Computer Vision domain in brief.

Ans. **Computer Vision:** Computer Vision (CV) is the scientific technology that obtains information from images, video, or any other visual data. CV involves methods of acquiring, processing, analyzing, and understanding digital images and extraction of data from the real and visual world to produce information.

Few Examples of Computer Vision:

(a) **Self-Driving cars/ Automatic Cars:** CV systems fitted in self-driving cars is able to scan live objects and analyze them based on whether the car decides to keep running or to stop.

Figure 6.19

(Photo courtesy: https://www.ntd.com/ford-self-driving-cars-to-launch-in-austin-in-2021_384352.html)

(b) **Face Lock in Smartphones:** Some smartphones come with the feature of face locks where the Smartphone's owner may set up his/her face as an unlocking mechanism for the same. The front camera of the Smartphone detects and captures the face to save its features during the initiation process. Next time onwards, whenever the features of the user match, the phone is unlocked.

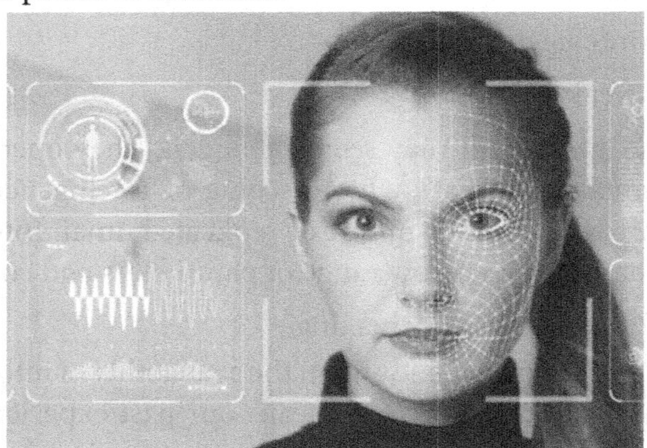

Figure 6.20
(Photo courtesy: https://face-id-face-lock-screen.en.softonic.com/android)

13. What is training data? Why is it used?

Ans. Machine learning algorithms usually build a model based on sample data, which is known as "training data." This is used to make predictions or decisions without being explicitly programmed to do so.

14. What are the different forms of data?

Ans. The data may be numeric, text, audio, video, image, etc., which is converted to numeric form for extraction, preparation, analysis, visualization, and maintenance of information.

15. What do you mean by Price Comparison Websites? Give some examples.

Ans. Price Comparison Websites are the websites that compare the price of a product from multiple vendors in one place.

Examples: PriceGrabber, Junglee, Shopzilla, PriceRunner, DealTime, etc.

16. Enlist three examples of AI Research areas.

Ans. The examples of Research areas of AI are:

a) **Expert Systems:** Related to those devices that can be trained for working like humans.
   Examples: flight-tracking systems, Clinical systems.

b) **Neural Networks:** Related to those devices that work the way human brain neurons work.
   Examples: Pattern recognition systems, like face recognition, character recognition, handwriting recognition.

c) **Natural Language Processing:** Related to those devices that use human language for operating.
   Examples: Google Now features, speech recognition, Automatic voice output.

17. Define and illustrate the function of Computer Vision (CV).

Ans. Computer Vision is a domain of AI that depicts the capability of a machine to get and analyze visual information to predict some decisions about it. The process involves image acquiring, screening, analyzing, identifying, and extracting information. This processing helps computers to understand the visual content for acting on it.

18. What is the input to machines in CV? Mention suitable examples.

Ans. In computer vision, input to machines may be images, photographs, videos, and pictures from thermal or infrared sensors, indicators, and different sources. Thus, CV is the technology for building artificial systems that obtain information from images, video, or any other visual data. Examples of Computer Vision include Self-Driving cars/ Automatic Cars.

19. Explain the meaning of AI Ethics.

Ans. Artificial Intelligence is the latest technology, but this technology is not accessible by everyone. Rather we can say that not everyone has the opportunity to access it. There are people who can interact with the device and use it effectively but still, a large part of society lack behind in using it. This gap between the people who can access and the ones who cannot process increasing day try day. This is due to the reason that those who access it are using it increasingly for performing many operations, whereas those who are not using it are still reluctant to use it in the future also.

20. Explain the main objective of Natural Language Processing

Ans. Natural Language Processing (NLP) is a domain of Artificial Intelligence that deals with the interaction between computers and human beings by using natural language. Natural language means a language that is used (spoken and written) by people. Natural language processing (NLP) enacts to extract information from the spoken and written word by using algorithms. The main objective of NLP is to read, decipher, understand, and make sense of human languages in a manner that is valuable.

21. Define the role of AI in the marketing sector.

Ans. Searching the products online is an easy way these days. Many online search sites have been available since the early 2000s. When we search for an item on an e-commerce website, we get all possible results related to the item. Searching for the product of your choice is just a click away. With AI technology, these search engines can now read our minds, and in a fraction of a second, we get a list of all relevant items based on our searches. An example of finding the movies of choice on Netflix. It examines millions of records to suggest this and films and based on your previous actions and choices of films. As the data set becomes larger, this technology is getting smarter and smarter every day.

Similarly, Amazon, Flipkart, Snapdeal, and many more commerce sites are using AI technology for selling products. AI has become an important part of selling goods online with various brands, and the features deployed in a structured manner are just a click away.

22. Explain two examples of Natural Language Processing.

Ans. (a) **Email filters:** Email filters are used to filter and classify emails using NLP. It started with spam filters, uncovering certain words or phrases that signal a spam message.

Figure 6.21

(b) **Smart assistants:** Smart assistants (Apple's Siri and Amazon's Alexa) recognize patterns in speech, then infer meaning and provide a useful response.

23. Explain "what is not AI" with the help of two examples.

Ans. All the devices that are automatically operated are not AI. We can understand this through the following examples:

   a) **An automatic car toy:** The car toy which is made nowadays by students as a part of a project is not AI. This car might be remote-driven, but it cannot run on its own. It needs to be operated by a remote, so it is not AI.

   b) **Automatic washing machine:** We feed the washing instruction in an automatic washing machine. The machine operates as per the instruction fed inside, but these instructions are not making it Artificial Intelligent. The machine is pre-programmed for doing the work. It is again not a part of AI as it is not doing any processing on its own rather, it is just following the instructions given, which is a part of automation.

24. How do you percieve AI in reference to ethics?

Ans. Artificial Intelligence can be sub-divided into a concern with the moral behaviour of human beings as they design, construct, use and treat artificial intelligent beings, and machine ethics, which is concerned with the moral behaviour of artificial moral agents (AMAs).

25. Discuss the use of data in the AI application.

Ans. All the new applications that are installed on your mobile or laptop need your permission to access your data in the form of audio-video, images, or contact. Once you allow, these applications are then ready to work on your devices using all the resources you allow. These resources are being accessed for data gathering, and then later, the Data is further analyzed. The best example is the online shopping app "AMAZON, which displays suggestions based on the search data given by you. Similarly, other online shopping apps Flipkart, Snapdeal also display suggestions based on the terms that you search online.

26. What is the importance of interpersonal Intelligence?

Ans. Interpersonal Intelligence is defined as the ability of a person to relate well with people and manage relationships, enabling people to understand the needs and motivations of those around them. This helps strengthen their overall influence.

27. When is a machine called to have artificial Intelligence?

Ans. When a machine has the ability to mimic human traits, i.e., learn, make decisions, predict the future, and improve on its own, it is said to have artificial Intelligence.

28. How does a machine get trained?

Ans. An AI machine gets trained first on the training data, and then it optimizes itself as per its own experiences, which makes AI different from any other technological device/machine.

29. How do you define Intelligence?

Ans. Intelligence involves abstract reasoning, mental representation, problem-solving, and decision-making, the ability to learn, creativity, emotional knowledge, and adaptation to meet the challenges of the environment effectively.

30. How has AI influenced human lives?

Ans. AI has changed the lives of human beings. It has changed the gaming world in terms of emotions and feelings. Some video games react to players' skill levels. Depending on how well a user does, adaptive AI changes the game's difficulty level and down to give the user a greater challenge. AI can also adapt to the user's playing style by making the game more exciting.

6.3.10 Long Answer Type Questions

1. Explain the meaning of Howard Gardner's Eight Specific bits of Intelligence.

Ans. Howard Gardener identified the following eight bits of intelligence:

Figure 6.22 Howard Gardener

i. **Linguistic Intelligence:** The ability to speak and write well

ii. **Logical-mathematical Intelligence:** The ability to use logic and mathematical skills to solve problems

iii. **Spatial Intelligence:** The ability to think and reason about objects in three dimensions

iv. **Musical Intelligence:** The ability to perform and enjoy music

v. **Kinaesthetic (bodily) Intelligence:** The ability to move the body in sports, dance, or other physical activities

vi. **Interpersonal Intelligence:** The ability to understand and interact effectively with other humans.

vii. **Intrapersonal Intelligence:** The ability to have insight into the self

viii. **Naturalistic Intelligence:** The ability to recognize, identify and understand animals, plants, and other living things.

2. What are the seven steps for decision-making?

Ans. Seven steps in decision making are as follows:

i.   Defining the problem

ii.   Gathering information and collecting data

iii. Identifying evidences / alternatives

iv.   Weighing each available option

v.   Choosing the best possible option

vi.   Planning and execution

vii. Taking follow up action

3. Enlist different challenges in the decision-making process.

Ans. The following are the challenges in decision making:

i.   Time Constraints

ii.   Biases

iii. Opinions and objectivity

iv.   Bounded Rationality

v.   Conflict

vi.   Overconfidence About the Future

vii. Impulsiveness (due to stress, time constraints, etc.)

viii. Uncertainty

ix.   Escalation of Commitment

x.   Short-term emotion tempts to Make the Wrong Choice.

xi.   Narrow framing prevents from seeing the options.

Figure 6.23

4. Differentiate between individual and group decision-making.

Ans. The main differences are enlisted in the following table:

Individual Decision Making	**Group Decision Making**
(i) An individual person normally makes prompt decisions and requires less time.	(i) A group is dominated by various people; decision-making is very time-consuming.

Individual Decision Making	Group Decision Making
(ii) Individuals do not escape responsibilities. Individuals are accountable for their acts and performance.	(ii) In a group, it is not easy to hold any one person accountable for a wrong decision.
(iii) The individual decision-making process saves time, money, and energy as individuals make prompt and logical decisions generally.	(iii) The group decision-making process consumes more time, money, and energy as group decision-making is not an easy task to make prompt and logical decisions.
(iv) Individual decisions are more focused and rational as compared to group decisions.	(iv) Group decisions are less focused and rational as compared to individual decisions.

5. Explain Artificial Intelligence as defined by different scientists and / organizations.

Ans. (a) Authors of the book 'Artificial Intelligence: A Modern Approach, Stuart Russell and Peter Norvig, describe the intelligent agents in machines and define AI as *"the study of agents that receive precepts from the environment and perform actions."*

(b) Norvig and Russell used four different approaches to define the field of AI:

- Thinking humanly
- Thinking rationally
- Acting rationally
- Acting humanly

The first two ideas are related to thought processes and reasoning, whereas the other two deal with behaviour.

(c) According to Patrick Winston (the professor of artificial Intelligence at MIT), "AI is algorithms that are enabled by constraints, exposed by representations that support models targeted at loops, and that tie thinking, perception and action together."

(d) **Jeremy Achin, CEO DataRobot** defined AI as follows:

'Artificial Intelligence is a computer system capable of performing various tasks that normally require human Intelligence. Some of these artificial intelligence systems are powered by machine learning, while some of them are powered by deep learning, and a very few are powered by very boring things like rules'.

(e) According to **NITI Aayog**, *"AI refers to the ability of machines to perform cognitive tasks like thinking, perceiving, learning, problem-solving, and decision making."*

(f) As per **World Economic Forum**, *"Artificial intelligence (AI) is the software engine that drives the Fourth Industrial Revolution, and its impact can already be seen in homes, businesses, and political processes."*

(g) According to **European Artificial Intelligence leadership (EUAIL),** *"AI is not a well-defined technology, and no universally agreed definition exists. It is a cover term used for techniques associated with data analysis and pattern recognition".*

Thus, AI can also be defined as follows:

"AI is a form of Intelligence, a type of technology, and a field of study, and development of computer systems (both machines and software) that enables machines to perform tasks that normally need human Intelligence."

Hence, it can be summarised that when a machine possesses the ability to mimic human traits, i.e., it makes decisions, predict the future, learn and improve on its own, it is said to possess artificial Intelligence. In other words, a machine is artificially intelligent when it can accomplish tasks by itself, such as collecting data, understanding it, analysing it, learning from it, and improving it.

6. Elaborate on the advantages of AI.

Ans. AI has the following advantages:

a) The chances of error are almost nil.

b) It can be used for reducing time in time-consuming tasks effectively.

c) It can be used to explore the space and depths of the ocean.

d) Smartphones are the greatest example of AI.

e) Algorithms can help doctors to assess patients and their health risks.

f) Machines do not require breaks or sleep, and thus, they are capable of functioning without stopping.

7. Give six examples of Narrow AI.

Ans. Some of the examples of ANI are enlisted below:

a) Virtual assistants, like Alexa by Amazon, IBM's Watson, Siri by Apple, Cortana by Microsoft, etc.

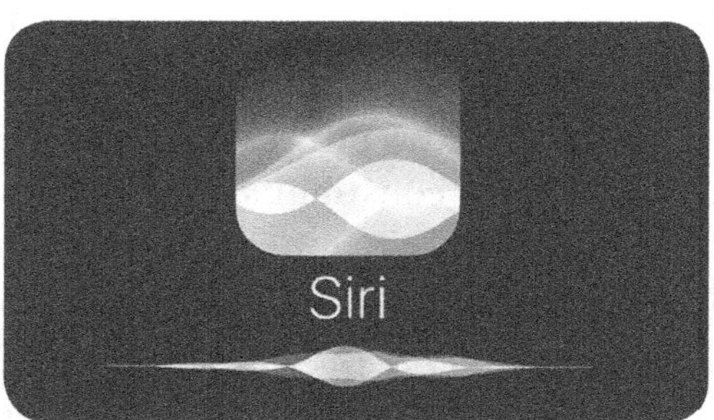

Figure 6.24

b) Self-driving cars

c) Google search

d) Drone robots

e) Email spam filters

f) Social media (like Facebook, Twitter, Instagram, etc.) monitoring tools for dangerous content/spams

g) Rank brain by Google

h) Image / facial recognition software

i) Disease mapping and prediction tools

j) Line manufacturing units

8. Discuss the various types of analysis used in ML.

Ans. Four different types of analysis are used in ML:

i. **Predictive Analysis:** It is used for using various AI techniques for different data processes, like data mining, data exploration, etc., to 'predict' the behaviour of possible outcomes.

ii. **Regression Analysis:** It is a kind of predictive technique that is based on the interaction between a dependent (target) and independent variable(s).

iii. **Action Analysis:** In this analysis, all the actions carried out by the two techniques mentioned above are analyzed, and then the outcome is fed into the machine learning memory for taking action.

iv. **Statistical Modelling:** It involves building a mathematical description of a real-world process and elaborating the uncertainties, if any, within that process.

9. Enlist the various fields of AI.

Ans. The various fields of AI are as follows:

a) Graphical User Interface

b) Automatic Storage management

c) Object-Oriented Programming (OOP)

d) Data mining

e) Speech Recognition

f) Computer gaming

g) Telecommunication

h) Automated Online Assistants

i) Voice dialing

10. Elaborate some common Machine Learning applications.

Ans. The following are the applications of ML:

a) Fraud detection (electricity pilferage, fraudulent transactions)

b) Cybersecurity

c) Customer-oriented Marketing

d) Targeted marketing

e) Sentiment analysis

f) Risk Management

g) Recommendation engine

h) Next best action

i) Customer churn prevention

j) Anti-money laundering

k) Know your customer Supply Chain Management

l) Reduction of freight costs/Optimal routing

m) Damage identification/Mechanical repair

11. Explain some of the applications of AI.

Ans. Human beings are using the applications of Artificial Intelligence in day-to-day life. They are surrounded by so many machines that work on AI. They are becoming an important part of our everyday life. They provide us with the ease of having even some of the most complicated and time-consuming tasks in a minute.

Some of the applications of Artificial Intelligence are as follows:

- Smartphones
- Self-driving cars
- Drones
- Smart assistants (like Siri and Alexa)
- Disease mapping and prediction tools
- Video games
- Manufacturing and drone robots
- Facial recognition devices
- E-banking and e-commerce
- Smart email Apps (Spam filters in email)
- Tools for Social media monitoring for dangerous content or false news
- Songs or TV shows recommendations from Spotify and Netflix
- Online Ads Network
- Smart speakers
- Expert Systems
- Online Games
- Rapid translation of foreign language
- Remote-controlled surgical procedures
- Decoding of enemy secret codes

12. How has AI affected our lives? Explain.

Ans. AI has made our lives easier, and at the same time, it has been taking care of our habits, likes, and dislikes. That's why platforms like YouTube, Netflix, Amazon, Spotify, etc., show us recommendations on the basis of what we like or visit on the net. These recommendations are not just limited to our preferences, but they even cater to our actual needs of connecting with old friends on social media platforms with apps like Facebook, COO, and Instagram. They also send us customized notifications about our online shopping details, auto-create playlists according to our requests and likes, and so on. Taking selfies has become fun as Snapchat filters make them look so cool. AI is also used to monitor our health, like the use of health watches. A number of chatbots and other health apps are available nowadays, which continuously monitor the physical and mental health of their users. These applications are not only limited to smart devices, but also they vary to humanoids like Sophia- the first humanoid robot to get citizenship of a country, biometric security systems like the face locks used in mobile phones, real-time language translators, weather forecasts, and so on.

Figure 6.25

13. What is AI and IoT but not AI? Explain with suitable examples.

Ans. Because we have a lot of different technologies that exist around us in today's real-time, it is common for us to misunderstand any other technology like AI. So, we need to have a clear distinction between what is AI and what is not. Any machine that has been trained with training data and can make decisions/predictions on its own can be termed AI. Here, the term 'training' is very important. A fully automatic washing machine may work on its own. But it requires human intervention for selecting the parameters of washing and to do the necessary preparation for it to function correctly before washing each time, which makes it an example of automation, not AI.

In smart homes, an air conditioner can be turned on and off remotely with the help of the internet but still needs a human touch. This is an example of the Internet of Things (IoT), not of AI.

Robotics and AI have definitely opened the doors to develop humanoids and self-driving cars. AI, when merged with the internet of things (IoT), gives rise to cloud computing of data and remote access of AI tools. Automation along with AI is used in achieving automated voice homes, etc. Such integrations may help us get the best of both worlds.

14. Enumerate the drawbacks/limitations of AI.

Ans. AI has the following drawbacks/limitations:

    a) Can't Handle Emergency Situation

    b) Limited Ability

    c) Difficult code

    d) High Cost

    e) Machine Ethics

    f) Slow Real-Time Response

    g) Decrease in demand for human labour

    h) AI may also be programmed to do something horrible/devastating.

    i) The storage and access are not as easy and effective as human brains.

    j) No improvement with experience

Figure 6.26

6.3.11 HOTS Questions

1. How can AI bias creep into algorithms?

Ans. AI Bias can creep into algorithms in many ways, like:

   a) Existing bias,

   b) Technical bias, and

   c) Emergent bias

2. Why is it necessary that training data should not be biased for Deep Learning (DL)?

Ans. It is a fact now that 'Deep Learning' depends on training data. Hence, if we train the model using biased data, then the results will be biased AI systems. Normally the training data is not always "clean," and it does not represent society as a whole. When we are going to use machine learning algorithms to make important decisions, then we must use clean data. Otherwise, it will end up in a biased situation.

3. What will happen when AI is programmed to do something beneficial to mankind but develops a destructive method for achieving its goal?

Ans. This may happen whenever we fail to program the AI's goals, and hence, there may be serious negative impacts on the environment or nature. Example: When a super intelligent system is tasked with an ambitious geoengineering project, then it might destroy our ecosystem as a side effect.

4. Where does the ethics of AI lie?

Ans. The ethics of AI lies in the ethical quality of its prediction, the ethical quality of the end outcomes drawn out of that, and the ethical quality of the impact it has on humans.

5. Discuss the four principles of AI Ethics used by AI companies to make AI products trustworthy.

Ans. The following principles of AI Ethics are used by AI companies to make AI products trustworthy:

   i. **Principle 1:** Ethical Purpose: How to make sure the AI's actions have a net good to society.

   ii. **Principle 2:** Fairness: Ensuring the AI's actions avoid entrenching historical disadvantage and avoid discriminating on sensitive features.

   iii. **Principle 3:** Disclosure: Disclosing sufficient information to an AI's stakeholders so that they can make informed decisions.

   iv. **Principle 4:** Governance: Where there is a risk, apply high standards of governance over the design, training, deployment, and operation of AIs.

6. Describe the relationship between AI and unemployment.

Ans. On the one hand, AI is making people's lives easier; it is creating unemployment on the other hand. Most of the things now are done in just a few clicks. In no time, AI will manage to do all the laborious tasks which humans have been doing for a long. Maybe in the coming few years, AI-enabled machines will replace all the labourers at workplaces. This process may start a problem of mass unemployment when people having little or no skills may live without jobs, and others who keep up with their skills according to what is required will flourish. This may bring humans to a crossroads.

7. How do you perceive the future of AI?

Ans. The future of AI is really uncertain as researchers do not agree on the issues related to AI. When we see the rate at which technology is improving, it is logical to say and believe that AI will continue to get more and more sophisticated. Over the years, AI is getting exponentially sophisticated. Personal assistants will become more personal and context-aware. More and more systems/robots will run autonomously. Hence, it may be concluded that AI research will have a positive impact on humanity.

8. How is ML considered as data analytics?

Ans. Machine learning is a data analytics technique that teaches computers to do what comes naturally to humans and animals.

9. How does a machine learn in deep learning?

Ans. Deep learning is a subset of machine learning where artificial neural networks, algorithms inspired by the human brain, learn from large amounts of data.

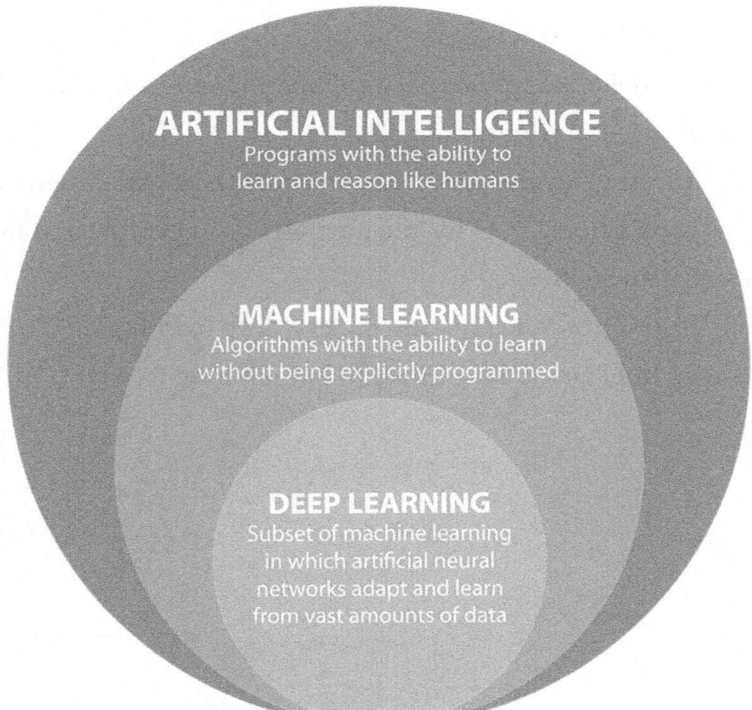

Figure 6.27

6.4 PRACTICE QUESTIONS

1. Differentiate between Intelligence and artificial Intelligence.

2. Define sustainable development.

3. What is the meaning of SDGs?

4. Define AI Ethics. Illustrate with suitable examples.

5. What do you mean by AI bias? Write main types of AI Bias.

6. Can someone steal/hack your personal information and sell it to others? How is it possible?

7. How do most companies collect data?

8. Is it right to share users' data collected by websites with other organizations/ companies? Justify your answer.

9. What will happen when your personal Data is leaked/hacked?

10. Differentiate among Data, CV, and NLP.

11. Define and illustrate Supervised Learning.

12. How has Al affected the financial sector of Indian society?

13. Explain with suitable example Reinforcement Learning.

14. Enlist three uses of Deep Learning.

15. How will AI ethics play an important role in the future?

16. Differentiate between Machine Learning and Deep Learning.

17. What is the future of AI? Express your opinion.

18. Explain the various fields where AI is helpful in our day-to-day life.

19. How far do social sites use Al technology?

20. How does deep learning depend on data? Explain with suitable examples.

21. Explain various applications of AI for the purpose of supporting sustainable development.

22. Enlist the names of any 6 SDGs.

23. Discuss the applications of Machine Learning or deep learning.

24. How can Artificial Intelligence be a threat to human Intelligence?

AI Project Cycle

7.1 UNIT IN BRIEF

✦ The components of an AI Project Cycle are Problem Scoping, Data acquisition, Data exploration, Modelling, and Evaluation.

✦ The problem statement gives a clear idea about the basic framework required to achieve the goal.

Figure 7.1

✦ Data Acquisition is a process to collect data for the problem scoped, which has to be correct, authentic, and reliable. It is the second component of the AI Project Cycle after the problem scoping.

✦ Data is defined as the raw fact, which is organised together to form information that needs to be processed further for analysis and data visualisation.

✦ Training data is used to give the AI machine a set of inputs on which the machine will be assessed later on.

✦ The training data needs to be reliable, authentic, and accurate for the AI machine to work efficiently.

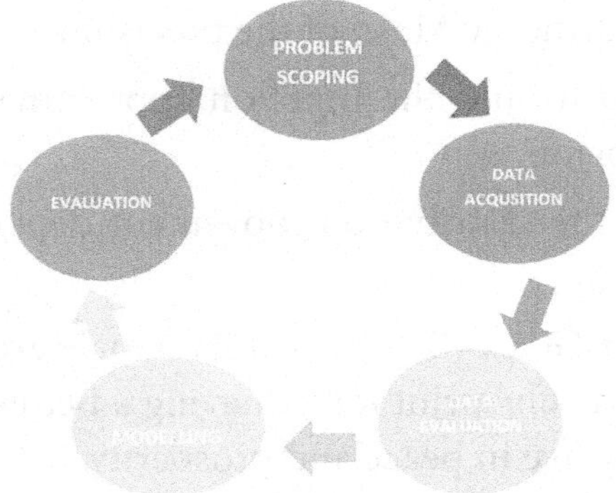

Figure 7.2

+ Testing data is used to assess the AI machine for its efficiency and performance too.

+ Data features can be collected from various sources like newspapers, cameras, observations, surveys, questionnaires, and so on.

+ Open-sourced websites are the government portals to provide the information to be used and referred to in data analytics. These websites/portals are authentic, accurate, and reliable.

+ Some of the open-sourced websites are as follows:

https://www.india.gov.in/data-portal-india

https://data.gov.in/

https://dbie.rbi.org.in/DBIE/dbie.rbi?site=home

http://mospi.nic.in/data

+ Neural Network is a mesh of one input layer and multiple hidden Layers.

+ All elements in the AI system are interconnected, and one has to understand the elements and relationships between the elements to understand the system.

+ The concept of a loop defines a chain of events in the system and relationships between them.

+ A testing dataset is a dataset provided to the model ML algorithm after training the algorithm.

+ The change in one element in an AI-based project affects the other elements. Moreover, the elements are interdependent, and hence, removing or changing any element in the system will imbalance the whole system.

+ LOOPY is defined as an interactive tool that can be used to play with simulations in real-time without using any coding.

+ The evaluation stage is to evaluate whether the ML algorithm is able to predict with high accuracy or not before deployment.

+ A decision tree is a simple graphical representation for classifying examples.

+ Decision tree learning is one of the most successful techniques for supervised classification learning.

+ Data analysis means a process of cleaning, transforming, and modelling data to discover useful information for business decision-making.

+ Recall indirectly tells us the model's ability to randomly identify an observation that belongs to the positive class.

+ F1 Score is also termed the Harmonic Mean of the precision and recall Evaluation Metrics.

+ Mathematically, one is trying to find the function approximation with the minimum error deviation in a regression problem.

+ Regression can also identify the distribution movement depending on the available data or historical data.

+ The Sustainable Development Goals (SDGs)/ Global Goals are a collection of 17 interlinked goals that were designed like a "blueprint for achieving a better and sustainable future for all" so that future generations may live in peace and prosperity.

✦ Regression is defined as the process of finding a model for defining the data into continuous real values instead of discrete values. It can also identify the distribution movement that depends on the historical data.

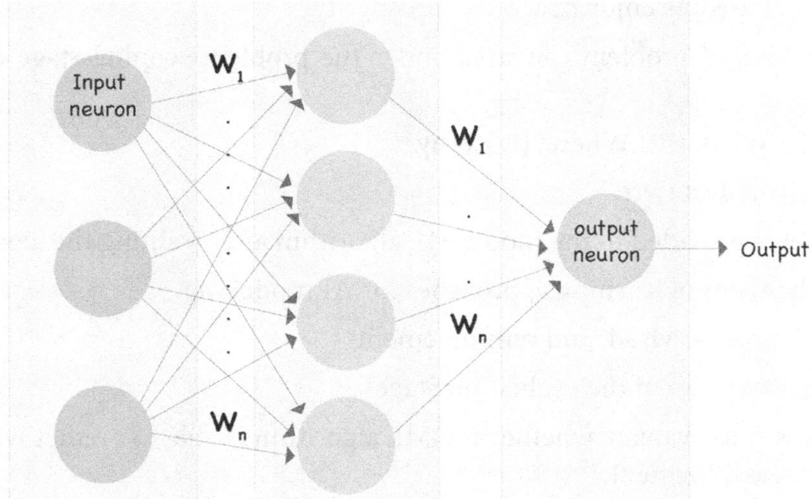

Figure 7.3

7.2 CBSE/NCERT SECTION (SOLVED CBSE/NCERT EXERCISE QUESTIONS)

(A) MCQs

1. Which source is not an authentic source for data acquisition?

   a) Sensors
   b) Surveys
   c) Web Scraping
   d) System Hacking

   Ans: d) System Hacking

(B) Fill in the Blanks

1. The analogy of an Artificial Neural Network can be made with ______________.

Ans. Parallel Processing.

2. Neural Network is a mesh of multiple ______________.

Ans. Hidden Layers

(C) VSA (One Mark Questions)

1. Which type of graphical representation suits best for the continuous type of data like monthly exam scores of a student?

Ans. Linear graph

2. Name all the stages of an AI Project cycle.

Ans. The stages of a Project Cycle are: Problem Scoping, Data Acquisition, Data Exploration, Modelling, Evaluation

3. What are sustainable development goals?

Ans. The Sustainable Development Goals (SDGs) were adopted by all the United Nations Member States in 2015 as a universal call to action to end poverty, protect the planet and ensure that all people enjoy peace and prosperity.

4. Name the 4Ws of problem canvases under the problem scoping stage of the AI Project Cycle.

Ans. (i) Who, (ii) What, (iii) Where, (iv) Why.

5. What is Testing Dataset?

Ans. The Dataset is provided to the model ML algorithm after training the algorithm.

6. Mention the types of learning approaches for AI modelling.

Ans. Supervised, unsupervised, and reinforcement

7. What is the objective of the evaluation stage?

Ans. This process is to evaluate whether the ML algorithm is able to predict with high accuracy or not before deployment.

(D) SAQs (Two Mark Questions)

1. Mention two precautions to be taken while acquiring data for developing an AI Project.

Ans. (i) It should be from an authentic source and accurate.

(ii) Look for redundant and irrelevant data parameters that do not take part in prediction.

2. What are the two different approaches to AI modelling? Define them.

Ans. There are two approaches for AI Modelling; Rule-Based and Learning Based.

The Rule-based Approach generates pre-defined outputs based on certain rules programmed by humans.

The Learning-based Approach has its own rules based on the output and data used to train the models.

3. What do you mean by Data Features?

Ans. The type of data to collect should be relevant and authentic data.

4. What is a problem statement template, and what is its significance?

Ans. The problem statement template refers to a clear idea about the basic framework required to achieve the goal. It is the 4Ws canvas that segregates; what is the problem, where does it arise, who is affected, why is it a problem? It takes us straight to the goal.

5. Explain any two SDGs in detail.

Ans. (a) **No Poverty:** This is SDGoal No 1 and strives to End poverty in all its forms from everywhere globally by the end of 2030. This goal has a total of seven targets to be achieved.

(b) **Quality Education:** This is Goal 4, which aspires to ensure inclusive and equitable quality education and promote lifelong learning opportunities for all. It has ten targets to achieve.

6. Write the names for missing stages in the given AI project cycle:

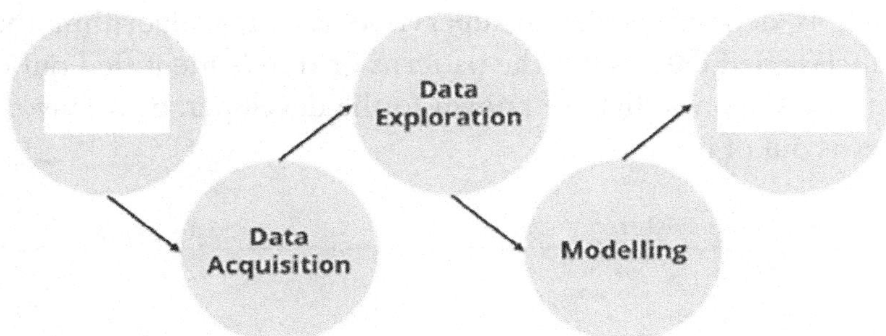

Figure 7.4

Ans. Problem Scoping, Evaluation.

7. Draw the icons of the following SDGs: Gender Equality, Clean Water and sanitation

Ans.

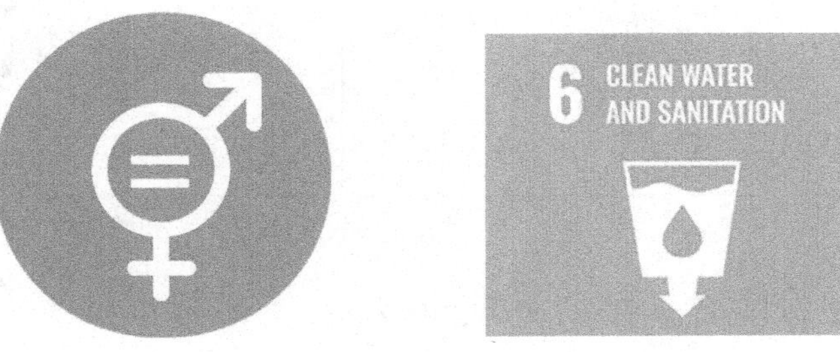

Figure 7.5   Figure 7.6

8. Draw the graphical representation of the Classification AI model. Explain in brief.

Ans. **Classification:** The classification Model works on the labeled data. For example, we have three coins of a different denomination that are labeled as per their weights; then, the model would look for the labeled features for predicting the output. This model works on a discrete dataset. It means the data need not be continuous.

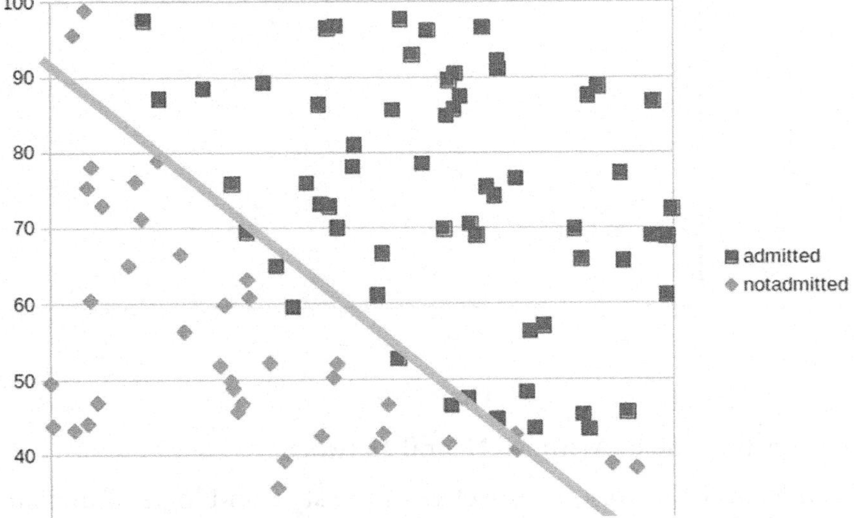

Figure 7.7

9. Draw the graphical representation of the Clustering AI model. Explain in brief.

Ans. **Clustering:** It is defined as the unsupervised learning algorithm that can cluster the unknown/unclassified data as per the patterns or trends identified out of it. The observed patterns must be the ones that are known to the developer, or it may come up with some special patterns out of it.

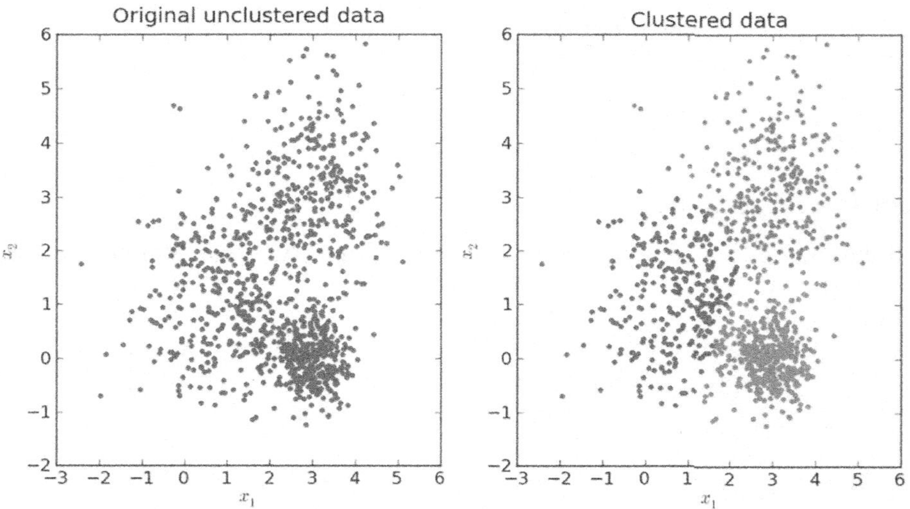

Figure 7.8

10. Draw the graphical representation of the Regression AI model. Explain in brief.

Ans. **Regression:** This model works on continuous data for predicting the output based on patterns. For example, when a user wishes to predict his/her next salary, then he/she would put in the data of his/her previous salary, any increments, etc., and would train the model. Here, the data that has been fed to the machine is continuous.

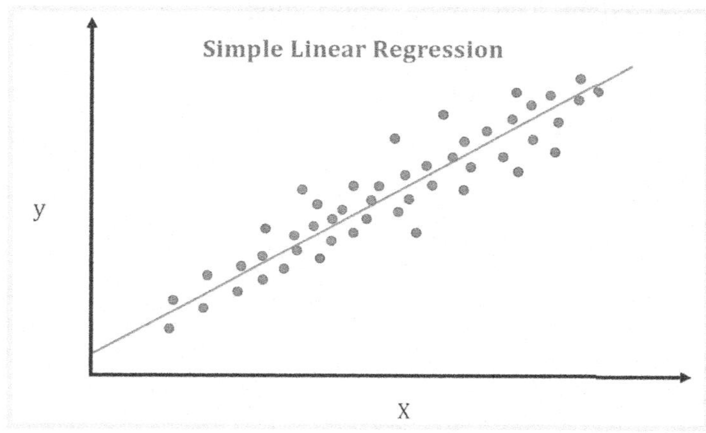

Figure 7.9

11. What are the features of an Artificial Neural Network?

Ans. An Artificial Neural Network, irrespective of the style and logic of implementation, has a few basic features as given below:

a) The Artificial Neural Network systems are modeled on the human brain and nervous system.

b) ANNs are able to automatically extract features without feeding the input by the programmer.

c) Every node of a layer of a Neural Network is compulsorily a machine learning algorithm.

d) It is useful to implement when solving problems for huge datasets.

12. Explain the Data Exploration stage.

Ans. In the Data exploration stage of the project cycle, we try to interpret some useful information out of the data we have collected. For this step, we need to explore the data and then try to put it uniformly for a better understanding. This stage deals with validating/ verification of the collected data and analyzing that:

a) The data is as per the specifications decided.

b) The data is free from errors.

c) The data is meeting our needs.

13. What is the main purpose of getting AI Ready?

Ans. The world is changing very fast each day, and we have huge data coming our way. The main purpose of getting AI-ready is taking steps to collect data around relevant systems, equipment, and procedures; and storing/curating that data in a way that makes it easily accessible to others for use in future AI applications.

14. What are the different modes of sources of data from where reliable and authentic datasets can be collected? Explain in brief.

Ans. Data may be a piece of information or facts and statistics collected together for reference/ analysis. When we want an AI project to be able to predict an output, we have to train it first by using training data. There may be many ways and sources from where we may collect reliable and authentic datasets. These may include Surveys, Web scrapping, Sensors, Cameras, Observations, Research, Investigation, API, etc. The data from the Internet should be taken from reliable and authentic websites. Some reliable data sources are UNO, Google scholar, Finance, CIA, Data.gov, etc.

(E) LAQs (Four Mark Questions)

1. Explain the AI Project Cycle with details.

Ans. The steps involved in the AI project cycle are as given:

The first step is to Scope the Problem by which we set the goal for our AI project by stating the problem which we wish to solve with it. Under problem scoping, we should look at various parameters which may affect the problem to be solved.

The next step is to acquire data that will become the base of your project as it will help you in understanding the parameters that are related to problem scoping.

Next, we go for data acquisition by collecting data from various reliable and authentic sources. Since the data we collect would be in large quantities, we can try to give it a visual image using different types of representations like graphs, databases, flow charts, maps, etc. This makes it easier for us to interpret the patterns in which our acquired data follows.

After exploring the patterns, we can decide upon the type of model we would build to achieve the goal. For this, we can research online and select various models which give a suitable output.

We can test the selected models to find out the most efficient one.

The most efficient model is now the base of our AI project, and you can develop your algorithm around it.

Once the modelling is complete, we need to test the model on some newly fetched data. The results will help us in evaluating the model and hence improving it. Finally, after Evaluation, the project cycle is complete and we get our AI project.

2. Draw the 4Ws problem canvas and explain each one of them briefly.

Ans. The 4Ws problem canvas is used as the basic template. When scoping a problem and using this canvas, the picture of the problem becomes clearer to solve.

a) **Who:** The "Who" block helps us in analysing the people getting affected directly or indirectly due to it? Under this, we find out who the 'stakeholders' to the problem area and what we know about them. Stakeholders are those people who face the problem and would be benefitted from the solution.

b) **Where:** In this block, we need to focus on the context/situation/location of the problem. It will help us look into the situation in which the problem arises, the context of it, and the locations where it is most prominent.

c) **What:** Under the "What" block, we need to look into what we have on hand. At this stage, we need to determine the nature of the problem. What is the problem, and how do we know that it is a problem?

d) **Why:** In the "Why" block, think about the benefits which the stakeholders would get from the solution and how it would benefit them as well as the society.

3. Explain the relation between data size and model performance of an Artificial Neural Network.

Ans. The basis for any AI development is Big DATASET. The performance of any AI-based application depends on the data entered. ANN models are also known as learning models, which are used for prediction purposes. These models are developed without paying much cognizance to the size of datasets. Although, a large Dataset is needed to construct a predictive learning model. Therefore, what constitutes a dataset to be considered as being big or small is vague. In fact, the quantity of data required for the purpose of training must be a good representation of the entire set. The Data must be authentic and relevant for giving a better model performance.

4. What do you mean by an Artificial Neural Network? Explain the functions of layers in an Artificial Neural Network.

Ans. Artificial Neural Network: Based on the functioning of the human brain, a Neural Network was built to copy the functionality of a human brain. The human brain is a neural network that is made up of multiple neurons. Similarly, an Artificial Neural Network (ANN) consists of multiple perceptrons. ANN consists of three important layers:

a) **Input Layer:** This layer accepts all the inputs provided by the programmer.

b) **Hidden Layers:** Between the input and the output layer, there is a set of layers known as Hidden layers. In these layers, computations are performed to get the output. There may be any number of hidden layers.

c) **Output Layer:** The inputs provided go through a series of transformations via the hidden layers, which finally transfer results in the output layer.

5. Five sustainable Development Goals are mentioned below. Write two problems under each goal that you think should be addressed for achieving the goal.

  a) Quality Education   b) Reduced Inequalities

  c) Life on Land   d) No Poverty

  e) Clean Water and Sanitation

Ans. a) **Quality Education:**
   i.   Providing education remotely, leveraging hi-tech, low-tech, and no-tech approaches;
   ii. Ensuring coordinated responses and avoiding overlapping efforts;
   iii. Ensuring the return of students to school when they reopen to avoid an upsurge in dropout rates.

  b) **Reduced inequalities:**
   i.   Reduction of relative economic inequalities, inequality in some countries having poorest and most vulnerable communities.
   ii. Improving the situations in countries with weaker health systems.

  c) **Life on land:**
   i.   Prevention of Deforestation caused by humans and restoration of land
   ii. Preventions and cures of diseases that are transmissible between animals and humans

  d) **No Poverty:**
   i.   Creation of Strong social protection systems to prevent people from falling into poverty.
   ii. Reduction of social exclusion and high vulnerability of certain populations to disasters and diseases.
   iii. Responsible distribution of natural resources.

  e) **Clean Water and Sanitation:**
   i.   To increase access to clean drinking water and sanitation, mostly in rural areas.
   ii. Managing water sustainably to manage the production of food and energy.

6. Explain the following: a). Supervised Learning b). Unsupervised Learning.

Ans. a) **Supervised Learning:** Supervised Learning is defined as an approach to creating Artificial Intelligence (AI), where the program is given labeled input data and the expected output results.

  b) **Unsupervised Learning:** An unsupervised learning model works on an unlabelled Dataset. This means that the data that is fed to the machine is random, and hence, there is a possibility that the user who is training the model does not have any clue/information regarding it. The unsupervised learning models are employed to identify relationships, patterns, and trends out of the data fed into them. It helps the user in understanding the major features as identified by the machine in it.

7. Differentiate between rule-based and learning-based AI modelling approaches.

Ans. a) **Rule-Based Approach:** It refers to the AI modelling where the relationship/patterns in data are defined by the developer. The machine/computer follows the rules/instructions mentioned by the developer(s) and performs its task accordingly. Example: suppose the user has a dataset comprising 500 images of apples and 500 images of bananas. To train the machine, the user feeds the training data into the machine and label each image as either apple or banana. Now, when the user tests the machine with the image of an apple, it will compare the image with the trained data. And it will identify the test image as an apple based on training data. This is known as the Rule-based Approach. The rules provided to the machine in this example are the labels provided to the machine for each image in the training dataset.

b) **Learning-Based Approach:** In this approach, the machine learns by itself. It refers to AI modelling where the relationship or patterns in data are not defined by the developer(s). Here, random data is fed to the machine, and it is left on the machine to find patterns and trends out of it. Normally, this approach is followed when the data is unlabelled and too random for a human being to make any decision out of it. For example, suppose the user has a dataset of 1000 images of random stray dogs of any area. He/she will put this into a learning approach-based AI machine, and the machine will come up with various patterns as observed in the features of these 1000 images, which he/she might not have even thought of!

8. What is the need for an AI Project Cycle? Explain.

Ans. A project cycle is a process of planning, organising, coordinating, and developing a project effectively through its phases, from planning through execution, then completion to achieve pre-defined objectives. The human mind makes up plans for every task for its which we have to accomplish, which is why things become clearer in our minds. Similarly, when we have to develop an AI project, then the AI Project Cycle provides us with an appropriate framework that can lead us towards the goal. The major role of the AI Project Cycle is to distribute the development of AI projects into various stages so that the development becomes easier, clearly understandable. The steps/stages should be more specific to efficiently get the best possible output. It mainly has five ordered stages which distribute the entire development in specific and clear steps. These steps are Problem Scoping, Data Acquisition, Data Exploration, Modelling, and Evaluation.

9. Do ethics in AI hamper the data acquisition stage? Justify your answer.

Ans. Data acquisition is the most important factor/stage as the entire project development is based on the acquired data. There are several ethical issues that must always be considered when planning any type of data collection. We should understand that the collected data is ethical only if the provider agrees to provide it. For example, in the case of smartphone/ mobile users, data is collected only by clicking on the 'allow' button when it asks for permission and by agreeing to all the terms and conditions. But, when someone does not want to share his/her data with anyone, then this ethical issue stops the acquisition process and lowers the accuracy or amount of data required. Hence, regardless of the type of data collection, it is a must to gain the approval of the community from which the data will be collected.

10. Differentiate between classification and clustering algorithms with the help of suitable examples.

Ans. **Classification** is defined as a process of finding a function that helps in dividing the Dataset into classes that are based on different parameters. In Classification, a computer program is trained on the training dataset. Based on that training, it categorises the data into different classes. The main task of the classification algorithm is to search the mapping function to map/plot the input(x) to the discrete output(y). Example: Email Spam Detection, where the model is trained on the basis of millions of emails on different parameters, and whenever the model receives a new email, it classifies the email into spam and important mail. When the email is spam, then it is moved to the Spam folder otherwise in Inbox mail.

Regression is defined as the process of finding the correlations between dependent and independent variables. It helps in predicting the continuous variables like the prediction of Market Trends, prediction of House prices, etc. The task of the Regression algorithm is used to find the mapping function to map/plot the input variable(x) to the continuous output variable(y). Example: If a user wants to do weather forecasting, so for this, he/she will use the Regression algorithm. For weather prediction, the model is trained on the past data, and after the training is completed, the model can easily predict the weather for future days.

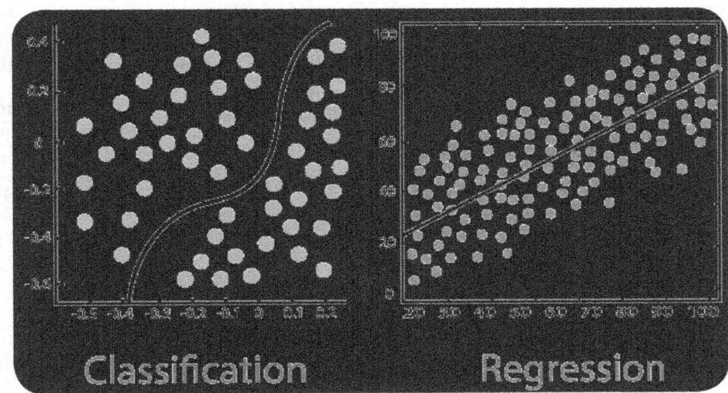

Figure 7.10

(Photo courtesy: https://seongjuhong.com/2019-12-08am-types-of-machine-learning/)

7.3 SOLVED EXERCISES

7.3.1 Multiple Choice Questions

1. What is Data?

   a) A piece of information

   b) A fact and/ visual

   c) A raw fact

   d) Any meaningful information

2. In the project cycle, data acquisition is the

   a) First phase

   b) Second phase

   c) Third phase

   d) Fifth phase

3. With which SDG, the following objective is associated:

   "Making the cities and human settlements inclusive, safe, resilient, and sustainable."
   a) Life on Land
   b) Sustainable Cities and Communities
   c) Responsible Consumption and Production
   d) Life Below Water

4. With which SDG, the following objective is associated?

   "To promote peaceful and inclusive societies for sustainable development; providing access to justice for all."
   a) Life on Land
   b) Peace and Justice Strong Institutions
   c) Sustainable Cities and Communities
   d) Responsible Consumption and Production

5. Which of the following project is related to SDG "No Poverty"?
   a) Creating Strong social protection systems to prevent people from falling into poverty
   b) Responsible distribution of resources.
   c) Reducing social exclusion and high vulnerability of certain populations to disasters and diseases.
   d) All of the above

6. Which of the following project is related to the SDG "Clean Water and sanitation"?
   a) Providing education remotely, leveraging hi-tech, low-cost, and no-tech approaches;
   b) Ensuring coordinated responses and avoiding overlapping efforts;
   c) Managing water sustainably to manage our production of food and energy.
   d) Ensuring the return of students to school when they reopen to avoid an upsurge in dropout rates.

7. Which of the following is a data quality measurement?
   a) Completeness
   b) Integrity
   c) Validity
   d) All of the above

8. Which of the following is not a data quality measurement?
   a) Completeness
   b) Uniqueness
   c) Non-valid
   d) Consistency

9. Which of the following is a source of data?
   a) Surveys, observations, Internet
   b) Web scrapping, API, Research
   c) Sensors, Cameras, Identity charts
   d) All of the above

10. Which of the following is not a source of data?
   a) Observations, API
   b) Search, DPI
   c) Investigation, Internet
   d) API, Identity Charts

11. How many types of AI models are used normally?

    a) Two   b) Three   c) Four   d) Ten

12. Which is not a part of problem scoping?
    a) Measurable objectives
    b) Failure criteria
    c) Project's purpose, vision, and mission
    d) Concerned stakeholders

13. In which step of the AI Project is data collected from different sources?
    a) Data Exploration   b) Data Modelling
    c) Data Evaluation   d) Project Scoping

14. Which one of the following stages is the second-last stage of the Al project cycle?
    a) Evaluation   b) Problem Scoping
    c) Data Acquisition   d) Data mining

16. For which purpose is the visualisation technique used?
    a) Enabling to make comparisons easily.
    b) Using order, layout, and hierarchy to prioritise
    c) Handling and understanding big data
    d) All of the above

17. Which of the following is an open-sourced data website?
    a) *https://www.india.gov.in/data-portal-india*
    b) *https://data.gov.in/*
    c) *https://dbie.rbi.org.in/DBIE/dbie.rbi?site=home*
    d) All of these

18. Which type of graphical representation suits best for a continuous type of data like the monthly income of an employee?
    a) Decision tree   b) Linear graph
    c) Identity chart   d) Pie chart

19. Which one of the following is not a Data Visualisation tool?
    a) F1 Score   b) Histogram
    c) Bar diagram   d) Fusion charts

20. ______________ is not included in sustainable development.
    a) Recycling and reuse of waste products/materials,
    b) Promoting deforestation
    c) Promoting green grassy patches between concrete buildings,
    d) Scientific management of renewable resources, especially bio-resources,

21. Which of the following sources is not an authentic one for data acquisition?
    a) Sensors   b) APIs
    c) System Hacking   d) Web Scraping

22. _______________ is a subset of artificial Intelligence.

    a) Data Mining
    b) Machine learning
    c) Data Modelling
    d) Data Visualisation

23. Which of the following sources is not used for data acquisition?

    a) Survey
    b) DPI
    c) API
    d) System map

24. Which of the following qualities is a must in the training data used for the AI machine?

    a) Authentic
    b) Reliable
    c) Accurate
    d) All of the above

25. Which one of the following is SDG as adopted by UNO?

    a) No Unemployment
    b) No Pollution
    c) No Poverty
    d) No Hunger

26. Which of the following is related to data visualization?

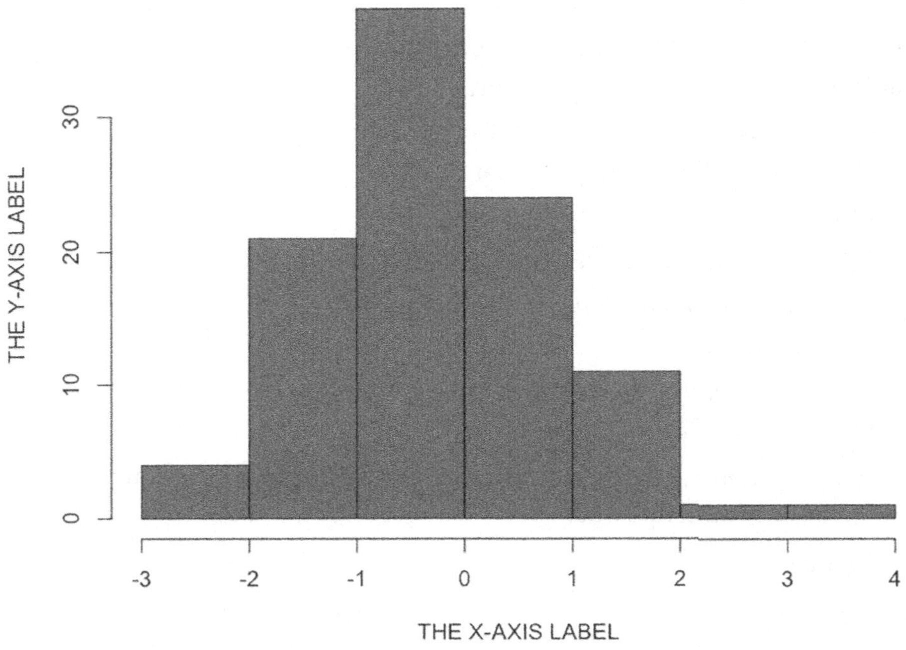

Figure 7.11

    a) System Mapping
    b) Histogram
    c) Sketchy graphs
    d) All the above

27. Which of the following Approach is used in AI models?

    a) Learning-based Approach
    b) Rule-based Approach
    c) both a and b
    d) Project-based Approach

28. In the Rule-Based Approach, who defines the relationships in patterns or data?

    a) User
    b) Coder/Programmer
    c) Computer Owner
    d) Buddy

29. In which process the model selected is evaluated for its efficiency on the basis of the results?

    a) Problem scoping
    b) Evaluation
    c) Data Visualisation
    d) Data Exploration

30. Which tool is used to formulate the information more meaningful for making decisions?

    a) QlikView
    b) Python
    c) MS Word
    d) All of the above

31. Which of the following features is associated with ANN?
    a) The neural network system is modeled on the human brain.
    b) Every Neural Network node is a machine learning algorithm.
    c) Neural networks are able to automatically extract features without input from the coder/programmer.
    d) All the above.

32. Which word is not a part of the 4Ws Problem Canvas?

    a) What
    b) Whom
    c) Who
    d) Why

33. For which purpose, Training Data is used in the AI-based machine?

    a) Testing the model
    b) Making Predictions
    c) Processing
    d) Giving input to the machined.

34. Which of the following feature is not related to ANN?
    a) A Neural Network has the ability to learn by itself to produce the output.
    b) ANN cannot work with incomplete knowledge and may not produce output with incomplete information.
    c) ANN is capable of automatically extracting features without feeding the input by the programmer.
    d) ANN has the ability to learn events and make decisions by commenting on similar events.

35. Consider the following statements about sustainable development and select the right set.
    i.   Reducing excessive use of natural resources,
    ii.   Enhancing natural resource conservation,
    iii. Recycling and reuse of waste products/materials,
    iv.   Using more environmentally friendly material promoting products made of biodegradable material
    v.   Scientific management of renewable resources, especially bio-resources.
    vi.   Promoting deforestation.
    vii. Use of environmental-friendly technologies based on the efficient use of resources.

    a) (ii) (iii) (iv)
    b) (ii) (iii) (iv) (v)
    c) (iii) (iv) (v) (vi)
    d) None of these

36. Consider the following statements about project charter and choose the correct set for project charter.
    i.   Project's purpose, vision, and mission

    ii. Measurable objectives

   iii. Elaborated project description, conditions, and risks

   iv. Success criteria

    v. Name and authority of the project sponsor, if any.

   vi. Concerned stakeholders

  a) (ii) (iii) (iv)   b) (i) (iii) (iv) (v)

  c) (i) (ii) (iv) (v) (vi)   d) (i) (ii) (iii) (iv) (v) (vi)

37. Which of the following is not a stage of the project cycle?

  a) Problem scoping   b) Data scoping

  c) Modelling   d) Evaluation

38. Which of the following pairs are mismatched?

i. Affordable and Clean Energy:	(a)	Ensuring access to affordable, reliable, sustainable, and green energy by all by 2030
ii. Decent Work and Economic Growth:	(b)	Promoting sustained, inclusive, and sustainable economic growth.
iii. Industry, Innovation, and	(c)	Building the resilient infrastructure, promoting
iv. Infrastructure	(d)	inclusive and sustainable industrialisation, and fostering innovation by 2030.
v. Reduced Inequality	(e)	Actions to reduce equality within and among countries by 2030.
vi. Climate Action	(f)	Taking urgent action globally to combat Climate change and its impacts
vii. Life on Land	(g)	Actions to protect, restore, and promote sustainable use of aquatic ecosystems; combating desertification, and halting biodiversity loss.

  a) (i) & (iii)   b) (ii) & (iv)   c) (iii) & (vii)   d) (iv) & (vi)

ANSWERS									
1. (d)	2. (b)	3. (b)	4. (b)	5. (d)	6. (c)	7. (d)	8. (c)	9. (d)	10. (b)
11. (a)	12. (b)	13. (a)	14. (b)	15. (d)	16. (d)	17. (d)	18. (b)	19. (a)	20. (b)
21. (c)	22. (b)	23. (b)	24. (d)	25. (b)	26. (d)	27. (c)	28. (b)	29. (b)	30. (a)
31. (d)	32. (b)	33. (a)	34. (b)	35. (d)	36. (d)	37. (b)	38. (d)		

7.3.2 Fill in the blanks

1. AI _____________ provides an appropriate framework that can lead us towards the goal.

2. _____________ is a skill where the learners need to focus on the relevant details related to the problem.

3. _____________ is the process of extracting useful and structured knowledge from unstructured documents to find useful associations and insights.

4. _____________ refers to the unsupervised learning algorithm that can cluster the unknown data according to the patterns or trends identified out of it.

5. A _____________ is a simple graphical representation for classifying examples.

6. _____________ may be a piece of information or facts and statistics collected together for reference or analysis purposes.

7. The _____________ Neural Network tends to perform better with large data.

8. _____________ is defined as the process of finding a model/ function for distinguishing the data into continuous real values in place classes.

9. Data acquisition is the _____________ stage in the AI project cycle.

10. _____________ is a testing technique where the model is installed in the real world, and it is tested in as many ways as possible.

11. _____________ are often called Transducers.

12. _____________ helps the machine to make decisions and learn from large Data sets.

13. The learning-based Approach performs algorithms on a sample Data set which is called _____________.

14. _____________ is used to collect data that has to be authentic and reliable.

15. The analogy of an _____________ can be made with Parallel Processing.

Figure 7.12

ANSWERS			
1. Project Cycle	2. Problem scoping	3. Text Analytics	4. Clustering
5. decision tree	6. Data	7. larger	8. Regression
9. second	10. Evaluation	11. Sensors	12. Deep Learning
13. training data	14. Data exploration	15. Artificial Neural Network	

7.3.3 True or False

State the following statements either as True (T) or false (F).

1. Sensors used in AI-enabled machines convert real-world phenomena like temperature, force, movement to voltage or current, etc., into signals.

2. Decision tree learning is the technique used for supervised classification learning.

3. A classification problem arises when the output variable is a category.

4. Classification is defined as the process of finding a model/ function for distinguishing the data into continuous real values in place classes.

5. Data modelling is the fifth stage in the AI project cycle.

6. The data is labeled when entered into the model in a rule-based approach.

7. Data analysis means a process of cleaning, transforming, and modelling data to discover useful information for business decision-making.

8. Text, Statistical, Diagnostic, Predictive, and Prescriptive Analysis are the types of Data Analysis.

9. LOOPY is an interactive tool that can be worked without any knowledge of coding.

10. Problem scoping is a skill where the learners need to focus on the relevant details related to the problem.

11. The training data need not be reliable, authentic, and accurate for the AI machine to work efficiently.

12. Semantic Analytics is the process of extracting useful and structured knowledge from unstructured documents to find useful associations and insights.

13. AI models can be classified either on Rule-based or learning-based approaches.

14. In regression, data is categorised under different labels based on some parameters mentioned in the input.

15. AI Project scoping provides an appropriate framework that can lead us towards the goal.

16. Stakeholders are all those humans who are affected the most by the model used in the AI project.

17. The Artificial Intelligent project cycle describes all steps required to convert a real-life problem or a challenge into a computer-based AI model.

18. AI Modelling refers to developing algorithms or AI models which can be trained to get intelligent output, i.e., writing codes to make a machine artificially intelligent.

19. The Training data must not be relevant and authentic for the better efficiency of an AI project.

20. Data may be a piece of information or facts and statistics collected together for reference or analysis purposes.

ANSWERS
1. (T) 2. T 3. (T) 4. F (Regression not classification) 5. F (fourth not fifth)
6. (T) 7. T 8. (T) 9. (T) 10. (T) 11. F 12. F (Text Analytics) 13. T
14. F (classification ..not regression) 15. F (Project cycle..not project scoping) 16. T
17. T 18. T 19. F (must be) 20. T

7.3.4 Matching type

(I) Match the items enlisted in column A with those of column b correctly.

(A) Goal /Objective	**(B) Description of goal**
(i) No Poverty	(a) Ensuring healthy lives and promoting well-being for all at all ages by 2030.
(ii) Zero Hunger	(b) Actions to ensure availability and sustainable management of water and sanitation for all by 2030.
(iii) Good Health and Well-being	(c) Initiating actions to eradicate extreme poverty for all people in the world by 2030.
(iv) Quality Education	(d) Actions to achieve gender equality, empowering all women and girls of the world
(v) Gender Equality	(e) Actions to ensure that all girls and boys complete free, equitable, and quality primary and secondary education by 2030.
(vi) Clean Water and Sanitation	(f) End hunger, achieving food security, and improved nutrition by 2030.

ANSWERS
(I) (i)-c, (ii)-f, (iii)-a, (iv)-e, (v)-d, (vi)-b

Figure 7.13

7.3.5 Assertion Reason Type Questions

1. Assertion (A): Testing data is used to assess the AI machine for its efficiency and performance, which depends on training data.

   Reason (R): The training data needs to be reliable, authentic, and accurate for the AI machine to work efficiently.

   a) Both A and R are correct and R is the correct reason for A.

   b) Both A and R are correct and R is not the correct reason for A.

   c) A is correct but R is incorrect.

   d) A is incorrect but R is correct.

2. Assertion (A): Data Modelling is defined as processing in which Al-Enabled algorithms are being designed as per the requirements of the system, and later, the model is implemented.

   Reason (R): Data Modelling is the fifth stage of the project cycle.

   a) Both A and R are correct and R is the correct reason for A.

   b) Both A and R are correct and R is not the correct reason for A.

   c) A is correct but R is incorrect.

   d) A is incorrect but R is correct.

3. Assertion (A): Decision tree learning is one of the most successful techniques for supervised classification learning.

   Reason (R): A decision tree is a simple graphical representation for classifying examples.

   a) Both A and R are correct and R is the correct reason for A.

   b) Both A and R are correct and R is not the correct reason for A.

   c) A is correct but R is incorrect.

   d) A is incorrect but R is correct.

4. Assertion (A): The semi-supervised learning models are employed to identify patterns, relationships, and trends out of the data which is fed into it.

   Reason (R): Semi-Supervised Learning is the set of learning algorithms in which both labeled and unlabelled data in the training dataset are directly used to train the classifier.

   a) Both A and R are correct and R is the correct reason for A.

   b) Both A and R are correct and R is not the correct reason for A.

   c) A is correct but R is incorrect.

   d) A is incorrect but R is correct.

5. Assertion (A): Visualization is like a form of visual art that grabs our interest and keeps our eyes on the message.

   Reason (R): F1 Score is the Arithmetic Mean of the precision and recall Evaluation Metrics.

   a) Both A and R are correct and R is the correct reason for A.

   b) Both A and R are correct and R is not the correct reason for A.

   c) A is correct but R is incorrect.

   d) A is incorrect but R is correct.

6. Assertion (A): The problem statement template provides a clear idea about the basic framework required to achieve the goal.

   Reason (R): ANN has numerical strength that can perform more than one job at the same time.

   a) Both A and R are correct and R is the correct reason for A.

   b) Both A and R are correct and R is not the correct reason for A.

   c) A is correct but R is incorrect.

   d) A is incorrect but R is correct.

7. Assertion (A): When an element in an AI-based project is removed or changed, it will imbalance the whole system.

   Reason (R): All elements in the AI system are interconnected

   a) Both A and R are correct and R is the correct reason for A.

   b) Both A and R are correct and R is not the correct reason for A.

   c) A is correct but R is incorrect.

   d) A is incorrect but R is correct.

ANSWERS						
1. (a)	2. (c)	3. (b)	4. (d)	5. (c)	6. (b)	7. (a)

7.3.6 Statements Based Questions

1. Statement 1: The components of the AI Project Cycle Problem are scoping, Data acquisition, Data exploration, Modelling, and Evaluation.

   Statement 2: Clustering is defined as the task of classifying the data points into a number of groups in such a manner that data points in the same groups are more similar and dissimilar data points in other groups.

   a) Statement 1 is correct but statement 2 is incorrect.

   b) Statement 1 is incorrect but statement 2 is correct.

   c) Both the statements are correct.

   d) Both the statements are incorrect.

2. Statement 1: The evaluation stage is to evaluate whether the ML algorithm is able to predict with high accuracy or not before deployment.

   Statement 2: Recall directly tells us the model's ability to randomly identify an observation that belongs to the positive class.

   a) Statement 1 is correct but statement 2 is incorrect.

   b) Statement 1 is incorrect but statement 2 is correct.

   c) Both the statements are correct.

   d) Both the statements are incorrect.

3. Statement 1: Data may not be a piece of information or facts and statistics collected together for reference or analysis purposes.

   Statement 2: Data Modelling is a process of collecting data from various sources for the purpose of analytical operations like training and predictions.

   a) Statement 1 is correct but statement 2 is incorrect.
   b) Statement 1 is incorrect but statement 2 is correct.
   c) Both the statements are correct.
   d) Both the statements are incorrect.

4. Statement 1: Data is defined as the raw fact, which is organised together to form information that needs to be processed further for analysis and data visualisation.

   Statement 2: Data analysis means a process of cleaning, transforming, and modelling data to discover useful information for business decision-making.
   a) Statement 1 is correct but statement 2 is incorrect.
   b) Statement 1 is incorrect but statement 2 is correct.
   c) Both the statements are correct.
   d) Both the statements are incorrect.

5. Statement 1: A decision tree is a simple textual representation for classifying examples.

   Statement 2: Recall indirectly tells us the model's ability to randomly identify an observation that belongs to the positive class.
   a) Statement 1 is correct but statement 2 is incorrect.
   b) Statement 1 is incorrect but statement 2 is correct.
   c) Both the statements are correct.
   d) Both the statements are incorrect.

6. Statement 1: Training data is used to give the AI machine a set of inputs on which the machine will be assessed later on.

   Statement 2: Regression is the process of finding a model for distinguishing the data into continuous real values instead of using discrete values.
   a) Statement 1 is correct but statement 2 is incorrect.
   b) Statement 1 is incorrect but statement 2 is correct.
   c) Both the statements are correct.
   d) Both the statements are incorrect.

7. Statement 1: Neural Network is a mesh of one input layer and multiple hidden Layers.

   Statement 2: Evaluation is a training technique where the model is installed in the real world, and it is tested in as many ways as possible.
   a) Statement 1 is correct but statement 2 is incorrect.
   b) Statement 1 is incorrect but statement 2 is correct.
   c) Both the statements are correct.
   d) Both the statements are incorrect.

8. Statement 1: The concept of a loop defines a chain of events in the system and relationships between them.

   Statement 2: Data features can be collected from various sources like newspapers, cameras, observations, surveys, questionnaires, and so on.
   a) Statement 1 is correct but statement 2 is incorrect.
   b) Statement 1 is incorrect but statement 2 is correct.

c) Both the statements are correct.

d) Both the statements are incorrect.

9. Statement 1: A training dataset is a dataset provided to the model after training the algorithm.
    Statement 2: Data mining is the process of extracting useful and structured knowledge from unstructured documents to extract useful associations and insights.
    a) Statement 1 is correct but statement 2 is incorrect.
    b) Statement 1 is incorrect but statement 2 is correct.
    c) Both the statements are correct.
    d) Both the statements are incorrect.

10. Statement 1: The components of an AI Project Cycle are Problem Scoping, Data acquisition, Data exploration, Modelling, and Evaluation.
    Statement 2: Training data is used to give the AI machine a set of inputs on which the machine will be assessed later on.
    a) Statement 1 is correct but statement 2 is incorrect.
    b) Statement 1 is incorrect but statement 2 is correct.
    c) Both the statements are correct.
    d) Both the statements are incorrect.

ANSWERS									
1. (c)	2. (a)	3. (d)	4. (c)	5. (b)	6. (c)	7. (a)	8. (c)	9. (b)	10. (c)

7.3.7 Competency-Based Questions

1. In the production of AI-enabled machines in a company called **'Surekha AI Enterprises'**, Rekhangana Sharma used tools/parts which convert real-world phenomena like temperature, force, movement to voltage or current, etc., into signals. These parts/tools are called:
    a) Fizzy Systems
    b) Transducers
    c) Transformers
    d) Translocators

2. Naundita was exploring websites for data collection that should be authentic, accurate, and reliable. She used the following government portals for the information to be used and referred to in data analytics.
    i.   https://www.india.gov.in/data-portal-india
    ii. https://data.gov.in/
    iii. https://dbie.rbi.org.in/DBIE/dbie.rbi?site=home
    iv. http://mospi.nic.in/data

    These websites/portals are called:
    a) Blogs
    b) Closed-sourced portals
    c) Open-sourced websites
    d) Landing pages

3. A network has the following characteristics:
    i.   It can work with incomplete information/knowledge and may produce output even with incomplete information.

 ii. It has Parallel processing capability. It means that it has numerical strength that can perform more than one job at the same time.

 iii. It has the capability to learn events and make decisions by commenting on similar events.

 iv. It has fault tolerance. It means that the corruption of one or more cells does not stop it from generating output.

This is all about:

a) ANN   b) BNN   c) CNN   d) NN

4. It is the learning in which humans teach or train the machine using well-labeled data. It means that some data is already tagged with the correct answers. Then, the machine is provided with a new set of information/data so that the supervised learning algorithm may analyze the training data to produce a correct outcome from labeled data. It is:

 a) Un-Supervised Learning   b) Semi-Supervised Learning

 c) Supervised Learning   d) Reinforcement Learning

5. A process has the following features:

 i. It is the process of creating a model to predict continuous quantity.

 ii. It predicts ordered data.

 iii. It may be evaluated using root mean square error.

The process is:

 a) System map   b) Decision tree

 c) Classification   d) Regression

ANSWERS
1. (b) 2. (c) 3. (a) 4. (c) 5. (d)

7.3.8 VSA

1. Define text analytics.

Ans. Text Analytics is defined as the process of extracting useful and structured knowledge from unstructured documents to find useful associations and insights.

2. Define data visualisation.

Ans. Data visualisation is like a form of visual art that grabs our interest and keeps our eyes on the message. To visualise data, we can use various types of visual representations.

3. What is data modelling?

Ans. Modelling is defined as processing in which Al-Enabled algorithms are being designed as per the requirements of the system, and later, the model is implemented. Modelling is the fourth stage of the project cycle.

4. Define data.

Ans. Data may be a piece of information or facts and statistics collected together for reference or analysis purposes.

5. What do you mean by data acquisition?

Ans. Data acquisition is defined as a process of collecting data from various sources for the purpose of analytical operations like training and predictions.

6. Define problem scoping.

Ans. Problem Scoping is to focus on the problem for which we are aiming to solve.

7. How is problem scoping considered a process?

Ans. Problem scoping is the process through which the problem is to be defined, and a detailed review of the problem is gathered for analysis.

8. Define AI model evaluation.

Ans. Evaluation in AI modelling is one of the testing techniques where the model is installed in the real world, and it is tested in as many ways as possible.

9. Define Semi-supervised Learning.

Ans. Semi-Supervised Learning is the set of learning algorithms in which both labeled and unlabelled data in the training dataset are directly used to train the classifier.

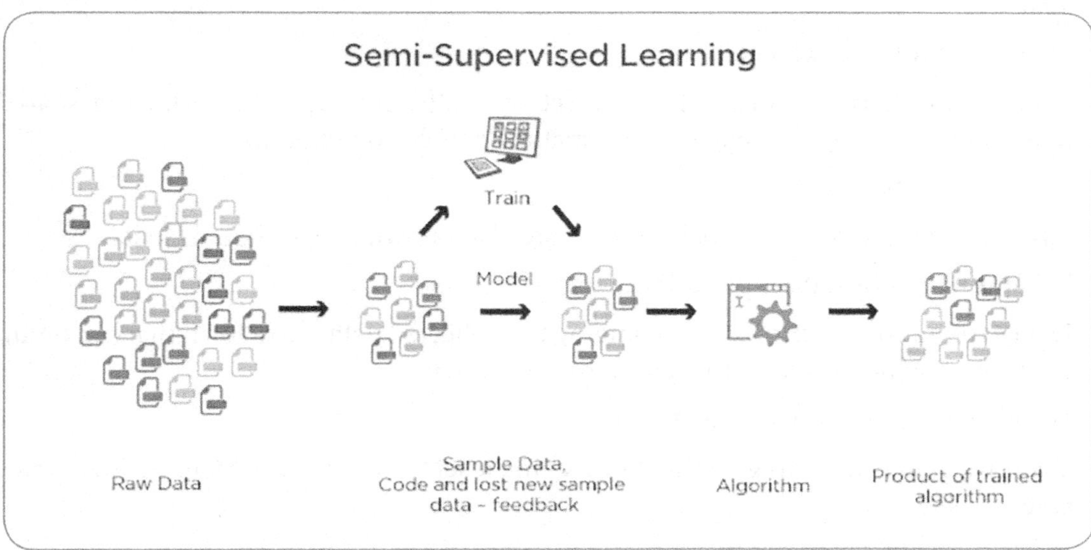

Figure 7.14

10. What is indicated by the problem statement template?

Ans. The problem statement template provides a clear idea about the basic framework required to achieve the goal.

11. What do you mean by the parallel processing capability of ANN?

Ans. ANN has numerical strength that can perform more than one job at the same time. This is called 'Parallel processing capability.

12. What is the 'Rule-Based Approach'?

Ans. The Rule-Based Approach refers to the AI modelling where the relationship or patterns in data are defined by the coder/programmer.

13. What is the learning-based Approach?

Ans. It refers to AI-modelling, where the machine learns by itself.

14. Define ANN.

Ans. An Artificial Neural Network (ANN) is defined as an Al algorithm that is based on the similarities in structure and functions of biological neural networks that might be applied in advanced supervised, unsupervised, or reinforcement learning.

15. What do you mean by data?

Ans. Data is defined as the raw fact, which is organised together to form information that needs to be processed further for analysis and data visualization.

16. What are the components of the Al project Cycle?

Ans. The components of the AI Project Cycle Problem are scoping, Data acquisition, Data exploration, Modelling, and Evaluation.

17. What does the problem statement signify?

Ans. The problem statement gives a clear idea about the basic framework required to achieve the goal.

18. Define convolution kernel.

Ans. Convolution kernel is defined as the set of coefficients used to perform a spatial filter operation over a digital image via the spatial convolution operator.

19. What are Global 'Goals'?

Ans. Sustainable Development Goals (SDGs) are also known as the Global Goals.

20. What is meant by data exploration?

Ans. Data exploration is a process of arranging the collected data into a form that can be analyzed or through which useful information can be drawn.

21. For what purpose is 'Training data' used?

Ans. Training data is used to give the AI machine a set of inputs on which the machine will be assessed later on.

22. What is the full form of API?

Ans. Application Programming Interface

23. Define loop.

Ans. The concept of a loop defines a chain of events in the system and relationships between them.

24. What is Data Acquisition?

Ans. Data Acquisition is a process to collect data for the problem scoped, which has to be correct, authentic, and reliable.

25. Define LOOPY.

Ans. LOOPY is defined as an interactive tool that can be used to play with simulations in real-time without using any coding.

26. Define testing dataset.

Ans. A testing dataset is a dataset provided to the model ML algorithm after training the algorithm.

27. Why are the unsupervised learning models used?

Ans. The unsupervised learning models are employed to identify patterns, relationships, and trends out of the data which is fed into it.

28. What do you mean by semi-supervised Learning?

Ans. Semi-Supervised Learning is the set of learning algorithms in which both labeled and unlabelled data in the training dataset are directly used to train the classifier.

29. What is the relationship between various elements in an AI-based project?

Ans. The elements in an AI-based project are interdependent, and hence, removing or changing any element in the system will imbalance the whole system.

30. Define data analysis.

Ans. Data analysis means a process of cleaning, transforming, and modelling data to discover useful information for business decision-making.

31. What do you mean by Evaluation in an AI-based project?

Ans. Evaluation is a testing technique where the model is installed in the real world, and it is tested in as many ways as possible.

32. What is the significance of Recall?

Ans. Recall indirectly tells us the model's ability to randomly identify an observation that belongs to the positive class.

33. What are the other names of F1-score?

Ans. The harmonic mean of the Precision and Recall is called the F-1 Score.

34. What are transducers?

Ans. Sensors are often called 'Transducers.'

35. What is the main objective of the evaluation stage?

Ans. The evaluation stage is to evaluate whether the ML algorithm is able to predict with high accuracy or not before deployment.

36. What is clustering?

Ans. Clustering refers to the unsupervised learning algorithm that can cluster the unknown data according to the patterns or trends identified out of it.

37. What is a decision tree?

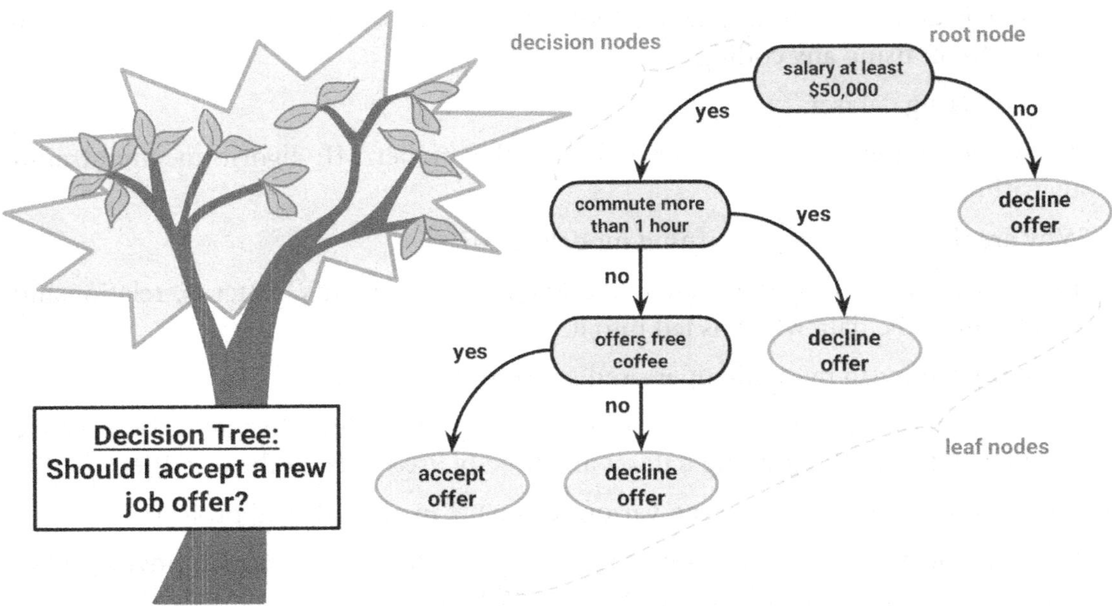

Figure 7.15 Decision Tree

Ans. A decision tree is a simple graphical representation for classifying examples.

38. Which stage is data evaluation in the AI Project cycle?

Ans. Fifth stage

39. What is sustainable development?

Ans. Sustainable development is defined as the development that satisfies the needs of the present generations as well as the future generations, ensuring the balance between economic growth, care for the environment, and social well-being.

40. What do you mean by data exploration?

Ans. Data exploration is a method to collect data that has to be authentic and reliable.

41. What is a learning-based approach?

Ans. The learning-based Approach performs algorithms on a sample Data set which is called training data.

42. What are the main functions of sensors in AI-based projects?

Ans. Sensors used in AI-enabled machines convert real-world phenomena like temperature, force, movement to voltage or current, etc., into signals.

43. Mention the different types of data analysis.

Ans. Text, Statistical, Diagnostic, Predictive, and Prescriptive Analysis

44. Define regression.

Ans. Regression is defined as the process of finding a model for distinguishing the data into continuous real values instead of using discrete values.

45. Mention the main qualities of training data.

Ans. The training data needs to be reliable, authentic, and accurate for the AI machine to work efficiently.

46. Why is testing data used?

Ans. Testing data is used to assess the AI machine for its efficiency and performance too.

47. What are the main qualities of an open-sourced data website (Govt portal)?

Ans. Open-sourced websites or government portals are authentic, accurate, and reliable.

48. Who are the stakeholders?

Ans. Stakeholders are all those human beings who are affected the most by the model used in the AI project.

49. What are the four W in 'The 4Ws Problem canvas'?

Ans. Who, what, where, and why.

50. What are the other names given for web scraping?

Ans. Web data extraction, web harvesting, and Screen Scraping.

51. Define web scraping.

Ans. Web scraping is defined as a technique used for extracting huge amounts of data from websites on the Internet by using a web browser.

52. What is an API?

Ans. Application programming interfaces (API) are the piece of code that helps to connect one application to another to collect data from it.

53. When is a system map used?

Ans. System Map is used to find relationships between different elements of the problem that is scoped.

54. What is indicated by an 'Identity Chart'?

Ans. Identity chart indicates the qualities, characteristics, or beliefs that make a person who he/she is and how does the world looks at them.

55. What do you mean by data modelling?

Ans. Data Modelling is defined as a process in which Al-Enabled algorithms are being designed as per the requirements of the system, and later, the model is implemented.

56. Define text analysis.

Ans. Text Analytics is the process of extracting useful and structured knowledge from unstructured documents to find useful associations and insights.

57. How many stages are there in an Al-project cycle?

Ans. Five stages

58. Define Classification.

Ans. Classification is defined as the process of finding/ discovering a model (function), which helps in separating the data into multiple categories/ classes.

59. What is data visualisation in an AI project?

Ans. Data visualization is like a form of visual art that grabs users' interest and keeps their eyes on the message.

60. Explain clustering.

Ans. Clustering is defined as the task of classifying the data points into a number of groups in such a manner that data points in the same groups are more similar and dissimilar data points in other groups.

7.3.9 Short Answer Type Questions

1. Explain Rule-based Approach in AI Modelling.

Ans. The rule-Based Approach Refers to the AI modelling where the relationship or patterns in data are defined by the coder. The machine follows the rules/ instructions mentioned by the developer(s) and performs its task accordingly. Whereas in the Learning-based Approach, the relationship/patterns in data are not defined by the developer(s). In this Approach, random/unclassified data is fed to the machine to find the patterns and trends out of it.

2. How is Classification different from clustering?

Ans. In Classification, data is classified under different labels according to some parameters as given in input for prediction of the data, while clustering is a collection of objects on the basis of similarity and dissimilarity among them.

3. Mention the specific features of ANN.

Ans. ANN has the following features:
   a) ANN can work with incomplete information/knowledge and may produce output even with incomplete information.
   b) It has the capability to learn events and make decisions by commenting on similar events.
   c) It has fault tolerance. It means that the corruption of one or more cells of ANN does not stop it from generating output.
   d) It has Parallel processing capability. It means that ANN has numerical strength that can perform more than one job at the same time.

4. What are the main features of Neural Networks (NN)?

Ans. Neural Networks have the following features:
   a) Neural Networks have the capability to learn by themselves and produce the output, and the output is not limited to the input provided to the NN.
   b) Moreover, the input is stored in its own networks in place of a database. Hence, the loss of data does not have any effect on its work.
   c) In case a neuron is not responding or a piece of information is missing, even then, the network can detect the fault and produce the output.
   d) These networks can learn from examples too and apply them when a similar event happens, making them able to work through real-time events.
   e) They can perform multiple tasks simultaneously without affecting the system performance.

5. Specify the purpose of getting AI-ready.

Ans. The purpose of getting AI-ready specifies the responsible and optimum use of the huge amount of data around humans to create and implement into such systems and applications, which will make the life of future generations organised and sustainable. This process will lead to better lives for mankind.

6. What is done in Supervised Learning (SL)?

Ans. Supervised Learning is the learning in which humans teach or train the machine using well-labeled data. It means that some data is already tagged with the correct answers. Then, the machine is provided with a new set of information/data so that the supervised learning algorithm may analyse the training data to produce a correct outcome from labeled data.

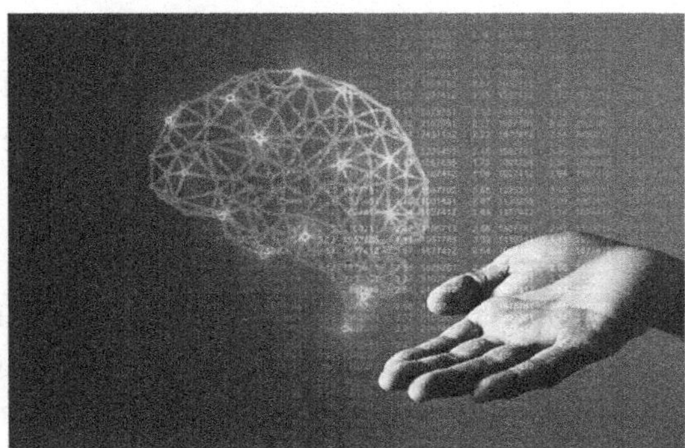

Figure 7.16

7. 'Dataset used in a supervised learning model is labeled'- What does it mean?

Ans. In a supervised learning model, the labeled Dataset is fed to the machine. It means that some data is tagged with the correct answers. In other words, the Dataset is known to the person who is giving training to the machine, then he/she is able to label the data.

8. Explain unsupervised Learning.

Ans. Unsupervised Learning is defined as the training of a machine using unclassified and non-labeled information and then allowing the algorithm to act on that information without any guidance. Here, the task of the machine is to group unsorted information according to similarities, patterns, and differences without any prior training of data.

9. Differentiate between classification and regression.

Ans.

Classification	Regression
(i) Classification is the process of finding or discovering a model (function) which helps in separating the data into multiple categorical classes.	(i) Regression is defined as the process of finding a model or function for distinguishing the data into continuous real values in place of using classes.
(ii) In Classification, the group membership of a problem is identified.	(ii) In regression, the numeric data dependency is predicted to distinguish it.
(iii) In Classification, the data is categorized under different labels according to some parameters, and then the labels are predicted for the data.	(iii) The Regression analysis is the statistical model used to predict the numeric data in place of labels.

10. Mention the main features of Classification.

Ans. The main features of Classification are as follows:

a) The Classification process models have a function through which the data is predicted in discrete class labels.

b) The classification algorithms involve decision trees, logistic regression, etc.

c) Classification predicts unordered data.

d) Classification is evaluated by measuring accuracy.

11. Enlist the main features of regression.

Ans. The main features of regression are as follows:

a) Regression is defined as the process of creating a model to predict continuous quantity.

b) Regression predicts ordered data.

c) Regression may be evaluated using root mean square error.

d) Examples: Regression Tree (e.g., Random Forest) and Linear Regression.

12. Explain the system map.

Ans. A system map exhibits the components and boundaries of a system at a specific point in time. With the help of System Maps, a relationship amongst different elements of a system can be understood. The use of '+' signs and '−' signs in the loops indicate the nature of the relationship between elements. The arrowhead depicts the direction of the effect. When the arrow goes from X to Y with a +sign, it indicates that both are directly related to each other. Thus, if X increases, then Y will also increase and vice versa. On the other hand, when the arrow goes from X to Y with a - sign, it shows that both the elements are inversely related to each other. It means if X increases, Y will decrease and vice-versa.

13. Explain the four main methods of acquiring data.

Ans. There are mainly four methods of acquiring data:

a) Collecting new data from employees/contractors

b) Converting/ transforming data

c) Sharing/exchanging data

d) Purchasing data

14. What is the main purpose of analysing the data? Explain.

Ans. To analyze the data, it is essential to visualise it in some user-friendly format. It will serve the following purposes:

a) Quickly have a look and make decisions about the trends, relationships, and patterns contained within the data.

b) Define strategy for which model is to be used at a later stage.

c) The data is free from errors.

d) Communicate the same to others effectively.

e) The Data Exploration stage deals with validating or verification of the collected data and analysing that:

f) The data is according to the pre-decided specifications.

g) The data is meeting the needs and requirements.

15. Explain Rule-based Approach in AI Modelling with an example.

Ans. In AI modelling, a Rule-based approach is based on the data and rules fed to the machine, where the machine reacts accordingly to deliver the desired output. Also, the Rule-Based Approach refers to the AI modelling where the relationship or patterns in data are defined by the coder/programmer. The machine is trained by using the rules laid down by the developer. The machine has to follow the rules/instructions mentioned to perform its task accordingly.

Example: A decision tree is an example of a Rule-based approach. In other words, the Rule-based Approach refers to the AI modelling where the rules are defined by the developer.

16. What is the main drawback of the Rule-based Approach of AI Modelling? Explain.

Ans. The main drawback/feature for the Rule-based Approach is that the learning is static. The machine, once trained, does not consider any changes made in the original training dataset. That means that if we try testing the machine on a dataset that is different from the rules and data we fed it at the training stage, the machine will not succeed and will not learn from its mistakes. The once trained model cannot improvise itself on the basis of feedback. Thus, machine learning is taken as an extension to this as the machine adapts for new changes in data and rules following the updated path only, whereas a rule-based model does what it has been taught once.

17. What is Leaning -Based Approach in AI Modelling? Explain.

Ans. The Learning-based Approach refers to AI-modelling, where the machine learns by itself. A learning approach is that the machine is fed with data, and the desired output is achieved when the machine designs its own algorithm (or set of rules) to match the data to the desired output. The Learning-based Approach refers to the AI modelling where the relationship or patterns in data are not defined by the programmer/ model developer. In this Approach, random data as input is fed to the machine, and the machine figures patterns and trends out it. Generally, this approach is used when the data is unlabelled and too random for humans to make sense out of it. Thus, the machine looks at the data, try to extract similar features out of it, and clusters the same data sets together. In the end, the machine tells us about the observed trends in the training data as output.

18. Explain Problem Scoping and project charter.

Ans. Problem Scoping aims to define the project and to create a Project Charter. The Project Charter enlists the primary requirements for the project and includes information, like:

- Project's purpose, vision, and mission
- Measurable objectives
- Elaborated project description, conditions, and risks
- Success criteria
- Name and authority of the project sponsor, if any.
- Concerned stakeholders

19. Enlist two projects related to SDG "Reduced Inequalities."

Ans. Two projects related to SDG "Reduced Inequalities" are as follows:

   a) Reducing relative economic inequalities and inequality in some countries having the poorest and most vulnerable communities.

   b) Improving the situations in countries having weaker health systems.

20. Enlist two projects related to SDG **"Life on Land"**.

Ans. Two projects related to SDG **"Life on Land"** are as follows:

   a) Preventing deforestation caused by human beings and restoration of land

   b) Preventing and curing diseases that are transmissible between animals and humans

21. What is data cleaning? Why is it required?

Ans. Data cleaning or data cleansing and data scrubbing is the process of removing incorrect, corrupted, incorrectly formatted, duplicate, or incomplete data within a dataset. This is required to create a culture around quality data decision-making.

22. Discuss the steps to be taken for data cleaning.

Ans. The following steps are employed to clean the data:

   a) Remove duplicate or irrelevant observations.

   b) Remove unwanted observations from the Dataset.

   c) Fix/ remove structural errors. Structural errors are when data is transferred and strange naming is noticed.

   d) Filter unwanted outliers which do not appear to fit.

   e) Handle missing data.

   f) Validate the data by answering the questions, like Does the data make sense? Does the data follow the appropriate rules for its field?

23. Mention four open-sourced Govt portals.

Ans. the open-sourced Govt portals are as follows:

   - https://www.india.gov.in/data-portal-india

   - http://mospi.nic.in/data

   - https://data.gov.in/

   - https://dbie.rbi.org.in/DBIE/dbie.rbi?site=home

24. Explain the term project cycle.

Ans. A project cycle is defined as the sequence of phases that a project goes through from its conception/initiation to its closure. Thus, the project cycle is the process of planning, organizing, coordinating, and finally developing a project effectively throughout its phases. It is related right from planning through execution, then completion and review to achieve pre-defined objectives.

25. What are the benefits of the project cycle?

Ans. Benefits of Project Cycle for any organization are enlisted as follows:

   a) It helps professional services teams to be more proficient and profitable.

   b) It helps the organization to achieve the targets on time.

c) It makes the flow of communication effective and easier.

d) It emphasises reporting and examining previous projects.

26. What are the three types of Learning-Based Approaches?

Ans. The learning-based Approach is subdivided into three types:

(a) Supervised Learning

(b) Unsupervised Learning

(c) Reinforcement Learning

27. Explain Reinforced Learning.

Ans. In reinforcement learning, the ability of an agent to interact with the environment is checked to find out the best outcome. Reinforcement learning is defined as Machine Learning that is associated with how software agents should take actions in an environment. It is a part of the deep learning method. It is a kind of hit and trial method, where the agent is rewarded or penalised with a point for a correct or a wrong answer; on the basis of the positive reward points gained, the model trains itself. After the training, it gets ready to predict the new data fed into the machine.

28. What is a neural network? What is the main advantage of neural networks?

Ans. (a) A neural network is a system of organizing machine learning algorithms to perform specific tasks. It is a fast and efficient method to solve problems for a very large dataset, like in images.

(b) The key advantage of neural networks is that they are capable of extracting data features automatically without any support for the input by the programmer.

29. How does a neural network work? Explain.

Ans. A Neural Network contains multiple layers, and each layer is divided into several blocks known as nodes. Every node has its own task to perform. Then, it is passed to the next layer. The first layer of a Neural Network is called the input layer. The main function of an input layer is to acquire data for feeding it to the Neural Network. No data processing occurs at the input layer.

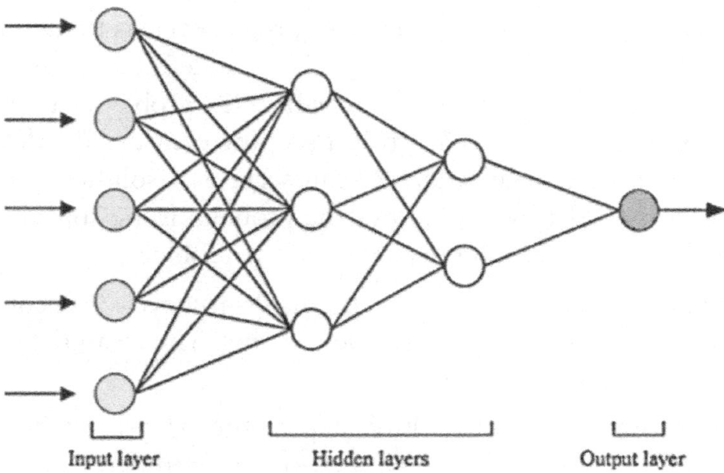

Figure 7.17 Structure of neural network

Next to the input layer, there are the hidden layers. Hidden layers are the layers wherein the whole processing occurs. The hidden layers are not visible to the users. Each node of the hidden layers has its own machine learning algorithm, which executes the data received from the input layer. The output is then fed to the subsequent hidden layer of the network. There may be multiple hidden layers in a neural network system. The number of hidden layers in any neural network depends upon the complexity of the function for which the network has been configured. Moreover, the number of nodes in each layer may vary accordingly. The final processed data is passed on by the last hidden layer to the output layer, which is made available to the user as the final output. Like the input layer, the output layer also does not process the data on acquiring it.

30. Enlist the main features of a Neural Network.

Ans. The main features of a Neural Network are listed as below:

   a) The neural network system is modeled on the human brain and nervous system.

   b) Each neural network node is essentially a machine learning algorithm.

   c) Neural networks are able to automatically extract features without input from the programmer.

   d) It is useful in solving problems for which a data set is very large.

31. Explain Artificial Neural Network (ANN).

Ans. An Artificial Neural Network is one of the information processing techniques. An Artificial Neural Network (ANN) is defined as an AI algorithm that is based on the similarities in structure and functions of biological neural networks (i.e., animal brains) that might be applied in advanced supervised, unsupervised, or reinforcement learning. ANN works like the way the human brain processes information. ANN includes a large number of connected processing units working together to process information. They also generate meaningful results from it.

7.3.10 Long Answer Type Questions

1. Discuss the stages of the AI Project.

Ans. The AI Project Cycle mainly has five stages, as mentioned below:

   a) **Problem Scoping:** The first step of the AI project cycle is to identify the problem to be solved. It is the process by which the problem is defined. Under problem scoping, we have to look at various parameters which affect the problem we wish to solve so that the picture becomes more clear. The project scoping provides the details of the challenges of the system and the areas where AI can serve as a solution. Thus, problem scoping is the process by which we figure out the problem to be solved. The key elements or factors are also considered in the context of the problem.

   b) **Data Acquisition:** The second step of the AI Project cycle is to collect and prepare all of the relevant data to be used in machine learning. The clean data is collected to ensure the proper operation of the system.

   c) **Data Exploration:** This is the third step of the AI project cycle in which the data collected is arranged in a proper manner for better understanding. The analysis of the data can be done after its arrangement in a systematic manner.

d) **Modelling:** This is the fourth step of the AI project cycle. It is the process in machine language that can be done either manually or automated by selecting a specific machine learning algorithm. Some software may be used for model preparation to work with our data.

e) **Evaluation:** In the final step, the Evaluation of the project on machine learning is done. The more accurate result of the model will be easier to meet the requirements of the stakeholders.

2. What is included in sustainable development? Explain.

Ans. Sustainable development includes:

   a) Reducing excessive use of natural resources,

   b) Enhancing natural resource conservation,

   c) Recycling and reuse of waste products/materials,

   d) Promoting green grassy patches between concrete buildings,

   e) Using more environmentally friendly material promoting products made of biodegradable material Scientific management of renewable resources, especially bio-resources,

   f) Promoting afforestation/planting more trees,

   g) Use of environmental-friendly technologies based on the efficient use of resources.

3. Discuss in detail the various data acquisition sources.

Ans. Various data acquisition sources are as follows:

   a) **Web Scraping:** Web data extraction or web scraping or web harvesting or Screen Scraping is defined as a technique used for extracting huge amounts of data from websites on the Internet by using a web browser. The data collected from the website is arranged in an organised format, like table, CSV file, spreadsheet, etc.

   b) **Surveys:** Surveys are one method to collect information directly by asking the details of the customers. A survey may collect either quantitative or qualitative data or both. A survey consists of a list of queries that are to be attended by the respondents in just one or two words. Thus, a survey can be conducted online, over email, the phone, or in-person for collecting data.

   c) **Cameras:** A camera is a crucial tool for the collection of data in the form of images. Live data can be acquired by using various devices, like web-camera, CCTV, chat-bot interface, etc. Images form a big part of data nowadays, as visual techniques are more important than numerical data.

   d) **Observations:** The process of careful and systematic viewing and recording of facts as they occur is termed observation. It requires movement of the eyes and careful listening. Observation serves the purpose of:

   ▲ studying collective behaviour and complex social situations;

   ▲ following up on individual elements of the situations;

   ▲ understanding the situation in their interrelation;

   ▲ getting the details of the situation.

e) **Sensors:** Sensors or Transducers are the devices used to convert real-world phenomena like temperature, force, and movement to current or voltage signals that may be used as inputs.

e) **API (Application Program Interface):** Application programming interfaces are used to collect data from other applications. API is the piece of code that helps to connect one application to another. For example, when we copy and paste text from one application to another, it is the API that allows that to work.

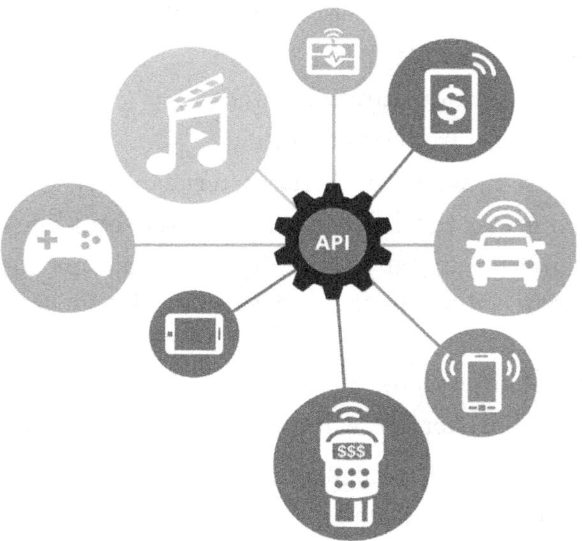

Figure 7.18

f) **System Map:** System Map is used to find relationships between different elements of the problem that is scoped. It helps us in strategizing the solution for achieving the goal of our project.

g) **IDENTITY charts:** These charts indicate the qualities, characteristics, or beliefs that make a person who they are and how does the world look at them.

4. Explain the Learning-based Approach with the help of a suitable example.

Ans. In the Learning-based Approach, the AI model gets trained on the data fed to it, and then a model is designed, which is adaptive to the change in data. Thus, when the model is trained with X type of data, and the machine designs the algorithm around it, then the model would modify itself according to the changes which occur in the data to handle all the exceptions in this case.

Example: Suppose we have a dataset comprising 200 images of pineapples and mangoes each. These images depict pineapples and mangoes in various shapes and sizes. These images are then labeled as either apple or banana so that all apple images are labeled 'pineapple,' and all the mango images have 'mango' as their label. Then, the AI model is trained with this Dataset, and the model is programmed in such a way so that it can distinguish between a pineapple image and a mango image according to their features. And it can predict the label of any image which is fed to it as pineapple or mango. After training, when the machine is fed with testing data, then the testing data might not have similar images to the ones on which the model has been trained. Hence, the model adapts to the features on which it has been trained, and accordingly, it predicts if the image is of pineapple or mango. In this way, the machine learns by itself by adapting to the new data which is flowing in. This is the learning-based Approach introducing the dynamicity in the model. The learning-based approach can further be divided into three parts: Supervised Learning, Unsupervised Learning, and Reinforced Learning.

5. Differentiate between Rule-Based Approach and Learning-based Approach for AI Modelling.

Ans. the difference between rule-based Approach and learning-based Approach is given below:

Rule-based Approach	Learning-based Approach
(i) The Rule-based Approach generates pre-defined outputs based on certain rules programmed by humans.	(i) Learning-based approach has its own rules based on the output and data used to train the models.
(ii) Rule-based Approach refers to the AI modelling where the relationship or patterns in data are defined by the developer.	(ii) In the Learning-based Approach, the relationship or patterns in data are not defined by the developer.
(iii) In the Rule-based Approach, the machine follows the rules or instructions mentioned by the developer and performs its task accordingly.	(iii) In the Learning-based Approach, random data as input is fed to the machine, and the machine figures out patterns and trends out.

6. Explain Supervised Learning with a suitable example.

Ans. In a normal classroom, supervised Learning occurs in the presence of a supervisor like a teacher. But in the case of a machine, supervised Learning is a learning in which the machine is trained by using data that is well labeled. It means that some data is already labeled with the correct answer. Later for training purposes, the machine is provided with a new dataset so that the supervised learning algorithm can analyze the training data and produces a correct outcome from labeled data.

Therefore, in a supervised learning model, the Dataset which is fed to the machine is labeled. A label is some information that can be used as a tag for data. Example: students get grades as per the marks secured in the examinations. These grades are labels that categorise the students according to their marks.

There are two types of Supervised Learning models:

a) **Classification:** In Classification, the data is classified according to the labels. Classification is defined as the process of finding/ discovering a model (function), which helps in separating the data into multiple categories/ classes. In Classification, the data is categorised under different labels according to some parameters, and then, the labels are predicted for the data. This model works on a discrete dataset. It means the data fed in the machine need not be continuous.

A classification problem will be when the output variable is a category, such as "Green or "Red," "disease" and "no disease," "spam" or "no spam" in email, etc.

Example: In the grading system, the students are classified based on the grades they obtain with respect to their marks in the annual examination.

b) **Regression:** Regression is defined as the process of finding a model/ function for distinguishing the data into continuous real values in place classes. Mathematically, one is trying to find the function approximation with the minimum error deviation in a regression problem. In regression, the numeric data dependency is predicted to distinguish it.

The Regression analysis is the statistical model that is used to predict the numeric data instead of labels. Regression can also identify the distribution movement depending on the available data or historical data. A regression problem will be when the output variable is a real value, such as "dollars" or "weight. Such models work on continuous data.

Consider this example: when we want to predict our next salary, then we have to put in the data of our previous salaries, all increments, etc. and would train the model. Here, the continuous data which has been fed to the machine is continuous.

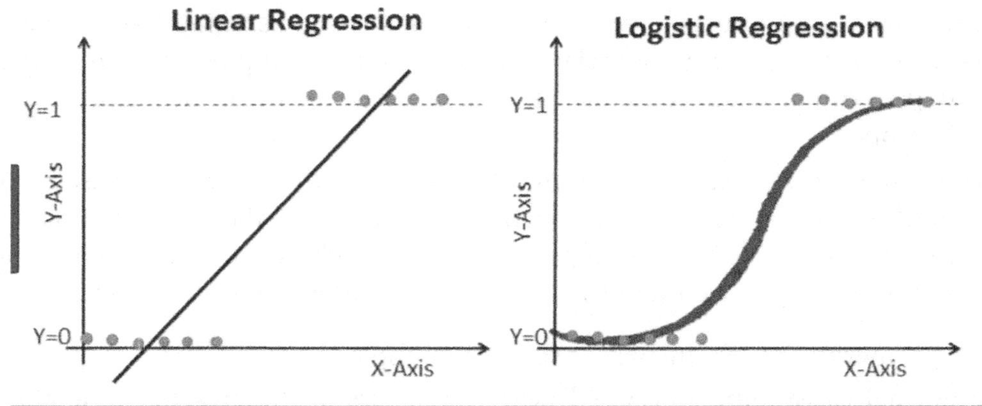

Figure 7.19

7. Differentiate between classification and clustering algorithms.

Ans.

Classification algorithm	Regression algorithm
(i) Classification is a process of finding a function that helps in dividing the Dataset into classes based on different parameters.	(i) Regression is the process of finding the correlations between dependent and independent variables.
(ii) In Classification, a computer program is trained using the training dataset and based on the training, it classifies the data into different classes.	(ii) In regression, it helps in predicting the continuous variables such as prediction of Market Trends, prediction of House prices, etc.
(iii) The task of the classification algorithm is to find the mapping function to map the input(x) to the discrete output(y).	(iii) The main function of the Regression algorithm is to search the mapping function to plot/map the input variable(x) to the continuous output variable(y).
Example: Classification of Email (Spam Detection)	*Example:* Weather forecasting

8. Discuss Unsupervised Learning with suitable examples.

Ans. Unsupervised Learning is defined as the training of a machine by using un-classified nor non-labeled information. It allows the algorithm to act on that information without any guidance or supervision. An unsupervised learning model works on an unlabelled dataset. Moreover, there is a possibility that the person who is training the model does not have any information regarding it. In this case, the machine has to classify/ group unsorted information according to similarities, patterns, and differences without any previous training of data, and no training will be given to the machine. Thus, the machine is restricted to finding the hidden structure in unlabelled data by itself. The unsupervised learning model identifies patterns, relationships, and trends out of the data which is fed into it. It helps the users in understanding what the data is about and what are the major features identified by the machine in it.

Example 1: Suppose an image having animals that have not been seen ever is fed into the machine, and the machine has no idea about the category of animals, so it won't be able to categorize them. But it can try to categorize them according to their similarities, patterns, and differences, i.e., it can easily categorize the animals belonging to the same group.

Example 2: Suppose we have random data of 1000 cat images, and you wish to understand some pattern out of it; you would feed this data into the unsupervised learning model and would train the machine on it. After training, the machine would come up with patterns which it was able to identify out of it. The machine might come up with patterns that are already known to the user, like colour, or it might even come up with something very unusual, like the size of the cats.

9. Explain two types of Unsupervised learning models with suitable examples.

Ans. Unsupervised learning models are divided into two categories: Clustering and Dimensionality Reduction.

a) **Clustering:** Clustering refers to the unsupervised learning algorithm which can cluster the unknown data according to the patterns or trends identified out of it. The patterns observed might be the ones that are known or unknown to the programmer /developer. Sometimes, it might even come up with some unique patterns out of it.

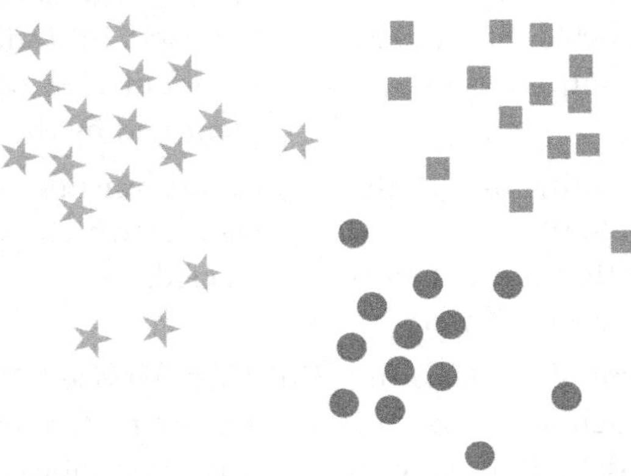

Figure 7.20 Clustering

A clustering problem is where we want to discover the characteristic groupings in the data, such as grouping customers by their purchasing behaviour or grouping customers using a library site by their reading behaviours or interest in different types of literature (novel/stories/science fiction/poetry, etc.).

b) ***Dimensionality Reduction:*** Humans can visualize up to three dimensions only, whereas a lot of theories and algorithms say that there are various entities in real life that exist beyond 3-Dimensions. But in real life, there are various entities that exist beyond the three dimensions. Dimensionality reduction is the process of transformation of data from high dimensional space into low dimensional space. The purpose of this transformation is to retain some meaningful properties of the original data that are close to the dimension. As we reduce the dimension of an entity, the information contained by it starts getting distorted.

For example, in Natural language Processing, the words are considered to be N-Dimensional entities. It means that we cannot visualize them as they exist beyond our visualization ability.

Consider this example: when we have a ball in our hand, it has 3-Dimensions right now. While clicking its picture, the data transform to 2-D as an image is a 2-Dimensional entity. On reducing one dimension, at least 50% of the information about the ball is lost. Don't we know whether the ball was of the same colour at the back or not? Or was it just a hemisphere? On reducing the dimensions further, more and more information will get lost.

Hence, we use Dimensionality Reduction to reduce the dimensions and still be able to make decisions out of the data.

10. Differentiate between Supervised and Unsupervised Learning.

Ans.

Supervised Learning	Unsupervised Learning
(i) Supervised Learning is an approach to creating Artificial Intelligence (AI), where the program is provided with labeled input data and the expected output results.	(i) The unsupervised learning models are used to identify relationships, patterns, and trends out of the data that is fed into them. It helps the users in understanding what the data is all about and what are the major features identified by the machine in the data.
(ii) In a supervised learning model, the Dataset that is fed to the machine is labeled. It means that some data is tagged with the correct answers.	(ii) In an unsupervised learning model, the Dataset which is fed to the machine is not labeled.
(iii) Supervised Learning is learning in which we teach or train the machine using data that is well labeled.	(iii) Unsupervised Learning is defined as the training of a machine using unclassified and non-labeled information. And then allowing the algorithm to act on that information without training/guidance.

(iv) In supervised Learning, the task of the machine is to group unsorted information according to similarities, patterns, and differences with some prior training of data.	(iv) the task of the machine is to group unsorted information according to similarities, patterns, and differences without any prior training of data.

11. Enlist the characteristics of different types of Machine Learning (ML).

Ans. The characteristics of three types of ML are given below:

a) **Supervised Learning:**
   - Labeled data
   - Direct feedback
   - Predict outcome/future

b) **Unsupervised Learning:**
   - Unsupervised Learning No labels
   - No feedbacks
   - Find hidden structure in data

c) **Reinforcement Learning:**
   - Decision process
   - Reward system
   - Learn a series of actions

12. Discuss the main Features of an Artificial Neural Network (ANN).

Ans. The Artificial Neural Network systems are modeled on the human brain and nervous system. The main features of an Artificial Neural Network (ANN) are as follows:

a) A Neural Network has the ability to learn by itself to produce the output and is not limited to the input provided to it.

b) It can work by using incomplete knowledge/information and may produce output.

c) In case a neuron is not responding, or a piece of information is missing, even then, the network can detect the fault and can produce the output.

d) It is capable of automatically extracting features without feeding the input by the programmer.

e) It has fault tolerance. It means that the corruption of one or more cells of ANN does not prevent it from generating output.

f) It has the capability to learn events and make decisions by commenting on similar events/data.

g) The loss of data does not affect it as the input is stored in its own networks instead of a database.

h) ANN has numerical strength that can perform more than one job at the same time (Parallel processing capability).

i) Able to work through real-time events, these networks can learn from examples and apply them when a similar event arises, making them.

j) Every node in the layer in a Neural Network is compulsorily a machine learning algorithm.

k) It is very useful to implement for solving problems for huge datasets.

13. On which basis is the efficiency of an AI Model calculated? Discuss.

Ans. The efficiency of a model is calculated on the following parameters:

a) **Accuracy:** Accuracy is a well-known performance metric that is used to tell about an AI-based model, whether it is a strong or weak model. While evaluating, we need to find out the accuracy of the results from the trained model.

b) **Precision:** It refers to the ratio of observations/predictions belonging to the positive class and are actually positive to the total number of all observations. It tells about that out of total predicted true output, what is the % of actual truth. How often is the model giving us correct results?

c) **Recall:** It indirectly tells us the model's ability to randomly identify an observation that belongs to the positive class.

d) **F1 Score:** F1 Score is an averaging Evaluation Metric used to generate a ratio. The F1 Score is also named the Harmonic Mean of the precision and recall Metrics. This is used as a measure of overall correctness that the model has achieved in a positive prediction environment.

7.3.11 HOTS Questions

1. How do the human neurons transmit information?

Ans. The human nervous system consists of millions of neurons. They use electrical impulses and chemical signals to transmit information between different areas of the brain and then between the brain and the rest of the nervous system.

2. Why is data acquiring considered a difficult task?

Ans. The data is a complex entity, and its acquiring is a difficult task as it is full of numbers, and if someone wants to make some sense out of it, he/she has to work some patterns out of it.

3. Why is a Project Cycle needed?

Ans. When we want to develop an AI-based project, the AI Project Cycle provides us with a complete and appropriate framework to lead us towards the desired goal. This makes our task easier, and the success rate in the project is ensured. The major role of the AI Project Cycle is to distribute the development of AI projects in various stages so that the execution of the project becomes easier, clearly understandable, and the steps/stages should become more specific to achieve the best possible output.

Figure 7.21

7.4 PRACTICE QUESTIONS

1. How do you define 'Testing Dataset'?
2. What is the main objective of the evaluation stage?
3. What are sustainable development goals?
4. Define Data Exploration.
5. What is the purpose of Unsupervised Learning?
6. Why are SDGs also known as 'Global Goals'?
7. Mention one example of clustering.
8. What is the main difference between 'Classification' and 'Regression'?
9. Define Data Features.
10. Define a problem statement template, and mention its significance.
11. Draw the icons of the following SDGs: No Poverty, Clean Water.
12. Explain any two SDGs.
13. Which precautions are to be taken while acquiring data for developing an AI Project?
14. What are the five stages of an AI Project cycle?
15. What are the types of learning approaches for AI modelling?
16. Define the role of a survey as a data acquisition source.
17. Difference between Biological Neural Network and Artificial Neural Network.
18. Mention the techniques that are used for data exploration.
19. Why are system maps used in data acquisition?
20. Why is it required to arrange the data in a systematic manner?
21. For which purpose artificial neural networks are used?
22. Observation is considered an appropriate tool for collecting data. Why?

23. What is the main purpose of Data Visualisation?

24. Enlist two types of Data Modelling.

25. Explain the necessary steps of an AI Project Cycle framework.

26. Explain an outline for scoping the following problem:

    "A growing concern of increased use of pesticides in farming by the farmers."

27. Differentiate among Artificial Intelligence, Machine Learning, and Deep Learning.

28. What is the 4W's canvas used in the Project cycle? Explain each of them with a suitable example.

29. Design an activity from real life to be used to make an AI project cycle.

30. Why is data acquired? From where is relevant data obtained?

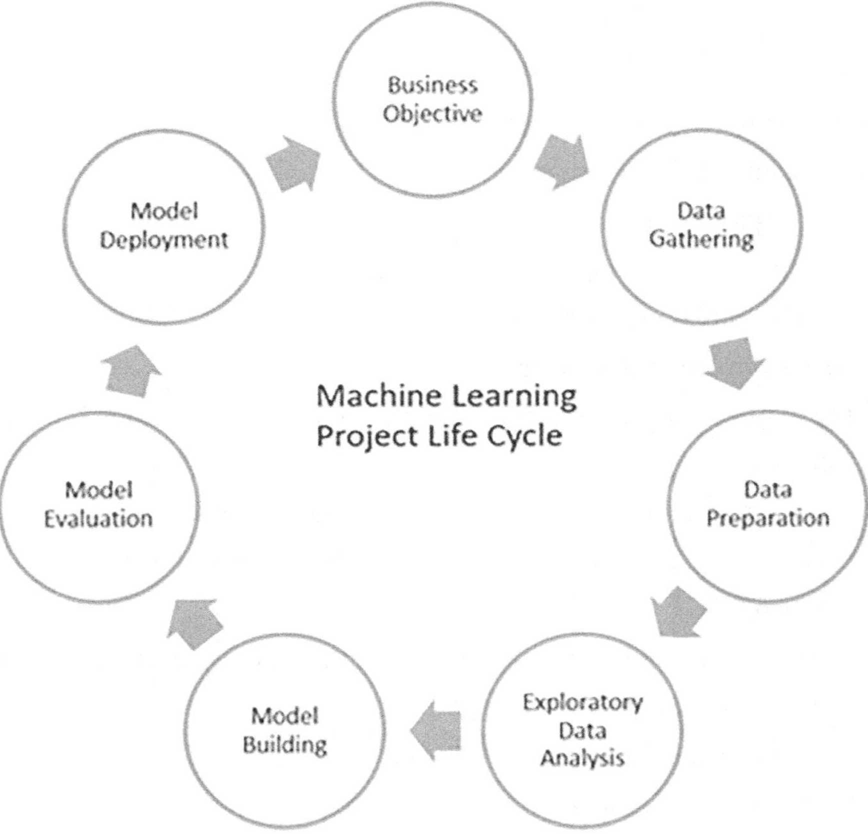

Figure 7.22

UNIT 8

Python Advance

8.1 UNIT IN BRIEF

✦ Python's support and ever-evolving libraries make it one of the best choices for all sorts of projects, like Web App, Mobile App, IoT, Data Science, AI, etc.

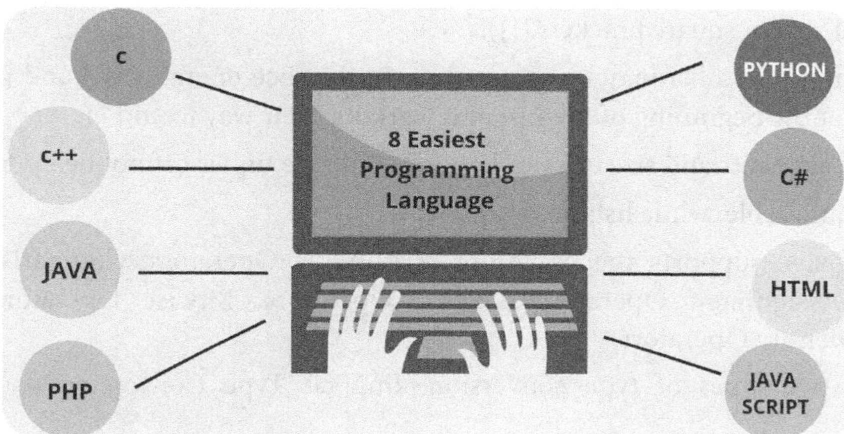

Figure 8.1

✦ Python is a high-level and interpreted programming language.

✦ Python is a case-sensitive programming language.

✦ OOPs means Object-Oriented Programs.

✦ The pseudocode in computer science is a plain language description of all the steps of an algorithm.

✦ The flow chart shows the logic of a program in a simple way.

✦ The flow chart is an easy and efficient tool to analyse a problem.

✦ It is easy to convert the flow chart into any programming language code.

✦ A diagrammatic/graphical representation of a sequence of steps to solve a problem is known as a flow chart.

✦ Website for installation of Python: https://www.python.org

✦ Weblink for downloading Python documentation: https://www.python.org/doc

✦ Python does not allow punctuation/special characters such as @, $, and % within identifiers.

✦ All other identifiers except class names start with a lowercase letter.

✦ An identifier starts with a single leading underscore signifies when the identifier is private.

✦ When an identifier starts with two leading underscores, it indicates that the identifier is a strongly private identifier.

✦ When the identifier also ends with two trailing underscores, then the identifier is a language-defined special name.

✦ A complex number may be defined as an ordered pair of real floating-point numbers denoted by x +yi, whereas x and y are the real numbers and 'i' is the imaginary unit.

✦ Strings in Python are identified as a contiguous set of characters represented in the quotation marks.

✦ The plus (+) sign is defined as the string concatenation operator, and the asterisk (*) is the repetition operator.

✦ Lists are an important data type of Python. A list contains items that are separated by commas and enclosed within square brackets ([]).

✦ The values stored in a list may be accessed using the slice operator ([ ] and [:]) with indexes starting at 0 at the beginning of the List and working their way to end -1.

✦ In lists, their elements and size can be changed while the tuples cannot be updated.

✦ Tuples are immutable, while lists are mutable.

✦ Python language supports the operators: Arithmetic Operators, Comparison (Relational) Operators, Assignment Operators, Logical Operators, Bitwise Operators, Membership Operators, Identity Operators.

✦ Python has two types of type conversion: Implicit Type Conversion and Explicit Type Conversion.

✦ A Jupyter notebook is a powerful tool used for interacting, developing, and presenting artificial intelligence-related projects.

Figure 8.2

✦ A package is a collection of Python modules. In other words, a package is a directory of Python modules containing an additional application environment.

✦ Matplotlib is a Python library meant for plotting the data and has NumPy as its numerical mathematics extension?

✦ NumPy is a Python library that will allow the user to handle multi-dimensional arrays and matrices. It also offers multiple high-level mathematical functions to operate on these.

✦ Loops are also known as iteration or iterative statements.

8.2 SOLVED EXAMPLES

8.2.1 Multiple Choice Questions

Tick (√) the correct option for each question.

1. Which statement is TRUE for the flowchart?
    a) A flowchart shows the logic of a program in a simple way.
    b) A flowchart is an easy and efficient tool to analyze the problem.
    c) Flow chart makes program or system maintenance easier.
    d) All the above

2. All other identifiers except _______________ start with a lowercase letter.
    a) Class names
    b) Private identifier
    c) Complex number
    d) None of the above

3. Which statement about Python is correct?
    a) It is a high-level and interpreted programming language.
    b) It is a highly useful language focused on rapid application development (RAD), and don't repeat yourself (DRY).
    c) It works to connect existing components together.
    d) All the above

4. Which of the following programming languages is considered the most popular programming language?
    a) Haskell   b) Python
    c) C++   d) Ruby

5. In which sorts of projects is Python used?
    a) Web App, and Mobile App   b) IoT, and Data Science
    c) AI   d) All the above

6. A complex number having an ordered pair of real floating-point numbers is denoted by x +yi, whereas x and y are the real numbers. What is 'i' in it?
    a) Identifier   b) Imaginary unit
    c) Both a and b   d) None of the above

7. Consider the following statements about the flowchart and choose the correct set.
    i.   It exhibits the individual steps and their interconnections.
    ii. It represents a workflow or process in a diagrammatic representation.
    iii. It exhibits the Sequence of instructions/happenings in a single program.

iv. It shows the logic of an algorithm from start to end.

v. It consists of standardised and acceptable symbols.

vi. It has a clear start point and End/Finish point.

vii. It exhibits the control from one activity to the next one.

a) (ii) (iii) (iv)

b) (iv) (v) (vi)

c) (iii) (v) (vii)

d) All the above

8. Which programming language is exhibited by the following logo?

Figure 8.3

a) Java

b) Prolog

c) Python

d) Pascal

9. Consider the following reasons for the selection of Python for AI Projects and choose the correct set.

i. A great library ecosystem

ii. Flexibility

iii. A low entry barrier

iv. Platform independence

v. Readability

vi. Good visualisation options

vii. Community support

a) (ii) (iii) (iv)

b) (ii) (iii) (vi) (vii)

c) (iii) (iv) (v) (vi)

d) All the above

10. Which application does not use Python?

a) Database Access

b) Network Programming

c) 2D Graphics

d) Desktop Applications

11. Which platform can be used to run Python?

a) Windows

b) macOS,

c) Linux

d) All of these

12. From which weblink can Python be downloaded for free?

a) www.python.com

b) www.python.org

c) www.python.in

d) None of the above

13. Which of the following is not a Python keyword?

a) except

b) Outcome

c) as

d) Def

14. Which of the following pairs is not a Python keyword?

    a) and, pass   b) Out, Accept   c) as, With   d) Del, if

15. A sequence of values of any type enclosed in square brackets is called:

    a) List   b) Tuple

    c) Set   d) None of the above

16. The full form of NLP with reference to AI is:

    a) Natural Language Processing   b) Neural Learning Program

    c) Natural Logic Program   d) Neuro-Linguistic Program

17. Which of the following languages is one of the most popular languages for AI nowadays?

    a) Java   b) Python   c) Ruby   d) C+

18. Which of the following properties of Python make it one of the fastest-growing programming languages?

    a) Ease of learning   b) Scalability

    c) Adaptability   d) All the above

19. Out of the following applications, which does not use Python?

    a) Web and Internet Development   b) Desktop GUI Applications

    c) Mobile development   d) Database Access

20. Which application is considered an application of AI?

    a) Remote-controlled Drone   b) Self-Driving Car

    c) Self-Watering Plant System   d) Self-Service Kiosk/ATM

21. What is the correct syntax to output the type of variable in python?

    a) print(type x)   b) print(type of x)

    c) print(type of (x))   d) print(type (x))

22. Which geometric shape is used for input and output operation in a flowchart?

    a) Oval   b) Rectangle

    c) Diamond   d) Parallelogram

23. Which command is used to open Jupyter Notebook in anaconda prompt?

    a) conda Jupiter notebook   b) open jupyter notebook

    c) jupyter notebook   d) activate Jupiter Notebook

24. Which Python library is meant for plotting the data and has NumPy as its numerical mathematics extension?

    a) NLTK   b) Pandas   c) Matplotlib   d) OpenCV

25. Which shape is used to represent the start and the end of the flowchart?

    a) Rectangle   b) Diamond   c) Oval   d) Arrow

26. Which shape is used for arithmetic operations and data manipulations in the flow chart?

    a) Oval　　　　　b) Rectangle　　　　c) Diamond　　　　d) Arrow

27. What is also known as iteration or iterative statements in Python?

    a) Loops　　　　b) Lists　　　　c) Tuple　　　　d) Operator

28. Which pair of operators is not supported by Python?

    a) Logical Operators, Bitwise Operators

    b) Membership Operators, Identity Operators

    c) Arithmetic Operators, Assignment Operators

    d) None of the above

29. How many types of type conversions are used in Python?

    a) 2　　　　　b) 3　　　　　c) 4　　　　　d) 5

30. In which type of projects is Python used?

    a) Web App, IoT　　　　　　　　b) Mobile App, AI

    c) Data Science,　　　　　　　　d) All the above

31. What command is used to open Jupyter Notebook in anaconda prompt?

    a) open jupyter notebook　　　　　　b) jupyter notebook

    c) conda Jupiter notebook　　　　　　d) activate Jupiter Notebook

32. For which reason is Python gaining maximum popularity?

    a) Easy in writing and Less execution of codes

    b) Availability of prebuilt libraries

    c) Flexibility in providing an API from an existing language

    d) All the above

33. Which of the following reasons make Python a suitable language for AI Projects?
    a) A great library ecosystem, Community support
    b) Flexibility, Readability, Good visualization options
    c) A low entry barrier, Platform independence
    d) All the above

34. Which of the following statements is INCORRECT?
    a) The flow chart shows the logic of a program in a simple way.
    b) It is difficult to convert the flow chart into any programming language code.
    c) The flow chart is an easy and efficient tool to analyze a problem.
    d) The flow chart makes program or system maintenance easier.

35. A diagrammatic/graphical representation of a sequence of steps to solve a problem is known
    as:

    a) Pie chart　　　　　　　　　b) Venn diagram

    c) Flowchart　　　　　　　　　d) None of the above

36. Which shape in a flowchart is used to represent the operation in which there are two/three alternatives, true and false, etc.?

    a) Oval   b) Rectangle

    c) Diamond   d) Parallelogram

37. Which shape is used to exhibit page connector in a flow chart?

    a) Circle   b) Rectangle

    c) Diamond   d) Parallelogram

38. What symbol is used to indicate the flow of logic by connecting symbols in a flow chart?

    a) Diamond   b) Oval

    c) Circle   d) Flowline or arrow

39. Which of the following is not standard data types in Python?

    a) Boolean   b) Numbers, List

    c) String, Tuple   d) Dictionary

40. Which statement is INCORRECT?

    a) Lists are enclosed in parentheses, whereas tuples are enclosed in brackets.

    b) In lists, their elements and size can be changed while the tuples cannot be updated.

    c) A tuple is a sequence data type that consists of a number of values separated by commas.

    d) Tuples are immutable, while lists are mutable.

ANSWERS									
1. (d)	2. (a)	3. (d)	4. (b)	5. (d)	6. (b)	7. (d)	8. (c)	9. (d)	10. (c)
11. (d)	12. (b)	13. (b)	14. (b)	15. (a)	16. (a)	17. (b)	18. (d)	19. (c)	20. (b)
21. (a)	22. (d)	23. (c)	24. (c)	25. (c)	26. (b)	27. (a)	28. (d)	29. (a)	30. (d)
31. (b)	32. (d)	33. (d)	34. (b)	35. (c)	36. (c)	37. (a)	38. (d)	39. (a)	40. (a)

8.2.2 Fill in the blanks

1. _______________ are immutable, while lists are mutable.

2. When an identifier starts with two leading underscores, it indicates that the identifier is strong _____________.

3. The plus (+) sign is defined as the _____________ concatenation operator, and the asterisk (*) is the repetition operator.

4. When the identifier also ends with two trailing underscores, then the identifier is a _____________ special name.

5. A complex number may be defined as an ordered pair of real floating-point numbers denoted by x + yi, whereas x and y are the real numbers and 'i' is the _____________ unit.

6. _____________ are an important data type of Python. A list contains items that are separated by commas and enclosed within square brackets ([]).

7. Python has two types of type conversion: _____________ Type Conversion and Explicit Type Conversion.

8. Starting an identifier with two leading _______________ indicates a strongly private identifier.

9. _______________ notebook is a powerful tool for interacting, developing, and presenting artificial intelligence-related projects.

10. _______________ in Python are identified as a contiguous set of characters represented in the quotation marks.

11. The values stored in a List may be accessed using the _______________ operator ([ ] and [:]) with indexes starting at 0 at the beginning of the List and working their way to end -1.

12. _______________ language supports the operators: Arithmetic Operators, Comparison (Relational) Operators, Assignment Operators, Logical Operators, Bitwise Operators, Membership Operators, Identity Operators.

13. It is easy to convert the _______________ into any programming language code.

14. _______________ are also known as iteration or iterative statements.

15. Class names start with an _______________ letter.

ANSWERS			
1. Tuples	2. private identifier	3. string	4. language-defined 5. imaginary
6. Lists	7. Implicit 8. underscores 9. Jupyter	10. Strings 11. slice	
12. Python	13. flowchart 14. Loops	15. uppercase	

8.2.3 True or False

1. In lists, the elements and size can be changed while the tuples cannot be updated.

2. Flow chart makes program or system maintenance easier.

3. Python has six standard data types.

4. Class names start with lowercase letters.

5. The flow chart shows the logic of a program in a difficult way.

6. Lists are an important data type of Python.

7. Tuples are enclosed in brackets.

8. SciPy also offers multiple high-level mathematical functions to operate on these.

9. Python does not allow punctuation/special characters such as @, $, and % within identifiers.

10. A list contains items that are separated by commas and enclosed within square brackets ([]).

11. Python has three types of type conversion.

12. A diagrammatic/graphical representation of a sequence of steps to solve a problem is known as a flowchart.

13. Starting an identifier with a double leading underscore indicates that the identifier is private.

14. The pseudocode in computer science is a plain language description of all the steps of an algorithm.

15. The flowchart is an easy and efficient tool to analyze a problem.

Figure 8.4

ANSWERS

1. T	2. T	3. F (five)	4. F (uppercase)	5. F (simple way)	6. T	7. T
8. F (NumPy)	9. T	10. T	11. F (two)	12. T		
13. F (single leading underscore)		14. T	15. T			

8.2.4 Matching type

Match the items of column A with those of column b correctly.

Column A

(i) Problem Scoping

(ii) Data Acquisition

(iii) Data Exploration

(iv) Modelling

(v) Evaluation

Column B

(a) Arranging the collected data in a proper manner for better understanding.

(b) Evaluation of the machine learning project to meet the requirements of the stake holders

(c) Selecting a specific machine learning algorithm

(d) Identification of the problem to be solved.

(e) Collection and preparation of all of the relevant data to be used in machine learning.

ANSWERS

| (i) -d | (ii) -e | (iii) -a | (iv) -c | (v) -b |

8.2.5 Assertion Reason Type Questions

1. Assertion (A): Python is platform-independent.

   Reason (R): Python can be used across different platforms and technologies with the basic coding.

   a) Both A and R are correct and R is the correct reason for A.

   b) Both A and R are correct and R is not the correct reason for A.

   c) A is correct but R is incorrect.

   d) A is incorrect but R is correct.

2. Assertion (A): In lists, their elements and size can be changed while the tuples cannot be updated.

    Reason (R): Tuples are mutable, while lists are immutable.
    a) Both A and R are correct and R is the correct reason for A.
    b) Both A and R are correct and R is not the correct reason for A.
    c) A is correct but R is incorrect.
    d) A is incorrect but R is correct.

3. Assertion (A): A code is a programming tool that uses different symbols to design a solution to a problem.

    Reason (R): A program is a collection of instructions used to perform a specific task when executed by a computer.
    a) Both A and R are correct and R is the correct reason for A.
    b) Both A and R are correct and R is not the correct reason for A.
    c) A is correct but R is incorrect.
    d) A is incorrect but R is correct.

4. Assertion (A): A list contains items that are separated by commas and enclosed within square brackets ([ ]).

    Reason (R): A package is a directory of Python modules containing an additional application environment.
    a) Both A and R are correct and R is the correct reason for A.
    b) Both A and R are correct and R is not the correct reason for A.
    c) A is correct but R is incorrect.
    d) A is incorrect but R is correct.

5. Assertion (A): Python is platform Independent.

    Reason (R): Python can be used across different platforms and technologies with basic coding.
    a) Both A and R are correct and R is the correct reason for A.
    b) Both A and R are correct and R is not the correct reason for A.
    c) A is correct but R is incorrect.
    d) A is incorrect but R is correct.

6. Assertion (A): Python is an object-oriented program.

    Reason (R): Python supports Object-Oriented style or technique programming that encapsulates code within objects.
    a) Both A and R are correct and R is the correct reason for A.
    b) Both A and R are correct and R is not the correct reason for A.
    c) A is correct but R is incorrect.
    d) A is incorrect but R is correct.

7. Assertion (A): A package is a directory of Python modules containing an additional application environment.

    Reason (R): Lists are enclosed in parentheses, whereas tuples are enclosed in brackets.

a) Both A and R are correct and R is the correct reason for A.

b) Both A and R are correct and R is not the correct reason for A.

c) A is correct but R is incorrect.

d) A is incorrect but R is correct.

<table>
<tr><td colspan="7" align="center">ANSWERS</td></tr>
<tr><td>1. (a)</td><td>2. (c)</td><td>3. (d)</td><td>4. (b)</td><td>5. (a)</td><td>6. (a)</td><td>7. (c)</td></tr>
</table>

8.2.6 Statements Based Questions

1. Statement 1: All other identifiers except class names start with a lowercase letter.

    Statement 2: Strings in Python are identified as a contiguous set of characters represented in the quotation marks.

    a) Statement 1 is correct but statement 2 is incorrect.

    b) Statement 1 is incorrect but statement 2 is correct.

    c) Both the statements are correct.

    d) Both the statements are incorrect.

2. Statement 1: Python allow punctuation/special characters such as @, $, and % within identifiers.

    Statement 2: A variable whose value cannot be changed even later on is called a 'Constant.'

    a) Statement 1 is correct but statement 2 is incorrect.

    b) Statement 1 is incorrect but statement 2 is correct.

    c) Both the statements are correct.

    d) Both the statements are incorrect.

3. Statement 1: The plus (+) sign is defined as the string concatenation operator, and the asterisk (*) is the repetition operator.

    Statement 2: A program is considered as a blueprint of a design used for solving any specific problem.

    a) Statement 1 is correct but statement 2 is incorrect.

    b) Statement 1 is incorrect but statement 2 is correct.

    c) Both the statements are correct.

    d) Both the statements are incorrect.

4. Statement 1: A notebook integrates code and its output into a single document that combines narrative text, visualisations, mathematical equations, and other rich media.

    Statement 2: An algorithm means a procedure or a technique. An algorithm is a sequence of steps to solve a specific problem.

    a) Statement 1 is correct but statement 2 is incorrect.

    b) Statement 1 is incorrect but statement 2 is correct.

    c) Both the statements are correct.

    d) Both the statements are incorrect.

5. Statement 1: A List contains items which are separated by commas and enclosed within square brackets ([]).

   Statement 2: Logical operators are used for comparing values. It either returns True or False as per the condition.

   a) Statement 1 is correct but statement 2 is incorrect.

   b) Statement 1 is incorrect but statement 2 is correct.

   c) Both the statements are correct.

   d) Both the statements are incorrect.

6. Statement 1: Strings in Python are identified as a contiguous set of characters represented in the quotation marks.

   Statement 2: Logical operators are three: and, or, not.

   a) Statement 1 is correct but statement 2 is incorrect.

   b) Statement 1 is incorrect but statement 2 is correct.

   c) Both the statements are correct.

   d) Both the statements are incorrect.

7. Statement 1: NumPy is a Python library meant for plotting the data and has NumPy as its numerical mathematics extension?

   Statement 2: Matplotlib is a Python library that will allow the user to handle multi-dimensional arrays and matrices. It also offers multiple high-level mathematical functions to operate on these.

   a) Statement 1 is correct, but statement 2 is incorrect.

   b) Statement 1 is incorrect, but statement 2 is correct.

   c) Both the statements are correct.

   d) Both the statements are incorrect.

8. Statement 1: The Loop or Repetition allows the statement(s) to be executed repeatedly based on certain loop conditions.

   Statement 2: A 'while' statement allows you to repeatedly execute a block of statements till the condition is true.

   a) Statement 1 is correct but statement 2 is incorrect.

   b) Statement 1 is incorrect but statement 2 is correct.

   c) Both the statements are correct.

   d) Both the statements are incorrect.

9. Statement 1: Matplotlib is a package that is used to plot 2D figures like lines, bars, histograms, pie charts, etc.

   Statement 2: NLTK is an open-source Python module that has been developed for CV.

   a) Statement 1 is correct, but statement 2 is incorrect.

   b) Statement 1 is incorrect, but statement 2 is correct.

   c) Both the statements are correct.

   d) Both the statements are incorrect.

10. Statement 1: Anaconda Navigator is a desktop graphical user interface(GUI) present in Anaconda that allows the users to manage conda packages, environments, Apps, and channels without the need to use command-line commands.

    Statement 2: In programming, Sequence means to place statements one after the other, and the execution takes place starting from top to bottom.

    a) Statement 1 is correct, but statement 2 is incorrect.

    b) Statement 1 is incorrect, but statement 2 is correct.

    c) Both the statements are correct.

    d) Both the statements are incorrect.

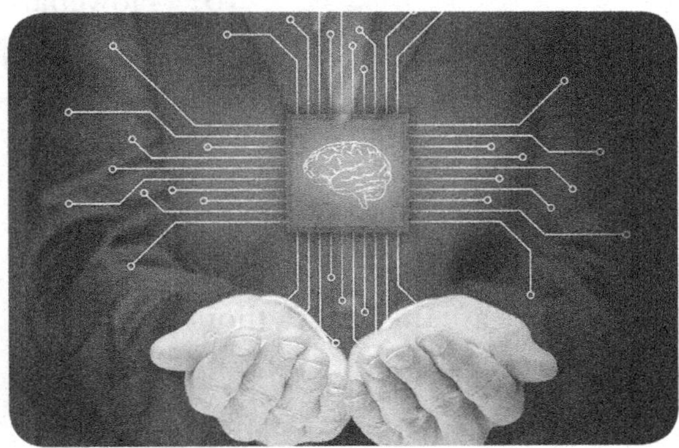

Figure 8.5

ANSWERS									
1. (c)	2. (b)	3. (a)	4. (c)	5. (a)	6. (c)	7. (d)	8. (c)	9. (a)	10. (c)

8.2.7 Competency-Based Questions

1. A process has the following steps
    i.   Define the inputs
    ii. Define the variables
    iii. Outline the algorithm's operations
    iv. Output the results of the operations

    Which of the following is associated with these steps?

    a) Algorithm   b) Code   c) Flowchart   d) Mentoring

2. A coding language has the following features:

    i.   It is a case-sensitive language.

    ii. Learning and using this language is easy.

    iii. It is portable and its codes are short.

    iv. It is Interpreted, interactive and OOP language.

    v.   It is a very simple high-level language with a vast library of add-on modules.

    This coding language is:

    a) Java   b) Python   c) C++   d) Maya

3. Consider the following properties:
   i. It exhibits the Sequence of instructions/happenings in a single program.
   ii. It consists of standardized and acceptable symbols.
   iii. It has a clear start point and End/Finish point.
   iv. It exhibits the individual steps and their interconnections.
   v. It shows the logic of an algorithm from start to end.
   vi. It has short, clear, and readable statements written inside the symbols.

   The above statements refer to:
   a) Algorithm
   b) Flowchart
   c) Code
   d) Coding language

ANSWERS
1. (a)   2. (b)   3. (b)

8.2.8 VSA

1. How many standard data types are there in Python?

Ans. Python has five standard data types.

2. Which website is used for the installation of Python?

Ans. https://www.python.org

3. Which weblink is used for downloading Python documentation?

Ans. https://www.python.org/doc

4. Which operator is used to store the values in a list?

Ans. The values stored in a list may be accessed using the slice operator ([ ] and [:]) with indexes starting with 0 at the beginning of the List and working their way to end -1.

5. How are strings identified in Python?

Ans. Strings in Python are defined as a contiguous set of characters represented in the quotation marks.

6. What is exhibited by a plus (+) sign and asterisk (*) in Python?

Ans. The plus (+) sign exhibits the string concatenation operator, and the asterisk (*) shows the repetition operator.

7. How items/elements in a list are displayed?

Ans. A list contains items that are separated by commas and enclosed within square brackets ([]).

8. Mention one difference between lists and tuples.

Ans. Lists are enclosed in brackets, whereas tuples are enclosed in parentheses. In lists, their elements and size can be changed while the tuples cannot be updated. Tuples are immutable, while lists are mutable.

9. How many types of conversions are present in Python?

Ans. Python has two types of type conversion: Implicit Type Conversion and Explicit Type Conversion.

10. What is a package in Python?

Ans. A package is a directory of Python modules containing an additional application environment.

11. What do you mean by Matplotlib?

Ans. Matplotlib is a Python library meant for plotting the data and has NumPy as its numerical mathematics extension?

12. Define constants in Python.

Ans. A variable whose value cannot be changed even later on is called a 'Constant.'

13. What is a flowchart?

Ans. A flowchart is a programming tool that uses different symbols to design a solution to a problem.

14. Define a program.

Ans. A program is a collection of instructions used to perform a specific task when executed by a computer.

15. Who designed the first flowchart?

Ans. John Von Neumann in 1945.

16. Which is considered a blueprint of a design?

Ans. A flowchart is considered as a blueprint of a design used for solving any specific problem.

17. What are Comparison operators?

Ans. Comparison operators are used for comparing values. It either returns True or False as per the condition.

18. How many Logical operators are used in Python?

Ans. Logical operators are three: and, or, not.

19. Define assignment operators.

Ans. Assignment operators are mainly used in Python to assign values to variables.

20. Define Anaconda.

Ans. Anaconda is a free and open-source distribution of the Python language for scientific computing (data science, machine learning applications, large-scale data processing, predictive analytics, etc.) that aims to simplify package management and deployment. It provides the facility to create different virtual environments, each having its own packages and settings, as per the user's need.

21. What do you mean by Anaconda Navigator?

Ans. Anaconda Navigator is a desktop graphical user interface(GUI) present in Anaconda that allows the users to manage conda packages, environments, Apps, and channels without the need to use command-line commands.

22. Define Notebook.

Ans. A notebook integrates code and its output into a single document that combines narrative text, visualisations, mathematical equations, and other rich media.

23. What is the meaning of the word 'algorithm'?

Ans. An algorithm means a procedure or a technique. An algorithm is a sequence of steps to solve a specific problem.

24. What do you mean by Sequence in programming?

Ans. In programming, Sequence means to place statements one after the other, and the execution takes place starting from top to bottom.

25. What is 'branching'?

Ans. In branch control, there will be a condition, and according to the condition, a decision of either TRUE or FALSE is evaluated. In the case of TRUE, one of the two options is mentioned, whereas, in the case of the FALSE condition, the other alternative is taken.

26. What do you mean by Loop (Repetition)?

Ans. The Loop or Repetition allows the statement(s) to be executed repeatedly based on certain loop conditions, e.g., WHILE, FOR loops.

27. Define the while loop in Python.

Ans. A 'while' statement allows you to repeatedly execute a block of statements till the condition is true. A while statement is also an example of a looping statement.

28. What is the Syntax of while Loop in Python?

Ans. while test_expression: statement (s)

29. How is test expression checked in while loop?

Ans. In a 'while' loop, test expression is checked in the first step. The body of the 'loop' is entered only when the test expression evaluates to be True. After each iteration, the test expression is checked again and again. This process continues until the test expression evaluates to False.

30. What is the main purpose of the python virtual environment?

Ans. The main purpose of the python virtual environment is to create an isolated environment for these projects. It means that each project may have its own dependencies, irrespective of what dependencies every other project has.

31. What is the use of a Jupyter Notebook?

Ans. A Jupyter notebook is a powerful tool used for interacting, developing, and presenting artificial intelligence-related projects.

32. What does it mean that Python is interpreted?

Ans. Python is processed at runtime by the interpreter, and we do not need to compile our program before executing it.

33. How is python interactive?

Ans. We can actually work at Python prompt and interact with the interpreter directly to write our programs. That's why Python is interactive.

34. How is Python Object-Oriented Program (OOP)?

Ans. Since Python supports Object-Oriented style or technique programming that encapsulates code within objects and hence, it is an object-oriented program.

35. Why is Python platform Independent?

Ans. Python can be used across different platforms and technologies with the basic coding, and hence, it is platform-independent.

36. What is the use of matplotlib?

Ans. Matplotlib is a package that is used to plot 2D figures like lines, bars, histograms, pie charts, etc.

37. What is the main use of NLTK?

Ans. NLTK is another open-source Python module that has been developed for natural language processing and text analytics.

38. Mention two commonly used Python AI libraries.

Ans. AIMA, pyDatalog, Simple AI, Open CV, Easy AI, etc.

39. Who was the first designer of a flowchart in 1945?

Ans. John Von Neumann.

Figure 8.6 John Von Neumann

40. What is a 'Flowchart'?

Ans. A flowchart is a programming tool that uses different symbols to design a solution to a problem.

41. What is often considered as a blueprint of a design used for solving a specific problem?

Ans. Flowchart

42. Which shape is used to exhibit page connector in a flowchart?

Ans. Circle

43. Which shape is used to represent the start and end of the flowchart?

Ans. Oval

44. What symbol is used to indicate the flow of logic by connecting symbols in a flowchart?

Ans. Flowline or arrow

45. Which shape is used for arithmetic operations and data manipulations in the flowchart?

Ans. Rectangle

46. Which geometric shape is used for input and output operation in a flowchart?

Ans. Parallelogram

47. Which shape in a flowchart is used to represent the operation in which there are two/three alternatives, true and false, etc.?

Ans. Diamond

48. From which website can Python be installed?

Ans. https://www.python.org

49. From which weblink can we download Python documentation?

Ans. https://www.python.org/doc

50. What is a python identifier?

Ans. A Python identifier is a name used to identify a variable, module, function, class, or other objects.

51. What may be the value of a python identifier?

Ans. An identifier starts with a letter A to Z or a to z or an underscore (followed by zero or more letters underscores and digits (0 to 9).

52. What are strings in Python?

Ans. Strings in Python are identified as a contiguous set of characters represented in the quotation marks.

53. Define Lists.

Ans. Lists are an important data type of Python. A List contains items which are separated by commas and enclosed within square brackets ([]).

54. What do you mean by a tuple?

Ans. A tuple is a sequence data type that consists of a number of values separated by commas.

55. Define comparison operators.

Ans. Comparison Operators (Relational Operator) compare the values on either side of them and decide the relation among them.

56. What are Membership Operators?

Ans. Python's membership operators test for membership in a sequence, like strings, lists, tuples, etc.

57. What do you mean by Identify Operators?

Ans. Identity operators compare the memory locations of two objects.

58. Define type conversion.

Ans. Type conversion is defined as the process of converting the value of one data type (integer, float, string, etc.) to another data type.

59. What is explicit type conversion?

Ans. In Explicit Type Conversion, users can convert the data type of an object to the required data type.

60. Which type of conversion in Python is called 'Type Casting'?

Ans. Explicit type conversion

61. Define Anaconda.

Ans. Anconda is a free and open-source distribution of the Python language for scientific computing that includes data science, machine learning applications, large-scale data processing, predictive analytics, etc.

62. What do you mean by Anaconda Navigator?

Ans. Anaconda Navigator is a desktop graphical user interface (GUI) present in Anaconda that allows the user to manage conda packages, apps, environments, and channels.

63. Define the Jupyter Notebook.

Ans. A Jupyter notebook is a powerful tool used for interacting, developing, and presenting artificial intelligence-related projects.

64. What is a package in Python?

Ans. A package is a collection of Python modules, i.e., a package is a directory of Python modules containing an additional application environment.

65. Which Python library is meant for plotting the data and has NumPy as its numerical mathematics extension?

Ans. Matplotlib

66. Define NumPy.

Ans. NumPy is a Python library that will allow the user to handle multi-dimensional arrays and matrices. It also offers multiple high-level mathematical functions to operate on these.

67. Define Loops.

Ans. Loops are also known as iteration or iterative statements.

8.2.9 Short Answer Type Questions

1. Name all the operators that are supported by Python.

Ans. Python language supports the operators: Arithmetic Operators, Comparison (Relational) Operators, Assignment Operators, Logical Operators, Bitwise Operators, Membership Operators, Identity Operators.

2. What are the two main functions of NumPy?

Ans. NumPy is a Python library that allows the user to handle multi-dimensional arrays and matrices. It also offers multiple high-level mathematical functions to operate on these.

Figure 8.7

3. Explain the steps used in writing algorithms.

Ans. The following steps are used in writing algorithms:

a) **Define the inputs for the algorithm:** Define the inputs required for the algorithm. Various algorithms take in data for processing. For example, while calculating the area of a circle, input will be the radius.

b) **Define the variables:** Variables in an algorithm may be used by the user for more than one place, and hence, variables are to be defined. While calculating the area and circumference of a circle, the users need to define radius (variable).

c) **Outline the algorithm's operations:** Outlining the operations of the algorithm is required to input variables for computation purposes. For example, to find the area of a circle, multiply the value of pie (3.14) with radius. Here, the radius is defined.

d) **Output the results of the operations of the algorithm:** Outline the result(s) of the operations of the algorithm. In the case of the area of a circle, the output will be the value stored in the variable AREA.

4. Write the characteristics of a flowchart.

Ans. A flowchart has the following characteristics:

i. It exhibits the Sequence of instructions/happenings in a single program.

ii. It consists of standardized and acceptable symbols.

iii. It has a clear start point and End/Finish point.

iv. It exhibits the individual steps and their interconnections.

v. It represents a workflow or process in a diagrammatic representation.

vi. It exhibits the control from one activity to the next one.

vii. It shows the logic of an algorithm from start to end.

viii. It has short, clear, and readable statements written inside the symbols.

5. Mention four applications in which Python is used.

Ans. Python is used for a large number of applications. Some of them are mentioned below:

a) Web and Internet Development
b) Desktop GUI Applications
c) Business Applications
d) Software Development
e) Games and 3D Graphics
f) Database Access

6. Explain script mode.

Ans. In script mode, the users type the Python program in a file, followed by the use of the interpreter to execute the content from that file. Working in interactive mode is easy and convenient for beginners and for testing small pieces of code, as users may test them immediately. For coding more than a few lines, the users should always save the code so that they may modify and reuse the code.

7. Explain Python Statements.

Ans. Statements are the instructions written in the source code for execution. There are various types of statements in the Python programming language, like Assignment statements, Conditional statements, Looping statements, etc. These statements help the user to get the required output. For example, n = 60 is an assignment statement.

8. Define keywords in Python. Give a list of Python (9.5.1) keywords.

Ans. Keywords are the reserved words in Python used by the Python interpreter to recognize the structure of the program. The list of all the keywords in Python 9.5.1 is given in the following Table:

False	Class	Finally	is	return	None	Nonlocal
Try	Continue	True	and	as	assert	Lambda
Break	Def	Del	elif	Else	except	Not
For	From	Global	if	import	in	or
pass	raise	While	With	Yield		

9. What do you mean by identifiers? Explain the properties of Python identifiers.

Ans. An identifier is a user-defined name given to a variable, a function, a class, a module, or any other object under consideration. It becomes a programmable entity in Python- one with a name. Thus, it is a name given to the fundamental building blocks in a program.

Properties of Identifiers are as follows:

a) Python identifier can contain English alphabet letters in a small case (a-z), upper case (A-Z), digits (0-9), and underscore (_).

b) Identifier names can't begin with a digit.

c) Keywords cannot be used as identifiers.

d) Python identifier can't contain only digits.

e) Special symbols, like !, @, #, $, %, ^, &, etc cannot be used in the identifier.

f) The name of a Python identifier may start with an underscore.

g) The identifier can be of any length.

10. Explain variables with the help of examples.

Ans. A variable is a named location that is used to store data in the memory of the computer. It is like that variable as a container that holds data that can be changed later throughout programming. For example,

x = 42

y = 39

z = 71

These declarations make sure that the program reserves memory for three variables with the names x, y, and z. The variable names stand for the memory location.

Some examples of variables are mentioned in the following table:

Task	Sample Code	Output
(i) Assigning a value to a variable	Website = "abc.com" print(Website)	abc.com
(ii) Changing value of a variable	Website = "xyz.com" print(Website) Website1 = "spr.org" print(Website1)	xyz.com spr.org

Task	Sample Code	Output
(iii) Assigning different values to different variables	a, b, c=5, 3, 2 print(a) print(b) print(c)	5 3 2
(iv) Assigning same value to different variable	x=y=z= "Shama" print(x) print(y) print(z)	Shama Shama Shama

11. What are the rules and naming conventions for variables and constants in Python?

Ans. The following are the rules and naming conventions for variables and constants in Python:

a) Create a name that makes sense. Example: 'vowel' makes more sense than 'v.'

b) Use camelCase notation to declare a variable. It starts with a lowercase letter. Example: myFriend

c) Using capital letters was possible to declare a constant. Example: PI

d) Never use special symbols, like * , !, @, #, $, %, etc.

e) Constant and variable names should have a combination of letters in lowercase or uppercase or digits or an underscore (_).

12. Mention different types of user's input (syntax and its meaning) in Python.

Ans.

Syntax	Meaning
=input()	For string input
=int(input())	For integer input
=float(input())	For float (Real no.) input

13. Explain Implicit Type Conversion by giving an example.

Ans. In Implicit type conversion, Python converts one data type to another data type automatically. This process doesn't need any user involvement.

Example:

```
# Code to calculate the Simple_ Interest
principle_amount = 2000
roi = 3.5
time = 6
simple_interest = (principle_amount * roi * time)/100
print("datatype of principle amount : ", type(principle_amount))
print("datatype of rate of interest : ", type(roi))
print("value of simple interest : ", simple_interest)
print("datatype of simple interest : ", type(simple_interest))
```

When we run the above-mentioned program, the output we get is:

```
datatype of principle amount : <class 'int'>
datatype of rate of interest : <class 'float'>
value of simple interest : 420

datatype of simple interest : <class 'float'>
```

14. Explain Explicit Type Conversion by giving an example.

Ans. In Explicit Type Conversion, the users convert the data type of an object to the required data type by using predefined functions, like int(), float(), str(), etc. Moreover, this type of conversion is known as typecasting because the user casts (changes) the data type of the objects.

Syntax:

```
(required_datatype)(expression)
```

Typecasting may be done by assigning the required data type function to the expression. Example: Adding of string and an integer using explicit conversion

```
Birth_day = 21
Birth_month = "July"
print("data type of Birth_day before type casting :", type(Birth_day))
print("data type of Birth_month : ", type(Birth_month))
Birth_day = str(Birth_day)
print("data type of Birth_day after type casting :",type(Birth_day))
Birth_date = Birth_day + Birth_month
print("birth date of the student : ", Birth_day)
print("data type of Birth_date : ", type(Birth_date))
```

When we run the above-mentioned program, the output will be as follows:

```
data type of Birth_day before type casting: <class 'int' >
data type of Birth_month: <class 'str' >
data type of Birth_day after type casting: <class 'str' >
birth date of the student: ' 21 July '
data type of Birth_date: <class 'str' >
```

In the above program,

We add Birth_day and Birth_month variables.

We converted Birth_day from integer(lower) to string(higher) type using str() function to perform the addition.

We got the Birth_date value and data type to be a string.

15. Explain Jupyter Notebook.

Ans. The Jupyter Notebook is a powerful tool for interactively developing and presenting AI-related projects. The Jupyter project is the successor to the earlier IPython Notebook, which was first published as a prototype in 2010. Although it is possible to use many programming languages within Jupyter Notebooks, Python remains the most commonly used language for it. In other words, the Jupyter Notebook is an open-source web application that we can use to create and share documents that contain equations, live code, visualisations, and text.

16. Why are 'Notebooks' becoming a popular choice of data science?

Ans. The intuitive workflow promotes iterative and rapid development, making notebooks an increasingly popular choice at the heart of contemporary data science, analysis, and increasingly science at large.

17. How do you create a list in Python?

Ans. In the Python program, a list is created by placing all the items (elements) inside a square bracket [ ] and separated by commas. A List can have any number of items, and they may be of different types (integer, float, string, etc.).

Example:

```
#empty list
empty_list = []


#list of integers
age = [13,19,11]


#list with mixed data types
candidate_height_weight = ["Kanshika", 5.2, 48]
```

18. Explain nested List with the help of an example.

Ans. A list may also have another list as an item. Such a List is called Nested List.

```
# nested list
learner marks = ["Samita Jain", "10-C", [ "Science",89]]
```

19. How do you access elements of a list?

Ans. A list is made up of various elements which need to be individually accessed on the basis of the application it is used for.

There are two ways to access an individual element of a list:

a) **List Index:** A list index is a position at which any element is present in the List. Index in the List starts from 0, so if a list has five elements, the index will start from 0 and go on till 4. In order to access an element in a list, we need to use the index operator [].

b) **Negative Indexing:** In Python, negative indexing for its sequences is allowed. The index of -1 indicates the last item while -2 to the second last item, and so on.

20. Explain Slicing of a Python List.

Ans. In Python List, there are many ways to print the whole List having all the elements, but to print a specific range of elements from the List, we use the Slice operation. Slice operation is performed on the Lists with the use of a colon(:).

a) To print elements from beginning to a range, use [: Index].

b) To print elements from the end, use [:-Index].

c) To print elements from a specific index till the end, use [Index:].

d) To print elements within a range, use [Start Index: End Index].

e) To print the full List with the use of slicing operation, use [:].

f) While, to print the whole List in reverse order, use [::-1].

21. Explain Tuples. Give an example.

Ans. A tuple is ordered and unchangeable and a collection of Python objects. The Sequence of values that are stored in a tuple may be of any type, and these values are indexed by integers. Values of a tuple are separated by 'commas.' To define a tuple, closing the Sequence of values in parentheses is used. This helps to understand the Python tuples easily.

Example:

```
fruits = ("apple", "pineapple", "banana", "mango", "orange")
```

22. How do you create a tuple?

Ans. In Python, tuples are created by putting a sequence of values separated by 'comma,' and it may be done with or without the use of parentheses for grouping of the data sequence. It can contain any number of elements and of any datatype (like strings, integers, List, etc.).

Example:

```
#Creating an empty Tuple
Tuple1 = ()
#Creating a Tuple with the use of string
Tuple2 = ('Satyam', 'Ruchika')
#Creating a Tuple with Mixed Datatype
Tuple3 = (5, 'Atharv', 8, 'Shelja')
```

23. How can you delete a Tuple?

Ans. Tuples are immutable. So, they do not allow deletion of a part of it. The entire tuple can be deleted by using the del() method.

Example:

```
num = (0, 1, 2, 3, 4, 5, 6)
del num
```

24. How many types of decision-making statements are used in Python?

Ans. Decision-making statements available in Python are:

i. if Statement

ii. if..else statements

iii. if-elif ladder

25. Draw a Python if Statement Flowchart.

Ans.

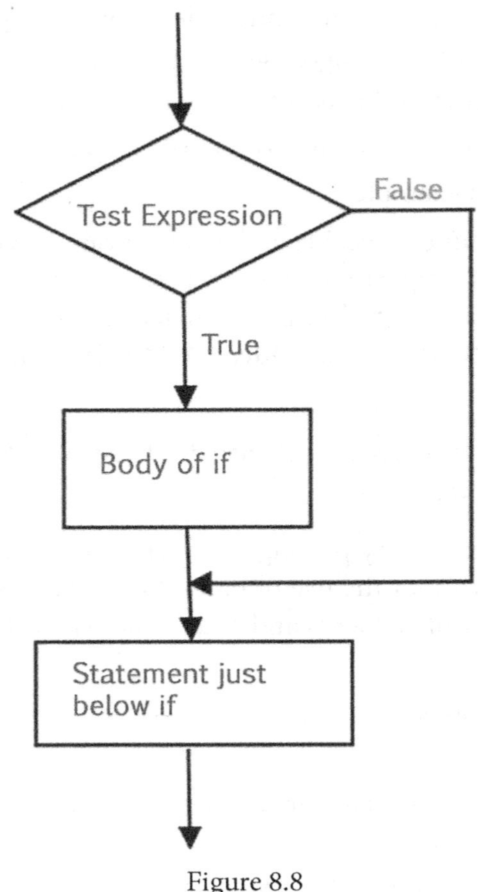

Figure 8.8

26. What is the syntax of the if…else statement?

Ans.
```
Syntax of if...else
if test expression:
Body of if
else:
Body of else
```

The if..else Statement evaluates test expression. It will execute the body of 'if' only when the test condition is True.

When the condition is False, the body of else is executed. Indentation is used to separate the blocks.

27. Draw if…else statement flowchart.

Ans.

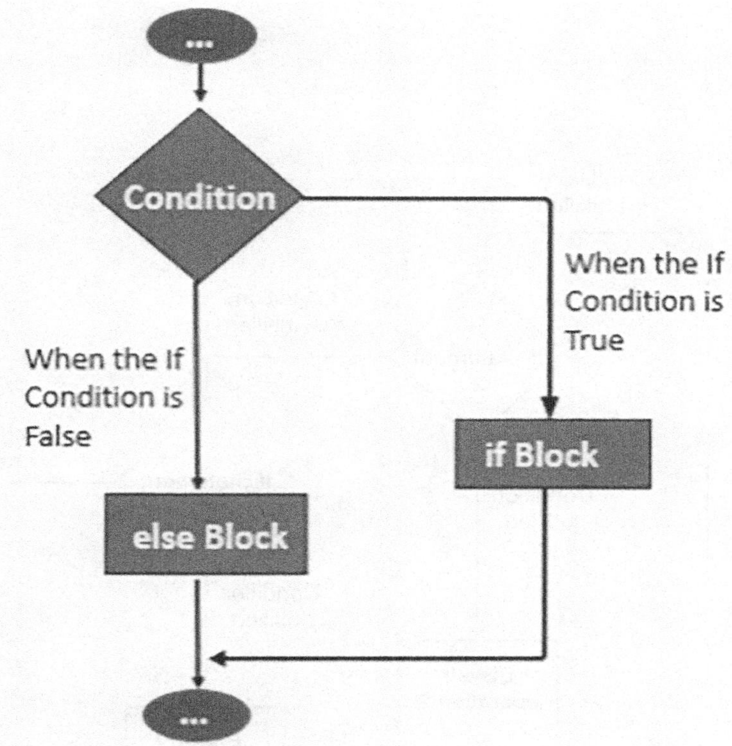

Figure 8.9

28. Write the syntax for Python if...elif...else Statement.

Ans. Syntax of if…Elif…else

```
if test expression:
Body of if
elif test expression:
Body of elif
else:

Body of else
```

The 'elif' is short for else if. It allows the user to check for multiple expressions.

When the condition for 'if' is False, it checks the condition of the next elif block and so on.

When all the conditions are False, the body of 'else' is executed.

Only one block among the several 'if…Elif…else' blocks are executed as per the condition. The 'if' block can have only one 'else block. But it can have multiple elif blocks.

29. Draw if…elif…else statement flowchart.

Ans.

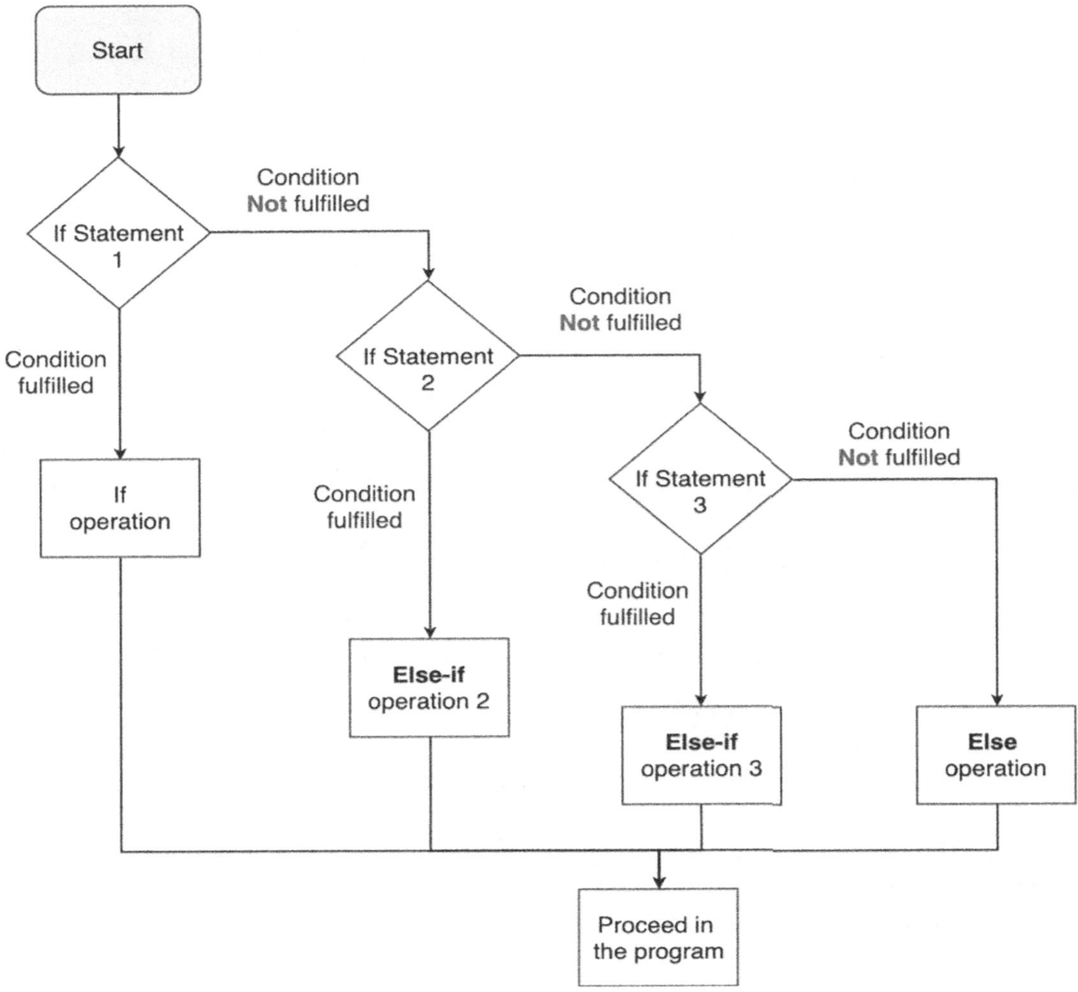

Figure 8.10

30. Write the syntax for a 'For' Loop.

Ans. The 'for' is a looping statement that iterates over a sequence of objects, i.e., go through each item in a sequence.

```
Syntax of For Loop

for val in Sequence:

Body of For
```

Here, Val is the variable that takes the value of the item inside the Sequence on each iteration.

Loop continues until the user reaches the last item in the Sequence. The body of the 'for' loop is separated from the rest of the code using indentation.

31. Draw the flowchart of the 'For' loop.

Ans.   Flowchart of for Loop

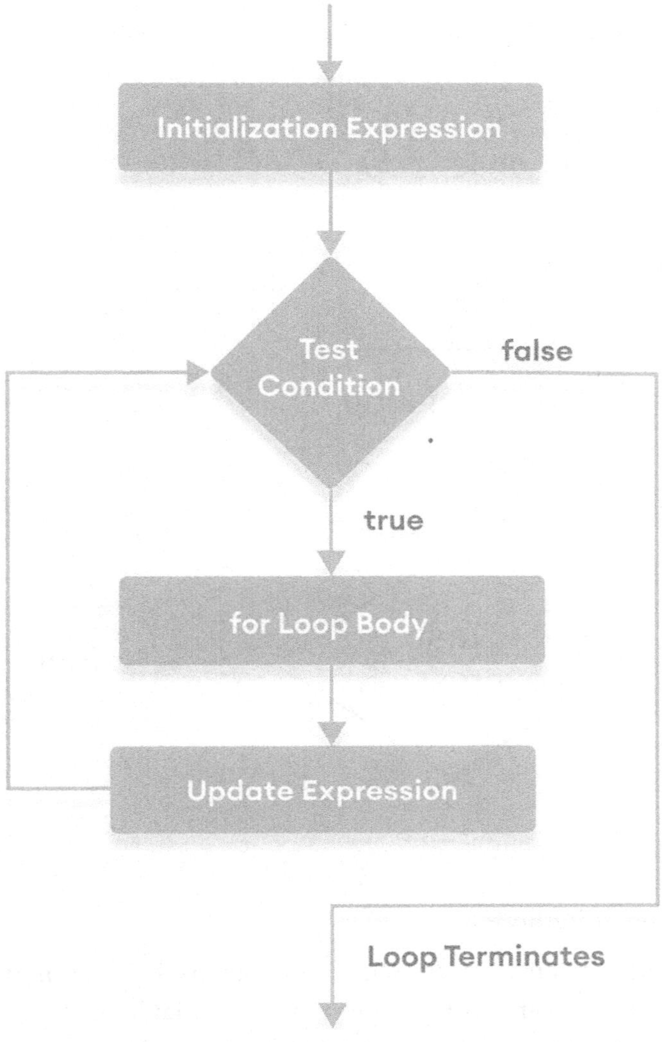

Figure 8.11

32. What is the syntax for the 'while' Statement?

Ans.   The 'while' statement allows the user to repeatedly execute a block of statements as long as a condition is to be True. A 'while' statement is an example of what is called a looping statement. A 'while' statement can have an optional 'else' clause.

Syntax of while Loop in Python

```
while test_expression:
```

```
Body of while
```

In a 'while' loop, test expression is checked in the first step. The body of the loop is entered when the test_expression evaluates to be True. After one iteration, the test expression is evaluated once again. This process continues until the test_expression is found to be False. In Python, the body of the 'while' loop is determined through indentation. The body starts with indentation, whereas the first unindented line marks the end. Python interprets any non-zero value as True. None and 0 are interpreted as False.

33. Draw the flowchart of the 'While' loop.

Ans. Flowchart of while Loop is below:

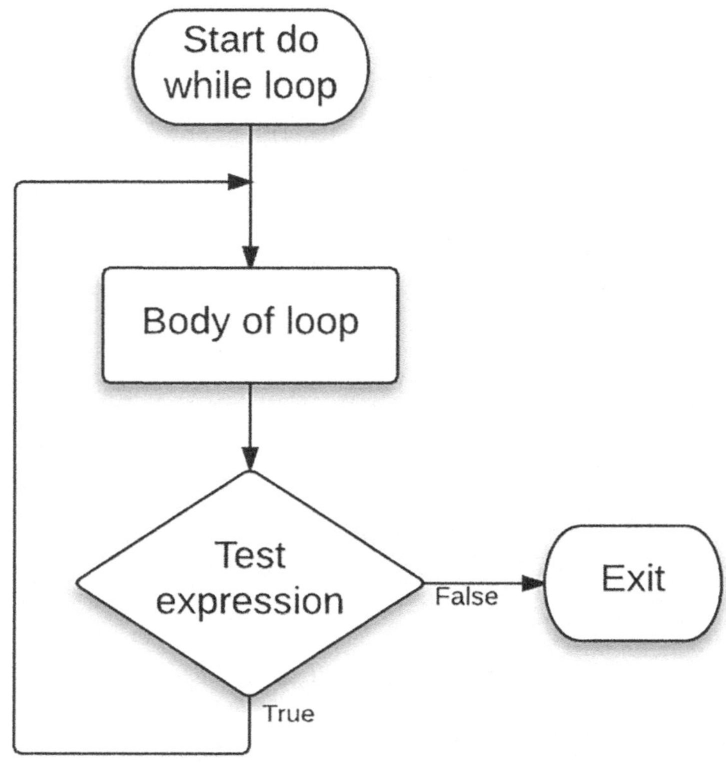

Figure 8.12

34. What is a Package in Python?

Ans. A package is nothing but a space where you can find codes or functions or modules of similar type. There are various packages readily available to use for free (perks of Python being an open-sourced language) for various purposes.

35. What do you mean by NumPy?

Ans. NumPy stands for Numerical Python and is the fundamental package for mathematical and logical operations on arrays in Python. It is a commonly used package when it comes to working around numbers. NumPy gives a wide range of arithmetic operations around numbers giving us an easier approach in working with them.

36. Explain the functioning of NumPy.

Ans. NumPy also works with arrays, which is nothing but a homogenous collection of data. An array is nothing but a set of multiple values which are of the same data type. They can be numbers, characters, Booleans, etc., but only one data type can be accessed through an array. In NumPy, the arrays used are known as ND arrays (N-Dimensional Arrays) as NumPy comes with a feature of creating n-dimensional arrays in Python. An array can easily be compared to a list. Look at Table 8.4 to find out how different they are.

37. Explain various methods for the creations of NumPy Arrays by giving examples.

Ans. Various methods for the creations of NumPy arrays are given below:

Function	Code/Example
(i) Creating a Numpy Array	numpy.array([1,2,3,4,5,6])
(ii) Creating a 2-Dimensional zero array (5X3 – 5 rows and 3 columns)	numpy.zeros((5,3))
(iii) Creating an array with 7 random values	numpy.random.random(7)
(iv) Creating a 2-Dimensional constant value array (5X3 – 5 rows and 3 columns) having all 6s	NumPy.full((5,3),6)
(v) Creating a sequential array from 0 to 20 with gaps of 3	numpy.arrange(0,20,3)

38. Explain various operations that can be implemented on an array.

Ans. Various operands that can be implemented on an array are given below:

Function	Code
(i) Adding 3 to each element	ARR + 3
(ii) Divide each element by 7	ARR / 7
(iii) Squaring each element	ARR ** 2
(iv) Accessing 3rd element of the array (element count starts from 0)	ARR[2]
(v) Multiplying 2 arrays {consider BRR = numpy.array([6,7,8,9,0]) }	ARR * BRR

It can be observed that direct arithmetical operations can be implemented on individual array elements just by manipulating the whole array variable.

39. Explain various functions and codes of an Array.

Ans.

Function	Code
(i) Type of an array	type(ARR)
(ii) Check the dimensions of an array	ARR.ndim
(iii) The shape of an array	ARR.shape
(iv) Size of an array	ARR.size
(v) The data type of elements stored in the array	ARR.dtype

40. Which mathematical functions are available with NumPy? Write their codes too.

Ans. The following mathematical functions are available with NumPy:

Function	Code
Function Code Finding out maximum element of an array	ARR.max()
Finding out row-wise maximum elements	ARR.max(axis = 1)

Function	Code
Finding out column-wise minimum elements	ARR.min(axis = 0)
Sum of all array elements	ARR.sum()

8.2.10 Long Answer Type Questions

1. Explain the different standard shapes used in a flowchart along with their functions.

Ans. The standard symbols used in the flowchart and their functions are given below:

   i.   **Oval:** It is used to represent the start and the end of the flowchart.
   ii. **Rectangle:** It is used to show processing; Used for arithmetic operations and data manipulations.
   iii. **Diamond:** It is used to show decision-making. It is used to represent the operation in which there are two/three alternatives, true and false, etc.
   iv. **Parallelogram:** it is used for input and output operation.
   v.   **Circle:** Page connector.
   vi. **Arrows:** Flowline is used to indicate the flow of logic by connecting symbols.

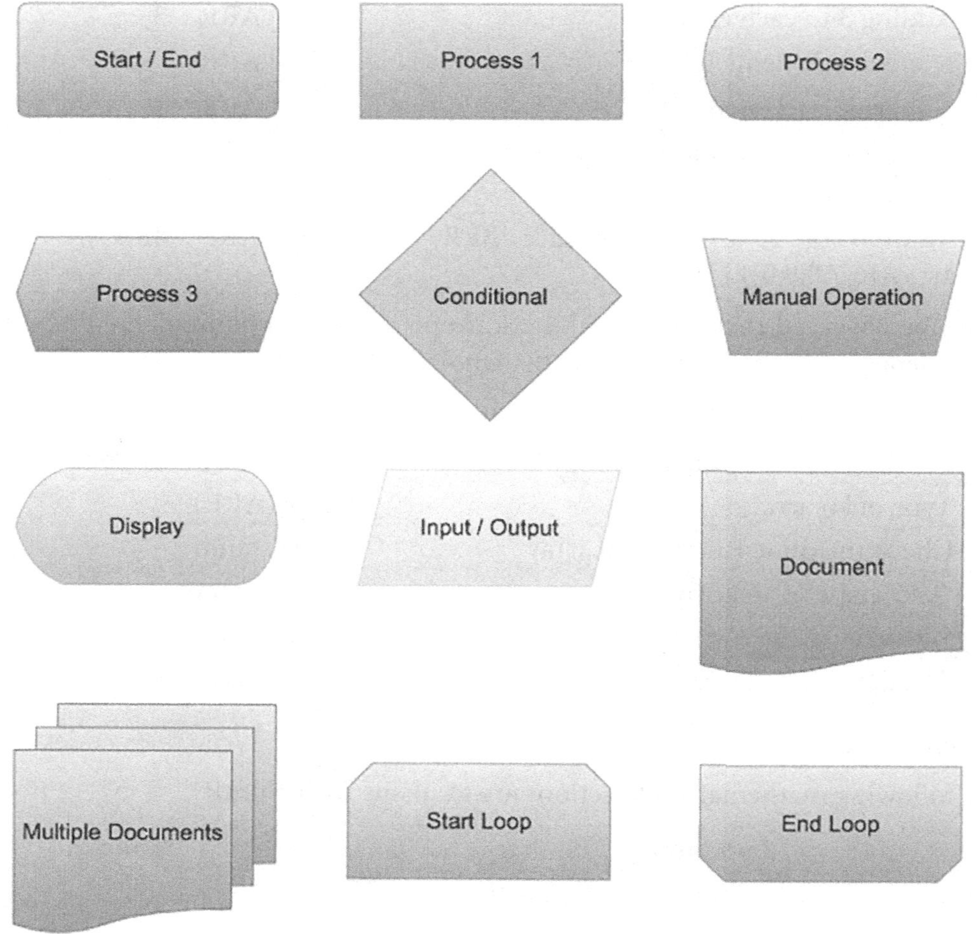

Figure 8.13

2. Enlist the main features of Python.

Ans. Python has the following features:

a) Python is a case-sensitive language because 'Node' and 'node' in Python is different.

b) Learning and using Python is easy.

c) Python is portable.

d) Python codes are short.

e) Python programs are easily readable and understandable.

f) Python is Interpreted. It means that Python is processed at runtime by the interpreter. The user does not need to compile our program before executing it.

g) Python is Interactive. The users can actually work at Python prompt and interact with the interpreter directly to write the programs.

h) Python is Object-Oriented. Python supports Object-Oriented style or technique programming that encapsulates code within objects.

i) Python is a very simple high-level language with a vast library of add-on modules.

3. Python has been gaining maximum popularity in recent times. Discuss the reasons behind it.

Ans. Python is gaining maximum popularity because of the following reasons:

i. **Less Code:** Python helps in the easy writing and execution of codes. Python has the ability to implement the same logic with about 1/5th of code as compared to other OOPs languages. Due to its interpreted approach, it enables check as the user code methodology.

ii. **Prebuilt Libraries:** Python contains a number of libraries for every need of AI projects. A few examples include NumPy for scientific computation, SciPy for advanced computing, and PyBrain for machine learning.

iii. **Support:** Python is an open-source resource with a great community. The host of resources available can get any developer up to speed in no time. Also, there is a huge community of active coders willing to help programmers in every stage of the developing cycle.

iv. **Platform Independence:** Python provides the flexibility to provide an API from an existing language which indeed provides extreme flexibility. It is also platform-independent. With just a few changes in codes, the user can get the app up and running in a new OS. This saves time for the developers in testing on different platforms and migrating code.

v. **Flexibility:** Flexibility is considered one of the core advantages of Python. With the option to choose between the OOPs approach and scripting, Python is suitable for every purpose. It works as a perfect backend and is also suitable for linking different data structures altogether. The option to check the validity of code in the IDLE is also a big plus point for developers who are struggling between different algorithms.

vi. **Popularity:** Python is winning the heart of millions of people. Its ease of learning is attracting millions of people. It is practically easier to find Python developers than LISP or Prolog programmers. Its extended libraries and active community have led it to be one of the best languages today.

4. Differentiate between NumPy Arrays and Lists.

Ans. The main difference between NumPy arrays and Lists are given below:

NumPy Arrays	Lists
(a) Homogenous collection of Data.	(a) Heterogenous collection of data.
(b) It can contain only one type of data, hence not flexible with datatypes.	(b) Can contain multiple types of data, hence flexible with datatypes.
(c) It cannot be directly initialized. It may be operated with the NumPy package only.	(c) It can be directly initialized as it is part of python syntax.
(d) Direct numerical operations can be done. For example, dividing the whole array by 3 divides every element by 3.	(d) Direct numerical operations are not possible. For example, dividing the whole List by 3 cannot divide every element by 3.
(e) They are widely used for arithmetic operations.	(e) They are widely used for data management.
(f) Arrays take less memory space.	(f) Lists acquire more memory space.
Example: To create a NumPy array 'A': import NumPy A=numpy.array([1,2,3,4,5,6,7,])	*Example:* To create a list: A = [1,2,3,4,5,6,7]

5. Explain Multi-line statements in Python. Give suitable examples.

Ans. In Python, a newline character is used to show the end of a statement. However, Statements in Python can be extended to one or more lines using parentheses (), braces {}, square brackets [], semi-colon (;), continuation character slash (\). When the user needs to do long calculations and cannot fit these statements into one line, he/she can make use of these characters.

The various methods and examples are enlisted below:

Type of Multi-line Statement	Usage
Using Continuation Character (\) s	= 1 + 2 + 3 + \
	4 + 5 + 6 + \
	7 + 8 + 9
Using Parentheses ()	n = (1 * 2 * 3 + 4 – 5)
Using Square Brackets []	footballer = ['MESSI',ISHAN, 'NEYMAR', 'SUNIL']
Using braces {}	x = {2 + 3 + 4 + 5 + 6 + 7 + 8 }
Using Semicolons (;)	flag = 3; ropes = 4; pole = 5

6. Explain Python Comments with the help of examples.

Ans. A comment is a text that doesn't affect the outcome of a code. It is just a piece of text to let someone know what the programmer has done in a program or what is being done in a block of code. In Python, the programmer uses the hash (#) symbol to start writing a comment.

(i) **Single Line Comments:** Python single-line comments start with a hashtag symbol with no white spaces (#) and may last till the end of the line. When the comment exceeds one line, then put a hashtag on the next line and continue the comment. Python's single-line comments are considered d useful for supplying short explanations for variables, function declarations, and expressions.

Example:

```
# This is a comment
# Print "ShailAnu" to console

print("ShailAnu ")
```

(ii) **Multi-Line Comments:** Python multi-line comments are pieces of text enclosed in a delimiter ("""") on each end of the comment. Moreover, there should not be any white space between delimiter (""""). These comments are useful when the comment text does not fit into one line and needs to spread across lines. Multi-line comments or paragraphs serve as documentation for others reading the code.

Example:

```
""""
This is a multi-line comment in Python that
has several lines and describes SatyamAI.com
An AI Science portal for the whole world. It contains
well written, well thought
and well-explained articles on AI
and programming articles,
quizzes, worksheets, projects, and more.
...
""""

print("SatyamAI.com ")
```

7. Discuss different Datatypes in Python with the help of examples.

Ans. Because everything is an object in Python programming, data types are actually classes, and variables are instances (object) of these classes. There are various data types in Python. Some of the types are discussed below.

(i) **Python Numbers:** Number data type stores Numerical Values. These are of four different types:

(a) **Integer and Long Integer:** The range of an integer in Python can be from -2147483648 to 2147483647, and a long integer has an unlimited range subject to available memory.

Integers are the whole numbers containing + or – sign, like 1000, -99, 0, 17. While writing a large integer value, don't use commas to separate digits. Also, integers should not have leading zeros.

(b) **Float/Floating Point Number:** Float () is a built-in Python function that converts a number or a string into a float value and then returns the result. When it fails for any invalid input, then an appropriate exception occurs. Numbers with fractions or decimal points are called floating-point numbers. A floating-point number will consist of a sign (+,-) sequence of decimals digits and a dot, like 0.0, -21.9, 0.98333328, 15.2963, etc. Such numbers may also be used to represent a number in engineering/ scientific notation.

-2.0×10^5 will be represented as -2.0e5

2.0×10^{-5} will be 2.0E-5

(c) **Complex numbers:** A complex number is represented by the expression " x + yi. "

Python converts the real numbers (x and y) into a complex number by using the function complex(x,y), and the real part can be accessed using the function real(), and the imaginary part can be represented by an image().

(d) **None:** 'None' is a special data type with a single value, which is used to signify the absence of value/false in a situation.

(ii) **Sequence:** A sequence is an ordered collection of items indexed by positive integers. It is a combination of mutable and non-mutable data types. Three types of sequence data types available in Python are: a) Strings, b) Lists c) Tuples.

(a) **String:** A string is defined as an ordered sequence of letters/characters. Strings are enclosed in single quotes (' ') or double (" "). The quotes are not part of a string, and they just tell the computer where the string constant begins and ends. They may have any character or sign, including space in them.

(b) **Lists:** The List is a sequence of values of any type. The values in a List are known as elements or items. These are indexed/ordered. The List is enclosed in square brackets. Example:

dob = [7,"January",1949]

(c) **Tuples:** A sequence of values of any type that are indexed by integers is called Tuples. They are immutable. Tuples are enclosed in ().

Example:

t = (3,'program',3.8) 5)

(iii) **Set:** A Set is a collection of unordered values, of any type, without any duplicate entry.

Example:

>>> a = {1,2,2,3,3,3} >>> a {1,2,3} 5)

(iv) **Mapping:** This data type is unordered. Dictionaries fall under Mappings. Dictionary contains an unordered collection of key-value pairs. It is used while dealing with a huge amount of data. Dictionaries are optimised for retrieving data. The key to retrieving the value should be known to the user. Python dictionaries are kept/defined within braces {} with each item being a pair in the form "key: value" while key and value can be of any type.

Example:

>>> d = {1:'Ajay','key':6}

>>> type(d)

<class 'dict'>

8. Explain Python Operators.

Ans. Operators are special symbols that represent computation. They are applied to operand(s), which can be values or variables. Same operators can behave differently on different data types. Operators, when applied to operands, form an expression. Operators are categorised as Arithmetic, Relational, Logical, and Assignment. Value and variables, when used with the operator, are known as operands.

Arithmetic operators are enlisted in the following table:

Operator	Meaning	Expression	Result
+	Addition	15 + 20	35
–	Subtraction	35 – 10	25
*	Multiplication	30 * 15	450
/	Division	50 / 10	5.0
		1 / 2	0.5
//	Integer Division	24 // 10	2
		1 // 2	0
%	Remainder	45 % 10	5
**	Raised to power	4 ** 2	16

9. What are the methods for adding an element to a List?

Ans. We can add an element to any list using the following methods:

a) **Using append() method:** Elements may be added to the List by using the built-in append() function. One element at a time may be added to the List by using the append() method; for the addition of a number of elements with the append() method, loops are used. Tuples are immutable, so they can be added to the List with the use of the append method. Additional Lists can also be added to the existing list with the use of the append() method.

b) **Using insert() Method:** Append() method only works for the Addition of elements at the end of the List; for the Addition of elements at the desired position, the insert() method is used. Unlike append(), which takes only one argument, the insert() method requires two arguments(position, value).

c) **Using extend() method:** Other than append() and insert() methods, extend() method is also there for the Addition of elements. This method is used to add many elements at the same time at the end of a List.

10. How can you remove elements from a List?

Ans. Elements from a list can be removed using two methods:

a) **Using remove() method:** Elements may be removed from a list using the built-in remove() function, but an Error arises when the element doesn't exist in the set. By this method, one element is removed at a time. For removing a range of elements, the iterator is used. The remove() method removes the specified item.

b) **Using pop() method:** The pop() function can also be used to remove and return an element from the set. By default, it removes the last element of the set. For removing an element from a specified position of the List, the index of the element is passed as an argument to the pop() method.

11. Explain various types of Packages used in Python.

Ans. Some of the readily available packages are:

a) **NumPy:** It is a package created to work around numerical arrays in Python. It is handy when it comes to working with large numerical databases and calculations around it.

b) **Matplotlib:** It is a package that helps in plotting the analytically (numerical) data in graphical form. It helps the users in visualizing the data in order to understand them better.

c) **OpenCV:** It is an image processing package that can explicitly work around images and can be used for image manipulation and processing like cropping, resizing, editing, etc.

d) **Pandas:** It is a package that helps in handling 2-Dimensional data tables in Python. It is useful when we are dealing with data in excel sheets and other databases.

e) **NLTK:** NLTK refers to Natural Language Tool Kit. It is a package that helps in tasks related to textual data. It is one of the most commonly used packages for NLP.

8.2.11 HOTS Questions

1. How will you prove that Python is a case-sensitive programming language?

Ans. Python is a case-sensitive programming language because in Python, 'SUMER' and 'sumer' have a different meanings.

2. How will you identify that an identifier is a language-defined special name?

Ans. When the identifier also ends with two trailing underscores, the identifier is a language-defined special name.

8.3 PRACTICE QUESTIONS

1. What is a package

2. Give some examples of a package with its use.

3. What is the command to install a package?

4. How can we use a package in a code? Explain.

5. What is a NumPy array? Give examples.

6. Differentiate between a NumPy array and a python list.

7. Define List in Python.

8. What do you mean by tuple?

9. Write the commands to install packages in Python.

10. Define loops.

11. What do you mean by Python nested if statements?

12. What are the main two types of Loops in Python?

13. What is OpenCV?

14. Define stringer in Python.

15. What is Anaconda?

16. What is the use of NumPy packages in Python?

17. Write the syntax of the 'for' loop.

18. Write two uses of NTLK packages in Python.

19. Differentiate between 'for loop and while loop.

20. Why is a flowchart used?

21. What are the two kinds of Type conversion?

22. What are the main uses of the OpenCV package in Python?

23. Write a program to find numbers that are divisible by 7 and multiple of 5 between 300 and 500.

24. Differentiate between Lists and Tuples.

25. Write the program to find simple interest using Jupyter notebook.

26. Write a program to find whether a number is prime or not using 'while loop.'

27. Discuss the main features of Python.

UNIT 9
Data Science

9.1 UNIT IN BRIEF

✦ Machine Learning is a subset of Artificial Intelligence that enables machines to improve at tasks with experience (Data).

Figure 9.1

✦ Deep Learning is considered the most advanced form of Artificial Intelligence.

✦ Deep learning is also defined as a subset of machine learning in which artificial neural networks, which are algorithms inspired by the human brain, learn from large data.

✦ Three domains of AI are Big Data, Computer Vision, and Natural Language Processing (NLP).

✦ Price Comparison Websites and Website Recommendations use data science.

✦ Data science is defined as the field of study that combines domain expertise, programming skills, and knowledge of mathematics and statistics for extracting meaningful insights from data.

✦ Computer Vision is a domain of AI that depicts the capability of a machine to get and analyze visual information.

✦ NLP is considered a subfield of Linguistics, Computer Science, Information Science, Engineering, and Artificial Intelligence dealing with the interactions between computers and natural languages.

✦ Data is collected from various sources, like Surveys, Sensors, Observations, Web scrapping (Internet), Interviews, Documents and records, Oral histories, etc.

✦ Data mining is the process of analyzing large data for extracting useful information from them.

✦ Data mining may be an automatic or semi-automatic technical process to analyze large amounts of scattered information to make sense of it.

✦ KDD is Knowledge Discovery in Data-another term for Data Mining.

✦ Proper and ethical handling of a company's own data or user data is called data privacy.

✦ Data privacy or information privacy is related to the proper handling of data -consent, notice, and regulatory obligations.

✦ AI bias is the prejudice in data that is used to create AI algorithms that can ultimately result in discrimination.

✦ Data privacy or information privacy focuses on how to collect, process, share, archive, and delete data in accordance with the law.

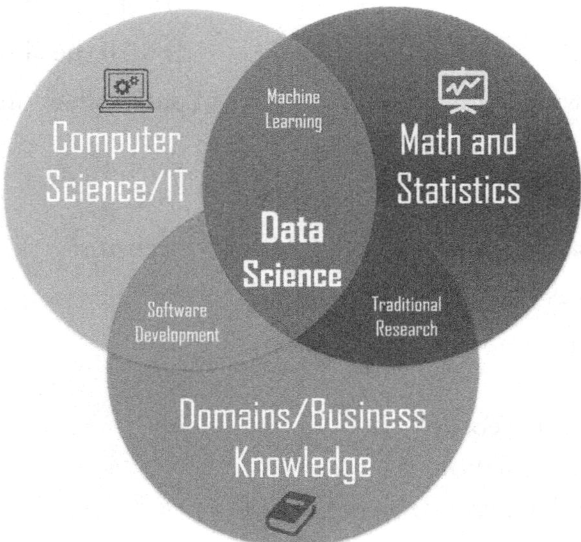

Figure 9.2

✦ Privacy is defined as the right of individuals, groups, or organizations to control who can access, observe, or use something they own, like their bodies, property, ideas, data, or information.

✦ In Deep Learning, the machine (computer) is trained with huge amounts of data that help it in training itself around the data.

✦ AI can automate most of the repetitive and physical tasks.

✦ The basic fact is that technology eliminates jobs, and not work.

9.2 SOLVED EXERCISES

9.2.1 Multiple Choice Questions

1. Which statistical tool is not used in Python?
   a) Mean and Median
   b) Mode and Variance
   c) Standard deviation
   d) None of these

2. Which of the following is not an offline source of data collection?

   a) Sensors   b) Surveys

   c) Interviews   d) None of these

3. Choose the correct set of examples of data.
   i.   Internet search,
   ii. Price Comparison Websites,
   iii. Self-Driving cars,
   iv. Website Recommendations,
   v.   Fraud and Risk detection,
   vi. Optimising Traffic routes in real-time,
   vii. Sentiment Analysis,

   a) (ii) (iv) (v) (vi)   b) (ii) (iv) (v) (vi) (vii)

   c) (iii) (v) (vi) (vii)   d) All the above

4. Which of the following is not an online source of data collection?

   a) Open-sourced Government Portals

   b) Observations

   c) World Organisations' open-sourced statistical websites

   d) Reliable Websites (Kaggle)

5. Which is not an application of data science?
   a) Email filter
   b) Price Comparison Websites
   c) Website Recommendations
   d) Fraud and Risk detection/ Internet search

6. Which of the following is not correct for neural networks?
   a) Training time for a neural network wholly depends on network size.
   b) Artificial neurons are very similar in operation to biological neurons.
   c) Neural networks may be simulated on conventional computers.
   d) The basic unit of a neural network is called a neuron.

7. Which of the following statements is not correct in the case of the KNN Algorithm?
   a) For a very large value of K, points from other classes may be included in the neighbourhood.
   b) The algorithm is very sensitive to noise for the very small value of K.
   c) KNN is utilised only for classification problem statements.
   d) KNN is a lazy learner.

8. Consider the following examples and choose the correct set of examples using CV.
   i.   Waste Management
   ii. Self-Driving cars
   iii. Face Lock in Smartphones

    iv. Medical Imaging,

    v.   Security Systems

    vi. Facial recognition

    vii. Automatic Summarisation

    a) (ii) (iv) (v) (vi)   b) (ii) (iii) (iv) (v) (vi)

    c) (iii) (v) (vi) (vii)   d) All of these

9. The robotic arm in an automobile company will be able to paint every corner in the automotive parts and minimise the quantity of paint wasted in the process. Which type of learning technique is used in this case?

    a) Supervised Learning   b) Unsupervised Learning

    c) Reinforcement Learning   d) Both (A) and (B).

10. Which is not an application of data science?

    a) Email filter   b) Price Comparison Websites

    c) Website Recommendations

    d) Fraud and Risk detection/ Internet search

11. Which of the following is not correct about Deep Learning and Machine Learning algorithms?

    a) Deep Learning algorithms work efficiently on large datasets.

    b) Feature Extraction is to be done manually in both ML and DL algorithms.

    c) Deep Learning algorithms are the best option for unstructured data.

    d) Deep Learning algorithms require high computational power.

12. Which of the following statement is TRUE?

    a) Outliers should be identified and always removed from a dataset.

    b) Outliers can never be present in the testing dataset.

    c) Outliers are data point that is significantly close to other data points.

    d) The nature of the business problem determines how outliers may be used.

13. Which of the following is not correct about Radial Basis Function Neural Network?

    a) It resembles Recurrent Neural Networks(RNNs) that have feedback loops.

    b) It uses the radial basis function as an activation function.

    c) While providing output, it considers the distance of a point with respect to the centre.

    d) The output given by the Radial basis function is always an absolute value.

14. Which of the following is not matched correctly?

    a) GPS: Location Data

    b) Gyroscope: Orientation Data

    c) Magnetometer: Running AR applications

    d) Biometric Sensors: Fingerprint and Face Data

15. Which of the following is present in smartphones?

    a) Magnetometer   b) Gyroscope

    c) GPS   d) All the above

16. Computer Vision is a domain of AI that depicts the capability of a machine to get and analyse ______________ information.

    a) Logical   b) Visual   c) Numerical   d) Authentic

17. Proper and ethical handling of a company's own data or users' data is called ____________.

    a) Data privacy   b) Data mining   c) Data science   d) Data piracy

18. Which of the following is used to focus on how to collect, process, share, archive, and delete data in accordance with the law?
    a) Information privacy   b) Data piracy
    c) CV   d) NLP

19. Select a game that is based on the Data Science domain of AI:
    a) Rock Paper and Scissors   b) Mystery Animal
    c) Emoji Scavenger Hunt   d) Pokémon

20. How many types of animals are suggested in the personality prediction quiz game?

    a) 2   b) 3   c) 4   d) 6

21. Which statement is incorrect about KNN?
    a) The KNN prediction model relies on the surrounding points or neighbours to determine its class or group.
    b) The KNN model is not a simple supervised machine learning algorithm.
    c) The KNN model utilises the properties of the majority of the nearest points to decide how to classify unknown points.
    d) The KNN model is based on the concept that similar data points should be close to each other.

22. Which tools are not a source of data collection?
    a) Surveys, Sensors,
    b) Observations, Web scrapping (Internet),
    c) Interviews, Documents, and records,
    d) Cinema, TV programmes

23. Which statement is not correct for neural networks?
    a) Artificial neurons are the same in operation as biological neurons.
    b) Training time for a neural network is dependent on the network size.
    c) Neural networks may be simulated on conventional computers.
    d) A neuron is called the basic unit of a neural network.

24. Which statement about Python is True?

    a) Python is relatively faster than any other programming language.

    b) The syntax roles in Python are both intuitive and easy to understand.

    c) A significant number of packages are available, which are developed by other users, which can be reused.

    d) All of the above

25. Which statement is not correct in the case of the KNN Algorithm?
    a) For a very small value of K, points from other classes may not be included in the neighbourhood.
    b) The algorithm is very sensitive to noise for the very small value of K.
    c) KNN is utilised only for classification problem statements.
    d) KNN is a lazy learner.

26. The robotic arm in an automobile company will be able to paint each corner in the automotive parts while minimising the wastage of paint wasted in the process. Which type of learning technique is used in this case?
    a) Supervised Learning
    b) Unsupervised Learning
    c) Reinforcement Learning
    d) Both (A) and (B).

27. Which of the following is not correct about Deep Learning and Machine Learning algorithms?
    a) Deep Learning algorithms work efficiently on large datasets.
    b) Feature Extraction is to be done manually in both ML and DL algorithms.
    c) Deep Learning algorithms are the best option for unstructured data.
    d) Deep Learning algorithms require high computational power.

28. Which of the following pairs are the correct applications of Python?
    a) Mobile development, Memory consumption devices
    b) Enterprise and business applications, Scraping the Web
    c) GUI based desktop applications, Visualising Data
    d) Data analysis, Game development

29. Which of the following tools is a simple way to depict a group of numerical data through their quartiles, and which is also used to visualize the shape of the data?

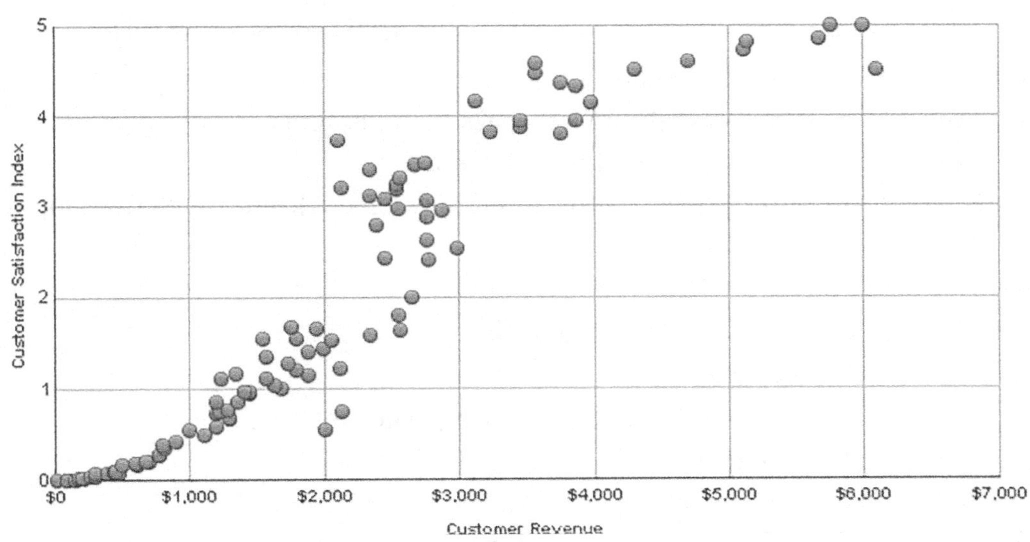

Figure 9.3 Scatter Chart

    a) Histogram
    b) Box Plot
    c) Scatter Chart
    d) Pie Chart

30. What is the term used for the number of pixels in an image?

    a) Quartiers   b) Resolution   c) CAD   d) NLP

31. Which statement is False about 'Lists'?

    a) Heterogenous collection of data   b) Non-flexible with datatypes
    c) Widely used for data management   d) Take more memory space

32. Which combination of statistical tools is not used in Python?

    a) Arithmetic Mean, Median   b) Mode, Standard deviation
    c) Variance, Harmonic mean   d) All of the above

33. Which of the following statements is TRUE?

    a) Outliers should be identified and always removed from a dataset.
    b) Outliers are never present in the testing dataset.
    c) Outliers are data points significantly close to other data points.
    d) The nature of the business problem determines how outliers may be used.

34. Which pair is not matched correctly?

    a) GPS: Location Data
    b) Gyroscope: Orientation Data
    c) Magnetometer: Running AR applications
    d) Biometric Sensors: Fingerprint and Face Data

35. Which of the following is present in smartphones?

    a) Magnetometer   b) Gyroscope
    c) GPS   d) All the above

36. Select a game that is based on the Data Science domain of AI:

    a) Pokémon   b) Rock Paper and Scissors
    c) Mystery Animal   d) Emoji Scavenger Hunt

37. Which of the following statements is incorrect?

    a) NumPy data structures take up less space than List and Series.
    b) NumPy arrays are faster than Lists and Series.
    c) Both list and NumPy have a numeric index (0,1,2, etc.), whereas Series supports custom index.
    d) The list supports the vectorised operation.

38. Which statement is not correct for Pandas?

    a) Keep track of the data.
    b) Use of different data types (float, int, string, date-time, etc.)
    c) Average IO capabilities
    d) Python MYSQL Connectivity

39. Which of the following statements is TRUE?

    a) AI can automate most of the repetitive and physical tasks.
    b) The technology eliminates jobs, not work.

   c) Price Comparison Websites and Website Recommendations use data science.

   d) All of the above

40. Which of the following statements is False?
   a) Data mining refers to the analysis of very large data sets and extracting useful information from them.
   b) Data is not the domain of AI.
   c) Data mining refers to an automatic or semi-automatic technical process.
   d) Privacy is defined as the right of individuals, groups, or organizations to control who can access, observe, or use something they own

41. ______________ refers to the field of study which combines programming skills, domain expertise, and knowledge of mathematics and statistics to get meaningful insights from data.
   a) Data Science
   b) Computer Vision
   c) NLP
   d) Data mining

42. During Deep Learning, the machine is trained with huge amounts of ____________ that help it in training itself around it.
   a) Raw facts
   b) Data
   c) Pictures and Figures
   d) None of these

43. Which example is not an example of the usage of data science?
   a) An Internet search, Price Comparison Websites
   b) Image tagging, Website Recommendations
   c) Fraud and Risk detection, Optimising Traffic routes
   d) CT scan, Face lock-in smartphone

44. Which example is an example of data science usage?
   a) Personalized healthcare recommendations
   b) Self-driven car
   c) Sentiment analysis
   d) Waste management

45. Why is data collection needed?
   a) To Manage business
   b) To make informed decisions for further analysis,
   c) To study the trends in the business.
   d) All of the above

46. For which of the following reasons, data collection is not required?
   a) For researching needs of customers for new products
   b) To find the ways on money frauds
   c) To provide answers to problems
   d) To analyse new insights to great effect

47. Which statement is NOT TRUE for NumPy arrays?
    a) Homogenous collection of Data
    b) Not flexible with datatypes
    c) Take more memory space
    d) Widely used for arithmetic operations

48. Which domain of AI depicts the capability of a machine to get and analyse visual information?
    a) Data
    b) CV
    c) NLP
    d) None of these

49. Which of the following is not correct about Radial Basis Function Neural Network?
    a) It resembles Recurrent Neural Networks(RNNs) that have feedback loops.
    b) It uses the radial basis function as an activation function.
    c) While giving output, it considers the distance of a point with respect to the centre.
    d) The output as given by the Radial basis function is always an absolute value.

50. Choose the correct set of examples of NLP.
    i.   Smart assistants,
    ii.   Email filters,
    iii. Digital phone calls,
    iv.   Automatic Summarisation
    v.   Optimising Traffic routes in real-time
    vi.   Sentiment Analysis
    vii. Self-Driving cars

    a) (ii) (iv) (v) (vi)
    b) (iii) (iv) (v) (vi)
    c) (ii) (iii) (iv) (vi)
    d) All of these

ANSWERS									
1. (d)	2. (d)	3. (a)	4. (b)	5. (a)	6. (a)	7. (c)	8. (b)	9. (c)	10. (a)
11. (b)	12. (d)	13. (a)	14. (c)	15. (d)	16. (b)	17. (a)	18. (a)	19. (a)	20. (c)
21. (b)	22. (d)	23. (a)	24. (d)	25. (c)	26. (c)	27. (b)	28. (a)	29. (b)	30. (b)
31. (b)	32. (c)	33. (d)	34. (c)	35. (d)	36. (b)	37. (d)	38. (c)	39. (d)	40. (b)
41. (a)	42. (b)	43. (d)	44. (a)	45. (d)	46. (b)	47. (c)	48. (b)	49. (a)	50. (c)

9.2.2 Fill in the blanks

1. _______________ is an automatic or semi-automatic technical process to analyse large amounts of scattered information to make sense of it.

2. In _______________, the machine is trained with large data that help it in training itself around the data.

3. _______________ can automate most of the repetitive and physical tasks.

4. _______________ or information privacy focuses on how to collect, process, share, archive, and delete data in accordance with the law.

5. ______________ is one of the major sources of data for many major companies.

6. ______________ uses techniques and theories taken from many fields within the context of Mathematics, Statistics, Computer Science, and Information Science.

7. Data mining is an interdisciplinary subfield of ______________ and statistics with an overall goal to extract information.

8. ______________ is a subset of Artificial Intelligence that enables machines to improve at tasks with data.

9. The output/information extracted through data science is used to make some ______________.

10. Proper and ethical handling of a company's own data or user data is called data ______________.

11. ______________ is considered a subfield of Linguistics, Computer Science, Information Engineering, and Artificial Intelligence dealing with the interactions between computers and natural languages.

12. The world of Artificial Intelligence revolves around ______________.

13. Three domains of AI are Data, ______________ and Natural Language Processing (NLP).

14. ______________ is considered the most advanced form of Artificial Intelligence.

15. Two important data structures of Pandas are Series and ______________.

ANSWERS			
1. Data mining	2. Deep Learning	3. AI	4. Data privacy
5. Smartphone	6. Data science	7. computer science	
8. Machine Learning	9. decisions	10. privacy	11. NLP
12. Data	13. Computer Vision	14. Deep Learning	15. DataFrame

9.2.3 True or False

1. Data privacy is also called Knowledge Discovery in Data.

2. Machine learning is defined as a data analytics technique that teaches computers to do what comes naturally to humans and animals, i.e., learning from experience.

3. Data Sciences is a combination of Python and Mathematical concepts like Statistics, Data Analysis, probability, etc.

4. The basic fact is that technology eliminates jobs, and not work.

5. Deep learning is considered a subset of machine learning where artificial neural networks, algorithms inspired by the human brain, learn from large data.

6. Price Comparison Websites and Website Recommendations use data science.

7. CV is the most advanced form of Artificial Intelligence.

8. The main purpose of Machine Learning is to enable machines to learn by themselves using the provided data and make accurate Predictions/ Decisions.

9. Data piracy is defined as a field of study that combines domain expertise, programming skills, and knowledge of mathematics and statistics for extracting meaningful insights from the given data.

10. AI cannot automate most repetitive and physical tasks.

11. Concepts of Data Science may be used in developing applications around AI as it gives a strong base for data analysis in Python.

12. Data mining is an automatic or semi-automatic technical process that analyses large amounts of scattered data to make sense of it.

13. All the apps in a smartphone collect some kind of data.

14. Data privacy is a branch of data security concerned with the proper handling of data -consent, notice, and regulatory obligations.

15. AI has a domain called NLP that depicts the capability of a machine to get and analyse visual information.

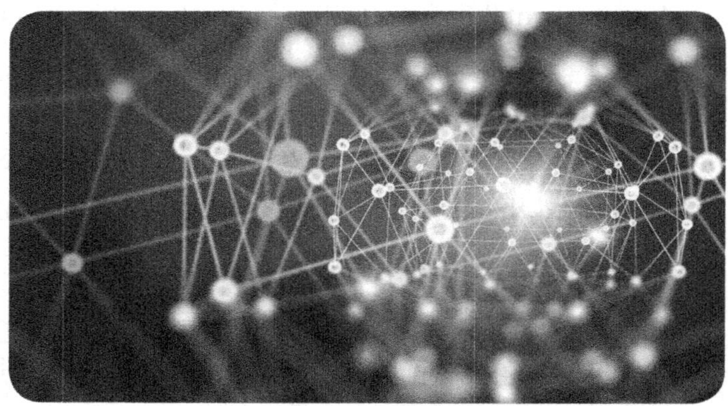

Figure 9.4

ANSWERS							
1. F (Data mining)	2. T	3. T	4. T	5. T		6. T	
7. F (Deep Learning not CV)		8. T	9. F (Data Science)		10. F	11. T	
12. T	13. T	14. T	15. F (CV not NLP)				

9.2.4 Matching type

(I). Match the sensor present in the smartphone with the correct function.

(A) Sensor	**(B) Function**
(i) GPS	(a) Orientation Data
(ii) Gyroscope	(b) Running AR applications and track steps
(iii) Biometric Sensors	(c) Direction and Magnetic Field Data
(iv) Magnetometer	(d) Location Data
(v) Accelerometer	(e) Fingerprint, Iris, Face Data

ANSWERS
(I) (i)-d,   (ii)-a,   (iii)- e,   (iv)-c,   (v)-b

9.2.5 Statements Based Questions

1. Statement 1: Computer Vision is a domain of AI that depicts the capability of a machine to get and analyse visual information.

   Statement 2: NLP is considered a subfield of Linguistics, Computer Science, Information Science, Engineering, and Artificial Intelligence dealing with the interactions between computers and natural languages.

   a) Statement 1 is correct but statement 2 is incorrect.
   b) Statement 1 is incorrect but statement 2 is correct.
   c) Both the statements are correct.
   d) Both the statements are incorrect.

2. Statement 1: Price Comparison Websites and Website Recommendations use CV.

   Statement 2: Data science is defined as the field of study that combines domain expertise, programming skills, and knowledge of mathematics and statistics for extracting meaningful conclusions from data.

   a) Statement 1 is correct but statement 2 is incorrect.
   b) Statement 1 is incorrect but statement 2 is correct.
   c) Both the statements are correct.
   d) Both the statements are incorrect.

3. Statement 1: Pandas is a programming language.

   Statement 2: SQL is a software library that provides data manipulation and analysis tools in the Python programming language.

   a) Statement 1 is correct but statement 2 is incorrect.
   b) Statement 1 is incorrect but statement 2 is correct.
   c) Both the statements are correct.
   d) Both the statements are incorrect.

4. Statement 1: Mode is defined as the arithmetic average of the data values.

   Statement 2: Mean is the data value(s) having the greatest frequency.

   a) Statement 1 is correct but statement 2 is incorrect.
   b) Statement 1 is incorrect but statement 2 is correct.
   c) Both the statements are correct.
   d) Both the statements are incorrect.

5. Statement 1: One application in which Python is used is Mobile development.

   Statement 2: Examples of the popular software programs written in Python are YouTube, Google, Instagram, Quora, and Dropbox.

   a) Statement 1 is correct but statement 2 is incorrect.
   b) Statement 1 is incorrect but statement 2 is correct.
   c) Both the statements are correct.
   d) Both the statements are incorrect.

6. Statement 1: The transducers not present in a smartphone include GPS, Gyroscope, Magnetometer, and Biometric Sensors.

   Statement 2: The data used for labeling variables without any type of quantitative value is called Nominal data.

   a) Statement 1 is correct but statement 2 is incorrect.

   b) Statement 1 is incorrect but statement 2 is correct.

   c) Both the statements are correct.

   d) Both the statements are incorrect.

7. Statement 1: In Deep Learning, the machine (computer) is trained with huge amounts of data that help it in training itself around the data.

   Statement 2: AI cannot automate most of the repetitive and physical tasks.

   a) Statement 1 is correct but statement 2 is incorrect.

   b) Statement 1 is incorrect but statement 2 is correct.

   c) Both the statements are correct.

   d) Both the statements are incorrect.

8. Statement 1: A spreadsheet is a computer program used for accounting and recording data using rows and columns to enter information.

   Statement 2: Application Programming Interfaces (API) are the piece of code that helps one application to connect to another.

   a) Statement 1 is correct but statement 2 is incorrect.

   b) Statement 1 is incorrect but statement 2 is correct.

   c) Both the statements are correct.

   d) Both the statements are incorrect.

9. Statement 1: The other term used for data acquisition is KDD (Knowledge Discovery in Data).

   Statement 2: Two important data structures of Pandas are Series and DataFrame.

   a) Statement 1 is correct but statement 2 is incorrect.

   b) Statement 1 is incorrect but statement 2 is correct.

   c) Both the statements are correct.

   d) Both the statements are incorrect.

10. Statement 1: Matplotlib in Python is an amazing visualisation library for 2D plots of arrays.

    Statement 2: Variance is the numerical values that describe the variability of the observations from its arithmetic mean.

    a) Statement 1 is correct but statement 2 is incorrect.

    b) Statement 1 is incorrect but statement 2 is correct.

    c) Both the statements are correct.

    d) Both the statements are incorrect.

ANSWERS									
1. (c)	2. (b)	3. (d)	4. (d)	5. (b)	6. (a)	7. (a)	8. (c)	9. (b)	10. (c)

9.2.6 Assertion Reason Type Questions

1. Assertion (A): AI bias is the prejudice in data that is used to create AI algorithms.

   Reason (R): The end result of prejudices in data to create AI algorithms ultimately results in creating discrimination.
   a) Both A and R are correct and R is the correct reason for A.
   b) Both A and R are correct and R is not the correct reason for A.
   c) A is correct but R is incorrect.
   d) A is incorrect but R is correct.

2. Assertion (A): A pie chart has points scattered over an area (2 D graph) representing the relationship between two values.

   Reason (R): A histogram is a chart/graph is used for the accurate representation of continuous data.
   a) Both A and R are correct and R is the correct reason for A.
   b) Both A and R are correct and R is not the correct reason for A.
   c) A is correct but R is incorrect.
   d) A is incorrect but R is correct.

3. Assertion (A): Privacy or information privacy focuses on how to collect, process, share, archive, and delete data in accordance with the law.

   Reason (R): Data Privacy is defined as the right of individuals, groups, or organizations to control who can access, observe, or use something they own, like their bodies, property, ideas, data, or information.
   a) Both A and R are correct and R is the correct reason for A.
   b) Both A and R are correct and R is not the correct reason for A.
   c) A is correct but R is incorrect.
   d) A is incorrect but R is correct.

4. Assertion (A): Quantitative data may be expressed as a number and can be measured by numerical variables only.

   Reason (R): Qualitative Data is also called categorical data.
   a) Both A and R are correct and R is the correct reason for A.
   b) Both A and R are correct and R is not the correct reason for A.
   c) A is correct but R is incorrect.
   d) A is incorrect but R is correct.

5. Assertion (A): Data is collected from various sources, like Surveys, Sensors, Observations, Web scrapping (Internet), Interviews, Documents and records, Oral histories, etc.

   Reason (R): Smartphone is the major source of data for many major companies, which all of us have in our hands all the time.
   a) Both A and R are correct and R is the correct reason for A.
   b) Both A and R are correct and R is not the correct reason for A.
   c) A is correct but R is incorrect.
   d) A is incorrect but R is correct.

6. Assertion (A): Price Comparison Websites and Website Recommendations use data science.

    Reason (R): Data science is defined as the field of study that combines domain expertise, programming skills, and knowledge of mathematics and statistics for extracting meaningful insights from data.

    a) Both A and R are correct and R is the correct reason for A.

    b) Both A and R are correct and R is not the correct reason for A.

    c) A is correct but R is incorrect.

    d) A is incorrect but R is correct.

7. Assertion (A): Web Scraping is the collection of web data from websites on the internet using a web browser.

    Reason (R): Sensors convert real-world phenomena like temperature, force, and movement to voltage or current signals that can be used as inputs.

    a) Both A and R are correct and R is the correct reason for A.

    b) Both A and R are correct and R is not the correct reason for A.

    c) A is correct but R is incorrect.

    d) A is incorrect but R is correct.

8. Assertion (A): Data piracy is related to the proper handling of data -consent, notice, and regulatory obligations.

    Reason (R): AI bias or information privacy is the prejudice in data that is used to create AI algorithms that can ultimately result in discrimination.

    a) Both A and R are correct and R is the correct reason for A.

    b) Both A and R are correct and R is not the correct reason for A.

    c) A is correct but R is incorrect.

    d) A is incorrect but R is correct.

9. Assertion (A): NumPy is the fundamental package for Mathematical and logical operations on arrays in Python.

    Reason (R): Data that is collected by various applications on websites or smartphones is not ethical in nature.

    a) Both A and R are correct and R is the correct reason for A.

    b) Both A and R are correct and R is not the correct reason for A.

    c) A is correct but R is incorrect.

    d) A is incorrect but R is correct.

10. Assertion (A): Deep Learning is considered the most advanced form of Artificial Intelligence.

    Reason (R): Deep learning is a subset of machine learning in which artificial neural networks, which are algorithms inspired by the human brain, learn from large data.

    a) Both A and R are correct and R is the correct reason for A.

    b) Both A and R are correct and R is not the correct reason for A.

    c) A is correct, but R is incorrect.

    d) A is incorrect but R is correct.

ANSWERS

1. (a)	2. (d)	3. (d)	4. (b)	5. (c)	6. (a)	7. (b)	8. (d)	9. (c)	10. (a)

9.2.7 Competency Based Questions

1. Consider the following domains:

   i.   Data,

   ii. Computer Vision (CV),

   iii. Natural Language Processing (NLP).

   To which field are these domains related?

   a) Linguistics   b) Science and Engineering

   c) AI   d) All of the above

2. Assume that Niharika Ganguly is using an algorithm that is a simple, easy-to-implement supervised machine learning algorithm and is used to solve both classification and regression problems. What actually is she using?

   a) CNN   b) KNN   c) ANN   d) ASI

3. Assume that Satyam AI Creations Inc. is an organization dealing with the research work involving identifying and predicting diseases, Personalised healthcare recommendations, Algorithms that help in finding genetic disorders, etc. Which of the following is used mainly by the firm?

   a) Data Science   b) Computer Vision (CV),

   c) Natural Language Processing (NLP)   d) Fuzzy Logic Systems

4. Consider the following actions/activities/decisions:

   i.   To Manage business,

   ii. To make informed decisions from further analysis,

   iii. To study the trends in the business

   iv. For researching the needs of customers for new products,

   v.   To provide answers to problems,

   Which of the following is required to manage all the above-mentioned processes?

   a) Data exploration   b) Data collection

   c) Data acquisition   d) Evaluation

5. Shailesh Mahapatra owns a firm, **"Shagufta AI Research Cell,"** which always needs a large data. In which form, the firm can collect data?

   a) Numeric & Text,   b) Audio & video

   c) Images   d) All of the above

ANSWERS

1. (c)	2. (b)	3. (a)	4. (b)	5. (d)

9.2.8 VSA

1. Define data science.

Ans. Data science is defined as the field of study that combines programming skills, domain expertise, and knowledge of mathematics and statistics for extracting meaningful insights from data.

2. From which sources are data collected?

Ans. Data is collected from various sources, like Surveys, Sensors, Observations, Web scrapping (Internet), Interviews, Documents and records, Oral histories, etc.

3. Define data mining.

Ans. The process of analyzing large data for extracting useful information from them is called data mining.

4. What is the major source of data for many major companies, which all of us have in our hands all the time?

Ans. Smartphone

5. Which is the most advanced form of Artificial Intelligence?

Ans. Deep Learning (DL)

6. What do you mean by data privacy?

Ans. Data privacy is defined as a branch of data security concerned with the proper handling of data -consent, notice, and regulatory obligations.

7. In which forms data may be collected?

Ans. Numeric, text, audio, video, or image

8. Where is the output/information extracted through data science is used?

Ans. The output/information extracted through data science is used to make some decisions.

9. Give two examples of data science applications.

Ans. Identifying and predicting diseases, Personalised healthcare recommendations, Stamping out tax fraud, Automating digital ad placement, Algorithms that help you find life partners, etc. (any two)

10. Why is Data collection required?

Ans. To Manage business, To make informed decisions from further analysis, To study the trends in the business. For researching needs of customers for new products, To provide answers to problems, etc.

11. Which AI domain is used by search engines like Google, Yahoo, Bing, Ask, and AOL?

Ans. Data science

12. What is the full form of CTR?

Ans. Call-Through Rate

13. Whether regression is a supervised learning model or an Unsupervised learning model?

Ans. Regression is a Supervised Learning model which takes continuous values of data over a period of time as input.

14. Define web scrapping.

Ans. Web Scraping is the collection of Web data from websites on the internet using a web browser.

15. What is the main function of sensors?

Ans. Sensors or Transducers convert real-world phenomena like temperature, force, and movement to voltage or current signals that can be used as inputs.

16. What do you mean by observations?

Ans. The process of careful and systematic viewing of facts as they occur is known as observation.

17. Define API.

Ans. Application programming interfaces are the piece of code that helps one application to connect to another.

18. Mention any two sensors present in a smartphone.

Ans. GPS, Gyroscope, Magnetometer, Biometric Sensors, etc

19. What is quantitative data?

Ans. Quantitative data may be expressed as a number and can be measured by numerical variables only.

20. What is categorical data?

Ans. Qualitative Data is also called categorical data.

21. Define nominal data.

Ans. The data used for labeling variables without any type of quantitative value is called nominal data.

22. What is the full form of CSV?

Ans. Comma-Separated Values.

23. What do you mean by a spreadsheet?

Ans. A spreadsheet is a computer program used for accounting and recording data using rows and columns to enter information.

24. What is the full form of SQL?

Ans. Structured Query Language.

25. What is SQL?

Ans. SQL is a programming language.

26. What do you mean by AI bias in data science?

Ans. The underlying prejudice in data used to create AI algorithms and that can ultimately result in discrimination is termed AI bias.

27. What is the focus area of data privacy?

Ans. Data privacy or information privacy focuses on how to collect, process, share, archive, and delete data in accordance with the law.

28. What is ML?

Ans. Machine Learning (ML) is a subset of Artificial Intelligence that enables machines to improve at tasks with experience (Data).

29. What is the other term used for data mining?

Ans. KDD (Knowledge Discovery in Data).

30. What is the end result of prejudices in data to create AI algorithms?

Ans. It ultimately results in creating discrimination.

31. Is data that is collected by various applications on websites or smartphones ethical in nature?

Ans. Yes

32. What is NumPy?

Ans. NumPy stands for Numerical Python. NumPy is the fundamental package for Mathematical and logical operations on arrays in Python.

33. What do you mean by 'Pandas'?

Ans. Pandas is a software library that provides data manipulation and analysis tools in the Python programming language.

34. What are the two important data structures of Pandas?

Ans. Series and DataFrame

35. What is Matplotlib?

Ans. Matplotlib in Python is an amazing visualization library for 2D plots of arrays.

36. Define Mean.

Ans. Mean is defined as the arithmetic average of the data values.

37. What do you mean by Mode?

Ans. Mode is the data value(s) having the greatest frequency.

38. What is Variance?

Ans. Variance is the numerical values that describe the variability of the observations from its arithmetic mean.

39. Which language is used in Machine learning, Artificial Intelligence, and Web applications and frameworks?

Ans. Python

40. Name any one application in which Python is not used.

Ans. Mobile development

41. Give two examples of the popular software programs written in Python.

Ans. YouTube, Google, Instagram, Quora, Dropbox.

42. What is a scatter chart?

Ans. A scatter chart has points scattered over an area (2 D graph) representing the relationship between two values.

43. Which chart/graph is used for the accurate representation of continuous data?

Ans.   Histogram

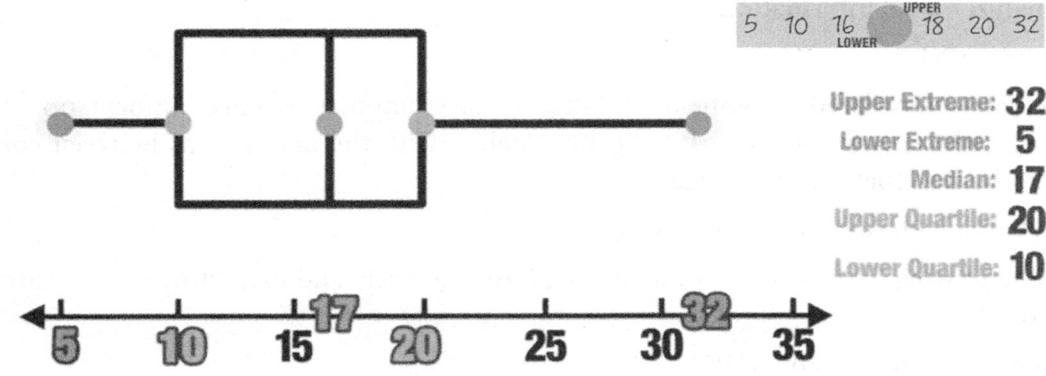

Figure 9.5 Box plots

44. Which graphical tool is used when the data is split according to its percentile throughout the range?

Ans.   Box plots.

45. What do you mean by KNN?

Ans.   The K-nearest neighbors (KNN) algorithm is a simple, easy-to-implement supervised machine learning algorithm that is used to solve both classification and regression problems.

46. Mention any one area where the KNN model is used.

Ans.   The banking system, Politics, calculating credit ratings, etc

47. What is privacy?

Ans.   Privacy refers to the right of individuals, groups, or organizations to control who can access, observe, or use something they own.

48. What is Machine Learning (ML)?

Ans.   Machine Learning is a subset of Artificial Intelligence that enables machines to improve at tasks with experience (Data).

49. Define Deep Learning.

Ans.   Deep learning is also defined as a subset of machine learning where artificial neural networks- algorithms inspired by the human brain, learn from large data.

50. What are the three domains of AI?

Ans.   Three domains of AI are Data, Computer Vision, and Natural Language Processing (NLP).

51. Mention two websites using data sciences.

Ans.   Price Comparison Websites and Website Recommendations use data science.

52. Define data science.

Ans.   Data science is defined as the field of study that combines domain expertise, programming skills, and knowledge of mathematics and statistics for extracting meaningful conclusions from data.

53. Define CV.

Ans. Computer Vision is a domain of AI that depicts the capability of a machine to get and analyze visual information.

54. Explain NLP.

Ans. NLP is considered a subfield of Linguistics, Computer Science, Information Science, Engineering, and Artificial Intelligence dealing with the interactions between computers and human (natural) languages.

55. What do you mean by data mining?

Ans. Data mining is the process of analyzing large data sets and extracting useful information from them.

56. What do you mean by KDD?

Ans. KDD is Knowledge Discovery in Data-another term for Data Mining.

57. What is data privacy?

Ans. Data privacy or information privacy refers to the proper handling of data -consent, notice, and regulatory obligations.

58. What is AI bias?

Ans. AI bias is the prejudice in data that is used to create AI algorithms that can ultimately result in discrimination.

59. What do you mean by privacy?

Ans. Privacy is defined as the right of individuals, groups, or organizations to control who can access, observe, or use something they own, like their bodies, property, ideas, data, or information.

Figure 9.6

9.2.9 Short Answer Type Questions

1. Mention different sources used for data collection.

Ans. Data is collected from various sources, like Surveys, Sensors, Observations, Web scrapping (Internet), Interviews, Documents and records, Oral histories, etc.

2. Why is data science regarded as a branch of science?

Ans. Data science is regarded as a branch of science having a multidisciplinary approach of mathematics, statistics, and computer science to apply machine learning algorithms to numbers, text, images, video, audio, etc., to produce artificial intelligence (AI) systems that may perform tasks as a human does.

3. In what forms may data be used in AI?

Ans. Data in AI may be as numeric, text, audio, video, or image, which is all converted to numeric form for extraction, preparation, analysis, visualization, and maintenance of information.

4. Differentiate among Data, CV, and NLP.

Ans.

Data Data Sciences	CV Computer Vision	NLP Natural Language Processing
(i) Working around numeric and alphanumeric data.	(i) Working around the image and visual data.	(i) Working around textual and speech-based data.
(ii) Examples: Internet search, Price Comparison Websites, Image tagging, Website Recommendations, Fraud, and Risk detection, Optimising Traffic routes in real-time, Personalised healthcare recommendations, etc.	(ii) Examples: Self-Driving cars, Facial recognition, Autonomous vehicles, Face Lock in Smartphones, Medical Imaging, Waste Management, Security Systems, Satellite imaging, etc.	(ii) Examples: Smart assistants, Email filters, Digital phone calls, Automatic Summarization, Search results, Sentiment Analysis, Language translation, etc.

5. Enlist the Data science examples and applications.

Ans. Data science is used in the following applications:

a) Stamping out tax fraud
b) Identifying and predicting diseases
c) Personalized healthcare recommendations
d) Predicting incarceration rates
e) Automating digital ad placement
f) Algorithms that help you find life partners
g) Optimizing shipping /sea routes in real-time
h) Finding the next slew of world-class athletes

6. What is the need for data collection?

Ans. Data collection is required for the following reasons:

a) To study the trends in the business.
b) To Manage business effectively.
c) To make informed decisions from further analysis.
d) For researching needs of customers for new products.

e) To provide answers to problems.

f) To analyze new insights to have a great effect.

7. Explain the application of data science in the field of 'Genetics and Genomics.'

Ans. Data Science enables an advanced level of treatment personalization through research in genetics and genomics. The data scientists' goal is to understand the impact of DNA on health to find out individual biological connections among en genetics, diseases, and drug response to diseases. Data science techniques use the integration of different kinds of data with genomic data in disease research, which provides a deeper understanding of issues related to genetic engineering in response to the administration of a particular drug. When will we acquire reliable personal genome data, we will achieve a deeper understanding of human DNA. In future, the advanced genetic risk prediction will be a crucial step towards more individual genetic health care.

8. Explain the use of data science in 'Fraud and Risk Detection.'

Ans. Data science was initially used in the field of finance. Many companies were fed up with bad debts and losses every year. However, the companies and banks had a lot of data that was used to get collected during the initial paperwork at the time of sanctioning loans. Data scientists were employed to rescue them from such losses. Data science helped in risk assessment and monitoring, potential fraudulent behaviour, payments, customer analysis, and experience, among many other utilisations. Over the years, banking companies learned how to divide and conquer data via customer profiling, past expenditures, past experiences , and other essential variables to analyze the probabilities of risk and default. Moreover, data science helped them to push their banking services and products based on customers' purchasing power. The data-driven decisions created a more stable financial environment, and now, data scientists make the backbone of the finance industry.

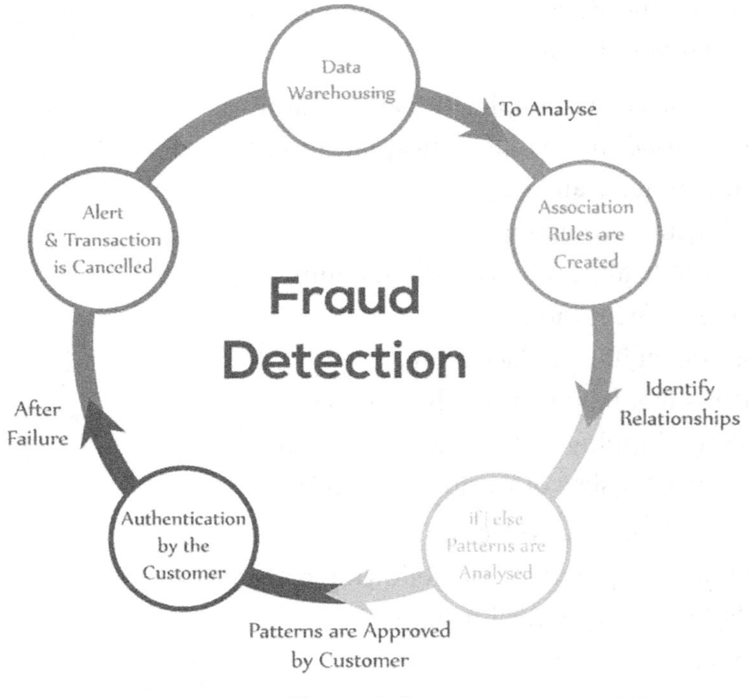

Figure 9.7

9. Explain data science applications in targeted advertising.

Ans. The biggest of all data science applications is used in the entire digital marketing spectrum. From the display banners on websites of different companies/organizations to the digital boards at the railway stations and airports, almost all of them are decided by using data science algorithms. That's why digital ads have been able to get a higher CTR (Call-Through Rate) than traditional advertisements by using and monitoring users' past behaviour.

10. Write a short note on 'Data science and Gaming.'

Ans. According to a research estimate, there are more than 2.5 billion gamers across the world. The gaming industry is progressing rapidly in the field of entertainment. Data science is used in the gaming industry to build models, analyze optimization points, make predictions, and/ identify patterns to improve gaming models. Data scientists work in monetization, where they need to identify the most valuable players and analyze general consumer behaviour to increase the profitability of the company. It is to be understood that the more the players spend, the higher the profitability. Another area where data scientists can check security levels in the gaming industry is to set the highest standards. Hence, machine learning algorithms allow faster identification of suspicious account activities during the process.

Figure 9.8

11. Mention three examples of datasets.

Ans. Three examples of datasets are given below:

a) **Banks:** Databases of loans issued, bank visitors, details of account holders, locker owners, employee registrations, etc.

b) **ATM Machines:** visitor details, Usage details per day, cash denominations transaction details, etc.

c) **Movie Theatres:** Movie details, tickets sold offline, tickets sold online, refreshment purchases, etc.

12. Enlist the types and functions of Sensors present in a smartphone.

Ans. Smartphone has the following sensors:

a) GPS (Location Data)

b) Gyroscope (Orientation Data)

c) Biometric Sensors (Fingerprint, Iris, Face Data)

    d) Magnetometer (Direction and Magnetic Field Data)

    e) Accelerometer (It helps run AR applications and track steps.)

13. Enlist the sources of data.

Ans. Data may be collected from various sources as listed below by two methods: Offline and Online.

    a) Cameras   b) Sensors

    c) Observations   d) API

    e) Web scrapping (Internet)   f) Surveys

    g) Interviews   h) Documents and records

    i) Oral histories

14. What are the different formats of datasets? Explain.

Ans. The tabular datasets can be stored in different formats. Some of the commonly used formats are:

    a) **CSV:** CSV stands for comma-separated values. It is a simple file format used to store tabular data. Each line of this file is a data record, and the reach record consisting of one or more fields separated by commas. Because the values of records are separated by a comma, so they are called CSV files.

    b) **Spreadsheet:** A Spreadsheet is a piece of paper or a computer program. It is used for accounting and recording data using rows and columns into which information can be entered. For example: Microsoft Excel is a program that helps in creating spreadsheets.

    c) **SQL:** SQL is a programming language also known as Structured Query Language. It is a domain-specific language that is used in programming and is designed for managing data held in different kinds of DBMS (Database Management System). It is useful in handling structured data mainly. A lot of other formats of databases also exist; you can explore them online!

15. For which purpose is Panda suitable package?

Ans. Pandas is suitable for different kinds of data, like

    a) Tabular data with heterogeneously-typed columns, like in an SQL table or Excel spreadsheet

    b) Ordered and non-ordered (not necessarily fixed-frequency) time-series data

    c) Arbitrary matrix data (homogeneously typed or heterogeneously typed) with row and column labels

    d) Any other form of observational/statistical data set

    e) The data actually need not be labeled at all for placing into a Pandas data structure.

16. Mention the 'Basic Features of Pandas.'

Ans. The important features of Pandas are listed below:

    a) Keep track of the data

    b) Use of different data types (float, int, string, date-time, etc.)

    c) Easy grouping and joins of data

    d) Good IO capabilities

    e) Python MYSQL Connectivity

    f) Label-based slicing, indexing, and sub-setting of large data sets

17. Why is Python preferred for Data Sciences?

Ans. There are various reasons for which Python is one of the most used programming languages for data science. Some of them are as follows:

    a) Python is relatively faster than any other programming language.

    b) There are a significant number of packages available that other users have developed, which can be reused.

    c) The syntax roles in Python are intuitive and easy to understand, thereby helping in building applications with a readable codebase.

18. Which statistical tools are used in Python?

Ans. The following statistical tools are used in Python:

    a) Mean

    b) Median

    c) Mode

    d) Standard deviation

    e) Variance

19. Mention the applications of Python packages.

Ans. Python packages are applied in the following applications:

    a) Data analysis

    b) Game development

    c) GUI based desktop applications

    d) Machine learning and artificial intelligence

    e) Visualising Data

    f) Web applications and frameworks

    g) Enterprise and business applications

    h) Automating things with scripts

    i) Scraping the Web

20. Explain a Bar Chart.

Ans. A 'Bar chart' is one of the most commonly used graphical methods. A bar chart / bar graph is a chart/ graph that is used to represent categorical data with rectangular bars with heights/ lengths proportional to the represented values. The bars may be plotted vertically or horizontally. Moreover, a vertical bar chart is called a column chart also.

The two axes depict two different parameters, while bars of different colours work with different entities. The bar chart also works on discontinuous data and is made at uniform intervals.

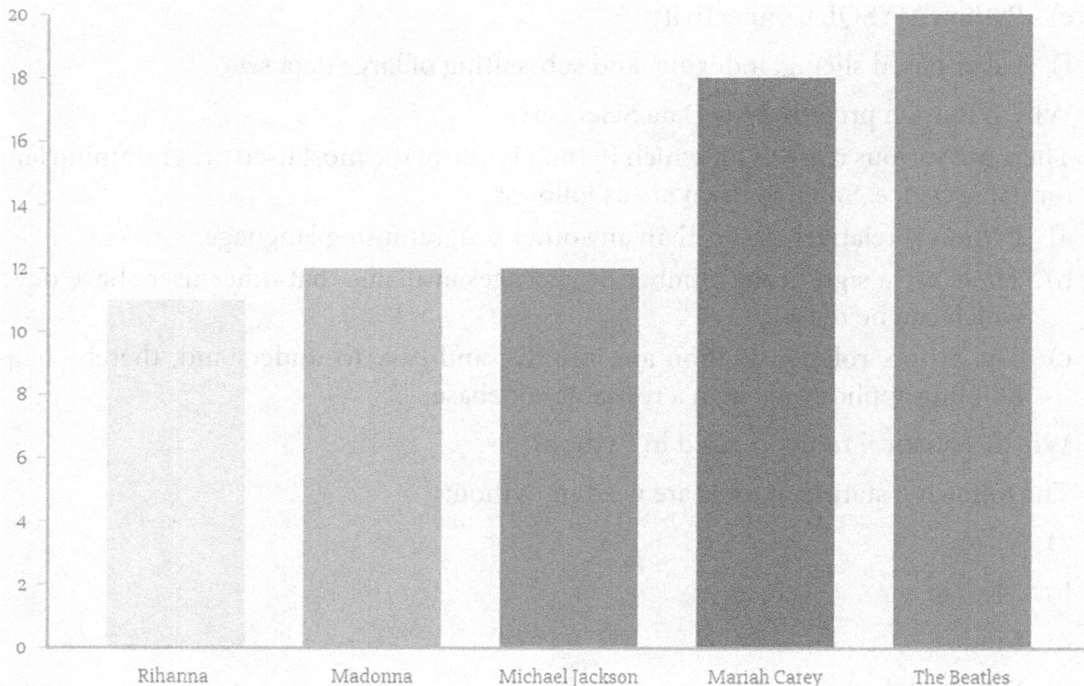

Figure 9.9 Bar chart

21. Explain histograms.

Ans. Histograms are the accurate representation of continuous data. A histogram or an area diagram is defined as a set of rectangles with bases along with the intervals between class boundaries and with areas proportional to frequencies in the corresponding classes. Here, all the rectangles are adjacent because the same base covers the intervals between class boundaries.

When it comes to plotting the variation in just one entity of a period of time, histogram is considered the best option. It displays the frequency of the variable at different points of time with the help of the bins.

9.2.10 Long Answer Type Questions

1. Discuss the applications of Data Science with the help of examples.

Ans. The various applications of Data Science are making our life easier as it is playing a crucial role in the tech-savvy world. The various applications of Data Science in today's world are discussed below:

a) **Fraud and Risk Detection:** Data science was initially used in the field of finance. Many companies were fed up with bad debts and losses every year. However, the companies and banks had a lot of data that was used to get collected during the initial paperwork at the time of sanctioning loans. Data scientists were employed to rescue them from such losses. Data science helped in risk assessment and monitoring, potential fraudulent behaviour, payments, customer analysis, and experience, among many other utilisations.

b) **Website Recommendations:** Data science is used to make suggestions about similar products on various websites like Amazon, based on the user's past behaivour and experience. Internet giants like Amazon, Twitter, Netflix,Google Play, LinkedIn, IMDB, etc., use this system to improve the user experience. Such recommendations are based on previous search results for a user.

c) **Gaming:** The gaming industry is progressing rapidly in the field of entertainment. Data science is used in the gaming industry to build models, analyze optimization points, make predictions, and/ identify patterns to improve gaming models. Data scientists work in monetisation, where they need to identify the most valuable players and analyse general consumer behaviour to increase the profitability of the company.

d) **Internet Search:** Many search engines like Google, Yahoo, Bing, Ask, AOL, etc., are using data science algorithms to deliver the best result for the searched query in a fraction of a second and considering the fact that Google processes more than 20 petabytes of data every day. Without data science, Google and other search engines wouldn't have been the same as we know today.

e) **Genetics and Genomics:** Data Science enables an advanced level of treatment personalisation through research in genetics and genomics. The data scientists' goal is to understand the impact of DNA on health to find out individual biological connections among genetics, diseases, and drug response. Data science techniques use the integration of different kinds of data with genomic data in disease research, which provides a deeper understanding of issues related to genetic engineering in response to the administration of a particular drug.

f) **Targeted Advertising:** The biggest of all data science applications is used in the entire digital marketing spectrum. From the display banners on websites of different companies/organisations to the digital boards at the railway stations and airports, almost all of them are decided by using data science algorithms. That's why digital ads have been able to get a higher CTR (Call-Through Rate) than traditional advertisements by using and monitoring users' past behaviour.

g) **Healthcare:** The demand for data analytics and scientists in the healthcare area is growing rapidly. By using the quick process of large volumes of data for clinical and laboratory reports, data scientists produce a more precise diagnosis report by utilising deep learning techniques. Thus, data scientists are helping to reduce the risk of health issues and directly impact the state of human wellbeing in the entire world.

h) **Energy:** Because the energy industry experiences major fluctuations in prices and higher costs of projects and hence, Data scientists help the energy industry in cutting costs, reducing risks, optimizing investments, and improving equipment maintenance. They use predicting models to monitor compressors' various processes. The data science tools used in extracting and evaluating data include Oracle, Hadoop, NoSQL, Python, and various other software.

i) **Travel industry:** Many people travel from one corner to the other corner of the world, and now, travel personalisation has become an increasingly deep process. The possibility to create customer profiles based on segmentation, offering personalised experiences according to the needs and preferences, has its foundations in data science. The travel industry is getting help from data scientists in forecasting the behaviour of travelers by knowing where they want to go next, what kind of prices they are ready to pay, and when to launch special promotions, etc.

Figure 9.10 Airline route planning

j) **Airline Route Planning:** Many airline companies are struggling to maintain their occupancy ratio and operating profits. With a high rise in air-fuel prices and the need to offer heavy discounts to customers, the situation is becoming worse. Data Science helps the industry to identify the strategic areas of improvements and the airline companies can:

- Predict flight delay.

- Effectively drive customer loyalty programs.

- Decide the type of airplanes to buy.

- Whether directly to land at the destination or take a halt in between the destinations.

k) **Manufacturing Industry:** The manufacturing industry keeps growing with the help of data scientists, where they can apply their knowledge of broad data management solutions through quality assurance, tracking defects, and increasing the quality of supplier relations. By utilising preventive maintenance, data scientists can help in avoiding delays in the production process, implementing artificial intelligence. Predictive analytics provides the solutions to manage frequent manufacturing issues, like overproduction of products, logistics, inventory, etc.

Figure 9.11

2. Explain various sources of data collection.

Ans. Some of the data acquisition sources are listed below:

a) **Surveys:** A survey consists of a list of queries that can be conducted online, over email, over the phone, or in-person for collecting data related to the project goal. A survey can collect either quantitative or qualitative data or both. Consider the example of Air Pollution. Through a survey, we can collect data from people about the number of people suffering from lung disease, hospitals, doctors, etc.

b) **Sensors:** Sensors are also called Transducers which convert real-world phenomena like force, temperature, and movement to current signals or changes in voltage that can be used as inputs. They are used to collect a variety of data for research and action.

c) **Web Scraping:** Web data extraction collects large amounts of data from websites on the internet using a web browser. The online product shopping trends, like a face masks, ventilators, oxygen cylinders, air purifiers, etc., can be gathered from websites, whereas the government's authentic data can be collected from the Govt's official websites.

d) **Observations:** The process of careful and systematic viewing of facts as they occur is known as observation. Observation requires movement of the eyes and carefully listening through the ears. Doctors can observe the sudden increase in the number of chest disease-infected patients.

e) **Cameras:** The camera plays an important part in data collection in the form of images. Live data can be acquired using the web camera, CCTV, chatbot interface, etc., for people showing problems due to air pollution.

f) **API (Application Program Interface):** Application programming interfaces are the piece of code that helps one application to connect to another. Examples: weather snippets used by Google, Pay with PayPal, Spotify to search different types of music, Twitter bots, Travel booking, etc.

g) **Smart Phone:** Main Source of data collection is smartphones used by a large population of a country. These devices collect various data, like user's face, browsing history, movement history, photographs, sentiment analysis, etc.

3. What type of information/data is collected through smartphones?

Ans. Smartphone collects the following data of users:

- User's face
- Browsing history
- Pictures/photographs
- User's geographic location
- Movement history
- Contact list
- Purchase interests/inclinations
- Purchase history
- Habits of viewing specific movies
- Reading habits
- Sentiment analysis, etc.

4. Which precautions are to be taken while accessing data from any source?

Ans. While accessing data from any of the data sources, the following points should be kept in mind:

   a) Data that is available for public usage only should be taken up.

   b) Personal datasets should only be used with the consent of the owner.

   c) One should never breach someone's privacy to collect data.

   d) Data should only be taken from reliable sources as the data collected from random sources can be wrong or unusable.

   e) Reliable sources of data ensure the authenticity of data that helps in the proper training of the AI model.

5. Explain the types of Data by giving some examples.

Ans. Data is classified as follows:

   a) **Quantitative data:** Quantitative Data answers key questions such as "how many, "how much," and "how often." It can be expressed as a number and can be measured by numerical variables only. Quantitative data is easily amenable to statistical manipulation. It can be represented by a wide variety of statistical types of graphs and charts, like line charts, bar graphs, scatter plots, and etc.

   Examples:

   - Scores on tests and exams: 93, 67, 25, etc.
   - The weight of a person
   - Shoe size of students of a school
   - The temperature in a room is recorded for a year.

   There are two types of quantitative data: discrete data and continuous data.

   (i) **Discrete data:** It is a count involving only integers, and the discrete values cannot be subdivided into parts. Discrete data can take certain values, and the data variables cannot be divided into smaller parts. For example, the number of teachers in a school is discrete data. You can count whole individuals. You can't count 4.5 teachers.

   Examples:

   - The number of boys/girls in a school.
   - The number of workers in a factory/company/organisation.
   - The number of runs made by bowlers in a cricket game
   - The number of test questions.

   (ii) **Continuous data:** Continuous Data can be meaningfully divided into finer levels. Continuous data can be measured on a scale or continuum and can have almost any numeric value. Continuous data can be recorded at so many different measurements, like width, temperature, time, and etc. The continuous variables may have any value between two numbers. For example, there are literally millions of possible values between 5 meters and 6 meters: 5.04762 m, 5.948376 m.

   Examples:

   - Time required to complete a project (in days/hours).
   - The height of children (in meter/inch).

    ⌃   The area of a two-bedroom house (in square foot/square meter).

    ⌃   The speed of cars (in km/h or m/s).

b) **Qualitative data:** It can't be expressed as a number and can't be quantified/ measured. It consists of words, pictures, and symbols, not numbers. Qualitative data can answer questions like "how this has happened" or and "why this has happened."

Examples:

    ⌃   Colours, like the colour of the sea, colour of flowers, etc

    ⌃   Various favourite holiday destinations, like Ajmer, Shimla, ISRO, New Zealand, Switzerland, etc.

    ⌃   Names such as Sudha, Imarti, Reshma, Jag Mohan, John, Amar Nath Singh Tyagi, etc

    ⌃   Ethnicity such as European, American, Indian, Asian, etc

6. What are the types of qualitative data? Explain by giving examples.

Ans. Two types of qualitative data are available: nominal data and ordinal data.

a) **Nominal data:** The data used for labeling variables without any type of quantitative value is called Nominal data. The name 'nominal' is originated from the Latin word "nomen," which means 'name.' Sometimes, the nominal data is just called "labels."

Examples of Nominal Data:

    ⌃   Gender (Women, Men)

    ⌃   Hair colour (Black, Brown, Brunette, Blonde, Red, etc.)

    ⌃   Marital status (Married, Single, Widowed, Divorcee)

    ⌃   Ethnicity (Hispanic, Asian)

    ⌃   Eye colour (Blue, Green, Brown)

b) **Ordinal data:** Ordinal data exhibits where a number is in order. Ordinal data is the data that is placed into some kind of order by their position on a scale. Ordinal data may indicate superiority. The ordinal variables only show sequence. The Ordinal Data is qualitative data in which the values are ordered.

Examples:

    ⌃   The first, second, and third position in a debate competition

    ⌃   Economic status: low, medium, and high

    ⌃   Letter grades: A, B, C, etc.

    ⌃   On a scale of 1-5, when a company asks a customer to rate the sales experience.

7. Discuss any three Python packages used for Data Access.

Ans. Various Python packages are used in accessing structured data (in tabular form) inside the Python code. Some of these packages are discussed below:

a) **NumPy:** NumPy stands for Numerical Python. NumPy is the fundamental package for Mathematical and logical operations on arrays in Python. It is a commonly used package when it comes to working around numbers. It is a library consisting of numbers in multidimensional array objects and a collection of methods for processing these arrays. It gives a wide range of arithmetic operations around numbers giving us an easier approach in working with them. NumPy also works with arrays, which is nothing but a homogenous collection of data. An array is nothing but a set of multiple values which are of the same data type, and they may be numbers, characters, Booleans, etc. One datatype can be accessed through an array. In NumPy, the arrays used are known as ND arrays (N-Dimensional Arrays) as NumPy comes with a feature of creating n-dimensional arrays in Python.

b) **Pandas:** Pandas is a software library that provides data manipulation and analysis tools in the Python programming language. It offers data structures and operations for manipulating numerical tables and time series. It provides special data structures and operations for the manipulation of numerical tables and time series. Pandas are expanded as panel data", which means data sets that include observations over multiple time periods for the same individuals.

c) **Matplotlib:** Matplotlib in Python is an amazing visualization library for 2D plots of arrays. Matplotlib is a multiplatform data visualization library built on NumPy arrays. One of the greatest benefits of visualization is that it allows us visual access to large data in easily digestible visuals. Matplotlib is available with a wide variety of plots. Plots help us to understand trends and patterns and to make correlations among them. They are typically instruments for reasoning about quantitative information.

8. Write important features of NumPy Arrays.

Ans. The important features of NumPy Arrays are as follows:

a) Homogenous collection of Data.

b) It may contain only one type of data, hence not flexible with datatypes.

c) It cannot be directly initialized. It may be operated with the Numpy package only.

d) Direct numerical operations can be done. For example, dividing the whole array by 3 divides every element by 3.

e) They are widely used for arithmetic operations.

f) Arrays take less memory space.

g) Functions like concatenation, appending, reshaping, etc., are not trivially possible with arrays.

9. What are the main features of Lists?

Ans. The important features of Lists are as follows:

a) Heterogenous collection of data.

b) It can contain multiple types of data, hence flexible with datatypes.

c) It can be directly initialised as it is a part of Python syntax.

d) Direct numerical operations are not possible. For example, dividing the whole list by three cannot divide every element by 3.

e) They are widely used for data management.

f) Lists acquire more memory space.

g) Functions like concatenation, appending, reshaping, etc., are trivially possible with lists.

10. Describe the usage of Pandas for handling different types of data.

Ans. Two primary data structures of Pandas are Series (1-dimensional) and DataFrame (2-dimensional) that handle the vast majority of typical use cases in statistics, finance, social science, and many areas of engineering. Pandas is built on top of NumPy. It intended to integrate well within a scientific computing environment with many other 3rd party libraries.

The following things can be done well by Pandas:

a) It is possible to handle missing data (represented as NaN) in floating point and non-floating- point data.

b) Intuitive merging and joining data sets

c) Columns can be easily inserted and deleted from DataFrame and higher dimensional objects (Size mutability).

d) Flexible reshaping and pivoting of data sets

e) Objects can be aligned to a set of labels, or the user can simply ignore the labels and let Series, DataFrame, etc., automatically align the data for the user in computations.

f) It is possible for Intelligent label-based slicing, fancy indexing, and sub-setting of large data sets.

g) Some types of graphs, like Bar graphs, histograms, pie charts, scatter plot, area plot, etc., can be drawn with this package.

11. Which types of errors may be found during data acquisition?

Ans. While collecting data, it is possible that the data might come with some errors. The following types of errors /issues may be found with data:

a) **Erroneous Data:** There are two ways in which the data can be erroneous:

(i) **Incorrect values:** The values in the dataset (at random places) are incorrect. For example, in the column of the phone number, there is a decimal value, or in the marks column, there is a name mentioned, etc. These are incorrect values that do not resemble the kind of data expected in that position.

(ii) **Invalid or Null values:** At some places, the values get corrupted, and hence they become invalid. Many times, we will find NaN values in the dataset. These are null values that do not hold any meaning and are not processible. That is why these values (as and when encountered) are removed from the database.

(iii) **Missing Data:** In some datasets, some cells are found empty. The values of these cells are missing, and hence, the cells remain empty. Missing data cannot be interpreted as an error as the values here are not erroneous or might not be missing because of any error.

(iv)**Outliers:** Data that do not fall in the range of a certain element are known as outliers. To understand it better, consider the example of the marks of students in a class. Suppose that a student was absent in the Annual exams and hence, has got zero marks in it. If his marks are taken into account, the whole class's average will go down. The average is taken for the range of marks from highest to lowest, keeping this particular result separate. This makes sure that the average marks of the class are true according to the data.

12. Explain Scatter Plot.

Ans. A scatter plot /scatter graph/scatter chart has points scattered over an area (2 D graph) representing the relationship between two values.

   i. Scatter plots are used to plot discontinuous data, i.e., the data which does not have any continuity inflow is termed as discontinuous. There exist gaps in data that introduce discontinuity. A 2D scatter plot can display information maximum of up to four parameters.

   ii. In the scatter plot, two axes (X and Y) are two different parameters. The colour of circles and the size both represent two different parameters. Thus, just through one coordinate on the graph, one can visualise four different parameters all at once.

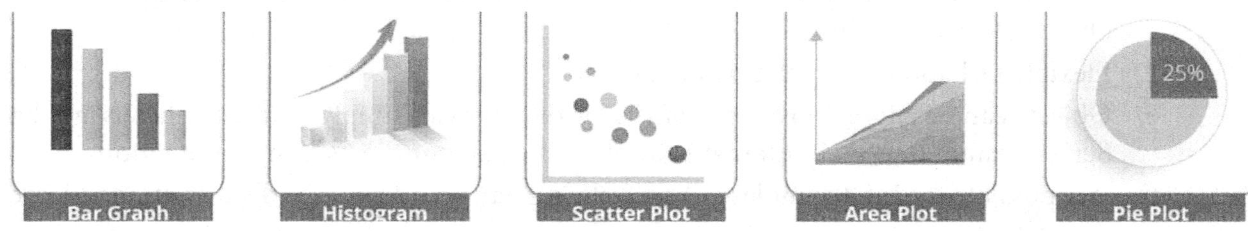

Figure 9.12

13. What do you mean by 'Box plot'? Explain.

Ans. Box Plot is a simple way to depict a group of numerical data through their quartiles, and it is used to visualise the shape of the data. Box plots divide the data into sections in such a manner that each contains approximately 25% of the data in that set. These plots are useful as they provide a visual summary of the data enabling researchers to quickly identify mean values, the dispersion of the data set, and signs of skewness. Inbox plot, it is very easy to compare the characteristics of data between categories.

When the data is split as per its percentile throughout the range, then box plots are used. Box plots (also known as Box and Whisker's plots) display the distribution of data throughout the range with the help of four quartiles.

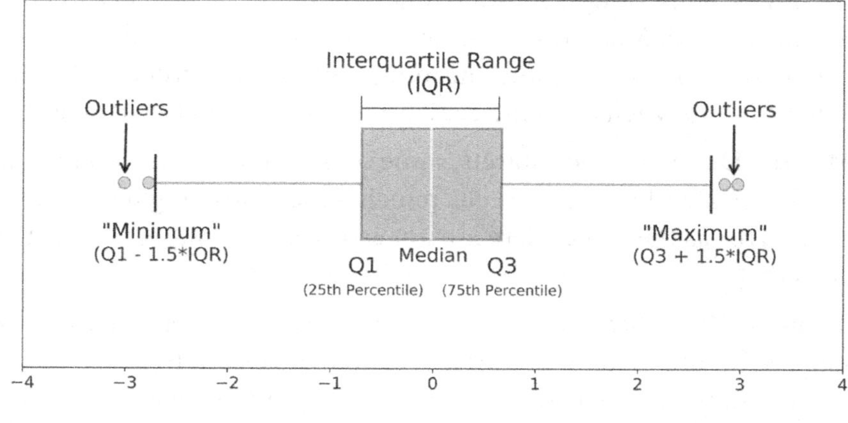

Figure 9.13

The plot contains a box and two lines at its left and right that are called whiskers. The plot has five different parts to it.

a) **Quartile 1:** (From 0 percentile to 25th percentile) Here, Data are lying between 0 and 25th percentile is plotted. When the data is close to each other, let's say 0 to 25th percentile data has been covered in just 20-30 marks range, then the whisker will be smaller because the range is smaller. When the range is large, i.e., 0-30 marks range; then the whisker would also get elongated as the range is longer.

b) **Quartile 2:** (From 25th Percentile to 50th percentile) 50th percentile is called the mean of the whole distribution, and because the data falling in the range of 25th percentile to 75th percentile has a minimum deviation from the mean, it is plotted inside the box.

c) **Quartile 3:** (From 50th percentile to 75th percentile) This range is again plotted in the box because its deviation from the mean is less. Quartile 2 & 3 (from 25th percentile to 75th percentile) together constitute the Inter Quartile Range (IQR). Also, depending upon the range of distribution, the length of the box varies if the data is less spread or more.

d) **Quartile 4:** (From 75th percentile to 100th percentile) It is the whiskers plot for the top 25 percentile data.

e) **Outliers:** The main advantage of box plots is that they clearly show the outliers in a data distribution. Points that do not lie in the range are plotted outside the graph as dots or circles and are termed as outliers because they do not belong to the range of data. Because being out of range is not an error, that is why they are still plotted on the graph for visualization.

Matplotlib library will help us in plotting all sorts of graphs, while Numpy and Pandas will help us in analysing the data.

14. Explain the K-Nearest Neighbour (KNN) model.

Ans. The K-Nearest Neighbours (KNN) algorithm is a simple, easy-to-implement supervised machine learning algorithm that can be used to solve both types of problems, i.e., classification and regression problems. The KNN algorithm uses the assumption that similar things exist in close proximity. It means that ds, similar things are near to each other.

Some features of KNN are:

▲ The KNN prediction model relies on the surrounding points or neighbours to determine its class or group.

▲ It utilises the properties of the majority of the nearest points to decide how to classify unknown points.

▲ Based on the concept that similar data points should be close to each other.

15. Discuss the significance of neighbours in the KNN prediction model.

Ans. The significance of the number of neighbours in the KNN prediction model may be understood as follows:

When we decrease the value of K to 1, the predictions become less stable. Take this example: suppose K=1, and we have X surrounded by several greens and one blue, but the blue is the single nearest neighbour. Reasonably, we would think X is most likely green, but because K=1, KNN incorrectly predicts that it is blue.

Inversely, when we increase the value of K, the predictions become more stable due to majority voting / averaging, and therefore, more likely to make more accurate predictions (up to a certain point). At this time, we begin to witness an increasing number of errors because we have pushed the value of K too far.

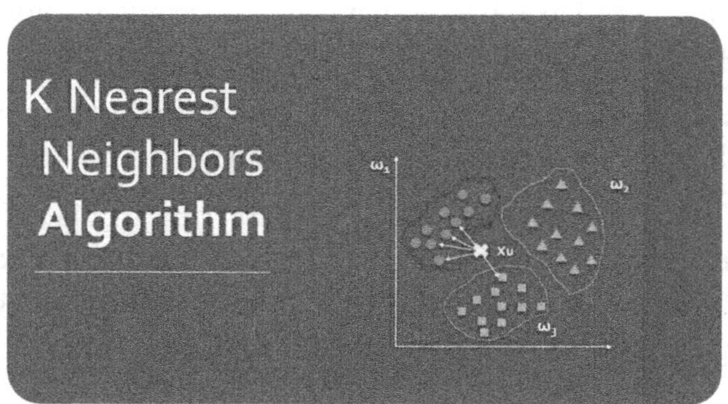

Figure 9.14

When we are taking a majority vote (e.g., picking the Mode in a classification problem) among labels, we normally make KNN odd number to have a tiebreaker.

16. Discuss any four applications of the KNN model.

Ans. Some of the areas where KNN is applied are enlisted as follows:

a) **Banking System:** KNN may be used in the banking system to predict whether an individual is fit for loan approval or not. We can find with the help of KNN that whether the individuals have the characteristics as that of a defaulter or the client will be able to pay the loan back successfully.

b) **Calculating Credit Ratings:** KNN algorithms are used to find an individual's credit rating by comparing with the persons having similar characteristics.

c) **Politics:** By using KNN algorithms, we can classify a potential voter into various classes like "Will Vote to Party' X', "Will Vote to Party' Y' " on the basis of his/her interest in politics and his/her opinion about the various parties.

d) **Other areas:** Other areas in which the KNN algorithm can be used are Speech Recognition, Handwriting Detection, Image Recognition, and Video Recognition.

17. What are the main ethical issues around Data Science?

Ans. There are some ethical challenges related to data and data science that are discussed below:

a) **Lack of Transparency:** Two areas that required transparency are as follows:

(i) **The step-by-step process, model, and its parameters by which a prediction is made:**

Depending on the model used, it can become very difficult as the exact functioning of certain models like the neural network is still not fully clear.

(ii) **Type of data that is being used in making a prediction:**

Statistical Models cannot differentiate between the predictive power of a single variable and that of a set of variables.

b) **Unfair Discrimination:** When data reflects unfair social biases against sensitive attributes, like Race or Gender, then the inferences drawn from the data might also be based on the said bias.

c) **Reinforcement of Human Biases:** This type of problem may arise when various computer models are used in making predictions in areas like Financial Loans, Insurance, Policing, etc. When the members of a certain racial group have historically been more likely to default on their loans, or when they have been more likely to be convicted of a crime, then the model may deem riskier.

It may be present during data selection, unintentional red-lining, re-inscription of existing biases, and reducing the discrimination already present in a training dataset.

18. Explain Data Privacy.

Ans. Artificial Intelligence mainly works dealing with data. Proper and ethical handling of a company's own data or user data is called data privacy. Privacy may be defined as the right of individuals, groups, or organisations to control who can access, observe, or use something they own, like their bodies, property, ideas, data, or information. Data privacy or information privacy is an area of data protection that deals with the proper handling of sensitive data, including personal data, confidential data (financial data, intellectual property data, etc.) to meet legal and regulatory requirements as well as protect the confidentiality and immutability of the data. It mainly focuses on how to collect, process, share, archive, and delete the data in accordance with the law.

Control on data usage is established through physical, social, or informational boundaries that help prevent unwanted access, observation, or use of data.

Examples:

▲ A physical boundary, like a locked front door, helps prevent others from entering a building without proper permission in the form of a key to unlock the door or a person inside opening the door.

▲ A social boundary, like a members-only club, only allows members to access and use club resources.

▲ An informational boundary, like a non-disclosure agreement, restricts what information can be disclosed to others.

19. Explain AI Bias with suitable examples.

Ans. AI bias is related to prejudice in data that's used to create AI algorithms, and this can create discrimination and other social consequences. AI Bias can also creep into algorithms in several ways. Moreover, AI systems learn to make decisions based on training data that may include biased human decisions, reflect historical or social inequities, sensitive variables such as gender, race, or sexual orientation, etc. Another source of bias is defective/biased data sampling, in which groups are over or underrepresented in the training data.

Examples:

(i) Almost all the virtual assistants are given a female voice. It is only now that some companies/organisations have understood this bias and have started giving options for male voice also. But because the virtual assistants came into practice, female voices are always preferred for them over any male voice.

(ii) When we search on Google for salons, the first few searches are mostly for female salons.

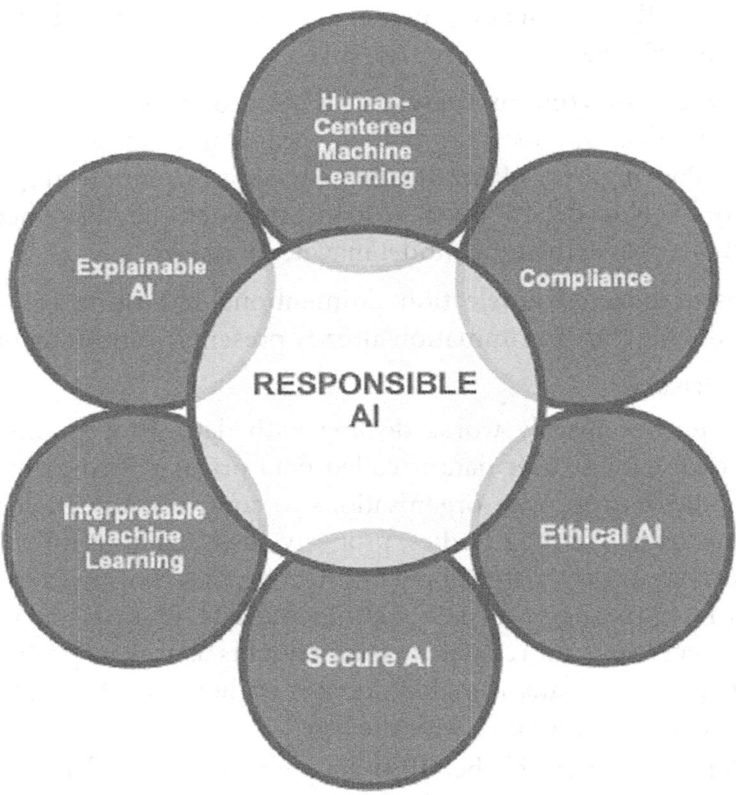

Figure 9.15

9.2.11 HOTS Questions

1. Why is qualitative data called categorical data?

Ans. Qualitative Data is called categorical data because the information can be sorted by category, not by number.

2. How does data science play an important role in airline route planning?

Ans. Many airline companies are struggling to maintain their occupancy ratio and operating profits. With a high rise in air-fuel prices and the need to offer heavy discounts to customers, the situation is becoming worse.

Data Science helps the industry to identify the strategic areas of improvements and the airline companies can:

- Predict flight delay
- Decide the class of airplanes to buy
- Effectively drive customer loyalty programs
- Whether directly land at the destination or take a halt in between.

3. Why is it important to preserve privacy?

Ans. Privacy of information is extremely important in the present digital age when everything is interconnected on the net and can be accessed and used easily. The possibilities of users' private information being extremely vulnerable are very real. That's why we require data privacy.

- Methods for handling sensitive data
- Uses of data science that undermine privacy
- Mitigating Malicious Attacks
- Intentional subversion of machine learning systems
- Hazards of learning from the open internet

4. How can we compare the properties of List, NumPy Array, and Series?

Ans. List, NumPy array, and Series have the following differences in properties:

Size: NumPy data structures take up less space than list and Series.

Performance: They are faster than lists and Series.

Indexing: Both List and NumPy have a numeric index (0,1,2,…), whereas Series supports custom index.

List does not support vectorised operation. Example: print(np.array([2,4])*2) $\Rightarrow$ [4,8]

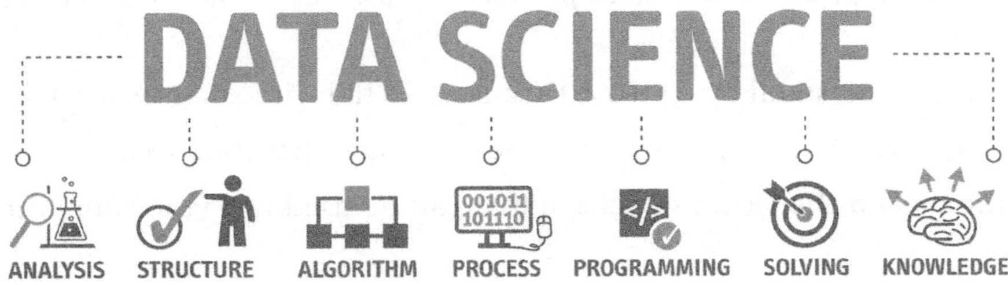

Figure 9.16

9.3 PRACTICE QUESTIONS

1. What is data exploration?
2. What do you understand by Data Privacy?
3. Define Machine Learning.
4. Define Deep Learning.
5. Mention any three examples of Natural Language Processing.
6. Name any three examples of CV.
7. What is the use of a box chart in data sciences?
8. Why does smartphone use different apps?
9. Explain data mining by giving two examples.
10. Differentiate between data science and computer science.
11. Mention any two examples of data.
12. Name four application areas of data sciences.

13. Why is data collected by companies?

14. What are the alternatives for major unemployment created by AI?

15. Differentiate among AI, ML, and DL.

16. Whether the Data collected by various applications is ethical in nature or not? Justify your answer.

17. Explain the working of sensors and cameras used for collecting the data.

18. Which statistical tools are used in Python?

19. Explain the NumPy package in Python.

20. What is data mining? Explain with a suitable example.

21. Define Data Privacy with suitable examples.

22. Why is personality prediction required? For which purpose do we use personality prediction?

23. AI should replace laborious jobs. Justify the statement.

24. List down different sensors present in a smartphone. What type of data is got collected through them?

25. Which type of approach is a better approach towards the ethical concern of data handling and why?

26. What do you understand by AI bias? Discuss in detail with some examples.

27. How is Data science used by the government in fraud detection cases?

28. Enlist and explain the various package that can be used in Python for working with data science.

UNIT 10

Computer Vision

10.1 UNIT IN BRIEF

✦ Computer Vision is the term for the hardware, software, and processes that allow computers to see and understand the physical world.

✦ The word "pixel" means a picture element.

Figure 10.1

✦ The pooling layer operates on every feature map independently.

✦ Semantic segmentation is the process of classifying each pixel belonging to a particular label.

✦ Classification+ Localisation involves both processes of identifying the object present in the image and at the same time also identifying the location that object is present in that image.

✦ Object Detection is the ability to detector identify objects in any given image correctly along with their three-dimensional position in the given image.

✦ Instance Segmentation basically identifies different instances given in the image with their boundaries intact.

✦ Grayscale images are images that have a range of shades of Gray without apparent colour.

✦ In an RGB image, each pixel has a set of three different values, which together give colour to that particular pixel.

✦ A convolution is a common tool used for image editing.

✦ Convolution is an element-wise multiplication of an image and a kernel to get the desired output.

✦ Convolution is used in Convolutional Neural Network (CNN) to extract image features in CV.

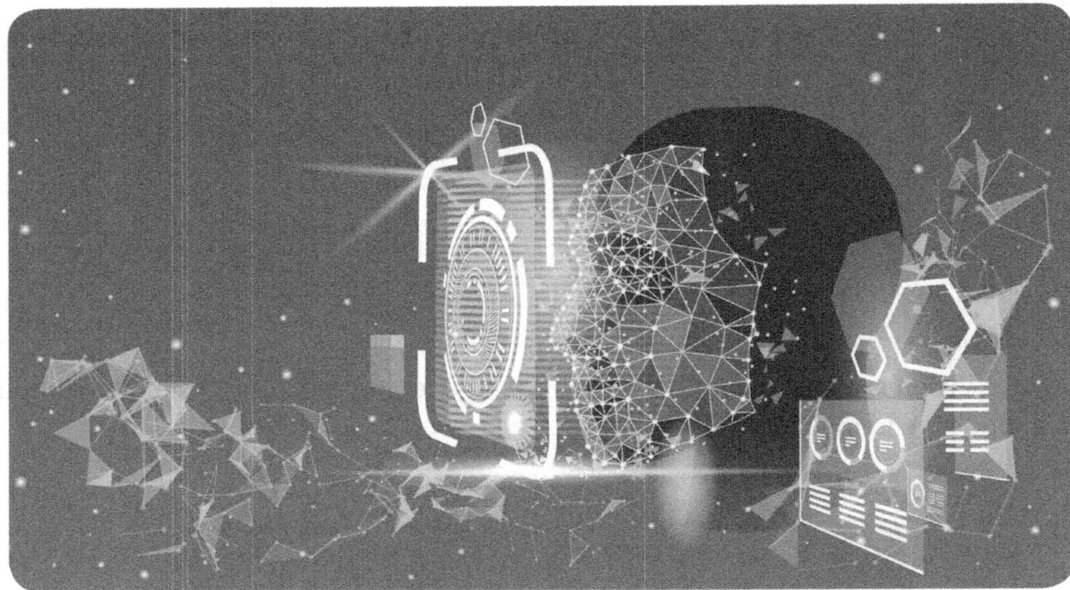

Figure 10.2

+ The main function of SVM is to divide the datasets into classes to find a maximum marginal hyperplane (MMH).

+ The goal of Computer vision is not only to see but also to process and provide useful results based on the observations.

+ Pixel value zero is given as no colour or black in the image.

+ The maximum pixel value is 255.

+ Grayscale images are images that have a range of shades of Gray without apparent colour.

+ The size of a grayscale image is the product of the Height by Width of that image.

+ Every RGB image is stored in the form of three different channels called the R channel, the G channel, and the B channel.

+ Convolution is a simple Mathematical operation and fundamental to many common image processing operators.

+ In CNN, we overlap the centre of the image with the centre of the Kernel to obtain the convolution output.

+ A Kernel is a matrix that slides across the image and multiplies with the input in such a manner that the output is enhanced in a certain desirable manner.

+ Monolithic Kernel is the Kernel where all operating system services operate in kernel space.

+ A convolution is a common tool used for image editing.

+ It is an element-wise multiplication of an image and a kernel to get the desired output.

+ Datapoints closest to the hyperplane are known as support vectors.

+ Margin is the gap between two lines on the closest data points of different classes.

+ Face Recognition application of CV may lead to ethical issues like Identity Theft, Discrimination, Espionage, Malicious Attacks, etc.

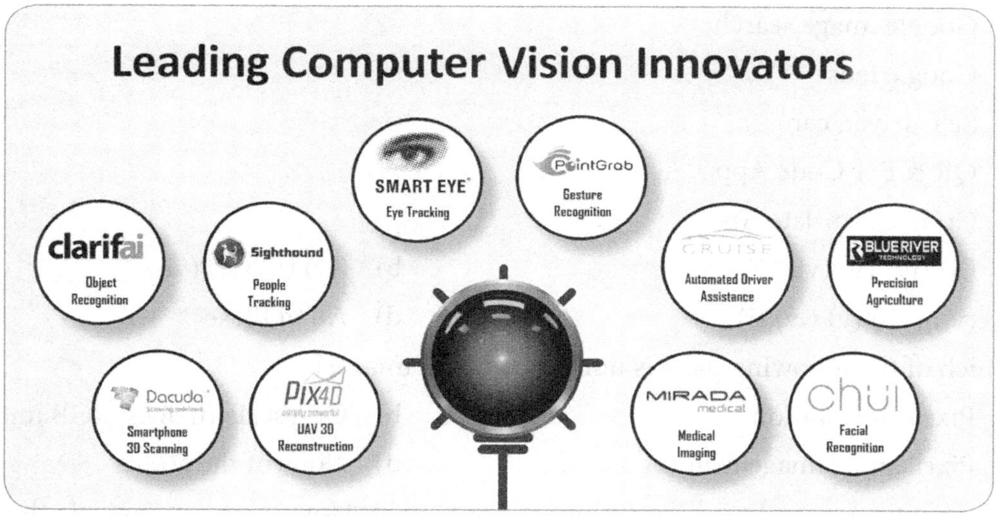

Figure 10.3

10.2 SOLVED EXERCISES

10.2.1 Multiple Choice Questions

1. Which of the following examples is NOT an application of CV?

   a) Traffic Control

   b) Population control

   c) Inventory management

   d) Google image search

2. Consider the following applications and choose the correct set of CV applications.

Figure 10.4

   i. Traffic Control

   ii. Inventory management

iii. Google image search

iv. Google lens

v. Self-driven car

vi. QR & Bar Code App

vii. Google translate App

a) (ii) (iii) (v) (vii)   b) (iv) (v) (vi) (vii)

c) (vi) (vii) (v) (iv) (i)   d) All of these

3. Which of the following pairs is not the basics of images?

a) Pixels, Resolution   b) Grayscale Images, RGB image

c) Pixel value, image features   d) None of the above

4. A computer screen has a resolution of 1280×1024. How many megapixels the computer monitor has?

a) 1.11 megapixels   b) 1.21 megapixels

c) 1.31 megapixels   d) 1.51 megapixels

5. What are the three primary colours?

a) Red, Green, Yellow   b) Red, Green, Blue

c) Green, Yellow, Blue   d) Blue, Green, Violet

6. What is the term used for the hardware, software, and processes that allow computers to see and understand the physical world?

a) Data   b) CV

c) NLP   d) Semantic analysis

7. Which one of the following examples is an application of CV?

a) Digital lock-in smartphone   b) ATM machine

c) Self-driven car   d) Mobile

8. Which is the process of classifying each pixel belonging to a particular label?

a) Classification   b) Instance Classification

c) Semantic classification   d) Object detection

9. Which application is not related to CV?

a) 2 D model building (photography)

b) Medical imaging, Biometrics

c) Retail automation, Automotive safety

d) Machine inspection, Automotive safety

10. Which statement is NOT TRUE?

a) A Convolutional Neural Network (CNN) is a Deep Learning algorithm.

b) There are three types of pooling that can be performed on an image.

   c) CNN may take in an input image for assigning importance (learnable weights and biases) to various aspects/objects in the image and be capable of differentiating one from the other.

   d) The pooling layer makes the image more resistant to small transformations, distortions, and translations in the input image.

11. Which of the following statements is TRUE?

   a) Convolution refers to a simple Mathematical operation that is fundamental to many common image processing operators.

   b) In CNN, we overlap the centre of the image with the centre of the Kernel to obtain the convolution output.

   c) Monolithic Kernel is the Kernel where all operating system services operate in kernel space.

   d) All the above

12. How many layers are present in a CNN?

   a) 3   b) 4   c) 5   d) 7

13. Which of the following Apps does use face filters?

   a) Instagram   b) Snapchat   c) Facebook   d) All of these

14. Which of the following layers is not associated with CNN?

   a) Fully Connected Layer.   b) Primary Layer

   c) Rectified Linear Unit (ReLU)   d) Pooling Layer

15. What is the name of the first layer of a CNN?

   a) Convolutional Layer   b) Rectified Linear Unit (ReLU)

   c) Pooling Layer   d) Fully Connected Layer.

16. Which layer in CNN makes the image smaller and more manageable?

   a) Pooling Layer   b) Convolution Layer

   c) Fully Connected Layer   d) ReLU

17. For which type of problems Support Vector Machine (SVM) is used?

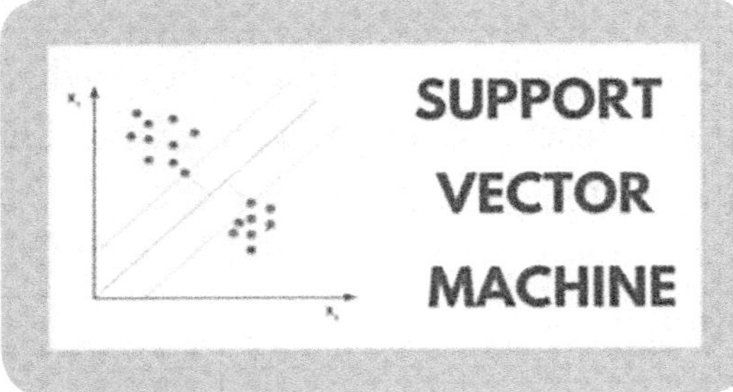

Figure 10.5

   a) Classification problems only

   b) Regression problems only

    c) Both classification and regression problems

    d) None of the above

18. What is the pixel value range for an image?

    a) 0 to 55   b) 0 to 255   c) 1 to 155   d) 1 to 255

19. ______________ is not a type of Kernel.

    a) Exo   b) Micro   c) Macro   d) Monolithic

20. What are activation maps also known as?

    a) Activity Map   b) Futuristic Map   c) Feature Map   d) Gole Map

21. Which of the following statements is INCORRECT?

    a) The pooling layer operates on every feature map independently.

    b) The word "pixel" means a picture element.

    c) In an RGB image, each pixel has a set of four different values, which together give colour to that particular pixel.

    d) Grayscale images are images that have a range of shades of Gray without apparent colour.

22. SVM is based on:

    a) Deep learning   b) Non-supervised learning

    c) Supervised machine learning   d) None of these

23. In the medical field, with the help of CV, a 2D image is converted into:

    a) 3D image   b) 4D image   c) 5D image   d) Both a and b

24. Which of the following is not a CV task?

    a) Object detection   b) Classification

    c) Resolution   d) Classification + Localisation

25. Which of the following statements is INCORRECT?

    a) The computer vision's goal is not only to see but also to process and provide useful results based on the observations.

    b) Convolution is used in Convolutional Neural Network (CNN) to extract image features in CV.

    c) The size of a grayscale image is the product of the Height and Width of that image.

    d) Computer vision is not closely associated with Artificial Intelligence.

26. Which function is not related to CV?

    a) Lie detector

    b) Motion Capture (Mocap)

    c) Fingerprint recognition

    d) Optical Character Recognition (OCR)

27. What is the pixel value for the black colour of an image?

    a) 155   b) 255   c) 355   d) Zero

28. What are the features of an image?
    a) Specific information about an image
    b) Specific structures in the image, like points, edges, or objects
    c) Pixels of an image
    d) Resolution of an image

29. Which of the following is not an objective of Kernel?
    a) To establish communication between user-level applications and hardware
    b) To decide the state of incoming processes
    c) To control disk and memory management
    d) All the above

30. Which statement is NOT TRUE?
    a) Computer Vision is the term for the hardware, software, and processes that allow computers to see and understand the physical world.
    b) The word "pixel" means a picture element.
    c) Classification involves both processes of identifying the object present in the image and at the same time also identifying the location that object is present in that image.
    d) Grayscale images are images that have a range of shades of Gray without apparent colour.

31. Which example is related to Exo Kernel?
    a) Nemesis   b) Linux   c) Mach   d) Open VMS

32. Which pair is an example of a Hybrid Kernel?
    a) Mach, L4   b) AmigaOS, Minix
    c) Nemesis, Unix   d) Both a and b

33. Which of the following statements is INCORRECT?
    a) Features of an image are defined as the specific structures in the image, such as points, edges, or objects.
    b) A convolution is a common tool used for image extraction.
    c) Convolution is an element-wise multiplication of an image and a kernel to get the desired output.
    d) In computer vision applications, convolution is used in Convolutional Neural Network (CNN) to extract image features.

34. What is the other name given to a feature map?
    a) Activity log   b) Activation map
    c) System map   d) None of these

35. Which example is related to monolithic Kernel?
    a) Unix,   b) Linux,   c) Open VMS,   d) All the above

36. Which of the following channels is not associated with a coloured picture?
    a) G Channel   b) X Channel   c) R Channel   d) B Channel

37. Study the following statements and mention the correct option.
    i.   SVM classifiers ensure great accuracy.
    ii. SVM classifiers need high training time and hence, in practice, are not suitable for large datasets.
    iii. SVM classifiers use a subset of training points; hence, they use very little memory.
    iv. SVM classifiers do not work efficiently with overlapping classes.

    a) and (ii)　　　　b) and (iii)　　　　c) and (iv)　　　d) (i),(ii), (iii) and (iv)

38. Which channel is not present in a colour image?
    a) R channel　　　　b) V channel　　　　c) B channel　　　　d) G channel

39. Which channels are present in a colour image?
    a) R, G, B　　　　b) V, R, Y　　　　c) B, Y, G　　　　d) G, O, R

40. Which of the following statements is INCORRECT?
    a) A convolution is a common tool used for image editing.
    b) It is an element-wise multiplication of an image and a kernel to get the desired output.
    c) Face Recognition application of CV may lead to ethical issues like Identity Theft, Discrimination, Espionage, etc.
    d) None of the above

41. Which one of the following parameters is not an advantage of using CV?
    a) Reliability　　　　　　　　　　　b) High cost
    c) Wide range of applications　　　　d) Accuracy

42. Which of the following statements is TRUE?
    a) Object Detection is the ability to detector identify objects in any given image correctly along with their three-dimensional position in the given image.
    b) Every RGB image is stored in the form of three different channels.
    c) Convolution is a simple Mathematical operation and fundamental to many common image processing operators.
    d) All the above

43. What is the command to install the OpenCV library after opening the an aconda prompt?

Computer Vision System

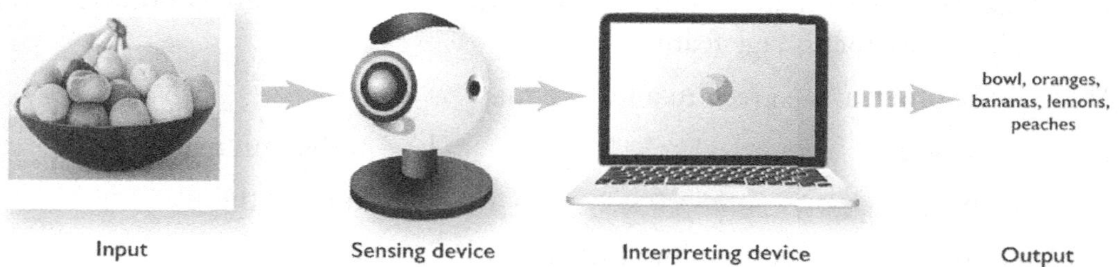

Figure 10.6

    a) install OpenCV-python　　　　　　　b) pip install OpenCV-python
    c) pip install OpenCV-jupyter　　　　　d) None of these

44. What are the smallest units of information that make up a picture?

    a) dpi   b) Resolution   c) Pixel   d) Kernel

ANSWERS

1. (b)	2. (d)	3. (d)	4. (c)	5. (b)	6. (b)	7. (c)	8. (c)	9. (a)	10. (b)
11. (d)	12. (b)	13. (d)	14. (b)	15. (a)	16. (a)	17. (c)	18. (b)	19. (c)	20. (c)
21. (c)	22. (c)	23. (a)	24. (a)	25. (d)	26. (a)	27. (d)	28. (b)	29. (d)	30. (c)
31. (a)	32. (d)	33. (b)	34. (b)	35. (d)	36. (b)	37. (d)	38. (b)	39. (a)	40. (d)
41. (b)	42. (d)	43. (b)	44. (b)						

10.2.2 Fill in the blanks

1. _______________ algorithm trains computers to interpret and understand the images in the visual world.

2. Computer Vision is a domain of AI that depicts the capability of a machine to get and analyse _______________ information to predict some decisions about it.

3. The darkest possible shade is black, i.e., the total absence of colour or _______________ value of a pixel.

4. Each pixel in the RGB image has _______________ values to form the complete colour.

5. The main function of SVM is to divide the _______________ into classes to find a maximum marginal hyperplane (MMH).

6. A _______________ is a matrix, which is slides across the image and multiplied with the input in such a manner that the output is enhanced in a certain desirable manner.

7. A _______________ is a common tool used for image editing.

8. _______________ segmentation is the process of classifying each pixel belonging to a particular label.

9. _______________ is defined the gap between two lines on the closet data points of different classes.

10. The _______________ pixels you have, the more closely the image resembles the original.

11. Datapoints closest to the hyperplane are known as _______________.

12. _______________ segmentation basically identifies different instances given in the image with their boundaries intact.

13. _______________ Kernel is a Kernel where all operating system services operate in kernel space.

14. _______________ images are images that have a range of shades of Gray without apparent colour.

15. _______________ the layer operates on each feature map independently.

ANSWERS
1. Computer vision   2. visual   3. zero   4. three   5. datasets
6. Kernel   7. convolution   8. Semantic   9. Margin   10. more
11. support vectors   12. Instance   13. Monolithic   14. Grayscale
15. Pooling

10.2.3 True or False

1. The Computer Vision (CV) domain of Artificial Intelligence enables machines to see-through images/ visual data, process and analyze them using algorithms and methods to analyze actual phenomena with images.

2. The word "pixel" means a picture element.

3. A convolution is a common tool used for image editing.

4. In an RGB image, each pixel has a set of five different values, which together give colour to that particular pixel.

5. The maximum pixel value is 365.

6. Convolution is an element-wise division of an image and a kernel to get the desired output.

7. In CNN, we overlap the centre of the image with the centre of the Kernel to obtain the convolution output.

8. Face Recognition application of CV may lead to ethical issues like Identity Theft, Discrimination, Espionage, Malicious Attacks, etc.

9. Classification+ Localisation involves both processes of identifying the object present in the image and at the same time also identifying the location that object is present in that image.

10. Convolution is a simple Mathematical operation and fundamental to many common image processing operators.

11. Convolution is used in Convolutional Neural Network (CNN) to extract image features in CV.

12. Object Detection is the ability to detector identify objects in any given image correctly along with their three-dimensional position in the given image.

13. The size of a grayscale image is defined as the product of the Height and Width of that image.

14. The computer vision's goal is not only to see but also to process and provide useful results based on the observations.

15. Computer vision is also defined as an interdisciplinary field dealing with how computers can be made to achieve high-level understanding from digital images or videos.

ANSWERS
1. T   2. T   3. T   4. F (three different values)   5. F (255)
6. F (multiplication not division)   7. T   8. ?   9. T   10. F   11. T   12. T
13. T   14. T   15. T

10.2.4 Matching type

(I) Match the items enlisted in column A with those of column b correctly.

Column A: **Column B:**

Computer Vision Application   **Ethical issue(s)**

(i) Face Recognition   (a) Espionage, Misinformation, Malicious attacks

(ii) Computational camera   (b) Malicious Attacks

(iii) Image Database   (c) Copyright Infringement, Espionage

(iv) Image classification   (d) Identity Theft, Discrimination, Espionage, Malicious Attacks

(v) Reverse Image Search   (e) Identity Theft, Espionage

ANSWERS				
(I) (i)-d,	(ii)-a,	(iii)-c,	(iv)-e	(v)-b

10.2.5 Statements Base Questions

1. Statement 1: In an RGB image, each pixel has a set of three different values, which together give colour to that particular pixel.

    Statement 2: Pixel count is defined as the number of pixels contained in an image sensor or the captured photograph is made up of.

    a) Statement 1 is correct but statement 2 is incorrect.

    b) Statement 1 is incorrect but statement 2 is correct.

    c) Both the statements are correct.

    d) Both the statements are incorrect.

2. Statement 1: Pixel value one is given as no colour or black in the image.

    Statement 2: The maximum pixel value is 275.

    a) Statement 1 is correct but statement 2 is incorrect.

    b) Statement 1 is incorrect but statement 2 is correct.

    c) Both the statements are correct.

    d) Both the statements are incorrect.

3. Statement 1: Segmentation basically identifies different instances given in the image with their boundaries intact.

    Statement 2: Convolution is a simple Mathematical operation and fundamental to many common image processing operators.

    a) Statement 1 is correct but statement 2 is incorrect.

    b) Statement 1 is incorrect but statement 2 is correct.

    c) Both the statements are correct.

    d) Both the statements are incorrect

4. Statement 1: Instance segmentation is the process of classifying each pixel belonging to a particular label.

    Statement 2: Face Recognition application of CV may lead to ethical issues like Identity Theft, Discrimination, Espionage, Malicious Attacks, etc.

a) Statement 1 is correct but statement 2 is incorrect.

b) Statement 1 is incorrect but statement 2 is correct.

c) Both the statements are correct.

d) Both the statements are incorrect

5. Statement 1: Object detection is the ability to detect/ identify objects in any given image correctly along with their three-dimensional position in the given image.

Statement 2: A convolutional network is a specialized type of neural network that uses convolution in place of general matrix multiplication in one of its layers.

a) Statement 1 is correct but statement 2 is incorrect.

b) Statement 1 is incorrect but statement 2 is correct.

c) Both the statements are correct.

d) Both the statements are incorrect

6. Statement 1: Convolution is used in BNN to extract image features in CV.

Statement 2: Classification plus Localisation involves both processes of identifying the object present in the image and at the same time also identifying the location that object is present in that image.

a) Statement 1 is correct but statement 2 is incorrect.

b) Statement 1 is incorrect but statement 2 is correct.

c) Both the statements are correct.

d) Both the statements are incorrect

7. Statement 1: Computer Vision is the term for the hardware, software, and processes that allow computers to see and understand the physical world.

Statement 2: Classification involves both processes of identifying the object present in the image and at the same time also identifying the location that object is present in that image.

a) Statement 1 is correct but statement 2 is incorrect.

b) Statement 1 is incorrect but statement 2 is correct.

c) Both the statements are correct.

d) Both the statements are incorrect

8. Statement 1: Every grey image is stored in the form of three different channels called the R channel, the G channel, and the B channel.

Statement 2: Grayscale images are images that have a range of shades of Gray without apparent colour.

a) Statement 1 is correct but statement 2 is incorrect.

b) Statement 1 is incorrect but statement 2 is correct.

c) Both the statements are correct.

d) Both the statements are incorrect

9. Statement 1: The word "pixel" means a picture element.

Statement 2: Grayscale images are images that have a range of shades of Gray without apparent colour.

a) Statement 1 is correct but statement 2 is incorrect.

b)   Statement 1 is incorrect but statement 2 is correct.

c)   Both the statements are correct.

d)   Both the statements are incorrect

10. Statement 1: The pooling layer operates on every feature map independently.

Statement 2: Semantic segmentation is the process of classifying each pixel belonging to a particular label.

a)   Statement 1 is correct but statement 2 is incorrect.

b)   Statement 1 is incorrect but statement 2 is correct.

c)   Both the statements are correct.

d)   Both the statements are incorrect

ANSWERS

1. (c)	2. (d)	3. (a)	4. (b)	5. (c)	6. (a)	7. (a)	8. (b)	9. (c)	10. (c)

10.2.6 Assertion Reason Type Questions

1. Assertion (A): A convolution is a common tool used for image editing.

Reason (R): A Kernel is a matrix that slides across the image and multiplies with the input in such a manner that the output is enhanced in a certain desirable manner.

a)   Both A and R are correct and R is the correct reason for A.

b)   Both A and R are correct and R is not the correct reason for A.

c)   A is correct but R is incorrect.

d)   A is incorrect but R is correct.

2. Assertion (A): Data sets closest to the hyperplane are known as support vectors.

Reason (R): Margin points are the gap between two lines on the closest data points of different classes.

a)   Both A and R are correct and R is the correct reason for A.

b)   Both A and R are correct and R is not the correct reason for A.

c)   A is correct but R is incorrect.

d)   A is incorrect but R is correct.

3. Assertion (A): The main function of SVM is to divide the datasets into classes to find a maximum marginal hyperplane (MMH).

Reason (R): The goal of Computer vision is not only to see but also to process and provide useful results based on the observations.

a)   Both A and R are correct and R is the correct reason for A.

b)   Both A and R are correct and R is not the correct reason for A.

c)   A is correct but R is incorrect.

d)   A is incorrect but R is correct.

4. Assertion (A): Monolithic Kernel is the Kernel where all operating system services operate in kernel space.

Reason (R): The hyperplane is a subspace whose dimensions are now less than that of its ambient space.

   a) Both A and R are correct and R is the correct reason for A.
   b) Both A and R are correct and R is not the correct reason for A.
   c) A is correct but R is incorrect.
   d) A is incorrect but R is correct.

5. Assertion (A): A convolution is a common tool used for image editing.

   Reason (R): Convolution is an element-wise multiplication of an image and a kernel to get the desired output.
   a) Both A and R are correct and R is the correct reason for A.
   b) Both A and R are correct and R is not the correct reason for A.
   c) A is correct but R is incorrect.
   d) A is incorrect but R is correct.

6. Assertion (A): CV is closely related to AI.

   Reason (R): Computer vision is closely associated with artificial intelligence because the computer must interpret what it sees and then perform appropriate analysis to act accordingly.
   a) Both A and R are correct and R is the correct reason for A.
   b) Both A and R are correct and R is not the correct reason for A.
   c) A is correct but R is incorrect.
   d) A is incorrect but R is correct.

7. Assertion (A): Zero pixel is taken as no colour or black.

   Reason (R): The main function of margin is to divide the datasets into classes to find a maximum marginal hyperplane (MMH).
   a) Both A and R are correct and R is the correct reason for A.
   b) Both A and R are correct and R is not the correct reason for A.
   c) A is correct but R is incorrect.
   d) A is incorrect but R is correct.

8. Assertion (A): In CNN, we overlap the centre of the image with the centre of the Kernel to obtain the convolution output.

   Reason (R): The size of a grayscale image is the product of the Height by Width of that image.
   a) Both A and R are correct and R is the correct reason for A.
   b) Both A and R are correct and R is not the correct reason for A.
   c) A is correct but R is incorrect.
   d) A is incorrect but R is correct.

9. Assertion (A): Resizing images is required when we want to train our model.

   Reason (R): When training a model, we want all our images to have the same size and aspect ratio.
   a) Both A and R are correct and R is the correct reason for A.
   b) Both A and R are correct and R is not the correct reason for A.
   c) A is correct but R is incorrect.
   d) A is incorrect but R is correct.

10. **Assertion (A):** Data detection basically identifies different instances given in the image with their boundaries intact.

    Reason (R): Object detection is the ability to detector identify objects in any given image correctly along with their three-dimensional position in the given image.

    a) Both A and R are correct and R is the correct reason for A.

    b) Both A and R are correct and R is not the correct reason for A.

    c) A is correct but R is incorrect.

    d) A is incorrect but R is correct.

ANSWERS

1. (a)	2. (d)	3. (b)	4. (b)	5. (a)	6. (a)	7. (c)	8. (b)	9. (a)	10. (d)

10.2.7 Competency-Based Questions

1. Consider the following functions of a domain of AI:
    i.   Surveillance
    ii.   Fingerprint recognition
    iii. Optical Character Recognition (OCR)
    iv.   Medical imaging
    v.   Biometrics
    vi.   Retail automation (Personalised research)
    vii. Machine inspection
    viii. Motion Capture (Mocap)

    The related domain is:

    a) Fuzzy Logic System   b) Data
    c) CV   d) NLP

2. Assume that Himanshu Dev is working on an improvised version of Convolutional Neural Network (CNN) that is a deep learning algorithm to be used in image processing, and it is largely inspired by the biological system for the connectivity pattern. Which of the following improvised versions based on CNN architecture may not be used by him?

    a) AlexNet   b) Maya   c) VGG-16   d) YOLO

3. Suppose Matin Ahmed is using a deep learning algorithm that can be used in image processing, and it is largely inspired by the biological system for the connectivity pattern. The algorithm has the following properties:
    i.   To establish communication between user-level applications and hardware.
    ii.   To decide the state of incoming processes.
    iii. To control disk management.
    iv.   To control memory management.
    v.   To control task management.

    This algorithm is known as:

    a) ANN   b) BNN   c) CNN   d) ASL

4. Suppose David works with a firm called Computer Vision Solutions and uses a matrix, which slides across the image and multiplies with the input such that the output is increased in a certain desirable manner. The matrix is used to fulfil the following objectives:

   i.   To establish communication between user-level applications and hardware.

   ii. To decide the state of incoming processes.

   iii. To control disk management.

   iv. To control memory management.

   Which matrix is used by him?

   a) Kernel

   b) Confusion Matrix

   c) SVM

   d) CNN

ANSWERS
1. (c)   2. (b)   3. (c)   4. (a)

10.2.8 VSA

1. How is CV closely related to AI?

Ans. Computer vision is closely associated with artificial intelligence because the computer must interpret what it sees and then perform appropriate analysis to act accordingly.

2. What is the main aim of CV?

Ans. Computer vision's aim is to make computers capable of performing the same kind of tasks as humans with the same or greater efficiency.

3. Define image classification in CV.

Ans. Image classification means identifying what class the object belongs to.

4. What do you mean by semantic segmentation?

Ans. Semantic segmentation is the process of classifying each pixel belonging to a particular label.

5. What is meant by classification plus Localisation?

Ans. Classification plus Localisation involves both processes of identifying the object present in the image and at the same time also identifying the location that object is present in that image.

6. For which type of objects classification plus localization is applied?

Ans. It is applied only for single objects.

7. What do you mean by object detection?

Ans. Object detection is the ability to detect/ identify objects in any given image correctly along with their three-dimensional position in the given image.

8. Define instance segmentation.

Ans. Instance Segmentation basically identifies different instances given in the image with their boundaries intact. Here, it is about finding objects in an image and about creating a mask for each detected object accurately as far as possible.

9. Define pixel count.

Ans. Pixel count is defined as the number of pixels contained in an image sensor, or the captured photograph is made up of.

10. A computer monitor has a resolution of 1280×1024. What does it mean?

Ans. This means that there are 1280 pixels from one side to the other and 1024 from top to bottom.

11. What does it mean when someone says that he has a 6-megapixel camera?

Ans. By saying that a person has a 6-megapixel camera refers that the product of the pixels along the width and the pixels along the height of the image taken by the camera is equal to 6 million pixels.

12. What is the pixel value for a black and white colour?

Ans. Typically, zero is taken as no colour or black, and 255 is taken to be full colour or white.

13. What are the three primary colours?

Ans. Red, green, and blue

14. What do you mean by an OpenCV?

Ans. OpenCV or OpenSource Computer Vision Library is a tool that helps a computer extract these features from the images.

15. When is resizing of images required?

Ans. Resizing images is required when we want to train our model. When training a model, we want all our images to have the same size and aspect ratio.

16. What is the base of image editing?

Ans. This process of changing pixel values is the base of image editing.

17. What are the pixel values while extending the edges in an image?

Ans. The pixel values are considered as zero while extending the edges in an image.

18. Mention one specific feature of CNN.

Ans. A convolutional network is a specialized type of neural network that uses convolution in place of general matrix multiplication in one of its layers.

19. What is the full form of CNN?

Ans. Convolutional Neural Network (CNN)

20. Define CNN.

Ans. A convolutional network is a specialized type of neural network that uses convolution in place of general matrix multiplication in one of its layers.

21. Give an application of a feature map.

Ans. We might only need to recognize someone's eyes, nose, and/ mouth to recognize the person and not need to see the whole face.

22. What are Support Vectors?

Ans. Datapoints closest to the hyperplane are known as support vectors. A separating line will be defined by using these data points.

23. What do you mean by hyperplane?

Ans. The hyperplane is a subspace whose dimensions are now less than that of its ambient space.

24. Define computer vision.

Ans. Computer Vision is a domain of AI that depicts the capability of a machine to get and analyze visual information to predict some decisions about it.

25. Name the process of classifying each pixel belonging to a particular label.

Ans. Semantic segmentation

26. Which process does involve both processes of identifying the object present in the image and at the same time also identifying the location that object is present in that image?

Ans. Classification+ Localisation

27. What do you mean by Object Detection?

Ans. Object detection is the ability to detector identify objects in any given image correctly along with their three-dimensional position in the given image.

28. What is identified by Instance Segmentation?

Ans. Instance Segmentation basically identifies different instances given in the image with their boundaries intact.

29. What is the goal of a CV?

Ans. The goal of Computer vision is not only to see but also to process and provide useful results based on the observations.

30. Mention two items in which CV is used.

Ans. Self-driven car, facial recognition device, face filter techniques, medical imaging, etc

31. What are Gray images?

Ans. Grayscale images are images that have a range of shades of Gray without apparent colour.

32. What do you mean by a convolution?

Ans. A convolution is a common tool used for image editing.

33. What is the main difference between convolution and Kernel?

Ans. Convolution is an element-wise multiplication of an image and a kernel to get the desired output.

34. Where is convolution used?

Ans. Convolution is used in Convolutional Neural Network (CNN) to extract image features in CV.

35. What is the main function of SVM?

Ans. The main function of SVM is to divide the datasets into classes to find a maximum marginal hyperplane (MMH).

36. Which Pixel value is given as no colour or black in the image?

Ans. Pixel value zero.

37. What is the maximum pixel value?

Ans. 255.

38. How is the size of a grayscale image defined?

Ans. The size of a grayscale image is defined as the product of the Height and Width of that image.

39. What are the three channels in which every RGB image is stored?

Ans. The R channel, the G channel, and the B channel.

40. What is the other name given to a feature map?

Ans. Activation map.

41. Mention two advantages of CV.

Ans. Accuracy, Simpler and Faster Process, Reliability, Cost Reduction, A wide range of applications, etc

42. What are Datapoints?

Ans. Datapoints closest to the hyperplane are known as support vectors.

43. What is Kernel?

Ans. A Kernel is a matrix that slides across the image and multiplies with the input so that the output is increased in a certain desirable manner.

44. Define margin.

Ans. Margin refers to the gap between two lines on the closest data points of different classes.

45. Mention two functions of CV.

Ans. Fingerprint recognition, Optical Character Recognition (OCR), Surveillance, Motion Capture (Mocap), Retail automation, Biometrics, etc.

46. What is image classification?

Ans. Image classification is defined as basically means identifying what class the object belongs to.

47. Give two examples of the monolithic Kernel.

Ans. Unix, Linux, Open VMS, XTS-400, etc.

48. What is identified by Instance Segmentation?

Ans. Instance segmentation basically identifies different instances given in the image with their boundaries intact. Define semantic classification.

49. What do you mean by Open CV?

Ans. OpenCV or OpenSource Computer Vision Library is a tool that helps a computer extract these features from the images.

50. Which tool is used to process images and videos to identify objects, faces, or even handwriting?

Ans. OpenCV

51. Mention two objectives of Kernel.

Ans. Two objectives of Kernel are given below:

   a) To decide the state of incoming processes;

   b) To control disk management;

52. What are the different types of Kernels?

Ans. Monolithic, Micro, Hybrid, Exo, and Nano kernel.

53. Mention two examples of Hybrid Kernel.

Ans. Mach, L4, AmigaOS, Minix, K42, etc.

54. Define pixel value.

Ans. Each of the pixels that represent an image and that is stored inside a computer has a pixel value that describes how bright that pixel is and/or what colour it should be.

55. What is pixel range?

Ans. 0 to 255.

56. What is the name of the first layer of a CNN?

Ans. Convolutional Layer.

57. What is the main objective of the Convolution Operation?

Ans. To extract the high-level features, like edges, from the input image.

58. What is the main function of Rectified Linear Unit Function (ReLU)?

Ans. ReLU simply removes all the negative numbers and zero in the feature map and lets the positive number stay as it is.

59. Which layer in CNN makes the image smaller and more manageable?

Ans. Pooling layer

60. What is the objective of a fully connected layer in CNN?

Ans. The objective of a fully connected layer in CNN is to take the results of the convolution/pooling process to use them to classify the image into a label (in a simple classification example).

61. For which type of problems Support Vector Machine (SVM) is used?

Ans. Classification as well as Regression problems.

62. What type of learning model is a support vector machine (SVM)?

Ans. A supervised Machine Learning model using classification algorithms for two-group classification problems.

63. Define Margin.

Ans. The gap between two lines on the closest data points of different classes is called margin.

64. What is the main function of SVM?

Ans To divide the datasets into classes to find a maximum marginal hyperplane (MMH).

65. Mention the function of the Pooling layer.

Ans. The pooling layer reduces the spatial size of the convolved feature while retaining its important features.

66. Give one example of Exo Kernel.

Ans. Nemesis, EXOS, etc.

67. What do you mean by a feature of an image?

Ans. A feature of an image is a piece of information that is relevant for solving the computational task related to a certain application.

68. Mention the names of different layers of convolutional neural networks.

Ans. Convolution Layer, Rectified Linear Unit (ReLU), Pooling Layer, and Fully Connected Layer.

69. What do you mean by Espionage?

Ans. Espionage (spying) involves the disclosure or theft of many types of information, especially secrets, political, military, business, or industrial information.

70. What is Identity theft?

Ans. Identity theft is defined as the use of an individual's personally identifying information by someone else (often a stranger) without that individual's permission or knowledge.

71. Define Data Retrieval.

Ans. The process of the identification and extraction data from a database as per the query provided by the users is called data retrieval.

72. Define Copyright infringement.

Ans. Copyright infringement is the use or reproduction of copyright-protected material without the permission of the copyright holder.

Figure 10.7

10.2.9 Short Answer Type Questions

1. What is involved in CV as a process?

Ans. The entire process of CV involves image acquiring, screening, analysing, identifying, and extracting information. Thus, Computer vision is a sub-field of artificial intelligence (AI) that enables computers and systems to derive meaningful information from digital images, videos, and other visual inputs, and based on those inputs, it can take action.

2. How could you search a particular picture, like that of a dog on Google search?

Ans. Search of a particular picture, like that of a dog on Google search, is possible because Google's unique search algorithms and tools have categorised images.

3. Give two examples of CV applications.

Ans. Self-Driving cars/ Automatic Cars, Face Lock in Smartphones.

4. Explain the goal of CV.

Ans. The goal of Computer vision is not only to see but also to process and provide useful results based on the observations. For example, a computer can create a 3D image from a 2D image (like those in cars), and provide important data to the car and/or driver. Now, cars can be fitted with computer vision which would be able to identify and distinguish objects on and around the road, like traffic lights, pedestrians, traffic signs, etc., to act accordingly.

5. How is CV helpful in self-driven cars?

Ans. The Computer Vision integrated intelligent device, like the self-driven car, could provide inputs to the driver or even make the car stop when there is a sudden obstacle on the road.

6. What actually happens when a human is driving a car and sees someone suddenly move into the path of the car?

Ans. When a human being who is driving a car sees someone suddenly move into the path of the car, the driver must respond instantly. In a fraction of a second, human vision has to complete a complex task, i.e., identifying the object, processing data in the brain, and deciding what to do.

7. Explain the basics of pixels.

Ans. The word 'pixel' means a picture element. Every photograph is made up of pixels in digital form. These are the smallest unit of information that make up a picture. Normally round or square in shape, these are typically arranged in a 2-dimensional grid. The more pixels the image has, the more closely the image resembles the original.

8. What is meant by resolution with reference to CV?

Ans. The number of pixels in an image is called the resolution. A resolution of a computer screen depends upon the graphics card and display monitor, the quantity, size, and colour combination of pixels. Usually round or square, they are arranged in a 2-dimensional grid. The more pixels you have, the more closely the image resembles the original.

9. What is Pixel value? Explain.

Ans. Each of the pixels that represent an image stored inside a computer has a pixel value that describes how bright that pixel is and/or what colour it should be. The common pixel format is the byte image, where this pixel number is stored as an 8-bit integer by giving a range of possible values from 0 to 255.

10. What is the reason for the maximum Pixel value of 255?

Ans. In computer science, computer data is in the form of ones and zeros, which is known as the binary system. Each bit in a computer system may have either a zero or a one because each pixel uses 1 byte of an image- equivalent to 8 bits of data. Because each bit can have two possible values, which tells us that the 8 bit can have 256 possibilities of values, and those values start from 0 and end at 255. Thus, the computers store the images we see in the form of these numbers.

11. What is a grayscale image? Explain.

Ans. Grayscale images are images that have a range of shades of gray without apparent colour. The darkest possible shade is black, i.e., the total absence of colour or zero value of a pixel. The lightest possible shade is white means the total presence of colour or 255 value of a pixel. Intermediate shades of gray colour are represented by equal brightness levels of all three primary colours. And a grayscale has each pixel of size 1 byte that has arranged in a single plane of 2d array of pixels. The size of a grayscale image is defined as the product of the Height and Width of the image.

12. Explain RGB Images.

Ans. All the images around us are coloured images (RGB). The RGB images are made up of three primary colours, i.e., Red, Green, and Blue. All the colours that are present may be made by combining different intensities of red, green, and blue colours. Every RGB image is stored in the form of three different channels called the R channel, the G channel, and the B channel.

Each plane separately has a number of pixels, with each pixel value varying from 0 to 255. All the three planes, when combined together, form a colour image. This means that in an RGB image, each pixel has a set of three different values, which together give colour to that particular pixel.

13. "All the three planes, when combined together, form a colour image." What is signified by this statement?

Ans. All the three planes, when combined together, form a colour image. This means that in an RGB image, each pixel has a set of three different values, which together give colour to that particular pixel.

14. How is the storage of images done by a computer?

Ans. Every RGB image is stored in a computer in the form of three different channels called the R channel, G channel, and the B channel. Each plane separately has a number of pixels, with each pixel value varying from 0 to 255. All the three planes, when combined together, form a colour image. This means that in an RGB image, each pixel has a set of three different values, which together give colour to that particular pixel. All three channels combine together to form a colour we see.

15. What are the three channels in an RGB image?

Ans. In an RGB image, there are three different channels, namely the Red (R), Green (G), and Blue (B) channels.

16. What are image features?

Ans. A feature of an image in computer vision and image processing is a piece of relevant information required for solving the computational task related to a certain application. Features of an image may also be defined as the specific structures in the image, such as points, edges, or objects. In image processing, we may get a lot of features from the image. It can be either a flat area, an edge, or a corner.

17. For which purpose is OpenCV used?

Ans. OpenCV is used for all kinds of images and video processing and analysis. It is capable of processing images and videos to identify objects, faces, or even handwriting.

18. What is the role of image features in CV?

Ans. Image Features are specific structures in the image, like points, edges, objects, etc. The image features help us to perform various tasks, like for identifying purposes, and then get the analysis done on the basis of the application.

19. How can cropping an image be done in OpenCV?

Ans. We can crop a certain area of the image, either to process the image and get rid of non-relevant parts or to draw a bounding box around a certain area, our region of interest (ROI).

20. Why are different filters used in Apps like Instagram?

Ans. Different filters applied to an image change the pixel values evenly throughout the image. This is achieved by using the process of convolution and the convolution operator, which is commonly used to create these effects.

21. What is a Kernel in CV?

Ans. A Kernel is a matrix, which slides across the image and multiplies with the input such that the output is increased in a certain desirable manner. Each Kernel has a different value for different kinds of effects that we want to apply to an image.

22. Where is CNN used?

Ans. Convolutional Neural Network is a deep learning algorithm used in image processing, and it is largely inspired by the biological system for the connectivity pattern. There are many improvised versions based on CNN architecture like AlexNet, VGG, YOLO, etc.

Figure 10.8

23. Enlist the main objectives of Kernel in CV?

Ans. The objectives of Kernel are listed as below:

a) To establish communication between user-level applications and hardware.

b) To decide the state of incoming processes.

c) To control disk management.

d) To control memory management.

e) To control task management.

24. Enlist the main functions of computer Vision (CV).

Ans. The main functions of Computer Vision (CV) are enlisted below:

a) Surveillance

b) Fingerprint recognition

c) Optical Character Recognition (OCR)

d) Medical imaging

e) Biometrics

f) Retail automation (Personalised research)

g) Machine inspection

h) 3 D model building (photography)

i) Motion Capture (Mocap)

j) Automotive safety

25. Discuss the functioning of CNN.

Ans. A convolutional network is a specialized type of neural network that uses convolution in place of general matrix multiplication in one of its layers.

In the convolution layer, there are several kernels that are used to produce several features. The output/result of processing by this layer is called the feature map. We reduce the image size so that it can be processed more efficiently. We only focus on the features of the image that can help us in processing the image further.

In a Convolution Neural Network, each neuron tells us a specific feature of the image, which is extracted by using the convolution operator, and that gives us the neurons or the information of the features of the image in the form of values arranged in a specific format. The values which are extracted are then passed through more complex processes to make its features easier to identify and hence, to make processing easier and better for us to make the choices as well.

26. How many types of layers are present in CNN?

Ans. A convolutional neural network consists of the following layers:

a) Convolution Layer

b) Rectified Linear unit (ReLU)

c) Pooling Layer

d) Fully Connected Layer.

27. Explain the convolutional layer of CNN.

Ans. The first layer of a CNN is called Convolutional Layer. The main objective of the Convolution Operation is to extract the high-level features, like edges, from the input image. CNN is not limited to only one Convolutional Layer. Conventionally, the first Convolution Layer is responsible for capturing the Low-Level features such as edges, colour, gradient orientation, etc.

It uses convolution operation on the images. In the convolution layer, there are several kernels that are used to produce several features. The output of this layer is known as the feature map. A feature map is also called the activation map. We can use these terms interchangeably.

28. Enlist two uses of the feature map.

Ans. Two uses we derive from the feature map are as follows:

a) We reduce the image size so that it can be processed more efficiently.

b) We only focus on the features of the image that can help us in processing the image further.

29. Discuss the function of Rectified Linear Unit (ReLU).

Ans. The second layer in the Convolution Neural Network is the Rectified Linear Unit function (the ReLU layer). After we get the feature map, it is then passed onto the ReLU layer. This layer simply removes all the negative numbers and zero in the feature map and lets the positive number stay as it is. Then, the process of passing it to the ReLU layer introduces non – linearity in the feature map.

30. What is the function of the pooling layer?

Ans. The Pooling layer is responsible for reducing the spatial size of the Convolved Feature while still retaining the important features. The pooling layer of CNN operates on each feature map independently.

31. What are the different types of pooling?

Ans. There are two types of pooling that can be performed on an image.

(*i*) **Max Pooling:** Max Pooling refers the returning of the maximum value from the portion of the image covered by the Kernel.

(*ii*) **Average Pooling:** Max Pooling returns the average value from the portion of the image covered by the Kernel.

32. Discuss the function of Fully Connected Layer (FCL) in CNN.

Ans. The Fully Connected Layer (FCL) is the final layer in the CNN. The main objective of a fully connected layer (FCL) is to take the results of the convolution/pooling process and use it to classify the image into a label (in a simple classification example). The output of convolution/pooling is flattened into a single vector of values, where each value represents a probability that a specific feature belongs to a label.

Example: When the image is of a cat, features representing things, like whiskers or fur, should have high probabilities for the label "cat."

33. What is Support Vector Machines (SVM)?

Ans. Support Vector Machine or SVM is one of the most popular Supervised Learning algorithms used for both classification and Regression problems, but primarily, it is used for Classification problems in Machine Learning.

34. Why are SVMs preferred over ML algorithms?

Ans. SVMs have their unique way of working as compared to other machine learning algorithms due to the ability to handle multiple continuous and categorical variables.

35. What are the main concepts in SVM?

Ans. The main concepts in SVM are as follows:

a) **Support Vectors:** Datapoints closest to the hyperplane are known as support vectors. A separating line will be defined using these data points.

b) **Hyperplane:** Hyperplanes are defined as the decision boundaries that help classify the data points.

c) **Margin:** Margin is the gap between two lines on the closest data points of different classes. It may be calculated as the perpendicular distance from the line to the support vectors. A large margin is known as a good margin, and a small margin is considered a bad margin.

36. Explain margin in SVM?

Ans. Margin in SVM is defined as the gap between two lines on the closest data points of different classes. It may be calculated as the perpendicular distance from the line to the support vectors. A large margin is known as a good margin, and a small margin is called a bad margin.

37. What is the main function of SVM? How is it achieved?

Ans. The main function of SVM is to divide the datasets into classes to find a maximum marginal hyperplane (MMH). It may be done in the following two steps:

First, SVM will generate hyperplanes iteratively to segregate the classes in the best way possible.

Then, it will choose the hyperplane for separating the classes correctly.

38. What are the pros and cons of SVM classifiers?

Ans. The pros and cons of the SVM classifier are as follows:

a) SVM classifiers ensure great accuracy.

b) They work well with high-dimensional space.

c) SVM classifiers use a subset of training points; hence, they use very little memory.

d) They need high training time and hence, in practice, are not suitable for large datasets.

e) SVM classifiers do not work efficiently with overlapping classes.

10.2.10 Long Answer Type Questions

1. Discuss the main advantages of using CV.

Ans. The use of Computer Imagining grows rapidly due to its main advantages as listed below:

a) **Accuracy:** The precision of Computer Imagining and Computer Vision ensures a better accuracy on the output/final product.

b) **Simpler and Faster Process:** It allows the clients, customers, and industries to check it. Moreover, it gives them access to their products. It is possible due to the presence of Computer Vision in fast computers.

c) **Cost Reduction:** Time and error rate are reduced in the process of computer Imagining to reduce the cost of hire and train the staff to do the activities that computers will do as hundreds of workers.

d) **Reducing human error:** CV is used to reduce human error in different industrial processes, like sorting of substandard potatoes in the potato industry, etc.

e) **Digital assistance:** CV provides digital assistance for getting things faster.

f) **Reliability:** The human factor of tiredness is not present in computers and cameras, and hence, the efficiency remains usually the same, which doesn't depend on external factors such as illness or sentimental status.

g) **A wide range of use:** A computer system can be utilized in several different fields and activities, like in factories with warehouse tracking and shipping of supplies, and in the medical industry through scanned images, among other multiple options.

h) **Social Acceptance:** It is more socially acceptable.

2. What are the disadvantages/limitations of using CV?

Ans. Computer vision has some disadvantages/ limitations as mentioned below:

a) **Failing of image processing:** When the device fails due to a virus or any other software issues, there is a probability that Computer Vision and image processing will fail. And when the problem is not solved, then the functions of the device may disappear. Sometimes, it can stop the entire services/production in the case of warehouses.

b) **The necessity of specialists:** A large number of specialists related to the field of Machine Learning and Artificial Intelligence is required. A professional that knows how these devices work and take full advantage of Computer Vision can repair them when required.

c) **Spoiling:** It eliminates the human factor, which may be good in some cases. When the machine or device fails, then it doesn't announce or anticipate that problem. At the same time, a human person can tell in advance when the person won't come.

d) **Potential of misuse:** CV may be misused in various industries.

3. Describe some applications of CV.

Ans. The concept of computer vision was first envisioned in the 1970s when new applications of computer vision excited everyone. Computer vision technology is advanced enough to make these applications available to everyone at ease today. Some of the applications of CV are mentioned as below:

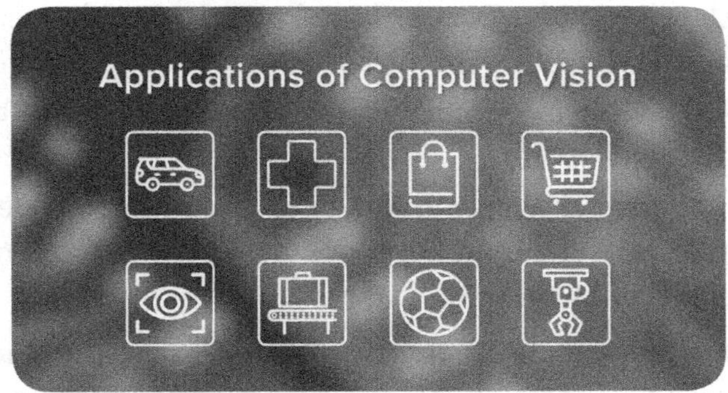

Figure 10.9

a) **Facial recognition:** Computer vision plays a very important role in providing security for smart cities and smart homes. Many applications used for home security require facial recognition when any guest or visitor arrives in the house. Facial recognition is used in smart schools to take attendance of students through Artificial intelligence using computer vision technology. Computer Vision plays a vital role in making the home smarter. Security is the most important application, involves the use of Computer Vision for facial recognition. It can be either guest recognition or log maintenance of the visitors.

b) **Medical Imaging:** Computer vision used in MRI is helpful in reconstruction, automatic pathology, diagnosis, machine aided surgeries, etc., for the help to physicians In the field of Medical Sciences, who are relying on medical imaging applications for their interpretation of patient's health condition. This application is used to read and convert 2D scanned images into interactive 3D models for enabling medical professionals to gain a detailed understanding of a patient's health condition.

c) **Computer vision through smartphones:** All the photo filters (including animation filters on social media), QR code scanners, panorama construction, Computational photography, face detectors, image detectors (Google Lens, Night Sight) that we use are computer vision applications.

d) **Search by using an image:** Google has come up with a new concept of searching data not only by using textual data as well as images. This uses Computer Vision as it compares different features of the input image to the database of images and gives us the search result while at the same time analysing various features of the image selected.

e) **Managing traffic control:** Computer vision can be used to detect the vehicles that break the traffic rules, read the number, and generate a fine slip for it.

f) **Self-driving cars:** Computer Vision is the fundamental technology used in developing autonomous vehicles or self-driven cars. Self-driven cars like tesla are already in use for traveling. These cars navigate on roads using GPRS and are helping the old people who cannot ride the vehicles. The technology involves the process of identifying the objects, getting navigational routes, and also, at the same time, environment monitoring.

g) **Face Filters:** The modern-day Apps like Instagram, Snapchat, Facebook, etc., use many features based on the usage of computer vision. These applications use the face filter technique for identifying the facial dynamics of the person for working on photographs. Facebook, through the camera or the algorithm, is able to identify the facial dynamics of the person and applies the facial filter.

h) **Google Translate App:** The Google Translate app is used to tell us what it means in our preferred language almost instantly. By using optical character recognition to see the image and augmented reality to overlay an accurate translation, this is a convenient tool that uses Computer Vision.

i) **Internet uses Computer Vision in many applications:** Image search, geo-localization image captioning, Ariel imaging for maps, video categorization, and more applications on the internet require Computer vision.

j) **Tracking customers in Retail:** Computer Vision is used by retailers to keep track of their customers' movement through stores, analyze their movement within the store, their shopping habits, and walking patterns. Retailers are keeping track of their inventory and can get an estimate of the items available in the store through the security camera.

k) **Inventory Management:** CV is used in security camera image analysis, where a Computer Vision algorithm can generate an accurate estimation of the items available in the store. Also, it can analyse the use of shelf space to identify suboptimal configurations and suggest better item placement.

4. Explain the main Computer Vision Tasks.

Ans. The various applications of Computer Vision are based on a certain number of tasks that are performed to get some information from the input image, which can be directly used for prediction or form the base for further analysis. The tasks used in a computer vision application are:

a) **Classification:** Image classification is the process of identifying what class the object belongs to. The machine or deep learning model will determine that the animal detected in the image belongs to a class cat with the highest probability.

b) **Semantic Segmentation:** Semantic segmentation is the process of classifying each pixel belonging to a particular label. It doesn't look different across different instances of the same object. For example, if there are three sheep in an image, semantic segmentation gives the same label to all the pixels of three sheep.

Figure 10.10 Semantic Segmentation

c) **Classification plus Localisation:** Classification+ Localisation involves both processes of identifying the object present in the image and at the same time also identifying the location that object is present in that image. It is applied only for single objects.

d) **Object Detection:** It is the ability to detect or identify objects in any given image correctly along with their three-dimensional position in the given image. The 3D image is shown in the form of rectangular boxes (known as Bounding Boxes), which bound the object within it. An example: detects objects such as laptops, glasses, notebooks, coffee, and iPhones in their Bounding Boxes.

e) **Instance Segmentation:** Instance Segmentation basically identifies different instances given in the image with their boundaries intact. Here, it is about finding objects in an image and about creating a mask for each detected object that is as accurately as far as possible.

5. Explain different types of Kernel?

Ans. There are five types of Kernel:

a) **Monolithic Kernel:** It is the Kernel where all operating system services operate in kernel space. It depends on system components. It has huge lines of code that are complex in nature. It has good performance. It depends on system components and lines of code in millions.

   Examples: Unix, Linux, Open VMS, XTS-400, etc.

b) **MicroKernel:** It is the Kernel that has a minimalist approach. It has virtual memory and thread scheduling. It is more stable with fewer services in kernel space. It puts to rest in userspace. It is more stable. There are many system calls and context switches.

   Examples: Mach, L4, AmigaOS, Minix, K42, etc.

c) **Hybrid Kernel:** It is the combination of both monolithic Kernel and micro-kernel. It has the speed and design of monolithic Kernel and modularity and stability of Microkernel. It combines both monolithic Kernel and Microkernel. It is still similar to the monolithic Kernel.

   Examples: Windows NT, Netware, BeOS, etc.

d) **Exo Kernel:** It is the type of Kernel that follows the end-to-end principle. It has the fewest hardware abstractions possible. It allocates physical resources to applications. It has the fewest hardware abstractions. There is more work for application developers.

   Examples: Nemesis, EXOS, etc.

e) **Nano Kernel:** It is the type of Kernel that offers hardware abstraction but without system services. MicroKernel also does not have system services; therefore, the MicroKernel and Nano Kernel have become analogous. It offers hardware abstractions without system services. It is almost the same as Microkernel; hence it is less used.

   Examples: EROS, etc.

6. Discuss the various ethical issues around CV.

Ans. The various ethical issues around CV are important to discuss. Some of them are given below:

Figure 10.11

a) **Espionage (spying):** It can involve the disclosure or theft of many types of information. This is defined as the activity of secretly collecting and reporting information, especially secret political, military, business, or industrial information.

b) **Identity theft:** It is the use of an individual's personally identifying information by someone else (often a stranger) without that individual's permission or knowledge. This form of impersonation is often used to commit fraud, generally resulting in financial harm to the individual.

c) **Discrimination:** It is defined as the act of making unjustified distinctions between human beings that may be based on the groups, classes, or other categories of the people. People may be discriminated against on the basis of race, gender, age, religion, as well as other categories.

d) **Malicious Attacks:** A malware attack is a common cyberattack where malware (normally malicious software) executes unauthorised actions on the victim's system. A firewall may act like a barrier between the internet and the IT infrastructure, blocking the malware attacks and other malicious activities.

e) **Data Retrieval:** It is the process of identifying and extracting data from a database based on a query provided by the user.

f) **Copyright infringement:** It is defined as the use or production of copyright-protected material without the permission of the copyright holder.

10.2.11 HOTS Questions

1. How are SVMs used for machine training?

Ans. A support vector machine (SVM) is a supervised Machine Learning model using classification algorithms for two-group classification problems. After giving an SVM model set of labeled training data for each category, they're able to categorise new text.

2. Why is the pooling layer so important in CNN?

Ans. The pooling layer is a very important layer in the CNN because it performs a series of tasks that are as follows:

    a) It makes the image smaller and more manageable.

    b) It makes the image more resistant to small transformations, distortions, and translations in the input image. A small difference in the input image will create a very similar pooled image.

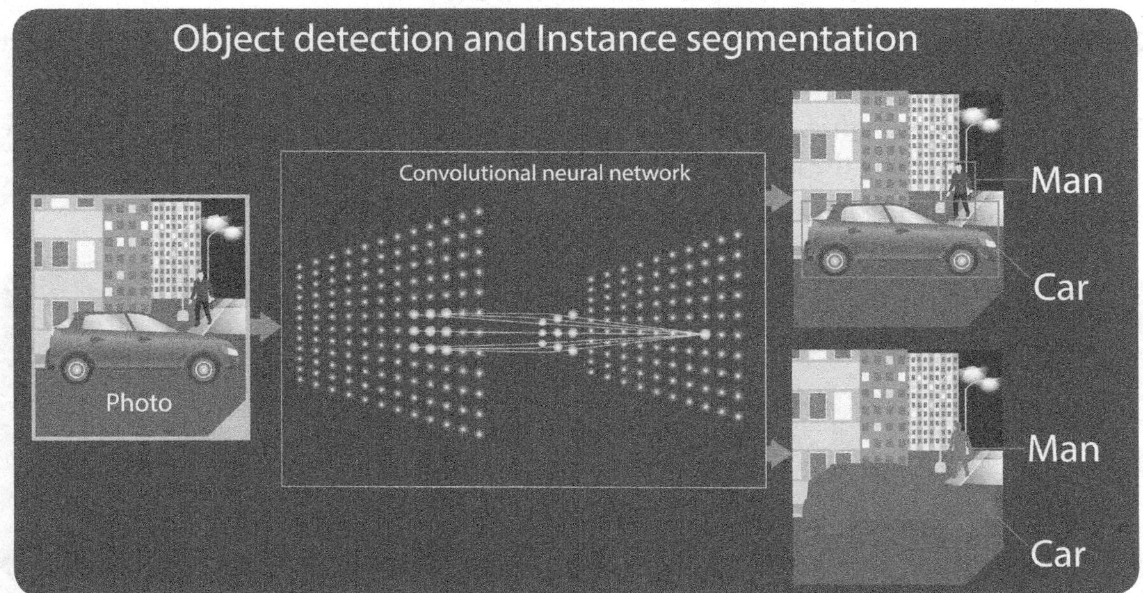

Figure 10.12

10.3 PRACTICE QUESTIONS

1. What do you mean by object detection in CV?

2. How is computer vision different from NLP?

3. Name the computer vision task related to one object and multiple objects.

4. Write the code in python to display any cropped part of the image.

5. What do you mean by convolution operator?

6. What is Kernel?

7. Define semantic classification in CV.

8. What do you mean by pixel?

9. What is the pixel range for an image?

10. Write names of the four layers of the convolution operator.

11. How does CNN play an important role in identifying the image?

12. How is CV used in facial recognition?

13. Differentiate between grayscale image and RGB image.

14. If an image has a pixel of 300 x 300, then what will be the dpi? Write its calculation.

15. Differentiate between instance segmentation and semantic segmentation?

16. Define and explain the four layers of the convolution operator.

17. How is computer vision helpful in the field of automation?

18. Name the four layers of CNN.

19. Explain the three channels of a coloured image.

20. What are the different types of kernels? Explain any two.

21. Draw an image and show classification, classification and Localisation, object detection, and image segmentation.

22. Take a fictitious matrix and show the max pooling and average pooling method. Write the steps of calculating the average and max pooling in your practical file.

23. Take an image and draw the diagram to show the CNN process.

Figure 10.13

Natural Language Processing

11.1 UNIT IN BRIEF

✦ The inner guiding, moral principles, and values of people and society are called ethics. Ethics is not in black and white, but there are grey areas. Both Ethics and NLP are Interdisciplinary Fields.

Figure 11.1

✦ A chatbot is defined as a computer program that can learn over time how to best interact with human beings.

✦ The grammatical structure of a sentence is called Syntax.

✦ Semantics refers to the meaning of the sentence.

✦ Stemming is defined as the process in which the affixes of words are removed to convert words into their base form.

✦ A large and structured set of texts can be read by machines and have been produced in a natural communicative setting, and this is called a corpus.

✦ Stemming is a technique used to extract the base forms of the words by removing affixes from them. It is similar to cutting down the branches of a tree to its stems.

✦ Lemmatisation is defined as the process of grouping together different forms of the same word.

✦ In search queries, Lemmatisation allows end-users to query any version of a base word and get relevant results.

✦ Thus, 'Stemming' is the process in which the affixes of words are removed to convert them to their base form.

✦ In Lemmatisation, the word we get after affix removal (also known as lemma) is a meaningful one.

✦ Lemmatisation takes a longer time to execute than stemming.

✦ In NLP, a dictionary is a list of all the unique words occurring in the corpus.

✦ Natural Language Toolkit (NLTK): It is one of the leading platforms for building Python programs that can work with human language data.

✦ Term frequency is defined as the frequency of a word in one document.

✦ A large and structured set of texts that can be read by machines and have been produced in a natural communicative setting is known as a corpus.

✦ A corpus can also be defined as a collection of text documents. It can also be taken as a bunch of text files in a directory, often alongside many other directories of text files.

✦ A table that contains the frequency of each word of the vocabulary in a document is called Document Vector Table.

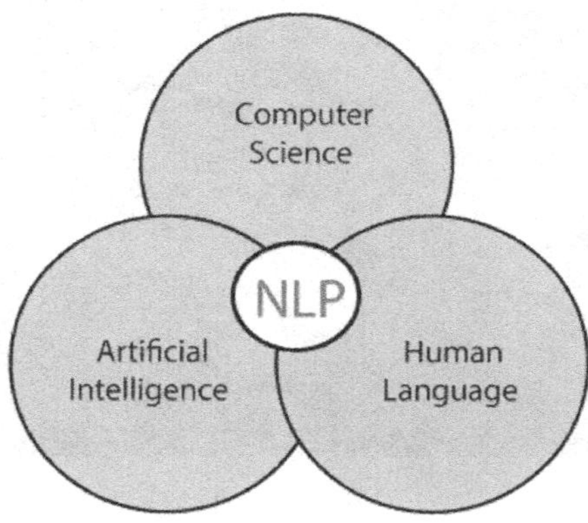

Figure 11.2

✦ Document Vector Table is used while implementing the 'Bag of Words' algorithm.

✦ The header row in a document vector table contains the vocabulary of the corpus while the other rows correspond to different documents.

✦ Term frequency is the frequency of a word in a document that can easily be found from the document vector table.

✦ Document Vector Table is used while implementing the Bag of Words algorithm.

✦ 'Bag of Words' is a Natural Language Processing model that helps in extracting features out of the text that may be helpful in machine learning algorithms.

✦ In a bag of words, we get the occurrences of each word and construct the vocabulary for the corpus.

✦ Bag of Words creates a set of vectors containing the frequency of each word in the document (reviews), which are easy to interpret.

✦ Words occurring in all the documents with high term frequencies have the least values and are called the stopwords.

✦ For a word having a high TFIDF value, the word will have a high term frequency but less document frequency. This shows that the word is important for one document but is not a common word for all documents.

✦ TFIDF values help the computer understand which words are to be considered while processing the natural language.

✦ The higher the value of TFIDF, the more important the word is for a given corpus.

✦ Natural Language Processing (NLP) is an AI domain concerned with the interaction between human language(s) and computers.

✦ Natural Language Processing is also defined as a component of artificial intelligence dealing with the interaction between machines/computers and humans' natural language.

✦ Natural language means speech analysis in both audible speeches and the text of a language.

✦ AI is a subfield of Linguistics, Technology and Engineering, Computer Science and Informatics. Artificial Intelligence deals with the interactions between computers and humans using natural languages, especially how to program computers to process and analyze big natural language data.

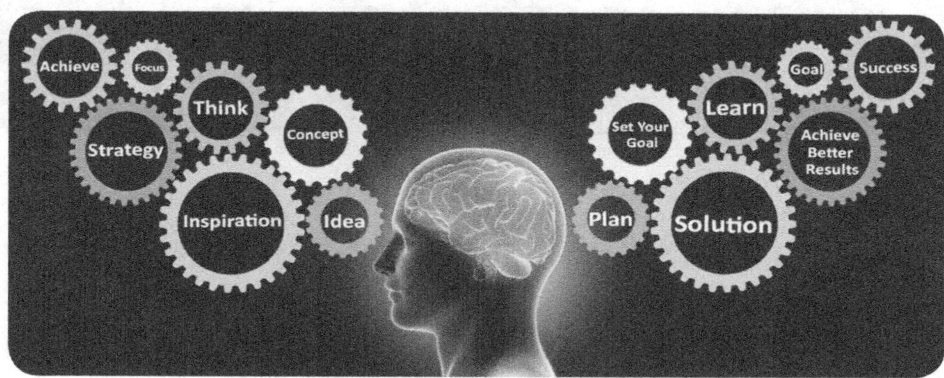

Figure 11.3

✦ By using Natural language processing, computers can extract keywords and phrases, understand the meaning of language, translate the content into another language, or generate response/output.

✦ The study of NLP involves the tasks like how to make computers perform useful tasks after processing the natural languages that humans use.

✦ A chatbot is a software application used to conduct an online chat/ conversation through text/ text-to-speech to provide direct contact with live humans.

✦ A chatbot is also defined as a computer program that can learn over time how to best interact with human beings. It can answer questions and solutions to customer problems, generate sales leads, evaluate and qualify prospects, and increase sales on an e-commerce site.

✦ A chatbot is defined as a computer program that is designed to simulate conversations with human beings.

✦ NLP is regarded as art to extract some information from the text.

✦ 'Bag of Words' is a Natural Language Processing model which helps in extracting features out of the text that is helpful in machine learning algorithms.

✦ The morphological analysis of the words with the help of detailed dictionaries is called Lemmatisation.

✦ Term frequency is defined as the frequency of a word in one document that can easily be found from the document vector table.

✦ TFIDF values help the computer understand which words are to be considered while processing the natural language.

✦ Machine learning" is taken as a subset of AI in which a computer works at a problem programmatically without being programmed to do something specific.

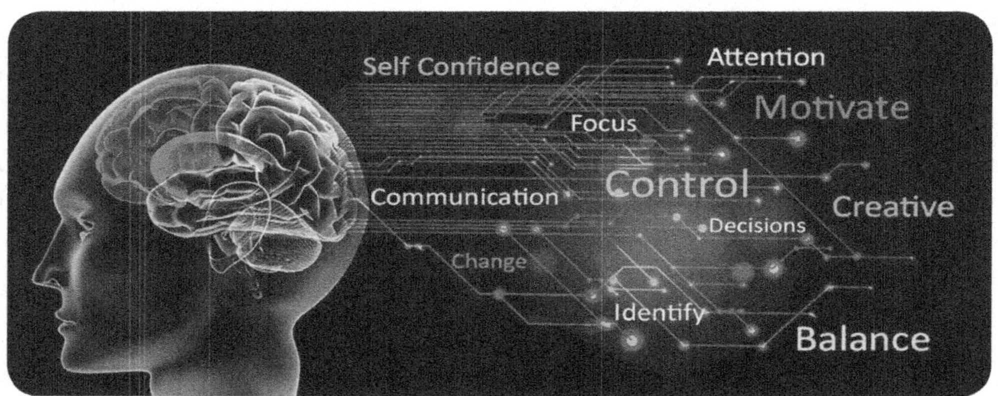

Figure 11.4

11.2 CBSE/NCERT SECTION (SOLVED CBSE/NCERT EXERCISE QUESTIONS)

(A) VSA (One Mark Questions)

1. What is a Chabot?

Ans. A computer program designed to simulate human conversation through voice commands or text chats, or both, is called a chatbot. Example: Mitsuku Bot, Jabberwacky, etc.

2. Mention the full form of NLP.

Ans. Natural Language Processing.

3. What is the meaning of Syntax and Semantics with reference to NLP?

Ans. Syntax deals with the grammatical structure of a sentence.
Semantics refers to the meaning of a sentence in a document.

4. What is the main difference between stemming and Lemmatization?

Ans. 'Stemming' is a technique used to extract the base form of the words by removing affixes from them, while 'Lemmatization' is the grouping together of different forms of the same word.

5. Write the full form of TFIDF.

Ans. Term Frequency and Inverse Document Frequency.

6. What do you mean by a dictionary in NLP?

Ans. Dictionary in NLP refers to a list of all the unique words occurring in the corpus. When some words are repeated in different documents, then they are all written just once during the creation the dictionary.

7.   What is term frequency?

Ans.   Term frequency is the frequency of a word in one document. Term frequency can easily be found in the document vector table.

8.   Name the package that is used for Natural Language Processing in Python programming.

Ans.   Natural Language Toolkit (NLTK).

9.   What is a document vector table?

Ans.   Document Vector Table is used while implementing the Bag of Words algorithm. The header row in a document vector table contains the vocabulary of the corpus, while other rows correspond to different documents. When the document contains a particular word, then it is represented by 1, and the absence of a word is represented by 0 value.

10.   What do you mean by corpus?

Ans.   The whole/full-textual data from all the documents put together is known as corpus.

(B) SAQs (Two Mark Questions)

1.   Which types of data are used for Natural Language Processing applications?

Ans.   Natural Language Processing takes in the data of Natural Languages (in the form of written words and spoken words), which humans use in their daily lives and operates on this.

2.   Differentiate between a script-bot and a smart-bot (Any two differences).

Ans.

Script-bot	Smart-bot
(i) A scripted chatbot doesn't carry even a glimpse of AI	(i) Smart bots are built on NLP and ML.
(ii) Script bots are easy to make.	(ii) Smart –bots are comparatively difficult to make.
(iii) Script bot functioning is very limited as they are less powerful.	(iii) Smart-bots are flexible and powerful.
(iv) Script bots work around a script that is programmed in them.	(iv) Smart bots work on bigger databases and other resources directly
(v) No or little language processing skills	(v) NLP and Machine learning skills are required.
(vi) Limited functionality.	(vi) Wide functionality

3.   Give an example of the following:

(a) Multiple meanings of a word

(b) Perfect Syntax, no meaning

Ans.   (a) Example of Multiple meanings of a word:

Ramita's face turns red after consuming the medicine. It may have two meanings: First Meaning: Is Ramita's having an allergic reaction?

Second Meaning: Is Ramita not able to bear the taste of that medicine?

(b) Example of Perfect Syntax, no meaning:

Lions feed extravagantly while the monkeys drink tea. This sentence is correct grammatically, but it does not carry any meaning/ any sense. In Human language, a perfect balance of Syntax and semantics is important for better understanding.

4. What is inverse document frequency?

Ans. Document Frequency is defined as the number of documents in which the frequencies of all words in a document are noted. In inverse document frequency, we put the document frequency in the denominator, and the total number of documents is the numerator. For example, when the document frequency of the word "CHAMAN" is 2 in a particular document (The total number of documents is 3), then its inverse document frequency will be 3/2.

5. Define the following:

(a) Stemming

(b) Lemmatisation

Ans. (a) Stemming: Stemming is a rule-based process of stripping the suffixes ("ing," "ly," "es," "s," etc.) from a word. In other words, 'Stemming ' is a process of converting words to their word stem, base, or root form (for example, looks — look, Cooked — Cook).

(b) Lemmatisation: Lemmatisation is an organised and step-by-step procedure to obtain the root form of the word by using vocabulary (dictionary importance of words) and morphological analysis (word structure and grammar relations).

6. What are document vectors?

Ans. Document Vectors contain the frequency of each word of the vocabulary in a particular document.

7. What is TFIDF? Write its formula.

Ans. The term TFIDF refers to frequency-inverse document frequency that is a numerical statistic intended to reflect the importance of a word in a document/ in a corpus. In TFEDF, the frequency of a word (the number of times a word appears in a document) is divided by the total number of words in the document. Each document has its specific term frequency.

$$tf_{i,j} = \frac{n_{i,j}}{\sum_k n_{i,j}}$$

Figure 11.5

8. Which words in a corpus have the highest values and which ones have the least?

Ans. Stop words like - and, this, is, the, etc., have the highest values in a corpus. But these words do not talk about the corpus at all. Hence, these are termed stopwords and are mostly removed at the pre-processing stage only. Rare or valuable words occur the least but add the most important to the corpus. Hence, when we look at the text, we take frequent and rare words into consideration.

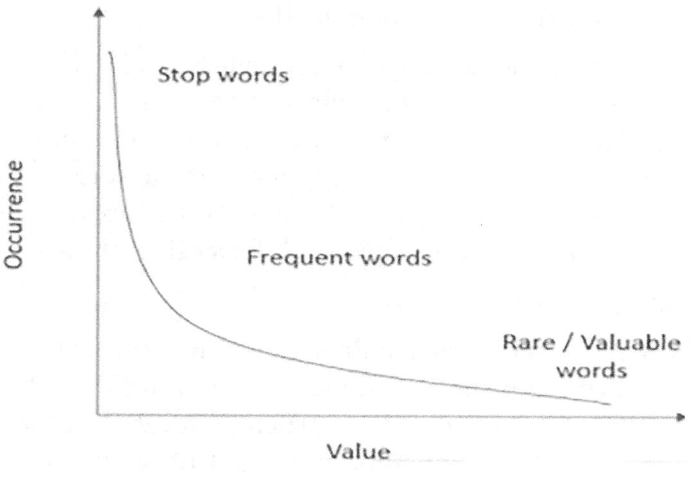

Figure 11.6

9. Does the vocabulary of a corpus remain the same before and after text normalisation? Why?

Ans. No, the vocabulary of a corpus does not remain the same before and after text normalization. Reasons are as follows:

In Normalisation, the text is normalised through various steps and is lowered to minimum vocabulary since the machine does not require grammatically correct statements but the essence of it.

In Normalisation, Stop words, Special Characters, and Numbers are removed.

In stemming, the affixes of words are removed, and the words are converted to their base form. So, after Normalisation, we get the reduced vocabulary.

10. What is the significance of converting the text into a common cause?

Ans. In-Text Normalisation, we undergo several steps to normalize the text to a lower level. After the removal of stop words, we convert the whole text into a similar case, preferably lower case. This ensures that the case sensitivity of the machine does not consider the same words as different just because of different cases.

11. Mention some applications of Natural Language Processing.

Ans. Applications of Natural Language Processing Applications are as follows:

- Sentiment Analysis.
- Chatbots and Virtual Assistants.
- Text Classification.
- Text Extraction.
- Machine Translation
- Text Summarization
- Market Intelligence
- Auto-Correct

12. What is the need for text normalisation in NLP?

Ans. Since we all know that the language of computers is Numerical, the very first step that comes to our mind is to convert our language to numbers. This conversion takes a few steps to happen. The first step to it is Text Normalisation. Since human languages are complex, we need to, first of all, simplify them in order to make sure that understanding becomes possible. Text Normalisation helps in cleaning up the textual data in such a way that it comes down to a level where its complexity is lower than the actual data.

13. Explain the concept of Bag of Words.

Ans. Bag of Words is a Natural Language Processing model which helps in extracting features out of the text, which can be helpful in machine learning algorithms. In a bag of words, we get the occurrences of each word and construct the vocabulary for the corpus. Bag of Words just creates a set of vectors containing the count of word occurrences in the document (reviews). Bag of Words vectors is easy to interpret.

14. Explain the relation between the occurrence and value of a word.

Ans.

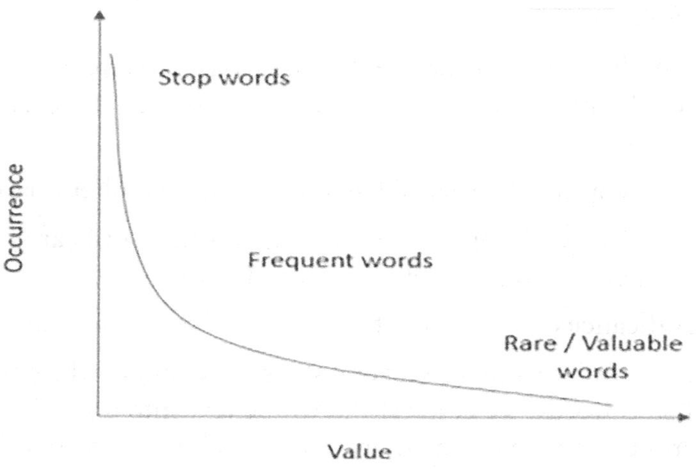

Figure 11.7

As shown in the graph, the occurrence and value of a word are inversely proportional. The words which occur most (like stop words) have negligible value as the occurrence of words drops, the value of such words rises. These words are termed rare or valuable words. These words occur the least but add the most value to the corpus.

15. What are the applications of TFIDF?

Ans. TFIDF is commonly used in the Natural Language Processing domain. Some of its applications are:

(*i*) **Document Classification:** Helps in classifying the type and genre of a document.

(*ii*) **Topic Modelling:** It helps in predicting the topic for a corpus.

(*iii*) **Information Retrieval System:** To extract the important information out of a corpus.

(*iv*) **Stop word filtering:** Helps in removing the unnecessary words out of a text body.

16. What are stop words? Explain with the help of examples.

Ans. "Stop words" are the most common words in a language like "the", "a", "on", "is", "all". These words do not carry important meaning and are usually removed from texts. It is possible to remove stop words using Natural Language Toolkit (NLTK), a suite of libraries and programs for symbolic and statistical natural language processing.

17. Differentiate between Human Language and Computer Language.

Ans. Humans communicate through language, which we process all the time. Our brain keeps on processing the sounds that it hears around itself and tries to make sense out of them all the time. On the other hand, the computer understands the language of numbers. Everything that is sent to the machine has to be converted to numbers. And while typing, if a single mistake is made, the computer throws an error and does not process that part. The communications made by the machines are very basic and simple.

(C) LAQs (Four Mark Questions)

1. Create a document vector table for the given corpus:

    Document 1: We are going to Mumbai

    Document 2: Mumbai is a famous place.

    Document 3: We are going to a famous place.

    Document 4: I am famous in Mumbai.

Ans.

We	Are	going	to	Mumbai	is	a	famous	place	I	am	in
1	1	1	1	1	0	0	0	0	0	0	0
0	0	0	0	1	1	1	1	1	0	0	0
1	1	1	1	0	0	1	1	1	0	0	0
0	0	0	0	1	0	0	1	0	1	1	1

Figure 11.8

2. Classify each of the images according to how well the model's output matches the data samples:

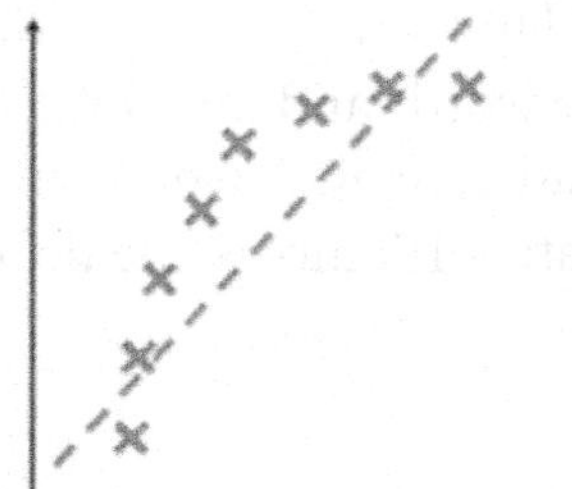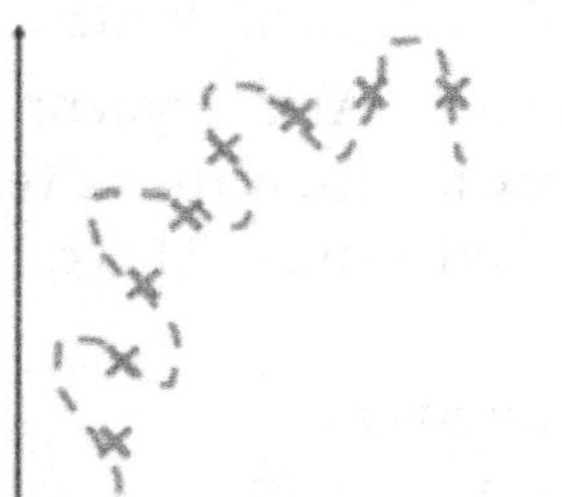

Figure 11.9

Ans. Here, the red dashed line is the model's output, while the blue crosses are actual data samples.

The model's output does not match the true function at all. Hence the model is said to be underfitting, and its accuracy is lower.

In the second case, model performance is trying to cover all the data samples even if they are out of alignment with the true function. This model is said to be overfitting, and this too has lower accuracy.

In the third one, the model's performance matches well with the true function, which states that the model has optimum accuracy and the model is called a perfect fit.

3. Explain how AI can play a role in the sentiment analysis of human beings?

Ans. The goal of sentiment analysis is to identify sentiment among several posts or even in the same post where emotion is not always explicitly expressed. Companies use Natural Language Processing applications, such as sentiment analysis, to identify opinions and sentiment online to help them understand what customers think about their products and services (i.e., "I love the new iPhone" and, a few lines later "But sometimes it doesn't work well" where the person is still talking about the iPhone) and overall * Beyond determining simple polarity, sentiment analysis understands sentiment in context to help better understand what's behind an expressed opinion, which can be extremely relevant in understanding and driving purchasing decisions.

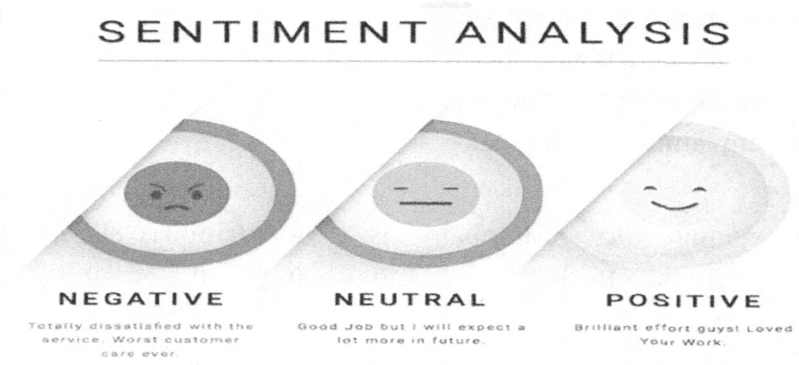

Figure 11.10

4. Why are human languages complicated for a computer to understand? Explain.

Ans. The communications made by the machines are very basic and simple. Human communication is complex. There are multiple characteristics of the human language that might be easy for a human to understand but extremely difficult for a computer to understand. For machines, it is difficult to understand our language.

Let us take a look at some of them here: Arrangement of the words and meaning - There are rules in human language. There are nouns, verbs, adverbs, adjectives. A word can be a noun at one time and an adjective some other time. This can create difficulty while processing by computers.

Analogy with a programming language:

Different syntax, same semantics: 2+3 = 3+2

Here the way these statements are written is different, but their meanings are the same that is 5.

Different semantics, same Syntax: 2/3 (Python 2.7) ≠ 2/3 (Python 3)

Here the statements written have the same Syntax, but their meanings are different. In Python 2.7, this statement would result in 1, while in Python 3, it would give an output of 1.5.

Multiple Meanings of a word: In natural language, it is important to understand that a word can have multiple meanings and the meanings fit into the statement according to its context.

Perfect Syntax, no Meaning: Sometimes, a statement may have perfectly correct Syntax, but it does not mean anything. In Human language, a perfect balance of Syntax and semantics is important for better understanding. These are some of the challenges we might have to face if we try to teach computers how to understand and interact in human language.

5. What are the steps of text Normalization? Explain them in brief.

Ans. In-Text Normalisation, we undergo several steps to normalise the text to a lower level. Sentence Segmentation - Under sentence segmentation, the whole corpus is divided into sentences. Each sentence is taken as different data, so now the whole corpus gets reduced to sentences. Tokenization- After segmenting the sentences, each sentence is then further divided into tokens. A Token is a term used for any word or number, or special character occurring in a sentence. Under Tokenization, every word, number, and special character is considered separately, and each of them is now a separate token. Removing Stop words, Special Characters, and Numbers - In this step, the tokens which are not necessary are removed from the token list. Converting text to a common case -After the stop words removal, we convert the whole text into a similar case, preferably lower case. This ensures that the case sensitivity of the machine does not consider the same words as different just because of different cases. Stemming In this step, the remaining words are reduced to their root words. In other words, stemming is the process in which the affixes of words are removed, and the words are converted to their base form. Lemmatization -in Lemmatisation, the word we get after affix removal (also known as lemma) is a meaningful one. With this, we have normalized our text to tokens which are the simplest form of words present in the corpus. Now it is time to convert the tokens into numbers. For this, we would use the Bag of Words algorithm.

6. Through a step-by-step process, calculate TFIDF for the given corpus and mention the word(s) having the highest value.

Document 1: We are going to Mumbai

Document 2: Mumbai is a famous place.

Document 3: We are going to a famous place.

Document 4: I am famous in Mumbai.

Ans. **Term Frequency:** Term frequency is the frequency of a word in one document. Term frequency can easily be found from the document vector table as in that table; we mention the frequency of each word of the vocabulary in each document.

We	Are	going	to	Mumbai	is	a	famous	place	I	am	in
1	1	1	1	1	0	0	0	0	0	0	0
0	0	0	0	1	1	1	1	1	0	0	0
1	1	1	1	0	0	1	1	1	0	0	0
0	0	0	0	1	0	0	1	0	1	1	1

Figure 11.11

Inverse Document Frequency: The other half of TFIDF is Inverse Document Frequency. For this, let us first understand what does document frequency means. Document Frequency is the number of documents in which the word occurs irrespective of how many times it has occurred in those documents. The document frequency for the exemplar vocabulary would be:

We	Are	going	to	Mumbai	is	a	Famous	place	I	am	in
2	2	2	2	3	1	2	3	2	1	1	1

Figure 11.12

Talking about inverse document frequency, we need to put the document frequency in the denominator while the total number of documents is the numerator. Here, the total number of documents is 3; hence inverse document frequency becomes:

We	Are	going	to	Mumbai	is	a	Famous	place	I	am	in
4/2	4/2	4/2	4/2	4/3	4/1	4/2	4/3	4/2	4/1	4/1	4/1

Figure 11.13

The formula of TFIDF for any word W becomes:

$$TFIDF(W) = TF(W) * \log(IDF(W))$$

The words having the highest value are Mumbai, Famous.

7. Normalise the following text and comment on the vocabulary before and after the Normalization:

Raj and Vijay are best friends. They play together with other friends. Raj likes to play football, but Vijay prefers to play online games. Raj wants to be a footballer. Vijay wants to become an online gamer.

Ans. Normalisation of the given text:

Sentence Segmentation:

1. Raj and Vijay are best friends.

2. They play together with other friends.

3. Raj likes to play football, but Vijay prefers to play online games.

4. Raj wants to be a footballer.

5. Vijay wants to become an online gamer.

a) **Tokenization:** Raj and Vijay are best friends. Raj and Vijay are best friends. They play together with other friends. They play Together with other friends. The same will be done for all sentences.

Tokenization:

Raj and Vijay are best friends.	Raj	and	Vijay	are	best	friends
They play together with other friends	They	play	Together	with	other	friends

Same will be done for all sentences.

Figure 11.14

b) **Removing Stop words, Special Characters, and Numbers:** In this step, the unnecessary tokens are removed from the token list. Hence, the words and, are, to, an, (Punctuation) will be removed.

c) **Converting text to a common cause:** After the stop words removal, we convert the whole text into a similar case, preferably lower case. Here, we don't have words in different cases, so this step is not required for a given text.

d) **Stemming:** Here, the remaining words are converted to their root words/base forms. In other words, stemming is a process in which the affixes of words are removed/chopped, and the words are converted to their base forms. Word Affixes Stem Likes -s Like Prefers -s Prefer Wants -s want

Word	Affixes	Stem
Likes	-s	Like
Prefers	-s	Prefer
Wants	-s	want

Figure 11.15

e) In the given text, **Lemmatisation is not required**.

f) **Given Text:** Raj and Vijay are best friends. They play together with other friends. Raj likes to play football but Vijay prefers to play online games. Raj wants to be a footballer. Vijay wants to become an online gamer.

g) **Normalised Text:** Raj and Vijay best friends They play together with other friends Raj likes to play football but Vijay prefers to play online games Raj wants to be a footballer Vijay wants to become an online gamer

11.3 SOLVED EXERCISES

11.3.1 Multiple Choice Questions

Choose the correct option.

1. Which of the following words are stopwords?

   a) A, an, the

   b) For, and, it

   c) There, in, such

   d) All of these

2. A technique used to extract the base forms of the words by removing affixes from them is called:

   a) Stemming

   b) Tokenization

   c) Lemmatization

   d) Data extraction

3. Which type of information is given by the 'Bag of Words' algorithm?

   a) Type of words

   b) Number of words

   c) Number of stopwords

   d) None of the above

4. Frequency of words in each document of the corpus

   a) TFIDF helps us in identifying:

   b) Number of words

   c) Value for each word

   d) Stopwords

5. The process of grouping different forms of the same word together is known as:

   a) Stemming

   b) Tokenization

   c) Lemmatization

   d) Data extraction

6. Which encoding technique is used during Text Processing?

   a) Bag of Word,

   b) Bi-gram, n-gram,

   c) TF-IDF, Word2Vec

   d) All of these

7. What is a large and structured set of texts that can be read by machines to produce in a natural communicative setting known as?

   a) Corpus

   b) Semantics

   c) Stemming

   d) Lemmatization

8. For a word having ______________ TFIDF value, the word will have a high term frequency with less document frequency.

   a) Zero

   b) Low

   c) high

   d) Negative

9. Which of the following names is NOT given to a chatbot?

   a) Artificial conversational entity (ACE),

   b) Chat robot,

   c) Talk bot,

   d) Chatterpatterbox

10. In which process is grouping together different forms of the same word do?

   a) Lemmatisation

   b) Semantics

   c) Corpus

   d) Stemming

11. Which chatbot is produced by IBM?

    a) ManyChat
    b) Watson Assistant
    c) Snatchbot
    d) Ada

12. Which example is not related to smart bots?

    a) Tesla's self-driven car
    b) Google Assistant, Siri
    c) Alexa, We Chat
    d) Cortana, Slack bots

13. Which term is used to refer to the grammatical structure of a sentence?

    a) Stemming
    b) Syntax
    c) Semantics
    d) None of the above

14. Which statement is INCORRECT?

    a) TFIDF values help the computer understand which words are to be considered while processing the natural language.

    b) Words occurring in all the documents with high term frequencies have the least values and are called the 'Stopwords.'

    c) The higher the value of TFIDF, the less important the word is for a given corpus.

    d) For a word having a high TFIDF value, the word will have a high term frequency but less document frequency. This shows that the word is important for one document but is not a common word for all documents.

15. Which statement is NOT TRUE?

    a) Script-bots are powered by sophisticated AI and big data processing.

    b) A Script Bot is capable of reading and executing an external script.

    c) Text Normalisation cleans the textual data in such a manner that it comes down to a level where its complexity becomes lower than the actual data.

    d) None of the above

16. What model in Natural Language Processing helps in extracting features out of the text and is helpful in machine learning algorithms?

    a) Chatbot
    b) Bag of words
    c) Stemming
    d) None of the above

17. Which TFIDF value exhibits that the word is important for one document, but it is not a common word for all documents?

    a) Negative   b) Zero   c) Low   d) High

18. Which technique is used to extract the base form of the words by removing affixes from them?

    a) Stemming   b) Lemmatisation   c) Semantics   d) Chatbots

19. Which package is used for Natural Language Processing in Python programming?

    a) NLTK   b) DLCK   c) MLTK   d) PLTK

20. Which term is used for the frequency of a word in one document?

    a) Echo

    b) Hertz

    c) Low frequency

    d) Term frequency

21. Which is the algorithm that works by cutting off the end of the beginning of the word and taking into account a list of common prefixes and suffixes that can be found in an inflected word?

    a) Lemmatisation   b) Stemming   c) Semantics   d) Stemming

22. It is a computer program that can learn over time how to best interact with human beings. What is it?

    a) Chatbot   b) Robot   c) Stemming   d) TFIDF

23. What is the step-by-step procedure of obtaining the root form of the word in NLP known as?

    a) Corpus   b) Stemming   c) Lemmatisation   d) Semantics

24. In the process of Stemming, the affixes of words are removed to convert them into their ______________ form.

    a) Super

    b) Base

    c) Adjective

    d) None of the above

25. Which device is not a grammar checker?

    a) Grammarly

    b) Siri

    c) WhiteSmoke

    d) ProWritingAid

26. What is the step-by-step procedure of obtaining the root form of the word called?

    a) Corpus

    b) Semantics

    c) Stemming

    d) Lemmatisation

27. Which of the following statements is INCORRECT?

    a) The Syntax is associated with the grammatical structure of a sentence, while Semantics refers to the meaning of the sentence.

    b) NLP makes use of text classification techniques to filter emails.

    c) Chatbots are created using NLP and Deep Learning.

    d) NLP is used to identify customers' needs and pain points.

28. What is the term used for the words occurring in all the documents with high term frequencies but having the least values?

    a) Stopwords   b) Good words   c) TRIDF   d) Qwords

29. What term is used for a table that contains the frequency of each word of the vocabulary in a document called?

    a) Document Vector Table

    b) Bag of words

    c) Stemming

    d) Lemmatisation

30. It is a computer program that is designed to simulate human conversation through voice commands or text chats or both. What is it?

    a) Stemming   b) A chatbot   c) Robot   d) Click

31. Natural language refers to speech analysis in:

    a) Audible speeches of a language   b) The text of a language

    c) Both (a) and (b)   d) None of the above

32. Which application is not related to NLP?

    a) Language Translator   b) Semantic analysis

    c) Sentiment analysis   d) Text Summarisation

33. Which of the following products is based on NLP?

    a) Grammar checkers   b) Chatbots

    c) Voice Assistants   d) All the above

34. Which of the following pairs of applications is not based on NLP?
    a) Targeted marketing, chatbots
    b) Survey Analysis, Voice assistants
    c) Autocomplete in Search Engines, Market Intelligence
    d) Email distribution, Surveillance

35. Which technique is not used in targeted marketing?
    a) Keyword analysis
    b) Semantic analysis
    c) Text mining tools
    d) Browsing patterns of the users on the internet, emails, and social media platforms

36. Study the following statements to choose the correct option stating the advantages of chatbots.
    i.   It saves users time, money and gives better customer satisfaction.
    ii. This application can deliver a near-human-like conversational experience.
    iii. It helps you to increase customer satisfaction.
    iv. It supports customisation without writing any code.

    a) (i) & (ii)   b) (ii) & (iii)

    c) (i), (ii) & (iii)   d) (i), (ii), (iii) & (iv)

37. Which of the following steps is involved wherein the whole corpus is divided into sentences?
    a) Sentence segmentation   b) Tokenization
    c) Stemming   d) None of the above

38. Which of the following words in a corpus has the highest value?

    a) Punctuation   b) Rare words   c) Stop words   d) Stemming

39. What is the term used for a collection of text documents in NLP?

    a) Chatbot   b) Corpus   c) Semantics   d) Stemming

40. 'Bag of Words' creates a set of _______________ containing the count of word occurrences in the document that is easy to interpret.

    a) Data

    b) Vectors

    c) Algorithms

    d) None of the above

41. Which term is used for the whole textual data from all the documents altogether during Text Normalisation?

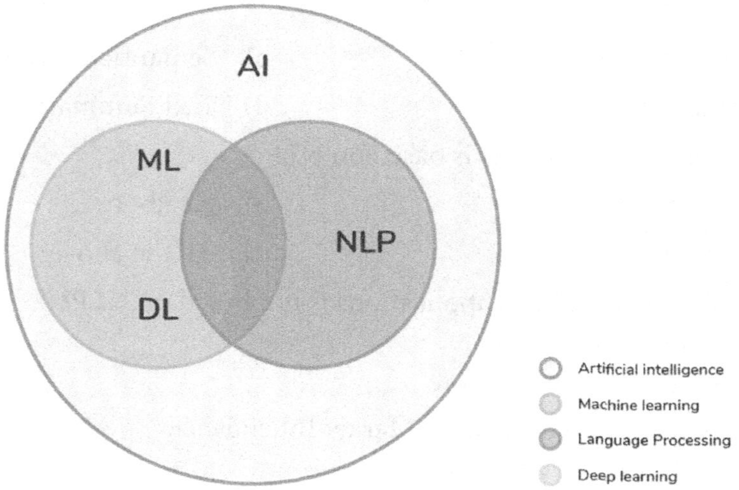

AI

ML

NLP

DL

Artificial intelligence

Machine learning

Language Processing

Deep learning

Figure 11.16

    a) Lotus

    b) Data

    c) Corpus.

    d) TextInput

ANSWERS									
1. (d)	2. (a)	3. (d)	4. (b)	5. (c)	6. (d)	7. (a)	8. (c)	9. (b)	10. (a)
11. (b)	12. (a)	13. (b)	14. (c)	15. (d)	16. (b)	17. (d)	18. (a)	19. (a)	20. (d)
21. (b)	22. (a)	23. (c)	24. (b)	25. (b)	26. (a)	27. (c)	28. (a)	29. (a)	30. (b)
31. (c)	32. (b)	33. (d)	34. (d)	35. (b)	36. (d)	37. (a)	38. (c)	39. (b)	40. (b)
41. (c)									

11.3.2 Fill in the blanks

1. _______________ is an AI domain concerned with the interaction between human language(s) and computers.

2. A _______________ is a software application used to conduct an online chat/conversation via text or text-to-speech to provide direct contact with live humans.

3. _______________ is a Natural Language Processing model that helps in extracting features out of the text that is helpful in machine learning algorithms.

4. Natural language means speech analysis in both audible speeches and the _______________ of a language.

5. _______________ is a technique used to obtain the base forms of the words by removing affixes from them.

6. _______________ takes a longer time to execute than stemming.

7. _______________ is defined as the frequency of a word in one document that can easily be found from the document vector table.

8. _______________ is used while implementing the Bag of Words algorithm.

9. _______________ is taken as a subset of AI in which a computer works at a problem programmatically without being programmed to perform a particular task.

10. _______________ values help the computer understand which words are to be considered while processing the natural language.

11. The morphological analysis of the words with the help of detailed dictionaries is called _______________.

12. A _______________ is a large and structured set of machine-readable texts that have been produced in a natural communicative setting.

13. NLTK is a platform for creating _______________ programs that can work with human language data.

14. Document Vector Table is a table that contains the _______________ of each word of the vocabulary in a document.

15. The _______________ the value of TFIDF, the more important the word is for a given corpus.

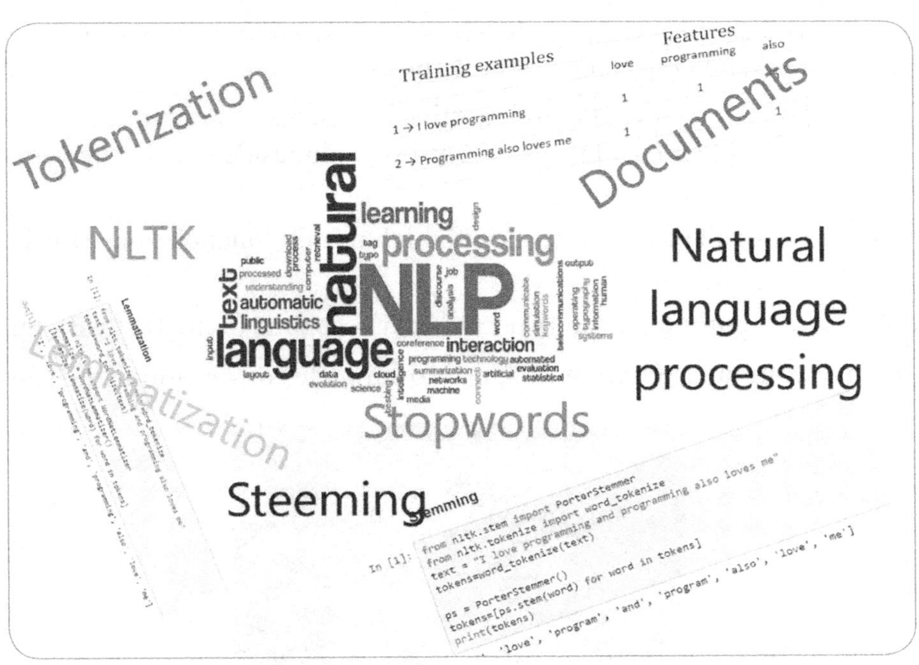

Figure 11.17

ANSWERS			
1. Natural Language Processing (NLP)	2. chatbot	3. 'Bag of Words'	4. text
5. Stemming	6. Lemmatisation	7. Term frequency	8. Document Vector Table
9. Machine learning	10. TFIDF	11. Lemmatisation	12. corpus
13. Python	14. frequency	15. higher	

11.3.3 True or False

1. AI is a subfield of Linguistics, Information Technology and Engineering, Computer Science, and Artificial Intelligence dealing with the interactions between computers and humans through natural languages, especially how to program computers to process and analyze big natural language data.

2. A corpus is a collection of textual documents that can be read by machines.

3. The frequency of a word in a document is called the Term Frequency.

4. NLP is regarded as art to extract some useful information from the text.

5. The grammatical structure of a sentence is called corpus.

6. A table having the frequency of each word of a vocabulary in a document is called Document Table.

7. By using Natural language processing, computers can extract keywords and phrases, understand the meaning of language, translate the content into another language, or generate response/output.

8. The meaning of the sentence is referred to as Syntax

9. Lemmatisation is the grouping together of different forms of the same word.

10. The lower the value of TFIDF, the more important the word is for a given corpus.

11. The study of NLP involves the tasks like how to make computers perform useful tasks after processing the natural languages that humans use.

12. A corpus is a collection of text documents that can be read by computers. It may be thought of as just a bunch of text files in a directory, often alongside many other directories of text files.

13. Words occurring in all the documents with high term frequencies have the least values and are called the 'Stopwords.'

14. A chatbot is a computer program that can learn over time to interact with human beings.

15. A chatbot is a computer program designed to simulate conversation with humans.

Figure 11.18

ANSWERS
1. T   2. T   3. T   4. T   5. F (Syntax not corpus)
6. F (Document Vector Table)   7. T   8. F (Semantics.)   9. T
10. F (higher not lower)   11. T   12. T   13. T   14. T   15. T

11.3.4 Matching type

Match the items of column A with those of column B correctly.

Column A	**Column B**
i. These bots are built on NLP and ML.	(a) Smart- bots
ii. These bots are easy to make.	(b) Script-bots
iii. These bot functioning is very limited as they are less powerful.	
iv. These bots work around a script which is programmed in them	
v. NLP and Machine learning skills are required.	
vi. Wide functionality	

ANSWERS
(i) -a   (ii) -b   (iii) -b   (iv) -b   (v) -a   (vi) -a

11.3.5 Assertion Reason Based Questions

1. Assertion (A): 'Bag of Words' is a Natural Language Processing model that helps in extracting features out of the text that may be helpful in machine learning algorithms.

   Reason (R): In a bag of words, we get the occurrences of each word and construct the vocabulary for the corpus.
   a) Both A and R are correct and R is the correct reason for A.
   b) Both A and R are correct and R is not the correct reason for A.
   c) A is correct but R is incorrect.
   d) A is incorrect but R is correct.

2. Assertion (A): A chatbot is helpful in interaction with humans?

   Reason (R): A chatbot is a software application used to have an online chat/ conversation via text /text-to-speech to provide indirect contact with live human beings.
   a) Both A and R are correct and R is the correct reason for A.
   b) Both A and R are correct and R is not the correct reason for A.
   c) A is correct but R is incorrect.
   d) A is incorrect but R is correct.

3. Assertion (A): Lemmatization is defined as the process of grouping together different forms of the same word.

   Reason (R): In search queries, Lemmatization allows end-users to query any version of a base word and get relevant results.
   a) Both A and R are correct and R is the correct reason for A.
   b) Both A and R are correct and R is not the correct reason for A.

    c) A is correct but R is incorrect.

    d) A is incorrect but R is correct.

4. Assertion (A): The grammatical structure of a sentence is called grammar.

    Reason (R): Semantics refers to the meaning of the sentence.

    a) Both A and R are correct and R is the correct reason for A.

    b) Both A and R are correct and R is not the correct reason for A.

    c) A is correct but R is incorrect.

    d) A is incorrect but R is correct.

5. Assertion (A): The inner guiding, moral principles, and values of people and society are called ethics. Ethics is not in black and white, but there are grey areas. Both Ethics and NLP are Interdisciplinary Fields.

    Reason (R): A chatbot is a computer program that can learn over time how to best interact with human beings.

    a) Both A and R are correct and R is the correct reason for A.

    b) Both A and R are correct and R is not the correct reason for A.

    c) A is correct but R is incorrect.

    d) A is incorrect but R is correct.

6. Assertion (A): Document Vector Table is used while implementing the 'Bag of Words' algorithm.

    Reason (R): A table that contains the frequency of each word of the vocabulary in a document is called Document Vector Table.

    a) Both A and R are correct and R is the correct reason for A.

    b) Both A and R are correct and R is not the correct reason for A.

    c) A is correct but R is incorrect.

    d) A is incorrect but R is correct.

7. Assertion (A): Document Vector Table is used while implementing the Bag of Words algorithm.

    Reason (R): Bag of Words creates a set of vectors containing the frequency of each word in the document (reviews), which are easy to interpret.

    a) Both A and R are correct and R is the correct reason for A.

    b) Both A and R are correct and R is not the correct reason for A.

    c) A is correct but R is incorrect.

    d) A is incorrect but R is correct.

8. Assertion (A): Lemmatization takes a longer time to execute than stemming.

    Reason (R): In NLP, a document is a list of all the unique words occurring in the corpus.

    a) Both A and R are correct and R is the correct reason for A.

    b) Both A and R are correct and R is not the correct reason for A.

    c) A is correct but R is incorrect.

    d) A is incorrect but R is correct.

9. Assertion (A): A large and structured set of texts can be read by machines and have been produced in a natural communicative setting, and this is called an algorithm.

   Reason (R): Words occurring in all the documents with high term frequencies have the least values and are called the stopwords.

   a) Both A and R are correct and R is the correct reason for A.

   b) Both A and R are correct and R is not the correct reason for A.

   c) A is correct but R is incorrect.

   d) A is incorrect but R is correct.

10. Assertion (A): Thus, 'Stemming' is the process in which the affixes of words are removed to convert them to their base form.

   Reason (R): In Stemming, the word we get after affix removal (also known as lemma) is a meaningful one.

   a) Both A and R are correct and R is the correct reason for A.

   b) Both A and R are correct and R is not the correct reason for A.

   c) A is correct but R is incorrect.

   d) A is incorrect but R is correct.

11. Assertion (A): Lemmatization takes more time than stemming.

   Reason (R): Lemmatization carries the morphological analysis of the words from detailed dictionaries that the algorithm can look the form back to its lemma.

   a) Both A and R are correct and R is the correct reason for A.

   b) Both A and R are correct and R is not the correct reason for A.

   c) A is correct but R is incorrect.

   d) A is incorrect but R is correct.

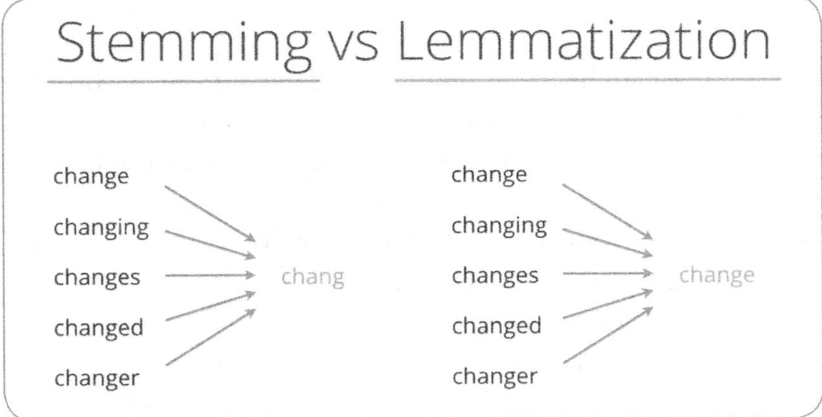

Figure 11.19

ANSWERS									
1. (b)	2. (a)	3. (b)	4. (d)	5. (b)	6. (a)	7. (b)	8. (c)	9. (d)	10. (c)
11. (a)									

11.3.6 Statements Based Questions

1. Statement 1: The lower the value of TFIDF, the more important the word is for a given corpus.

   Statement 2: Natural Language Processing (NLP) is an AI domain concerned with the interaction between human language(s) and computers.
   a) Statement 1 is correct but statement 2 is incorrect.
   b) Statement 1 is incorrect but statement 2 is correct.
   c) Both the statements are correct.
   d) Both the statements are incorrect.

2. Statement 1: Stemming is a technique used to extract the base forms of the words by removing affixes from them. It is similar to cutting down the branches of a tree to its stems.

   Statement 2: Term frequency is defined as the frequency of a word in one document that can easily be found from the document vector table.
   a) Statement 1 is correct but statement 2 is incorrect.
   b) Statement 1 is incorrect but statement 2 is correct.
   c) Both the statements are correct.
   d) Both the statements are incorrect.

3. Statement 1: 'Bag of Words' is a CV model which helps in extracting features out of the text that is helpful in machine learning algorithms.

   Statement 2: The morphological analysis of the words with the help of detailed dictionaries is called Stemming.
   a) Statement 1 is correct but statement 2 is incorrect.
   b) Statement 1 is incorrect but statement 2 is correct.
   c) Both the statements are correct.
   d) Both the statements are incorrect.

4. Statement 1: TFIDF values help the computer understand which words are to be considered while processing the natural language.

   Statement 2: The higher the value of TFIDF, the more important the word is for a given corpus.
   a) Statement 1 is correct but statement 2 is incorrect.
   b) Statement 1 is incorrect but statement 2 is correct.
   c) Both the statements are correct.
   d) Both the statements are incorrect.

5. Statement 1: Script-bots is a cohesive bot development platform that designs, develops, validates, and deploys AI-powered conversational chatbots that suit the user's unique needs.

   Statement 2: A smart bot simply completes a set of predefined tasks once triggered and cutting-edge software.
   a) Statement 1 is correct but statement 2 is incorrect.
   b) Statement 1 is incorrect but statement 2 is correct.
   c) Both the statements are correct.
   d) Both the statements are incorrect.

6. Statement 1: Natural Language Processing (NLP) refers to extracting information from the spoken and written word using algorithms.

   Statement 2: A corpus is defined as a collection of text documents.

   a) Statement 1 is correct but statement 2 is incorrect.

   b) Statement 1 is incorrect but statement 2 is correct.

   c) Both the statements are correct.

   d) Both the statements are incorrect.

7. Statement 1: A chatbot is defined as a computer program that is designed to simulate conversations with human beings.

   Statement 2: NLP is regarded as art to extract some information from the text.

   a) Statement 1 is correct but statement 2 is incorrect.

   b) Statement 1 is incorrect but statement 2 is correct.

   c) Both the statements are correct.

   d) Both the statements are incorrect.

8. Statement 1: A corpus can be taken as a bunch of image files in a directory, often alongside many other directories of text files.

   Statement 2: The header row in a document vector table contains the vocabulary of the corpus while the other rows correspond to different documents.

   a) Statement 1 is correct but statement 2 is incorrect.

   b) Statement 1 is incorrect but statement 2 is correct.

   c) Both the statements are correct.

   d) Both the statements are incorrect.

9. Statement 1: By using Natural language processing, computers can extract keywords and phrases, understand the meaning of language, translate the content into another language, or generate response/output.

   Statement 2: The study of CV involves the tasks like how to make computers perform useful tasks after processing the natural languages that humans use.

   a) Statement 1 is correct but statement 2 is incorrect.

   b) Statement 1 is incorrect but statement 2 is correct.

   c) Both the statements are correct.

   d) Both the statements are incorrect.

10. Statement 1: A dictionary in NLP is a list of all the unique words occurring in the corpus.

    Statement 2: A table that contains the frequency of each word of the vocabulary in a document is called Document Vector Table.

    a) Statement 1 is correct but statement 2 is incorrect.

    b) Statement 1 is incorrect but statement 2 is correct.

    c) Both the statements are correct.

    d) Both the statements are incorrect.

11. Statement 1: Term frequency is defined as the frequency of a word in one document.

    Statement 2: A large and structured set of texts that can be read by machines and have been produced in a natural communicative setting is known as a corpus.

    a) Statement 1 is correct but statement 2 is incorrect.

    b) Statement 1 is incorrect but statement 2 is correct.

    c) Both the statements are correct.

    d) Both the statements are incorrect.

<table>
<tr><td colspan="10" align="center">ANSWERS</td></tr>
<tr><td>1. (b)</td><td>2. (c)</td><td>3. (d)</td><td>4. (c)</td><td>5. (d)</td><td>6. (c)</td><td>7. (c)</td><td>8. (b)</td><td>9. (a)</td><td>10. (c)</td></tr>
<tr><td>11. (c)</td><td></td><td></td><td></td><td></td><td></td><td></td><td></td><td></td><td></td></tr>
</table>

11.3.7 Competency-Based Questions

1. Suppose Vibha Deshmukh is using Alexa chatbot in her home, that is very powerful, flexible, and has wide functionality. The chatbot is capable of performing various tasks, like playing music, etc. What type of bot she is using?

    a) Script bot

    b) Smart bot

    c) May be smart bot or script bot

    d) None of the above

2. Consider the following features of a chatbot:

    i.   It is used to build relationships with customers through interactive and tailored content.

    ii. It books appointments, sell products, capture contact details, and build relationships through Messenger.

    iii. It connects to many tools, including Google Sheets, MailChimp, Shopify, Zapier, HubSpot, ConvertKit, etc.

    This Facebook Messenger is meant for e-commerce and support use. This is called:

    a) Alexa

    b) Flow XO

    c) ManyChat

    d) Amplify

3. Suppose Radhika S Chandran is typing a manuscript using a computer. She is using "Grammarly" to type grammatical error free text with improvised syntax. Which of the following is used in this algorithm that is also known as 'Grammar and Spell Checker'?

    a) CV

    b) Data Science

    c) Fuzzy Logic

    d) NLP

4. Assume that Sugandh Gogai owns ***Saumya World Tours & Travels Pvt Ltd***. He is using a computer program that can learn over time how to best interact with human beings. It can answer questions and solutions to customer problems, generate sales leads, evaluate and qualify prospects, and increase sales on his eCommerce site. It is used to answer questions and troubleshoot customer problems, evaluate and qualify prospects, generate sales leads, and increase sales on an e-commerce site. He is using:

    a) Artificial bot

    b) Artificial Conversational Entity (ACE)

    c) Chat Bot

    d) Chatter mail

ANSWERS
1. (b)   2. (c)   3. (d)   4. (c)

11.3.8 VSA

1. What is contained in Document Vector Table?

Ans. Document Vector Table is a table having the frequency of each word of the vocabulary in each document.

2. Can a chatbot learn with interaction with humans?

Ans. Yes. A chatbot is a computer program designed to interact with humans.

3. What can be done by a chatbot?

Ans. A chatbot can answer questions and troubleshoot customer problems, evaluate and qualify prospects, generate sales leads, and increase sales on an e-commerce site.

4. Write other names given to chatbot.

Ans. A chatbot is known as an 'Artificial Conversational Entity' (ACE), talk bot, chat robot, chatterbot, or chatterbox.

5. How is a chatbot helpful in interaction with humans?

Ans. A chatbot is a software application used to have an online chat/ conversation via text /text-to-speech to provide indirect contact with live human beings.

6. In what form are words converted during Stemming?

Ans. Stemming is defined as the process in which the affixes of words are removed, and the words are converted to their base form.

7. What is a lemma?

Ans. In Lemmatization, the meaningful word we get after affix removal is known as a lemma.

8. Why does Lemmatization take more time in execution than stemming?

Ans. Lemmatisation makes sure that lemma (a word we get after affix removal) is a word with some meaning, and hence, it takes a longer time to execute than stemming.

9. How do Stemming algorithms work?

Ans. Stemming algorithms work by chopping/cutting off the end of the beginning of the word after considering a list of common prefixes and suffixes found in an inflected word.

10. Why does Lemmatisation take more time than stemming?

Ans. Lemmatisation carries the morphological analysis of the words from detailed dictionaries that the algorithm can look the form back to its lemma. So, it takes more time than stemming.

11. Which term is used for a large and structured set of machine-readable texts that have been produced in a natural communicative setting?

Ans. Corpus.

12. How do you compare a corpus with text files in a directory?

Ans. A corpus is defined as a collection of text documents.

13. What is the term used for an AI domain that refers to a method that communicates with an intelligent system using a natural language such as English?

Ans.   Natural Language Processing (NLP).

14. When is the processing of NLP required?

Ans.   Processing of Natural Language is required when we want an intelligent system like a robot to perform according to our instructions.

15. Define dictionary in NLP.

Ans.   In NLP, a list of all the unique words occurring in the corpus is called a dictionary.

16. What happens when some words are repeated in different documents to make a dictionary in NLP?

Ans.   When some words are repeated in different documents, then they are all written just once during the creation of the dictionary.

17. What is a natural language?

Ans.   Natural language refers to a language that is spoken and written by humans, and Natural Language Processing (NLP) refers to extracting information from the spoken and written word using algorithms.

18. Mention one difference between Syntax and semantics?

Ans.   The Syntax is associated with the grammatical structure of a sentence, while Semantics refers to the meaning of the sentence.

19. What is Cognitive Behavioural Therapy (CBT)?

Ans.   CBT therapy includes understanding the behaviour and mindset of a person in their normal life, and the therapists help people overcome their stress to live a happy life.

20. What are the other names given to chatbot?

Ans.   Other names for an artificial conversational entity (ACE), chat robot, talk bot, chatterbot, and chatterbox are other names given to a chatbot.

21. Mention one of the most common applications of Natural Language Processing.

Ans.   A chatbot.

22. How many types of chatbots are there?

Ans.   There are two types of chatbots around us: Script-bot and Smart-bot.

23. What is done during Text Normalisation?

Ans.   Text Normalisation cleans up the textual data in such a manner to lower down its complexity.

24. Define Text processing.

Ans.   Machines need data in the numeric form, for which humans basically use encoding techniques (Bag of Word, Bi-gram, n-gram, TF-IDF, Word2Vec) to encode text into numeric vectors.

25. Write two examples of encoding techniques used during Text Processing.

Ans.   Bag of Word, n-gram, Bi-gram, TF-IDF, Word2Vec, etc.

26. Which term is used for the whole textual data from all the documents altogether during Text Normalisation?

Ans. Corpus.

27. Define Stemming.

Ans. Stemming is a process in which the affixes of words are chopped/removed, and the words are converted to their base form.

28. What is the common feature of Lemmatisation and Stemming?

Ans. Stemming and Lemmatisation are both alternative processes to each other as the role of both the processes is the same – removal of affixes.

29. What is done during the Sentence Segmentation step?

Ans. Under sentence segmentation, the full corpus is divided into sentences. Each sentence is taken as different data, so now the whole corpus gets reduced to sentences.

30. What do you mean by 'Token' in NLP?

Ans. The token is a term used for any word or number, or special character occurring in a sentence.

31. What is the main feature of Tokenisation?

Ans. During Tokenisation, every word, number, and special character is considered separately, and each of them is now a separate token.

32. What are stopwords?

Ans. Stopwords are the words that occur very frequently in the corpus but do not add any value to it.

33. What is the full form of TFIDF?

Ans. Term Frequency and Inverse Document Frequency

34. Which type of information is given by the 'Bag of Words' algorithm?

Ans. The 'Bag of Words' algorithm gives us the frequency of words in each document we have in the corpus. It gives us an idea that if the word is occurring more in a document, its value is more for that document.

35. Define chatbot.

Ans. Any computer program designed to simulate human conversation through voice commands or text chats, or both is called a chatbot.

36. What do you mean by Syntax?

Ans. The grammatical structure of a sentence is called Syntax.

37. What is Semantics?

Ans. Semantics refers to the meaning of the sentence.

38. What do you mean by stemming?

Ans. Stemming is defined as the process in which the affixes of words are removed to convert words into their base form.

39. What is a corpus?

Ans.   A structured but large set of texts that can be read by machines and have been produced in a natural communicative setting is called a corpus.

40. What is Lemmatisation?

Ans.   Lemmatisation is the process of grouping together different forms of the same word.

41. What is the function of Lemmatisation in search queries?

Ans.   In search queries, Lemmatisation allows end-users to query any version of a base word and get relevant results.

42. In Lemmatisation, what is the name given to the meaningful word we get after affix removal?

Ans.   Lemma

43. Out of Lemmatisation and stemming, which takes a long time to execute?

Ans.   Lemmatisation

44. What is a dictionary in NLP?

Ans.   It is a list of all the unique words occurring in the corpus.

45. What is the full form of NLTK?

Ans.   Natural Language Toolkit

46. What do you mean by Natural Language Toolkit?

Figure 11.20

Ans.   It is one of the leading platforms for building Python programs that can work with human language data.

47. Define Term frequency.

Ans.   Term frequency is defined as the frequency of a word in one document.

48. Define Document Vector Table.

Ans.   A table that contains the frequency of each word of the vocabulary in a document is called Document Vector Table.

49. When is Document Vector Table used?

Ans.   Document Vector Table is used while implementing the 'Bag of Words' algorithm.

50. What is contained in the header row in a document vector table?

Ans.   The vocabulary of the corpus.

51. What do you mean by 'Bag of Words'?

Ans.   'Bag of Words' is a Natural Language Processing model which helps in extracting features out of the text that can be helpful in machine learning algorithms.

52. What shall we find in a bag of words?

Ans. In a bag of words, we get the occurrences of each word and construct the vocabulary for the corpus.

53. What is created by 'Bag of Words'?

Ans. Bag of Words creates a set of vectors containing the frequency of each word in the document (reviews), which are easy to interpret.

54. What do you mean by 'Stopwords'?

Ans. Words occurring in all the documents with high term frequencies have the least values and are known as the 'stopwords.'

55. When a word has a high TFIDF value, then the word will have a high term frequency but less document frequency. What does this signify?

Ans. This shows that the word is important for one document but is not a common word for all documents.

56. What do you mean by extraction-based summarisation?

Ans. The summarisation that extracts key phrases and creates a summary without adding any extra information is called extraction-based summarisation.

57. What is abstraction-based summarisation?

Ans. The summarisation that paraphrases the original content to create new phrases is called abstraction-based summarisation.

58. What is the full form of NMT?

Ans. Neural Machine Translation

59. What do you mean by Neural Machine Translation?

Ans. When a machine translation uses a neural network to translate low-impact content and speed up communication with its partners, it is called Neural Machine Translation.

60. What is the importance of TFIDF values?

Ans. TFIDF values help the computer understand which words are to be considered while processing the natural language.

61. What is the significance of the higher value of TRIDF?

Ans. The higher the value of TFIDF, the more important the word is for a given corpus.

62. Define a smart bot.

Ans. Smart-bots is a cohesive bot development platform that designs, develops, validates, and deploys AI-powered conversational chatbots that suit the user's unique needs.

63. What is Script-bot?

Ans. A script bot simply completes a set of predefined tasks once triggered and cutting-edge software.

64. Define Tokenisation.

Ans. In Tokenisation, during text normalization, every word, number, and special character of each sentence is considered separately for a separate token.

65. What do you mean by Tokens?

Ans. 'Tokens' is a term used for any word or number or special character occurring in a sentence.

66. What is the full form of TFIDF?

Ans. Term Frequency and Inverse Document Frequency

67. What is the formula of TFIDF for any word?

Ans. TFIDF(W) = T.F. (W) * log(IDF(W)) Here, log is to the base of 10.

68. What term is used for a computer program that can learn over time how to best interact with human beings?

Ans. A chatbot

69. Which term is used for a table containing the frequency of each word of the vocabulary in a document?

Ans. Bag of Words algorithm.

11.3.9 Short Answer Type Questions

1. Compare Stemming and Lemmatization.

Ans. **Stemming** is defined as a technique used to extract the base form of the words by removing affixes from them. Example: the stem of the words eats, eating, eaten is eat.

Lemmatisation is the grouping together of different forms of the same word. In search queries, Lemmatisation allows end-users to query any version of a base word and get relevant results.

2. Out of Stemming and Lemmatisation, which one will take a longer time and why?

Ans. Stemming is a process in which the affixes of words are removed, and the words are converted to their base forms. In Lemmatisation, the word obtained after affix removal is a meaningful one (lemma).

Lemmatisation confirms that lemma is a word with a meaning, and hence it takes a longer time to execute than stemming.

3. Enlist the common features of AI Chatbot.

Ans. The common features of AI Chatbot are as follows:

i. It directs the optimal path for solving any problem automatically.

ii. It offers custom integration and development.

iii. It enables the user to build, connect, and publish bots to interact with users wherever they are.

4. Enlist the important advantages of AI chatbots.

Ans. The important advantages of AI Chatbot are as follows:

i. It saves users time, money and gives better customer satisfaction.

ii. This application can deliver a near-human-like conversational experience.

iii. It helps you to increase customer satisfaction.

iv. It supports customisation without writing any code.

5. What is Ada? What are its two main features?

Ans. Ada is an AI-powered customer service chatbot that makes it easy for the team to solve customer inquiries quickly.

It has the following features:

(i) One of the best chatbots to provide On-demand and multi-channel engagement for customers.

(ii) Customise every conversation with content tailored to their interests, information, and intent.

6. What are Script-bots? Give two examples.

Ans. Script-bots are the bots that simply complete a set of predefined tasks once triggered (no intelligence required), and cutting-edge software, like Tesla self-driving software, that can adapt their behaviour dynamically according to the context. These are powered by sophisticated AI and big data processing. A Script Bot is capable of reading and executing an external script. The scripts are fully customisable. These are easy to make with limited functionality.

Examples: ELIZA, ALICE, etc.

7. What are Smart-bots? Give two examples.

Ans. Smart-bots is a cohesive bot development platform that designs, develops, validates, and deploys AI-powered conversational chatbots that suit the user's unique needs. It is very powerful, flexible, and has wide functionality.

Examples: Google Assistant, Alexa, Cortana, Siri, We Chat, Slack bots, etc.

8. Give an example of a different Syntax but the same semantics.

Ans. Statement 1: 5+4

Statement 2: 4+5

Here, the way these two statements are written is different, but their meanings are the same, that is 9.

9. Give an example of different semantics but the same Syntax.

Ans. 2/3 (Python 2.7)

$\neq$ 2/3 (Python 3)

The statements written here have the same Syntax, but their meanings are different.

In Python 2.7, this statement results in 1, while in Python 3, it gives an output of 1.5.

10. Give an example of perfect Syntax but no Meaning.

Ans. Sometimes, a statement can have perfectly correct Syntax, but it does not mean anything. *Example:* Peacocks feed extravagantly while Venus drinks milk.

This statement is correct grammatically but does make any sense. In natural language, a perfect balance of Syntax and Semantics is very important for better understanding.

11. What are the reasons for non-remaining the same vocabulary after Normalisation? Explain.

Ans. The following are the reasons for non-remaining the same vocabulary after Normalization:

In Normalisation, the text is converted/normalized through various steps and is lowered to minimum vocabulary because the machine does not require grammatically correct statements but only the essence of it.

In Normalisation, Stopwords, Numbers, and Special Characters are removed.

In Stemming, the words are converted to their base form after cutting the affixes of words, and after Normalisation, we get the reduced vocabulary.

12. What is the meaning of the term frequency? Where is it found?

Ans. Term Frequency is the frequency of a word in a document. Term frequency can be found from the document vector table where the frequency of each word of the vocabulary in each document.

13. Enlist the key benefits of TFIDF over word embeddings.

Ans. The following are the benefits of TFIDF over word embeddings:

a) They do not require a large external corpus and can be trained on the documents at hand.

b) They are less computationally expensive and memory intensive.

c) They perform exceptionally well in the context of large data sets /document files, like in text classification or topic modelling, whereas word embeddings focus on single words and do well in things like text generation or translation.

14. What are the applications of TFIDF?

Ans. The following are the applications of TFIDF:

a) Document Classification helps in classifying the type and genre of a document.

b) Topic Modelling helps in predicting the topic for a corpus.

c) Information Retrieval System (IRS) to extract the important information out of a corpus.

d) Stop word filtering that helps in removing the unnecessary words out of a text body.

15. Why is there a need for detailed dictionaries in Lemmatisation and not in stemming?

Ans. Stemming algorithms work by chopping/cutting off the end of the beginning of the word. It takes into account a list of common prefixes and suffixes that can be found in an inflected word. In contrast, 'Lemmatisation' considers the morphological analysis of the words. For this, it is necessary to have detailed dictionaries which the algorithm can look through to link the form back to its lemma.

16. Explain Sentiment Analysis.

Ans. Human beings throughout the world are using social media, where they have the gift of being sarcastic and ironic during conversations. Sentiment analysis is done by many companies on a periodic basis to understand the deeper aspects of the business. With sentiment analysis in real-time, these sentiments about any product or campaign launched by a company can be monitored on social media and can be tackled before they escalate. This application of NLP gives the company the power to sense the pulse of the clients/customers. Companies may use sentiment analysis in many ways, like to understand product reviews, to find out the emotions of their target audience, to gauge their brand sentiment, etc. Even sometimes, governments use sentiment analysis to find popular opinion and also catch out any threats to the security of the nation.

17. What do you mean by Amplify? Write any two features of Amplify.

Ans. Amplify is a new generation conversational artificial intelligence chatbot tool that offers personalised and persistent messaging-based experiences across large data.

It has the following features:

(i) One of the best AI chatbots to provide branded virtual assistants.

(ii) Easy to create and manage client's own branded virtual assistant.

18. What is the main aim of Lemmatisation?

Ans. The main aim of Lemmatisation is to reduce inflectional forms (words) to a common base form. Lemmatization does not simply chop off inflections, but it uses lexical knowledge bases to get the correct base forms of words.

Figure 11.21

11.3.10 Long Answer Type Questions

1. Discuss NLP Applications in our daily life.

Ans. The applications of Natural Language Processing are listed below:

i. **Email Classification and Filtering:** NLP makes use of text classification techniques to filter emails. This technique refers to the process of classification of a piece of text into predefined categories. The emails are automatically divided into three sections, namely, Primary, Social, and Promotions. Moreover, the classification of various articles into different categories is done using NLP so that we can choose to read the material of our choice. In more advanced cases, many companies use specialty anti-virus software with NLP scan the Emails to find out the patterns and phrases that may indicate a phishing attempt on the employees.

ii. **Chatbots:** A form of artificial intelligence that is programmed to interact with humans in such a manner that it sounds like a human being is called a chatbot. These are created using Natural Language Processing and Machine Learning. These chatbots may understand the complexities of the English language and find the actual meaning of the sentence. Moreover, they learn from their conversations with humans and become better with time. Chatbots work in two simple steps: They identify the meaning of the question asked and collect all the required data from the user to answer the question, and then, they answer the question appropriately.

iii. **Autocomplete in Search Engines:** The search engines tend to guess what you are typing and automatically complete the sentences, and use Natural Language Processing (NLP) to make sense of these words. When a user types "games" in Google, he may get many suggestions like "game for girls," "games download." All such types of suggestions are provided using autocomplete that uses NPL to guess what the user wants to ask. Search engines are using enormous data sets to analyze the customer's needs and suggest the most common possibilities using NPL.

iv. **Market Intelligence:** Many marketing personnel is using natural language processing to understand their customers in a better way for creating effective strategies. The power of NLP equips them for analyzing topics, keywords and making proper use of unstructured data. It is used to identify customers' needs and pain points and helps in keeping an eye on the competitors.

v. **Voice Assistants:** Many voice assistants, like Siri, Alexa, or Google Assistant, etc., are playing an important role in making calls, placing reminders, scheduling meetings, setting alarms, surfing the internet, etc. They have made life much easier. These devices use a complex combination of speech recognition, natural language understanding, and NPL to understand what humans are communicating and then act accordingly. They are becoming a bridge between humans and the internet by providing all manner of services based on just voice interaction.

Figure 11.22

vi. **Language Translator:** Many language translators based on NPL, like Google Translator, are used to translate a text from one language to other. Of course, it is not exactly 100% accurate. It allows the algorithm to change a sequence of words (phrase or sentence) from one language to another, which is called translation.

vii. **Sentiment Analysis:** Humans throughout the world are using social media, where they have the gift of being sarcastic and ironic during conversations. With sentiment analysis in real-time, these sentiments about any product or campaign launched by a company can be monitored on social media and can be tackled before they escalate. This application of NLP gives the company the power to sense the pulse of the clients/ customers. Companies may use sentiment analysis in many ways, like to find out the emotions of their target audience, to understand product reviews, to gauge their brand sentiment, etc. Sentiment analysis is done by many companies on a periodic basis to understand the deeper aspects of the business. Even sometimes, governments use sentiment analysis to find popular opinion and also catch out any threats to the security of the nation.

viii. **Survey Analysis:** Many companies use surveys as an important means of evaluating the performance of their products/services /employees. Survey analysis plays a crucial role in understanding the loopholes and helping the companies improve their products and services. The exceptionally large data size is dealt with natural language processing to get accurate information about the customer's opinion and improve their performance.

ix. **Grammar Checkers:** Grammar and spell checkers, like 'Grammarly', 'WhiteSmoke', 'ProWritingAid', etc., are used to check grammar and spelling that are very important factors for writing professional reports, assignments, developing content for books, newsletters, brochures, etc. These devices use NLP to suggest better synonyms and improve the overall readability of the content. The NLP algorithm is formally trained on millions of sentences to understand the correct format. NLP is a boon for content writers, copywriters, and editors because it can suggest the correct verb tense, a better synonym, or a clearer sentence structure than what is written.

x. **Hiring and Recruitment:** Human Resource (HR) department of a company/ organization recruits and hires employees from a big dataset after filtering resumes and shortlisting the candidates using NLP. HR professionals use techniques such as information extraction along with named entity recognition to extract information, like names, skills, locations, and educational backgrounds of the candidate. This technique allows for unbiased filtering of resumes and the selection of the right candidate for the desired post in the company.

xi. **Targeted Advertising:** Natural Language Processing is an excellent amazing resource for placing the right advertisement, in the right place, at the right time for attracting targeted customers. The techniques, like keyword analysis, Text mining tools, browsing patterns of users over the internet, emails, and social media platforms are used.

Figure 11.23

xii. **Text Summarisation:** NLP application is used to summarise text by extracting the most important information after reducing the process of going through large data in news content, legal documentation, scientific papers, etc. This is done in either of the two ways: here are two ways of using natural language processing for text summarisation: (a) extraction-based summarisation, which extracts key phrases and creates a summary without adding any extra information, (b) abstraction-based summarisation, which paraphrases the original content to create new phrases.

xiii. **Neural Machine Translation:** In NMT, a machine translation uses a neural network to translate low-impact content and speed up communication with its partners. A recurrent bidirectional network known as an encoder processes a source sentence to give vectors for another recurrent neural network, known as the decoder. This process helps to predict words in the target language as it is done in 'Google Translate.'

2. Compare the main features of some chatbots.

Ans.

Chatbot	Features
(a) **ManyChat:** This Facebook Messenger is meant for e-commerce and support use. It helps small businesses grow by simplifying the marketing stuff, like acquiring leads or launching campaigns. ManyChat Figure 11.24	(i) It is used to build relationships with customers through interactive and tailored content. (ii) It books appointments, sell products, capture contact details, and build relationships through Messenger. (iii) ManyChat connects to many tools, including Google Sheets, MailChimp, Shopify, Zapier, HubSpot, ConvertKit, etc.
(b) **Flow XO:** It is an automation software to build chatbots to help clients to engage and communicate with their customers across social media platforms, different sites, and applications. Figure 11.25	(i) Chatbot welcomes new visitors virtually to the eCommerce website by providing greetings. (ii) It gathers the user's details by asking simple questions and validating the answer provided. (iii) A chatbot can answer simple questions or provide a link to any article. (iv) It is one of the best chatbots that accepts payment by identifying a particular service or product your customer likes to purchase. (v) The client's bot can clarify and pre-filter customer data while they are on the site to receive higher-quality leads.

Chatbot	Features
(c) **Amplify:** A new generation conversational artificial intelligence chatbot-Amplify that offers personalized and persistent messaging-based experiences across a large and ever-expanding diversity of conversational surfaces.	(i) One of the best AI chatbots to provide branded virtual assistants. (ii) Easy to create and manage client's own branded virtual assistant.
(d) **Ada:** It is an AI-powered customer service chatbot that makes it easy for your team to solve customer inquiries quickly. Figure 11.26	(i) One of the best chatbots to provide On-demand and multi-channel engagement for customers. (ii) Customise every conversation with content tailored to their interests, information, and intent.
(e) **Watson Assistant:** It is one of the best chatbot applications that allow clients to build conversational interfaces into any device, channel, use of any cloud. Figure 11.27	(i) Integrate directly with Facebook Messenger or Slack. (ii) Direct optimal path for solving any problem automatically. (iii) Provide session management for the personalized experience.
(f) Snatchbot: It helps the clients to create smart chatbots for multi-channel messaging, having enterprise-grade security and robust administrative features. Figure 11.28	(i) Enable the clients to build, connect, and publish bots to interact with users. (ii) Offer rapid intelligent chatbot development for everyone. (iii) Help the clients to create a bot or Human chatbot without any coding or technical skills. (iv) Design conversations to utilize simple or something complex like translation, action buttons, collect payments, send receipts, and more.

3. Explain the main features of Snatchbot.

Ans. Snatchbot helps the clients to create smart chatbots for multi-channel messaging, having enterprise-grade security and robust administrative features.

It has the following features:

(i) Enable the clients to build, connect, and publish bots to interact with users.

(ii) Offer rapid intelligent chatbot development for everyone.

(iii) Help the clients to create a bot or Human chatbot without any coding or technical skills.

(iv) Design conversations to utilize simple or something complex like translation, action buttons, collect payments, send receipts, and more.

4. Differentiate between script-bot and smart-bot.

Ans. The features of both types of chatbots are given:

Script-bot	Smart-bot
(i) A script chatbot doesn't carry even a glimpse of AI.	(i) Smart bot is built on NLP and ML.
(ii) Script bots are easy to make	(ii) Smart – bot is comparatively difficult to make.
(iii) Smart-bot is flexible and powerful.	(iii) Script bot functioning is limited as it is they are less powerful.
(iv) Smart bot works on bigger databases and other resources directly.	(iv) Script bots work around a script that is programmed in them
(v) No or little language processing skills are required.	(v) NLP and Machine learning skills are required.
(vi) Limited functionality.	(vi) Wide functionality

5. Differentiate between Human language and Computer language.

Ans. The main points of difference between human language and computer language are given below:

Human language	Computer language
(i) Human language is 'context-sensitive language.'	(i) Computer language needs a 'context-free grammar,' i.e., there should be only one way to interpret one statement.
(ii) The meaning of a word depends on the other words in the sentence as well as its relative placement to other words.	(ii) This is independent of the "tokens" (or words) in the statement.
(iii) Vocabulary is very rich.	(iii) Vocabulary is very limited and restricted to a few number words in a very specific domain.
(iv) Human languages are tolerant of imprecise Syntax and ambiguous semantics.	(iv) Computer languages must have precise Syntax and semantics.

Human language	Computer language
(v) Human languages are supported by non-verbal communication to enrich and clarify the meaning of the words.	(v) Computer language is not supported by non-verbal communication.
(vi) The communications made by humans are very complex.	(vi) The communications made by the machines are basic and very simple.
(vii) Both the speaker and the audience understand the same language.	(vii) With programming languages, only the human understands the language, which has to be translated into something else (machine code) that the machine does understand (and which few human beings bother to learn).
(viii) There are local dialects in the human language.	(viii) There is no local dialect in the computer language.
(ix) Some useless words may be present in human language.	(ix) There is nothing useless in a computer language.
(x) Humans have some language as their mother tongue.	(x) No one has computer language as their mother tongue.
(xi) Humans communicate through language, which they process all the time. Their brain keeps on processing the sounds that it hears around itself and tries to make sense out of them all the time.	(xi) The computer understands the language of numbers. Everything that is sent to the machine is to be converted to numbers.

6. What are the pre-processing steps for dealing with raw text?

Ans. Pre-processing the raw text has the following steps:

   a) Removing URL.
   b) Removing all irrelevant characters (Numbers and Punctuation).
   c) Convert all characters into lowercase.
   d) Tokenization
   e) Removing Stopwords
   f) Stemming and Lemmatisation
   g) Remove the words having length <= 2
   h) Convert the list of tokens into the back to the string

7. Differentiate between Stemming and Lemmatisation.

Ans. The difference between stemming and Lemmatization is given below:

Stemming	Lemmatisation
(i) Stemming is a technique used to extract the base forms of the words by removing affixes from them.	(i) Lemmatisation is the grouping together of different forms of the same word.

Stemming	Lemmatisation
(ii) Stemming is a process in which the affixes of words are removed, and the words are converted to their base forms.	(ii) The word obtained after affix removal (also known as lemma) is a meaningful one.
(iii) It takes a shorter time to execute than Lemmatisation.	(iii) Lemmatization takes a longer time to execute than stemming.
(iv) In search queries, stemming does not allow end-users to query any question.	(iv) In search queries, Lemmatization allows end-users to query any version of a base word and get relevant results.

8. Explain the steps of Text Normalisation.

Ans. The following are the steps of Text Normalisation:

a) **Sentence Segmentation:** Here, the whole corpus is divided into sentences. Each sentence is taken as different data. Hence, now the whole corpus gets reduced to sentences.

b) **Tokenization:** Here, every word, number, and special character of each sentence is considered separately for a separate token. 'Tokens' is a term used for any word or number or special character occurring in a sentence.

c) **Removing Stop words, Numbers, and Special Characters:** In this step, the unnecessary tokens are removed from the token list.

d) **Converting text to a common cause:** In this step, the whole text is converted into a similar case, preferably lower case, to ensure that the case sensitivity of the machine does not consider the same words as different due to different cases.

e) **Stemming:** In this process, the remaining words are reduced to their root words by removing the affixes of words.

f) **Lemmatisation:** In Lemmatisation, the word we get after affix removal (also known as lemma) is a meaningful one.

g) **Converting tokens into numbers:** In this step, tokens are converted into numbers by using the Bag of Words algorithm.

9. Explain the step-by-step approach to implement the bag of words algorithm.

Ans. Here is the step-by-step approach to implement bag of words algorithm:

a) **Text Normalisation:** Collect data and pre-process it

b) **Create Dictionary:** Make a list of all the unique words occurring in the corpus. (Vocabulary)

c) **Create document vectors:** For each document in the corpus, find out how many times the word from the unique list of words has occurred.

d) Create document vectors for all the documents.

11.3.11 HOTS Questions

1. Why are stopwords removed from the corpus?

Ans. Because the stopwords occur the most in any given corpus but talk very little or nothing about the context or the meaning of it, and hence, to make it easier for the computer to focus on meaningful terms, these words are removed.

2. After the stopwords removal, the whole text is converted into a similar case, preferably lower case. Why?

Ans. After the removal of stopwords, the whole text is converted into a similar case, preferably lower case. This ensures that the case sensitivity of the machine does not consider the same words as different just because of different cases.

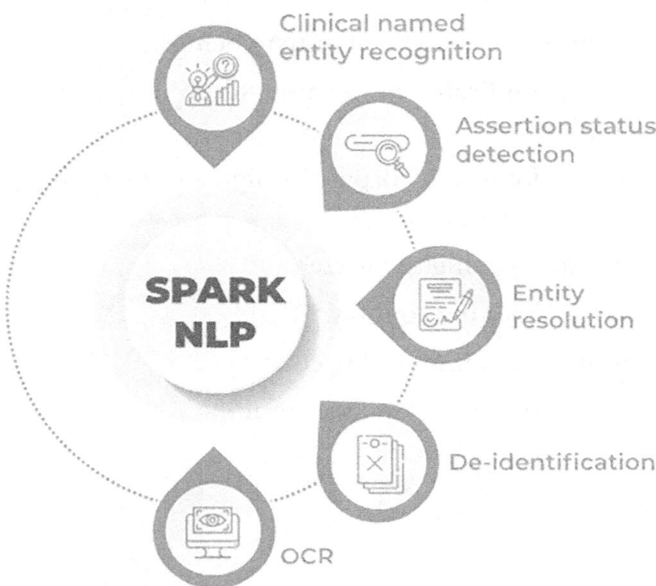

Figure 11.29

11.4 PRACTICE QUESTIONS

1. Give two examples of Chabot.

2. Define the word frequency.

3. What is inverse document frequency?

4. What are the data types used in NPL applications?

5. What is Lemmatisation?

6. What are document vectors?

7. Which package is used for NPL in Python programming?

8. What do you mean by a document vector table?

9. Write four applications of Natural Language Processing.

10. Mention any three differences between a script-bot and a smart-bot.

11. Whether the vocabulary of a corpus remains the same before and after text normalization and why?

12. Give an example of each: Multiple meanings of a word, and Perfect Syntax, no meaning.

13. Explain the relationship between the occurrence and value of a word.

14. Define and illustrate stopwords.

15. Define TFIDF? Mention its formula too.

16. What is the importance of converting the text into a common cause?

17. Which type of words in a corpus has the highest values, and which ones have the least?

18. Why is the text normalization in NLP needed?

19. Mention three applications of TFIDF.

20. Explain the role of sentiment analysis of human beings.

21. Human languages are complicated for a computer to understand. Justify the statement by giving suitable examples.

22. Calculate TFIDF for the following corpus through a step-by-step process and mention the word(s) having the highest value.

    Document 1: Team India is going to Switzerland.

    Document 2: Switzerland is a big country.

    Document 3: Team India is going to a big country.

    Document 4: Team India is famous in Switzerland.

UNIT 12

Evaluation

12.1 UNIT IN BRIEF

+ Prediction and Reality are the two essential parameters that are considered for the Evaluation of an AI model.

+ "Prediction" is the output that is given by the machine.

+ Models using the training dataset during testing will always result in correct output. This is called Overfitting.

+ "Reality" is the real scenario when the Prediction is made.

+ Confusion Matrix is a table used to describe the performance of a classification model.

+ An Overfitted Model is a statistical model containing more parameters than those that can be justified by the data.

+ Models using the training dataset during testing will always result in correct output. This is known as Overfitting.

+ Accuracy is defined as the ratio of correct predictions out of all the labels/observations.

+ A prediction is said to be correct when it matches Reality.

+ Precision is defined as the ratio of true positive cases out of all the cases where the Prediction is true.

+ Recall is defined as the ratio of positive cases that are correctly identified.

+ F1 Score maintains a balance between the 'Precision' and 'Recall' for the classifier.

+ When the Precision is low, then the F1 is low, and when the Recall is low again, then the F1 Score is low.

+ An F1 Score is a number between 0 and 1.

+ F1 Score is the harmonic mean of Precision and Recall.

+ When F1=1, it is known as the perfect value for the F1 Score.

+ F1 Score is the weighted average of Precision and Recall.

+ F1 Score is a single score that balances the concerns of Precision and Recall in one number.

+ Evaluation of the performance of an AI classification model is based on the counts of test records correctly and incorrectly predicted by the model.

+ All AI Models that use the training dataset during testing will always result in correct output. This is termed Overfitting.

+ Model Evaluation is considered an integral part of the model development process.

+ The stage of testing the models is called Model Evaluation.
+ Evaluation refers to the process of understanding the reliability of any AI model, which is based on outputs by feeding the testing dataset into the model and comparing it with actual answers.
+ The four elements of the matrix represent the four metrics that count the number of correct and incorrect predictions made by the model.
+ Each element in Prediction is given a label that consists of two words: Positive and Negative.
+ Each element in Reality is given a label that consists of two words: True and False.
+ The process of critically examining a program that involves collecting and analyzing information about a program's characteristics, activities, and outcomes is called Evaluation.
+ The Recall is the probability that a randomly retrieved relevant document is retrieved.
+ The target variable mayhas two values: Positive or Negative.
+ In the Confusion Matrix, the columns represent the actual values of the target variable.
+ Accuracy is the ratio of the number of correct predictions to the total number of predictions.
+ Accuracy percentage is defined as the percentage of correct predictions out of all the observations.
+ Accuracy is not always taken as the right method to measure the success of an AI model.

Figure 12.1

12.2 CBSE/NCERT SECTION (SOLVED CBSE/NCERT EXERCISE QUESTIONS)

(A) VSA (One Mark Questions)

1. Define Evaluation.

Ans. Before deploying the model in the real world, it is tested in as many ways as possible. The stage of testing the model is known as Evaluation.

2. Which two parameters are considered for the Evaluation of a model?

Ans. Prediction and Reality are the two parameters that are considered necessary for the Evaluation of a model. The "Prediction" is the output that is given by the machine, and the "Reality" is the real scenario when the Prediction was made.

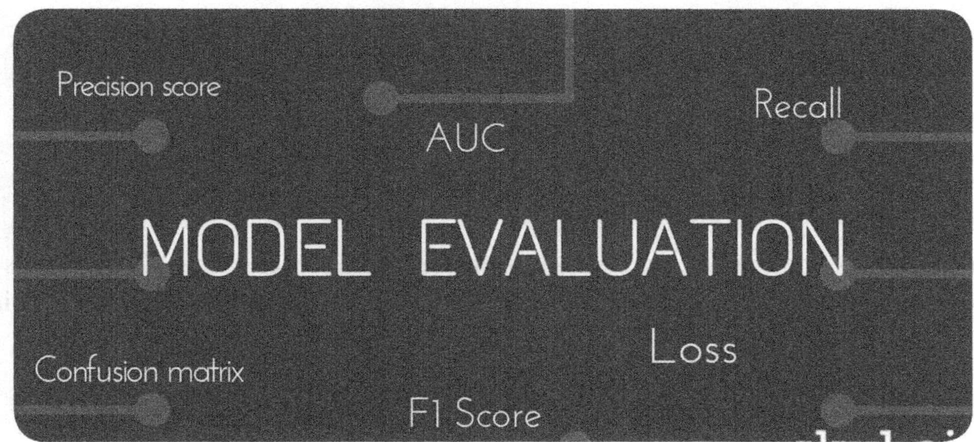

Figure 12.2

3. What is True Positive?

Ans. When the predicted value matches the actual value, it is called True Positive (TP). In this case, the actual value was positive, and the model predicted a positive value.

4. What is True Negative?

Ans. When the predicted value matches the actual value, it is called True Negative. In this case, the actual value was negative, and the model predicted a negative value.

5. What is False Positive?

Ans. When the predicted value is falsely predicted, it is called False Positive (FP). In this case, the actual value was negative, but the model predicted a positive value. It is also known as the Type 1 error.

6. What is a False Negative?

Ans. When the predicted value is falsely predicted, it is called False Negative (FN). In this case, the actual value was positive, but the model predicted a negative value. It is also known as the Type 2 error.

(B) SAQs (Two Mark Questions)

1. What is meant by Overfitting Data?

Ans. Overfitting refers to "the production of an analysis that corresponds too closely or exactly to any particular set of data, and may fail to fit additional data or predict future observations reliably."

2. What is Accuracy? Mention its formula.

Ans. Accuracy is defined as the ratio of correct predictions out of all the observations. A prediction is called correct when it matches Reality. Now, there may be two conditions where the Prediction matches with the Reality, i.e., True Positive and True Negative.

Therefore, the Formula for Accuracy is:

Accuracy = (TP+TN) / (TP+TN+FP+FN)

Where, TP = True Positives,

TN = True Negatives,

FP = False Positives, and

FN = False Negatives.

3. What is Precision? Mention its formula.

Ans. Precision is defined as the percentage of true positive cases versus all the cases where the Prediction is true. That is, it takes into account the True Positives and False Positives.

Precision= TP/ (TP+FP)

4. What is Recall? Mention its formula.

Ans. Recall is defined as the fraction of positive cases that are correctly identified.

Recall= TP/ (TP+FN)

5. Why is Evaluation important? Explain.

Ans. Importance of Evaluation: Evaluation is a process that critically examines a program.

a) It involves collecting and analysing information about a program's activities, characteristics, and outcomes.

b) Its purpose is to make judgments about a program, to improve its effectiveness, and/or to inform programming decisions.

c) Evaluation is important to ensure that the model is operating correctly and optimally.

d) Evaluation is an initiative to understand how well it achieves its goals.

e) Evaluations help to determine what works well and what could be improved in a program.

6. How do you suggest which evaluation metric is more important for any case?

Ans. F 1 Score is an Evaluation metric that is more important in any case. F1 Score maintains a balance between the Precision and Recall for the classifier. When the Precision is low, then F1 is low, and if the Recall is low again, the F1 Score is low. The F1 Score is a number between 0 and 1 and is the harmonic mean of Precision and recall.

F1 Score = 2 * (Precision*Recall) / (Precision + Recall)

When we have a value of 1 (that is 100%) for both Precision and Recall, then F1 Score would also be an ideal 1 (100%). It is known as the perfect value for the F1 Score. Because the values of both Precision and Recall ranges from 0 to 1; hence the F1 Score also ranges from 0 to 1.

7. Which evaluation metric would be crucial in the following cases? Justify your answer.

a. Mail Spamming   b. Gold Mining   c. Viral Outbreak

Ans. Out of the three cases, Mail Spamming and Gold Mining are related to False Positive cases, which are expensive. But Viral Outbreak is a False Negative case that infects a lot of people and leads to expenditure of money too for check-ups and medication. Hence, False Negative cases (Viral Outbreaks) are more crucial and dangerous when compared to False Positive cases.

b. A model stating that there exists treasure at a particular point, and the user keeps on digging that point, but it turns out that it is a false alarm. False Positive case is very costly as predicting that there is a treasure, but there is no treasure.

c. A deadly virus has started spreading, and the model that is supposed to predict a viral outbreak does not detect it. The virus might spread widely and infect a lot of people. Here, False Negative can become dangerous.

8. What are the possible reasons for an AI model not being efficient? Explain.

Ans. The following are the reasons for an AI model not being efficient:

a) **Unauthenticated Data / Wrong Data:** If the data is not authenticated and correct, then the model will not give good results.

b) **Lack of Training Data:** When the data is not sufficient for developing an AI Model, or when the data is missed while training the model, it will not be efficient.

c) **Not Easy:** If it is not easy to be implemented in production or scalable.

d) **Inefficient coding / Wrong Algorithms:** If the written algorithms are not correct and relevant, the model will not give the desired output.

e) **Not Tested:** When the model is not tested properly, then it will not be efficient.

f) **Less Accuracy:** A model will not be efficient when it gives fewer accuracy scores in production/test data or if it is not able to generalise well on unseen data.

9. Answer the following:
a. Give an example where High Accuracy is not usable.
b. Give an example where High Precision is not usable.

Ans. a) An example when High Accuracy is not usable:

Consider this case: An expensive robotic car toy crosses a very busy road two thousand times per day. An ML model evaluates traffic patterns and predicts when this toy can safely cross the road with an accuracy of 99.89%.

Explanation: A 99.89% accuracy value on a very busy road strongly shows that the ML model is far better than chance. But, in some settings, the cost of making even a small number of mistakes is still too high. 99.89% accuracy means that the expensive car toy may need to be replaced after every 3 days. The cost of damage to other vehicles due to accidents may also be added.

b) An example where High Precision is not usable:

Consider this case: "Predicting email as Spam or Not Spam."

False Positive: Email is predicted as "spam," but it is "not spam."

False Negative: Email is predicted as "not spam," but it is "spam."

Of course, so many False Negatives will make the spam filter ineffective, but False Positives may cause important emails to be missed, and hence Precision is not usable.

(C) LAQs (Four Mark Questions)

1. Deduce the formula of F1 Score? What is the need for its formulation?

Ans. The F1 Score, also called the F score or F measure is a measure of a test's accuracy. It is calculated from the Precision and Recall of the test, where the Precision is the number of correctly identified positive results divided by the number of all positive results, including those not identified correctly, and the Recall is the number of correctly identified positive results divided by the number of all samples that should have been identified as positive. The F1 Score is defined as the weighted harmonic mean of the test's Precision and Recall. This Score is calculated according to the formula.

$$\textbf{F1 = 2*(Precision*Recall) / (Precision+Recall)}$$

$$\textbf{F1 = 2*TP / (2TP+FP+FN)}$$

Necessary: F-1 Score provides a single score that balances both the concerns of Precision and Recall in one number. A good F1 score means that you have low false positives and low false negatives, so you're correctly identifying real threats, and you are not disturbed by false alarms. An F1 score is considered perfect when it's 1, while the model is a total failure when it's 0. F1 Score is a better metric to evaluate our model on real-life classification problems and when imbalanced class distribution exists.

2. What is a confusion matrix? Explain in detail with the help of an example.

Ans. **Confusion Matrix:** Confusion Matrix is a 2x2 table used to describe the performance of an AI classification model /classifier on a set of testing data. This matrix is called the Confusion Matrix. Evaluation of the performance of an AI classification model is based on the counts of test records correctly and incorrectly as predicted by the model. Therefore, the confusion matrix is useful for measuring Recall (also known as Sensitivity), Accuracy, Precision, and F1 Score.

The following confusion matrix table for calculation of the 4-classification metrics (TP, TN, FN, TN) and to predict value compared to the actual value in a confusion matrix:

The Confusion Matrix		Reality	
		Yes	No
Prediction	Yes	True Positive (TP)	False Positive (FP)
	No	False Negative (FN)	True Negative (TN)

Figure 12.3

The features of the confusion matrix are as below:

- The target variable may have two values: Positive or Negative.
- The rows represent the predicted values for the target variable.
- The columns represent the actual values of the target variable.
- True Positive, True Negative, False Positive, and False Negative are in a Confusion Matrix.
    a) **True Positive (TP):** When the predicted value matches the actual value, it is called True Positive. The actual value was positive, and the model predicted a positive value.

b) **True Negative (TN):** When the predicted value matches the actual negative value, then it is called True Negative. The actual value was negative, and the model also predicted a negative value.

c) **False Positive (FP):** When the predicted value was falsely predicted, then it is called False Positive. Thus, the actual value was negative, but the model predicted a positive value. This is also known as the Type 1 error.

d) **False Negative (FN):** When the predicted value was falsely predicted, then it is called False Negative. Thus, the actual value was positive, but the model predicted a negative value. This is also known as the Type 2 error.

Example: Case of Loan given by banks (Good loan & Bad loan)

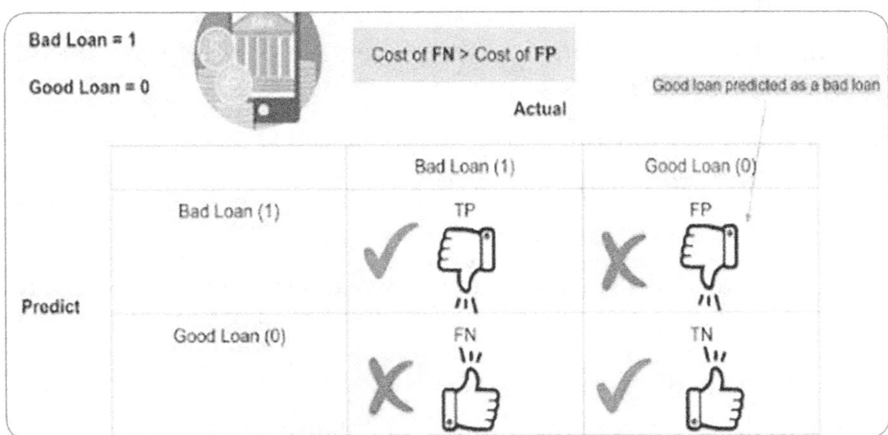

Figure 12.4

▲ Here, the result of TP will be that bad loans are correctly predicted as bad loans.

▲ While the value of TN will be that good loans are correctly predicted as good loans.

▲ The value of FP will be that (actual) good loans are incorrectly predicted as bad loans.

▲ The value of FN will be that (actual) bad loans are incorrectly predicted as good loans.

Therefore, the bank will lose a bunch of money when the actual bad loans are predicted as good loans because loans are not being repaid. On the other hand, banks won't be capable of making more revenue when the actual good loans are predicted as bad loans. Thus, in this case, the cost of False Negatives is much higher than the cost of False Positives(FN).

3. Calculate Accuracy, Precision, Recall, and F1 Score for the following Confusion Matrix on Heart Attack Risk. Also, suggest which Metric would not be a good evaluation parameter here and why?

The Confusion Matrix	Reality: 1	Reality: 0
Prediction: 1	50	20
Prediction: 0	10	20

The Confusion Matrix	Reality: 1	Reality: 0	
Prediction: 1	50	20	70
Prediction: 0	10	20	30
	60	40	100

Figure 12.5

Ans.   Calculations are as follows:

Here, TP=50, FP=20, FN=10, TN= 20

(a) **Accuracy:** Accuracy is defined as the percentage of correct predictions out of all the observations

Accuracy = (TP+TN) / (TP+TN+FP+FN)

Where TP=True Positive, TN=True Negative, FP= False Positive, and FN=False Negative

Accuracy = (50+20) / (50+20+20+10)

$$= (70/100)$$

$$= 0.7$$

(b) **Precision:** Precision is defined as the percentage of true positive cases versus all the cases where the prediction is true.

Precision = TP / (TP+FP)

$$= (50 / (50 + 20))$$

$$= (50/70) = 0.714$$

(c) **Recall:** It is defined as the fraction of positive cases that are correctly identified.

Recall = TP / (TP+FN)

$$= 50 / (50 + 10) = 50 / 60 = 0.83$$

(d) **F1 Score:** F1 score refers to the measure of balance between precision and recall.

F1 = 2* (Precision*Recall) / (Precision + Recall)

F1= 2 * (0.71 *0.83) / (0.714 + 0.83)

$$= 2 * (0.59 / 1.54)$$

$$=1.18/1.54 = 0.77$$

Therefore,

Accuracy= 0.7

Precision=0.714

Recall=0.83

F1 Score=0.77

Here, within the test, there is a tradeoff. Recall is not a good Evaluation metric. Recall metric needs to be improved more.

False Positive (impacts precision): When a person is predicted as high risk but has a low risk of heart.

False Negative (impacts Recall): A person is predicted as low risk but has a high risk of a heart attack. Thus, False Negatives miss actual heart patients; hence recall metrics need more improvement because False Negatives (FN) are more dangerous than False Positives (FP).

4. Calculate Accuracy, Recall, Precision, and F1 Score for the following Confusion Matrix on Water Shortage in Schools. Also, suggest which Metric would not be a good evaluation parameter in this case and why?

The Confusion Matrix (Water Shortage in School)	Reality: 1	Reality: 0
Prediction: 1	75	5
Prediction: 0	5	15

	Reality: 1	Reality: 0	
Prediction: 1	75	5	80
Prediction: 0	5	15	20
	80	20	100

Figure 12.6

Ans. Calculations are as follows:

Here, TP=75, FP=5, FN=5, TN=15

(a) **Accuracy:** Accuracy is defined as the ratio of correct predictions to all the predictions/ observations.

Accuracy = (TP+TN) / (TP+TN+FP+FN)

Where TP=True Positive, TN=True Negative, FP= False Positive, and FN=False Negative

Accuracy = (75+15) / (75+15+5+5)

= (90 / 100)

= 0.9

(b) **Precision:** Precision is defined as the percentage of true positive cases versus all the cases where the prediction is true.

Precision = TP / (TP+FP)

Precision = 75 / (75+5)

= 75 /80 = 0.9375

(c) **Recall:** It is defined as the fraction of positive cases that are correctly identified.

Recall = TP / (TP+FN)

= 75 / (75+5)

= 75 /80 = 0.9375

(d) **F1 Score:** F1 score refers to the measure to balance between precision and recall.

F1 = 2* (Precision*Recall) / (Precision +Recall)

= 2 * ((0.9375 *0.9375) / (0.9375+0.9375)

= 2 * (0.8789 / 1.875)

= 2 * 0.46875 = 0.9375

Therefore,

Accuracy= 0.9

Precision=0.9375

Recall=0.9375

F1 Score=0.937

Here, Precision, Recall, accuracy, F1 Score- all are same.

5. Calculate Accuracy, Precision, Recall, and F1 Score for the following Confusion Matrix on Spam Filtering. Also, suggest which Evaluation Metric would not be a good evaluation parameter here and why?

Confusion Matrix on SPAM SPAM Filtering:	Reality: 1	Reality: 0
Prediction: 1	10	55
Prediction: 0	10	25

Confusion Matrix on SPAM SPAM Filtering:	Reality: 1	Reality: 0	
Prediction: 1	10	55	65
Prediction: 0	10	25	35
	20	80	100

Figure 12.7

Ans. (a) **Accuracy:** Accuracy is defined as the ratio of correct predictions to all the observations.

Accuracy = (TP+TN) / (TP+TN+FP+FN)

Where TP=True Positive, TN=True Negative, FP= False Positive, and FN=False Negative

Accuracy = (10 + 25) / (10+25+55+10)

= 35 / 100 = 0.35

(b) **Precision:** Precision is defined as the percentage of true positive cases versus all the cases where the prediction is true.

Precision = TP / (TP+FP)

= 10 / (10 +55)

= 10 /65 = 0.15

(c) **Recall:** It is defined as the fraction of positive cases that are correctly identified to the total positive cases.

Recall = TP / (TP+FN)

= 10 / (10 + 10)

= 10 / 20 = 0.5

(d) **F1 Score:** F1 score refers to the measure of balance between precision and recall and it is harmonic mean of Precision and Recall.

F1 = 2* (Precision*Recall) / (Precision + Recall)

$$F1 = 2 * ((0.15 * 0.5) / (0.15 + 0.5))$$
$$= 2 * (0.075 / 0.65)$$
$$= 2 * 0.115 = 0.23$$

Therefore,

Accuracy = 0.35,

Precision = 0.15,

Recall = 0.5,

F1 Score = 0.23

Here, within the test, there is a tradeoff. Recall and Precision metric needs to be improved more.

False Positive (impacts Precision): Email is predicted as "spam," but it is not.

False Negative (impacts Recall): Email is predicted as "not spam," but it is spam.

Thus, so many False Negatives will make the Spam Filter ineffective. But False Positives may cause important emails to be missed. Hence, Precision is more important to improve.

12.3 SOLVED EXERCISES

12.3.1 Multiple Choice Questions

Tick (√) the correct option.

1. The process of understanding the reliability of an AI model, which is based on outputs by feeding the testing dataset into the model and comparing it with actual answers, is known as:

   a) Evaluation
   b) Overfitting
   c) Modelling
   d) Confusion matrix

2. The process of production of an analysis that corresponds too closely or exactly to a particular set of data, and may thus fail to fit additional data or predict future observations reliably, is known as:

   a) Evaluation
   b) Modelling
   c) Overfitting
   d) None of these

3. Which parameter reflects how reliable the model is in classifying samples as Positive?

   a) Accuracy
   b) F1 Score
   c) Precision
   d) Recall

4. Which is a metric that describes how the model performs across all classes?

   a) Accuracy
   b) F1 Score
   c) Precision
   d) Misclassification

5. Which statement is NOT TRUE?

   a) In binary classification, Recall is called Sensitivity.

   b) The Recall is defined as the ratio between the number of Positive samples correctly classified as Positive by the model to the total number of Positive samples.
   c) Precision is defined as the ratio between the number of Positive samples correctly classified to the total number of samples classified as Negative (either correctly or incorrectly).
   d) In information retrieval, Recall is the fraction of the relevant documents to the total documents that are successfully retrieved.

6. Which of the following statements is correct?
   a) When a model has a low recall but high Precision, then the model classifies most of the positive samples correctly.
   b) If a model has high Precision and high Recall, then the model is accurate.
   c) The Precision measures the model's trustiness in classifying positive samples, and the Recall measures how many positive samples were correctly classified as positive by the model.
   d) All the above

7. Models using the training dataset during testing will always result in incorrect output. This is called:
   a) Overfitting   b) Over lifting   c) Evaluation   d) Recall

8. Which statement is NOT TRUE?
   a) Recall cares about correctly classifying all positive samples, while it does not care if a negative sample is classified as positive.
   b) F1 Score refers to the measure of the balance between Precision and Accuracy.
   c) 'Precision' is dependent on both the negative and positive predictions, whereas 'Recall' is dependent only on the positive predictions.
   d) Accuracy works best when false positives and false negatives have almost similar costs.

9. Which are the two parameters that are considered for the Evaluation of a model?
   a) Prediction and Overfitting   b) Prediction and Reality
   c) Reality and Precision   d) None of them

10. F1 Score is the harmonic mean of:
   a) Recall and Accuracy   b) Recall and Precision
   c) Accuracy and Precision   d) None of the above

11. For which value of the F1 Score will the model be a total failure?
   a) 0   b) -1   c) 1   d) 4

12. What is the correct formula for the F1 Score?
   a) F1 = (2*Recall *Accuracy)/(Recall+ Accuracy)
   b) F1 = (Recall *Precision)/ (2Recall+ Precision)
   c) F1 = (2*Recall *Precision)/(Recall+ Precision)
   d) F1 = (2*Accuracy *Precision)/(Accuracy+ Precision)

13. What is the size of the confusion matrix?
   a) 3x4   b) 3x3   c) 2x2   d) 2x3

14. What is the range of the F1 Score?

    a) -1 to 0   b) 0 to +1   c) -1 to +1   d) -1 to +2

15. On which values F1 Score is dependent?

    a) Accuracy and Precision   b) Accuracy and Recall
    c) Precision and Recall   d) Accuracy, Precision, and Recall

16. Which of the following defines the ratio of the number of Positive samples correctly classified as Positive to the total number of Positive samples?

    a) Accuracy   b) Recall   c) F1 Score   d) Precision

17. What is the stage of the project cycle in which the AI model is evaluated?

    a) 2nd stage   b) 3rd stage   c) 4th stage   d) 5th stage

18. Which of the following statements is Incorrect?

    a) The 'Prediction' is the output that is given by the machine.
    b) The F1 Score is the harmonic mean of Precision and Recall.
    c) An Overfitted Model is a statistical model which contains more parameters than can be justified by the data.
    d) Precision is defined as the ratio of true positive cases and all the cases where the Prediction is false.

19. What is the term used for (1-Accuracy)?

    a) Accuracy   b) F1 Score   c) Misclassification   d) Recall

20. Study the following statements about the Evaluation to choose the true statements.
    i.   It is used to improve the effectiveness of the program.
    ii. It also informs about programming decisions.
    iii. It is used to ensure that the model is operating correctly and optimally.
    iv. It is an initiative to understand how well the program achieves its goals.

    a) (i) & (ii)   b) (i) & (iii)
    c) (ii), (iii) & (iv)   d) (i) (ii) (iii) & (iv)

21. Which term is used for a table that is often used to describe the performance of a classification model?

    a) Confusion Matrix   b) Histogram
    c) F1 Score   d) All of the above

22. Which of the following features of the confusion matrix is INCORRECT?

    a) Prediction and Reality are easily mapped together with the help of the confusion matrix.
    b) The column labels "True Positive" and " True Negative" refer to the ground reality labels in the data set.
    c) The entries inside of a confusion matrix (TPs, FPs, FNs, TNs) are exhibited in the form of Yes/No.
    d) The row labels "False Positive" and "False Negative" refer to the model's predictions, i.e., what the model thinks the label is.

23. Which of the formulae is correct?
    a) Accuracy= (TP+TN)/Total labels(samples)
    b) Misclassification= (1-Accuracy)
    c) Precision= TP/(TP+FP)
    d) Recall/ Sensitivity/TPR= TP/(TP-+FN)

24. _____________ is also known as Type 2 error.
    a) TP   b) TN   c) FP   d) FN

25. Which of the following statements is TRUE?
    a) Prediction and Reality are the two parameters to be considered for the Evaluation of a model.
    b) 'A statistical model that contains more parameters than can be justified by the data is called an overfitted model.'
    c) Evaluation helps to determine what works well and what could be improved in a program.
    d) All the above

26. The predicted value matches the actual value. When the actual value was negative, and the model predicted a negative value, then it is:
    a) TP   b) TN   c) FP   d) FN

27. _____________ is also known as Type 1 error.
    a) TP   b) TN   c) FP   d) FN

28. Which of the following statements is INCORRECT?
    a) Prediction and Reality may be easily mapped together with the help of this confusion matrix.
    b) The confusion matrix is a 2x3 matrix denoting the right and wrong predictions, and it is helpful to analyze the rate of success.
    c) For a model to perform well, the values of TPR and TNR should be high, and those of FPR and FNR should go low.
    d) F1 Score is the harmonic mean of Recall and Precision.

29. What can be calculated from a confusion matrix?
    a) Accuracy and Precision   b) Recall and F1 Score
    c) Both a and b   d) None of the above

30. The predicted value was falsely predicted. In other words, the actual value was positive, but the model predicted a negative value. It is:
    a) Type 1 error   b) Type 2 error   c) Type 3 error   d) Zero error

31. The result of the comparison between the Prediction and Reality can be recorded in a table which is known as:
    a) Prediction Table   b) Bag of words
    c) Confusion matrix   d) None of the above

32. What can be predicted with the help of a confusion matrix?
    a) Prediction
    b) Prediction and Reality
    c) Reality
    d) None of the above

33. For a model to perform well, which values should be high?
    a) TPR
    b) TNR
    c) FPR and FNR
    d) TPR and TNR

34. The ratio of 'Correct predictions' to the 'Total cases or samples' is called:
    a) Accuracy
    b) F1 Score
    c) Precision
    d) Misclassification

Figure 12.8

ANSWERS									
1. (a)	2. (c)	3. (c)	4. (a)	5. (c)	6. (d)	7. (a)	8. (c)	9. (b)	10. (b)
11. (c)	12. (a)	13. (c)	14. (b)	15. (c)	16. (b)	17. (d)	18. (d)	19. (c)	20. (d)
21. (a)	22. (c)	23. (b)	24. (d)	25. (d)	26. (b)	27. (c)	28. (b)	29. (c)	30. (b)
31. (c)	32. (b)	33. (d)	34. (a)						

12.3.2 Fill in the blanks

1. _____________ is defined as the ratio of the number of correct predictions to the total number of predictions.

2. _____________ is defined as the fraction of positive cases that are correctly identified.

3. F1 Score is the weighted average of _____________ and Recall.

4. An _____________ Model is a statistical model containing more parameters than can be justified by the data.

5. _____________ is defined as the process of understanding the reliability of any AI model, which is based on outputs by feeding the testing dataset into the model and comparing it with actual answers.

6. The F1 Score is the harmonic mean of Precision and _____________.

7. Each element in Prediction is given a label that consists of two words: _____________ and _____________.

8. _____________ refers to a balance between the Precision and Recall for the classifier.

9. The F1 Score ranges between zero and _____________.

10. Each element in Reality is given a label that consists of two words: _____________ and _____________.

11. When a model has high Recall and _____________ Precision, then the model classifies most of the positive samples correctly.

12. A Prediction is said to be correct when it matches _____________.

13. F1 Score maintains a balance between the Precision and Recall for the _____________.

14. _____________ is not always taken as the right method to measure the success of an AI model.

15. _____________ is defined as the ratio of true positive cases out of all the cases where the Prediction is true.

ANSWERS			
1. Accuracy	2. Recall	3. Precision	4. Overfitted
5. Evaluation	6. Recall	7. Positive, Negative	8. F1 score
9. one	10. True, False	11. low	12. Reality
13. classifier	14. Accuracy	15. Precision	

12.3.3 True or False

1. F1 Score is defined as the arithmetic mean of Recall and Precision.

2. Prediction and Reality are the two parameters to be considered necessary for the Evaluation of a model.

3. The columns in a confusion matrix represent the actual values of the target variable.

4. The four elements of the matrix represent the four metrics that count the number of correct and incorrect predictions made by the model.

5. F1 Score is a single score that balances the concerns of Precision and recall in one number.

6. When the Precision is low, the F1 is low, and if the Recall is high, the F1 Score is low.

7. Evaluation of the performance of an AI classification model is based on the counts of test records predicted (correctly and incorrectly) by the model.

8. When F1 Score =0, then it is known as the perfect value for F1 Score.

9. A prediction is said to be correct when it does not match Reality.

10. All AI Models that use the training dataset during testing will always result in correct output. This is termed Overfitting.

11. Model Evaluation is considered an integral part of the model development process.

12. The process of critically examining a program that involves collecting and analyzing information about a program's characteristics, activities, and outcomes is called Evaluation.

13. Accuracy percentage is defined as the percentage of correct predictions out of all the observations multiplied by 100.

14. The 'Reality is the real scenario when the Prediction has been made?

15. Precision is defined as the ratio of true positive cases out of all the cases where the prediction is not true.

<table>
<tr><td colspan="8" align="center">ANSWERS</td></tr>
<tr><td>1. F (harmonic mean)</td><td>2. T</td><td>3. T</td><td>4. T.</td><td>5. T</td><td>6. F (recall is low)</td><td>7. T</td></tr>
<tr><td>8. F (F1 score=1) 9. F (matches)</td><td>10. T</td><td>11. T</td><td>12. T</td><td>13. T</td><td>14. T</td><td>15. F</td></tr>
</table>

12.3.4 Matching type

Match the items of column A and Column B to complete the formulae.

Column A	**Column B**
i. Precision=	(a) (2*Recall Precision)/(Recall+ Precision)
ii. Accuracy=	(b) (TN+TP)/Total cases
iii. Recall=	(c) TP/TP+FP
iv. F1 =	(d) TP/TP+FN

<table>
<tr><td colspan="4" align="center">ANSWERS</td></tr>
<tr><td>(i) -c</td><td>(ii) -b</td><td>(iii) -d</td><td>(iv) -a</td></tr>
</table>

12.3.5 Assertion Reason Based Questions

1. Assertion (A): F1Score is more important than accuracy.

   Reason (R): F1 is usually more useful than accuracy, especially when we have an uneven class distribution.
   a) Both A and R are correct and R is the correct reason for A.
   b) Both A and R are correct and R is not the correct reason for A.
   c) A is correct but R is incorrect.
   d) A is incorrect but R is correct.

2. Assertion (A): A prediction is said to be correct when it matches reality.

   Reason (R): Precision is defined as the ratio of true positive cases out of all the cases where the Prediction is true.
   a) Both A and R are correct and R is the correct reason for A.
   b) Both A and R are correct and R is not the correct reason for A.
   c) A is correct but R is incorrect.
   d) A is incorrect but R is correct.

3. Assertion (A): When F1=0, it is known as the perfect value for the F1 Score.

   Reason (R): F1 Score is the harmonic mean of Precision and Recall.
   a) Both A and R are correct and R is the correct reason for A.
   b) Both A and R are correct and R is not the correct reason for A.
   c) A is correct but R is incorrect.
   d) A is incorrect but R is correct.

4. Assertion (A): The stage of testing the models is called Model Evaluation.

   Reason (R): Segmentation refers to the process of understanding the reliability of any AI model, which is based on outputs by feeding the testing dataset into the model and comparing it with actual answers.

   a) Both A and R are correct and R is the correct reason for A.

   b) Both A and R are correct and R is not the correct reason for A.

   c) A is correct but R is incorrect.

   d) A is incorrect but R is correct.

5. Assertion (A): The maximum value of the F1 Score is +2.0

   Reason (R): The lowest value of F1 score may be zero.

   a) Both A and R are correct and R is the correct reason for A.

   b) Both A and R are correct and R is not the correct reason for A.

   c) A is correct but R is incorrect.

   d) A is incorrect but R is correct.

6. Assertion (A): In the Confusion Matrix, the columns represent the actual values of the target variable.

   Reason (R): Accuracy is the ratio of the number of correct predictions to the total number of predictions.

   a) Both A and R are correct and R is the correct reason for A.

   b) Both A and R are correct and R is not the correct reason for A.

   c) A is correct but R is incorrect.

   d) A is incorrect but R is correct.

7. Assertion (A): Precision = TP/(TP-FP)

   Reason (R): Recall = TP/(TP-FN)

   a) Both A and R are correct and R is the correct reason for A.

   b) Both A and R are correct and R is not the correct reason for A.

   c) A is correct but R is incorrect.

   d) A is incorrect but R is correct.

8. Assertion (A): Recall is one of the parameters for evaluating the model's performance.

   Reason (R): In binary classification, Recall is called Sensitivity.

   a) Both A and R are correct and R is the correct reason for A.

   b) Both A and R are correct and R is not the correct reason for A.

   c) A is correct but R is incorrect.

   d) A is incorrect but R is correct.

9. Assertion (A): F1 Score is the harmonic mean of Precision and Recall.

   Reason (R): F1 Score is a single score that balances the concerns of Precision and Recall in one number.

   a) Both A and R are correct and R is the correct reason for A.

   b) Both A and R are correct and R is not the correct reason for A.

   c) A is correct but R is incorrect.

   d) A is incorrect but R is correct.

10. Assertion (A): Accuracy is useful only if all classes are given equal importance.

   Reason (R): A prediction may be said to be incorrect when it matches reality.

   a) Both A and R are correct and R is the correct reason for A.

   b) Both A and R are correct and R is not the correct reason for A.

   c) A is correct but R is incorrect.

   d) A is incorrect but R is correct.

ANSWERS									
1. (a)	2. (b)	3. (d)	4. (c)	5. (d)	6. (b)	7. (d)	8. (b)	9. (b)	10. (c)

12.3.6 Statements Based Questions

1. Statement 1: An F1 Score is a number between 0 and 1.

   Statement 2: Evaluation of the performance of an AI classification model is based on the counts of test records correctly and incorrectly predicted by the model.

   a) Statement 1 is correct but statement 2 is incorrect.

   b) Statement 1 is incorrect but statement 2 is correct.

   c) Both the statements are correct.

   d) Both the statements are incorrect

2. Statement 1: The size of the confusion matrix is a 3x3 matrix denoting the right and wrong predictions.

   Statement 2: The confusion matrix is useful for measuring Precision, Accuracy, Recall (also known as Sensitivity), and F1 Score.

   a) Statement 1 is correct but statement 2 is incorrect.

   b) Statement 1 is incorrect but statement 2 is correct.

   c) Both the statements are correct.

   d) Both the statements are incorrect

3. Statement 1: Recall is defined as the fraction of positive cases that are correctly identified of the total number of positive samples.

   Statement 2: Recall is used to measure the model's ability to detect positive samples.

   a) Statement 1 is correct but statement 2 is incorrect.

   b) Statement 1 is incorrect but statement 2 is correct.

   c) Both the statements are correct.

   d) Both the statements are incorrect

4. Statement 1: Precision is used for such a task when it is really important to avoid false positives.

   Statement 2: The lower value of Recall represents that the more positive samples are detected.

   a) Statement 1 is correct but statement 2 is incorrect.

   b) Statement 1 is incorrect but statement 2 is correct.

   c) Both the statements are correct.

   d) Both the statements are incorrect

5. Statement 1: When the predicted value was falsely predicted, it is called False Positive.

   Statement 2: In information retrieval, Recall is the fraction of the relevant documents to the total documents that are successfully retrieved.

   a) Statement 1 is correct but statement 2 is incorrect.

   b) Statement 1 is incorrect but statement 2 is correct.

   c) Both the statements are correct.

   d) Both the statements are incorrect

6. Statement 1: Accuracy is always taken as the right method to measure the success of an AI model.

   Statement 2: The confusion matrix is also called the 'Error-free matrix.'

   a) Statement 1 is correct but statement 2 is incorrect.

   b) Statement 1 is incorrect but statement 2 is correct.

   c) Both the statements are correct.

   d) Both the statements are incorrect.

7. Statement 1: Each element in Prediction is given a label that consists of two words: Positive and Negative.

   Statement 2: The Recall is the probability that a randomly retrieved relevant document is retrieved.

   a) Statement 1 is correct but statement 2 is incorrect.

   b) Statement 1 is incorrect but statement 2 is correct.

   c) Both the statements are correct.

   d) Both the statements are incorrect

8. Statement 1: The other name given for False Negative is Type 1 error

   Statement 2: The other name given for False Positive is Type 2 error

   a) Statement 1 is correct but statement 2 is incorrect.

   b) Statement 1 is incorrect but statement 2 is correct.

   c) Both the statements are correct.

   d) Both the statements are incorrect

9. Statement 1: The "Reality" is the real scenario when the Prediction is made.

   Statement 2: Confusion Matrix is a table used to describe the performance of a classification model.

   a) Statement 1 is correct but statement 2 is incorrect.

   b) Statement 1 is incorrect but statement 2 is correct.

   c) Both the statements are correct.

   d) Both the statements are incorrect

10. Statement 1: The model is a total failure when the F1 Score is 0.

   Statement 2: The formula for F1 Score is F1 score=(3*Recall* Precision)/(Recall+ Precision)

a)   Statement 1 is correct but statement 2 is incorrect.

b)   Statement 1 is incorrect but statement 2 is correct.

c)   Both the statements are correct.

d)   Both the statements are incorrect

ANSWERS									
1. (c)	2. (b)	3. (c)	4. (a)	5. (b)	6. (d)	7. (c)	8. (d)	9. (c)	10. (a)

12.3.7 Competency-Based Questions

1.   Shikhar Saikia owns an AI firm called **Antriksh AI Solutions** involved in developing programs for providing AI solutions to the problems of the clients. Before handing over the program to the client, he uses a process of critically examining a program that involves collecting and analysing information about a program's characteristics, activities, and outcomes. This is called:

   a)   Data Acquisition

   b)   Data mining

   c)   Evaluation

   d)   Modelling

2.   Consider the following metrics:

   i.   Accuracy

   ii.   Confusion matrix

   iii.   Precision

   iv.   Recall

   v.   F1 Score

   These are called:

   a)   Assessment metrics

   b)   Classification evaluation metrics

   c)   Modelling metrices

   d)   None of the above

3.   Suppose Zeenat Ahmed developed an AI Model which was found non efficient on evaluation. Which of the following reasons may be responsible for its non-efficiency?

   a)   Lack of Training Data, and Not Tested

   b)   Inefficient coding and Less Accuracy

   c)   Unauthenticated Data, and Not Easy

   d)   All of these

4.   Suppose Ishika Pushkarna uses a process that critically examines a program and involves collecting and analysing information about the program's activities, characteristics, and outcomes. The purpose of this process are as follows:

   i.   It is used to improve the effectiveness of the program.

   ii.   It also informs about programming decisions.

   iii.   It is used to ensure that the model is operating correctly and optimally.

   iv.   It is an initiative to understand how well it achieves its goals.

   The name of this process is:

   a)   Modelling

   b)   Mining

   c)   Evaluation

   d)   Prediction

5. Which of the following is used to calculate Recall, Precision, Accuracy and F1 Score?

    a) Confusion matrix   b) Evaluation Table

    c) Algorithm   d) None of the above

ANSWERS
1. (c)   2. (b)   3. (d)   4. (c)   5. (a)

12.3.8 VSA

1. **Why is the model evaluation done?**

Ans. Model evaluation is done to make judgments about a program, to improve its effectiveness, and/or to inform programming decisions.

2. **Define an overfitted model.**

Ans. A statistical model containing more parameters than can be justified by the data is called an overfitted model.

3. **Define Prediction in Evaluation.**

Ans. Prediction is the output that is given by the machine, and Reality is the real scenario in the forest when the Prediction is made.

4. **Define Reality in Evaluation.**

Ans. Reality is the real scenario when the Prediction is made.

5. **What are the two essential parameters for the Evaluation of an AI model?**

Ans. Two essential parameters for the Evaluation of a model are Prediction and Reality.

6. **Mention one important difference between Prediction and Reality.**

Ans. The "Prediction" is the output that is given by the machine, and the "Reality" is the real scenario when the Prediction is made.

7. **What is the other name given to the confusion matrix?**

Ans. The confusion matrix is also called the 'Error matrix'.

8. **What is the size of the confusion matrix?**

Ans. It is a 2x2 matrix denoting the right and wrong predictions.

9. **What can be measured by the confusion matrix?**

Ans. The confusion matrix is useful for measuring Precision, Accuracy, Recall (also known as Sensitivity), and F1 Score.

10. **Write the formula of the accuracy of an AI model.**

Ans. Accuracy= (TP+TN)/Total labels or samples

11. **How will you calculate misclassification?**

Ans. Misclassification: (FP+FN)/total labels/samples or Misclassification= (1-Accuracy)

12. **What is the formula for Precision?**

Ans. Precision= TP/(TP+FP)

13. What is the formula for Recall or Sensitivity?

Ans.   Recall/ Sensitivity/TPR= TP/(TP-+FN)

14. Write the formula for FPR or Specificity?

Ans.   False Positive Rate (FPR)/Specificity= FP/(FP+TN)

15. What is the formula used for calculating F1 Score?

Ans.   F1 score=(2*Recall Precision)/(Recall+ Precision)

16. What is the formula for accuracy percentage?

Ans.   Precision percentage is defined as the ratio of true positive cases multiplied by 100 and then divided by all the cases where the Prediction is true.

17. When is the calculation of accuracy useful?

Ans.   Accuracy is useful if all classes are given equal importance.

18. When is a prediction called to be correct?

Ans.   A prediction may be said to be correct when it matches Reality.

19. When is Precision used?

Ans.   Precision is used for such a task when it is really important to avoid false positives.

20. What is Recall?

Ans.   Recall is one of the parameters for evaluating the model's performance.

21. What is sensitivity in binary classification?

Ans.   In binary classification, Recall is called Sensitivity.

22. How will you define Recall?

Ans.   Recall is defined as the fraction of positive cases that are correctly identified of the total number of positive samples. It is defined as the ratio of the number of Positive samples correctly classified as Positive by the model to the total number of Positive samples.

23. For what purpose is Recall used?

Ans.   Recall is used to measure the model's ability to detect positive samples.

24. What is represented by the higher value of Recall?

Ans.   The higher value of Recall represents that the more positive samples are detected.

25. How will you define Recall with reference to information retrieval?

Ans.   In information retrieval, Recall is the fraction of the relevant documents to the total documents that are successfully retrieved.

26. Which parameter is taken as the measure of the balance between Precision and Recall?

Ans.   F1 Score.

27. Define F1 Score.

Ans.   F1 Score is defined as the measure of the balance between Precision and Recall.

28. When is F1Score is more important than accuracy?

Ans.   F1 is usually more useful than accuracy, especially when we have an uneven class distribution.

29. When will an AI model exhibit high performance?

Ans.   An AI model will have good performance if the F1 Score for that model is high.

30. What are the two parameters that are considered for the Evaluation of an AI model?

Ans.   Prediction and Reality.

31. What do you mean by outfitting?

Ans.   Models using the training dataset during testing will always result in incorrect output. This is called Overfitting.

32. What do you mean by 'Reality?

Ans.   The "Reality" is the real scenario for which the Prediction has been made.

33. What is a confusion matrix?

Ans.   A table used to describe the performance of a classification model is called a confusion matrix.

34. What is True Positive?

Ans.   When the predicted value matches the actual value, then it is called True Positive. When the actual value was positive, and the model also predicted a positive value, then it is True positive.

35. Define True Negative.

Ans.   When the predicted value matches the actual value, then it is called True Negative. When the actual value was negative, and the model predicted a negative value, it is called True Negative.

36. What is a False Positive?

Ans.   When the predicted value was falsely predicted, then it is called False Positive. Then the actual value was negative, but the model predicted a positive value, then it is False Positive.

37. What do you mean by False Negative?

Ans.   When the predicted value was falsely predicted, it is called False Negative. When the actual value was positive, and the model predicted a negative value, then it is False Negative.

38. Define accuracy.

Ans.   The ratio of correct predictions and the total labels/observations is called accuracy.

39. When is a prediction called to be correct?

Ans.   A prediction is called to be correct when it matches Reality.

40. What is the other name given for False Negative?

Ans.   Type 2 error

41. What is the other name given for False Positive?

Ans.   Type 1 error

42. Define Precision.

Ans. The ratio of true positive cases out of all the cases where the Prediction is true is called Precision.

43. What do you mean by Recall?

Ans. Recall is defined as the ratio of positive cases that are correctly identified.

44. What is the main function of the F1 Score?

Ans. It maintains a balance between the Precision and Recall for the classifier.

45. What happens to the F1 Score when the Precision is low?

Ans. If the Precision is low, then F1 is low.

46. What happens to the F1 Score when the Recall is low?

Ans. If the Recall is low, the F1 Score is low.

47. What is the range of the F1 Score?

Ans. An F1 score is a number between 0 and 1.

48. How do you define F1Score?

Ans. F1 Score is defined as the harmonic mean of Precision and Recall.

49. What is the perfect value for the F1 Score?

Ans. When F1=1, it is known as the perfect value for the F1 Score.

50. When is a prediction is said to be incorrect?

Ans. A prediction is said to be incorrect if it does not match Reality.

51. What is a formula for accuracy?

Ans. Accuracy= (TP+TN)/Total labels(samples)

52. What is the purpose of Evaluation?

Ans. Evaluation is done to make judgments about a program, to improve its effectiveness, and/or to inform programming decisions.

53. What is the formula for Recall?

Ans. Recall/ Sensitivity/TPR= TP/(TP-+FN)

54. What is the formula for F1 Score?

Ans. F1 score=(2*Recall* Precision)/(Recall+ Precision)

55. What does a good F1 Score signify?

Ans. A good F1 score means that we have low false positives and low false negatives; thus, correctly identifying real threats is possible without any disturbance by false alarms.

56. Define Evaluation.

Ans. Evaluation is defined as a process of understanding the reliability of an AI model, which is based on outputs by feeding the testing dataset into the model and comparing it with actual answers.

57. What is the maximum value of the F1 Score?

Ans. +1.0

58. What is the formula for misclassification?

Ans. Misclassification= (FP+FN)/total labels/samples or Misclassification= 1-Accuracy

59. Mention the formula of Precision.

Ans. Precision= TP/(TP+FP)

60. The harmonic mean of which two parameters are called F1 Score?

Ans. Recall and Precision

61. When is a model considered a total failure?

Ans. The model is a total failure when the F1 Score is 0.

62. What do you mean by seaborn package?

Ans. Seaborn is a Python data visualisation library based on matplotlib.

63. What is the command given to install the seaborne package on the anaconda prompt?

Ans. (env)PS C: \Users\user> Conda install seaborn

12.3.9 Short Answer Type Questions

1. Why is it necessary to test the model developed before its deployment in the real world?

Ans. Before deploying the model developed in the real world, we have to test it in as many ways as possible for its effectiveness and efficiency.

2. Explain the importance of Evaluation.

Ans. Evaluation is defined as a process that critically examines a program and involves collecting and analyzing information about the program's activities, characteristics, and outcomes. The purpose of Evaluation is to make judgments about a program.

   a) It is used to improve the effectiveness of the program.
   b) It also informs about programming decisions.
   c) It is used to ensure that the model is operating correctly and optimally.
   d) It is an initiative to understand how well it achieves its goals.
   e) It tells to determine what works well and what could be improved in a program.

3. What are the different types of classification evaluation metrics?

Ans. The following are the classification evaluation metrics:

   a) Accuracy   b) Confusion matrix   c) Precision   d) Recall
   e) F1 Score   f) Log Loss

4. Explain the features of a Confusion Matrix.

Ans. The main features of a confusion matrix are as follows:

   a) Prediction and Reality are easily mapped together with the help of this confusion matrix.
   b) The column labels "True Positive" and " True Negative" refer to the ground reality labels in the data set.

    c) The row labels "False Positive" and "False Negative" refer to your model's predictions, i.e., what your model thinks the label is.

    d) The entries inside of a confusion matrix (TPs, FPs, FNs, TNs) are exhibited in the form of counts:

5. What are the four important measures that are calculated using TP, FP, FP, and FN?

Ans. The four important measures are calculated using the above notations, which are very useful for model performance estimation. They are as follows:

    a) True Positive Rate (TPR): True Positive / Total Positive (TP/P)

    b) True Negative Rate (TNR): True Negative/ Total Negative (TN/N)

    c) False Positive Rate (FPR): False Positive / Total Negative (FP/N)

    d) False Negative Rate (FNR): False Negative/ Total Positive (FN/P)

6. What is the main difference between Precision and Recall?

Ans. Precision measures the model's trustiness in classifying positive samples, and the Recall measures how many positive samples were correctly classified as positive by the model.

7. Differentiate between Precision and Recall.

Ans. The points of difference between Precision and Recall are given below:

Precision	Recall
(i) Precision measures the model's trustiness in classifying positive samples.	(i) Recall counts how many positive samples were correctly classified as positive by the model.
(ii) During the calculation of the Precision, how both the positive and negative samples were classified is taken care of.	(ii) Recall considers the positive samples only in its calculations.
(iii) Precision is used when a sample is classified as Positive, while it does not care about correctly classifying all positive samples.	(iii) Recall cares about correctly classifying all positive samples, while it does not care if a negative sample is classified as positive.
(iv) When a model has a high recall but low Precision, then the model classifies most of the positive samples correctly, whereas it may have many false positives (i.e., it classifies many Negative samples as Positive).	(iv) When a model has high Precision but low Recall, then the model is accurate when it classifies a sample as Positive correctly, but it can only classify a few positive samples.

8. Explain the significance of F1 Score.

Ans. F1 Score is a single score that balances the concerns of Precision and recall in one number. A good F1 score means that we have low false positives and low false negatives; thus, correctly identifying real threats is possible without any disturbance by false alarms. An F1 score is considered perfect when it is 1, while the model is a total failure when it is 0 (zero). F1 Score is the best metric to evaluate the model on real-life classification problems and for the imbalanced class distribution.

9. How is Evaluation associated with the reliability of an AI Model?

Ans. Evaluation is a process of understanding the reliability of any AI model based on outputs after feeding/providing inputs the test dataset to the model and comparing it with the actual answers.

10. How is the Evaluation of an AI Model carried out? What is its purpose?

Ans. Evaluation is a process that critically examines a program. It involves collecting and analysing information about a program's activities, characteristics, and outcomes. Its purpose is to make judgments about a program, to improve its effectiveness, and/or to inform programming decisions.

11. What do you mean by an 'Overfitted Model' and 'Overfitting'?

Ans. An Overfitted Model is a statistical model containing more parameters than can be justified by the data. Because AI Model remembers the whole training data set, hence it always predicts the correct label for any point in the training dataset. This is known as Overfitting.

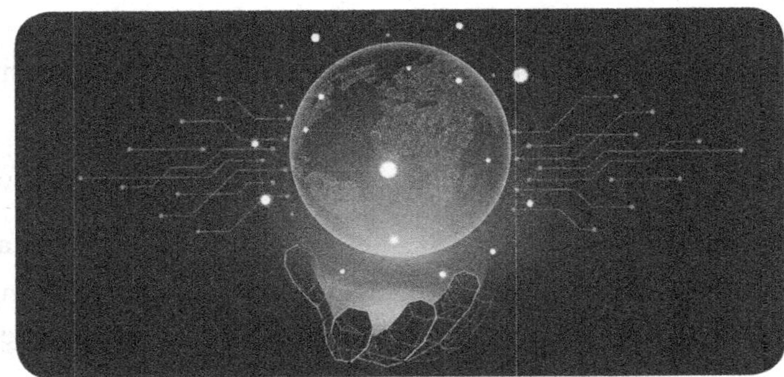

Figure 12.9

12.3.10 Long Answer Type Questions

1. What are the reasons for an AI model not being efficient?

Ans. Some of the reasons for an AI model not being efficient are enlisted as below:

   a) **Lack of Training Data:** When the data is not sufficient for developing an AI Model, or when the data is missed while training the model, then it will not be efficient.

   b) **Inefficient coding / Wrong Algorithms:** When the written algorithms are not correct and relevant, then the model will not give the desired output.

   c) **Unauthenticated Data / Wrong Data:** When the data is not authenticated and correct, then the model will not give authentic results.

   d) **Not Tested:** When the model is not tested properly, then it will not be efficient.

   e) **Less Accuracy:** A model is not efficient when it gives fewer accuracy scores in production/ test data or if it is not able to generalize well on unseen data.

   f) **Not Easy:** If it is not easy to be implemented in production or scalable. e.

2. Explain the four Metrics in the Confusion Matrix.

Ans. The four metrics in the confusion table are as follows:

   i. **True Positive (Top-Left):** How many times did the model under testing correctly classify a Positive sample as Positive?

   ii. **False Negative (Top-Right):** How many times did the model under testing incorrectly classify a Positive sample as Negative?

   iii. **False Positive(Bottom-Left):** How many times did the model under testing incorrectly classify a Negative sample as Positive?

   iv. **True Negative(Bottom-Right):** How many times did the model under testing correctly classify a Negative sample as Negative?

3. What is represented by the rows and columns in a confusion matrix?

Ans. The rows represent the predicted values of the target variable True Positive, True Negative, False Positive, and False Negative in a Confusion Matrix.

   i. **True Positive (TP):** The predicted value matches the actual value. The actual value was positive, and the model predicted a positive value.

   ii. **True Negative (TN):** The predicted value matches the actual value. The actual value was negative, and the model predicted a negative value.

   iii. **False Positive (FP) (Type 1 error):** The predicted value was falsely predicted. The actual value was negative, but the model predicted a positive value. It is also known as the Type 1 error.

   iv. **False Negative (FN) (Type 2 error):** The predicted value was falsely predicted. The actual value was positive, but the model predicted a negative value. It is also known as the Type 2 error.

4. Compare the features of TP, TN, FP, and FN.

Ans. The features of TP, TN, FP, and FN are compared as follows:

True Positive	True Negative	False Positive	False Negative
* The predicted value matches the actual value. * The actual value was positive, and the model predicted a positive value.	* The predicted value matches the actual value. * The actual value was negative, and the model predicted a negative value.	* The predicted value was falsely predicted. * The actual value was negative, but the model predicted a positive value. * It is also known as the Type 1 error.	* The predicted value was falsely predicted * The actual value was positive, but the model predicted a negative value * It is Also known as the Type 2 error

5. Calculate Recall, Precision, and Accuracy for the following case.

In medical research for the Zeta virus, scientists got the following confusion matrix. Calculate Recall, Precision, and accuracy for the following confusion matrix on coronavirus:

Confusion Matrix on Zeta virus	Reality: True	Reality: False
Prediction: Positive	200	10
Prediction: Negative	25	15

Ans. (i) Recall = TP/(TP+FN)

$$= 200/200+15$$

Recall = 200/215 = 0.93

(ii) Precision = TP/(TP+FP)

$$= 200/200+10$$

Precision = 200/210 = 0.95

(iii) Accuracy for this scenario is calculated as below:

Accuracy = (TN+TP)/Total cases

$$= (15+200)/250$$

Accuracy = 0.86

6. Out of Precision and Recall, which Metric is more important? Explain with the help of examples.

Ans. Choosing the best metric out of the Precision and Recall depends on the condition in which the model has been used. In a case like Forest Fire or covid virus detection case, a False Negative can cost us a lot and is risky too. Let's imagine that no alert is given even when there is a Forest Fire; then, the whole forest might burn down. Similarly, consider the case of coronavirus detection where a False Negative can be dangerous. Suppose that a deadly coronavirus has begun spreading, and the model that is supposed to predict a viral outbreak could not detect it, then the virus might spread widely to infect a lot of people.

On the contrary, there may be cases in which the False Positive condition costs more than False Negatives. Consider the case of Mining. Let's imagine that a model telling us that there exists petroleum at a point, and we keep on digging out there without getting petroleum. So, it turns out that it is a false alarm. Here, the False Positive case (predicting there is petroleum but there is no petroleum) may be very costly. Consider the case of a model that predicts whether a mail is spam or not. When the model always predicts that the mail is spam, people would not look at it and eventually might lose some important information. Here, the False Positive condition (Predicting the mail as spam while the mail is not spam) would have a high cost.

We may conclude that when we want to know if our model's performance is good, we need two measures: Recall and Precision. In some cases, we might have a High Precision but Low Recall, while in some cases, we might require Low Precision but High Recall. So, both the measures are important.

7. Give an example of Low Recall and High Precision.

Ans. Consider the following Table:

TP = 110	FP = 0
TN = 20	FN = 35

F1 is based on Precision and Recall, whereas

Precision = TP/(TP+FP), and

Recall = TP/(TP+FN).

For this table,

Recall= 0.76

Precision = 1

This is achieved if we have FP =0

8.   Give an example of High Recall and Low Precision.

Ans.   Consider the following Table:

TP = 110	FP = 25
TN = 20	FN = 0

For this table,

Recall=1

Precision = 110/110+25= 0.81

Thus, this is achieved if we have FN = 0.

12.3.11 HOTS Questions

1.   Why is F1 Score preferred over accuracy?

Ans.   Accuracy works best when false positives and false negatives have almost similar costs. But if the cost of false positives and false negatives are very different, then it is better to use both Precision and Recall values for which F1 Score is used.

2.   How is F1 Score calculated?

Ans.   F1 is based on Precision and Recall. When one (precision or recall) increases, the other one goes down. Hence, Fl score combines precision-recall into a single number where F1 is calculated as:

F1 = (2*Recall Precision)/(Recall+ Precision)

It is clear that the F1 Score is the harmonic mean of Recall and Precision.

We can rewrite the Fl score in terms of the values that we saw in the confusion matrix: true positives, false negatives, and false positives.

3.   When can we get a perfect F1 score?

Ans.   An ideal situation will be when both Precision and Recall have a value of 1 (i.e., 100%). Here, the F1 Score will also be an ideal 1 (i.e., 100%). This value is called the perfect value for the F1 Score. As the values of both Precision and Recall range from 0 to 1, and hence the F1 Score also ranges from 0 to 1.

Figure 12.10

12.4 PRACTICE QUESTIONS

1. Which parameters are considered for the Evaluation of a model?
2. What is True Positive and True Negative?
3. What is a False Positive and a False Negative?
4. What is the other name given for False Negative?
5. What is the other name given for False Positive?
6. Differentiate between Accuracy and Recall in evaluation methods.
7. What is Accuracy? Mention its formula.
8. How can you calculate F1 Score?
9. Why do we need evaluation methods?
10. Explain the difference between TP and FP in the confusion matrix.
11. How will you prove that Evaluation is important?
12. What is the difference between Reality and Prediction?
13. How can Precision and Recall be considered as a correct measures for Evaluation?
14. Which are the possible reasons for an AI model not being efficient? Explain.
15. What are the full forms of these abbreviations: TP, FP TN, FN, TPR, FPR, TNR, FNR.
16. Deduce the formula of F1 Score? What is the need for its formulation?
17. Define and explain the confusion matrix with the help of an example.
18. Calculate Accuracy, Recall, Precision, and F1 Score for the following Confusion Matrix on Covid Risk. Also, suggest which Metric would not be a good evaluation parameter in this case and why?

Confusion Matrix (on Covid Risk)	Reality: True	Reality: False
Prediction: Positive	70	15
Prediction: Negative	10	25

19. Calculate Accuracy, Recall, Precision, and F1 Score for the following Confusion Matrix on Water Shortage in a colony: Also suggest which Metric would not be a good evaluation parameter in this case and why?

Confusion Matrix (Water Shortage in a colony-Panchwati Enclave)	Reality: True	Reality: False
Prediction: Positive	75	5
Prediction: Negative	15	35

20. Calculate Accuracy, Recall, Precision, and F1 Score for the following Confusion Matrix on SPAM FILTERING. Also, suggest which Evaluation Metric would not be a good evaluation parameter in this case and why?

Confusion Matrix on SPAM FILTERING	Reality: True	Reality: False
Prediction: Positive	20	50
Prediction: Negative	15	15

21. In many schools, it happens that there is no water to drink. In a few places, cases of water shortage in schools (like in Rajasthan and Gujarat) are very common. Hence, an AI model is created/designed to predict whether there is going to be a water shortage in the school in the near future or not. A confusion matrix for the same problem is given below. Calculate Accuracy, Recall, Precision, and F1 Score for this problem.

Confusion Matrix on Shortage of Water in Schools	Reality: True	Reality: False
Prediction: Positive	85	10
Prediction: Negative	20	35

22. The problem of floods in the Bihar region of the country has worsened during the rainy season. It damages the whole area/place, and it also forces people to move out of their homes and relocate. To address the problem, an AI model is designed to predict the flood prediction in the Bihar region. The confusion matrix for the same problem is given below. Calculate Accuracy, Precision, Recall, and F1 Score for this problem.

Confusion Matrix on Floods in Bihar Region	Reality: True	Reality: False
Prediction: Positive	55	15
Prediction: Negative	10	25

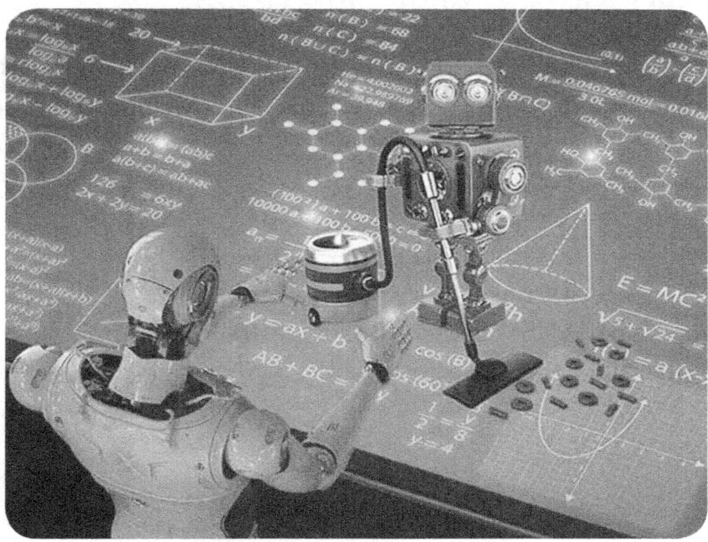

Figure 12.11

CBSE | DEPARTMENT OF SKILL EDUCATION
ARTIFICIAL INTELLIGENCE (SUBJECT CODE 417)
CLASS X (SESSION 2021-2022)
SAMPLE QUESTION PAPER FOR TERM – 1
BLUE PRINT

Max. Time Allowed: 1 Hour **Max. Marks: 25**

PART A – EMPLOYABILITY SKILLS (05 MARKS):

UNIT NO.	NAME OF THE UNIT	NO. OF QUESTIONS (1 MARK EACH)
1	Communication Skills-II	2
2	Self-Management Skills-II	2
3	Information and Communication Technology Skills-II	2

TOTAL QUESTIONS **6 Questions**
NO. OF QUESTIONS TO BE ANSWERED **Any 5 Questions**
TOTAL MARKS 1 x 5 = **5 Marks**

PART B – SUBJECT SPECIFIC SKILLS (20 MARKS):

UNIT NO.	NAME OF THE UNIT	NO. OF QUESTIONS (1 MARK EACH)
1	Introduction to AI II	12
2	AI Project cycle II	15

TOTAL QUESTIONS **27 Questions**
NO. OF QUESTIONS TO BE ANSWERED **20 Questions**
TOTAL MARKS 1 x 20 = **20 MARKS**

SAMPLE QUESTION PAPER FOR TERM – 2
BLUE PRINT

Max. Time Allowed: 1 Hour   **Max. Marks: 25**

PART A – EMPLOYABILITY SKILLS (05 MARKS):

UNIT NO.	NAME OF THE UNIT	NO. OF QUESTIONS (1 MARK EACH)
1	Entrepreneurial Skills-II	4
2	Green Skills-II	2

TOTAL QUESTIONS **6 Questions**

NO. OF QUESTIONS TO BE ANSWERED Any **5 Questions**

TOTAL MARKS 1 x 5 = **5 Marks**

PART B – SUBJECT SPECIFIC SKILLS (20 MARKS):

UNIT NO.	NAME OF THE UNIT	NO. OF QUESTIONS (1 MARK EACH)
1	NLP	13
2	Evaluation	14

TOTAL QUESTIONS **27 Questions**

NO. OF QUESTIONS TO BE ANSWERED **20 Questions**

TOTAL MARKS 1 x 20 = **20 MARKS**

CLASS X (SESSION 2021-2022)

CBSE SAMPLE QUESTION PAPER FOR TERM – 1 (2021)

Max. Time Allowed: 1 Hour   **Max. Marks: 25**

General Instructions:

1. Please read the instructions carefully

2. This Question Paper is divided into 03 sections, viz., Section A, Section B and Section C.

3. Section A is of 05 marks and has 06 questions on Employability Skills.

4. Section B is of 15 marks and has 20 questions on Subject specific Skills.

5. Section C is of 05 marks and has 07 competency-based questions.

6. Do as per the instructions given in the respective sections.

7. Marks allotted are mentioned against each section/question.

8. All questions must be attempted in the correct order

SECTION – A

Answer any 5 questions out of the given 6 questions on Employability Skills (1 × 5 = 5 marks)

1. Some American and Israeli managers were on a conference call. The topic of the call was transitioning from an on-premise product to a cloud-native product. In the middle of the discussion, one Israeli manager said that the R&D staff in Israel 'don't care' about some of the changes. An American manager, although usually polite, couldn't restrain himself when he heard that statement. "What's that supposed to mean, they DON'T CARE??" he thundered. This is an example of

   a) Organisational Barrier   b) Interpersonal Barrier

   c) Linguistic Barrier   d) Cultural Barrier

2. Identify the object, verb and subject in the sentence, 'The car crashed into a tree.'

   a) Object: a tree; Verb: crashed; Subject: the car

   b) Object: The car; Verb: crashed; Subject: a tree

   c) Object: crashed; Verb: the tree; Subject: the car

   d) Object: crashed; Verb: the car; Subject: the tree

3. There was a young boy who was fond of playing football and wanted to become a football player. He joined a football academy and came regularly to practice but never made it to the team. For four days, the boy didn't show up for practice. The matches had begun and his team was playing the finals. He showed up for the finals. He went up to the coach and pleaded him to let him play for the match. The coach had never seen the boy plead like this before. The Game started and the boy played like a ball on fire. Every time he got the ball,

he shot a goal. Needless to say, he was the star of the game and his team won. What type of motivation did the boy demonstrate?

a) External

b) Internal

c) Both internal and external

d) Not any specific type of motivation

4. Statement 1: A realistic goal is one that has no timeline or plans for execution.

Statement 2: Breaking down big goals into smaller parts will make the goal achievable.

a) Both Statement I and Statement II are correct

b) Both Statement I and Statement II are incorrect

c) Statement I is correct but Statement II is incorrect

d) Statement I is incorrect but Statement II is correct 1

5. Here are the steps that take place when starting a computer. Rearrange the steps in the correct order.

i) Desktop appears after login

ii) Login screen appears

iii) Power on Self-Test (POST) starts

iv) Operating system starts

v) Welcome screen appears

a) i) -> ii) -> iii) -> iv) -> v)

b) ii) -> iv) -> iii) -> v) -> i)

c) iii) -> iv) -> v) -> ii) -> i)

d) iii) -> v) -> iv) -> ii) -> i) 1

6. Which one of the following is an example of Operating System?

a) Microsoft Word

b) Microsoft Windows

c) Microsoft Excel

d) Microsoft Access

SECTION – B

Answer any 15 questions out of the given 20 questions (1 x 15 = 15 marks)

7. Which of the following is correct about the rule based approach?

a) We cannot provide enough rules to the machine.

b) A drawback/feature for this approach is that the learning is static.

c) Once the rules are fed into the system, it takes into consideration any changes made in the original training dataset.

d) It can improve itself based on the feedbacks.

8. Choose the five stages of AI project cycle in correct order

a) Evaluation -> Problem Scoping -> Data Exploration -> Data Acquisition -> Modelling

b) Problem Scoping -> Data Exploration -> Data Acquisition -> Evaluation -> Modelling

c) Data Acquisition -> Problem Scoping -> Data Exploration -> Modelling -> Evaluation

d) Problem Scoping -> Data Acquisition -> Data Exploration -> Modelling -> Evaluation

9. Unscramble the letters and find the name the first humanoid robot with a citizenship

    a) TERBHER OXEVE

    b) IAOHSP

    c) IRIS

    d) ACTROAN

10. When a machine possesses the ability to mimic the following human traits, it is said to have artificial intelligence. Identify the positive traits that an AI machine should possess. i. make decisions ii. bias iii. predict iv. learn and improve on its own

    (a) i), and iii) only

    (b) i) , iii) and iv) only

    (c) ii) and iv) only

    (d) i) ,ii), and iv) only

11. **Assertion(A):** Neural networks are the backbone of deep learning algorithms

    Reason(R): Neural networks use vast amounts of data

    (a) Both A and R are correct and R is the correct explanation of A

    (b) Both A and R are correct but R is NOT the correct explanation of A

    (c) A is correct but R is not correct

    (d) A is not correct but R is correct.

12. A business problem wherein we categorize whether an observation is "Safe," "AtRisk," or "Unsafe" is an example of

    (a) Classification

    (b) Clustering

    (c) Regression

    (d) Dimensionality Reduction

13. ________________ helps us to summarise all the key points into one single outline so that in future, whenever there is need to look back at the basis of the problem, we can take a look at it and understand the key elements of it.

    (a) 4W Problem canvas

    (b) Problem Statement Template

    (c) Data Acquisition

    (d) Algorithm

14. Tom is a student of grade five. He likes to move constantly at his desk. He plays with pencils and taps his fingers, stands up in his place any time he gets a chance. He enjoys playing basketball, and likes to play in the classroom. Which of the following intelligence does he demonstrate?

    (a) Linguistic

    (b) Logical-Mathematical

    (c) Musical

    (d) Kinesthetic

15. The basis of decision making depends upon

    (i) availability of information

    (ii) past experience

    (iii) positive attitude

    (iv) self-awareness

    (a) i) and ii)

    (b) ii) and iv)

    (c) i), ii) and iv)

    (d) i), ii) and iii) 1

16. Unscramble the letters and find the correct answer DATA + _________ = AI MACHINE

    (a) SMEGSEA   (b) IMLHOMRGAT   (c) RROER   (d) TSMMCOE

17. Infrared sensors detect infrared energy that is emitted by one's body heat. When hands are placed in the proximity of the sensor, the infrared energy quickly fluctuates. This fluctuation triggers the pump to activate and dispense the designated amount of sanitizer. This is an example of

    (a) Automated machine   (b) AI machine

    (c) Semi-automatic machine   (d) Deep Learning machine

18. Match Column A with Column B:

    Column A   **Column B**

    1. Face recognition machine   (i) Not AI

    2. Automatic door   (ii) AI

    3. Gesture recognition

    4. Automatic toy car

    (a) 1 -> (i) ; 2 -> (ii) ; 3 -> (i) ; 4 -> (ii)   (b) 1 -> (ii) ; 2 -> (i) ; 3 -> (ii) ; 4 -> (i)

    (c) 1 -> (i) ; 2 -> (i) ; 3 -> (ii) ; 4 -> (i)   (d) 1 -> (ii) ; 2 -> (i) ; 3 -> (i) ; 4 -> (ii)

19. **Assertion(A):** Anyone can kick an artificially intelligent machine

    Reason (R): They have no pain receptors

    (a) Both A and R are correct and R is the correct explanation of A

    (b) Both A and R are correct but R is NOT the correct explanation of A

    (c) A is correct but R is not correct

    (d) A is not correct but R is correct.

20. If Data is represented as "Answer", Processing is represented as "Data" and Answer is represented as "Processing", which of the following can be related to the description of layers in a neural network? Choose the correct options

    (a) Input Layer -> Data; Output layer -> Processing; Hidden Layer -> Answer

    (b) Input Layer -> Processing; Output layer -> Data; Hidden Layer -> Answer

    (c) Input Layer -> Answer; Output layer -> Processing; Hidden Layer -> Data

    (d) Input Layer -> Answer; Output layer ->Data; Hidden Layer -> Processing

21. Which of the following is incorrect?

    (i) Testing data is the one on which we train and fit our model basically to fit the parameters

    (ii) Training data is used only to assess performance of model

    (iii) Testing data is the unseen data for which predictions have to be made

    (a) i) and iii) only   (b) i) and ii) only

    (c) ii) and iii) only   (d) i), ii) and iii) 1

22. Unscramble the letters and find the parameter that is NOT used in evaluation stage

    (a) CMVETEEHAIN   (b) ONSIPRICE   (c) RYAUACCC   (d) ECLARL

23. **Assertion (A):** We can use histograms when data is in categories (such as "Pop", "Rock", "Jazz","Hip-Hop" etc)

    Reason (R): We use bar charts when we have continuous data (such as a person's height or weight)

    (a) (A) is false but (R) is true   (b) (A) is true but (R) is false

    (c) Both (A) and (R) are true   (d) Both (A) and (R) are false

24. Which of the following is true about neural networks?

    (a) Neural Networks tend to perform better with larger amounts of data.

    (b) Neural Networks tend to perform poorer with larger amounts of data.

    (c) Neural Networks tend to perform better with smaller amounts of data.

    (d) Neural Networks need no data

25. Choose the correct option

    (a) Unsupervised learning ->labelled dataset, Regression

    (b) Supervised learning -> labelled data set, Regression

    (c) Unsupervised learning ->unlabelled dataset, Classification

    (d) Supervised learning -> unlabelled data set, Regression

26. Google Translate is Google's free service that instantly translates words, phrases, and web pages between English and over 100 other languages. Google translate uses -----

    (a) 4w problem canvas   (b) Neural Networks

    (c) KWLH chart   (d) System maps 1

SECTION – C (COMPETENCY BASED QUESTIONS)

Answer any 5 questions out of the given 7 questions (1 x 5 = 5 marks)

27. Assume that you are working at MyFlight which is a major airlines company and that you have noticed that the way passengers board your planes is an inefficient use of time and resources. On an average, the current boarding system wastes about four minutes per boarding. This wastes about 35000 rupees per day across all flights. The boarding protocols make the company less competitive and thus create an unfavourable brand image. Using a modified boarding, passengers can board the plane from the sides rather than from the back to the front. This will eliminate four minutes of waste.

    Taking this as the problem, choose which of the following would be the ideal problem statement template.

    (a) Our passengers have a problem that it takes more time when one has to board the plane. An ideal solution would be to use different airlines.

(b) Our passengers have a problem that the current boarding system wastes time while waiting in the airport. An ideal solution would be to board the plane before the airline crew gets into the plane.

(c) Our airlines have a problem that the current boarding system wastes four minutes of time when passengers aboard the plane. An ideal solution would be to board the plane from the sides rather than from the back to the front.

(d) Our airlines have a problem that it takes more time when passengers have to board the plane. An ideal solution would be to sell the airlines.

28. a.   Understand and inspect the web page to find the HTML markers associated with the information we want.

   b.   Use Python libraries to pull out data from the HTML page.

   c.   Manipulate the collected data to get it in the form we need.

The above given steps are for collecting data from which of the following data sources?

(a) Cameras   (b) Sensors   (c) Surveys   (d) Web scraping

29. A leading multinational company operates on a chain of hypermarkets and grocery stores deployed an AI application to make it easier for employees to keep their stores running smoothly. They used thousands of video cameras, weighted sensors on shelves, and other technologies that can tell employees when certain products is starting to go bad. One of the task of the application is to identify bananas that had started to turn brown, eliminating the need for employees to manually inspect fruit. Which of the following domain is used to achieve this?

(a) Data sciences   (b) Computer vision

(c) Natural Language Processing   (d) Fuzzy logic

30. An AI system uses two broad classes of data namely content data which includes the raw video streams title, description, etc, and user activity data that includes rating a video, favoriting/liking a video, or subscribing to an uploader, and watch time. Based on this, the AI system measures a user's engagement and happiness. It then starts computing personalized recommendations to the user.

Which of the following applications can you relate to this?

(a) Self-driving car   (b) Siri   (c) email filters   (d) YouTube 1

31. Data about the houses such as square footage, number of rooms, features, whether a house has a garden or not, and the prices of these houses, i.e., the corresponding labels are fed into an AI machine. By leveraging data coming from thousands of houses, their features and prices, we can now train the model to predict a new house's price.

This is an example of:

(a) Reinforcement learning   (b) Supervised learning

(c) Unsupervised learning   (d) None of the above

32. A scenario is given to you below. Read it and answer the questions that follow:

   Late one night, a car ran over a pedestrian in a narrow by street and drove away without stopping. A policeman who saw the vehicle leave the scene of the accident reported it moving at very high speed. The accident itself was witnessed by six bystanders. They provided the following conflicting accounts of what had happened:

   - It was a Toyota and its headlights were turned off;

   - It was a grey Audi.

   - It was a red car driven by a woman;

   - The car was moving at high speed and its headlights were turned off;

   - The car did have license plates; it wasn't going very fast;

   - The car didn't have license plates; the driver was a man;

   When the car and its driver were finally apprehended, it turned out that only one of the six eyewitnesses gave a fully correct description. Each of the other five provided one true and one false piece of information.

   Keeping that in mind, can you determine the following:

   (i) What was the car's brand?

   (ii) What was the colour of the car?

   (iii) Was the car going fast or slow?

   (iv) Did it have license plates?

   (v) Were its headlights turned on?

   (vi) Was the driver a man or a woman?

   (a) i) -> TOYOTA ; ii) -> GREY ; iii) -> FAST ; iv) -> NO ; v) -> NO ; vi) -> WOMAN

   (b) i) -> AUDI ; ii) -> RED ; iii) -> SLOW ; iv) -> NO ; v) -> YES ; vi) -> WOMAN

   (c) i) -> AUDI ; ii) -> RED ; iii) -> FAST ; iv) -> YES ; v) -> NO ; vi) -> MAN

   (d) i) -> TOYOTA ; ii) -> RED ; iii) -> SLOW ; iv) -> NO ; v) -> NO ; vi) -> MAN

33. Amazon had been working on a secret AI recruiting tool. The machine-learning specialists uncovered a big problem: their new recruiting engine did not like women. The system taught itself that male candidates were preferable. It penalised resumes that included the word "women". This led to the failure of the tool. This is an example of

   (a) Data Privacy   (b) AI access

   (c) AI Bias   (d) Data Exploration

ANSWERS									
1. (c)	2. (a)	3. (b)	4. (d)	5. (c)	6. (b)	7. (b)	8. (d)	9. (b)	10. (b)
11. (a)	12. (a)	13. (b)	14. (d)	15. (c)	16. (b)	17. (a)	18. (b)	19. (d)	20. (c)
21. (b)	22. (a)	23. (d)	24. (a)	25. (b)	26. (b)	27. (c)	28. (d)	29. (b)	30. (d)
31. (b)	32. (c)	33. (c)							

Max. Time: 2 Hours   **Max. Marks: 50**

PART A – EMPLOYABILITY SKILLS (10 MARKS):

Unit No.	Name Of The Unit	Objective Type Questions 1 Mark Each	Short Answer Type Questions 2 Marks Each	Total Questions
1	Communication Skills-II	1	1	2
2	Self-Management Skills-II	2	1	3
3	Information and Communication Technology Skills-II	1	1	2
4	Entrepreneurial Skills-II	1	1	2
5	Green Skills-II	1	1	2
	TOTAL QUESTIONS	6	5	11
	NO. OF QUESTIONS TO BE ANSWERED	Any 4	Any 3	Any 7
	TOTAL MARKS	1 x 4 = 4	2 x 3 = 6	10 MARKS

PART B – SUBJECT SPECIFIC SKILLS (40 MARKS):

Unit No.	Name Of The Unit	Objective Type Questions 1 Mark Each	Short Answer Type Questions 2 Marks Each	Descriptive/ Long Ans. Type Questions 4 Marks Each	Total Questions
1	Introduction to Artificial Intelligence (AI)	6	1	1	8
2	AI Project Cycle	6	2	1	9
3	Natural Language Processing	6	2	2	10
4	Evaluation	6	1	1	8
	TOTAL QUESTIONS	24	6	5	35
	NO. OF QUESTIONS TO BE ANSWERED	Any 20	Any 4	Any 3	Any 27
	TOTAL MARKS	1 x 20 =20	2 x 4 = 8	4x3= 12	40 MARKS

ARTIFICIAL INTELLIGENCE (SUBJECT CODE: 417)

CBSE Sample Question Paper For Class X (Session 2020-2021)

Max. Time: 2 Hours   **Max. Marks: 50**

General Instructions:

1. Please read the instructions carefully.

2. This Question Paper consists of 21 questions in two sections: Section A & Section B.

3. Section A has Objective type questions whereas Section B contains Subjective type questions.

4. Out of the given (5 + 16 =) 21 questions, a candidate has to answer (5 + 10 =) 15 questions in the allotted (maximum) time of 2 hours.

5. All questions of a particular section must be attempted in the correct order.

6. SECTION A - OBJECTIVE TYPE QUESTIONS (24 MARKS):

    (i) This section has 05 questions.

    (ii) Marks allotted are mentioned against each question/part.

    (iii) There is no negative marking.

    (iv) Do as per the instructions given.

7. SECTION B – SUBJECTIVE TYPE QUESTIONS (26 MARKS):

    (i) This section has 16 questions.

    (ii) A candidate has to do 10 questions.

    (iii) Do as per the instructions given.

    (iv) Marks allotted are mentioned against each question/part.

SECTION A: OBJECTIVE TYPE QUESTIONS

Q. 1 Answer any 4 out of the given 6 questions on Employability Skills   **(1 × 4 = 4 marks)**

    i. ____________ is the final component in the process of communication as it defines the response given by the receiver to the sender.

        a) Response   b) Request

        c) Feedback   d) Notice

  Ans: c) Feedback

    ii. ____________ refers to focusing human efforts for maintaining a healthy body and mind capable of better withstanding stressful situations

        a) Mental Health   b) Emotional Health

        c) Self-Management   d) Stress Management

  Ans: d) Stress Management

iii. Having conscious knowledge of your own self, capabilities, feelings and one's own character is called ______________.

    a) Self-awareness   b) Self-motivation   c) Self-control   d) Independence

Ans: a) Self-awareness

iv. A ________________is a software program that attaches itself to other programs and alters their behaviour.

    a) Operating system   b) Firewall   c) Antivirus   d) Computer Virus

Ans: d) Computer Virus

v. ______________ refers to recruitment, employment, selection, training, development and compensation of the employees with an organization.

    a) Entrepreneurs   b) Management

    c) Human Resource Management   d) Employer

Ans: c) Human Resource Management

vi. ______________ is caused when natural or a man-made disturbance disrupts the natural balance of an ecosystem.

    a) Pollution   b) Damage

    c) Natural disaster   d) Ecological Imbalance

Ans: d) Ecological Imbalance

Q.2 Answer any 5 out of the given 6 questions   **(1 × 5 = 5 marks)**

i. A ______________ is divided into multiple layers and each layer is further divided into several blocks called nodes.

    a) Neural Networks   b) Convolutional Neural Network (CNN)

    c) Machine learning algorithm   d) Hidden Layers

Ans: a) Neural Network

ii. The ______________ canvas helps you in identifying the key elements related to the problem.

    a) Problem scoping   b) 4Ws Problem

    c) Project cycle   d) Algorithm

Ans: b) 4Ws Problem

iii. ______________ is a domain of AI that depicts the capability of a machine to get and analyse visual information and afterwards predict some decisions about it.

    a) NLP   b) Data Sciences

    c) Augmented Reality   d) Computer Vision

Ans: d) Computer Vision

iv. ______________ is defined as the percentage of correct predictions out of all the observations.

    a) Predictions   b) Accuracy   c) Reality   d) F1 Score

Ans: b) Accuracy

v. ______________ is the sub-field of AI that is focused on enabling computers to understand and process human languages.

   a) Deep Learning   b) Machine Learning   c) NLP   d) Data Sciences

Ans: c) NLP

vi. In ______________, the machine is trained with huge amounts of data which helps it in training itself around the data.

   a) Supervised Learning   b) Deep Learning

   c) Classification   d) Unsupervised Learning

Ans: b) Deep Learning

Q. 3 Answer any 5 out of the given 6 questions   **(1 × 5 = 5 marks)**

   i. Expand CBT ______________

   a) Computer Behaved Training   b) Cognitive Behavioural Therapy

   c) Consolidated Batch of trainers   d) Combined Basic Training

Ans: b) Cognitive Behavioural Therapy

   ii. Name any 2 methods of collecting data.

   a) Surveys and Interviews   b) Rumours and Myths

   c) AI models and applications   d) Imagination and thoughts

Ans: a) Surveys and Interviews

   iii. What is the role of modelling in an NLP based AI model?

   a) Modelling in NLP helps in processing of AI model

   b) Modelling is required to make an AI model

   c) In NLP, modelling requires data pre-processing only after which the data is fed to the machine.

   d) Modelling is used in simplification of data acquisition

Ans: c) In NLP, modelling requires data pre-processing only after which the data is fed to the machine.

   iv. What will be the outcome, if the Prediction is "Yes" and it matches with the Reality? What will be the outcome, if the Prediction is "Yes" and it does not match the Reality?

   a) True Positive, True Negative   b) True Negative, False Negative

   c) True Negative, False Positive   d) True Positive, False Positive

Ans: d) True Positive, False Positive

   v. Recall-Evaluation method is:

   a) defined as the fraction of positive cases that are correctly identified.

   b) defined as the percentage of true positive cases versus all the cases where the prediction is true.

c)   defined as the percentage of correct predictions out of all the observations.

d)   comparison between the prediction and reality

Ans: a) defined as the fraction of positive cases that are correctly identified.

vi.   Give 2 examples of Supervised Learning models.

a) Classification and Regression

b) Clustering and Dimensionality Reduction

c) Rule Based and Learning Based

d) Classification and Clustering

Ans: a) Classification and Regression

Q. 4 Answer any 5 out of the given 6 questions   **(1 × 5 = 5 marks)**

i.   Define Machine Learning.

a)   Machine learning is the study of computer algorithms that improve automatically through experience.

b)   Refers to any technique that enables computers to mimic human intelligence.

c)   Machine learning refers to computer systems (both machines and software) enables machines to perform tasks for which it is programmed.

d)   Machine Learning refers to projects that allow the machine to work on a particular logic.

Ans: a)   Machine learning is the study of computer algorithms that improve automatically through experience.

ii.   Give one example of an application which uses augmented reality.

Ans: Self Driving Cars

iii.   Differentiate between Prediction and Reality.

a)   Prediction is the input given to the machine to receive the expected result of the reality.

b)   Prediction is the output given to match the reality.

c)   The prediction is the output which is given by the machine and the reality is the real scenario in which the prediction has been made.

d)   Prediction and reality both can be used interchangeably.

Ans: c)   The prediction is the output which is given by the machine and the reality is the real scenario in which the prediction has been made.

iv.   The term Sentence Segmentation is

a) the whole corpus is divided into sentences

b) to undergo several steps to normalise the text to a lower level

c) in which each sentence is then further divided into tokens

d) the process in which the affixes of words are removed

Ans: a) the whole corpus is divided into sentences.

   v.   Which of the following statements is true for the term Evaluation?

   a) Helps in classifying the type and genre of a document.

   b) It helps in predicting the topic for a corpus.

   c) Helps in understanding the reliability of any AI model

   d) Process to extract the important information out of a corpus.

Ans: (c) Helps in understanding the reliability of any AI model 1

   vi.   Which of the following is not part of the AI Project Cycle?

   a)   Data Exploration   b) Modelling

   c) Testing   d) Problem Scoping

Ans: (c) Testing 1 Page No. 6 of 11

Q. 5 Answer any 5 out of the given 6 questions   **(1 × 5 = 5 marks)**

   i.   _______________ refers to the AI modelling where the machine learns by itself.

   a) Learning Based   b) Rule Based   c) Machine Learning   d) Data Sciences

Ans: (a) Learning Based

   ii.   Prediction and Reality can be easily mapped together with the help of:

   a)   Prediction   b) Reality

   c)   Accuracy   d) Confusion Matrix

Ans: (d) Confusion Matrix

   iii.   _______________ is an example of Applications of Natural Language Processing.

   a) Evaluation   b) Automatic Summarization

   c) Deep Learning   d) Problem Scoping

Ans: (b) Automatic Summarization

   iv.   _______________ is the last stage of the AI project Life cycle.

   a) Problem Scoping   b) Evaluation   c) Modelling   d) Data Acquisition

Ans: (b) Evaluation

   v.   In _______________, the machine is trained with huge amounts of data which helps it in training itself around the data.

   a) Machine Learning   b) Artificial Intelligence

   c) NLP   d) Deep Learning

Ans: (d) Deep Learning

   vi.   In _______________, input to machines can be photographs, videos and pictures from thermal or infrared sensors, indicators and different sources.

   a) Computer Vision   b) Data Acquisition

   c) Data Collection   d) Machine learning

Ans: (a) Computer Vision

SECTION – B: SUBJECTIVE TYPE QUESTIONS

Answer any 3 out of the given 5 questions on Employability Skills   **(2 × 3 = 6 marks)**

Part A: Employability Skills

Q. 6 Name the four main categories of Communication Styles.

Ans: Verbal, Non - Verbal, Written and Visual 2

Q. 7 List any 4 activities that help in stress management.

Ans: (Any 4 out of the following or any other appropriate activity)

- Positive Thinking,
- Physical Exercise,
- Yoga,
- Meditation,
- Nature Walks,
- Vacations,
- Laughing aloud,
- Listening to good music

Q. 8 What are antivirus? Name any 2 antiviruses.

Ans: Antivirus software is a program designed to detect and remove malicious programs from the computer.

Examples: (Any 2 out of the following or any other correct name of the antivirus):

- Microsoft Security essentials,
- Microsoft Defender,
- McAfee Virus Scan,
- Norton AntiVirus,
- Quick Heal.

Q. 9 Name any 4 qualities of an entrepreneur.

Ans: (Any 4 out of the following)

- Hard working,
- Optimistic,
- Independent,
- Energetic,
- Self-confident,
- Perseverant

Q. 10 Name any 4 man-made disruptions that cause ecological imbalance.

Ans: (Any 4 out of the following)

- Deforestation,
- Degradation of Land and Soil Erosion,
- Overexploitation of Resources,
- Industrial and Atmospheric Pollution,
- Faulty Mining Practices,
- E waste generation

Answer any 4 out of the given 6 questions in 20 – 30 words each   **(2 × 4 = 8 marks)**

Q. 11 Give 2 points of difference between a script-bot and a smart-bot

Ans:

Script-bot	Smart-bot
(i) Script bots are easy to make	(i) Smart-bots are flexible and powerful
(ii) Script bots work around a script with instructions of program stored inside them	(ii) Smart bots work on bigger databases and other resources directly
(iii) Mostly are Free and are Easy to Integrate	(iii) Smart bots learn on its own with more data
(iv) No or very little language processing skills	(iv) Coding is required to take this up on board
(v) Limited functionality	(v) Has wide functionality

Q. 12 Define the term Machine Learning. Also give 2 applications of Machine Learning in our daily lives.

Ans: Machine Learning: It is a subset of Artificial Intelligence which enables machines to improve at tasks with experience (data).

The intention of Machine Learning is to enable machines to learn by themselves using the provided data and make accurate Predictions/ Decisions. Machine Learning is used in Snapchat Filters, NETFLIX recommendation system.

Q. 13 Differentiate between Classification and Regression.

Ans:

Classification	Regression
(i) This model works on a discrete dataset which means the data need not be continuous.	(i) This type of models work on continuous data.
(ii) For example, in the grading system, students are classified on the basis of the grades they obtain with respect to their marks in the examination.	(ii) For example, if you wish to predict your next salary, then you would put in the data of your previous salary, any increments, etc and would train the model.

Q. 14 Explain the term Text Normalisation in Data Processing.

Ans: The first step in Data processing is Text Normalisation. Text Normalisation helps in cleaning up the textual data in such a way that it comes down to a level where its complexity is lower than the actual data. In this we undergo several steps to normalise the text to a lower level. We work on text from multiple documents and the term used for the whole textual data from all the documents altogether is known as corpus.

Q. 15 Name any 2 applications of Natural Language Processing which are used in the real-life scenario.

Ans: (Any 2 out of the following)

- Automatic Summarization,
- Sentiment Analysis,
- Text classification,
- Virtual Assistants

Q. 16 What is F1 Score in Evaluation?

Ans: F1 score can be defined as the measure of balance between precision and recall. It is defined as the harmonic mean of recall and precision.

F1Score = 2 * Precision * Recall/ (Precision + Recall)

Answer any 3 out of the given 5 questions in 50– 80 words each   **(4 × 3 = 12 marks)**

Q. 17 Categorize the following under Data Sciences, Machine Learning, Computer Vision and NLP. The latest technological advancements have made our lives convenient. Google Home, Alexa and Siri have been a huge help to non-tech savvy people. Features like Facial recognition and Facelock have added additional security to our gadgets. These advancements have also contributed in making our needs more approachable and convenient. Now you can even check the prices with Price comparison websites and order groceries online with chatbots. Did you know that you can even find how you are going to look when you grow old? Faceapps and Snapchat filters have made this possible!

Ans: a) Alexa, Siri-NLP, Facial Recognition - Computer Vision

  b) Facelock - Computer Vision

  c) Price comparison websites - Data Sciences

  d) Chatbots - NLP

  e) Faceapps -NLP

  f) Snapchat Filters - Machine Learning

Q. 18 Create a 4W Project Canvas for the following. As more and more new technologies get into play, risks will get more concentrated into a common network. Cybersecurity becomes extremely complicated in such scenarios and goes beyond the control of firewalls. It will not be able to detect unusual activity and patterns including the movement of data. Think how AI algorithms can scrape through vast amounts of logs to identify susceptible user behaviour. Use an AI project cycle to clearly identify the scope, how you will collect data, model and evaluation parameters.

Ans:

OUR	[stakeholders] People who are using the new technology	WHO
HAS/ HAVE PROBLEM THAT	[issue, problem, need] Cyber security is the need when so much of the flow of data is not monitored or escapes the antiviruses/ firewall systems.	WHAT
WHEN/ WHILE	[context/situation] The problem is in the use of the latest technology where vast amounts of data is at risk.	WHERE
AN IDEAL SOLUTION WOULD	[benefit of solution to them] An effective AI system which is able to detect the flow of data and also report unusual activity	WHY

Q. 19 Differentiate between stemming and lemmatization. Explain with the help of an example.

Ans: Stemming is the process in which the affixes of words are removed and the words are converted to their base form. In lemmatization, the word we get after affix removal (also known as lemma) is a meaningful one.

Lemmatization makes sure that lemma is a word with meaning and hence it takes a longer time to execute than stemming. The difference between the stemming and lemmatization can be depicted by the following example:

CARING .... **Stemming** .... CAR

CARING .... **Lemmatization**... CARE

Q. 20 Write the applications of NLP (Natural Language Processing). (Any four)

Ans: The applications of NLP are as follows:

a) **Automatic Summarization:** Automatic summarization is relevant not only for summarizing the meaning of documents and information, but also to understand the emotional meanings within the information, such as in collecting data from social media.

b) **Sentiment Analysis:** The goal of sentiment analysis is to identify sentiment among several posts or even in the same post where emotion is not always explicitly expressed.

c) **Text classification:** Text classification makes it possible to assign predefined categories to a document and organise it to help you find the information you need or simplify some activities.

d) **Virtual Assistants:** With the help of speech recognition, these assistants can not only detect our speech but can also make sense out of it.

Q. 21 Imagine that you have come up with an AI based prediction model which has been deployed on the roads to check traffic jams. Now, the objective of the model is to predict whether there will be a traffic jam or not. Now, to understand the efficiency of this model, we need to check if the predictions which it makes are correct or not. Thus, there exist two conditions which we need to ponder upon: Prediction and Reality. Traffic Jams have become a common part of our lives nowadays. Living in an urban area means you have to face traffic each and every time you get out on the road. Mostly, school students opt for buses to go to school. Many times, the bus gets late due to such jams and the students are not able to reach their school on time. Considering all the possible situations make a Confusion Matrix for the above situation.

Ans: Case 1: Is there a traffic Jam?

Prediction: Yes

Reality: Yes

True Positive

Case 2: Is there a traffic Jam?

Prediction: No

Reality: No

True Negative

Case 3: Is there a traffic Jam?

Prediction: Yes

Reality: No

False Positive

Case 4: Is there a traffic Jam?

Prediction: No

Reality: Yes

False Negative

Confusion Matrix		Reality	
		Yes	No
Prediction	Yes	True Positive	False positive
	No	False Negative	True Negative

SOLVED CBSE BOARD QUESTION PAPER
FOR TERM – 1 (2021)

CLASS X (SESSION 2021-2022)

Max. Time Allowed: 1 Hour   **Max. Marks: 25**

General Instructions:

1. Please read the instructions carefully

2. This Question Paper is divided into 03 sections, viz., Section A, Section B and Section C.

3. Section A is of 05 marks and has 06 questions on Employability Skills.

4. Section B is of 15 marks and has 20 questions on Subject specific Skills.

5. Section C is of 05 marks and has 07 competency-based questions.

6. Do as per the instructions given in the respective sections.

7. Marks allotted are mentioned against each section/question.

8. All questions must be attempted in the correct order

SECTION – A

Answer any 5 questions out of the given 6 questions on Employability Skills (1 × 5 = 5 marks)

1. ______________ is the inner urge to do something, achieve goals without any external pressure/lure for award or appreciation.

   a) Self-awareness

   b) Self-motivation

   c) Self-regulation

   d) self-control

2. Stress management is vital because it leads to the following benefit/s:

   a) Improves mood

   b) Boosts immune system

   c) Promotes longevity

   d) All of the above

3. ______________ in communication implies "stepping into the shoes of others".

   a) Consideration   b) Courtesy   c) Concreteness   d) Clarity

4. ______________ communication takes place between two individuals and is thus a one-to-one conversation. It can be formal or informal.

   a) Interpersonal   b) Written   c) Small group   d) Public

5. GUI stands for ______________.

   a) Graphical user Interaction

   b) Graphical User Interface

   c) Graphical Upper Interface

   d) Geographical User Interaction

6. The shortcut used for copying is:

   a) Ctrl + c   b) Ctrl + v   c) Ctrl + s   d) Ctrl + p

SECTION – B

Answer any 15 questions out of the given 20 questions   **(1 × 15 = 15 marks)**

7. Radha is good at singing since childhood, she understands key notes and is composing a song for her college festival but her father wants her to focus on science exam. She possesses ______________ Skills but her father is not finding it lucrative.

   a) Naturalist Intelligence
   b) Interpersonal Intelligence
   c) Musical Intelligence
   d) Spatial Visual Intelligence

8. Email filters is an application of:

   a) Computer Vision
   b) Data Science
   c) Natural Language Processing
   d) Neural Network

9. Computer Vision acquires, screens, ______________, identifies and extracts information.

   a) does price comparison
   b) analyses
   c) collects
   d) labels

10. ______________ involves collecting data from various authentic sources such as reliable websites, observations, surveys.

    a) Data Acquisition
    b) Data Evaluation
    c) Data Testing
    d) Data Modelling

11. Assertion(A): The training data should be authentic and relevant to the problem statement scoped.

    Reason(R): It increases the AI Project efficiency.

    a) Both Assertion (A) and Reason (R) are correct and R is the correct explanation of A.
    b) Both Assertion (A)   and Reason(R) are correct but Reason(R) is NOT the correct explanation of Assertion (A) .
    c) Assertion (A) s correct but Reason(R) is not correct.
    d) Assertion (A)   is not correct but Reason(R) is correct.

12. Accuracy, Recall, Precision, F1 Score are the parameters to calculate the efficiency under ______________

    a) Data Acquisition
    b) Data Evaluation
    c) Data Testing
    d) Data Modelling

13. Drawback/s of Rule-based approach is/are:

    i.   The learning is static.

    ii. Any changes made to the original data will not be considered.

    iii. Once trained the model cannot improvise on the basis of feedback.

    a) All the above statements are correct.
    b) Statements i and ii are correct.
    c) Statements ii and iii are correct.
    d) Statements i and iii are correct.

14. In ______________, design is adaptive to change in data, which results in dynamicity of a model.

    a) Learning-based Approach

    b) Rule-based Approach

    c) Data Acquisition

    d) Data Modelling

15. ______________ are modelled on human brain, it is essentially a machine learning algorithm, useful for solving problems when the dataset is large.

    a) Computer Vision

    b) Data Science

    c) Natural Language Processing

    d) Neural Network

16. ______________ is not a Learning-based Approach where AI model gets trained on the data fed to it and then is able to design a model which is adaptive to the change in data.

    a) Supervised Learning

    b) Unsupervised Learning

    c) Reinforcement Learning

    d) Enforcement Learning

17. Unsupervised Learning is divided into the following two categories. Identify the correct one.

    a) Rule -based and Learning -based

    b) Classification and Clustering

    c) Clustering and Dimensionality Reduction

    d) Classification and Regression

18. The 4Ws Problem canvas helps in identifying the key elements related to the problem. 4ws Problem canvas is a part of:

    a) Problem scoping   b) Data Acquisition   c) Modelling   d) Evaluation

19. The ______________ block of 4 Ws problem canvas helps in analysing the people getting affected directly or indirectly due to it.

    a) Who   b) What   c) Where   d) Why

20. During Data Acquisition feeding previous data into the machine is called:

    a) Training Data

    b) Predicting Data

    c) Testing Data

    d) Evaluating Data

21. ______________ is one of the types of Supervised Learning Model, where data is classified according to labels and data need not be continuous.

    a) Regression

    b) Classification

    c) Clustering

    d) Dimensionality reduction

22. Self-driving Car is an example of ______________.

    a) Data Science

    b) Computer Vision

    c) NLP

    d) Augmented Reality

23. Evaluation is the process of understanding the reliability of any AI model, based on outputs by feeding test dataset into the model and comparing with actual answers. Therefore, it must be followed by:

    a) Problem Scoping

    b) Data Acquisition

    c) Data Exploration

    d) Modelling

24. Radha was searching for new shoes online. Now she is fed up with mails, popups, advertisements related to shoes on her social media accounts, email inbox, and SMS on her phone. This is an issue related to:

    a) Gender bias

    b) Data Privacy

    c) Poor training

    d) Lack of access

25. Classification and Regression are _____________, and approach followed is _____________.

    a) Supervised, Learning

    b) Unsupervised, Learning

    c) Reinforcement, Learning

    d) Supervised, Rule-based

26. _____________ Refers to the unsupervised learning algorithm which can cluster the unknown data according to the patterns or trends identified out of it.

    a) Regression

    b) Classification

    c) Clustering

    d) Dimensionality Reduction

SECTION – C (COMPETENCY BASED QUESTIONS)

Answer any 5 questions out of the given 7 questions   **(1 × 5 = 5 marks)**

27. Choose the correct option describing the features of Neural Network.

    These are systems modelled on human Brain and Nervous System.

    i.   It is essentially a machine learning algorithm.

    ii. It is useful when solving the problems for which the data set is very large.

    iii. They are able to extract feature without input from the programmer.

    a) Statements i and ii are correct.

    b) Statements i and iii are correct.

    c) Statements ii and iii are correct.

    d) All of the above statements are correct.

28. Choose the correct statement related to Machine Learning.

    Statement i: It is a subset of Artificial Intelligence which enables machines to improve at tasks with experience.

    Statement ii: It enables machines to learn by themselves using the provided data and make accurate Predictions/Decisions.

    a) Only statement i is correct.

    b) Both the statements i and ii are correct.

    c) Both the statements i and ii are incorrect.

    d) Only statement ii is correct.

29. Vijender has to maintain inventory on a daily basis, it usually takes 3-4 hours for a helper to take out raw material, which in turns delays the production cycle and also delays the updation of stock. His manager has identified the problem and looking for a possible solution. This is a task under

    a) Problem Scoping

    b) Data Exploration

    c) Data Evaluation

    d) Neural Network

30. Statement i: In Deep Learning, the machine is trained with huge amounts of data which helps it in training itself around the data.

    Statement ii: Everything which is Machine Learning is also Deep Learning.

    a) Both the statements i and ii are correct.

    b) Only statement i is correct.

    c) Only statement ii is correct.

    d) Both the statements i and ii are incorrect.

31. Jhanvi loves traveling and makes wonderful travel vlogs. She was planning to take this as a profession and wanted to buy a good camera with other accessories for her vlogs. Her friend had suggested her to look for various options online which is giving her comparison from various vendors. She was happy to purchase the camera at a best price. Which domain of AI is working behind that has helped her to take decision on this?

    a) Computer Vision

    b) Data Science

    c) Natural Language Processing

    d) Neural network

32. Ananya has recently bought a robot to do cleaning including mopping. The robot senses the dirty floor, calculates the average time taken to mop, senses the obstacles and changes the direction, also goes for auto charging. Her housemaid was feeling insecure as if she would not be required in the near future. This is a problem related to:

    a) AI Bias

    b) AI Ethics

    c) AI Creating Unemployment

    d) Data Privacy

33. The following are the key elements of _______________.

    i.   Who are the stakeholders?

    ii. What is the problem?

    iii. Where does the problem arise?

    iv. Why do you believe that the problem is worth solving?

    a) 4 Ws Problem Canvas

    b) Accuracy

    c) Prediction

    d) Recall

ANSWERS									
1. (b)	2. (d)	3. (a)	4. (a)	5. (b)	6. (a)	7. (c)	8. (c)	9. (b)	10. (a)
11. (a)	12. (b)	13. (a)	14. (a)	15. (d)	16. (a)	17. (c)	18. (a)	19. (a)	20. (a)
21. (b)	22. (b)	23. (d)	24. (b)	25. (a)	26. (b)	27. (d)	28. (b)	29. (a)	30. (b)
31. (b)	32. (c)	33. (a)							

SOLVED SAMPLE QUESTION PAPER 1

FOR TERM – 1

Max. Time Allowed: 1 Hour   **Max. Marks: 25**

General Instructions:

1. Please read the instructions carefully

2. This Question Paper is divided into 03 sections, viz., Section A, Section B and Section C.

3. Section A is of 05 marks and has 06 questions on Employability Skills.

4. Section B is of 15 marks and has 20 questions on Subject specific Skills.

5. Section C is of 05 marks and has 07 competency-based questions.

6. Do as per the instructions given in the respective sections.

7. Marks allotted are mentioned against each section/question.

8. All questions must be attempted in the correct order

SECTION – A

Answer any 5 questions out of the given 6 questions on Employability Skills (1 × 5 = 5 marks)

1. Assume that a Russian group visited *GolumJa AIProducts Ltd.* The Indian team of the company communicated with Russian group using different prompts like body movements, gestures, facial expressions, symbols, images, signals charts, and soon to express sentiments, attitudes, or information. This type of communication is called:

    a) Verbal Communication

    b) Non-verbal Communication

    c) Visual Communication

    d) None of the above

2. Which of these is an imperative sentence?

    a) Switch off the fan.

    b) Sheila has gone to the market.

    c) Where are my pen colours?

    d) Oh no! I missed my flight.

3. Benson George won first prize at Inter-School Karate Tournament. Now, he is more focused on getting the same prize at State level Tournament. Which type of motivation does Benson George have?

    a) External

    b) Internal

    c) Intermediate

    d) Both internal and external

4. Statement 1: Stress means pressure, tensions, worries, and problems of life, affecting the balance in life.

    Statement 2: Setting realistic goals with proper time management may produce less stress.

    a) Statement 1 is correct but statement 2 is incorrect.

    b) Statement 1 is incorrect but statement 2 is correct.

    c) Both the statements are correct.

   d) Both the statements are incorrect.

5. Consider the following are the functions performed by an OS?

   i.   It keeps track of the status of the device, whether it is busy or not.

   ii. It makes users capable of sharing data among themselves.

   iii. It prevents users from interfering with one another.

   iv. It facilitates making errors.

   v.   It implements the user interface.

   a) (ii) (iii) (iv)   b) (iii) (iv) (v)   c) (v) (iii) (ii) (i)   d) All of these

6. Which function is not performed by using a mouse?

   a) Hover   b) Turn on   c) Right-click   d) Drag and Drop

SECTION – B

Answer any 15 questions out of the given 20 questions   **(1 × 15 = 15 marks)**

7. Which of the following feature is not related to ANN?

   a) A Neural Network has the ability to learn by itself to produce the output.

   b) ANN cannot work with incomplete knowledge and may not produce output with incomplete information.

   c) ANN is capable to automatically extract features without feeding the input by the programmer.

   d) Ann has the ability to learn events and make decisions by commenting on similar events.

8. Which of the following is not a source of data?

   a) Observations, API   b) Investigation, Internet

   c) Search, DPI   d) API, Identity Charts

9. Unscramble the letters and find the name of India's first 3D printed humanoid robot that was developed in 2014 by Diwakar Vaish-an alumni of Sharada University, Noida, UP?

   a) IMRAHS   b) AYTAS   c) UALHS   d) VANAM

10. Which type of Artificial Intelligence is used in Chatbots (Alexa, Siri, Cortana, Watson) and image / facial recognition software?

   a) ANI   b) AGI   c) ASI   d) None of the above

11. **Assertion (A):** When an element in an AI-based project is removed or changed, it will imbalance the whole system.

   Reason (R): All elements in the AI system are interconnected

   a) Both A and R are correct and R is the correct reason for A.

   b) Both A and R are correct and R is not the correct reason for A.

   c) A is correct but R is incorrect.

   d) Both A and R are incorrect

12. For which purpose is visualisation technique used?

    a) Enabling to make comparisons easily

    b) Using order, layout, and hierarchy to prioritise

    c) Handling and understanding big data

    d) All of the above

13. _____________ like Google assistant, Apple's Siri, Amazon's Alexa, etc., recognize patterns in speech and then understand its meaning and provide a useful response.

    a) Histograms   b) Smart Assistants   c) System maps   d) Algorithm

14. Which Intelligence is about a person's ability to recognize and create sounds, rhythms, and sound patterns?

    a) Spatial Intelligence   b) Kinaesthetic Intelligence

    c) Musical Intelligence   d) None of the above

15. Select a game which is based on Data Science domain of AI:

    a) Rock Paper and Scissors   b) Mystery Animal

    c) Emoji Scavenger Hunt   d) Pokémon

16. Which type of graphical representation suits best for a continuous type of data like the monthly income of an employee?

    a) Decision tree   b) Linear graph   c) Identity chart   d) Pie chart

17. Which of the following is associated with the study of computer algorithms that improve their efficiency automatically through experience?

    a) Data science   b) Machine Learning (ML)

    c) Deep Learning (DL)   d) None of the above

18. **Assertion (A):** Data Modelling is defined as processing in which Al-Enabled algorithms are being designed as per the requirements of the system, and later, the model is implemented.

    Reason (R): Data Modelling is the fifth stage of the project cycle.

    a) Both A and R are correct and R is the correct reason for A.

    b) Both A and R are correct and R is not the correct reason for A.

    c) A is correct but R is incorrect.

    d) Both A and R are incorrect.

19. Statement 1: Neural Network is a mesh of one input layer and multiple hidden Layers.

    Statement 2: Evaluation is a training technique where the model is installed in the real world, and it is tested in as many ways as possible.

    a) Statement 1 is correct but statement 2 is incorrect.

    b) Statement 1 is incorrect but statement 2 is correct.

    c) Both the statements are correct.

    d) Both the statements are incorrect.

20. What is a common method of processing meaning from a natural language known as?

    a) CV

    b) Semantic indexing

    c) Semantic analysis

    d) HB

21. Which of the following is incorrect?

    i.   Artificial intelligence must mean a human-made interface with the power to reason and integrate knowledge.

    ii. The AI devices need to be trained with information / Big data to produce the best possible accurate results.

    iii. The main objective of CV is to teach machines to collect information from pixels.

    iv. Rashmi is a humanoid robot developed in 2015 by "Hanson Robotics", Hong Kong.

    a) (i) only
    b) (ii) and iii) only
    c) (iii) and iv) only
    d) (iv) only

22. Which tool is used to formulate the information more meaningful for making decisions?

    a) QlikView
    b) Python
    c) MS Word
    d) All of the above

23. Assertion (A): Artificial Intelligence (AI) may be defined as the simulation of human intelligence by machines. It has the ability to solve problems, the ability to act rationally, and the ability to act like humans.

    Reason (R): Intelligence may be defined as the capacity to learn and solve problems.

    a) Both A and R are correct and R is the correct reason for A.

    b) Both A and R are correct and R is not the correct reason for A.

    c) A is correct but R is incorrect.

    d) Both A and R are incorrect.

24. Which of the following statement(s) is/are true?

    i.   Sensors used in AI-enabled machines convert real-world phenomena like temperature, force, movement to voltage or current, etc., into signals.

    ii. Decision tree learning is the technique used for supervised classification learning.

    iii. A classification problem is when the output variable is a category.

    iv. Classification is defined as the process of finding a model/ function for distinguishing the data into continuous real values in place classes.

    v.   Data modelling is the fifth stage in the AI project cycle.

    a) (i) only
    b) (i) (ii) (iii) only
    c) (i) (iii) (v) only
    d) (i) (ii) (iv) (v) only

25. Statement 1: NLP is defined as the ability of a machine to extract information from an image that is necessary to solve a task.

    Statement 2: Shalu is the first humanoid robot of India that can communicate in 37 languages.

    a) Statement 1 is correct but statement 2 is incorrect.

b) Statement 1 is incorrect but statement 2 is correct.

c) Both the statements are correct.

d) Both the statements are incorrect.

26. Assertion (A): The problem statement template provides a clear idea about the basic framework required to achieve the goal.

Reason (R): ANN has numerical strength that can perform more than one job at the same time.

a) Both A and R are correct and R is the correct reason for A.

b) Both A and R are correct and R is not the correct reason for A.

c) A is correct but R is incorrect.

d) Both A and R are incorrect.

SECTION – C (COMPETENCY BASED QUESTIONS)

Answer any 5 questions out of the given 7 questions   **(1 × 5 = 5 marks)**

27. Assume that in *'AnuJa AI RoboCreations'*, Prof RK Patel is working on the hypothetical concept where machines become self-aware and surpass the capacity of human intelligence and ability. These machines will supersede the humans in intelligence. With which of the following intelligence is he working?

a) ASI   b) ANI   c) AGI   d) None of the above

28. Which of the following pairs are mismatched?

i. Affordable and Clean Energy:	(a)	Ensuring access to affordable, reliable, sustainable, and green energy by all by 2030
ii. Decent Work and Economic Growth:	(b)	Promoting sustained, inclusive, and sustainable economic growth.
iii. Industry, Innovation, and	(c)	Building the resilient infrastructure, promoting
iv. Infrastructure	(d)	inclusive and sustainable industrialisation, and fostering innovation by 2030.
v. Reduced Inequality	(e)	Actions to reduce equality within and among countries by 2030.
vi. Climate Action	(f)	Taking urgent action globally to combat Climate change and its impacts
vii. Life on Land	(g)	Actions to protect, restore, and promote sustainable use of aquatic ecosystems; combating desertification, and halting biodiversity loss.

   a) (i) & (iii)   b) (ii) & (iv)   c) (iii) & (vii)   **d) (iv) & (vi)**

29. Assume that during the production of AI-enabled machines in a company called *'Surekha AI Enterprises'*, Rekha Dutt used tools/parts which convert real-world phenomena like temperature, force, movement to voltage or current, etc., into signals. These parts/tools are called:

   a) Fizzy Systems   b) Transducers

   c) Transformers   d) Translocators

30. A network has the following characteristics:

   i. It can work with incomplete information/knowledge and may produce output even with incomplete information.

   ii. It has Parallel processing capability. It means that it has numerical strength that can perform more than one job at the same time.

   iii. It has the capability to learn events and make decisions by commenting on similar events.

   iv. It has fault tolerance. It means that the corruption of one or more cells does not stop it from generating output.

   This is all about:

   a) ANN   b) BNN   c) CNN   d) NN

31. Suppose Ramita Nagpal is efficient in the process involving the selection of a course of action from among two or more possible options in order to arrive at a solution for a given problem. Which skills are possessed by her?

   a) Critical Thinking   b) Creative Thinking

   c) Empathy   d) Decision-making

32. Assume that *TriptaAgro Products* is a leading multinational company that operates a chain of Agro-stores. The company has deployed an AI application to make it easier for employees to keep their Agro-stores running smoothly. They used a large number of video cameras, fitted sensors on shelves, and other technologies that can tell employees when some products are starting to go bad. One of the tasks of the application is to identify apples that had started to turn pale-brown, eliminating the need for employees to manually inspect fruits. Which of the following domains is used to achieve this correct decision?

   a) Fuzzy logic   b) Natural Language Processing

   c) Data sciences   d) Computer vision

33. Read the following scenario and answer the questions that follow:

   Late one night, a truck ran over a pedestrian in a narrow street and drove away without stopping. A policeman who saw the vehicle leave the scene of the accident reported it was covered with a red coloured sheet. Six bystanders witnessed this accident. They provided the following conflicting statements as follows:

- ▲ It was a Mahindra Truck, and its headlights were turned off;

- ▲ The truck did have license plates; it wasn't going very fast;

- ▲ It was a Tata truck. It was covered with a blue sheet.

- ▲ It was a Mahindra truck driven by a woman;

- ▲ The truck was moving at high speed, and its roof was covered with a red sheet;

- ▲ The truck was covered with a red sheet; the driver was a man;

When the truck and its driver were finally caught, it was revealed that only one of the six eyewitnesses gave a fully correct description of the incident. Each of the other five provided one true and one false piece of information.

Keeping that in mind, can you determine the following:

i.   What was the truck's brand?

ii. Was the truck going fast or slow?

iii. Did it have license plates?

iv. Were its headlights turned on?

v.   Was the driver a man or a woman?

a) i) -> Tata; ii) -> Slow; iii) ->Yes ; iv) -> NO ;v) -> Woman

b) i) -> Mahindra; ii) -> Slow ; iv) -> NO ; v) -> YES ; vi) -> Man

c) i) -> Tata ; ii) -> Fast ; iii) -> YES ; iv) -> NO ; v) -> Woman

d) i) -> Mahindra ; ii) -> SLOW ; iii) -> NO ; iv) -> NO ; v) -> Man

ANSWERS									
1. (b)	2. (d)	3. (a)	4. (c)	5. (c)	6. (b)	7. (b)	8. (c)	9. (d)	10. (b)
11. (a)	12. (d)	13. (b)	14. (c)	15. (a)	16. (b)	17. (b)	18. (c)	19. (a)	20. (b)
21. (d)	22. (a)	23. (a)	24. (b)	25. (b)	26. (b)	27. (a)	28. (d)	29. (b)	30. (a)
31. (d)	32. (c)	33. (c)							

SOLVED SAMPLE QUESTION PAPER 2

FOR TERM – 1

Max. Time Allowed: 1 Hour · **Max. Marks: 25**

General Instructions:

1. Please read the instructions carefully
2. This Question Paper is divided into 03 sections, viz., Section A, Section B and Section C.
3. Section A is of 05 marks and has 06 questions on Employability Skills.
4. Section B is of 15 marks and has 20 questions on Subject specific Skills.
5. Section C is of 05 marks and has 07 competency-based questions.
6. Do as per the instructions given in the respective sections.
7. Marks allotted are mentioned against each section/question.
8. All questions must be attempted in the correct order

SECTION – A

Answer any 5 questions out of the given 6 questions on Employability Skills (1 × 5 = 5 marks)

1. Assume that Surjeet Khumman belongs to Manipur and he has a friend AK Unni Krishanan from Kerala. Both have ethnic, religious, and social differences that can often create misunderstandings during communication. These differences can also affect one's perception and create confusion in getting a message correctly. This type of communication barrier is known as:

   a) Linguistic barriers   b) Cultural barriers

   c) Attitudinal barriers   d) Perceptual barriers

2. Which of the following words does refer to a word or phrase that expresses a strong emotion?

   a) Interjection   b) Conjunction   c) Verb   d) Preposition

3. Suppose Narendra Pratap Bansal is more confident in handling problems affecting their lives, tends to rely less on others, easily makes decisions, and is emotionally independent. He represents:

   a) Confident people   b) Stressed people

   c) Independent people   d) Democratic people

4. Assertion (A): Stressors are factors that have an adverse effect on the physical, emotional, behavioural, and mental health of a human being.

   Reason(R): Vacation with friends and family can be a refreshing experience that can help in relieving stress.

   a) Both A and R are correct and R is the correct reason for A.

   b) Both A and R are correct and R is not the correct reason for A.

c) A is correct but R is incorrect.

d) Both A and R are incorrect.

5. Assume that Dinesh Pathak owns *Sai CompuSolutions* and he carries a process that is meant for the following tasks:

i.   For keeping them in proper running condition

ii. For enhancing their efficiency

iii. For finding problems and issues at an early stage

iv. For their safety and enhancing their life span

v.   For prevention against viruses and malware

vi. For increasing the working speed of the computers

vii. For maximising the computer software efficiency

viii. For preventing data loss

This process is known as:

a) Up dation of computers

b) Corrective measures for computers

c) Evaluation of computers

d) Maintenance of computers

6. Which of the following keys is not a command key?

a) Insert   b) Backspace   c) Delete   d) Home

SECTION – B

Answer any 15 questions out of the given 20 questions   **(1 × 15 = 15 marks)**

7. Which of the following project is related with the SDG "Clean Water and sanitation"?

a) Providing education remotely, leveraging hi-tech, low-cost, and no-tech approaches;

b) Ensuring coordinated responses and avoiding overlapping efforts;

c) Managing water sustainably to manage our production of food and energy.

d) Ensuring the return of students to school when they reopen to avoid an upsurge in dropout rates.

8. Which Intelligence has the capacity and capability to understand or learn any intellectual task that a human being can.?

a) Artificial Narrow Intelligence (ANI)

b) Artificial General Intelligence (AGI)

c) Artificial Super Intelligence (ASI)

d) None of the above

9. Unscramble the letters and find the second-last stage of the AI project cycle?

a) NOITAULAVE   b) NOITISUQCA ATAD

c) GNINIM ATAD   d) GNIPOCS MELBORP

10. In the Rule-Based Approach, who defines the relationships in patterns or data?

    a) User

    b) Coder/Programmer

    c) Computer Owner

    d) Buddy

11. **Assertion (A):** Artificial Intelligence (AI) may be defined as the simulation of human intelligence by machines. It has the ability to solve problems, the ability to act rationally, and the ability to act like humans.

    Reason (R): Intelligence may be defined as the capacity to learn and solve problems.

    a) Both A and R are correct and R is the correct reason for A.

    b) Both A and R are correct and R is not the correct reason for A.

    c) A is correct but R is incorrect.

    d) Both A and R are incorrect.

12. For which purpose, Training Data is used in the AI-based machine?

    a) Testing the model

    b) Making Predictions

    c) Processing

    d) Giving input to the machined.

13. ________________ is not included in sustainable development.

    a) Recycling and reuse of waste products/materials,

    b) Promoting deforestation

    c) Promoting green grassy patches between concrete buildings,

    d) Scientific management of renewable resources, especially bio-resources,

14. With which SDG, the following objective is associated:

    "Making the cities and human settlements inclusive, safe, resilient, and sustainable".

    a) Life on Land

    b) Responsible Consumption and Production

    c) Life Below Water

    d) Sustainable Cities and Communities

15. Assertion (A): When an element in an AI-based project is removed or changed, it will imbalance the whole system.

    Reason (R): All elements in the AI system are interconnected

    a) Both A and R are correct and R is the correct reason for A.

    b) Both A and R are correct and R is not the correct reason for A.

    c) A is correct but R is incorrect.

    d) Both A and R are incorrect

16. Unscramble the letters and find the correct answer for fill in the blank.

    AI machines also keep updating their knowledge to optimize their ______________.

    a) TINUP
    b) TPUUOT
    c) RPOCSSE
    d) EDOC

17. Statement 1: A decision tree is a simple textual representation for classifying examples.

    Statement 2: Recall indirectly tells us the model's ability to randomly identify an observation that belongs to the positive class.

    a) Statement 1 is correct but statement 2 is incorrect.

    b) Statement 1 is incorrect but statement 2 is correct.

    c) Both the statements are correct.

    d) Both the statements are incorrect.

18. Which one of the following applications is not considered an application of AI?

    a) Robot drones   b) Google search

    c) Remote-controlled Drone   d) Self-Driving Car

19. Statement 1: Intrapersonal Intelligence is the ability of humans to communicate with others after understanding other people's feelings & influence on the person.

    Statement 2: Intelligence is not needed for robots to handle tasks like object manipulation and navigation.

    a) Statement 1 is correct but statement 2 is incorrect.

    b) Statement 1 is incorrect but statement 2 is correct.

    c) Both the statements are correct.

    d) Both the statements are incorrect.

20. Suppose Jevelson wants to search a website for price comparison for a product. Which of the following websites should he not visit ?

    a) Junglee   b) Facebook   c) Shopzilla   d) DealTime

21. Assertion (A): The main objective of CV is to teach machines to collect information from pixels.

    Reason (R): Computer Vision (CV) related projects translate digital visual data into descriptions.

    a) Both A and R are correct and R is the correct reason for A.

    b) Both A and R are correct and R is not the correct reason for A.

    c) A is correct but R is incorrect.

    d) Both A and R are incorrect.

22. Which of the following statements is Not Correct?

    a) Deep Learning is considered the most advanced form of Artificial Intelligence.

    b) Artificial Intelligence may be defined as a technique that enables computers to mimic human Intelligence.

    c) CV inputs machine the ability to read and understand human language.

    d) Speech Recognition is the process of converting sound signals captured by a microphone or mobile/telephone to a set of words (70-100 words/minute with an accuracy of 90%).

23. Statement 1: Semantic indexing is a common method of processing meaning from natural language.

    Statement 2: Affective computing is the development of such systems that can recognize, interpret, simulate human effects.

    a) Statement 1 is correct but statement 2 is incorrect.

    b) Statement 1 is incorrect but statement 2 is correct.

    c) Both the statements are correct.

    d) Both the statements are incorrect.

24. Consider the following statements. Which of the statement(s) is/are INCORRECT?

    i. Stakeholders are all those humans who are affected the most by the model used in the AI project.

    ii. The Artificial Intelligent project cycle describes all steps required to convert a real-life problem or a challenge into a computer-based AI model.

    iii. AI Modelling refers to developing algorithms or AI models which can be trained to get intelligent output, i.e., writing codes to make a machine artificially intelligent.

    iv. The Training data must not be relevant and authentic for the better efficiency of an AI project.

    v. Data may be a piece of information or facts and statistics collected together for reference or analysis purposes.

    a) (i) only

    b) (iv) only

    c) (ii) (iv) only

    d) (iii) (iv) (v) only

25. In which analysis ML is not used?

    a) Predictive analysis

    b) Regression analysis

    c) Reaction analysis

    d) Action analysis

26. Consider the following statements about project charter and choose the correct set for project charter.

    i. Project's purpose, vision, and mission

    ii. Measurable objectives

    iii. Elaborated project description, conditions, and risks

    iv. Success criteria

    v. Name and authority of the project sponsor, if any.

    vi. Concerned stakeholders

    a) (ii) (iii) (iv)

    b) (i) (iii) (iv) (v)

    c) (i) (ii) (iv) (v) (vi)

    d) (i) (ii) (iii) (iv) (v) (vi)

SECTION – C (COMPETENCY BASED QUESTIONS)

Answer any 5 questions out of the given 7 questions   **(1 × 5 = 5 marks)**

27. Suppose Sakshi Agrawal Pandey owns an AI firm "Saksham AI Solutions," where the firm imparts training to the machines with the help of huge amounts of data (training data) for helping it in training itself around the data. After the training, the machines become intelligent enough to develop algorithms for themselves. This is an example of:

    a) NLP   b) Deep Learning

    c) Data Sciences   d) Advance Learning

28. Suppose Naundita and Rabina Khatoon are working as data analysts in **Galaxy Data Analytics Pvt Ltd**. They were exploring websites for data collection that should be authentic, accurate, and reliable. They used the following government portals for the information to be used and referred to in data analytics.

    i.   https://www.india.gov.in/data-portal-india

    ii. https://data.gov.in/

    iii. https://dbie.rbi.org.in/DBIE/dbie.rbi?site=home

    iv. http://mospi.nic.in/data

    These websites/portals are also called:

    a) Blogs   b) Closed-sourced portals

    c) Open-sourced websites   d) Landing pages

29. Assume that **Infinity Infra Pvt Ltd** is a project company dealing with the construction of new schools. The company uses an AI machine, which is fed the Data about the schools, like square footage, number of class-rooms and labs, number of playgrounds, features, whether a school has a swimming pool or not, and the construction costs of these schools, i.e., the corresponding labels. By leveraging data coming from a large number of schools, their features and costs, the company can now train the model to predict a new school's construction cost.

    Which of the following is an associated term with the AI machine used?

    a) Unsupervised learning   b) Supervised learning

    c) Reinforcement learning   d) CV

30. Consider the following pairs of sensors used in mobile phone.

    i.   **Accelerometer:** Fingerprint, Iris data

    ii. **GPS:** Location Data

    iii. **Gyroscope:** Orientation Data

    iv. **Magnetometer:** Direction and Magnetic Field Data

    v.   **Biometric Sensors:** Tracking steps

    Which of the above is/are mismatched?

    a) (i) only   b) (ii) and (v) only

    c) (iii) and (iv) only   d) (i) and (v) only

31. Assume that Sangeeta Deshmukh is working as Floor Manager at *AnuShail Automobiles Ltd*, which is a major automobile company producing Automatic cars. She has noticed that the way workers reach their working place is an inefficient use of time and resources. The workers waste, on average five minutes on clearing the safety checks, producing their id proofs and reaching their workplace. This wastes about 45,000 rupees per day. Using a modified automatic id proof identification machine at the gate, workers can enter the factory within a few seconds, which will eliminate about four minutes of waste per worker.

    Taking this as the problem, choose which of the following would be the ideal problem statement template.

    a) Our workers have a problem that it takes more time when one has to enter the factory. An ideal solution would be to use different methods.

    b) Our workers have a problem that it takes more time when one has to enter the factory. An ideal solution would be to use an id identification machine at the gate of the factory.

    c) Our workers have a problem that it takes more time when one has to enter the factory. An ideal solution would be to replace security guards with robots.

    d) Our workers have a problem that it takes more time when one has to enter the factory. An ideal solution would be to sell the factory.

32. Assume that *Jumbo Selection Pvt Ltd* is a recruitment agency dealing with the recruitment of teachers for schools and colleges. It uses an AI recruiting tool. The machine-learning specialists of the company found that their AI recruiting engine did not like men. The system taught itself that female candidates were preferable for schools and colleges and it started penalizing resumes that included the word "man". This is an example of:

    a) Data Exploration   b) Data Privacy   c) AI access   d) AI Bias

33. Which of the following steps is not related to web scrapping data source for collecting data?

    a) Understand and inspect the web page to find the HTML markers associated with the information we want.

    b) Use Python libraries to pull out data from the HTML page.

    c) Meet people to know their opinion to get the information.

    d) Manipulate the collected data to get it in the form we need.

ANSWERS									
1. (b)	2. (a)	3. (c)	4. (b)	5. (d)	6. (d)	7. (c)	8. (b)	9. (d)	10. (b)
11. (a)	12. (a)	13. (b)	14. (d)	15. (a)	16. (b)	17. (b)	18. (c)	19. (a)	20. (b)
21. (b)	22. (c)	23. (c)	24. (b)	25. (c)	26. (d)	27. (c)	28. (c)	29. (b)	30. (d)
31. (b)	32. (d)	33. (c)							

SOLVED SAMPLE QUESTION PAPER 1

FOR TERM – 2

Max. Time Allowed: 1 Hour   **Max. Marks: 25**

General Instructions:

1. Please read the instructions carefully
2. This Question Paper is divided into 03 sections, viz., Section A, Section B and Section C.
3. Section A is of 05 marks and has 06 questions on Employability Skills.
4. Section B is of 15 marks and has 20 questions on Subject specific Skills.
5. Section C is of 05 marks and has 07 competency-based questions.
6. Do as per the instructions given in the respective sections.
7. Marks allotted are mentioned against each section/question.
8. All questions must be attempted in the correct order

SECTION – A

Answer any 5 questions out of the given 6 questions on Employability Skills (1 × 5 = 5 marks)

1. Consider the following actions:

    i. Use energy-efficient lights (LED bulbs) and appliances.

    ii. Save energy by switching off electrical appliances, like tube lights and fans, when these items are not used.

    iii. Use energy-saving and water-saving techniques.

    iv. Use biodegradable items.

    v. Use natural light as much as possible.

    The actions required for developing 'Sustainable Cities' are:

    a) (i) (ii) (iii)   b) (ii) (iii) (iv)

    c) (ii) (iii) (iv) (v)   d) (i) (ii) (iii) (iv) (v)

2. Which factor is not responsible for causing soil erosion?

    a) Uncontrolled runoff of surface water   b) Grazing of land

    c) Deforestation   d) Improper farming techniques

3. Which of the following options is the correct set of tasks of an entrepreneur?

    i. Owning the full income/profit

    ii. Creating a New Method, Idea, or Product

    iii. Making Effective Decisions

    iv. Managing the Business

    v. Taking Risk

    vi. Distributing the dividend

a) (i) (ii) (iii) (iv) (v)　　　　　　b) (ii) (iii) (iv) (v) (vi)

c) (i) (iii) (iv) (v) (vi)　　　　　　d) All of the above

4. Statement 1: The principles of sustainable development does not require the integration of environmental, social, and economic concerns into all aspects of decision-making.

Statement 2: Sustainable Development Goals (SDGs) are the collection of 17 global goals set by the United Nations General Assembly in 2015, which are to be achieved by the year 2030.

a) Statement 1 is correct, but statement 2 is incorrect.

b) Statement 1 is incorrect, but statement 2 is correct.

c) Both the statements are correct.

d) Both the statements are incorrect.

5. Which of the following statements are related to sustainable development?

    i.   Use of digital media instead of paper

    ii.   Deforestation

    iii. Use of energy-saving devices like LED.

    iv. Use of drip irrigation

    v.   The practice of crop rotation

a) (i) (ii) (iii) (iv)　　　　　　b) (ii)(iii)(iv)(v)

c) (i) (iii) (iv) (v)　　　　　　d) All of these

6. Assertion (A): Sustainable development is defined as the development that ensures the needs of the present generation without compromising the needs of future generations too.

Reason (R): Sustainable development is meant for economic growth, environmental protection, social inclusion, and cultural diversity.

a) Both A and R are correct, and R is the correct reason for A.

b) Both A and R are correct, and R is not the correct reason for A.

c) A is correct but R is incorrect.

d) Both A and R are correct.

SECTION – B

Answer any 15 questions out of the given 20 questions　　　　　　**(1 × 15 = 15 marks)**

7. Which type of information is given by 'Bag of Words' algorithm?

a) Type of words

b) Number of words

c) Number of stopwords

d) Frequency of words in each document of the corpus

8. Which statement is NOT TRUE?
   a) In binary classification, recall is called Sensitivity.
   b) The recall is defined as the ratio between the number of Positive samples correctly classified as Positive by the model to the total number of Positive samples.
   c) Precision is defined as the ratio between the number of Positive samples correctly classified to the total number of samples classified as negative (either correctly or incorrectly).
   d) In information retrieval, recall is the fraction of the relevant documents that are successfully retrieved.

9. Unscramble the letters and find the name of the process of grouping together different forms of the same word.
   a) GNIMMETS
   b) NOITASINEKOT
   c) NOITASITAMMEL
   d) ATAD

10. Which of the following statements is Incorrect?
   a) Precision is defined as the ratio of true positive cases and all the cases where the Prediction is false.
   b) The 'Prediction' is the output that is given by the machine.
   c) The F1 Score is the harmonic mean of Precision and recall.
   d) An Overfitted Model is a statistical model which contains more parameters than can be justified by the data.

11. Statement 1: A corpus can be taken as a bunch of image files in a directory, often alongside many other directories of text files.
   Statement 2: The header row in a document vector table contains the vocabulary of the corpus while the other rows correspond to different documents.
   a) Statement 1 is correct but statement 2 is incorrect.
   b) Statement 1 is incorrect but statement 2 is correct.
   c) Both the statements are correct.
   d) Both the statements are incorrect

12. Which term is used for a table that is often used to describe the performance of a classification model?
   a) Histogram
   b) Confusion Matrix
   c) F1 Score
   d) Bar diagram

13. For a word having _______________ TFIDF value, the word will have a high term frequency with less document frequency.
   a) Zero
   b) Low
   c) high
   d) Negative

14. Suppose Unni Krishanan is using an algorithm that works by cutting off the end of the beginning of the word, and taking into account a list of common prefixes and suffixes that can be found in an inflected word. This process is called:
   a) Lemmatisation
   b) Stemming
   c) Semantics
   d) Stemming

15. The predicted value was falsely predicted. In other words, the actual value was positive, but the model predicted a negative value. It is:

    a) Type 1 error　　　b) Type 2 error　　　c) Type 3 error　　　d) Zero error

16. Unscramble the letters and find the parameter that reflects how reliable the model is in classifying samples as Positive.

    a) CAACCRUY　　　b) LLERCA　　　c) CISOINPRE　　　d) 1F ORESC

17. Which statement is INCORRECT?

    a) TFIDF values help the computer understand which words are to be considered while processing the natural language.

    b) Words occurring in all the documents with high term frequencies have the least values and are called the 'Stopwords.'

    c) The higher the value of TFIDF, the less important the word is for a given corpus.

    d) For a word having a high TFIDF value, the word will have a high term frequency but less document frequency. This shows that the word is important for one document but is not a common word for all documents.

18. Which of the following pairs of applications is not based on NLP?

    a) Targeted marketing, chatbots

    b) Survey Analysis, Voice assistants

    c) Autocomplete in Search Engines, Market Intelligence

    d) Email distribution, Surveillance

19. Statement 1: The "Reality" is the real scenario when the Prediction is made.

    Statement 2: Confusion Matrix is a table used to describe the performance of a classification model.

    a) Statement 1 is correct but statement 2 is incorrect.

    b) Statement 1 is incorrect but statement 2 is correct.

    c) Both the statements are correct.

    d) Both the statements are incorrect

20. Which of the following statements is correct?

    a) When a model has a low recall but high Precision, then the model classifies most of the positive samples correctly.

    b) If a model has high precision and high recall, then the model is accurate.

    c) The Precision measures the model's trustiness in classifying positive samples, and the recall measures how many positive samples were correctly classified as positive by the model.

    d) All the above

21. Study the following statements and choose the correct option stating the advantages of chatbots.

    i.   It saves users time, money and gives better customer satisfaction.

    ii. This application can deliver a near-human-like conversational experience.

    iii. It helps you to increase customer satisfaction.

    iv. It supports customisation without writing any code.

    (a) (i) & (ii)   (b) (ii) & (iii)
    (c) (i), (ii) & (iii)   (d) (i), (ii), (iii) & (iv)

22. Unscramble the letters and find the process of understanding the reliability of an AI model, which is based on outputs by feeding the testing dataset into the model and comparing it with actual answers.

    a) TTFIINGEROV   b) ANTIOELAVU
    c) LENGIDMO   d) TRIXMA FNSUINOUCO

23. Assertion (A): Lemmatization takes more time than stemming.

    Reason (R): Lemmatization carries the morphological analysis of the words from detailed dictionaries that the algorithm can look the form back to its lemma.

    a) Both A and R are correct and R is the correct reason for A.

    b) Both A and R are correct and R is not the correct reason for A.

    c) A is correct but R is incorrect.

    d) Both A and R are incorrect.

24. The result of the comparison between the Prediction and Reality can be recorded in a table which is known as:

    a) Prediction Table   b) Bag of words
    c) Confusion matrix   d) None of the above

25. Assertion (A): F1 Score is the harmonic mean of Precision and Recall.

    Reason (R): F1 Score is a single score that balances the concerns of Precision and Recall in one number.

    a) Both A and R are correct and R is the correct reason for A.

    b) Both A and R are correct and R is not the correct reason for A.

    c) A is correct but R is incorrect.

    d) Both A and R are incorrect.

26. Which term is used for the whole textual data from all the documents altogether during Text Normalisation?

    a) Lotus   b) Data   c) Corpus.   d) TextInput

SECTION – C (COMPETENCY BASED QUESTIONS)

Answer any 5 questions out of the given 7 questions   **(1 × 5 = 5 marks)**

27. Suppose Radhika S Chandran is typing a manuscript using a computer. She is using " Grammarly" to type grammatical error free text with improvised syntax. Which of the following is used in this algorithm that is also known as 'Grammar and Spell Checker'?

    a) CV   b) Data Science   c) Fuzzy Logic   d) NLP

28. Assume that Sugandh Gogai owns ***Saumya World Tours & Travels Pvt Ltd***. He is using a computer program that can learn over time how to best interact with human beings. It can answer questions and solutions to customer problems, generate sales leads, evaluate and qualify prospects, and increase sales on his eCommerce site. It is used to answer questions and troubleshoot customer problems, evaluate and qualify prospects, generate sales leads, and increase sales on an eCommerce site. He is using:

    a) Artificial bot   b) Artificial Conversational Bot (ACB)

    c) Chat Bot   d) Chatter mail

29. Suppose Zeenat Ahmed developed an AI Model which was found non efficient on evaluation. Which of the following reasons may be responsible for its non-efficiency?

    a) Lack of Training Data, and Not Tested   b) Inefficient coding and Less Accuracy

    c) Unauthenticated Data, and Not Easy   d) All of these

30. Suppose Ishika Pushkarna uses a process that critically examines a program and involves collecting and analyzing information about the program's activities, characteristics, and outcomes. The purpose of this process are as follows:

    i.   It is used to improve the effectiveness of the program.

    ii. It also informs about programming decisions.

    iii. It is used to ensure that the model is operating correctly and optimally.

    iv. It is an initiative to understand how well it achieves its goals.

    The name of this process is:

    a) Modelling   b) Mining   c) Evaluation   d) Prediction

31. Which of the following is used to calculate Recall, Precision, Accuracy and F1 Score?

    a) Confusion matrix   b) Evaluation Table

    c) Algorithm   d) None of the above

32. Study the following statements to choose the correct option stating the advantages of chatbots.

    i.   It saves users time, money and gives better customer satisfaction.

    ii. This application can deliver a near-human-like conversational experience.

    iii. It helps you to increase customer satisfaction.

    iv. It supports customization without writing any code.

a) (i) & (ii)

b) (ii) & (iii)

c) (i), (ii) & (iii)

d) (i), (ii), (iii) & (iv)

33. Assume that David is considering the following statements about the purpose of a process:

i.   It is used to improve the effectiveness of the program.

ii. It also informs about programming decisions.

iii. It is used to ensure that the model is operating correctly and optimally.

iv. It is an initiative to understand how well it achieves its goals.

v.   It tells to determine what works well and what could be improved in a program.

The process under review is:

a) Coding

b) Modelling

c) Evaluation

d) Data mining

ANSWERS

1. (d)	2. (a)	3. (b)	4. (b)	5. (c)	6. (a)	7. (d)	8. (c)	9. (c)	10. (a)
11. (d)	12. (b)	13. (c)	14. (b)	15. (b)	16. (c)	17. (c)	18. (d)	19. (c)	20. (d)
21. (d)	22. (b)	23. (a)	24. (c)	25. (b)	26. (c)	27. (d)	28. (c)	29. (d)	30. (c)
31. (a)	32. (d)	33. (c)							

SOLVED SAMPLE QUESTION PAPER 2

FOR TERM – 2

Max. Time Allowed: 1 Hour **Max. Marks: 25**

General Instructions:

1. Please read the instructions carefully
2. This Question Paper is divided into 03 sections, viz., Section A, Section B and Section C.
3. Section A is of 05 marks and has 06 questions on Employability Skills.
4. Section B is of 15 marks and has 20 questions on Subject specific Skills.
5. Section C is of 05 marks and has 07 competency-based questions.
6. Do as per the instructions given in the respective sections.
7. Marks allotted are mentioned against each section/question.
8. All questions must be attempted in the correct order

SECTION – A

Answer any 5 questions out of the given 6 questions on Employability Skills (1 × 5 = 5 marks)

1. Consider the following actions:
   i.   Use energy-efficient lights (LED bulbs) and appliances.
   ii. Save energy by switching off electrical appliances, like tube lights and fans, when these items are not used.
   iii. Use energy-saving and water-saving techniques.
   iv. Use biodegradable items.
   v.   Use natural light as much as possible.

   The actions required for developing 'Sustainable Cities' are:

   a) (i) (ii) (iii) b) (ii) (iii) (iv) c) (iii) (iv) (v) d) All of these

2. Government of India launched a policy whose objective is to meet the challenge of skilling at scale with speed and standard, and it aims to provide an umbrella framework to all skilling activities being carried out within the country, for aligning them to common standards and link the skilling with demand centres. This is called:

   a) Ujjavala Yojana

   b) PMJDY

   c) Pradhan Mantri Yuva Udyamita Vikas Abhiyan

   d) Start-up India

3. What is the process of building sensitivity towards all cultures and celebrating diversity called?

   a) Social inclusion b) Cultural diversity

   c) Cultural inclusion d) Environmental protection

4. Assertion (A): Development was not used as a term for describing political goals and economic progress.

   Reason (R):: The major challenges of sustainable growth are eradicating extreme poverty, promoting consumption and production, and managing the planet's natural resource base.

   a) Both A and R are correct, and R is the correct reason for A.

   b) Both A and R are correct, and R is not the correct reason for A.

   c) A is correct but R is incorrect.

   d) Both A is incorrect and R is correct.

5. Statement 1: The two important personality traits that entrepreneurs possess are critical thinking and laziness.

   Statement 2: Developed countries are moving from ' entrepreneurial ' to 'managerial ' economies.

   a) Statement 1 is correct, but statement 2 is incorrect.

   b) Statement 1 is incorrect, but statement 2 is correct.

   c) Both the statements are incorrect.

   d) Both the statements are correct.

6. Study the following statements to choose the correct set of myths about entrepreneurs.

   i.   A person who has a big business is an entrepreneur.

   ii. Entrepreneurs are not in the industry for the money.

   iii. Entrepreneurs take lots of risks.

   iv. An entrepreneur cannot borrow from banks.

   v.   A new business always flourishes.

   vi. One must be young and restless to be an entrepreneur.

   vii. The only requirement to become an entrepreneur is a good idea.

   a) (ii) (iii) (iv) (v)   b) (iii) (iv) (v) (vi)

   c) (iii) (iv) (v) (vii)   d) All of the above

SECTION – B

Answer any 15 questions out of the given 20 questions   **(1 × 15 = 15 marks)**

7. Which statement is NOT TRUE?

   a) In binary classification, recall is called Sensitivity.

   b) The recall is defined as the ratio between the number of Positive samples correctly classified as Positive by the model to the total number of Positive samples.

   c) Precision is defined as the ratio between the number of Positive samples correctly classified to the total number of samples classified as negative (either correctly or incorrectly).

   d) In information retrieval, recall is the fraction of the relevant documents that are successfully retrieved.

8. Which of the following statements is TRUE?

   a) Prediction and Reality are the two parameters to be considered for the Evaluation of a model.

   b) 'A statistical model that contains more parameters than can be justified by the data is called an overfitted model.'

   c) Evaluation helps to determine what works well and what could be improved in a program.

   d) All the above

9. Unscramble the letters and find the term that is used for the whole textual data from all the documents altogether during Text Normalisation.

   a) TUSOL   b) DAAT   c) PSUROC   d) TINTUPXET

10. Consider the following formulae and choose the incorrect formulae.

    i.   Accuracy= (TP+TN)/Total labels(samples)

    ii. Misclassification= (1-Accuracy)

    iii. Precision= TP/(TP-FP)

    iv. Recall/ Sensitivity/TPR= TP/(TP+FN)

    a) i), and iii) only   b) ii) and iii) only

    c) iii) and iv) only   d) ii), and iv) only

11. Statement 1: By using Natural language processing, computers can extract keywords and phrases, understand the meaning of language, translate the content into another language, or generate response/output.

    Statement 2: The study of CV involves the tasks like how to make computers perform useful tasks after processing the natural languages that humans use.

    a) Statement 1 is correct but statement 2 is incorrect.

    b) Statement 1 is incorrect but statement 2 is correct.

    c) Both the statements are correct.

    d) Both the statements are incorrect

12. What is the term used for (1-Accuracy)?

    a) Accuracy   b) F1 Score   c) Misclassification   d) Recall

13. ______________ is a computer program that can learn over time how to best interact with human beings.

    a) Chatbot   b) Robot

    c) Stemming   d) None of the above   a) TFIDF

14. Which of the following statements is TRUE?

    a) Script-bots are powered by sophisticated AI and big data processing.

    b) A Script Bot is capable of reading and executing an external script.

    c) Text Normalisation cleans the textual data in such a manner that it comes down to a level where its complexity becomes lower than the actual data.

    d) All of the above

15. Which of the following statements are CORRECT?

    i. Prediction and Reality can be easily mapped together with the help of this confusion matrix.

    ii. The confusion matrix is a 2x3 matrix denoting the right and wrong predictions, and it is helpful to analyse the rate of success.

    iii. For a model to perform well, the values of TPR and TNR should be high, and those of FPR and FNR should go low.

    iv. F1 Score refers to the harmonic mean of recall and Precision.

    a) i) and ii)   b) ii) and iv)   c) i), iii) and iv)   d) i), ii) and iii)

16. Which of the following names is NOT given to a chatbot?

    a) Artificial conversational entity (ACE)   b) Chat robot

    c) Talk bot   d) Chatterpatterbox

17. 'Bag of Words' creates a set of ______________ containing the count of word occurrences in the document, that is easy to interpret.

    a) Data   b) Vectors

    c) Algorithms   d) None of the above

18. The result of the comparison between the Prediction and Reality can be recorded in a table which is known as:

    a) Prediction Table   b) Bag of words

    c) Confusion matrix   d) None of the above

19. Assertion (A): 'Bag of Words' is a Natural Language Processing model that helps in extracting features out of the text that may be helpful in machine learning algorithms.

    Reason (R): In a bag of words, we get the occurrences of each word and construct the vocabulary for the corpus.

    a) Both A and R are correct and R is the correct reason for A.

    b) Both A and R are correct and R is not the correct reason for A.

    c) A is correct but R is incorrect.

    d) Both A and R are incorrect.

20. Assertion (A): A prediction is said to be correct when it matches reality.

    Reason (R): Precision is defined as the ratio of true positive cases out of all the cases where the Prediction is true.

    a) Both A and R are correct and R is the correct reason for A.

    b) Both A and R are correct and R is not the correct reason for A.

    c) A is correct but R is incorrect.

    d) Both A and R are incorrect.

21. Which of the following statements is Incorrect?
    i.   False positive is also called Type 2 Error.
    ii. The 'Prediction' is the output that is given by the machine.
    iii. The F1 Score is the harmonic mean of Precision and recall.
    iv. An Overfitted Model is a statistical model which contains more parameters than can be justified by the data.
    v.   Precision is defined as the ratio of true positive cases and all the cases where the Prediction is false.

    a) iv) and v) only
    b) i) and iii) only
    c) i) and v) only
    d) ii) and iii) only

22. Unscramble the letters and find the term used for a collection of text documents in NLP.

    a) SUCPOR   b) TOBATHC   c) SCTIMAESN   d) MMNGITES

23. Statement 1: Accuracy is always taken as the right method to measure the success of an AI model.
    Statement 2: The confusion matrix is also called the 'Error-free matrix.'
    a) Statement 1 is correct but statement 2 is incorrect.
    b) Statement 1 is incorrect but statement 2 is correct.
    c) Both the statements are correct.
    d) Both the statements are incorrect.

24. Which is the algorithm that works by cutting off the end of the beginning of the word, and taking into account a list of common prefixes and suffixes that can be found in an inflected word?
    a) Lemmatisation   b) Stemming   c) Semantics   d) Stemming

25. F1 Score is the harmonic mean of ______________ and ______________.
    a) Recall and Accuracy
    b) Recall and Precision
    c) Accuracy and Precision
    d) Precision and Programming

26. Which of the following devices is not a grammar checker?
    a) Siri
    b) Grammarly
    c) WhiteSmoke
    d) ProWritingAid

SECTION – C (COMPETENCY BASED QUESTIONS)

Answer any 5 questions out of the given 7 questions   **(1 × 5 = 5 marks)**

27. Which two words will be used to fill up the following sentence correctly:

    ______________ is a technique used to extract the base form of the words by removing affixes from them, while ______________ is the grouping together of different forms of the same word.

    a) Lemmatization, Stemming
    b) Stemming, Bag of words
    c) Stemming, Lemmatization
    d) SVM, Stemming

28. Shikhar Saikia owns an AI firm called **Antriksh AI Solutions** involved in developing programs for providing AI solutions to the problems of the clients. Before handing over the program to the client, he uses a process of critically examining a program that involves collecting and analyzing information about a program's characteristics, activities, and outcomes. This is called:

    a) Data Acquisition   b) Data mining   c) Evaluation   d) Modelling

29. Suppose Javelson is studying the following statements related to evaluation of an AI Model. Which of the statements are found correct by him?

    i.   F1 Score is defined as the arithmetic mean of Recall and Precision.

    ii.   Prediction and Reality are the two parameters to be considered necessary for the Evaluation of a model.

    iii. The columns in a confusion matrix represent the actual values of the target variable.

    iv.   The four elements of the matrix represent the four metrics that count the number of correct and incorrect predictions made by the model.

    v.   F1 Score is a single score that balances the concerns of Precision and accuracy in one number.

    a) (i), (iv) and (v)   b) (ii) (iii) and (iv)   c) (i) and (v) only   d) (ii) only

30. Suppose Vibha Deshmukh is using Alexa chatbot in her home, that is very powerful, flexible, and has wide functionality. The chatbot is capable of performing various tasks, like playing music, etc. What type of bot she is using?

    a) Script bot   b) Smart bot

    c) May be smart bot or script bot   d) None of the above

31. Consider the following features of a chatbot:

    i.   It is used to build relationships with customers through interactive and tailored content.

    ii.   It books appointments, sell products, capture contact details, and build relationships through Messenger.

    iii. It connects to many tools, including Google Sheets, MailChimp, Shopify, Zapier, HubSpot, ConvertKit, etc.

    The above-mentioned Facebook Messenger is meant for e-commerce and support use. This is called:

    a) Alexa   b) Flow XO   c) ManyChat   d) Amplify

32. Study the following statements about the Evaluation to choose the true statements.

    i.   It is used to improve the effectiveness of the program.

    ii.   It also informs about programming decisions.

    iii. It is used to ensure that the model is operating correctly and optimally.

    iv.   It is an initiative to understand how well the program achieves its goals.

    a) (i) & (ii)   b) (i) & (iii)

    c) (ii), (iii) & (iv)   d) (i) (ii) (iii) & (iv)

33. Consider the following metrics:

    i.   Accuracy   ii. Confusion matrix   iii. Precision   iv. Recall

    v.   F1 Score

These are called:

    a) Assessment metrics   b) Classification evaluation metrics

    c) Modelling metrices   d) None of the above

ANSWERS									
1. (d)	2. (c)	3. (b)	4. (d)	5. (c)	6. (d)	7. (c)	8. (d)	9. (c)	10. (b)
11. (a)	12. (c)	13. (a)	14. (d)	15. (c)	16. (b)	17. (b)	18. (c)	19. (b)	20. (b)
21. (c)	22. (a)	23. (d)	24. (b)	25. (b)	26. (a)	27. (c)	28. (c)	29. (b)	30. (b)
31. (b)	32. (c)	33. (d)							

UNSOLVED SAMPLE QUESTION PAPER 1 TERM 1
CLASS X
ARTIFICIAL INTELLIGENCE (417)

Maximum Marks: 25   **Time: 60 Minutes**

General Instructions:

1. Please read the instructions carefully.
2. This Question Paper is divided into 3 sections, viz., Section A, Section B and Section C.
3. Section A is of 5 marks and has 6 questions on Employability Skills.
4. Section B is of 15 marks and has 20 questions on Subject-specific Skills.
5. Section C is of 5 marks and has 7 Competency-based questions.
6. Do as per the instructions given in the respective sections.
7. Marks allotted are mentioned against each section/question.
8. All questions must be attempted in the correct order.

Section – A

Answer any 5 questions out of the given 6 questions.

1. Assume that Sucheta Nag attended online classes during pandemic. Her teacher Mrs Huma Abid asked her to create a video in which she can make people aware of protecting themselves against the Coronavirus for uploading it on YouTube. She used her own voice in the video and added a few photographs and background sound to make it more effective. After sharing it on YouTube and with her friends, relatives and teachers, she received feedback as follows:

   i.   Awesome video!

   ii. Wonderful! Keep it up!

   iii. Fantastic work! You have done an excellent job by choosing accurate images with awesome background music.

   iv. Excellent Video! Your explanation of the topic with perfect pronunciation is quite effective.

   v.   Very Nice work!

   vi. Awesome informative video!

   Which of the feedbacks are considered descriptive?

   a) (i) (ii)   b) (ii) (iii)

   c) (iii) (iv)   d) (v) (vi)

2. Which of the following is not an imperative sentence?

   a) Read many magazines to improve your reading skills.

   b) Which mall do you visit?

   c) Don't go there.

   d) Wash your cycle.

3. Assume that Heena Chaturvedi had put on weight as a result of her poor eating habits and unhealthy lifestyle. She was a big foodie who never worried about her weight. Looking at her increasing weight, people started mentioning it to her. So, she decided to change her daily routine and started going on walk, playing, doing exercise and yoga followed by taking a healthy diet. Now he maintains his weight and lives a healthy lifestyle. What type of motivation did Heena demonstrate?

   a) Diet management   b) Self-awareness

   c) Work independently   d) Empathy

4. Statement 1: Individuals experience increased anxiety and boredom when they motivate themselves.

   Statement 2: Self-motivation teaches you self-discipline and hard work to achieve your goals.

   a) Statement 1 is correct but Statement 2 is incorrect.

   b) Statement 1 is incorrect but Statement 2 is correct.

   c) Both Statement 1 and Statement 2 are correct.

   d) Both Statement 1 and Statement 2 are incorrect.

5. Given below are the steps to make a copy of folder 'E:\Myfolder' in 'D:\Documents'. Rearrange the steps in the correct order.

   i. Select the D: drive and locate Documents folder.

   ii. Right click anywhere in the folder and select Paste option from the shortcut menu or use Ctrl+V keyboard keys.

   iii. Select the E: drive and locate Myfolder.

   iv. Right click on Myfolder and select Paste option from the shortcut menu or use Ctrl+C keyboard keys.

   a) (iii) -> (i) -> (ii) -> (iv)   b) (iv) -> (ii) -> (iii) -> (i)

   c) (iii) -> (iv) -> (i) -> (ii)   d) (i) -> (ii) -> (iii) -> (iv)

6. Which of the following is an example of Antivirus software?

   a) McAfee   b) Norton

   c) Kaspersky   d) All of the above

SECTION – B

Answer any 15 questions out of the given 20 questions.

7. Which of the following statements is incorrect about the unsupervised learning-based model?

   a) The algorithm itself analyzes the data set and determines relationship within that data.

   b) We can provide a very large data set.

   c) It lets make predictions and improves the algorithms on its own.

   d) The labelled data is fed with some rules by the developers.

8. Suppose Shailesh Saxena is going to build an AI-based system in his company 'Goyal Traders' to predict profit outcomes in the next 6 years. Choose the stages of AI project cycle in the correct order.

   a) Data cleaning -> 4Ws canvas -> choosing the algorithm -> collecting data -> Evaluating the model

   b) Choosing the algorithm -> Evaluating the model -> data cleaning -> collecting data -> 4Ws canvas

   c) 4Ws canvas -> collecting data-> data cleaning -> choosing the algorithm-> Evaluating the model

   d) 4Ws canvas -> data cleaning -> collecting data -> choosing the algorithm-> Evaluating the model

9. Unscramble the letters to find which is not a virtual assistant.

   a) LAEAX   b) ULHSA   c) IIRS   d) AACTRON

10. Artificial Intelligence (AI) is a discipline that aims to create robots that are intelligent enough to do jobs that are typically performed by humans only. Identify which of the following aspects is still beyond the capabilities of artificial intelligence.

    i.   Numerical ability

    ii. Emotional intelligence

    iii. High processing power

    iv. Speech recognition

    a) (i) only   b) (ii) only

    c) (ii) and (iii) only   d) (i), (iii) and (iv) only

11. Assertion (A): A Neural Network helps in building predictive models based on huge data sets.

    Reason (R): Semantation is one of the techniques used to train an Artificial Neural Network.

    a) Both A and R are correct and R is the correct explanation of A.

    b) Both A and R are correct but R is NOT the correct explanation of A.

    c) A is correct but R is incorrect.

    d) A is incorrect but R is correct.

12. In SAS Sr Secondary School, Ms Ankita Deshmukh grouped her students according to their level of achievements in monthly test (like below 40%, attaining upto 60%, attaining up to 75%, attaining 90% and above) for participation in some activities. This is an example of:

    a) Classification   b) Clustering   c) Decision Tree   d) Regression

13. _____________ is a technique used to solve a problem using computation processes in a structured sequence of computer-implementable instructions.

    a) Coding   b) Algorithm

    c) Programming   d) Data visualisation

14. Assume that Neha Chanchad, professional psychologist, runs 'Anubhav Psycho Help Clinic' where she helps people with mental health issues. She has a natural capability to read human behaviour, temperament and mood, which helps her in quickly diagnosing and treating the problem. Which of the following intelligence quality does Neha possess?

    a) Intrapersonal Intelligence   b) Interpersonal Intelligence

    c) Musical Intelligence   d) Logical Intelligence

15. A machine is called an intelligent machine only if it can:

    i.   Click photos

    ii. Do complex decision-making

    iii. Do speech recognition

    iv. Mimic human intelligence

    a) (i) and (ii)   b) (ii) and (iii)

    c) (i), (iii) and (iv)   d) (ii), (iii) and (iv)

16. Unscramble the letters and find the correct answer.

    Machine Learning + _____________ = Artificial Intelligence

    a) TRNUALA GNLAGAUE CPSISEROGN

    b) UTECPOMR ISOVNI

    c) EPED RIGLENAN

    d) URAENL KNWTEOR

17. Life support systems and ventilators are equipped with multiple sensors that are designed to monitor and observe body signals in order to activate the device's features. For example, as soon as it senses a drop in the level of oxygen in a person's body, it turns on the artificial oxygen supply. Ventilators are an example of:

    a) Machine with emotional intelligence   b) Artificial general intelligence

    c) Automated machine   d) Computer vision technology

18. Match Column A with Column B:

    Column A

    1. Regression
    2. K-NN (K-Nearest Neighbour)
    3. Clustering
    4. Decision Tree

    Column B

    (i) Unsupervised Learning
    (ii) Supervised Learning

    a) 1 -> (i); 2 -> (ii); 3 -> (i); 4 -> (ii)
    b) 1 -> (ii); 2 -> (ii); 3 -> (i); 4 -> (ii)
    c) 1 -> (i); 2 -> (i); 3 -> (ii); 4 -> (i)
    d) 1 -> (ii); 2 -> (ii); 3 -> (ii); 4 -> (i)

19. Assertion (A): The car producer isnot liable if a self-driving car is involved in an accident.

    Reason (R): A self-driving car is made up of a combination of sensors, cameras, radar and AI.

    a) Both A and R are correct and R is the correct explanation of A.
    b) Both A and R are correct but R is NOT the correct explanation of A.
    c) A is correct but R is incorrect.
    d) A is incorrect but R is correct.

20. Which of the following is related to function of layers in a neural network?

    a) Input Layer -> Output Layer -> Algorithms
    b) Information -> Input Layer -> Output Layer
    c) Input Layer-> Hidden Layer -> Algorithms -> Output Layer
    d) Bias -> Output layer -> Hidden Layer

21. Which of the following statement(s) are correct?

    i. Data collection helps us in determining the nature of the problem.
    ii. Modelling is the process of implementing AI-enabled algorithms on a chosen model.
    iii. Evaluation is the process of putting our model to test by using AI-enabled algorithms to generate accurate real time results.
    iv. Data acquisition ensures that data obtained from many sources is accurate, dependable and traceable.

    a) (i) and (ii) only
    b) (i), (ii) and (iii)
    c) (ii) and (iii) only
    d) (ii), (iii) and (iv)

22. Unscramble the letters and find the parameter through which machine learning understands data?

    a) VEROEPLDE   b) IASB   c) TRPETAN   d) ONTKEWR

23. Assertion (A): System maps tool helps figure out the relationship of elements with the project's goal.

    Reason (R): Positive arrows determine a direct relationship of elements while the negative arrows show an inverse relationship of elements.

    a) A is false but R is true.

    b) A is true but R is false.

    c) Both A and R are true.

    d) Both A and R are false.

24. Which of the following statements is false?

    a) A perceptron consists of weights, summation processor and an activation function.

    b) Neural network can be trained by backpropagation method.

    c) Input and output layers of neural network process data.

    d) Neural networks work on approximations and iterative improvements.

25. Choose the correct option:

    a) Classification -> continuous data

    b) Regression -> discrete data sets

    c) Clustering -> unknown data set

    d) Decision Tree -> Only discrete data

26. Amazon Alexa is a voice-controlled digital or virtual assistant software that takes voice commands to make to-do lists, place online orders, schedule reminders and answer queries through internet searches. Alexa uses__________

    a) Decision Tree

    b) NLP

    c) Classification

    d) Data Visualization

SECTION – C (Competency-Based Questions)

Answer any 5 questions out of the given 7 questions.

27. Assume that Yogesh Ram Chandran is working as Head (IT) at ***Omega Coding Pvt Ltd***, which is an AI learning app manufacturing company. During Covid pandemic, all employees were working from home. Remote employees throughout the company should be able to connect with one another in a smooth and simple manner, without being bombarded with irrelevant or unwanted communications. As so many professionals working there, emails could get mixed up and even lost, which created some problems and confusions among employees. Mr Yogesh suggested that all employees should use an instant communication app for sending only official mails over the email. Taking this as a problem, which of the following would be the ideal problem statement template?

    a) The employees working from home during Covid pandemic having a problem that they are getting irrelevant and unwanted mails frequently from different departments. An ideal solution is to block everyone.

    b) The employees working from home during Covid pandemic have a problem that sometimes they are getting irrelevant and unwanted mails frequently from different departments. An ideal solution is to use the communication app for sending only official email.

c) The employees working from home during Covid pandemic having a problem that they are getting irrelevant and unwanted mails frequently from different departments. An ideal solution is to remove some professionals.

d) The employees working from home during Covid pandemic have a problem that they are getting irrelevant and unwanted mails frequently from different departments. An ideal solution is to write letters and post them in the letterbox.

28. The given below files are examples of structured data. Which of the following steps are involved in converting data from various sources into digital format?

    i. CSV is a simple file format used to store tabular data.

    ii. A spreadsheet is used for managing data using rows and columns.

    iii. SQL is used for managing data stored in Database Management Systems (DBMS).

a) Problem Scoping   b) Data Acquisition

c) Data Modelling   d) Data Exploration

29. Ambika Talukdar has started **"News in Air"** channel -a news channel that broadcasts news and information on a wide range of topics, including politics, government, foreign affairs, science & technology, games & sports, wild-life and the latest movie and television news. Reporters are in charge of gathering, evaluating and transmitting information about current events too. Additionally, this channel permits people to submit breaking news, which is subject to verification by the channel's reporters. However, it may be difficult to distinguish between real news and fake news, which can lead to confusion among readers and threaten a news organization's reputation. Which of the following domains is used to detect fake news for getting a high level of trust by the audience in the news channel?

a) Matrices   b) Data Science

c) Computer Vision   d) Natural Language Processing

30. Suppose Devika Murthy -owner of **"Devika Customer Support Systems"**, possesses an AI application that has a higher level of intelligence. This app is capable of understanding open-ended questions too to provide assistance in finding the most relevant replies beyond the pre-scripted responses it learns over time using NLP. This app is ideal for dealing with customer support concerns, resolving typical issues, aiding account administration and offering general assistance. What is possessed by her?

a) Spam filter

b) Smart Chatbot

c) ANPR (Automatic Number Plate Recognition)

d) Voice filter

31. Suppose Sumit Anand, an AI & IT expert uses an AI model to input only from the dynamic environment that does not include any labelled data. It uses a behavioural learning model and improves as it learns about the environment. During the process, as the learning agent interacts with the environment while moving from one state to another, it is rewarded for success but penalized for failure. Which type of the learning model is used by him?

a) Unsupervised Learning

b) Supervised Learning

c) Reinforcement Learning

d) Semi-Supervised Learning

32. Which of the following is/are not related to smart bots?

   i. Google Assistant,

   ii. Siri

   iii. Tesla's self-driven car

   iv. Alexa,

   v. We Chat

   vi. Cortana

   a) (i) only

   b) (iii) only

   c) (i) (ii) (iii) only

   d) (iv) (v) (vi) only

33. Suppose **Satyakaam International Vidyapeeth** uses an AI-based system to manage the learning process by delivering customized study materials. To assign appropriate subjects to students, the system takes into consideration all the factors such as gender, race, ongoing learning, economic level, minority status and details of previous educational institute. But it ignores a fundamental aspect of learning as an ongoing process based on an individual's abilities and knowledge. What is the related term to be used for this scenario?

   a) Algorithm bias

   b) Cultural bias

   c) Safety concerns

   d) Gender bias

UNSOLVED SAMPLE QUESTION PAPER 2 TERM 2
CLASS X
ARTIFICIAL INTELLIGENCE (417)

Maximum Marks: 25   **Time: 60 Minutes**

General Instructions:

1. Please read the instructions carefully.
2. This Question Paper is divided into 3 sections, viz., Section A, Section B and Section C.
3. Section A is of 5 marks and has 6 questions on Employability Skills.
4. Section B is of 15 marks and has 20 questions on Subject-specific Skills.
5. Section C is of 5 marks and has 7 Competency-based questions.
6. Do as per the instructions given in the respective sections.
7. Marks allotted are mentioned against each section/question.
8. All questions must be attempted in the correct order.

SECTION – A

Answer any 5 questions out of the given 6 questions.   **(1 × 5 = 5 marks)**

1. Consider the following statements:

    i.   Use of hybrid cars instead of conventional cars to reduce air pollution

    ii. Use of biofuels (biogas in the kitchen)

    iii. Treatment of Industrial waste and sewage before releasing in the water bodies

    Which statement is related to the promotion of sustainable development?

    a) (i) only
    b) (iii) only
    c) (i) (iii) only
    d) (i) (ii) (iii) only

2. Entrepreneurship is not only beneficial for the Entrepreneur itself, but it is also essential for the _____________ of the economy.

    a) Decline
    b) Flexibility
    c) Growth
    d) None of the above

3. Assertion (A): The principles of sustainable development are based on the integration of environmental, social, and economic concerns into all aspects of decision-making.

    Reason (R): The projects which are initiated to manufacture products or to do something by harnessing the environment are called green projects.

    a) Both A and R are correct, and R is the correct reason for A.

    b) Both A and R are correct, and R is not the correct reason for A.

    c) A is correct but R is incorrect.

    d) A is incorrect but R is correct.

4. Jeet Singh Raina lives in Jammu and buys bulbs for his business from Noida. He finds that bulbs are cheaper in Pathakot than in Noida. Hence, he decides to start buying bulbs from there. He:

   a) is creative. b) Takes risk

   c) Makes decisions d) Divides income

5. Statement 1: The two important personality traits that entrepreneurs possess are critical thinking and decision making.

   Statement 2: Developed countries are moving from ' entrepreneurial ' to 'managerial ' economies.

   a) Statement 1 is correct, but statement 2 is incorrect.

   b) Statement 1 is incorrect, but statement 2 is correct.

   c) Both the statements are correct.

   d) Both the statements are incorrect.

6. Choose the option which defines sustainable development.

   a) Taking care of future generations

   b) Taking care of only ourselves

   c) Taking care of ourselves and the future generations

   d) Wellbeing of all

SECTION – B

Answer any 15 questions out of the given 20 questions. **(1 × 15 = 15 marks)**

7. Which statement is INCORRECT?

   a) TFIDF values help the computer understand which words are to be considered while processing the natural language.

   b) Words occurring in all the documents with high term frequencies have the least values and are called the 'Stopwords.'

   c) The higher the value of TFIDF, the less important the word is for a given corpus.

   d) For a word having a high TFIDF value, the word will have a high term frequency but less document frequency. This shows that the word is important for one document but is not a common word for all documents.

8. Which type of information is given by the 'Bag of Words' algorithm?

   a) Type of words b) Number of words

   c) Number of stopwords d) None of the above

9. Unscramble the letters to find out the term used for words in a corpus having the highest value.

   a) NPUONCTTUAI b) WRDSO ERAR

   c) WDRSO TOPS d) GNISTMME

10. Which is the algorithm that works by cutting off the end of the beginning of the word and taking into account a list of common prefixes and suffixes that can be found in an inflected word?

    a) Lemmatisation   b) Stemming   c) Semantics   d) Stemming

11. Assertion (A): When F1=1, it is known as the perfect value for the F1 Score.

    Reason (R): F1 Score is the average of Precision and Recall.

    a) Both A and R are correct and R is the correct reason for A.

    b) Both A and R are correct and R is not the correct reason for A.

    c) A is correct but R is incorrect.

    d) Both A and R are incorrect.

12. Which of the following statements is INCORRECT?

    a) Prediction and Reality can be easily mapped together with the help of this confusion matrix.

    b) The confusion matrix is a 2x3 matrix denoting the right and wrong predictions, and it is helpful to analyse the rate of success.

    c) For a model to perform well, the values of TPR and TNR should be high, and those of FPR and FNR should go low.

    d) F1 Score refers to the harmonic mean of recall and Precision.

13. ______________ assists in analyzing the outcome of each algorithm utilized and selecting the best method to produce the most efficient and accurate outcome.

    a) Data Exploration   b) 4Ws Canvas   c) Modelling   d) Evaluation

14. Statement 1: A chatbot is defined as a computer program that is designed to simulate conversations with human beings.

    Statement 2: NLP is regarded as art to extract some useful information from the text.

    a) Statement 1 is correct but statement 2 is incorrect.

    b) Statement 1 is incorrect but statement 2 is correct.

    c) Both the statements are correct.

    d) Both the statements are incorrect.

15. On which parameters do you calculate the efficiency of the model?

    i. Speed   ii. Precision   iii. Accuracy   iv. F1 Score

    a) (i) and (ii) only   b) (ii) and (iii) only

    c) (ii), (iii) and (iv)   d) (i), (ii) and (iii)

16. What can be calculated from a confusion matrix?

    a) Accuracy and Precision   b) Recall and F1 Score

    c) Both a and b   d) None of the above

17. Statement 1: The model is a total failure when the F1 Score is 0.

    Statement 2: The formula for F1 Score is F1 score=(3*Recall* Precision)/(Recall+ Precision)

    a)   Statement 1 is correct but statement 2 is incorrect.

    b)   Statement 1 is incorrect but statement 2 is correct.

    c)   Both the statements are correct.

    d)   Both the statements are incorrect

18. Match Column A with Column B:

    Column A   **Column B**

    1. Siri   (i)   CV

    2. Self-driving car   (ii) NLP

    3. Snapchat filters

    4. Alexa

    a)   1 -> (ii); 2 -> (i); 3 -> (i); 4 -> (ii)   b)   1 -> (i); 2 -> (ii); 3 -> (ii); 4 -> (i)

    c)   1 -> (i); 2 -> (i); 3 -> (ii); 4 -> (i)   d)   1 -> (i); 2 -> (i); 3 -> (ii); 4 -> (ii)

19. ______________ is not always taken as the right method to measure the success of an AI model.

    a)   Accuracy   b)   Precision   c)   F1 Score   d)   Recall

20. Which of the following statements is incorrect?

    i.   Snapchat filters use augmented reality and machine learning.

    ii.   Siri uses NLP and machine learning.

    iii. Netflix uses CV and machine learning.

    iv.   The predicted value was falsely predicted. It is called Type 1 error.

    v.   Self-driving cars use CV and deep learning.

    a)   (i) and (ii) only   b)   (ii) and (iv) only

    c)   (iii) and (iv) only   d)   (iv) and (v) only

21. Which of the following statements is incorrect?

    i.   An AI model is a computer program that has been taught to identify specific patterns.

    ii.   An AI model is a robot that has been programmed to instruct humans.

    iii. An AI model is a human who has been trained to instruct machines.

    iv.   An AI model requires a large amount of data to derive a relationship in the data.

    a)   (i) and (iv) only   b)   (ii) and (iv) only

    c)   (ii) and (iii) only   d)   (i), (iii) and (iv)

22. Assertion (A): The maximum value of the F1 Score is +2.0

    Reason (R): The lowest value of the F1 score is 0.

    a)   Both A and R are correct and R is the correct reason for A.

b) Both A and R are correct and R is not the correct reason for A.

c) A is correct but R is incorrect.

d) Both A and R are incorrect.

23. Assertion (A): Recall is one of the parameters for evaluating the model's performance.

Reason (R): In binary classification, Recall is called Sensitivity.

a) Both A and R are correct and R is the correct reason for A.

b) Both A and R are correct and R is not the correct reason for A.

c) A is correct but R is incorrect.

d) Both A and R are incorrect.

24. Which term is used for the frequency of a word in one document?

a) Echo

b) Hertz

c) Low frequency

d) Term frequency

25. Which of the following statements is NOT TRUE?

a) The recall cares about correctly classifying all positive samples, while it does not care if a negative sample is classified as positive.

b) F1 Score is defined as the measure of the balance between Precision and Accuracy.

c) The Precision is dependent on both the negative and positive samples, but the recall is dependent only on the positive samples.

d) Accuracy works best when false positives and false negatives have almost similar costs.

26. It is a computer program that is designed to simulate human conversation through voice commands or text chats, or both. What is it?

a) Stemming   b) Chatbot   c) Robot   d) Qlick

SECTION – C (Competency-Based Questions)

Answer any 5 questions out of the given 7 questions.   **(1 × 5 = 5 marks)**

27. Consider the following points regarding algorithms: With more and more data, an algorithm becomes better and more accurate.

   i.   We can choose from various techniques such as Regression, Classification, Clustering, etc depending on the data set.

   ii. Algorithms are mainly used in pattern recognition which help in deriving meaningful insights and describe the data better to the users.

   Which stage of AI project life cycle requires algorithms?

   a) Evaluation   b) Problem Scoping   c) Data Acquisition   d) Modelling

28. Suppose **AnuRekha AI Productions Pvt Ltd** uses a process that critically examines a program and involves collecting and analyzing information about the program's activities, characteristics, and outcomes. The purpose of this process are as follows:

   i.   It informs about programming decisions.

   ii. It is used to ensure that the model is operating correctly and optimally.

   iii. It is used to improve the effectiveness of the program.

   iv. It is an initiative to understand how well it achieves its goals.

What is the name of the process used by the company?

a) Evaluation   b) Prediction   c) Modelling   d) Mining

29. Assume that Sagar Khan has joined as a librarian in **Anand Vidyashram School**. The school library doesn't have any database system and all books are mixed up. Thus, he faces several problems when looking for a particular book. In order to find a book, the library requires an effective technique. Hence, he suggested to the management for the creation of a database of books, after which the books are categorized into shelves so that students and teachers can quickly search for them. Taking this as a problem, which of the following would be the ideal problem statement template?

a) Librarian and users (students & teachers) are facing problem regarding searching for books in a library. An ideal solution would be to close the library.

b) Librarian and users (students & teachers) are facing problem regarding searching for books in a library. An ideal solution would be to assign a duty to the student to find books in the library.

c) Librarian and users (students & teachers) are facing problem regarding searching for books in a library. An ideal solution would be to create a database of books and place books on shelves according to category.

d) Librarian and users (students & teachers) are facing problem regarding searching for books in a library. An ideal solution would be to restrict the entry of students in the library.

30. Assume that **Dhananjay Mathur** uses an application, during the surfing of internet, which offers appropriate results on the basis of the same search behaviour or user intention. Hence, he will find what he needs. It not only supports voice-enabled queries but also offers real-time auto-complete suggestions based on factors such as browsing history, the intention commonly associated with the words used and best ranked contents from comparable searches. What is the name of the application used by him?

a) Web Browser   b) Search Engine   c) Chatbot   d) Voice filter

31. Assume that **Chitnis AI Solutions** is using a chatbot that has the following properties/features:

   i. Enable the clients to build, connect, and publish bots to interact with users.

   ii. Offer rapid intelligent chatbot development for everyone.

   iii. Help the clients to create a bot or Human chatbot without any coding or technical skills.

   iv. Design conversations to utilize simple or something complex like translation, action buttons, collect payments, send receipts, and more.

Which bot is used by the company?

a) Snatchbot   b) Ada   c) Watson Assistant   d) Amplify

32. Assume that Latha Sridharan, CEO, Otopia Social Site directed to run a video on her social site. The users who viewed a video of Black males on an American tabloid were asked, "Would you like to keep viewing videos of primates (apes and monkeys)?" after seeing this video. But the company disabled the AI function that made the recommendation, apologized for the "unacceptable error" and began an investigation into what went wrong. What is the possible reason of this incident?

a) Cultural bias

b) Technological bias

c) Biased data fed into the machine

d) Data Privacy

33. Suppose *XtraMile AI Predictions* uses the following metrics:

i.   Accuracy

ii. Confusion matrix

iii. Precision

iv. Recall

v.   F1 Score

What are these metrics known as?

a) Assessment metrics

b) Classification evaluation metrics

c) Modelling metrices

d) Prediction Metrices

REFERENCES
(Pictures/Figures/Photographs)

1.1   https://www.wallpaperflare.com/hands-earth-next-generation-climate-protection-space-universe-wallpaper-akbfy

1.3   https://pt.slideshare.net/tempestperson/barriers-to-effective-communication-16441084/6

1.4   https://extraessay.com/?key_wpg=661d4f6b1bb32966c024dce66bbade5c

1.5   https://www.ambyrne.com/2018/01/22/we-lose-much-of-the-non-verbal-language-over-the-phone/

1.11   https://www.nationalmlm.com/barriers-of-communication/

1.13   https://www.youtube.com/watch?v=hhTK9Yobz-Q

1.15   https://teachologi.blogspot.com/

1.17   https://www.usa.edu/blog/communication-in-nursing/

1.18   https://www.helpwithmen.com/how-much-of-communication-is-really-nonverbal/

1.19   ·https://www.lakeheadu.ca/teaching-commons

1.20   https://kingz0925.blogspot.com/2013/04/visual-communication-classs-publication.html

1.21   https://www.it402.com/communication-cycle

1.22   http://www.iibmindialms.com/library/operation-management/production-management/barriers-effective-communication/

1.23   http://keplarllp.com/a-good-topic-sentence-for-a-paragraph.html

2.1   https://reba.global/content/why-wellbeing-and-stress-management-matters-when-it-comes-to-staff-retention

2.2   https://www.yourtherapysource.com/product/student-self-regulation-rubrics/

2.3   http://www.russellhouse.co.uk/book-categories/management/?Page_ID=3610&ref-pid=66383&id=749780

2.4   https://www.manomaya.in/services/stress-management

2.5   http://ureadthis.com/an-overview-of-stress-management/

2.6   https://www.crewhu.com/blog/smart-goal-examples-for-employees

2.7   https://www.thebalance.com/money-milestones-you-need-to-hit-at-every-age-4147835

2.8   https://kiddosmagazine.com/the-benefits-of-yoga-for-kids/

2.10   https://yourdost.com/blog/2016/05/feeling-stressed-in-twenties.html

2.11   https://www.cognitiveinstitute.org/get-smart-about-emotional-intelligence/

2.14   http://robertjrgraham.com/time-mastery-or-time-management-its-your-choice/

2.15   https://midwest-center.tumblr.com/post/93855148651/symptoms-of-stress-what-is-stress-stress-is

2.16   https://mamaslegacycookbooks.com/healthy-eating-is-not-a-diet/

2.17   https://www.marketing91.com/strategy-definition/

2.18   http://leanblitzconsulting.com/2012/01/new-years-resolutions-smart-goals/

2.19   https://blog.mbeforyou.com/management/time-management-top-11-tips-that-work/

2.20   https://www.shimmeringcareers.com/blog/time-management-tips-help-manage-your-job-search/

3.1   https://www.secfull.com/ict-products/

3.2   https://idevie.com/other/top-5-types-of-social-media-users

3.4   http://www.informationsecuritybuzz.com/study/data-protection-day/

3.5   https://www.silicon.co.uk/e-regulation/legal/gdpr-data-protection-212947

3.9   https://news.softpedia.com/news/pear-os-has-just-been-brought-to-life-based-on-ubuntu-14-04-lts-screenshot-tour-494344.shtml

3.10   https://ecomputernotes.com/software-engineering/types-of-software-maintenance

3.12   https://www.createwebquest.com/webquest/computer-viruses

3.13   https://cantoncomputers.com/2018/10/24/1492/

4.1   https://www.morebusiness.com/marketing-plan-example/

4.2   https://www.dreamstime.com/startup-rocket-words-illustration-image123448285

4.3   https://www.opstart.ca/what-makes-an-entrepreneur-10-key-qualities-of-successful-entrepreneurs/

4.5   https://blog.ipleaders.in/need-know-make-india/

4.6   https://www.papertyari.com/government-schemes/pradhan-mantri-yuva-yojana/

4.8   https://digitallearning.eletsonline.com/2018/01/nsdc-imparting-skills-to-propel-economic-growth/

4.9   http://www.bms.co.in/what-is-the-meaning-of-entrepreneurship-2/

4.10   https://www.slideshare.net/MediaSocial/the-importance-of-entrepreneurship-for-society

4.11   https://www.paggu.com/entrepreneurship/top-5-contributions-of-entrepreneurship-in-society/

4.12   http://www.atalpensionyojana.co.in/atal-innovation-mission-aim/

4.13   https://www.makedigitalindian.com/list-of-most-successful-entrepreneur-in-india/

5.1   https://www.denbow.com/sustainable-development-strategy/

5.2   https://wrytin.com/lijins1/environment-sustainable-development-ju5mljtb

5.3   http://www.globaleducationmagazine.com/sustainable-development-goals/

5.4   https://www.tumblr.com/tagged/Save-the-Earth?sort=top

5.5   https://www.researchgate.net/figure/A-sustainable-development-has-to-involve-economy-social-community-and-environment_fig5_271766042

5.6   https://www.quora.com/How-can-sustainable-development-be-achieved

5.8 https://leverageedublog.s3.ap-south-1.amazonaws.com/blog/wp-content/up-loads/2020/04/29203536/3Rs-Reduce-Reuse-Recycle.jpg

5.9 https://www.dreamstime.com/stock-photo-human-hands-holding-green-planet-tree-first-second-growing-plant-shape-heart-soil-rainy-over-blurred-beautiful-image58808050

5.10 https://twitter.com/ossap_sdgs/status/980729203288170497

6.1 https://brands2life.com/views/artificial-intelligence/

6.2 https://artist.com/art-recognition-and-education/art-and-the-singularity-how-will-artificial-intelligence-creative-robots-change-art/

6.3 https://www.hindustantimes.com/budget/budget-2019-govt-plans-ai-push-with-national-centre/story-fdqlbqfOZMdruQ5GxEaU6M.html

6.10 https://www.jagranjosh.com/articles/kv-teacher-turns-innovator-develops-social-humanoid-robot-shalu-that-can-speak-9-indian-36-foreign-languages-1612431262-1

6.11 https://oneteamsolutions.in/blogoneteam/it-software-training/artificial-intelligence-machine-learning/

6.12 https://geomarketing.com/what-do-brands-need-to-know-about-how-the-rise-of-voice-will-impact-advertising

6.13 https://www.youtube.com/watch?v=FvPeT_-JlEM

6.15 https://hubpages.com/education/Edcuation-Discussion-The-History--Evolution--and-Acceptance-of-Standardized-Testing

6.16 https://tridenstechnology.com/all-about-the-internet-of-things-iot/

6.18 https://frontender.com/blog/enablers/data-mining/

6.19 https://www.ntd.com/ford-self-driving-cars-to-launch-in-austin-in-2021_384352.html

6.20 https://newsroom.unsw.edu.au/news/science-tech/human-plus-machine-%E2%80%93-face-recognition-its-best

6.21 https://www.lifewire.com/k9-spam-email-filter-1164807

6.22 https://bigthink.com/politics-current-affairs/howard-gardner-on-obamas-educaiton-speech/

6.25 https://evaconconsulting.com/

6.26 https://openiun.com/top-5-reasons-why-artificial-intelligence-can-be-dangerous/

6.27 https://creativefuture.co/what-is-artificial-intelligence-machine-learning-deep-learning/

7.2 https://innolabindia.co.in/wp-content/uploads/2020/10/39.jpg.png

7.7 https://www.practicalai.io/implementing-classification-using-logistic-regression-in-ruby/

7.8 https://www.andlearning.org/visualizing-the-clusters-with-machine-learning-algorithm/

7.9 https://towardsai.net/p/data-science/linear-regression-basics-for-absolute-beginners

7.10 https://www.javatpoint.com/regression-vs-classification-in-machine-learning

7.11 http://stats4stem.weebly.com/r-histograms-and-density-plots.html

7.12 https://savvytower.com/types-of-sensors/

7.13   https://www.slideshare.net/ThomasKellyPMP/semantic-analytics-51868190

7.14   https://www.simplilearn.com/tutorials/machine-learning-tutorial/what-is-machine-learning

7.15   https://dataaspirant.com/how-decision-tree-algorithm-works/

7.18   https://www.redwoodlogistics.com/edi-vs-api/

7.19   https://medium.datadriveninvestor.com/logistic-regression-18afd48779ce

7.20   https://www.datavedas.com/clustering-problems/

7.22   https://pianalytix.com/machine-learning-project-life-cycle/

8.1   https://www.pinterest.com/?show_error=true

8.4   https://www.pinterest.com/pin/88172105183619028/

8.5   https://www.mygreatlearning.com/blog/expert-systems-in-artificial-intelligence/

8.9   https://www.imagesshirt.com/generate-flowchart-from-python/

8.10   https://code-knowledge.com/python-elif-statement/

8.11   https://www.programiz.com/java-programming/for-loop

8.12   http://codepanel.blogspot.com/2013/07/do-while-loop-syntax.html

8.13   https://cacoo.com/resources/flowchart-guide/

9.1   https://www.datanami.com/2016/01/07/what-data-science-skills-employers-want-now/

9.2   https://towardsdatascience.com/introduction-to-statistics-e9d72d818745?gi=49a63ea921d6

9.3   https://www.sampleformats.org/scatter-chart-template

9.5   https://www.blendspace.com/lessons/dqjScZBM1vwiRw/box-plots-3-10-4-5-7th-grade-math-2020

9.7   https://www.omnisci.com/technical-glossary/fraud-detection-and-prevention

9.9   https://vizzlo.com/data-viz-guide/bar-chart/how-to-create-a-more-impressive-bar-chart

9.11   https://blog.datixinc.com/blog/ai-manufacturing

9.13   https://medium.com/@agarwal.vishal819/outlier-detection-with-boxplots-1b6757fafa21

9.14   https://medium.com/@agarwal.vishal819/outlier-detection-with-boxplots-1b6757fafa21

9.15   https://www.hitechies.com/what-is-ai-bias-interesting-examples-of-ai-bias/

9.16   https://www.datanami.com/2018/09/17/improving-your-odds-with-data-science-hiring/

9.17   https://www.datanami.com/2020/04/06/brief-perspective-on-key-terms-and-ideas-in-responsible-ai/

10.1   https://www.geekboots.com/story/computer-vision-and-its-possibility

10.3   http://blog.ventureradar.com/2015/10/21/top-10-innovative-companies-in-computer-vision/

10.4   https://7starlake.com/SOLUTION/SmartCity/V2X

10.5   https://learnopencv.com/support-vector-machines-svm/

10.6	https://manningbooks.medium.com/computer-vision-pipeline-part-1-the-big-picture-5d6a6964913a
10.8	https://www.youtube.com/watch?v=1-EDeIxM4ow
10.9	https://www.digipen.edu.sg/showcase/news/7-amazing-applications-of-computer-vision
10.10	https://tariq-hasan.github.io/concepts/computer-vision-semantic-segmentation/
10.12	https://www.dreamstime.com/convolutional-neural-network-work-scheme-object-detection-instant-segmentation-performs-task-recognition-picture-image142451357
10.13	https://artificialintelligence.oodles.io/blogs/computer-vision-applications-improve-customer-satisfaction/
11.1	https://www.newson6.com/story/5e6fc971f86011d4820c3b88/natural-language-processing-algorithms-nlp-ai
11.2	https://www.javatpoint.com/nlp
11.3	https://www.dayofdubai.com/event/4-days-nlp-practitioner-program
11.4	https://medium.com/@anilthomasnlp/five-core-nlp-techniques-for-self-improvement-164c62a8d7b0
11.5	https://devopedia.org/natural-language-processing
11.16	https://devopedia.org/natural-language-processing
11.17	https://www.veribilimiokulu.com/natural-language-toolkitnltk/
11.18	https://herobot.app/messenger-chatbot/best-chatbot-app-you-should-have-on-your-phone/
11.19	https://medium.com/swlh/introduction-to-stemming-vs-lemmatization-nlp-8c69eb43ecfe
11.20	https://towardsdatascience.com/nltk-applications-for-nlp-and-python-dc8c5381668a
11.22	https://www.germanautolabs.com/blog/how-to-build-better-voice-assistants-arbitrate
11.29	https://datascience.foundation/datatalk/release-update-for-spark-nlp-for-healthcare-2-6
12.1	https://hiringtek.com/ai-evaluation/
12.2	https://medium.com/@skyl/evaluating-a-machine-learning-model-7cab1f597046
12.9	https://www.vecteezy.com/vector-art/622573-ai-concept

Made in the USA
Monee, IL
07 July 2026